International Finance
A Markets Approach

International Finance
A Markets Approach

■

John S. Evans
University of Alabama

The Dryden Press
A Harcourt Brace Jovanovich College Publisher

Fort Worth Philadelphia San Diego New York Orlando Austin San Antonio
Toronto Montreal London Sydney Tokyo

Acquisitions Editor: Mike Roche
Developmental Editor: Paula Dempsey
Project Editor: Teresa Chartos
Production Manager: Barb Bahnsen
Director of Editing, Design, and Production: Jane Perkins
Cover Designer: Mercedes Santos
Copy Editor: David Talley
Indexer: Leoni McVey
Compositor: The Clarinda Company
Text Type: 10/12 Sabon

Library of Congress Cataloging-in-Publication Data

Evans, John S. (John Sidney), 1930–
    International finance : a markets approach / John S. Evans.
      p.   cm.
    Includes bibliographical references and index.
    ISBN 0-03-073226-3
    1. International finance.   I. Title.
  HG3881.E844   1992
  332'.042—dc20
                                            91-8843
                                             CIP

Printed in the United States of America
234-90-987654321
Copyright © 1992 by The Dryden Press

Address orders:
The Dryden Press
Orlando, Florida 32887

Address editorial correspondence:
The Dryden Press
301 Commerce Street, Suite 3700
Fort Worth, TX 76102

The Dryden Press
Harcourt Brace Jovanovich

Cover: © Alan Klehn/Tony Stone Worldwide (Trading Floor, Chicago);
© Mark Segal/Tony Stone Worldwide (Trading Floor, Paris);
© Julian Calder/Tony Stone Worldwide (Stock Exchange, Japan)

To Janet, whose patience and support have been appreciated more than she can ever know.

The Dryden Press Series in Finance

Preface

■

Longer ago than I like to admit, a representative of a publishing firm challenged me to write an international finance textbook that would focus on financial markets. I had been teaching the international finance course at the University of Alabama for several years and had become frustrated by the existing textbooks' poor coverage of the financial markets in which multinational firms operate. I felt I could not expect my students to understand international financial management without first understanding the markets in which multinational firms make their financial decisions.

In addition, I thought that the focus of existing texts on the operations of nonfinancial multinational firms gave students an unbalanced introduction to the subject of international finance. I believed that the operations and motivations of internationally oriented banking firms were as worthy of study as those of nonfinancial corporations. Also, because governments greatly influence the international financial environment, I thought their role deserved a deeper look. My students were more likely to wind up working for financial firms than for multinational companies, and some of them would probably wind up working for government.

From such considerations emerged the firm conviction that the academic orientations of courses in international finance were certain to change. Events of the past few years have done nothing to persuade me that I was wrong.

Much has changed in the years since I first began to put my ideas about international finance on paper. New markets have materialized, and institutional arrangements have been altered. Some financial techniques for managing the exchange risk have become so complicated that acquiring even a rudimentary understanding of them requires considerable effort. Developments in the body of theory pertaining to exchange rate determination and other matters of interest to international financial managers have challenged our ability to achieve a coherent and consistent overview of how the international financial system operates. Under these fluid circumstances, to write a textbook about international finance is an audacious undertaking. I hope that the fruits of my efforts will be recognized as a significant step in the right direction.

Interest in the study of international finance has grown with the fall of communism and resulting political realignments, the continuing evolution of the European Economic Community, the growing international integration of the U.S. economy, and the astounding expansion of international financial markets. The AACSB has recommended that all business courses include international coverage where appropriate. In addition to this emphasis, internationally oriented students of business and economics need a core course that brings together concepts and details that would be glossed over when presented in conjunction with other topics. This book is designed to meet the requirements for such a course.

This text offers a comprehensive look at international financial markets, including the foreign exchange market, international banking, international securities markets, and markets for financial swaps. It also covers the features of international macroeconomics and monetary theory that are most relevant to international financial markets. Throughout the book, the discussion strongly emphasizes the application of theories, concepts, and techniques to real-world situations.

Features of the Book

This text provides a wealth of detail on the operation of the foreign exchange market. For example, Chapter 6 goes beyond the standard observation that most forward transactions are interbank swaps and explains why this is the case. Chapter 7 shows how to interpret currency futures trading data in *The Wall Street Journal* and covers how the leading futures contracts are actually traded and processed. Chapter 8 provides similar information for currency options, emphasizing such topics as the role of specialists in trading currency options at the Philadelphia Stock Exchange.

The book provides up-to-date information on international banking and international securities markets. Included in the coverage of international banking are such topics as International Banking Facilities (IBFs), private banking, Euronotes, the role of interbank transactions in the Eurocurrency market, syndicated lending, and the management of the sovereign debt problem. The coverage of international securities markets includes such topics as choosing between fixed-rate and floating-rate bond financing, the process of bringing Eurobonds to market, the growing role of private placements, the growth of trading in international equities, and portfolio gains from international investment.

In its coverage of international financial markets, the book includes important features of these markets that other textbooks commonly omit or mention only in passing. Examples include the use of currency warrants, how synthetic option positions can be constructed to lock in desired positions and improve exchange risk management, and the extensive coverage of such topics as forfaiting, commodity swaps, and swaptions.

The book's coverage of international macroeconomics provides an overview of the international economy's financial side that is designed to give financial managers information about how this economy works. Past and present international economic policy issues are examined to provide a broad understanding of matters that are likely to be of continuing importance. Examples of the coverage provided include an explanation for fluctuations in the statistical discrepancy account of the U.S. balance of payments and why they are important; an investigation of the extent to which the United States is a net debtor nation; an explanation of the exchange rate mechanism (ERM) of the European Monetary System; and the effects of central bank intervention in the foreign exchange market on exchange rates and domestic money supplies.

The book's realistic coverage of exchange rate theories highlights their key features without getting bogged down in time-consuming analysis of theoretical models. This coverage is intended to make the reader conversant with the features of economic theory that bear most directly on the determination of exchange rates and the conduct of international economic policy. Both the strengths and the limitations of the leading theories are brought out. In addition, the uses and limitations of exchange rate forecasts are considered.

Numerous questions at the end of each chapter facilitate student learning and review. Where appropriate, chapters contain problems that help to improve students' understanding of quantitative relationships. Each chapter has a summary that highlights the chief points covered.

The text is supplemented by a complete *Instructor's Manual and Test Bank* that provides solutions and answers to all of the problems and many of the questions. In addition, the *Instructor's Manual and Test Bank* includes comments on how to present the textbook that are based on several years' experience in teaching international finance from the same material in manuscript form.

The material in this text is drawn from many years of teaching international economics and international finance and from several years of intensive reading about contemporary international financial theory and practice. With the vast literature about these matters, it has been an enormous challenge to distill out those features that are most relevant to a balanced and comprehensive understanding of international finance. I am sure that I have overlooked some important works that I should have read, and I hope to correct such omissions in the future.

Acknowledgments

I am indebted to a number of people for their help in getting this project under way and bringing it, at last, to a conclusion. J. B. Yowell, formerly of West Publishing, provided great encouragement at the start, assuring me that I had sound ideas and the talent to put them into effect. Among early reviewers of parts of the manuscript, Peggy Swanson of the University of Texas at Arlington should be singled out for her strong encouragement.

At The Dryden Press, I have received strong support from three acquisitions editors. Liz Widdicombe encouraged me by giving my ideas a hearing and indicating that she thought I was on the right track. Ann Heath, her successor, put her company on the line by offering me a contract. Finally, Mike Roche has provided both encouragement and strong direction. Among others at Dryden, I wish to thank Paula Dempsey, who held the responsibility for directing this project for several months, and Karen Shaw, in whose capable hands the project rested for a briefer period. At Elm Street Publishing Services, which has readied this book for printing, I wish to thank Cate Rzasa and Teresa Chartos, who have kept the pressure on in an agreeable fashion. During the final stages of this project, Dryden was undergoing a consolidation that involved changes of personnel and a move from Hinsdale, Illinois, to Fort Worth, Texas, but at no time did I feel that my project suffered as a consequence. My relationship with Dryden has been positive in every respect.

To four reviewers of the previous version of my manuscript, I owe a considerable debt: Robert Driskill of Ohio State, Boyden E. Lee of New Mexico State, S. Ghon Rhee of the University of Rhode Island, and Ahmad Sohrabian of California Polytechnic at Pomona. I have benefitted from their commentary and have tried to take advantage of it. Their reviews were thoroughly professional and, in many cases, incisive. I hope that the final product measures up to their expectations.

I have also benefitted from support, moral and otherwise, from colleagues at the University of Alabama, namely Eric Baklanoff, Bob Brooks, Benton Gup, Charles Leathers, Bob McLeod, and H. K. Wu. Three of my graduate assistants, Rick Marchand, Joseph Fung, and Davinder K. Malhotra have given me considerable help along the way.

As this project comes to a close, however, I cannot help but recall that my decision to write a textbook coincided with the adoption by my department and college of a rigid policy rewarding journal articles above other writing. In the environment in which I have worked, a textbook project, particularly one destined to be long and drawn out, has held a very low position on the departmental priority list. From the outset, however, I have sensed that writing a textbook was the best way for me to make a meaningful professional contribution. The market will determine whether or not I have been correct.

John S. Evans
Tuscaloosa, Alabama
February 1992

Contents in Brief

Contents

CHAPTER 1

Introduction to International Finance

■

The Scope of International Finance

The field of international finance is divided into two conceptually distinct, but highly interrelated parts: international financial economics and international financial management. The former is concerned with the causes and effects of financial flows among nations and is built on the application of macroeconomic theory and policy to the world economy. The latter is concerned with how individual economic units, especially nonfinancial multinational firms, cope with the complex financial environment of international business in their efforts to gain profits and realize any other objectives that condition their behavior.

Considerable confusion exists about the scope of international finance because of a tendency to identify the field with one or the other of its component parts. Those who approach the field from the economics side tend to focus on the size and efficiency of international financial markets and their ability to promote the attainment of national and world objectives. Those who approach the field from the financial management side tend to fasten upon the material that seems most relevant to making sound business decisions. Inevitably, matters that are important to one side are relegated to secondary importance or even ignored by those on the other side.

Neither the economist nor the financial manager can afford to be totally ignorant about aspects of international finance that lie outside his or her primary area of interest. Keeping everything else the same, an internationally oriented economist who is intimately familiar with the operations of international financial markets and the managerial strategies of multinational firms is more valuable than one who is not; also, keeping everything else the same, a financial manager for a multinational firm who is intimately familiar with international macroeconomic theory and policy is more valuable than one who is not. It follows, therefore, that there is a common core of subject matter in international finance that should be studied by both those who aspire to become internationally oriented economists and those who aspire to approach international finance from the managerial perspective.

| E X H I B I T | 1.1 | *The Subject Matter of International Finance*

I. *International Macroeconomics*

    A. Data collection and interpretation (balance of payments; balance of international indebtedness; other data on international financial flows; other data on real investment flows; comparative statistics on economic growth, inflation, interest rates, and other important economic variables)

    B. International monetary history (gold standard, Bretton Woods System, experience with managed floating, European Monetary System, International Monetary Fund, evolution of international reserve assets)

    C. Parity relationships (purchasing power parity, interest rate parity, international Fisher effect, expected exchange rate relationship, operation of arbitrage processes)

    D. Theory of payments adjustment and exchange rate determination (Keynesian, absorption, elasticities, monetary, portfolio balance, and equilibrium theories; exchange rate forecasting)

    E. Open economy macroeconomic policy (with fixed exchange rates, with floating exchange rates, exchange control and other restrictions on international capital flows, export financing programs, treatment of foreign investors, policies toward international banking)

    F. International investment (theory and effects, direct investment flows, portfolio investment flows, development financing institutions)

    G. Issues and problems (sovereign debt crisis, international monetary reform, limiting exchange rate instability, financial protectionism, promoting financial integration, achieving uniformity of regulations and practices pertaining to international financial operations)

II. *International Financial Markets*

    A. Foreign exchange market (basic organization; characteristics of spot, forward, futures, and options trading; interbank trading; exchange risk management; details of arbitrage processes; linkages to other markets; details of trading at futures and options exchanges; central bank intervention and government regulation)

    B. International banking (traditional operations, structure of the Eurocurrency market, syndicated lending, managing the sovereign debt problem, government promotion of international banking, securitization of international banking operations, offshore banking operations, government regulation, multinational banking, role of banks in trade finance)

Exhibit 1.1 outlines the subject matter of international finance. It breaks the field down into three parts, not two: international macroeconomics, international financial markets, and international financial management. The markets category is inserted between the other two in recognition of the fact that its subject matter weaves materials from economics and financial management together to produce a mix that is not clearly dominated by either. Taken together, the economics elements of international financial markets and

C. International securities markets (foreign bonds, structure of the Eurobond market, types of international bond issues, role of the managing syndicate, trends in international bond financing, internationalization of stock markets, portfolio considerations)

D. Financial swaps (reasons for their emergence, currency swaps and their uses, interest-rate swaps and their uses, swap pricing, issues and problems, commodity swaps, swaptions)

III. International Financial Management

A. Exchange risk management (types of forex exposure, determining and measuring economic exposure, strategies and techniques of exposure management, accounting and tax considerations, diversifying against the exchange risk)

B. Political risk management (nature of political risks, political risk analysis, potential and actual conflicts, political risk insurance, strategies and techniques of political risk management)

C. Managing direct foreign investment (motivations for direct investment, theory of multinational firms, capital budgeting—its theory and implementation, cost of capital analysis, diversification strategies, determining the financial structure of affiliates)

D. Managing portfolio investment (portfolio theory and the role of diversification, empirical analysis of portfolio strategies and results, implementing derivative instruments into portfolio management, hedging strategies and techniques)

E. Working capital management (short-term financing alternatives, financing foreign trade, current asset management, transfer pricing and intracorporate flows)

F. Long-term management and control (evaluation of results of international operations, alternative control systems, comparative studies of multinationals' long-term performance)

G. International taxation (general principles of international taxation, role of tax treaties, tax havens and multinational companies, effects of international taxation on corporate structures and financing techniques)

the subject matter of international macroeconomics constitute what is called international financial economics.

Whether one's central concern is international macroeconomics or international financial management, there is a common core of subject matter that pertains to international financial markets. These markets fall into four categories: the foreign exchange (forex) market, international banking markets, international securities markets, and financial swaps.

The forex market deals with exchanges of monetary units. These monetary units, known as currencies, are generally national monetary units, such as the U.S. dollar and the pound sterling, but they also include two supranational monetary units, European currency units (Ecus) and special drawing rights (SDRs). In terms of transaction volume, the forex market is by far the world's largest market. Because of this market's size and complexity, a major portion of any textbook on international finance must focus on its activities, which fall into three main categories: spot transactions, forward transactions, and transactions in futures and options contracts.

Included within the scope of international banking markets are the lending and related operations of domestic banks, to the extent that they are international, and the activities of the Eurocurrency market, a bank-driven market that operates on a worldwide basis outside the traditional framework of commercial banking. International bank operations that are related to lending include the acquisition of deposits by banks and the generation of fee income when banks do not actually extend credit, but serve as intermediaries between borrowers and lenders.

International securities markets are primarily concerned with the creation and trading of debt instruments, but they also handle a large volume of business in equities. To some extent, international securities markets are simply extensions of countries' domestic trading in securities to encompass foreign participation. Just as commercial banks developed the Eurocurrency market to operate outside the boundaries of traditional banking, however, investment banking firms have also developed the Eurobond market and the Euroequities market to operate outside the boundaries of traditional securities markets.

Financial swaps make up a market category that has attained major status only since the 1980s. There are two main types of financial swaps: **currency swaps** and **interest-rate swaps.** The former consist of exchanges of currencies that are later reversed, while the latter involve exchanges of interest payments. A party with an existing obligation to make fixed-rate interest payments may agree to make floating-rate interest payments to another party in return for receiving fixed-rate interest payments from this second party (which is likely to have an outstanding floating-rate obligation). Because of the similarities between currency swaps and interest-rate swaps and the fact that both may be combined into a single swap agreement, it is advisable to consider financial swaps to be a distinct international financial markets category. The links between financial swaps and other financial markets are very strong, however. Thus, currency swaps can be viewed as forex market transactions; and the transactions associated with both currency swaps and interest-rate swaps often include bank borrowings or security issues.

Since the end of World War II, there has been a pronounced trend toward greater financial openness. Despite strong resistance from some governments and private interest groups, which have tried to maintain segmented financial markets, this trend has accelerated during the past 2 decades. Associated with it has been an unprecedented wave of innovations in products and practices. Financial instruments that were unusual or virtually unknown a dozen years ago now account for hundreds of billions of dollars of business annually, and sophisticated new techniques of financial management have emerged to challenge the abilities of financial managers to adapt to rapid changes. It is little wonder, therefore, that the field of international finance is wide open for new practitioners who have the requisite knowledge and ability required to master its latest developments.

From its financial markets heartland, international finance fans out to encompass a wide range of subject matter. Because international financial transactions are often intimately connected with real transfers of goods and services across national boundaries, there is considerable contact between international finance and the fields of international trade theory and policy and international marketing. International financial management comes into frequent contract with international accounting and the international dimensions of law. Political science also has important links with international finance. Thus, in one area of international finance, political risk analysis, the talents of political scientists help to evaluate the creditworthiness of foreign borrowers and the investment climate of specific foreign countries. History also has important linkages with international finance, for contemporary financial institutions and practices were shaped by historical trends and developments.

International finance is a highly technical field, one that cannot be mastered without a thorough understanding of macroeconomics, the institutional details of international financial markets, and the principles of international financial management. In acquiring this understanding, it is essential to have an easy familiarity with the mathematics of finance, and it is desirable to have considerable familiarity with statistical methods. Yet for all its quantitative aspects, it is a field in which a broad familiarity with social sciences other than economics is often advantageous. Breadth of background and training is particularly advantageous for those who either have or seek to have broad responsibilities.

Distinguishing Features of International Finance

That international finance is regarded as a distinct field of study reflects the fact that certain features set it apart from other fields within economics and finance. There are at least four of these distinguishing features, and most of the subject matter of international finance is rooted in them.

First and most important, international finance is distinguished by its great emphasis on **exchange risk,** the risk of loss (or gain) from unforeseen changes in exchange rates (the prices at which currencies trade for each other). In domestically oriented economics and finance, this risk is generally ignored because a single national monetary unit customarily serves as the sole or primary medium of exchange within a country. When a party exchanges national currency units for the same national currency units, as happens, for example, when you cash a check or shift your checking account from one bank to another, the units are exchanged on a one-for-one basis. You ordinarily don't have to worry that dollars you obtain will decline in value relative to other dollars before you use them.[1]

When different national currencies are exchanged for each other, however, the situation is quite different. While exchange rates have sometimes been held constant, or fixed, for substantial periods of time, the general pattern today is one of great variability. Indeed, this variability of exchange rates is widely regarded as the most serious international financial problem facing policymakers and corporate managers.

Exchange risk is obviously a problem for those who engage in international transactions, but it may also be a problem for parties that conduct all their business in a domestic currency and have little participation, if any, in international trade and investment. Consider, for example, the case of a U.S. firm that trades and sells used cars. If the Japanese yen declines substantially against the dollar, imports of Japanese-made cars will tend to increase. Since new cars compete against used ones, the firm's profits may well decline. What is true for the car dealer is true for many other U.S. firms that do not participate directly in international trade or engage in international financial transactions. In principle, if exchange rate changes have a significant impact on the profitability of a domestically oriented firm, the firm's managers probably have good reason to hedge the exchange risk, provided they know how the firm's profits are affected by exchange rate variations. Indeed, many U.S. automobile dealers whose primary activity is the sale of cars of U.S. manufacture hedge exchange risk by including imported models among their offerings. Many domestically oriented U.S. firms completely ignore exchange risk, however, either because their managers do not comprehend its nature or because its effects are considered to be either insignificant or too difficult to measure with confidence.

A second distinguishing feature of international finance is its concern with **political risk,** the risk of loss (or gain) from unforeseen government action or other events of political character, such as acts of terrorism. The types of government action may range from imposing mild restraints on firms' operations, such as easily satisfied domestic content requirements on manufactured goods, to the extreme of expropriation without compensation. There is political risk associated with strictly domestic business operations, of course, but the political risk associated with international operations is generally greater than that associated with domestic operations. It is not unusual,

---

[1]There have been exceptions to the general rule that a single currency is not subject to the exchange risk. For example, from 1862 to 1879, U.S. Notes ("greenbacks"), a type of paper money lacking convertibility into gold, circulated at a discount relative to gold coins and paper money with the gold conversion privilege. Furthermore, during the wildcat banking era that preceded the Civil War, it was common for paper money issued by many banks to circulate at various discounts relative to gold and gold-convertible paper money, with the size of the discount being a function of the cost and probability of obtaining gold conversion. Even today, minor departures from the rule of one-for-one exchanges of the national monetary unit sometimes occur. For example, a person cashing a check at a bank where he or she does not have an account may be charged a fee for the service.

however, for the political risk associated with international operations to be *less* than that associated with domestic operations, as is shown by the fact that capital often flows from less developed countries (LDCs) to highly developed countries because of the safety of investments there. In any event, the political risk associated with international operations differs from that associated with domestic operations and is often far more complicated.

A third distinguishing feature of international finance is that it must deal with the fact that macroeconomic fluctuations among nations are less uniform than those among regions of the same nation. Within a nation, economic and financial integration and the ability of the central government to unify and control economic policy mean that economic fluctuations tend to affect all parts of the nation in similar ways. A recession may affect some regions of a nation more severely than others, but all regions will tend to feel its effects. Financial integration assures a high degree of uniformity of interest rates and the rates at which regional money supplies expand or contract. Also, while lesser units of government, i.e., those of states, provinces, counties, etc., may exercise some autonomy in the conduct of fiscal policy, such autonomy is generally very limited.

Internationally, economic integration is generally less complete than domestic economic integration. The ability of national governments to conduct macroeconomic policy with considerable autonomy means that even though economic fluctuations tend to be transmitted from country to country, price levels, interest rates, real income, and employment tend to vary more internationally than they vary interregionally within a country. It is true that economic and financial integration among nations has moved forward rapidly in recent years, but national economies are still generally more integrated than the world economy or the economies of groups of nations, even those like the European Economic Community (EEC) that promote economic integration with each other.

Given that macroeconomic variability is greater internationally than domestically, it follows that the world of international finance differs from that of domestic finance with respect to the risks associated with macroeconomic fluctuations. These risks include the business risk and the credit risk, which may be combined to constitute the commercial risk. Business risk is the risk of loss or gain due to unforeseen changes in general business conditions, and credit risk is the risk of loss or gain due to unforeseen changes in the performance by debtors of their contractual obligations.

These risks are not necessarily greater internationally than domestically. Indeed, to the extent that macroeconomic fluctuations are imperfectly correlated internationally, it may be that these risks can be reduced by diversifying through international financial operations. If, for example, a domestic economy is experiencing a recession, conditions in other countries may be different enough that a domestically based firm that diversifies internationally may have more stable earnings than firms that remain strictly domestic.

The final feature of international finance that distinguishes it from domestic finance is that international finance deals with the consequences of the profound differences among nations' laws, institutionalized business practices, and general cultural environments. Differences in tax systems, for example, have important implications for the volume and locations of international financial activity, as do variations in the restrictions imposed by law and custom on the operational flexibility of internationally oriented firms. There are risks and costs in coping with this cultural, legal, and institutional diversity, but there are also abundant opportunities. The opportunities are sometimes overestimated, of course, but the very fact that investors, lenders, and producers often prefer the known and safe to the unknown and risky means that, for those possessing the right combination of skill and audacity, the returns from international operations often compensate for the risks incurred.

Plan of the Book

The study of international finance leans heavily on economic and financial theory and the application of the techniques of financial analysis, but, like other fields of applied economics and finance, it has an institutional environment whose essentials need to be understood before attempting to apply the relevant theory and techniques. Some readers of this book may be quite familiar with the institutional environment of international finance, but it is probably safe to assume that many are not.

Accordingly, Part I of the book presents an overview of the international monetary system emphasizing its institutional underpinning. Chapter 2 surveys the history of the international monetary system from the heyday of the gold standard from the period 1880–1914 to the present time. It gives particular attention to the period of the Bretton Woods System (from 1944 to 1973) and to developments since the "fixed" exchange rates of that period gave way to the managed floating system that prevails today. Chapter 3 examines the contemporary international monetary scene and considers such matters as the nature and uses of international reserves, the International Monetary Fund, the European Monetary System, and the different types of exchange rate systems that governments employ. Chapter 4 explains the financial statement known as the balance of payments (BOP). It gives particular attention to the BOP of the United States and explores such concerns as the U.S. trade deficit and its financing. It also examines the overall international investment position of the United States and the extent to which it is, as is widely believed, a debtor nation.

Part II is devoted entirely to the forex market. Chapter 5 provides an overview of this market, with emphasis on its organization and the fundamentals of spot forex trading. Chapter 6 deals with the forward market in foreign exchange and explains the nature of interest rate parity and the related process of interest arbitrage. Chapter 7 examines two alternatives to the forward market: the money market, which relies on spot trades, and the market in forex futures, which works through organized exchanges. Chapter 8 deals with forex option contracts, both those that are traded on organized exchanges and those that are arranged informally on the over-the-counter market.

Part III brings in the elements of macroeconomic theory and policy that are most central to international finance, namely those pertaining to the determination of exchange rates. Chapter 9 examines four fundamental relationships that affect exchange rage determination: purchasing power parity, the International Fisher effect, interest rate parity (again), and the expected exchange rate. It also provides a look at exchange rate forecasting. Chapter 10 surveys several theories of exchange rate determination. They are not all center stage, but they illuminate the process of exchange rate determination and continue to influence policymakers. Chapter 11 examines some of the latest ideas on the theory of exchange rate determination and addresses the question of the limits to the desirability of exchange rate flexibility.

Part IV consists of five chapters that deal with international financial markets other than the forex market. Chapter 12 deals with the general features of international banking and the international aspects of domestic banking, such as lending to foreigners and issuing commercial paper on behalf of foreign borrowers. Particular emphasis is given to the internationalization of banking in the United States. In addition, Chapter 12 takes up the sovereign debt problem of the governments of less developed countries and explains how banks have managed to cope with it. Chapter 13 examines the Eurocurrency market, in which banks' deposit and lending operations are denominated in currencies other than those of the countries in which these operations take place. Most international lending by banks takes place in this market. Chapter 14 shifts the focus from international banking to international securities markets. The Eurobond market receives the greatest amount of attention, but consideration is also given to international borrowing through domestic bond markets and international markets in equities. Chapter 15 is concerned with the financing of international trade, which is largely accomplished through banks, but which also is greatly influenced by the export promotion agencies of governments. The final chapter, Chapter 16, is devoted to the subject of internationally oriented financial swaps. The basics of using currency swaps and interest-rate swaps are explained, some attention is given to commodity swaps, and some moderately complicated applications of these remarkably flexible financial tools are presented.

A Few Words of Advice and Encouragement

International finance is an important field and, for many people, an exciting one. A great deal of what happens in the world economically and politically is closely connected with international finance, which makes it an intellectually stimulating field for people with a strong interest in understanding how the world works. Furthermore, it is a field that offers potentially large financial rewards to those who become experts in it. It is not, however, a field that is easy to master. Its subject matter is extensive in scope and can be technically challenging, and it is constantly changing. If it were an easy field to master, the financial rewards for mastery would hardly be as great as they are for many of its practitioners.

This book is fundamentally designed to serve as an introduction to the study of international financial markets for readers with little previous exposure to the details of those markets. The author assumes that while some readers will have taken courses in international economics, many others will not. Accordingly, some of the material, particularly that in Chapters 2, 3, 4, 5, 9, and 10, will be somewhat familiar to readers who have had courses in international economics. Not all of the material in these chapters will have been covered in such a course, however, and much of the material covered is complex enough or new enough that readers who have taken an international economics course should resist the temptation to coast through them.

International finance places great emphasis on fundamental concepts of economics and finance and the application of techniques of financial analysis that are, in some cases, rather sophisticated. Mastering the quantitative aspects of the subject is such a formidable task (and often brings such large financial rewards) that there is a temptation to focus on quantitative matters to the exclusion of the institutional and qualitative. Such an exclusive focus is of questionable desirability, however, because successful career performance often hinges more on familiarity with institutional details and a broad understanding of concepts and strategies than on the ability to handle narrowly applicable tools of analysis. For this reason, even those who aspire to become specialists in the application of particular quantitative skills to international financial operations are well-advised to allocate some time to reading pertinent articles in *The Wall Street Journal,* the *Financial Times, Euromoney,* the *Economist,* and other publications that deal with the fast-moving events of the international financial world. At the other end of the scale, those who aspire to international financial careers that do not involve technical specialties need some familiarity with the quantitative techniques used in international finance. Thus, while you do not necessarily have to be an expert on the mathematics of pricing options to understand how forex options are used, you should have *some* understanding of the fundamentals of option pricing if you intend to make any use of this type of financial instrument.

With the exception of this introductory chapter, a list of questions appears at the end of each chapter. Chapters that contain considerable quantitative material have sample problems for you to work. Be sure that your study plan for the course in which you use this book allows some time for answering the questions and solving the problems.

| APPENDIX | *1.1* |

The Growing Importance of International Finance

An obvious trend in the world today is the growing integration of national economies and financial systems into the world economy. Increasingly business and economic news deals with such matters as exchange rate movements, the performance of European and Japanese stocks, discussions on economic policy among representatives of the leading industrial countries, doing business in Eastern Europe, the push toward free trade among the nations of North America, and the issues raised by the growing presence of foreign firms in the U.S. economy. On college campuses, one finds an expansion of course offerings in international business; a strong tendency (at last!) for macroeconomics textbooks to discard the closed economy model; a growth in international exchange programs and conferences; and a renewed interest in foreign language courses, particularly those with business applications.

There are various ways to demonstrate statistically the expansion of international activity that has been taking place. One such way is illustrated by Exhibit 1.2, which looks at the growth of various stocks and flows pertaining to the internationalization of the U.S. economy from 1972 through 1989 and relates figures for them to nominal or current GNP in those years. The year 1972 was chosen as the starting point because of dramatic developments in 1973 that produced lasting changes in the structure of international trade and the scope and focus of international financial activity. These developments ended the post-World War II set of exchange rate arrangements known as the Bretton Woods System and included the unprecedented increases in oil prices that soon followed its demise.

From 1972 through 1989, the United States experienced an enormous expansion of its international trade, with the result that total exports and total imports both nearly doubled as percentages of GNP. In 1989 total exports were 12 percent of GNP, while total imports were 12.9 percent of GNP. Contributing to this expansion were increases in the relative importance of income from U.S. investment abroad and foreign income from investment in the United States. The growth in the foreign-source income of the United States was particularly large in what is known as portfolio investment, which appears as "other private U.S. investment income" in Exhibit 1.2. Income from direct foreign investment, i.e., investment that provides a substantial element of control, was relatively stagnant, but even it increased slightly relative to GNP. Foreigners' income from investment in the United States grew spectacularly, from only $6.6 billion in 1972 to $128.4 billion in 1989. In 1989, about seven-eighths of this income was derived from portfolio investment ("foreigners' income from other investment in the United States").

The lower half of Exhibit 1.2 presents data on reciprocal claims between the United States and the rest of the world at year's end in 1972 and 1989. With one exception, there were increases relative to GNP in each of the nine

| E X H I B I T | 1.2 | *The Internationalization of the U.S.*
Economy, 1972 to 1989

Flow or end-of-year amount	Amounts (in billions of current dollars)		Percentage of GNP	
	1972	1989	1972	1989
GNP	1,158.0	5,200.8	—	—
Trade flows				
Exports of goods and services	72.4	626.2	6.3	12.0
Imports of goods and services	78.4	672.3	6.8	12.9
U.S. income from direct investment	10.9	53.6	0.9	1.0
Other private U.S. investment income	2.9	68.4	0.3	1.3
Foreigners' income from direct investment in the United States	1.3	14.0	0.1	0.3
Foreigners' income from other investment in the United States	5.3	114.4	0.5	2.2
End-of-year claims				
U.S. claims on foreigners				
Direct investment	94.3	373.4	8.1	7.2
Portfolio holdings of securities				
Bonds	15.9	98.5	1.4	1.9
Stocks	9.0	91.1	0.8	1.8
Claims of U.S. banks	20.7	658.0	1.8	12.7
Foreign claims on the United States				
Direct investment	14.3	400.8	1.2	7.7
Private portfolio holdings of securities				
Bonds	10.9	364.4	0.9	7.0
Stocks	27.8	260.2	2.4	5.0
Claims of foreign official agencies	61.6	337.2	5.3	6.5
Other claims on U.S. banks	22.3[a]	674.8	1.9	13.0

[a]This figure is slightly overstated because of the inclusion of some liquid claims by international agencies and private foreigners that were not on U.S. banks.

Source: *Survey of Currency Business,* various issues.

items shown, and most of the increases were large. The one exception was U.S. direct foreign investment, with relative value declining from 8.1 percent of GNP in 1972 to 7.2 percent of GNP in 1989. This decline is deceptive, for as is explained in Chapter 4, official estimates of U.S. direct foreign investment understate its actual market value by a large margin, and the understatement has increased over time. On the other hand, U.S. portfolio holdings of foreign securities grew very rapidly from 1972 to 1989. Also exhibiting spectacular growth were the reciprocal claims of banks. Exhibit 1.2 indicates that the claims of U.S. banks against foreigners rose from $20.7 billion in 1972 to $658.0 billion in 1989, while the claims of foreigners (mainly banks) against U.S. banks rose from $22.3 billion in 1972 to $674.8 billion in 1989.

The dollar is widely used by foreign governments as an **international reserve asset**, i.e., an asset that can be used to support a currency's value in the forex market. The volume of dollar assets held by foreign governments tends, over time, to mirror the growth in the overall volume of international payments for the world as a whole. At the end of 1972, however, the volume of dollars held by foreign governments exceeded what they desired to hold because some of these governments had acquired large amounts of dollars in order to prevent their currencies from rising against the dollar. Moreover, from 1972 to 1989, such currencies as the mark and the yen gained greatly in importance as international reserve assets. These two factors worked to slow the growth in foreign governments' demand for the dollar as a reserve asset, yet Exhibit 1.2 shows that their dollar holdings went from $61.6 billion in 1972 to $337.2 billion in 1989, which was enough to raise them from 5.3 percent of U.S. GNP in 1972 to 6.5 percent of U.S. GNP in 1989. An implication of this growth is that the volume of international transactions must surely have grown considerably more rapidly than nominal U.S. GNP. Incidentally, in the exhibit the dollar claims of foreign governments are excluded from the other categories of foreign claims on the United States.

Exhibit 1.2 contains no data on the volume of forex transactions, the volume of internationally oriented financial swaps, or numerous other international transactions with either spectacular or impressive growth since 1972. Data on such transactions appear elsewhere in this book. The general impression conveyed by such data is that international financial transactions have grown much more rapidly than the underlying "real" flows of goods and assets on which international financial transactions are based. Some idea of the magnitude of the growth of international financial transactions is provided by the large increases in the reciprocal claims of banks shown in Exhibit 1.2.

PART 1

The International
Monetary System

■

| CHAPTER | *2* |

The Historical Background

| CHAPTER | *3* |

The Contemporary International Monetary System

| CHAPTER | *4* |

The Measurement of International
Trade and Investment

The Historical Background

■

The various arrangements that have been devised to organize the environment in which financial flows among nations occur are collectively known as the international monetary system. This system has evolved over the course of centuries, and it is impossible to understand its present structure without some familiarity with this evolution. Accordingly, we shall focus on that process in this chapter.

Although the contemporary international monetary system is the product of long experience, we need go back no further than the 1870s to begin our survey, for at that time the world could truly be said to have developed an international gold standard. The gold standard passed from the scene in the 1930s, but gold has continued to play a role in international monetary affairs. Moreover, many knowledgeable people believe that some features of the gold standard were superior to what we have today. For this reason, the world's experience with the gold standard is relevant to the subject of international monetary reform.

After a brief period of monetary autarky, when governments conducted monetary policy independently of each other, the gold standard gave way to the Bretton Woods System shortly after World War II. This system, which was designed to achieve a high degree of exchange rate stability without the gold standard's disadvantages, remained fundamentally intact until 1971 when the U.S. government was forced to abandon its long-standing policy of selling gold to foreign governments at a fixed price. From late 1971 until early 1973, governments attempted to retain the Bretton Woods System in slightly modified form, but they abandoned the effort in the face of continued speculative pressure. This chapter records the history of the Bretton Woods System and the failed attempt to retain it. In Chapter 3, we shall examine the international monetary system as it has evolved since 1973.

The Gold Standard

During most of the world's history, money has consisted of commodities, among which gold and silver have been preeminent. During the nineteenth century, paper money and bank deposits developed rapidly as substitutes for such "hard money," but their acceptability was long conditioned on convertibility into gold or silver at fixed prices maintained by governments. Although gold has always commanded a higher price than silver, during much of the nineteenth century its market price tended to decline relative to that of silver. In general, however, governments were reluctant to respond to gold's growing relative abundance by lowering the price, known as the **mint price,** at which they bought it. As a result, gold tended to flow into the hands of governments, and the monetary role of silver diminished. When the market price of silver fell in the last quarter of the century, governments were generally unwilling to make their paper money convertible into silver at fixed prices out of fear of inflation and the possible consequences of undermining the monetary role of gold.

By the late 1870s, most leading nations had formally adopted the gold standard; because so many governments did so, it is customary to say that the world was at that time on an *international* gold standard. This system remained in effect until the outbreak of World War I. The gold standard was restored in a much weaker form for a brief interval in the 1920s and 1930s, but it could not weather the Great Depression of the 1930s.

The Operation of the Gold Standard

The gold standard had three fundamental characteristics for countries that were full participants in it. First, the government of each such country defined its national monetary unit in terms of gold. Second, each government stood ready to buy and sell gold in unlimited quantities at the price inferred from the definition of its monetary unit. Third, the government allowed a free private gold market in which firms and individuals could export or import gold as they saw fit. In addition, especially before World War I, the governments of gold standard countries customarily minted coins with a gold content equal in value to their monetary values. The countries minting and circulating such coins were said to be on the **gold coin standard.** Some governments chose, however, to refrain from minting gold coins and instead adopted the **gold bullion standard.**

Under either the gold coin standard or the gold bullion standard, governments routinely issued paper money that was fully convertible into gold on demand. In turn, commercial banks generally allowed their deposit liabilities and any paper money that they issued to be converted on demand into gold or gold-convertible paper money issued by governments. In effect, therefore, the entire national money supply of a gold standard country was gold-convertible.

The total amount of money convertible either directly or indirectly into gold typically far exceeded the amount of a government's gold holdings (reserves). This meant that governments were under pressure to maintain confidence in their monetary integrity.

The Gold Points Why the gold standard resulted in fixed exchange rates is shown by the following example. From 1837 until 1934, the dollar was defined in terms of gold to establish an official gold price of $20.672 per ounce. The

U.S. government was obligated to exchange gold coins or gold bullion at this price for gold-convertible paper money.[1] Because commercial banks stood ready to convert their demand deposit liabilities and their own paper money issues (bank notes) into gold-convertible paper money and gold coins or gold bullion, the entire money supply of the United States was effectively gold-convertible. Arbitrage assured that the free market price of gold was virtually equal to the official price.

During this same period, the British government defined the pound to establish an official gold price of £4.248 per ounce. The ratio between the two official prices, $20.672/£4.248 = $4.866/£, established the mint parity between the two currencies; and the mint parity defined the currencies' approximate exchange rate.

Assume that the cost of shipping gold across the Atlantic averaged $0.020 for the amount of gold in a British pound (approximately as it did around 1931). If the exchange rate rose above $4.886/£ in New York, arbitrage became profitable when gold would be purchased in the United States, shipped to England, and exchanged for pounds. The pounds would then be exchanged for dollars, providing a net profit. The exchange rate of approximately $4.89/£ would thus serve as the gold export point, the price above which it became profitable to export gold from the United States. Similarly, if the exchange rate in New York dipped below $4.846/£, it became profitable to ship gold from England to the United States. The exchange rate of approximately $4.85/£ would thus serve as the gold import point.

The dollar/pound exchange rate could vary by a small amount from the mint parity rate of approximately $4.87/£; so gold standard exchange rates were not completely fixed. The range of possible variation was so small, however, that it is customary to regard the gold standard as a fixed exchange rate system. Incidentally, the fixed exchange rate label is also commonly applied to the Bretton Woods System, which allowed greater exchange rate flexibility than the gold standard.

The Adjustment Mechanism   The gold standard would not have lasted as long as it did had there been large and persistent one-way gold flows among the participating nations. On some occasions, as during the American Civil War, a participating country was forced to suspend the gold convertibility of its currency, but in only a few instances did a gold standard government severely restrict or eliminate the right of individuals to export gold. The United Kingdom, which was the world's dominant financial power during the nineteenth century, held gold reserves that were but a small fraction of the potential claims against them, and yet it remained firmly on gold from 1821

---

[1]During the Civil War, the U.S. government suspended the convertibility of paper money into gold except for a relatively minor type of money known as gold certificates. The Civil War ended in 1865, but the full convertibility of paper money into gold was not resumed until 1879 because the U.S. government opted to deflate the price level until gold could be made convertible at the price of $20.672 per ounce instead of opting to increase gold's official price.

until the outbreak of World War I in 1914. Evidently, something about the gold standard's operation prevented large and persistent gold outflows. This factor, the **gold standard adjustment mechanism,** worked through changes in money supplies and interest rates that occurred in response to international gold flows.

When a gold-standard country lost or gained gold, its national money supply tended to adjust automatically either downward or upward since the changes in gold holdings directly affected monetary reserves. A change in money supply, in turn, tended to affect interest rates. To reinforce these automatic effects, exchange rate speculation tended to stabilize exchange rates and governments often accelerated adjustments through their monetary policy.

A government gained or lost gold when the exchange rate between its currency and another currency passed the gold import or export points in response to a large enough gap between the quantity of foreign exchange demanded and the quantity supplied at those points. The resulting gold flow would tend to equate the exchange rate with either its gold export or gold import point. As long as the gap between supply and demand existed, however, the exchange rate would tend to keep changing so as to induce a gold flow. In principle, therefore, a gold-losing country would eventually exhaust its gold reserves unless something happened to correct the imbalance between supply and demand.

Exhibit 2.1 provides a greatly simplified illustration of a gold-losing situation in the United States. The graph employs the assumptions that the dollar/pound exchange rate is a proxy for the exchange rates of the dollar with other currencies, and that the gold export point coincides with the mint parity exchange rate, i.e., gold exports are costless.

Exhibit 2.1 also assumes that $4.87/£ is the mint parity exchange rate and that the demand for and the supply of foreign exchange (from the U.S. perspective) are originally D_1 and S_1, respectively. Given D_1 and S_1, the equilibrium exchange rate is $4.92/£, the exchange rate that would tend to hold in the absence of gold flows. Gold would be exported, however, in sufficient volume to keep the exchange rate at $4.87/£. The gap between D_1 and S_1 at the exchange rate of $4.87/£, equal to the distance AB, measures the **balance-of-payments deficit** of the United States, the amount by which the demand for foreign exchange exceeds its supply at the fixed exchange rate $4.87/£. Unless something happens to correct this deficit, it will eventually exhaust the gold reserves of the U.S. government, which must sell an amount of gold equal to the balance-of-payments deficit in order to prevent the free market price of gold from rising.

Because the U.S. money supply is, it is assumed, a function of its monetary gold stock, the U.S. money supply contracts as gold flows out. Simultaneously, the United Kingdom's money supply increases, since it depends on the U.K. monetary gold stock. Since price levels are assumed to vary directly with changes in money supplies, the U.S. price level tends to decline and the United Kingdom's price level tends to rise. These price level changes boost U.S. exports and reduce U.S. imports. Correspondingly, the U.S. demand for foreign exchange decreases from D_1 to D_2, while the U.S. supply of foreign

| E X H I B I T | 2.1 | *Balance-of-Payments Adjustment*
                           under the Gold Standard

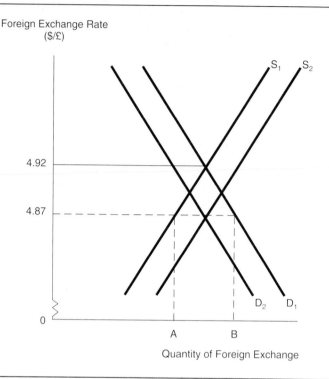

Foreign Exchange Rate
($/£)

Quantity of Foreign Exchange

exchange increases from S_1 to S_2. Together, these shifts produce a new equilibrium at the mint parity exchange rate. The U.S. economy is thus forced to adjust to the exchange rate.

The shifts in the demand and supply curves of Exhibit 2.1 can be explained in terms of capital flows as well as trade flows. The prevailing free-market ideology at the time kept capital flows much less restricted during the years of the gold standard than they became later under the onslaught of nationalism and socialism. Even though the technologies of communication and information processing were in their infancy by comparison with today, many savers and investors were interested in obtaining high returns from exchange rate changes and a well-developed network of financial intermediaries (largely British) were eager to accommodate them. Accordingly, international capital flows were of considerable importance during the gold standard period, and they responded to interest rate differentials, though hardly with the lightning-like speed that we take for granted today.

The gold flows and money supply changes associated with balance-of-payments disequilibria tended to cause interest rate changes that brought capital flows into the adjustment process. Referring to Exhibit 2.1, the *real* interest rate of the United States would tend to increase as gold flowed out, because the lower money supply would tend to reduce the supply of loanable funds. This increase, however, might not increase the *nominal* interest rate of the United States, which approximately equals the real interest rate plus the expected inflation rate, because the inflation premium incorporated into the nominal rate would tend to decrease. Simultaneously, the real interest rate of the United Kingdom would tend to decline as its money supply expanded. These real interest rate changes would tend to induce a flow of capital from the United Kingdom to the United States and to reduce the outflow of capital from the United States to the United Kingdom. In the United States, therefore, the supply of foreign exchange would tend to increase and the demand for foreign exchange would tend to decrease. Thus, as capital flows adjusted to the interest rate changes, they would contribute to the adjustment shown in Exhibit 2.1 just as the changes in trade flows did.

A possible objection to this line of analysis is that in a world of fixed exchange rates, it is nominal interest rate changes, not real interest changes, that govern international capital flows. In the case at hand, for example, a British investor considering the purchase of U.S. assets who intended to eventually convert any such purchase back into pounds would be guided by the nominal U.S. interest rate, not the real rate, in making the investment decision. As explained in the last paragraph, however, any increase in the nominal U.S. interest rate would also be an increase in the real rate. Moreover, even if the nominal U.S. interest rate failed to rise, the fall in the real interest rate of the United Kingdom associated with the inflow of gold would tip the scales in favor of purchasing U.S. assets. It seems clear, therefore, that the interest rate changes that contributed to the gold standard adjustment mechanism should be viewed as real interest changes, not nominal interest rate changes.

Because capital flows tended, even in gold standard days, to adjust more rapidly to interest rate changes than trade flows adjusted to price level changes, governments could minimize gold flows and changes in production patterns associated with changes in international trade by accelerating the adjustment process through appropriate monetary measures. For example, the government of a gold-losing country could actively apply a tight money policy to rapidly increase the real interest rate.

The adjustment process also relied on speculation, which tended to stabilize exchange rates under the gold standard. As long as potential speculators were convinced that a gold-losing country could maintain the mint parity of its currency, it made sense for them to buy that currency since they could anticipate that its price would not fall any further below its gold export point and would probably tend to move back toward the mint parity. Speculation thus tended to increase the supply of foreign exchange in the gold-losing country.

The Demise of the Gold Standard

The outbreak of war in August 1914 led immediately to the general suspension of gold convertibility of national currencies. Among the major belligerents, only the United States maintained the gold standard essentially intact. When World War I ended, the eventual restoration of the international gold standard was taken for granted, but restoration was impeded by large increases in national money supplies since 1914. For restoration to occur, therefore, either nations had to deflate their price levels, as the United States had done after the Civil War, or else they had to reduce the gold content of their monetary units, an action known as **devaluation.** Deflation encountered strong political resistance in countries where it was technically feasible, while in those countries where price inflation had rendered devaluation totally out of the question, there was uncertainty about its proper extent. As a result, many exchange rates were allowed to fluctuate subject to government controls and central bank intervention, a situation known as **floating exchange rates.**

The Restored Gold Standard of the 1920s   The key currency involved in the attempt to restore the international gold standard was the pound sterling, which returned to gold in 1925 at the old mint parity exchange rate of $4.87/£. This proved to be a great mistake. Because the United Kingdom had experienced considerably more inflation than the United States, and because most of Britain's foreign investments had been liquidated in the course of financing the war, drastically reducing an important flow of forex earnings, the return to gold at $4.87/£ subjected Britain to severe deflationary pressure. Britain's gold reserves were very small relative to the potential claims against them, including claims from a large volume of pounds held by governments that had adopted the **gold exchange standard,** in which a currency that was not itself gold-convertible was exchangeable at a fixed price for one that was gold-convertible.

The British government's decision to come back to $4.87/£ did not lack plausibility. Previously, the British economy had adjusted quickly to a deflationary monetary policy without grave economic or political consequences. Further, many Britons shared the feeling of Winston Churchill, Chancellor of the Exchequer (the British finance minister), that for London to avoid being displaced by New York as the world's greatest financial center, it was essential to maintain the pound's exchange value. Moreover, maintaining the pound had symbolic importance for the preservation of the British Empire. It was understood that Britain would initially tend to incur balance-of-payments deficits, but it was hoped that American capital, lured by attractive interest rates and confidence in the pound, would provide sufficient financing to stabilize the pound at $4.87/£ until the adjustment process could be completed.

There were vigorous critics of the British government's decision, most notably John Maynard Keynes, who had earlier denounced the gold standard as a "barbarous relic" and who now proclaimed that the government's slavish adherence to outmoded ideas would lead to disaster.[2] Events proved Keynes to be correct. Both prices and wages proved resistant to the deflationary pressure

---

[2]John Maynard Keynes, *The Economic Consequences of Mr. Churchill* (London: Macmillan, 1925). The reference to the gold standard as a "barbarous relic" is found in Keynes's *Tract on Monetary Reform* (London: Macmillan, 1924), p. 138.

produced by the pound's overvaluation. As a result, real output and employment in Britain declined. Nevertheless, after more than 60 years since the United Kingdom's return to gold, some are not yet convinced that the gold standard is irrelevant to the contemporary scene. To the contrary, recent exchange rate instability has sparked renewed interest in what Keynes called a "barbarous relic."

The pound's overvaluation was not the only major problem of the restored gold standard. Other problems included the failure of the United States to act responsibly, the reparation payments imposed on Germany by the victorious Allies, the undervaluation of the French franc, and a general decrease in nations' willingness and ability to rely on the gold standard adjustment mechanism.

Unlike most European nations, the United States emerged from World War I with a strong and expanding economy. Together the government and the private sector in the United States provided a large volume of loans to the Allies during the war, and the outflow of U.S. capital continued when the war ended. Unfortunately, at the very moment when the United States strode forward as the world's economic colossus, its people and leadership turned their thoughts inward. Rather than encourage international trade, as suited the creditor status of the United States, the U.S. Congress increased tariffs during the 1920s and ultimately, in 1930, passed the infamous Smoot–Hawley Tariff Act. This swing toward protectionism occurred even though the United States had a trade surplus, i.e., exports exceeded imports of goods and services. Under the circumstances, governments that were indebted to the United States could hardly reduce their overall dollar indebtedness since it was difficult for *them* to develop trade surpluses. During most of the 1920s, the debtor nations effectively financed the U.S. trade surplus by borrowing dollars from the U.S. private sector and spending them for imports. Their borrowings also allowed them to meet existing debt service obligations.

The result was the erection of a financial house of cards whose collapse was certain should the United States ever scale down its capital outflows to the rest of the world. This occurred with the U.S. stock market boom of 1928 to 1929, which siphoned away dollars that would otherwise have been available for international loans and investments. Once the stock boom began, only massive international lending by the U.S. government could have preserved the fixed exchange rates of the restored gold standard; such lending was politically out of the question.

The German reparations problem stemmed from the Treaty of Versailles in 1919, which imposed punitive damages on Germany over the opposition of President Woodrow Wilson.[3] The total amount of the reparations was set in 1921 at abut $33 billion, with payment to be made over a long period. It is

---

[3]There was, unfortunately, historical precedent for this action. The victorious Germans had imposed (much smaller) reparations payments on France after the Franco–Prussian War of 1870 as the price for getting the occupying Prussian army to leave France. It is hardly surprising, therefore, that France insisted on obtaining reparations from Germany after World War I.

doubtful that Germany could have developed trade surpluses large enough to finance the reparations payments in any event, but the weak Weimar Republic government of a demoralized Germany lacked the strength and the will to develop them. For a while, Germany kept up a pretense of meeting its reparations obligations by borrowing internationally from private sources. These funds came largely from the British, who, in turn, borrowed heavily from the United States. When the Americans shut off the credit spigot in the late 1920s, however, this financing channel dried up and Germany defaulted on its obligations. When the Great Depression began in 1929, any hope that remained for their partial resumption evaporated. The nations that were to have received reparations payments offset their losses in part by defaulting on obligations due to the U.S. government. Americans reacted to these developments by becoming even more isolationist than before.

The French promoted the gold standard's collapse by returning to gold in 1928 with a greatly undervalued franc. Whether the undervaluation was deliberate is questionable, but in any event it gave France a sizable trade surplus and an illusion of prosperity based on an export boom. Rather than take the necessary steps to correct the undervaluation, the French government elected to add to its gold holdings, largely at British expense. The loss of British gold reserves further undermined confidence in the pound sterling.

In general, governments were less willing after World War I than before to abide by what had become known as the gold standard's **rules of the game.** They were increasingly reluctant to allow the gold standard adjustment mechanism to operate. Moreover, prices and wages were less flexible after World War I than they had been a few decades earlier, which meant that the adjustment mechanism would not have worked smoothly even if governments had been willing to allow it to operate freely. In the years immediately after the war, there was a general shift of political power from society's upper classes to other social groups who were profoundly disillusioned with the old order. To many, the gold standard was not only a "barbarous relic" that inhibited the proper conduct of macroeconomic policy, but an instrument of oppression by the creditor class. Politically and psychologically, the gold standard had lost the social support that was essential to its survival.

The Last Days of the Gold Standard   The gold standard did not collapse immediately with the onset of the Great Depression, but by the end of 1931 its days were clearly numbered. In that year, a wave of bank failures began in Austria and spread to Germany, starting a panic that forced the United Kingdom off gold. The United States abandoned the gold standard de facto in 1933 and de jure in 1934. A few countries, most notably France, struggled on with the gold standard a bit longer, but by 1937 no major country allowed its citizens to convert domestic paper money into gold at a fixed price.

Although the international gold standard came to an end in the 1930s, governments continued using gold as an international reserve asset, relying on their gold holdings to support their currencies in the forex market. Thus, if the exchange value of a country's currency began to decline, its government could support the currency by selling gold for dollars and using the dollars to buy the currency. Intervention to support a currency usually involved the purchase of dollars with gold because the dollar was the world's leading currency and because the U.S. government continued buying gold at a fixed price. That price, however, was no longer $20.672 per ounce.

In the Gold Reserve Act of 1934, the U.S. government redefined the dollar to raise the official price of gold to $35 per ounce. At this price, the U.S. government committed itself to buy gold in unlimited amounts from all suppliers and to sell gold to foreign *governments*. Private trading of gold in the United States was abolished, as was the domestic convertibility of paper money into gold. Nevertheless, the act preserved a cosmetic linkage between the U.S. money supply and the government's gold holdings by requiring the Federal Reserve Banks to hold specified percentages of gold certificates to back their paper money issues and deposit liabilities to banks. This requirement preserved a theoretical link between the government's gold holdings and the U.S. money supply because: (1) the M1 money supply consisted of currency in circulation and the demand deposit liabilities of commercial banks; (2) most currency was issued by the Federal Reserve Banks; and (3) the deposits of commercial banks with the Federal Reserve Banks were the reserves used by the member banks of the Federal Reserve System in determining the volume of their deposit liabilities. The gold certificates, which are still used, were warehouse receipts giving the Federal Reserve Banks title to gold held by the U.S. Treasury, but they could not be converted into gold or sold.[4]

In practice, the gold certificate reserve requirement was not allowed to restrict the Fed's expansion of the money supply. In the 1960s, when the combination of gold outflows and money supply expansion threatened to exhaust the Fed's excess reserves of gold certificates, the reserve requirement was quietly eliminated. On the other hand, the commitment of the U.S. government to buy and sell gold at a fixed price proved to be extremely important, for it meant that gold would continue to play a major role in the international monetary system.

From the End of the Gold Standard to Bretton Woods

Since governments continued to define their monetary units in terms of gold, the increase in the U.S. government's gold price amounted to a devaluation of the dollar relative to other currencies. The dollar was devalued even though it remained a strong currency in the erroneous belief that increasing the price of gold would somehow bring about an approximately proportionate increase in the U.S. price level and promote economic recovery. Predictably, other nations responded by devaluing their own currencies, raising trade barriers, and restricting international payments. However, these actions did not prevent a

---

[4]The gold certificates held by the Federal Reserve Banks are not the same thing as a type of paper money of the same name which circulated before the passage of the Gold Reserve Act. The Federal Reserve Banks receive gold certificates from the Treasury when the Treasury sells them the title to gold in exchange for deposit credit.

massive transfer of gold to the United States, whose gold reserves rose from $6.8 billion immediately after the dollar's devaluation to $21.9 billion by the end of 1940.[5]

In part, this "golden avalanche" reflected growing political turmoil in Europe and Asia. In any event, the U.S. government acquired most of the world's monetary gold. Ironically, in spending billions of dollars to obtain its treasure, the government sacrificed opportunities for domestic spending that would have contributed far more to economic recovery.

After passing the Gold Reserve Act, the U.S. government began to reverse its pattern of irresponsible behavior. Its first important step toward international economic rationality was the enactment of the Reciprocal Trade Agreements Act in 1934, which authorized the president to lower tariffs in exchange for tariff reductions by other countries. In 1936, the governments of Britain, France, and the United States entered into the Tripartite Agreement, which provided for stable exchange rates among their currencies, mutual assistance to maintain them, and relaxed restrictions on international trade and payments. The agreement was not entirely successful, but it began a movement toward international monetary reform.

Despite some encouraging developments beginning in 1934, the general picture during the 1930s was one of chaos. International trade had shrunk drastically since the 1920s, and international capital flows had become a trickle. Many governments sought to stabilize their currencies against the dollar, the pound, or even the French franc, but this was difficult without access to sizable borrowings of foreign exchange. Devaluations were frequent and uncoordinated, and restrictions on international payments were widespread. While the gold standard may have been a "barbarous relic," the days when it reigned supreme looked idyllic by comparison with what followed it.

The Bretton Woods System

Tragedy often draws people together, and the catastrophic events of the years 1929 through 1945 propelled nations and their leaders to accept the ideal of international economic cooperation far more willingly than ever before. Well before the end of World War II, the leaders of the nations allied against the Axis powers of Germany and Japan began planning for the reconstruction of Europe and Asia. In the summer of 1944, delegates from more than 40 nations met at a famous resort hotel in Bretton Woods, New Hampshire to work out arrangements that would expand international trade, promote international capital flows, and contribute to monetary stability. Because the International Monetary Fund (IMF) and the monetary arrangements under its supervision grew out of this conference, the monetary system that subsequently emerged is

---

[5]Lawrence Smith, *Money, Credit, and Public Policy* (Boston: Houghton Mifflin, 1959), p. 286.

known as the Bretton Woods System.[6] This system operated from 1946 until 1973, and much of its structure has been retained. Accordingly, it is essential to know something about it to understand the contemporary international monetary system.

The Bretton Woods Conference

Although many nations were represented at Bretton Woods, only two proposals for international monetary reform received serious attention there. These were the British plan, which was largely the brainchild of John Maynard Keynes, head of the British delegation, and the plan of the U.S. Treasury's delegation, headed by Harry Dexter White. The British plan derived support from the immense prestige of Keynes, while the American plan's support rested primarily on the immense political and economic power of the United States. Fundamentally, it can be argued, power triumphed over intellect.

There was general agreement that restoring the gold standard was out of the question, that exchange rates should be basically stable, that governments needed access to credits in convertible currencies if they were to stabilize exchange rates, and that governments should make major adjustments in exchange rates only after consultation with other countries. On specifics, however, opinion was divided. The British wanted a reduced role for gold, more exchange rate flexibility than had existed with the gold standard, a large pool of lendable resources at the disposal of a proposed international monetary organization, and acceptance of the principle that the burden of correcting payment disequilibria should be shared by both surplus countries and deficit countries. The Americans favored a major role for gold, highly stable exchange rates, a small pool of lendable resources, and the principle that the burden of adjustment to payment imbalances should fall primarily on deficit countries.

The differences in the American and British positions reflected different perceptions about the desired degree of government control over the world economy and differences in the two nations' economic positions. While Keynes argued that gold's monetary role should be eliminated, the U.S. government, which held most of the world's monetary gold, contended that gold should have an important role. Keynes proposed the creation of a new type of international reserve asset called "bancor" that would be added as needed to governments' reserve asset holdings by a new international agency that would serve as a central bank for central banks. Bancor would be used in basically the same ways as commercial banks used their reserve deposits with central banks,

---

[6]The Bretton Woods Conference also led to the establishment of the International Bank for Reconstruction and Development (World Bank), which has long played a major role in development financing. In addition, the conference called for the establishment of the International Trade Organization (ITO). The ITO never materialized, primarily because the U.S. Senate refused to ratify the agreement providing for it. Subsequently, however, an informal trade organization emerged, the General Agreement on Tariffs and Trade (GATT), which promotes the expansion of international trade through the reciprocal reduction of trade barriers.

and were to be created in much the same manner as such domestic reserve assets. Congressional reaction to the bancor proposal led to its outright rejection by the Treasury delegation. Congress could not accept the idea of diminishing the role of an asset the United States owned in abundance, and it had doubts that a *world* central bank could withstand pressure from financially weak nations to expand the quantity of bancor at a rate that would foster inflation.

In the American view, nations with severe international financial problems might deserve sympathy and even some aid, but they should not be allowed to escape the discipline of the marketplace and the consequences of profligate behavior. As a general rule, American officials believed, nations that accumulated international reserves by developing balance-of-payments surpluses in open competition with other nations were more efficient and more virtuous than nations with chronic balance-of-payments deficits. Why, then, punish virtue by making nations with surpluses share the burden of bailing out nations whose problems arose from their own behavior?

The plan for monetary reform that emerged from Bretton Woods was basically in line with the U.S. position, with some concessions to the British position in the spirit of compromise. Ironically, 20 years later when the United States appeared to have developed a chronic balance-of-payments deficit, its government adopted a position on international monetary reform that remarkably resembled Keynes's proposals of 1944.

The Structure of the Bretton Woods System

The Bretton Woods delegates endorsed an "adjustable peg" system in which a country could make a major change in exchange rates, but only in response to a "fundamental disequilibrium" and after consultation with the IMF. The IMF never formally explained what made a disequilibrium fundamental, but the concept clearly encompassed persistent payment imbalances whose correction without exchange rate adjustments would have entailed excessive costs.

Each member nation of the IMF set a par value for its currency as an amount of its currency per dollar or ounce of gold. Since the U.S. government continued to sell gold to other governments at $35 per ounce, a par value referenced to gold was equivalent to one referenced to the dollar. Member governments were obligated to keep the market values of their currencies within 1 percent of par value. Changes in par values were to occur after consultation with the IMF, but changes in par value were permissible without IMF approval as long as net changes did not exceed 10 percent of the initial par values. Any nation violating this 10 percent rule could be denied access to IMF credit.

The IMF's lendable resources were composed mainly of paid subscriptions based on members' quotas, which were assigned to member governments in accordance with their countries' economic importance. Quotas were payable 25 percent in gold or dollars and 75 percent in the currencies of the subscribing governments. Because quota payments were largely in inconvertible currencies, the total lendable resources at the Fund's disposal when it began operating (in 1947) fell well short of the aggregate quota amount of $8 billion.

The first 25 percent of a quota, known originally as the "gold tranche," was treated as part of the contributing government's reserves because it could be borrowed back at any time. Beyond this amount, borrowings were to be contingent on the ability of the borrowing government to satisfy the IMF's lending criteria. All loans were to be repaid within 3 to 5 years from the time they were disbursed.

When borrowing from the IMF, a government was required to turn over to the fund an amount of its currency equal in value to the amount borrowed. For this reason, borrowings from the IMF have always been officially termed "purchases." Until the 1970s, purchases normally could not exceed 25 percent of a borrower's quota during a 12-month period, and the cumulative total of purchases could not exceed the point at which the IMF's holdings of the borrower's currency equalled 200 percent of its quota.

The agreement establishing the IMF provided for a code of forex practices to be administered by the Fund. The code was designed to promote exchange rate stability while simultaneously restraining governments from interfering with forex transactions. The rules for maintaining exchange rates were part of the code. In general, the code encouraged members to avoid exchange controls on transactions in goods and services and to abjure discriminatory forex practices. It was recognized, however, that exchange controls on *capital* transactions might sometimes be essential to the preservation of exchange rate stability.

When the IMF began operating, currency convertibility was much more a dream than a reality. Realistically, therefore, the Fund was unable to require all of its members to make their currencies convertible. Article XIV of the IMF agreement provided that existing exchange controls on transactions in goods and services could be retained during an indefinite transition period and that these restrictions could be adapted to changing economic circumstances. In practice, Article XIV has been interpreted to allow ongoing transition periods for many less developed countries. In other words, while exchange controls on international trade remain an important feature of the international monetary system, among developed countries they are largely confined to capital transactions, and even these are generally not comprehensive.

The Operation of the Bretton Woods System to 1967

The Bretton Woods System operated without major structural changes from 1947 until 1971. During that time, international trade expanded in real terms at a faster rate than world output; the currencies of many nations, particularly those of developed countries, became convertible; international financial integration made enormous strides; and changes in par value exchange rates among leading currencies were few. Much criticism has targeted the system, and it was, no doubt, defective in important respects, but it is difficult to make a really convincing case that it was a failure.

Ironically, the Bretton Woods System was undermined by success. Its fundamental problem was that, as international financial integration progressed, maintaining stable exchange rates required governments to sacrifice more and more monetary autonomy. While governments of financially powerful nations often exhibited a willingness to cooperate economically, they strongly resisted the idea of subordinating domestic monetary policy to the goal of preserving exchange rate stability. With the benefit of hindsight, it is clear that this reluctance assured the system's eventual failure.

The Bretton Woods System would probably have lasted a little longer than it did had it not been so dependent on a gold-convertible U.S. dollar. Its operation required increases in international reserves over time, but these increases required increasing the quantity of dollars held by foreign governments. At some point, it was inevitable that governments' accumulation of dollars would exceed the gold reserves of the U.S. government and lead to a crisis that the system could not manage.

Gold and the Dollar   In the first few years of its existence, the IMF's resources were insufficient for it to exercise much influence over the course of events. Fortunately, the severe dollar shortage that resulted from World War II and persisted for about a decade after the war's end was alleviated by rapid economic growth in many countries, the expansion of U.S. imports, and large capital outflows from the United States. These capital outflows included unprecedented amounts of foreign aid loans and grants from the U.S. government. As the dollars flowed out from the United States, other countries rapidly expanded their imports, and their central banks simultaneously added to their dollar reserves.

Although the dollar holdings of central banks increased, governments still required access to dependable sources of credit to finance balance-of-payments deficits if they were to allow their currencies to become freely convertible at fixed exchange rates. By the middle of the 1950s, the need for balance-of-payments financing was increasingly being met by the IMF, which moved in to fill the partial vacuum that developed as the United States scaled down its foreign aid programs. Nevertheless, most western European governments retained extensive exchange controls for more than a dozen years after World War II ended (probably longer than necessary), and their currencies were not made generally convertible for foreigners until December 1958. General convertibility for western European residents was delayed until 1961, and Japan did not allow the yen to become convertible until 1964.

Once currency convertibility was established in western Europe, it was evident that the dollar shortage had ended among developed countries. In fact, the perception quickly developed that the central problem of the Bretton Woods System was to prevent a dollar glut. Gold continued serving as a reserve asset, but the combination of its fixed price and rising production costs caused by creeping inflation led to declines in the annual increments to the world's gold stock. Moreover, much of the addition to that stock disappeared into private hands.

Since governments' needs for additional reserves were not being satisfied by gold, they had to rely more heavily on convertible currencies as reserve assets. There were, however, only two currencies that could be widely used as reserve assets—the dollar and the pound sterling—and the postwar weaknesses of the latter discouraged reliance on it. The role of meeting govern-

| EXHIBIT | 2.2 | *International Reserves: 1948 to 1970*
(in Billions of U.S. Dollars)

End of Year	Gold (Valued at $35 per Ounce)	Other Reserves	Total Reserves	Percentage Change in Total Reserves	Gold as a Percentage of Total Reserves
1948	34.5	15.0	49.5	—	69.7%
1950	35.3	15.0	50.3	1.6%	70.2
1952	35.8	16.0	51.8	3.0	69.1
1954	36.9	18.5	55.4	6.9	66.6
1956	38.1	20.1	58.2	5.1	65.5
1958	38.0	19.6	57.6	−1.0	66.0
1960	38.0	22.2	60.2	4.5	63.1
1962	39.3	23.8	63.1	4.8	62.3
1964	40.8	29.1	69.9	10.8	58.4
1966	40.9	30.8	71.7	2.6	57.0
1968	38.9	38.5	77.4	7.9	50.3
1970	37.2	55.6	92.8	19.9	40.1

Source: *IMF Annual Reports*, various issues.

ments' needs for reserves thus fell to the U.S. dollar, but by 1960 the quantity of gold-convertible dollars exceeded the gold holdings of the U.S. government. As the 1960s progressed, the gold holdings of the U.S. government declined while the potential claims against them grew. The pressure against the dollar accumulated slowly enough, however, that the Bretton Woods System was held together through the decade.

Exhibit 2.2 summarizes governments' reserve holdings during the years 1948 through 1970. The other reserves in the third column consisted primarily of dollars. Overall, Exhibit 2.2 indicates modest growth of total reserves considering that the percentage changes in the fifth column are for 2-year intervals. Only in the years 1963 to 1964 and 1969 to 1970 did total reserves increase at rates that could be regarded as excessive. From 1950 on, gold's relative importance as a reserve asset declined except during the interval 1957 to 1958, and it declined rapidly after 1966.

National Currencies as Reserve Assets One pertinent question about the Bretton Woods System is why national currencies other than the dollar were not widely used as reserve assets. In part, this was because it was difficult for other currencies to compete with the dollar as long as it remained gold-convertible. Another part to the answer is that the pound sterling, which had been a major reserve currency before World War II, was perceived as being subject to periodic devaluations that made holding it risky. Some currencies, however, such as the mark, the Swiss franc, the Dutch guilder, the Canadian dollar, and the yen developed strength as the Bretton Woods System evolved, and yet not one of them emerged as a genuine reserve currency. We should try to understand why this was the case.

When a country's currency serves as a reserve asset, that country derives the seeming advantage of procuring what amount to low-cost loans from other countries. It can, within limits, acquire both assets and goods from foreigners simply by allowing its banking system to create enough money for their purchase. To the extent that the amount of its money supplied to foreigners exceeds what other nations require for their international transactions, the country's currency tends to be accumulated by foreign governments as a reserve asset. These reserves are held in the form of highly liquid, low-yielding assets such as short-term Treasury securities.

As long as foreign governments do not reduce the quantity of the currency they hold, the funds that are effectively borrowed do not have to be repaid. It might seem that governments would be eager to have their currencies serve as reserve assets, especially when, as they usually do, they run budgetary deficits. Understandably, therefore, critics of the U.S. government claimed that it was taking advantage of the dollar's special status in the Bretton Woods System to run, as French spokesmen commonly put it, "deficits without tears," i.e., persistent balance-of-payments deficits financed without accompanying measures of fiscal and monetary restraint.

As the U.S. government of the Bretton Woods era discovered, there is a major drawback to having one's currency be a reserve currency. The country's government must ultimately take that status into account in framing economic policy. For example, an easy money policy to stimulate the domestic economy may have to be ruled out if other countries' governments are unwilling to increase their holdings of the country's currency. The pressure on the government of a reserve currency is particularly great if any other national currency serves as an important reserve asset. During the 1960s, the U.S. government was fortunate that no other currency could seriously challenge the dollar.

During the nineteenth century, the Bank of England felt pressure to raise short-term interest rates whenever the British government was threatened with losses of gold reserves. Similarly today, the central bank of a reserve currency country is under pressure to push up short-term interest rates whenever foreign governments are accumulating the country's currency faster than desired. Whereas the British government of the last century did not have to worry very much about speculation against the pound in favor of another currency, the central bank of a reserve currency country in today's world must worry about the possibility of a wholesale dumping of its currency in favor of one or more other currencies. Avoiding such a wholesale dumping, or coping with it once it has begun, may force a central bank to greatly alter its monetary policy from the desired course. This is particularly troublesome if the economy of the reserve currency country is small relative to the quantity of its currency held as reserve assets by foreign governments. For this reason, reserve currencies have tended to be the currencies of nations with relatively large economies and well-developed money markets. During the Bretton Woods period, however, few countries could satisfy these criteria.

The Defense of the Dollar   At the beginning of the 1960s, the government of the United States faced a dollar management problem that seemed to require nothing less than the overhaul of the Bretton Woods System. If it followed policies that increased the quantity of dollars held by foreign governments, it would have risked a run on its gold reserves, but if it prevented the quantity of dollars controlled by foreign governments from increasing, the world would have lacked sufficient reserves to lubricate the international financial engine. It chose the middle course of allowing the quantity of dollars controlled by foreign governments to increase at a modest pace while buying time through piecemeal measures and simultaneously pushing for structural reforms of the Bretton Woods System.

Toward the end of 1960, a rise in the free market price of gold induced the U.S. government to supply gold to the market through the Bank of England. Recognizing that the price of gold would probably tend to rise and that the lack of a gold market in the United States limited its ability to affect the world market, the U.S. government arranged with Britain and other western European nations to form the London Gold Pool with the purpose of stabilizing the price of gold at $35 per ounce by market intervention. This arrangement succeeded for several years in keeping the price of gold at the desired level, but it was clearly temporary because it required the U.S. government to sell gold to foreign central banks. Meanwhile, the dollar liabilities of the government continued to increase.

In 1961, the U.S. government took the first of a series of unilateral actions to defend the dollar. This was Operation Twist, in which the Treasury announced that it was shifting the maturity structure of its debt to raise short-term interest relative to long-term rates, hoping to simultaneously diminish short-term capital outflows and stimulate real investment.[7] During Operation Twist (from 1961 to 1964), short-term interest rates did rise relative to long-term rates, but it is doubtful that this development owed much to the operation because the Treasury did not, in fact, pursue it vigorously. When a general rise in interest rates occurs, as happened in the 1960s, short-term rates normally rise initially by more than long-term rates, and it is likely that this normal pattern rather than Treasury policy explains the relative increase in short-term rates.[8] In any event, the shift in the term structure of interest rates did not solve the problem of the weakening dollar.

The U.S. government adopted various other measures for the dollar's defense during the 1960s, some of which were directed at the promotion of

---

[7]The name came from a popular dance whose contortions sometimes produced muscular pains and/or spinal dislocations for the participants.

[8]John H. Wood and Norma L. Wood, *Financial Markets* (San Diego: Harcourt Brace Jovanovich, 1985), pp. 643–644. Any effect on the term structure of interest rates caused by Operation Twist was probably temporary. In the highly efficient financial markets of the United States, borrowers and lenders are often able to respond quickly to changes in the relative levels of short-term and long-term interest rates, thereby tending to restore the normal differential between them. Moreover, any relative reduction in long-term rates added to the already strong incentive for multinational firms and governments to borrow long-term in the United States even when the funds were to be spent elsewhere.

exports. Particularly significant were two programs designed to directly curb dollar outflows: the **Interest Equalization Tax** (IET) of 1963 and the voluntary **Foreign Credit Restraint Program** (FCRP) of 1965. The IET was levied on U.S. residents' purchases of bonds issued by foreign borrowers in the United States and (in 1964) on foreign loans by U.S. financial institutions with maturities of 1 to 3 years. This effectively raised the interest rates paid by foreign borrowers, thereby discouraging them from borrowing. The FCRP was implemented by the Federal Reserve System to restrain U.S. banks from lending to multinational firms to finance their acquisitions of foreign firms and properties.[9]

While these measures may have bought a little time for the dollar, they were short-sighted and even naive. Most significantly, they stimulated the development of the Eurodollar and Eurobond markets, whose origins are examined later in the chapter and whose operations are examined in later chapters. The United States lost the income, employment, and tax revenues that would have been generated had its government not provided powerful incentives to locate financial activity in more hospitable environments.

Almost as soon as the IET went into effect, a boom began in both the Eurodollar and Eurobond markets. Nevertheless, the U.S. government persisted in its chosen course by widening the scope of the IET, introducing the FCRP on a voluntary basis in 1965, and making the FCRP mandatory in 1968. Only in 1974, after the dollar had become a floating currency and the Eurodollar and Eurobond markets had become solidly established, were these ill-conceived measures eliminated.

Another course of action adopted by the U.S. government for the dollar's defense, this time a sensible one, was to increase monetary cooperation with other governments. It became standard practice for the Treasury and the Fed to arrange swaps with foreign central banks providing for reciprocal exchanges of currencies that were to be reversed at a later date. This technique improved governments' defenses against speculative assaults on their currencies.

In a similar vein, the governments of 10 developed nations formed a loose association known as the **Group of Ten** (G-10) to discuss and improve the international economic environment. Among other accomplishments, the G-10 established the General Agreements to Borrow (GAB) in 1962, which provided that G-10 members would lend up to about $6 billion to the IMF for relending to GAB contributors for the mutual defense of their currencies. Because it has been continuously renewed, the GAB has become a permanent feature of the international monetary system.[10]

Additional measures for the dollar's defense included persuading some foreign governments to exchange surplus dollars for nonmarketable, dollar-

---

[9]Capital outflows to Canada, the LDCs, and international agencies were exempted from these measures and from the mandatory investment controls introduced in 1968.

[10]The members of the G-10 are the United States, Canada, Japan, Belgium, France, Italy, the Netherlands, Sweden, the United Kingdom, and Germany. Switzerland agreed to contribute to the GAB in 1964, but it chose not to officially join the group. Subsequently, Saudi Arabia made a commitment to contribute to the GAB if the funds were needed. At present, total commitments to the GAB are SDR 18.5 billion, but this facility is seldom used.

denominated Treasury securities or Treasury securities denominated in foreign currencies. Neither of these expedients was adopted on a large scale, however, nor did the U.S. government attempt to dissuade other countries from cashing in dollars for gold by offering to compensate them in the event that it should become necessary to raise the official price of gold above $35 per ounce.

Throughout the 1960s, there was much discussion about the reform of the Bretton Woods System. Numerous plausible reform proposals were advanced, some of them coming from the academic world. Indeed, one problem was that there were so many plausible proposals to consider that it was difficult to build a consensus around any of them. At one extreme, it was suggested (primarily by academics) that the leading countries should adopt freely fluctuating exchange rates, i.e., allow exchange rates to be completely market-determined. At the other extreme were proposals for the adoption of some form of gold standard. In between were such ideas as the creation of a new reserve asset along the lines of Keynes's bancor, a simultaneous and uniform increase in official gold prices by IMF members, allowing more national currencies to serve as international reserves, and allowing greater exchange rate flexibility within the adjustable peg framework.

A concrete result of the discussions about international monetary reform was the creation of a new international reserve asset, similar in conception to bancor, known as special drawing rights (SDRs). The basic plan for SDRs was worked out by the G-10, and at IMF meetings in Rio de Janeiro in 1967, the fund announced that it intended to introduce them and oversee their use. No SDRs were created until 1970, however, and their impact on the Bretton Woods System was minuscule. Accordingly, SDRs are not examined until the next chapter, which deals with the international monetary system since 1973.

On the whole, the debate on the restructuring of the international monetary system during the 1960s was unproductive because national governments could not agree on what should be done. As a result, the dollar was left without adequate defenses against potential speculative attacks.

The IMF under the Bretton Woods System   During the 1950s and 1960s, the IMF expanded and improved its operations to preserve the Bretton Woods System and assure itself of a secure place in the world, whatever the future might bring. By the late 1950s, it routinely lent funds in connection with **standby agreements,** in which it would extend a line of credit to a borrowing government specifying the maximum amount of "credit tranche" borrowing during a specified time period, provided that the borrower met conditions laid down by the IMF. Credit tranche borrowing covered (and still covers) funding needs in excess of 25 percent of a borrower's quota. A strong incentive for satisfying the conditions laid down by the IMF was the fact that both government and private lenders were more likely to lend to a government with an IMF standby agreement than to a government without one.

In 1963, the IMF established the first of several special "facilities" designed to provide assistance to certain classes of borrowers beyond that normally available. This compensatory financial facility aided countries experiencing temporary declines in export earnings. The amount that could be borrowed under this facility was quota-based, but a compensatory financial facility loan did not diminish the borrower's eligibility for other IMF loans.

The expansion of IMF lending was fueled by increases in its resources. In 1959, the quotas of IMF members were raised by 50 percent, and in 1965 these enlarged quotas were raised by 25 percent more. In addition, the IMF added new members and, as was mentioned earlier, absorbed the GAB.

Even these large increases in the IMF's resources failed to match the growth of governments' demand for short-term financial assistance. A major problem was that, as currencies were made convertible and international financial integration advanced, the potential for currency speculation also grew. Another problem was that governments generally failed to adjust their exchange rate parities in response to changing supply and demand conditions in the forex market, with the result that large gaps developed between supply and demand at the existing parities.

The Bretton Woods System was intended to be an *adjustable* peg system in which a nation would alter its par value exchange rate when faced with fundamental disequilibrium. In practice, however, governments were often unwilling to alter their parities even when it seemed clear that fundamental disequilibria existed. In deficit countries, governments generally rejected devaluation because of inflation fears and the appearance of policy failure. In surplus countries, governments were even more adamantly opposed to increases in their currencies' parities (**revaluations**) because they believed that payments surpluses stimulated their economies and because they were willing to accumulate dollars. In some cases, the IMF could compel devaluation by withholding financial support. Critics have charged that in its eagerness to be involved, the IMF often lent to governments that should have been devalued. The IMF could do little to force revaluations since surplus countries did not need to borrow from it.

Because governments tended to postpone devaluation, often with IMF support, devaluations tended to be large when they finally occurred. Also, since governments were required by IMF rules to keep exchange rates within 1 percent of parity, speculators saw that they had little to lose and much to gain by betting on devaluation whenever it seemed a good possibility.

The Final Phase: 1967 to 1973

By 1967, it was clear to many people that the Bretton Woods System had a short remaining life expectancy. The Vietnam War had induced the U.S. government to pursue policies that allowed the quantity of dollars held by foreign governments to grow at a rapid rate. Further, the SDR experiment was on too small a scale to make much difference, and surplus countries, most notably Germany and Japan, were averse to come to the dollar's aid by revaluing their currencies. Speculators saw a wonderful opportunity to let the good times roll. Never before had chances for large, low-risk speculative gains been available on such a grand scale. The strategy of the speculators was simple—find a weak currency and bet against it. Those who wanted speculative variety could play the gold game; sooner or later, the price of gold had to rise. The only question was when.

| EXHIBIT | 2.3 | *U.S. Gold Reserves and Liquid Dollar Liabilities to Foreign Governments and Banks: 1960 to 1971 (in Billions of Dollars)*

End of Year	Gold Reserves[a]	Dollar Liabilities[b]	Ratio of Dollar Liabilities to Gold
1960	17.8	18.7	1.05
1961	17.0	20.2	1.18
1962	16.1	21.1	1.31
1963	15.6	22.5	1.44
1964	15.5	25.0	1.61
1965	14.1	25.0	1.77
1966	13.2	25.4	1.89
1967	12.1	28.4	2.35
1968	10.9	28.5	2.61
1969	11.9	37.1	3.12
1970	11.1	38.5	3.47
1971	11.1	50.0	4.50

[a]Valued at $35 per ounce.

[b]Includes short-term liabilities to foreign commercial banks, many of which were available for government use.

Source: *International Financial Statistics*, various issues.

The Golden Years of Speculation: 1967 to 1971   As is shown in Exhibit 2.3, the ratio of liquid dollar liabilities to foreign governments and banks to the U.S. government's gold reserves rose throughout the period from 1960 to 1971, and the increases in this ratio were particularly large after 1966. The growing gap between these liabilities and the U.S. government's gold reserves encouraged speculation against the dollar, but as long as governments supported the dollar and the U.S. government could sweet-talk them into refraining from cashing in dollars for gold on a massive scale, the dollar's immediate prospects were favorable enough to keep most speculators content, for a while, to seek other game.

The first major currency to be subjected to massive speculative pressure in the late 1960s was the pound sterling, which was devalued from $2.80/£ to $2.40/£ late in 1967 after a spirited contest. This led to the permanent shrinkage of the Sterling Area, a group of nations pegging their currencies to the pound.

The speculators next turned to gold, whose price started rising once more. Because the speculation in gold proved too massive to be contained by the London Gold Pool, the governments of the leading financial powers agreed in March 1968 to establish a "two-tiered gold market, in which official intervention in the private gold market ended and intergovernmental transactions in gold took place at $35 per ounce. This relieved some of the pressure on the U.S.

government's gold reserves, but it was clear that any pronounced rise in gold's free-market price would create an irresistible inducement for governments to arbitrage between the official and private markets. The U.S. government's best tactic in this situation was quiet pressure on governments to refrain from asking it for gold.

Soon after the two-tiered gold market emerged, the private market price of gold rose to over $40 per ounce, but it then fell back to almost $35 per ounce when speculators shifted their attention back to currencies, notably the French franc. When the speculation against the franc began in November 1968, the French government vigorously defended its currency and even forced some speculators to absorb losses. Finally, however, in August 1969, the franc was devalued by 11.1 percent, catching the forex market by surprise. This move also surprised the IMF, which had not been notified in advance, as it should have been since the devaluation was in excess of 10 percent.

The favored currency for speculators to buy in the late 1960s was the mark. Prior to that time, the only significant currency revaluations under the Bretton Woods System had been 5 percent increases in both the mark and the guilder in 1961. By 1968, the mark appeared to be more undervalued than it had been in 1961. Another revaluation seemed logical. West Germany's political leaders vehemently debunked the idea that the mark might be revalued, and the Bundesbank (the German central bank) intervened in the forex market to prevent the mark from rising. In October 1969, however, inflationary pressure from the Bundesbank's purchases of foreign currencies and the failure of the franc's devaluation to end speculation led to a 9.1 percent mark revaluation.

Speculators favored the mark over other strong currencies such as the Swiss franc and the yen because of the greater ease with which marks could be acquired and held in short-term earning assets. Both Switzerland and Japan had long vigorously discouraged speculative purchases of their currencies, and each had kept the exchange rate of its currency with the dollar stable throughout the Bretton Woods period. Nevertheless, by the end of the 1960s speculative money was moving into both Swiss francs and yen in anticipation of a major currency realignment.

The 1969 revaluation of the mark failed to convince the forex market that the dollar's overvaluation had been eliminated, but it did temporarily divert speculative buying into other currencies, most notably the Canadian dollar. The Canadian government responded in June 1970 by deciding to float its currency in a reversion to a practice followed from 1950 until 1962.[11] After this development, speculators shifted back to the mark, and the West German government reacted by prohibiting banks from paying interest on foreign-owned deposits and making such deposits subject to a 100 percent reserve

---

[11]During this earlier period, the Canadian dollar had floated against the U.S. dollar with little intervention, yet the exchange rate between the two currencies had remained basically stable. This experience was widely (and wrongly) interpreted as supporting the idea that a general system of floating rates would not necessarily exhibit great exchange rate instability.

| EXHIBIT | 2.4 | *Currency Realignments: May 5, 1971,*
to December 18, 1971

| | Currency Units per U.S. Dollar | | Percentage Change against the |
Currency	May 5, 1971	December 18, 1971	U.S. Dollar
Japanese yen	360.00	308.00	+16.9
Swiss franc	4.37	3.84	+13.8
German deutschemark	3.66	3.22	+13.7
Netherlands guilder	3.62	3.24	+11.7
Austrian schilling	26.00	23.30	+11.6
Belgian franc	50.00	44.82	+11.6
Pound sterling[a]	2.40	2.61	+8.8
French franc	5.56	5.12	+8.6
Italian lira	625.00	581.50	+7.5
Swedish krona	5.17	4.81	+7.5

[a]Dollars per pound sterling.

Source: Bank for International Settlements, *Forty-First Annual Report, 1971*, p. 30.

requirement. Still, dollars continued to flow in. In May 1971, after buying billions of dollars in a futile effort to prevent the mark's appreciation, the German government allowed its currency to float. At about the same time, the government of the Netherlands floated the guilder and the governments of Switzerland and Austria revalued their currencies. The stage was thus set for the decisive blow to the Bretton Woods System, the floating of the dollar.

August 1971 to March 1973 Although President Richard Nixon had previously insisted that his government would neither devalue the dollar nor invoke the wage and price controls that Congress had authorized, he reversed himself on August 15, 1971. He not only allowed the dollar to float, but also imposed a 10 percent surcharge on most dutiable imports in order to provide the U.S. government with a large bargaining chip for the negotiations that were sure to follow.

In taking these actions, the U.S. government failed to consult beforehand with the IMF and made it clear that it preferred working within the G-10 framework rather than with a larger body. In December 1971, after harsh verbal exchanges between U.S. officials and the officials of other G-10 nations, representatives of these nations met in Washington, D.C. and hammered out the Smithsonian Agreement. Under its provisions, the dollar was devalued by 7.9 percent by raising the official price of gold to $38 per ounce. Simultaneously, except for the Canadian dollar (which continued to float), the currencies of the other G-10 nations were redefined relative to the dollar so that their values against it rose by amounts ranging from 16.9 percent for the yen to 7.5 percent for the Swedish krona and the Italian lira. Exhibit 2.4 details the currency realignments of the Smithsonian Agreement, which included the currencies of two nations, Switzerland and Austria, that were not G-10 members.

The Smithsonian Agreement discarded the 1 percent rule for market fluctuations of exchange rates in favor of a rule allowing fluctuations of 2.25 percent on either side of a currency's official parity. This widened the band of permissible variations between any two currencies, excluding the dollar, from 2 percent to 4.5 percent. Against the dollar, however, a currency could fluctuate by only 2.25 percent. In addition, the U.S. government agreed to rescind the 10 percent import surcharge. Very quickly, the IMF approved the Smithsonian Agreement, in which it had played no role.

The 4.5 percent band exceeded what the nations of the European Economic Community (EEC) desired among their own currencies. Accordingly, in April 1972, the EEC's members entered into an arrangement known as the "snake within the tunnel" that limited the variations among their currencies to 2.25 percent, the same as their permitted variations against the dollar and half of the Smithsonian band of 4.5 percent.

The architects of the Smithsonian Agreement hoped that the wider band would deter speculation and, in combination with the currency realignments, keep matters under control until any other needed reforms of the Bretton Woods System could be negotiated. These hopes were dashed, however, when the agreement came apart a little more than a year after it was reached. The agreement did have a calming effect at first, but after a few months speculators showed a marked inclination (no pun intended) to believe that the recent histories of individual currencies would be repeated sufficiently closely to justify accepting the slightly greater risk that had been introduced into the speculative game. The resulting speculative wave swept away the Smithsonian Agreement early in 1973.

This speculative wave actually began revealing itself in June 1972, when the pound sterling was floated. Except for this event, the agreement remained intact until January 1973, when the government of Italy began floating the lira in capital transactions. Soon afterward, the Swiss franc was floated. On February 12, 1973, the dollar was formally devalued by 10 percent in terms of gold and SDRs,[12] and in March the dollar once more became a floating currency. With the floating of the dollar, the world's long romance with fixed exchange rates had ended, or at least passed into a lengthy suspension.

Eurodollars and Eurobonds

The fundamental problem of the Bretton Woods System was that it could not reconcile fixed exchange rates and progress toward international financial integration with governments' insistence on autonomy in the conduct of monetary policy. By and large, the governments of the most economically

---

[12]The official price of gold was raised to $42.22 per ounce, where it has remained. Since the U.S. government neither buys nor sells gold at this price, it has mainly accounting significance, and little of that.

advanced countries were committed to maintaining economies that combined great reliance on private enterprise with extensive governmental direction and control. The governments of these countries all espoused the principle of currency convertibility, but all of them, in varying degrees, were also committed to the principle of government intervention to affect exchange rates.

Every industrialized country of the West, and Japan even more so, has strongly resisted international financial integration almost every step of the way. Nationalistic sentiments have blended with the influence of various special interest groups and faith in socialistic planning and a corresponding skepticism about free markets to foster the attitude that international financial integration should be very limited. Notwithstanding such opposition, international financial integration has surged onward, affecting even those countries in which resistance to it has been strongest.

Its momentum has come in part from debtors, including governments themselves, who have wanted to obtain credit on the best terms possible. In part, the momentum has come from lenders and investors who have perceived that the international mobility of capital gives them opportunities to increase their risk-adjusted rates of return. Much of the momentum has been supplied by financial intermediaries with the ability to rapidly expand their internationally oriented operations. Over short periods of time, the outcome between these two sets of contending forces has sometimes been in doubt. Over the long run, however, the forces favoring integration have won because practical experience and economic theory weigh in heavily on their side.

International financial integration is contagious, and once it has proceeded very far, preventing its further spread is difficult. One thing leads to another, producing a pattern of growth that appears to be virtually exponential, leading to developments that were not clearly foreseen, if they were foreseen at all. Among the largely unforeseen developments affecting the international monetary system during the Bretton Woods era, none have had a more lasting impact than the emergence of the Eurodollar and Eurobond markets.

The Eurodollar Market   The standard definition states that **Eurodollars** are dollar-denominated deposits (almost always time deposits) in banks located outside the United States.[13] The banks in which the deposits are located may be branches of U.S. banks, but they do not have to be. **Eurocurrencies** are any deposit liabilities of banks, including Eurodollars, that are denominated in currencies other than the national currencies of the banks in which they are held. Such foreign currency deposits were sometimes used by European banks before World War II, but it was during the Bretton Woods period that they became a major factor in the international financial world.

Some say the Soviets started the Eurodollar market to protect their dollar deposits in U.S. banks from seizure. That the Soviet government even had such holdings during the Bretton Woods and Cold War years reflected the fact that

---

[13]As is explained in Chapter 13, certain bank accounts in the United States, known as international banking facilities (IBFs), are considered to be Eurodollars.

the dollar was indisputably the world's vehicle currency and, until 1958, one of the few convertible currencies. Although the Soviet government conducted much of its international trade on a barter basis, it needed convertible currency for some of its trade and for other international activities. The Soviet government feared that after the incorporation of East Germany into the Soviet Bloc, the Berlin airlift, the communist attack on Greece, and the invasion of South Korea, the U.S. government might retaliate by seizing Soviet-owned bank deposits in the United States, either on the U.S. government's own behalf or on behalf of aggrieved parties who achieved court judgments against the Soviet government. To safeguard its assets, the Soviet government transferred them to banks in London and Paris that it owned, reasoning that the U.S. government would be reluctant to seize deposits owned by these banks, which were legally incorporated under British and French law. In return for its dollar deposits in U.S. banks, the Soviet government received dollar-denominated time deposits in its London and Paris banks that could be converted into dollar demand deposits in the United States as necessary to make international payments.

In reality, it was British-owned banks, not Soviet-owned ones, that took the crucial step of turning foreign currency deposits into a lending medium. They did so around the beginning of 1957 in order to save business that was endangered by exchange controls on transactions in pounds sterling. The incipient Eurodollar market then grew rapidly once the exchange controls were removed because of restrictions imposed by the U.S. government on banking operations in the United States.

In the fall of 1956, the government of Egypt, under the leadership of Gamal Abdel Nasser, seized the Suez Canal, which had long been operated by a company that was largely owned by the British and French governments. In the ensuing turmoil, Israel invaded Egypt while Britain and France seized the canal. The Anglo–French intervention was met by the strong disapproval of the U.S. government, which proceeded to sell pounds and to block British efforts to support the pound by borrowing from the IMF. The Bank of England sought to protect the pound by prohibiting British banks from lending internationally in pounds. Threatened with a large loss of earnings, some British banks offered dollar-denominated time deposits with attractive interest rates. As dollars flowed into these deposits, the banks obtained dollar *demand* deposits in U.S. banks that they could lend as they saw fit.[14]

After the Suez crisis passed and the pound had weathered the attack on it, British banks found that they could continue to earn good profits by offering dollar-denominated deposits. For a while, however, the developing Eurodollar market operated virtually unnoticed by government officials, academics, and even top-level bank executives. By 1959, however, Paul Einzig, a writer for the *Financial Times,* perceived what was happening and brought it to the attention of his readers. Einzig christened a new phenomenon, the "Eurodollar market," and the name stuck.

---

[14]J. Orlin Grabbe, *International Financial Markets* (New York: Elsevier, 1986), p. 16.

During the 1960s, the Eurodollar market expanded rapidly, in large part by restrictions imposed on banks by the U.S. government. Thus, beginning in 1966, U.S. interest rates on time and savings deposits began to push against the ceilings on such deposits imposed by the Federal Reserve System's Regulation Q. Since Eurobanks (as the banks with Eurodollar liabilities came to be called) were subject to no such restrictions, they could offer interest rates on time deposits that substantially exceeded those offered in the United States. A large migration of funds to Eurobanks then occurred, to which U.S. banks responded by establishing Eurobanking branches, which could attract funds that could be lent to their home offices in the United States. In some cases, especially when the size of the branches was too small to meet the minimum capital requirements in London, the branches were established in such offshore locations as the Bahamas, which offered low capital requirements, minuscule fees and taxes, and virtually no regulation.

In 1969, the Fed acted to restrain the movement of funds into the Eurodollar market by passing Regulation Q by subjecting the liabilities of U.S. banks to foreign banks, including their own branches, to reserve requirements. Not until 1973, however, when the Fed freed single-maturity time deposits of more than $100,000 from Regulation Q restrictions, was the incentive to circumvent the regulation eliminated.

The IET and the FCRP provided additional incentives for the expansion of the Eurodollar market. When the IET was extended to bank loans in 1964, many banks simply transferred funds to their Eurobank branches and made loans to foreigners as they saw fit. Evidently being slow to appreciate the ease with which the Eurodollar market could be used to avoid such restrictions, the U.S. government introduced the FCRP in 1965 and made it mandatory at the beginning of 1968. U.S. firms wanting to use bank loans to finance equity investments abroad avoided the FCRP by simply borrowing from Eurobanks.

The IET and the FCRP were eliminated in 1974, by which time the Eurodollar market had become well-established and was offering deposits in other foreign currencies than the dollar. Correspondingly, the term Eurocurrency market increasingly replaced the term Eurodollar market. Since 1974, this market has continued to flourish despite the removal of the restrictions that spurred its early growth. Evidently, these restrictions accelerated a process that would probably have ultimately occurred in any event, for even after their removal, the absence of reserve requirements and other restrictions gave Eurobanks a competitive edge over more traditional forms of banking.

Eurobonds   In the early 1960s, the Eurobond market began accomplishing for international securities markets what the Eurodollar market had started accomplishing for international banking—providing advantages to both borrowers and lenders by circumventing laws and regulations. Like the Eurodollar market, the Eurobond market has grown rapidly and become a permanent feature of the international financial system.

Eurobonds differ from other international bonds in that they are initially distributed outside the country in whose currency they are denominated. Until the Eurobond market materialized, a foreign firm or government wanting to issue dollar bonds had to do so in the U.S. domestic bond market. The Eurobond market allowed such borrowers to issue dollar-denominated bonds outside the United States.

The Eurobond market offered two important advantages over issuing bonds in the United States. First, with Eurobonds, a borrower could avoid the financial disclosure rules of the Securities and Exchange Commission (SEC). Avoiding these rules meant avoiding the costs of complying with them and the disclosure of information that a borrower might prefer to keep confidential. Moreover, lax regulations on Eurobond issues meant that the time consumed in floating a bond issue could be substantially shortened so firms could acquire funds more quickly.

The second major advantage of Eurobond financing was that it offered somewhat lower interest rates than the domestic U.S. bond market. This advantage stemmed largely from the fact that the interest paid on Eurobonds was, for the most part, effectively nontaxable. From the outset, Eurobonds were generally bearer bonds, i.e., the identities of their owners did not appear in any legal record, and the interest on them was payable to whoever presented the proper coupons at the correct times and places. Since the governments of the countries in which Eurobonds were issued did not require tax withholding on the interest payments, Eurobond owners could often escape paying taxes on the resulting interest income. This was particularly true when (as was usually the case) the bondholders were individuals rather than corporations. Since the interest income went largely untaxed, the issuers of Eurobonds could generally borrow at slightly lower interest rates than those prevailing on comparable U.S. bond issues.

The first dollar-denominated Eurobond issue was a 1957 borrowing by Petrofina, a Belgian petroleum company.[15] For the next few years after that, the Eurobond market developed slowly. As the 1960s progressed, however, the combination of a growing volume of investment dollars owned outside the United States and the introduction by the U.S. government of restrictions on foreign borrowing in the United States gave a decided push to the market's development. The chief factor tending to limit growth was the refusal of the U.S. government to allow newly issued Eurobonds to be sold in the United States.

The government did not, however, attempt to prevent the bonds from being sold to foreign buyers outside the United States, as it could have done by prohibiting dollar deposits in U.S. banks from being used for Eurobond purchases. Moreover, it permitted Eurobonds to be sold in secondary trading in the United States after 90 days had elapsed from their dates of issue. Further, in 1964 the SEC ruled that U.S. investment banking firms could participate in the initial distribution of Eurobonds as long as the bonds were not sold to U.S. nationals. In other words, the SEC decided that since the government was

---

[15]David S. Kidwell, M. Wayne Marr, and G. Rodney Thompson, "Eurodollar Bonds: Alternative Financing for U.S. Companies," *Financial Management*, Winter 1985, p. 19.

willing to tolerate the existence of Eurobonds, it should allow U.S. investment banks to receive part of the action. In short order, several of these firms became major Eurobond underwriters.

Borrowers in the Eurobond market included well-known firms, governments and their agencies, and international organizations. Because of the lack of disclosure requirements, borrowers needed to have high credit ratings and name recognition. Because the distribution of Eurobonds to U.S. buyers was restricted, the market's development required the existence of a large pool of portfolio (income only) investors located outside the United States. Such a pool materialized during the 1960s.

In the early 1970s, the Eurobond market's growth slowed because of the weakness of the dollar. To some degree, the slowdown stimulated the issuance of Eurobonds denominated in other currencies, notably the mark. In any event, by 1974, the Eurobond market was so well-established that the elimination of the IET and the FCRP seemed to have little effect on it. To the contrary, the market grew rapidly during the late 1970s. Inevitably, that growth, like the growth of the Eurocurrency market, was to lead to a loosening of government restrictions on international financial activity.

Summary

This chapter has surveyed the evolution of the international monetary system from the days of the international gold standard until the final breakdown of the Bretton Woods System in 1973. The international gold standard dominated the world economy from the late 1870s until 1914 and established fixed exchange rates among the leading currencies. The ability of nations to retain this system hinged on a number of factors working collectively to minimize gold flows between countries. The outbreak of World War I in 1914 led to its general suspension, and a restored gold standard in the 1920s failed because of structural weaknesses and the onset of the Great Depression of the 1930s.

The Bretton Woods System emerged after World War II as an attempt to establish a monetary system that offered a high degree of exchange rate stability without the perceived disadvantages of the gold standard, most notably the loss of national monetary authority associated with a full-fledged gold standard. Over time, however, structural weaknesses accumulated that ultimately assured its demise. Governments tended to resist needed exchange rate adjustments, the dollar's position as the key international reserve asset was undermined, and speculative attacks on currencies became more frequent. The system finally passed into history in 1973 when the Smithsonian Agreement of 1971 proved insufficient to repair its flaws.

Great advances in international financial integration were achieved under the Bretton Woods System, and these advances opened up opportunities to take advantage of differences in the laws and regulations pertaining to financial operations. The Eurocurrency and Eurobond markets developed in response to these opportunities and grew rapidly from around 1960 through the remainder of the Bretton Woods period.

References

Bloomfield, Arthur I. *Monetary Policy under the International Gold Standard, 1880–1914.* New York: Federal Reserve Bank of New York, 1959.

Bordo, Michael David. "The Classical Gold Standard: Some Lessons for Today." *Federal Reserve Bank of St. Louis Review,* May 1981, pp. 2–17.

Grabbe, J. Orlin. *International Financial Markets.* New York: Elsevier, 1986, Chapter 1.

International Monetary Fund. *Annual Report,* various issues.

McKinnon, Ronald I. *Money in International Exchange.* New York: Oxford University Press, 1979.

Nurkse, Ragnar. *International Currency Experience.* Princeton, N.J.: League of Nations, 1944.

Rolfe, Sidney E., and James L. Burtle. *The Great Wheel.* New York: McGraw-Hill, 1975.

Smith, Lawrence. *Money, Credit, and Public Policy.* Boston: Houghton Mifflin, 1959.

Triffin, Robert. *Gold and the Dollar Crisis,* rev. ed. New Haven, Conn.: Yale University Press, 1961.

————. *The Evolution of the International Monetary System: Historical Reappraisal and Future Perspectives.* Princeton, N.J.: Princeton University Press, 1964.

Yeager, Leland B. *International Monetary Relations,* 2d. ed. New York: Harper & Row, 1976.

Questions

1. From the late 1870s until 1914, the exchange rates among the currencies of the economically most advanced nations remained stable. Why did none of these nations ever lose enough gold to force it to suspend the gold standard?
2. The British decision to return to gold at the old mint parity in 1925 is considered to have been a major error. Why was this decision made, and why was it a mistake?
3. How did U.S. economic policy contribute to the weaknesses of the international monetary system during the 1920s and 1930s?
4. What were the consequences of the Gold Reserve Act of 1934?
5. What were the British delegation's monetary proposals at the Bretton Woods Conference? How do you explain the fact that 20 years later, the U.S. position on international monetary reform bore close resemblances to the British position at Bretton Woods?
6. What has been the IMF's position with regard to the use of exchange controls?
7. What was it about the structure of the Bretton Woods System that encouraged currency speculation, and why did such speculation become more serious as the system evolved?
8. What actions were taken by the U.S. government to protect the dollar during the 1960s, and why did these actions ultimately fail?
9. It is often said that the Bretton Woods System failed ultimately because the U.S. government allowed the quantity of dollars in the hands of foreign governments to rise too rapidly. Do you think this criticism is valid? Explain.

10. What did the Smithsonian Agreement of December 1971 do, and why did it fail?

11. Why are countries with strong currencies often reluctant to allow their currencies to be widely used as reserve currencies?

12. People commonly compare the performance of the gold standard with that of the international monetary situation today and recommend the restoration of some form of gold standard. Do you think a modern gold standard could work? Explain.

13. What historical circumstances led to the development of the Eurodollar market?

14. What historical circumstances led to the development of the Eurobond market? How did the development of this market affect the operations of U.S. investment banks?

The Contemporary International Monetary System

■

Early in 1973 when the predominantly fixed exchange rates of the Bretton Woods System gave way to generalized floating among the leading currencies, the world entered a new monetary era. There had been brief periods of floating in the past—during the 1920s and 1930s some currencies had floated temporarily, and Canada had experimented extensively with floating rates during the 1950s and 1960s—but never before had so many nations simultaneously abandoned their commitments to exchange rate stability. The U.S. dollar, the Canadian dollar, the yen, the pound sterling, and the Swiss franc all began to float in 1973. While the French franc and the mark were being stabilized against each other at that time, they were floating against the other listed currencies, and it was doubtful that the franc could be kept from depreciating against the mark for long.

As the world entered this new era, many doubted that the rapid growth of international trade and investment that had characterized the Bretton Woods era could be sustained in a floating rate environment. Against such doubts, some, particularly an increasingly influential group of economists known as "monetarists," argued forcefully that if markets were allowed to adapt freely to the new environment, the exchange risk would not necessarily prevent the continued expansion of the international economy. Private ingenuity, they argued, could be counted on to develop suitable techniques of exchange risk management, and they doubted that either the exchange risk or the political risk would be greater with floating rates than with the adjustable peg of Bretton Woods. Devaluations had occurred infrequently under that system, while revaluations were rare; also, when exchange rate adjustments had occurred, they had tended to be large. The advocates of flexible exchange rates believed that the small, day-to-day variations associated with floating rates would, in the long run, disturb trade and investment less than the much larger variations that periodically occurred under the Bretton Woods System.

In the years since 1973, private ingenuity has indeed devised techniques for exchange risk management, and international trade and investment have grown more rapidly than the world economy as a whole. Floating rates have removed much of the pressure on governments to defend the exchange values of their currencies, and this has reduced their motivation to erect and maintain restrictions on trade and investment since.

On the negative side, exchange risk management is not costless, and exchange rates have been more volatile than the proponents of floating rates had predicted. Moreover, the problem of exchange rate volatility appears to have grown more serious with the passage of time. These negative aspects of the floating rate experience are serious enough to lead many observers of the international monetary scene to envision a return to some sort of fixed exchange rate system at some time in the future.

Exchange Rate Behavior Since 1973

The exchange rate instability that has existed since 1973 has made it clear that exchange rate determination is a very imperfectly understood process. If it were perfectly understood, one would expect to find a high degree of uniformity of opinion about proper exchange rate levels under given conditions, and opinions about future exchange rates would differ only to the degree that opinions differed about the probabilities and magnitudes of future events affecting them. In reality, however, opinions widely diverge about what exchange rates should be at any given time, and opinions also differ about how exchange rates are likely to be affected by different events. Add to this mix the fact that the events affecting exchange rates are largely random in nature, and you have a situation in which they can fluctuate widely in the absence of massive government intervention. That is the situation that confronts the world today.

Long-term Exchange Rate Behavior

In financial analysis, it is customary to distinguish between short-term and long-term periods. **Short-term** means a period of a year or less, while **long-term** can mean any period longer than a year, but may mean a period longer than 5 or even more years. An **intermediate** or **medium-term period** is commonly interposed between the two. Such a period can range from 1 year (or even slightly less) to 5 or 7 years. In the material at hand, *long-term* means a period longer than a year.

As is explained in detail in Chapter 9, a relationship known as **purchasing power parity (PPP)** indicates that, over time, exchange rates tend to vary so as to offset variations in nations' relative price levels. If, for example, country B's price level doubles relative to country A's price level, PPP means that, everything else remaining the same, the exchange value of B's currency in terms of A's currency should tend to fall to about one-half of its original level. Formally, this relationship can be expressed as follows:

$$e_t = e_0 \times \frac{p_{a,0}^t}{p_{b,0}^t} \qquad (3-1)$$

where e_t is the PPP exchange rate at time t, expressed in units of country A's currency per unit of country B's currency, e_0 is the exchange rate, preferably an equilibrium rate, at the initial time 0, expressed in the same manner; $P_{a,0}^t$ is the price index of country A at time t based on time 0; and $P_{b,0}^t$ is the price index of country B at time t based on time 0.

To the extent that PPP holds, one would expect that, over time, the currencies of nations with relatively low inflation rates should tend to rise in exchange value against the currencies of nations with relatively high inflation rates. In actuality, the currencies of nations with relatively low inflation rates do exhibit a long-term tendency to rise in value against other currencies. Thus, since 1973, the currencies of Japan, Germany, Switzerland, and the Netherlands have all risen against the U.S. dollar, and all of these countries have had less inflation than the United States. Conversely, the U.S. dollar has risen against the currencies of the United Kingdom, France, Italy, and Canada, all of which have had more inflation than the United States.

While there can be no doubt that an important causal linkage holds between exchange rates and price levels, exchange rates frequently depart widely from PPP for substantial periods of time. For example, while the U.S. dollar has lost ground against the mark and the yen since 1973, during lengthy periods it has risen against these currencies despite the relatively high U.S. inflation rate compared to Germany and Japan. During other lengthy periods, however, the dollar has fallen against the mark and the yen by much more than was to be expected on the basis of PPP. It is clear, therefore, that long-term exchange rate variations can be independent of price level changes.

Because market exchange rates can vary independently of price levels, corresponding changes occur in **real exchange rates,** which are nominal (market or actual) exchange rates adjusted for changes in relative price levels. A real exchange rate can be expressed as follows:

$$v_t = a_t \times \frac{p_{b,0}^t}{p_{a,0}^t} \tag{3-2}$$

where v_t is the real exchange rate between the currencies of countries A and B on date t expressed as the quantity of A's currency per unit of B's currency; a_t is the actual exchange rate on date t; $P_{a,0}^t$ is country A's price index on date t based on date 0; and $P_{b,0}^t$ is country B's price index on date t based on date 0. Note that by comparison with equation (3-1), equation (3-2) substitutes a_t for the base period exchange rate e_0 and inverts the numerator and denominator of the first equation.

A real exchange rate changes if actual exchange rates depart from PPP exchange rates. Changes in real exchange rates indicate variations in nations' levels of competitiveness in international trade and in their returns from investments denominated in various currencies. If, for example, the real exchange value of the U.S. dollar increases over a period of several years, this means that U.S. exports have become less competitive in international trade since their inflation-adjusted prices have risen relative to prices in other countries. It also means that, in real terms, a given quantity of U.S. investment

| E X H I B I T | 3.1 | *The Nominal and Real Effective Exchange Rates of the U.S. Dollar*

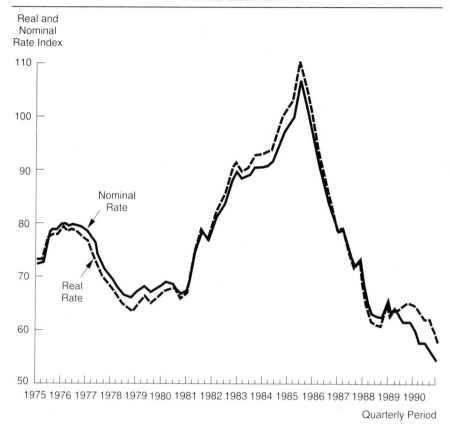

Source: *International Financial Statistics*, various issues.

in interest-yielding assets denominated in foreign currencies provides a lower rate of return in terms of dollars than would have been the case had the real exchange value of the dollar remained the same.

It is not necessarily true, however, that a rise in the dollar's real exchange value lowers the real rate of return in dollars on *equity* investments in foreign assets. For example, such investments include the ownership by U.S. parent companies of foreign subsidiaries whose income is largely derived from exports to the United States. It is conceivable that an increase in the dollar's real exchange value could lead to such a large increase in the subsidiaries' earnings that the dollar rates of return obtained by the parent companies from their investments would actually increase. Other cases can be envisioned, however, in which a rise in the dollar's real exchange value would lower the dollar rate of return from equity investments in foreign assets.

Exhibits 3.1 and 3.2 provide information on long-term exchange rates with a focus on the U.S. dollar. Exhibit 3.1 plots the nominal effective

| E X H I B I T | 3.2 | **_Nominal and Real Exchange Indexes of the U.S. Dollar against Other Currencies (1973 = 100)_**

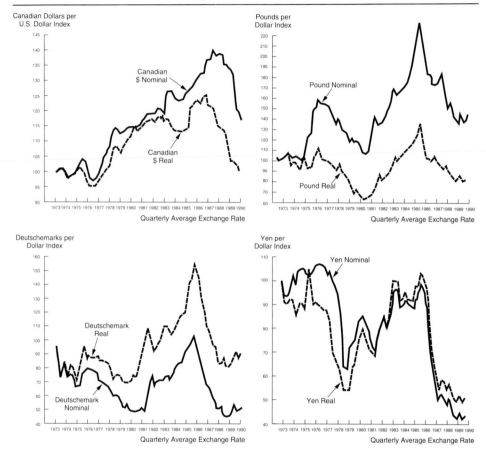

Source: _International Financial Statistics,_ various issues.

exchange rate and the real effective exchange rate of the U.S. dollar, as calculated by the IMF, from the beginning of 1975 through the end of 1990. The **nominal effective exchange rate** of the dollar is a price index obtained by averaging exchange rate indexes between the dollar and the currencies of 16 other developed countries. The currency indexes are weighted to reflect the relative importance of currencies in international transactions. The real effective exchange rate of the dollar is derived from the nominal effective exchange rate, adjusted for price indexes composed of labor costs and several other factors. Both exchange rate indexes in Exhibit 3.1 have been plotted using quarterly averages, and both use the year 1985 as the base of 100. An upward movement indicates a rise in the dollar's exchange value, and a downward movement indicates a fall in that value.

Exhibit 3.1 reveals the existence of a close correlation between the dollar's effective nominal exchange rate and its effective real exchange rate. A change in the nominal rate normally indicates a parallel change in the real rate. This fact has enormous implications for both international trade and international investment and helps to explain why exchange rate behavior rightly looms so large in the study of international finance.

Exhibit 3.2 presents four charts plotting nominal and real exchange rate indexes that pair the U.S. dollar with four other currencies from early in 1973 through the end of 1990 (the Canadian dollar, the mark, the pound sterling, and the yen). Each index is referenced to the first quarter of 1973 in order to highlight the divergence between nominal and real exchange rates since the end of the Bretton Woods System. The indexes are expressed in U.S. dollars per other currency unit, so that an upward movement means a rise in the dollar and a downward movement means a decline. Each nominal exchange rate index plots quarterly movements in the market exchange rate between the U.S. dollar and the designated other currency since the first quarter of 1973. The corresponding real exchange rate indexes were obtained by adjusting the nominal indexes by the ratios of quarterly averages of consumer price indexes based on the first quarter of 1973 in the manner indicated by equation 3–2. Consumer price indexes were used for the adjustments of nominal exchange rate indexes because the more sophisticated IMF indexes have not been extended all the way back to 1973. The use of consumer price indexes instead of the more sophisticated IMF indexes does not significantly alter the pattern of exchange rate behavior revealed in Exhibit 3.2.

If PPP had held perfectly at all times, the real exchange rate indexes of both Exhibits 3.1 and 3.2 would have been horizontal lines at the value of 100. Obviously, however, PPP has not held closely either short-term or long-term. Exhibit 3.2 indicates, like Exhibit 3.1, that nominal exchange rate variations have closely paralleled those of real exchange rates. Exhibit 3.2 also indicates, however, that when the U.S. dollar is paired against individual currencies, large gaps have existed between real and nominal exchange rates. This pattern contrasts strongly with that of Exhibit 3.1. The gaps such as those in Exhibit 3.2 have tended to offset each other so as to produce the remarkable correlation between the multiple-currency real and nominal exchange rate indexes of Exhibit 3.1.

The different patterns of the gaps between the real and nominal exchange rate indexes of Exhibit 3.2 simply indicate that countries have had different inflation rates. The gaps measure differences in inflation rates and do not imply, for example, that the dollar's real exchange value tends to rise against the currencies of low-inflation countries or to fall against the currencies of high-inflation countries. Incidentally, the gap between the indexes of Exhibit 3.1 that emerged in 1989 and 1990 indicates that the United States had a relatively high inflation rate in those years.

Beginning with Chapter 9, we shall examine the determination of exchange rates and the explanations that have been offered for exchange rate variability. For the time being, it is sufficient that you know what real exchange rates are, that they show a good deal of variability, that this variability is often long-term, and that you have some idea about why the variability is significant.

Short-term Exchange Rate Behavior

The long-term exchange rate variability that stands out so clearly in Exhibits 3.1 and 3.2 has been accompanied by a high degree of short-term exchange rate variability and volatility. Exchange rate volatility increased noticeably during the 1980s from its range during the 1970s, placing great pressure on central banks to intervene forcefully in the forex market. Extensive experience with central banks' intervention demonstrates, however, that their ability to influence exchange rate behavior through forex sales and purchases is limited. While central banks do intervene frequently, exchange rates may still move several percentage points in one direction during a few days' time, or they may move sharply in one direction one day and equally sharply in the other direction the next.

During the 1970s, central bank intervention to stabilize exchange rates was generally unsuccessful, primarily because governments attempted to hold currencies at unsustainable levels, given the strength of exchange rate trends and the resources at the disposal of speculators. During the first half of the 1980s, central bank intervention became less common, in part because of the failures of the 1970s, but largely because the Reagan administration was opposed to it.

By late 1985, however, the U.S. government had shifted its position, and since that time, massive and coordinated central bank intervention has become common. When central banks intervene these days, however, they choose their ground more carefully than during the 1970s. They avoid attempting to deflect exchange rates from their fundamental trends, and, more than they did during the 1970s, they attempt to secure international cooperation in the conduct of monetary policy. This improved monetary coordination has largely been brought about through meetings and consultations among officials of the G-7 countries: the United States, Canada, Japan, the United Kingdom, France, Italy, and Germany. Nevertheless, day-to-day, week-to-week, and month-to-month, exchange rates between freely traded currencies are often highly variable.

| E X H I B I T | 3.3 | *Daily Exchange Rate Variability: January and August 1988*

	West German Mark	Swiss Franc	British Pound	Japanese Yen	Canadian Dollar
January 1988					
Number of trading days	20	19	20	19	20
Number of daily variations					
0.0 percent	2	1	0	1	1
0.1 to 0.4 percent	9	11	10	6	18
0.5 to 0.9 percent	5	1	5	4	1
1.0 to 1.9 percent	2	4	3	4	0
2.0 percent or more	2	2	2	4	0
Direction of movement					
Number of days with exchange rate increase	9	7	9	11	12
Number of days with exchange rate decrease	9	11	11	7	7
Cumulative exchange rate change during the month	−5.6%	−6.3%	−5.4%	−2.9%	+1.9%
August 1988					
Number of trading days	23	22	22	23	22
Number of daily variations					
0.0 percent	1	1	0	1	1
0.1 to 0.4 percent	11	11	11	16	20
0.5 to 0.9 percent	8	4	9	4	1
1.0 to 1.9 percent	3	6	2	2	0
2.0 percent or more	0	0	0	0	0
Direction of movement					
Number of days with exchange rate increase	10	8	10	9	7
Number of days with exchange rate decrease	12	13	12	13	14
Cumulative exchange rate change during the month	+0.3%	−1.2%	−1.5%	−1.8%	−2.4%

Source: IMF, *International Financial Statistics*, various issues. The daily exchange rates reported by this source are market rates, as reported by central banks.

Daily Exchange Rate Variations Exhibit 3.3 sheds some light on short-term exchange rate variability by providing summaries of daily exchange rate variations during the months of January and August 1988 between the U.S. dollar and the five currencies that are most heavily traded against it: the mark, the Swiss franc, the British pound, the yen, and the Canadian dollar. August 1988 represents a relatively quiet trading month, while January 1988 illustrates a month of frantic forex market activity.

In January 1988, the U.S. dollar rose sharply against most other currencies, reversing a downward trend. For the month as a whole, it rose against all the other currencies except the Canadian dollar. The U.S. dollar price against the mark and the Swiss franc fell by more than 5 percent during the month, and even the yen, the currency that has shown the strongest long-term tendency to rise against the dollar, fell in its dollar price by 2.9 percent.

The dollar's upward movement in January 1988 was accompanied by great day-to-day volatility. For the five currencies included in Exhibit 3.3, there were 23 cases in which the variation from the previous trading day's price was 1.0 percent or more. On four occasions, an exchange rate changed by 3.0 percent or more in a single day. Despite the generally downward drift of four of the currencies, there were many days on which their dollar prices increased. The yen increased in price on 11 trading days and fell on only 7, notwithstanding its net downward movement. The currency whose U.S. dollar price exhibited by far the greatest stability during the month was the Canadian dollar. On 18 out of 20 trading days, its price varied within the narrow range of 0.1 to 0.4 percent.

August 1988 was much quieter on the forex front. Even so, there was considerable day-to-day movement, and there was a significant cumulative change during the month. As in January 1988, the U.S. dollar rose against four of the five currencies, but this time the currency that rose against the dollar was the mark. The mark's cumulative rise for the month was, however, only 0.3 percent. The cumulative declines of the other currencies ranged from 1.2 percent for the Swiss franc to 2.4 percent for the Canadian dollar. Even in this comparatively tranquil month, there were still 13 occasions on which one of the currencies rose by 1.0 percent or more in a single day. Although the Canadian dollar had the greatest cumulative slide against the U.S. dollar, it retained its usual status as the most stable currency against the U.S. dollar on a day-to-day basis.

Central Bank Policy since the Plaza Agreement   Since 1985, the central banks of the leading industrial nations have been more actively involved in forex market intervention than they were before then. Given that the resources at the command of potential speculators exceed those available for central bank intervention, central bankers realize that they can favorably influence exchange rates through market intervention only if the intervention is consistent with prevailing market expectations. If, however, it is widely believed that central bank intervention is, or is going to be, supported by governments' macroeconomic policies, it can have a definite influence on expectations. The key to the success or failure of intervention, therefore, is its effect on expectations.

From early 1980 to the end of February 1985, the exchange value of the U.S. dollar had a sustained rise that central bankers became anxious to reverse; although the dollar's exchange value moved downward from its February high point, the consensus among central bankers was that it needed to fall still more during the next few months. In September 1985, representatives of the Group of Five (G-5) nations (the United States, Japan, the United Kingdom, France, and Germany) met at the Plaza Hotel in New York City and agreed on a program to lower the dollar's exchange value. The U.S. government then reversed its previous policy of avoiding forex market intervention and adopted an expansionary monetary policy motivated in large part by the desire to lower the dollar's exchange value.

The Plaza Agreement's objective of a cheaper dollar was subsequently achieved. In fact, it was overachieved! By the beginning of 1987, the dollar had fallen so far that a new exchange rate strategy was deemed necessary. In February 1987, representatives from the now-enlarged inner circle of industrial nations known as the G-7 (adding Canada and Italy) met at the Louvre in Paris to revise their strategy. The Louvre Accord brought a commitment from the participating nations to support the dollar within narrow, unannounced limits. The government of the United States promised to reduce its budget deficit and the governments of Japan and Germany indicated that they would take action to stimulate their economies.

It proved politically difficult for G-7 nations to honor the promises they made in the Louvre Accord, and in October 1987, the financial world was rocked by a drastic decline in stock market prices that began in the United States. Reacting to the resulting uncertainty, representatives of the G-7 nations met in November and December 1987 and negotiated secret agreements that, it soon became clear, pledged their governments to seek to maintain exchange rates among G-7 countries within *broad* limits. In effect, governments recognized that sizable exchange rate fluctuations might be unavoidable, but they hoped to avoid repeating the "roller-coaster" pattern of the years 1980 to 1987 (see Exhibits 3.1 and 3.2). Just what the permitted limits were to be was not announced officially, but many believe they specified that the market exchange rates of the dollar with the mark and the yen should be kept within bands of DM1.60 to 1.90/$ and ¥ 120 to 140/$, respectively.

On the whole, long-term exchange rate fluctuations have been smaller since 1987 than in the period 1980 to 1987, but this does not mean that they have been small. Notwithstanding massive and frequent central bank interventions, exchange rates have continued to exhibit a high degree of day-to-day volatility, and their short-term and long-term variations have tended to be large enough to warrant a continued preoccupation with exchange rates by financial managers, economists, and other interested parties.

During most of 1988 and 1989, the dollar generally performed strongly. For example, in the second and third quarters of 1980, its exchange value against the mark and the yen averaged slightly more than the presumed upper limits of the G-7 bands of DM 1.90/$ and ¥ 140/$, respectively. The dollar then continued its upward movement against the yen, with the result that the yen/dollar exchange rate averaged about ¥ 155/$ during the second quarter of 1990. From that level the dollar then sank rapidly to an average of about ¥ 131/$ in the fourth quarter of 1990. Against the mark, the dollar started moving downward in the fourth quarter of 1989 and reached an average exchange rate of only about DM1.50/$ in the fourth quarter of 1990. During the early months of 1991, the dollar moved generally upward against both currencies.

Although G-7 exchange rates have generally remained within their prescribed bands since the end of 1987, there have obviously been occasions when the bands' limits have been substantially exceeded. Moreover, while G-7 consultations occur frequently, the coordination of economic policy achieved has disappointed many observers. The European countries have succeeded in reducing exchange rate fluctuations among their currencies, and Canada and the United States appear to be achieving a greater harmonization of economic policy with each other. When it comes to harmonization among the three power centers of Europe, North America, and Japan, however, the story is very different. Each center sets its economic policy with a high degree of independence from the other two. This means, for example, that central bank intervention in the forex market is often not coordinated among the three centers. Under these circumstances, the probability is high that exchange rate variability will continue to be a major factor of economic life in the years ahead.

The IMF under Floating Exchange Rates

Because the IMF was set up to support an adjustable peg system of exchange rates, some observers predicted around 1973 that floating rates would lead to a diminution in its role in the international monetary system. They underestimated the bureaucratic imperative of survival (which is not necessarily a bad thing). In actuality, the IMF has found an important role for itself in the present scheme of things, though that role has changed substantially since 1973. Before 1973, the IMF lent primarily to developed countries. In the contemporary international monetary system, however, it is primarily concerned with lending to LDCs.

Changes in the Rules

Because the IMF's rules were originally designed to accommodate the needs of an adjustable peg system, floating rates forced the fund to conduct policy on an ad hoc basis until its Articles of Agreement could be formally amended. Early in 1976, the Interim Committee of the IMF met in Kingston, Jamaica and reached agreement on how the rules should be changed. This agreement, known as the Second Amendment, became effective in 1978.[1]

Article IV of the Second Amendment sets forth the general principles that IMF members are expected to follow in conducting exchange rate policy.[2] Its language and subsequent interpretation permit several generalizations about the IMF's current guidelines. First, the fund exercises "firm surveillance" over exchange rates. Second, firm surveillance is based on three general principles: (1) members should avoid manipulating exchange rates so as to obtain unfair competitive advantages in international trade; (2) they are expected to

---

[1]The First Amendment, which went into effect in 1969, authorized the use of SDRs, whose role is examined a little later in the chapter.

[2]See *IMF Survey: Supplement on the Fund,* September 1988, pp. 7–8.

intervene in the forex market to counter disruptive exchange rate fluctuations; and (3) when they intervene, they should take into account the interests of other countries. Third, the fund encourages its members to coordinate their economic policies with those of other members so as to minimize exchange rate fluctuations.

Article IV requires regular consultations between the IMF and its members about their forex practices. Members who maintain exchange controls on current account transactions (goods and services) by availing themselves of Article XIV of the Articles of Agreement, as they are still permitted to do, are required to consult more frequently with the IMF than members who have accepted Article VIII of the Articles of Agreement, which requires the avoidance of exchange controls on current account transactions.[3]

The IMF thus concedes the right to float, provided that members exercise it in harmony with their own economic welfare and that of other nations. It rejects the idea that exchange rates should fluctuate freely, and it strives to promote conditions that minimize exchange rate instability. In pursuing its objectives, it can obviously bring greater pressure to bear on countries that need to borrow from it than on countries that do not, which means that it has more power over LDCs than over wealthy countries. It should be noted, however, that the latter are not immune to world opinion and that the IMF reflects that opinion.

IMF Lending

Since 1973, the IMF's operations have increasingly focused on the LDCs. In part, the change in focus has occurred because the wealthier countries haven't needed IMF financing. Floating exchange rates have lowered the pressure on them to intervene in the forex market; they have greatly augmented their holdings of intervention assets; and they have improved on mechanisms for the mutual support of their currencies outside IMF channels, such as reciprocal lines of credit. By contrast, the LDCs have tended to become more dependent on the IMF. They have generally been reluctant to allow their currencies to float, which means they often confront serious payment problems. Moreover, their alternative financing channels have tended to dry up.

The drying up of the LDCs' alternative financing channels is largely a consequence of the sovereign debt problem, whose origins and consequences are examined in Chapter 12. Beginning in 1982, a number of LDC governments revealed that they could no longer fully service their foreign debt, most of which they owed to commercial banks in wealthy countries. Ever since this problem emerged, the flow of credits to LDCs has tended to be tightly constricted, and the risk premiums on the loans made have tended to be high. Some countries that encountered serious debt service difficulties have improved

---

[3]Of the Fund's 155 members, 68 have accepted Article VIII. The members who have accepted Article VIII account for the vast majority of the world's forex transactions and include all members whose currencies are freely traded.

their credit standing, and some LDCs avoided such difficulties in the first place. In general, however, private parties have less interest in lending to LDCs than they had before 1982. Accordingly, the IMF has been under pressure to use its facilities to transfer resources from countries that have to countries that have not.

The end of the 1980s brought with it the rapid dismantling of the Soviet Bloc. As part of the dismantling process, former Bloc members have turned to the IMF for assistance and shown themselves willing to accept the restrictions that the IMF imposes on borrowers. As these countries have become more effectively integrated into the world economy, they have added to the pressure on the Fund to expand its assistance to have-not nations.

As its focus has changed, the IMF has progressively expanded its resources and liberalized its loan terms. Credit tranche lending through stand-by agreements continues to be important, but other lending arrangements with more lenient conditions now account for most IMF loans. These other arrangements are known generally as "facilities."

Exhibit 3.4 summarizes IMF lending by loan type and geographical distribution as of March 31, 1991. The loan amounts are actual disbursements minus repayments, not authorized amounts. At any given time, there are large amounts of authorized borrowings that have not been disbursed. On March 31, 1991, for example, the undisbursed amounts of authorized loans totaled almost $9.5 billion. Note that the amounts shown in Exhibit 3.4 are, following IMF custom, in millions of SDRs, a currency unit whose nature is examined a little later in the chapter. Had those amounts been in dollars, they would have totaled approximately $33.5 billion instead of the approximately SDR 25 billion actually indicated.

As of March 31, 1991, 63.4 percent of the IMF's loans were financed from its own resources (mainly members' quota subscriptions). These loans fall into three categories: the stand-by credit tranche, the compensatory and contingency financing facility (CCFF), and the extended fund facility. Stand-by borrowing in credit tranches equal to 25 percent of members' quotas is the traditional IMF lending technique mentioned in Chapter 2 and requires repayment within 3-1/4 to 5 years after disbursement. The CCFF evolved from the compensatory financing facility, which originated in 1963 for the purpose of assisting countries with temporary shortfalls in their earnings from exports. The CCFF is used not only for this purpose, but also for maintaining vital food imports and sustaining structural adjustment programs worked out under IMF auspices. Extended facility loans, which date from 1974, are designed to overcome structural balance of payments problems and generally have longer payback periods (4-1/2 to 10 years) than credit tranche or CCFF loans.

These three types of loans carry a uniform interest rate. While it is common to say that this rate is a market or commercial rate, it is generally slightly below the interest rates charged by commercial banks on loans to governments with high credit ratings. The loans are subject to **conditionality,** which means that the borrowers must accept restrictions imposed by the IMF to receive loans and continue to abide by these restrictions in order to receive undisbursed amounts. In general, the restrictions imposed on extended facility loans are more stringent than those imposed on the other types.

| EXHIBIT | 3.4 | *Outstanding IMF Loans: March 31, 1991*

Loan Classification	Outstanding Loans (in Millions of SDRs)	Percentage of Total
Total loans outstanding[a]	25,036.6	100.0%
From the general resources account[b]	22,409.9	89.5
Ordinary Resources	15,867.9	63.4
Compensatory and contingency financing facility	5,007.7	20.0
Stand-by credit tranche	5,073.7	20.3
Extended fund facility	5,786.5	23.1
Borrowed resources	6,542.0	26.1
Supplementary financing facility	268.4	1.1
Enlarged access resources	6,273.6	25.1
From special accounts and trusteeship Arrangements[c]	2,626.5	10.5
Structural adjustment facility	1,359.1	5.4
Enhanced structural adjustment facility	1,101.3	4.4
Trust fund	166.1	0.7
Geographical Distribution of IMF Loans		
Africa	5,670.5	22.6
Asia	4,772.2	19.1
Middle East	138.9	0.6
Western hemisphere	12,306.0	49.2
Europe	2,149.0	8.6

[a]Excludes the use of the reserve tranche.

[b]General resources loans are financed from the IMF's own resources and its borrowings. None of these loans are on concessionary terms

[c]These loans are on a concessionary basis and are financed by contributions from member governments.

Source: *International Financial Statistics,* May 1991, pp. 23, 26, and 27.

Exhibit 3.4 indicates that 26.1 percent of the IMF's outstanding loans on March 31, 1991, were financed by IMF borrowings. The use of this lending technique can be traced back to 1974, when it developed in response to the crisis caused by steep increases in petroleum prices. The financing has come from member governments, most notably the government of Saudi Arabia, and the loans are used to fund credit tranche and extended facility borrowings in excess of the normal limits.

The remaining 10.5 percent of the IMF's outstanding loans on March 31, 1991, consisted of loans on concessionary terms. Some of these funds have been contributed by member governments, and some were obtained when the IMF sold most of its gold and used the proceeds to establish a trust fund. Loans under these subsidized arrangements are generally at the interest rate of 0.5 percent. The IMF's use of concessionary lending dates from 1976.

IMF lending continues to be quota based, but the quota percentages that borrowings may reach have substantially increased over the years. Stand-by credit tranche borrowing has always had a ceiling of 100 percent of a government's quota, but when stand-by loans are supplemented with funds that the IMF has borrowed, they may substantially exceed 100 percent of quotas. Extended facility loans may be made to countries with outstanding stand-by loans, and vice versa. Extended facility loans have more generous limits than stand-by credits, and CCFF loans and loans on concessionary terms may be made without diminishing a member's eligibility for stand-by and extended facility loans.

It is now possible for a government's outstanding borrowings from the IMF to exceed 500 percent of its quota. As of March 31, 1991, however, few governments had borrowings in excess of 200 percent of their quotas. The most heavily indebted governments in this sense were the Sudan and Mexico, whose borrowings totaled 395.8 percent and 378.0 percent, respectively, of their quotas.[4]

The data in Exhibit 3.4 on the geographical distribution of IMF loans indicates that 49.2 percent of the loans outstanding on March 31, 1991, were to Latin American governments. The SDR 2,149.0 billion in loans to European borrowers were all to either Yugoslavia or former members of the Soviet Bloc. Not a single outstanding IMF loan was to the government of a developed country.

Quotas and Other Loan-Related Matters

As of March 31, 1991, there were 155 IMF member countries with total quotas of SDR 91.1 billion.[5] Since their total IMF borrowings of SDR 25.0 billion equalled less than 27 percent of their overall quotas, it may seem initially that the IMF's lending capacity is greatly underutilized. The IMF maintains, however, that there are members who could service additional borrowings but are constrained by existing quota limits. Moreover, since only 25 percent of a nation's quota must be paid in currencies that the Fund classifies as reserve assets, while the rest is paid in the member's currency, a large part of the IMF's currency holdings are made up of currencies that are not widely used internationally. While someone occasionally borrows Malaysian ringgits from the IMF, for example, borrowers normally want dollars or some other widely used convertible currency.

Although repaying IMF loans tends to carry a high priority for borrowers, in recent years some borrowers have fallen into arrears in their payments to the Fund. When this happens, a member becomes almost totally cut off from access to external credit sources. With some of its loans in arrears, the IMF is under pressure to lend cautiously and to insist on structural reforms with beneficial long-term effects before providing additional credits.

Under the Articles of Agreement, the Board of Governors of the IMF must conduct general reviews of quotas at intervals that do not exceed 5 years. Such reviews usually lead to recommendations that quotas be increased. In June

---

[4]*International Financial Statistics*, May 1991, pp. 24–25.
[5]*Ibid.*

1990, the Board recommended that quotas be raised by approximately 50 percent. Simultaneously, it proposed a Third Amendment to the Articles of Agreement to provide for the suspension of the voting and other rights of members who fail to fulfill their obligations. No increase in quotas is to take effect until the Third Amendment has been implemented. Members have until December 31, 1991, to approve or reject the proposed quota increases, and the review period may be extended if that is deemed necessary.[6]

The proposed quota increases would raise the quota of the United States from SDR 17.9 billion to SDR 26.5 billion. Germany and Japan are to share second place with quotas of SDR 8.2 billion each, and Britain and France are to share fourth place with identical quotas of SDR 7.4 billion. Sixth place would go to Saudi Arabia, at SDR 5.1 billion. At the other end of the list are such countries as the Republic of Kiribati (SDR 4.0 million) and Bhutan (SDR 4.5 million).[7]

Prior to the dissolution of the Soviet Union in 1991, all the members of the former Soviet Bloc except the Soviet Union itself has joined the IMF. Albania also joined the IMF. Now that the Soviet Union has officially dissolved itself, its constituent republics are in the process of affiliating with the IMF, whose financial assistance they badly need. Switzerland, which is not officially an IMF member, is likely to formally join the IMF in the next few years. The last two holdouts will probably be Cuba and North Korea.

The chief executive of the IMF, known as its Managing Director, is invariably a European. The IMF's Deputy Director is customarily an American. To date, few Japanese have held important executive positions with the IMF, but this situation can be expected to change.

Special Drawing Rights (SDRs)

The SDR is an international reserve asset composed of parts of five currencies (the U.S. dollar, the mark, the yen, the French franc, and the pound sterling). The agreement to create SDRs was reached in 1967 and implemented at the beginning of 1970. To date, 21.4 billion SDRs have been created in six allocations occurring in two rounds of 3 years each. The first round created 9.3 billion SDRs, which were distributed in approximately equal amounts in January 1970, 1971, and 1972. The other 12.1 billion SDRs were allocated in January 1979, 1980, and 1981. All allocations were made through the IMF in proportion to members' IMF quotas at the time of allocation.

SDRs can be held only by IMF members, the IMF itself, and (as of 1984) designated official (government-sponsored) agencies. They are used to a limited extent as a medium of exchange, but since they can only be held officially, they cannot be exchanged in transactions between private parties. Governments that have received SDRs from the IMF, i.e., the vast majority of IMF members, are obligated to accept them from other SDR holders under

---

[6]*IMF Survey: Supplement on the Fund,* August 1990, p. 5.
[7]*Ibid,* p. 4.

certain conditions. Specifically, the IMF may require the acceptance of SDRs in a "transaction with designation," in which the IMF informs a government that it must receive a certain quantity of SDRs and give up an equivalent quantity of convertible currency. This requirement is subject to the restriction that no member can be required to hold additional SDRs when its current holdings equal three times its original allocations.

In reality, the SDR has become good enough as an international reserve asset so that it has not been necessary for the IMF to employ transactions with designation since 1987. Almost all SDR transactions now fall under the classification of "transactions by agreement," which means that two authorized holders of them agree, at their own initiative, to a spot exchange of SDRs for an equivalent amount of foreign exchange. In addition, the use of SDRs in forward transactions and swap arrangements is permissible, provided they are not exchanged for gold.

Governments are willing to accept SDRs for two reasons. First, if a government had refused to agree to accept them, it would not have received them from the IMF. Second, when a government holds SDRs in excess of its total allocation, it collects interest on the excess. The interest rate paid equals 100 percent of a weighted-average interest rate based on the interest rates of designated money market instruments in the five countries whose currencies determine the SDR's value.[8] The interest received by accepting countries is paid by the countries whose SDR holdings fall below their allocations.

A Brief History of SDRs   When the SDR came into being, it was defined in gold to establish an official gold price of SDR35 per ounce. This meant that its value exactly equalled that of the dollar. The gold definition of the SDR was retained when the dollar was devalued in terms of gold in 1971 and 1973, with the result that the SDR's value rose substantially above that of the dollar. In 1974, the IMF cut the tie between the SDR and gold by redefining it as a basket of 16 currencies.[9] This decision resulted from the IMF's threefold desire to eliminate the SDR's tie to gold, to discourage the monetary use of gold, and to make the SDR a reserve asset with greater stability of value than a national currency.

Because the basket of 16 currencies proved unduly cumbersome, the IMF limited the SDR's components, effective January 1, 1981, to the five currencies that were listed earlier. Accompanying this revision, it changed the interest rate paid on the use of SDRs from 80 percent of the weighted average of interest rates to 100 percent in order to increase the attractiveness of holding SDRs.

The SDR's composition is revised every 5 years unless the IMF's Executive Board should deem an earlier revision to be desirable. The last revision became

---

[8]The weights assigned to the interest rates of the five countries are the same as the weights of their currencies in the SDR.

[9]The decision to redefine the SDR coincided with the renaming of the gold tranche as the "reserve tranche." From that time, the reserve tranche was to be payable in reserve assets (currencies) other than gold.

| EXHIBIT | 3.5 | *SDR Composition and Valuation: March 28, 1991*

Currency	Currency Amount in One SDR	Exchange Rate on March 28, 1991[a]	U.S. Dollar Equivalent[b]
Deutsche mark	0.4530	1.7170	$0.2638
French franc	0.8000	5.8160	0.1376
Japanese yen	31.8000	139.80	0.2275
Pound sterling	0.0812	0.576203	0.1409
U.S. dollar	0.5720	1.0000	0.5720
Valuation of one SDR in terms of U.S. dollars			$1.3418[c]

[a]The exchange rates are market exchange rates in currency units per dollar as reported to the IMF by central banks and are usually the noon rates of the London forex market.

[b]The U.S. dollar equivalents are obtained by dividing the first column by the second column.

[c]The value of the SDR reported on this date by the IMF was actually $1.34085. The discrepancy between this rate and the rate shown above can be attributed to the IMF's using slightly different rates from those given in calculating the SDR's official value.

Sources: The currency amounts are from *IMF Survey*, January 21, 1991, p. 23. The exchange rates were obtained from *International Financial Statistics*, May 1991, p. 18.

effective on January 1, 1991. As can be seen in Exhibit 3.5, which gives the composition and valuation of the SDR as of March 28, 1991 (the last regular trading day of the month), the percentage of each component currency in the SDR's value depends on the quantity of it in the SDR and (for currencies other than the dollar) its exchange value against the dollar. In the basket revision of 1991, the amount of each currency was adjusted to compensate for exchange rate changes since the last previous revision (January 1, 1986). The dollar quantity was raised from $0.452 to $0.572, and the quantities of the other currencies were correspondingly reduced. The change in the SDR's composition was implemented so as not to disturb the SDR's existing exchange value. In time, of course, such a change does have an impact on the SDR's value.

Since the basket simplification of 1981, there has been some tendency to use the SDR as a unit of account in private transactions. A few international trade transactions have been SDR-denominated, but the settlement of such transactions usually requires payment in an equivalent amount of a national currency. More popular is the use of SDRs in financial transactions. Thus, some time deposits, private loan contracts, and securities are SDR-denominated. In addition, some governments have pegged the exchange values of their currencies to the SDR.

The primary appeal of the SDR as a unit of account, including its use for pegging purposes, is that since its value is a weighted average of currencies that vary in value against each other, it tends to have a more stable value than a national currency. To illustrate the point, consider that from August 6, 1990, to March 28, 1991, the mark, the French franc, and the pound sterling fell in terms of the dollar by 8.2 percent, 9.1 percent, and 7.3 percent, respectively, while the yen rose against the dollar by 7.2 percent. During the same period, the dollar value of the SDR declined by 2.1 percent.

The Future of SDRs   Although SDRs are used as a reserve asset and in some private transactions, and although a few countries peg their monetary units to the SDR, they are a long way from becoming a major factor in the international monetary system. They constitute about 3 percent of total reserve assets excluding gold, and, while there have been some interesting developments in their private use, they rank far behind the Ecu in this respect.

An argument can be made for increasing the role of SDRs. With the exceptions of gold, which has been reduced to inactive status, and Ecus, the SDR is the only reserve asset that is not a national currency. Despite considerable monetary cooperation among the leading financial powers, namely the United States, Japan, and Germany, no supranational mechanism can now control the overall growth of reserve assets. There is danger, therefore, that the overall growth rate of these assets may be too high or too low. Given the world's proclivity toward inflation, the former eventuality is the more probable; it is conceivable, however, that, at times such as worldwide recessions, the growth of reserve assets may prove inadequate. On such occasions, it might be desirable to inject more SDRs into the international monetary system.

The distribution of governments' reserves troubles many observers. In general, low-income countries have small reserve holdings, while high-income countries have large reserve holdings. One way to deal with this distribution problem is to increase IMF quotas, enabling LDCs to borrow more heavily, but an alternative is to issue more SDRs. Since SDRs are distributed free of charge, increasing their quantity would allow the LDCs to increase their reserves without incurring additional interest costs. Moreover, the distribution of SDRs in any new allocation could be based in part on the criterion of need rather than on the proportion of members' IMF quotas.

Against such arguments, some counter that the world is not suffering from insufficient reserve growth at present, that it is not likely to do so in the future, and that it is dangerous to provide large financial subsidies to LDCs that lack the structural political and economic conditions to assure that additional financial resources would be used productively. As such cases as South Korea and Taiwan demonstrate, the existing international financial order can accommodate the reserve needs of countries that have made the necessary structural adjustments.

The European Monetary System and the Ecu

The stormy financial weather of the early months of 1973 subjected the European snake to a furious pounding, from which it emerged with its backbone bruised but intact. During the next few years, the snake held loosely together around the mark, and even two non-EEC countries, Norway and

Sweden, participated in it for a while. Most of the snake's would-be participants found, however, that they could not keep their currencies within 2.25 percent of the mark because of Germany's low inflation rate and the tendency of speculators to flock to marks at the slightest hint of exchange rate disequilibrium. By 1978, the snake's only participants were Germany, the Benelux countries, and Denmark. At that juncture, however, the desire to achieve greater regional monetary stability and dissatisfaction with the dollar as the region's primary reserve asset induced the EEC's members to enter into a formal arrangement to promote regional monetary integration and financial integration. This arrangement, known as the **European Monetary System (EMS)**, began operating in 1979. Its most eye-catching features have been the creation of a new reserve asset, the **European currency unit (Ecu)**, and its maintenance of a joint float against the dollar and other non-EEC currencies. This joint float is commonly called the exchange rate mechanism (ERM).

At present, the membership of the EEC consists of Belgium, Denmark, France, Germany, Greece, Ireland, Italy, Luxembourg, the Netherlands, Portugal, Spain, and the United Kingdom. All of these nations participate in the EMS, but Greece and Portugal do not participate in the ERM.

The Exchange Rate Mechanism

The ERM relies heavily on the Ecu, whose components include all the monetary units of EEC members, including Greece and Portugal. Each ERM currency has a central rate, which is expressed in currency units per Ecu. From the central rates are derived **bilateral par value exchange rates** between each pair of ERM currencies. Most of the float's participants are required to maintain bilateral market exchange rates that are within approximately 2.25 percent above or below the corresponding bilateral par values, but the Spanish peseta and the pound sterling (the two newest additions to the ERM) are allowed to fluctuate approximately 6 percent above or below their bilateral par value rates with the other ERM currencies.[10] If a bilateral market exchange rate moves to either of its limits, the central banks of *both* countries must intervene to keep the rate within its prescribed bounds.

Intervention may also be required because of a complicated procedure based on divergences of currencies' Ecu market rates from their Ecu central rates. It is desirable to have some idea of what this procedure is and what it

---

[10]The reason for writing *approximately* 2.25 percent and *approximately* 6 percent is that the allowable fluctuations differ slightly from these figures because of adjustments that take into account the fact that when an exchange rate changes, the percentage change in one currency does not exactly equal, with signs reversed, the percentage change in the other. For example, the pound sterling's market value relative to another ERM currency is allowed to increase by as much as 6.18 percent, but the maximum decrease allowed the pound is 5.82 percent. Similarly, the maximum increase allowed the mark against an ERM currency other than the peseta or the pound sterling is 2.28 percent. While the maximum decrease allowed the mark is 2.25 percent in one case (the lira), it is 2.24 percent against most currencies and 2.22 percent against one (the Danish krone).

means. The basic idea is that, if the Ecu market rate of a currency moves beyond a point known as the "threshold of divergence," the government of the country with that currency must act to reverse the currency's movement against the Ecu. Such action may take the form of forex market intervention, but it may also involve raising or lowering money market interest rates in order to encourage or discourage capital inflows.

The **threshold of divergence** equals 75 percent of the allowable divergence of a currency's Ecu market rate from its Ecu central rate after certain adjustments to both rates. These adjustments refine both the market rate and the central rate by eliminating from them those parts of the Ecu consisting of the currencies of EMS members who do not participate in the ERM. Another adjustment takes into account the greater allowable deviations of the peseta and the pound sterling from their Ecu central rates. Furthermore, in calculating the allowable divergence of a currency's Ecu market rate from its Ecu central rate, an adjustment is made that removes from the central rate the currency for which the allowable divergence is being calculated. This adjustment takes into account the fact that a currency cannot diverge against itself. The resulting adjusted central rate is then multiplied by 2.25 percent or, in the case of the peseta and the pound sterling, by 6 percent to determine the maximum allowable divergence of the Ecu market rate from the corresponding central rate. If the adjusted Ecu market rate differs from the adjusted Ecu central rate by 75 percent or more of the maximum allowable divergence, the threshold of divergence has been reached or crossed, and corrective action becomes mandatory as noted earlier.

Exhibit 3.6 illustrates how this procedure works in practice. It is essentially a reproduction of a table appearing in the *Financial Times* of March 28, 1991. The first column of figures gives the Ecu central rates of each of the nine currencies in the ERM. (The Luxembourg franc is excluded because it exchanges one-for-one with the Belgian franc and is treated as the same currency in divergence calculations.) The second column gives the market exchange rates of individual currencies with the Ecu, and the third column measures the differences between the first two columns in percentages. The fourth column shows the percentages by which the market exchange rates of eight of the currencies differed from their bilateral par values with the French franc, the weakest of the nine currencies on the chosen date. These bilateral percentages are calculated from the Ecu rates of the first two columns. The last column gives the divergence indicator, which is the percentage of the maximum allowable divergence from its adjusted Ecu central rate that the adjusted Ecu market value of a currency has reached.

Exhibit 3.6 indicates that on March 27, 1991, the peseta's Ecu market rate had a divergence indicator of 78 and was, therefore, past the divergence threshold of 75. Presumably, therefore, the Spanish government was acting to lower the peseta's Ecu market value. Exhibit 3.6 also indicates that the bilateral market value of the peseta against the French franc was 5.99 percent above its bilateral par value with the franc. This is so close to the maximum allowable divergence of approximately 6 percent that it can be presumed that

| EXHIBIT | 3.6 | *Status of the ERM: March 27, 1991*

EMS European Currency Unit Rates

Currency	Ecu Central Rates	Currency Amounts against the Ecu, March 27, 1991	Percentage Change from Central Rate[a]	Percentage spread vs. Weakest Currency[b]	Divergence Indicator[c]
Spanish peseta	133.631	127.669	−4.46	5.99	78
Italian lira	1538.24	1527.84	−0.68	1.95	41
Pound sterling	0.696904	0.693687	−0.46	1.73	8
Belgian franc	42.4032	42.3683	−0.08	1.34	11
Deutsche mark	2.05586	2.05804	0.11	1.15	3
Dutch guilder	2.31643	2.32028	0.17	1.09	−1
Irish punt	0.767417	0.771380	0.52	0.74	−17
Danish krone	7.84195	7.89366	0.66	0.59	−23
French franc	6.89509	6.98179	1.26	0.00	−61

[a]A negative sign indicates that a currency has risen relative to the Ecu central rate, and the absence of a negative sign indicates that a currency has fallen relative to the Ecu central rate.

[b]This is the percentage by which the market value of a currency exceeded its bilateral par value with the French franc, the currency with the greatest decline against the Ecu as of this date.

[c]This is the percentage of its maximum permissible divergence from its Ecu central rate that the market value of a currency has actually diverged. In calculating this percentage, certain adjustments are made that cause this percentage to differ from the ratio between the third column of figures above and the maximum amounts (6 percent for the pound sterling and the peseta and 2.25 percent for the other currencies) by which bilateral market exchange rates are permitted to diverge from bilateral par value rates. See the text for further explanation.

Source: *Financial Times*, March 28, 1991, p. 40.

the central banks of Spain and France were either acting to lower this rate or preparing to act to lower it.[11] Although the franc was close to its divergence limit against the peseta, the divergence indicator of the franc (minus 61) was considerably short of its divergence threshold, which means that the French government was not yet required to act to raise the franc's Ecu market value.

---

[11]According to the parity grid under which the central banks of the ERM operate (see, for example, the *Financial Times*, October 9, 1990, p. 10 for an illustration of the grid), the central bank of Spain must buy French francs when the franc's market value falls to Ptas 18.2530/FF, and the central bank of France must sell pesetas when the peseta's market value reaches FF 0.054785/Pta. From Exhibit 3.6 it can be determined that the market rate between these two currencies on March 27, 1991, was Ptas 18.2860/FF or FF 0.5479/Pta (divergences of minus 5.82 percent and plus 6.18 percent, respectively, from their bilateral par value). This means that neither central bank was yet required to enter the market between the two currencies.

The Key Role of the Mark While Exhibit 3.6 shows the mark resting comfortably in the middle position among the nine currencies with a divergence indicator of plus 3, the point should be noted that the mark is allowed smaller variations against the Ecu than any other ERM currency. The adjusted Ecu market value of the mark may diverge by 2.25 percent from its adjusted Ecu central rate, but because of the nature of the adjustments, the actual Ecu market value of the mark is allowed to vary by considerably *less* than 2.25 percent of its actual Ecu central rate.[12] This situation follows from the nature of the adjustments and the fact that the mark has, by a considerable margin, the greatest weight of any currency in the Ecu.

The technical aspects of calculating the divergence limits for the mark need not concern us, but the practical significance of the mark's relatively small allowable divergence from its adjusted Ecu central rate is another matter. It means that the Bundesbank, Germany's central bank, is often required to intervene to steer the mark away from its divergence threshold. This fact explains, in part, why the mark is the ERM's key currency. More fundamentally, however, the mark is the key currency in the ERM because of its importance as a reserve currency and because the German government's dogged insistence on maintaining a low inflation rate puts great pressure on the governments of other ERM countries to do likewise.

Realignments of Ecu Central Rates The Ecu central rates of the currencies in the ERM are subject to periodic realignments. As of June 1991, there have been 12 of these, the last one having occurred in August 1990. Their frequency has caused some observers to assert that the joint float has failed in its mission to stabilize exchange rates among the participating currencies.

There is, however, abundant evidence that the ERM has been a success. Since 1979, its members have achieved a much greater convergence of monetary policies than they had previously achieved, the differences in their inflation rates have diminished sharply, and their overall inflation rate has fallen. As a result, Ecu central rate adjustments have tended to become smaller over time. No major changes in Ecu central rates have occurred since 1987—the adjustments of 1990 were minor ones designed to accommodate the lira's switch from a 6 percent band of allowable fluctuations to a narrow band of 2.25 percent. Spain (in 1989) and the United Kingdom (in 1990) have recently elected to join the ERM, and other European countries are now pegging their currencies to the Ecu and exploring the possibility of becoming EMS participants. There will undoubtedly be further Ecu central rate realignments, but the evidence warrants optimism about the joint float's future.

---

[12]Exhibit 3.6 can be used to shed some light on the point being made here. Observe that it indicates that, on March 27, 1991, the Ecu market value of the mark was 11 percent less than its Ecu central rate value, but that the divergence indicator for the mark was plus 3. Without the adjustments referred to, the divergence indicator for the mark would have been −0.11/2.25 or −4.9 percent.

| E X H I B I T | 3.7 | *Ecu Composition and Valuation: March 28, 1991*

Currency	Currency Amount in One Ecu	Exchange Rate on March 28, 1991[a]	U.S. Dollar Equivalent[b]
Belgian franc	3.301	35.10	0.0940
Danish frone	0.1976	6.5363	0.0302
Deutsche mark	0.6242	1.7055	0.3660
French franc	1.332	5.7725	0.2307
Greek drachma	1.44	177.00	0.0081
Irish punt	0.008552	1.5664	0.0134
Italian lira	151.8	1269.33	0.1196
Luxembourg franc	0.13	35.10	0.0037
Netherlands guilder	0.2198	1.9224	0.1143
Portuguese escudo	1.303	149.55	0.0087
Pound sterling	0.08784	1.7405	0.1529
Spanish peseta	6.885	105.71	0.0651
Valuation of one Ecu in terms of U.S. dollars			$1.2067[c]

[a]The exchange rates are interbank selling rates for foreign currencies as quoted at 3 p.m. Eastern time in the New York foreign exchange market. All exchange rates except those for the Irish punt and the pound sterling are in currency units per dollar, but these two rates are in dollars per currency unit.

[b]The U.S. dollar equivalents are obtained by dividing the first column by the second except for the Irish punt and the pound sterling, for which the first column is multiplied by the second.

[c]The actual selling rate for the Ecu being quoted was $1.20018. The difference between that rate and the rate calculated above was probably due primarily to the incorporation of multiple dealer spreads into the currency selling rates.

Sources: The currency amounts were supplied by the Office of the European Economic Community in Washington, D.C. The exchange rates are from *The Wall Street Journal*, March 29, 1991, p. C10.

Composition and Valuation of the Ecu

Exhibit 3.7 presents the composition and valuation of the Ecu as of March 28, 1991, using the exchange rates published in *The Wall Street Journal* on the following day. The amounts of each of the 12 currencies in the Ecu were last revised in September 1989. Thus, when in October 1990 the government of the United Kingdom announced that it was joining the ERM, the Ecu's composition remained intact.

From Exhibit 3.7 it can be determined that, on March 28, 1991, the mark accounted for 30.3 percent of the Ecu's dollar value and that the corresponding percentages for the French franc and the pound sterling were, respectively, 19.1 percent and 12.7 percent. The seemingly small percentage for the pound can be attributed to Britain's being a latecomer to the ERM. At the other end of the scale were the Luxembourg franc (0.3 percent), the Greek drachma (0.7 percent), the Portuguese escudo (0.7 percent), and the Irish punt (1.1 percent). In between, in descending order, were the lira (9.9 percent), the guilder (9.5 percent), the Belgian franc (7.8 percent), the peseta (5.4 percent), and the Danish krone (2.5 percent). Note that the drachma and the escudo, the two currencies not included in the ERM, accounted for only 1.4 percent of the Ecu's value.

The Role of the Ecu

When the ERM came into being, it required a monetary unit to serve as the common denominator or *numeraire* for the determination of official exchange rates. The role of numeraire could have been performed by the mark or any other currency in the float, but it was deemed advisable to create a currency composite to perform this role.

From the outset, however, the Ecu was intended to be more than just a numeraire, for it was to be an official reserve asset similar to the SDR. Each participant in the ERM turned over 20 percent of its gold and dollar reserves to the European Monetary Cooperation Fund (EMCF), receiving an equivalent quantity of Ecus in return. Although Britain did not participate in the ERM, it also exchanged 20 percent of its gold and dollar reserves for Ecus. It was intended that each government receiving Ecus would use them to obtain currencies from other EMS governments to support forex market intervention. Such transfers are recorded on the books of the Bank for International Settlements (BIS), which was designated to serve as the EMCF's agent. The BIS, a long-established bank for central banks, is jointly owned and operated by the central banks of European countries.[13]

Notice that this method for creating Ecus means that their quantity is variable, because it depends not only on the quantity of gold and dollars exchanged for Ecus, but also on the dollar/Ecu exchange rate and the price of gold. If, for example, the dollar's Ecu value increases, the Ecu deposits of EMS members with the BIS automatically increase. The purpose of allowing the

---

[13]The BIS is located in Basle, Switzerland. The Federal Reserve owns stock in it but plays no managerial role. It came into existence in 1930 in order to facilitate transfers of funds among European countries whose currencies lacked full convertibility into other currencies, and it exercised a similar role after World War II. Its primary duties now are: (1) to foster international monetary cooperation by holding meetings of central bankers; (2) to provide support for the EMS and the EEC; (3) to provide emergency assistance (bridge financing) to central banks, including those of LDCs and former Soviet Bloc members, until these institutions can arrange credits from other sources; and (4) to serve as an agent for the private Ecu clearing system.

In supporting the EEC, the BIS serves as the financial agent for the EMCF, in which capacity it administers financial operations denominated in Ecus that are connected with the operations of the EMS. In connection with this duty, it holds Ecu balances for EMS members and records transfers of Ecus between members. It also executes financial operations approved by the EEC, including operations designed to assist EEC central banks in supporting the exchange values of their currencies in accordance with EMS rules.

quantity of Ecus to vary directly with the dollar/Ecu exchange rate and the price of gold was to make the Ecu a more attractive reserve asset.

In practice, the official use of Ecus has been very limited. In fact, the Ecu ranks behind the SDR in this regard. The official use of Ecus is subject to severe restrictions, such as the fact that only EMS members can receive them in official transactions. On the other hand, the Ecu has come to be used extensively as both a medium of exchange and a unit of account in private transactions and in government transactions that are not between central banks. So extensive is its use in these ways that it now probably ranks fourth among the world's currencies in terms of the external positions in foreign currencies reported by banks, and the volume of Ecu-denominated bonds has recently been so large as to give the Ecu at least a temporary second place as the currency of denomination for new international bond issues. Hundreds of European banks offer Ecu deposits, and the volume of transactions in these deposits exceeds that of most European currencies. While the uses of Ecu deposits are overwhelmingly financial rather than for purchases of goods and services, the Ecu is clearly a major world currency.

Obviously, the Ecu has helped to meet an important need—the need for a European currency with a more stable value than any single national currency—for, like the SDR, the Ecu's value fluctuates less than the values of the individual currencies of which it is composed. This means, for example, that a firm with operations scattered over the face of Europe can modestly reduce its exchange risk by conducting its operations in Ecus. While the Ecu *has* tended to decline against the mark since 1979, this decline has been small enough relative to the normally prevailing excess of Ecu interest rates over mark interest rates that the holders of Ecu assets have generally not had reason to regret their choice.

The Future of the EMS and the Ecu

The members of the EEC have targeted the end of 1992 for the creation of a common market among them. Their goal of a common market entails the complete integration of financial markets, but a common market is not a monetary union. Accordingly, each member country will retain its currency and its national central bank, which will, with obvious limitations, conduct an autonomous national monetary policy. It is widely believed, however, that the formation of the common market will lead, in the space of a few years, to the formation of a European monetary union with a supranational central banking structure resembling the Federal Reserve System and a common currency. It is also widely believed that the Ecu will be that currency.

Ecu-skepticism was voiced when the Ecu materialized in 1979, and some such skepticism continues to be voiced today. It is pointed out, for example, that as exchange rates among European currencies have become more stable, there has been less reason to hedge the exchange risk by using Ecus rather than a national currency. It is sometimes claimed that including such historically weak currencies in the Ecu as the lira, the peseta, the escudo, and the drachma reduces the Ecu's appeal as a store of value since this implies that the Ecu may depreciate against the stronger currencies of the ERM. It is also pointed out that, at present, no central bank controls the quantity of Ecu deposits or stands ready to lend Ecus to banks needing additional reserves.

Beyond such questions about the quality of the Ecu, there are questions about the prospects of the EMS. For example, considerable tension exists between Britain and Germany over the powers and location of a proposed European central bank. The British would like assurance that the establishment of such an institution will not undermine the preeminence of London among European banking centers, while the Germans tend to feel that their economic power, their location, and their long-term success as inflation fighters entitle them to have the proposed central bank's operations based primarily in Germany.

Other questions about the EMS are whether it can whittle away the remaining differences in members' inflation rates and whether it is causing interest rates to be excessively volatile. As things now stand, such countries as Italy, Spain, and the United Kingdom have lowered their inflation rates in comparison with earlier years, but they continue to inflate more rapidly than Germany and other EMS members. To date, these countries have staved off declines in their Ecu central rates by maintaining relatively high interest rates. It is argued, however, that these high rates discourage investment and that, ultimately, PPP must prevail and bring about large cumulative currency realignments. Moreover, it is argued, because the maintenance of the ERM rests on the use of interest rate flexibility to preserve exchange rate stability, all ERM members are paying a price for membership in terms of interest rate uncertainty.

While the EMS obviously faces tough challenges, its success to date and the momentum it has achieved argue powerfully for its future success. The fact that the Ecu is composed in part of the currencies of countries with an inflation problem does not seem to be seriously retarding the expansion of its use. Indeed, Norway and Sweden have recently elected to peg their currencies firmly to the Ecu, and other countries are expected to follow suit. As things currently stand, European countries with relatively high inflation rates are anticipating that pegging their currencies to the Ecu will help them to reduce inflation and that the reduction of inflation will bring about reductions in the inflation premiums incorporated into interest rate structures. It is quite conceivable, therefore, that the pegging of their currencies to the Ecu will ultimately give them lower interest rates.

As things now stand, Ecu interest rates tend to be more stable than the interest rates of the individual nations that belong to the ERM or peg to the Ecu from outside the ERM framework. This fact is tending to increase the use of Ecus in financial transactions. As far as the problem of interest rate instability among the Ecu-pegging countries is concerned, this provides a rationale for developing a true monetary union in Europe in which the Ecu is the common currency. The obstacles to the formation of such a union are certain to be formidable, but the logic of having it may soon tip the scales in its favor.

Exchange Rate Arrangements and Reserve Holdings

Two final topics remain for consideration in this chapter: the exchange rate arrangements used by different countries and the volumes and distributions of governments' holdings of international reserve assets. Brief examinations of both follow.

Contemporary Exchange Rate Arrangements

While the contemporary international monetary system is often called a managed floating system, most nations have chosen to peg their currencies either to a single national currency or to a currency composite. This means, among other things, that while the gold standard and the Bretton Woods System have been discarded onto the historical scrap heap, the mechanics of their operation are still relevant to existing monetary arrangements. This is most obvious with the nations of the EMS, but the point also applies to many LDCs that have chosen to peg their currencies. It even applies, to a degree, to countries like the United States, which allows its currency to float, but attempts to confine the fluctuations within broad limits.

Exhibit 3.8 presents the exchange rate arrangements of IMF members as of December 31, 1990, as they appeared in *International Financial Statistics*. It indicates that, out of 153 reporting nations, 45 currencies were pegged to a national currency, 6 were pegged to the SDR, 35 were pegged to some other currency composite devised by governments to meet their particular needs, and 10 participated in the joint float of the EMS. In addition, the currencies of four Arabian peninsula countries listed in the single currency category were loosely pegged to the dollar.

When a government chooses to peg its currency to a particular national currency, it is because most or many of its international transactions are denominated in that currency. The U.S. dollar is by far the most widely used currency in international transactions, and this explains why 25 currencies were closely pegged to it and 4 currencies of Arabian Peninsula countries (that price their oil exports in dollars) were loosely pegged to it. Another 14 currencies, all those of former French colonies in Africa, were pegged to the French franc (and thus, indirectly, to the Ecu). In six other cases, the most notable one being Yugoslavia, a currency was pegged to a national currency other than the dollar or the franc. For example, Swaziland, a country surrounded by South Africa, pegged to the South African rand, and Yugoslavia pegged to the mark.

The decision to peg to the SDR or to some other currency composite is generally taken when a nation's international transactions are not predominantly in a single currency. Two of the 35 countries listed in the other composite category of Exhibit 3.8, Norway and Sweden, peg to the Ecu, and it is likely that a few other countries in this category will soon join them. Norway pegs to the Ecu within a 2.25 percent band, but Sweden (effective May 1991) has chosen to give up a 15-currency composite in which the dollar had a weight of about 22 percent in favor of a 1.5 percent Ecu band.

| E X H I B I T | 3.8 | *Exchange Rate Arrangements: March 31, 1991*[a]

Currency pegged to

U.S. Dollar	French Franc	Other Currency	SDR	Other Composite[b]
Afghanistan	Benin	Bhutan (Indian	Burundi	Algeria
Angola	Burkina Faso	rupee)	Iran	Austria
Antigua and	Cameroon	Kiribati	Libya	Bangladesh
Barbuda	Central	(Australian	Myanmar	Botswana
Bahamas	African	dollar)	Rwanda	Bulgaria
Barbados	Republic	Lesotho (South	Seychelles	Cape Verde
Belize	Chad	African rand)		Cyprus
Djibouti	Comoros	Swaziland		Czechoslovakia
Dominica	Congo	(South		Fiji
Dominican	Cote d'Ivoire	African		Finland
Republic	Equatorial	rand)		Hungary
Ethiopia	Guinea	Tonga		Iceland
Grenada	Gabon	(Australian		Israel
Guyana	Mali	dollar)		Jordan
Haiti	Niger	Yugoslavia		Kenya
Iraq	Senegal	(deutsche		Kuwait
Liberia	Togo	mark)		Malawi
Oman				Malaysia
Panama				Malta
St. Kitts and				Mauritius
Nevis				Morocco
St. Lucia				Nepal
St. Vincent				Norway
and the				Papua,
Grenadines				New Guinea
Sudan				Poland
Suriname				Romania
Syrian Arab				Sao Tome
Republic				and Principe
Trinidad and				Solomon
Tobago				Islands
Yemen, Republic of				Sweden
				Tanzania
				Thailand
				Uganda
				Vanuatu
				Western Samoa
				Zimbabwe

[a]Excluding the currency of Democratic Kampuchea, for which no current information is available. For members with dual or multiple exchange markets, the arrangement shown is that of the major market.

[b]Composed of currencies pegged to various baskets of currencies of the members' own choices, as distinct from the SDR basket.

Flexibility Limited in Terms of Single Currency or Group of Currencies		More Flexible		
Single Currency[c]	Cooperative Arrangements[d]	Adjusted According to Set of Indicators[e]	Other Managed Floating	Independently Floating
Bahrain	Belgium	Chile	China, People's	Argentina
Qatar	Denmark	Colombia	Republic of	Australia
Saudi Arabia	France	Madagascar	Costa Rica	Bolivia
United Arab	Germany	Mozambique	Ecuador	Brazil
Emirates	Ireland	Zambía	Egypt	Canada
	Italy		Greece	El Salvador
	Luxembourg		Guinea	Gambia
	Netherlands		Guinea–Bissau	Ghana
	Spain		Honduras	Guatemala
	United		India	Jamaica
	Kingdom		Indonesia	Japan
			Korea	Lebanon
			Lao, People's	Maldives
			Democratic Republic	Namibia
			Mauritania	New Zealand
			Mexico	Nigeria
			Nicaragua	Paraguay
			Pakistan	Peru
			Portugal	Philippines
			Singapore	Sierra Leone
			Somalia	South Africa
			Sri Lanka	United States
			Tunisia	Uruguay
			Turkey	Venezuela
			Vietnam	Zaire

[c]Exchange rates of all currencies shown have limited flexibility in terms of the U.S. dollar.

[d]Cooperative arrangements maintained under the European Monetary System.

[e]Includes exchange arrangements under which exchange rates are adjusted at relatively frequent intervals, on the basis of indicators determined by the respective member countries.

Source: *International Financial Statistics*, May 1991.

The five countries adjusting their currencies according to sets of economic indicators are relatively inflation-prone countries that depreciate their currencies periodically on the basis of a formula. By depreciating in this manner, they add an element of predictability to exchange rates which, it is hoped, reduces the disruption caused by exchange rate changes.

The countries in the other managed floating and independently floating categories are difficult to separate from each other with precision. On the whole, the countries in the former category have much more governmental intervention, including exchange controls, than the countries in the independently floating category. The other managed floating category includes a number of relatively prominent LDCs, a few small LDCs, and the two members of the EMS (Greece and Portugal) that do not participate in the ERM. The independently floating category also includes some relatively prominent LDCs and some small LDCs, but in addition, it includes most of the developed countries that do not peg their currencies to the Ecu. Thus, Australia, Canada, Japan, New Zealand, and the United States all belong to this category.

Summing up, small LDCs generally choose to peg their currencies to a national currency or a currency composite, while most countries with freely traded currencies either participate in the joint float of the EMS or permit their currencies to fluctuate relatively freely against all leading currencies. The larger LDCs tend not to peg their currencies to other national currencies or currency composites, but subject them, nevertheless, to a great deal of governmental control.

International Reserve Assets

International reserve assets consist of gold, freely convertible currencies, SDRs, and Ecus. The reserve tranche portions of IMF members' quotas are considered to be international reserves because members can borrow (purchase) them from the IMF at any time. In effect, they are pools of readily available forex reserves on loan to the IMF. Accordingly, IMF publications designate them as "reserve positions in the IMF."

Exhibit 3.9 presents IMF data on the year-end reserve assets of all IMF members, Switzerland, and Taiwan in 1984 and 1990. The amounts shown are in billions of SDRs. Exhibit 3.9 indicates that during these six years, total reserves, excluding gold, increased by 56.6 percent, which is equivalent to an annual growth rate of almost 8 percent. Moreover, since the reserve amounts are given in SDRs, and since the dollar value of the SDR increased by 45.1 percent during the period, the annual growth rate of international reserves in dollar terms was almost 15 percent. Measured either way, the growth of international reserves was rapid, but the growth in dollar terms was particularly rapid.

When reserves are allocated between industrial (or developed) and developing countries, a profound difference in reserve growth is evident. Measured in SDRs, the developed countries' reserves grew by 83 percent, but the reserves of the LDCs grew by only a little over 23 percent.

| E X H I B I T | 3.9 | *Governments' International Reserve Assets:*
December 31, 1984, and December 31, 1990
(in Billions of SDRs)

Classification	December 31, 1984	December 31, 1990	Percentage Change
IMF members plus Switzerland and Taiwan			
Total reserves, excluding gold	407.5	637.8	56.6
Reserve positions in the IMF	41.6	23.7	−43.0
SDRs	16.5	20.4	23.6
Foreign exchange	349.4	593.7	69.9
Gold (valued at SDR 35 per ounce)	33.1	32.9	−0.6
Industrial countries, including Switzerland			
Total reserves, excluding gold	226.0	414.1	83.2
Reserve positions in the IMF	27.4	20.0	−27.0
SDRs	13.4	17.6	30.6
Foreign exchange[a]	185.3	376.5	103.2
Gold (valued at SDR 35 per ounce)	28.4	27.9	−1.8
Developing countries, including Taiwan			
Total reserves, excluding gold	181.5	223.7	23.3
Reserve positions in the IMF	14.2	3.8	−73.2
SDRs	3.1	2.8	−9.7
Foreign exchange	164.2	217.2	32.3
Gold (valued at SDR 35 per ounce)	4.7	5.0	6.4
Memorandum: Dollars per SDR	0.9802	1.4227	45.1

[a]Included with the foreign exchange holdings of industrial countries are the Ecu holdings of EMS members. To avoid double counting, the dollars and gold deposited with the EMCF in exchange for Ecus are excluded from the industrial countries' gold and foreign exchange holdings.

Source: *International Financial Statistics*, May 1991, various pages.

Exhibit 3.9 makes it clear that, when gold is excluded, governments' reserve holdings consist overwhelmingly of forex holdings other than those represented by their reserve positions in the IMF. These reserve positions actually decreased, and they did so for both developed and developing countries. The explanation for this is twofold. First, many LDC governments drew down their reserve positions. Second, these countries reduced their total borrowings from the IMF by repaying loans in convertible currencies. Their loan repayments had the effect of reducing the IMF positions of *industrial* countries. The reason for this is that, when a currency such as the U.S. dollar is borrowed from the IMF, the country whose currency is borrowed gets an increase in its IMF reserve position, but when the loan is repaid, that position decreases.

There was some increase in SDR holdings from 1984 through 1990, even though no new SDRs were created. SDRs held by the IMF in 1984 were released to member countries during the intervening years. No Ecu holdings are shown in Exhibit 3.9 because Ecus held by EMS members are reflected in their gold and forex reserves.

The gold reserves shown in Exhibit 3.9 are valued at only SDR 35 per ounce, which is far below gold's market price in both 1984 and 1990. As of the end of 1990, if the gold reserves were shown at gold's market price, SDR 270.62 per ounce, their total value would have been SDR 254.4 billion, not SDR 32.9 billion. The market valuation would be more realistic than a valuation of SDR per ounce, but it is still advisable to value gold reserves below gold's market price because if governments attempted to make much use of their gold reserves, the market price of gold would tend to drop like the proverbial rock. At present, because gold's market price is not government-controlled, governments make little use of their gold reserves. It is conceivable, however, that at some point in the future, governments may decide once again to promote the use of gold as a reserve asset and support its price. For this reason, and because gold is still generally acceptable in settling international obligations, it is customary to show governments' gold holdings in compilations of reserve assets.

Exhibit 3.9 does not present data on the reserve holdings of individual governments. Most governments of developed countries have large reserve holdings. In billions of SDRs, the developed countries with the largest reserve holdings, excluding gold, as of the end of 1990 were: Japan (55.2), the United States (50.8), Germany (47.7), Italy (44.2), Spain (36.0), France (25.9), and the United Kingdom (25.2). One LDC ranks very high in terms of its reserve holdings; Taiwan, whose total reserves, excluding gold, were SDR 50.9 billion, slightly ahead of the United States and second only to Japan.

The United States is a comparatively recent arrival among the ranks of countries with large reserve holdings. In the past, its government did not feel that it needed large forex holdings because it could finance payments deficits by increasing foreign governments' holdings of dollars rather than by supplying foreign currencies to the forex market. Recently, however, the U.S. government has altered its policy in recognition of the fact that the defense of the dollar requires frequent forex market intervention with large foreign currency sales. At times, specifically when the dollar's forex value tends to increase, this new policy means that the U.S. government buys large amounts of foreign currencies and adds them to its reserve holdings.

For a long time, the U.S. dollar has been by far the most important currency in terms of governments' forex reserve holdings. Gradually, however, the dollar's dominance in this respect has diminished. It is estimated that from the end of 1973 to the end of 1989, the dollar's share in governments' total forex reserves decreased from about 76 percent to less than 60 percent. Over the same time span, the mark's share rose from about 9 percent to 20 percent.[14] It is generally expected that this trend toward a declining dominance of the dollar will continue.

---

[14]Bank for International Settlements, *60th Annual Report* (Basle, Switzerland, 1990), pp. 207–208.

Summary

Exchange rates have characteristically exhibited a high degree of variability, over both the short term and the long term, since they were allowed to float in 1973. Central bank intervention may have reduced the short-term variability slightly since the Plaza Agreement of 1985, but its effect appears to have been modest. On a long-term basis, exchange rate variations have been both real and nominal, and the variability of real exchange rates has had important consequences for international trade and investment.

Since 1973, lending to LDCs has become the dominant concern of the IMF. Relatively recently, the IMF has become concerned with providing financial assistance to countries that were formerly affiliated with the Soviet Bloc. As its focus has changed, the IMF has progressively expanded its resources and liberalized its loan terms. It is in the process of expanding its resources further so as to substantially increase its ability to lend to have-not nations with promising economic prospects. While the vast majority of IMF loans are on terms that at least approximate those of commercial loans, a significant proportion of the loans are on concessionary terms that provide a large interest subsidy.

The IMF exercises influence on the overall character of the international monetary system through its efforts to maintain generally accepted rules of monetary behavior. In addition, it has provided the international monetary system with SDRs, which represent a modest addition to nations' stocks of reserve assets.

The EMS has existed since 1979 and has achieved considerable success. Most of its members participate in a joint float, the ERM, that relies on the Ecu as a reserve asset and as the float's reference unit. The Ecu, like the SDR, is a currency composite. Although the Ecu is composed of elements of 12 currencies, the mark (as of 1991) accounts for over 36 percent of its value and plays the dominant role in the ERM.

While the Ecu has not developed great importance as a reserve asset, it has, nevertheless, become one of the world's leading currencies because of its widespread use in financial transactions. Spain and the United Kingdom have recently joined the ERM within the framework of the EMS, and other European countries are now pegging their currencies to the Ecu. It is widely perceived that pegging to the Ecu lowers the exchange risk, reduces inflation, and fosters economic integration. It is distinctly possible, though not yet a certainty, that most of Europe will form a monetary union in which the Ecu serves as the members' common currency.

While the contemporary international monetary system is often said to rely on managed floating, most nations peg their currencies to either a national currency or some type of currency composite. With the exception of the nations that peg to the Ecu, the pegging of currencies is particularly widespread among relatively small LDCs. The greatest degree of exchange rate flexibility is found in the currencies of developed countries.

Governments' international reserve holdings consist primarily of convertible foreign currencies. In recent years, the overall growth of governments' reserve holdings has been rapid. For the LDCs, however, reserve growth has been modest. The U.S. dollar remains the leading reserve currency, but its relative dominance has been declining.

References

Alogoskoufis, George, and Richard Portes. "International Costs and Benefits from EMU." National Bureau of Economic Research (NBER) *Working Paper* No. 3384, 1990.

Bank for International Settlements. *Annual Report.* Basle: BIS.

Belongia, Michael T. "Prospects for International Policy Coordination: Some Lessons from the EMS." Federal Reserve Bank of St. Louis *Review,* July–August 1988, pp. 19–29.

Bordo, Michael D., and Anna J. Schwartz. "What Has Foreign Exchange Market Intervention since the Plaza Agreement Accomplished?" NBER *Working Paper* No. 3562, 1990.

DeGrauwe, Paul. "Exchange Rate Variability and the Slowdown in Growth of International Trade." *IMF Staff Papers,* March 1988, pp. 63–84.

De Vries, Margaret. "The IMF: 40 Years of Challenge and Change." *Finance and Development,* September 1985, pp. 7–10.

Dooley, Michael P., J. Saul Lizondo, and Donald J. Mathieson. "The Currency Composition of Foreign Exchange Reserves." *IMF Staff Papers,* June 1989, pp. 385–434.

Fair, D. C., and C. de Boisseau, eds. *International Monetary and Financial Integration—The European Dimension.* Dordrecht, Netherlands: Kluver Academic, 1988.

Fieleke, Norman S. *The International Economy under Stress.* Cambridge, Mass.: Ballinger, 1988, Chapter 5.

Financial Times. Daily newspaper.

Frenkel, Jacob A. "The International Monetary System: Should It Be Reformed?" *American Economic Review Papers and Proceedings,* May 1987, pp. 205–210.

Frenkel, Jeffrey A. "The Making of Exchange Rate Policy in the 1980s." NBER *Working Paper* No. 3539, 1990.

International Financial Statistics. Monthly.

International Monetary Fund. *IMF Survey.* Washington, D.C. Biweekly.

———. *IMF Survey: Supplement on the Fund.* Annual.

Krugman, Paul, and Julio Rotemberg. "Target Zones with Limited Reserves." NBER *Working Paper* No. 3418, 1990.

McKinnon, Ronald. "Monetary and Exchange Rate Policies for International Financial Stability: A Proposal." *Journal of Economic Perspectives,* Winter 1988, pp. 83–103.

Obstfeld, Maurice. "The Effectiveness of Foreign Exchange Intervention: Recent Experience." NBER *Working Paper* No. 2796, 1988.

Shirsell, Howard. "Tell Me How It Works, Again . . ." *Euromoney,* September 1988, pp. 241–247.

Takagi, Shinji. "Pegging to a Currency Basket." *Finance and Development,* September 1986, pp. 41–44.

Williamson, John. "Exchange Rate Management: The Role of Target Zones." *American Economic Review Papers and Proceedings,* May 1987, pp. 200–204.

———. "The Case for Roughly Stabilizing the Real Value of the Dollar." *American Economic Review Papers and Proceedings,* May 1989, pp. 41–45.

Questions

1. According to *International Financial Statistics,* the nominal effective exchange rate of the U.S. dollar went from an average of 100 in 1985 to an average of 65.0 in 1990, while the dollar's real effective exchange rate went from 100 to 58.6 during the same period.
   a. Explain the implications of these changes for U.S. exporters, for U.S. investors in interest-bearing foreign assets, and for U.S. investors in the stocks of foreign companies during this period.
   b. Did the United States have, on the average, more inflation or less inflation than other countries during this period?
2. Assume that during a certain time period, the French franc/U.S. dollar market exchange rate moves from FF 5.7840/$ to FF 6.9260/$. Also assume that the U.S. wholesale price index (producer price index) rises by 10 percent and that the comparable French price index rises by 16 percent. On the assumption that these indexes and exchange rates are the appropriate ones, calculate the PPP exchange rate and the real exchange rate at the end of the period.
3. What did the Plaza Agreement and the Louvre Accord attempt to do, and what has been the general nature of G-7 exchange rate policy since the latter?
4. With respect to the IMF's rules of operation, explain the significance of Article IV of the Second Amendment and Articles XIV and VIII of the Articles of Agreement.
5. Since 1973, the terms on which IMF lending is available have become more generous. Summarize the primary ways in which the generosity of lending terms has increased.
6. Inasmuch as some of the IMF's loans are in arrears and the IMF has actually reduced the outstanding volume of its loans in recent years, how can it be argued that the IMF is justified in asking for a 50 percent increase in members' quotas?
7. On what basis have SDRs been allocated to IMF members, and why have governments been willing to accept them from the IMF? What does a government become obligated to do as a result of accepting an allocation of SDRs?
8. Compared to the dollar and other currencies that serve as international reserve assets, what are the strengths of the SDR as a reserve asset? What is the most plausible line of argument to justify creating more SDRs?
9. How are the bilateral par value exchange rates between currencies of the members of the ERM determined, and what are the limits to their fluctuations? When a bilateral exchange rate reaches one of its limits, what happens?
10. In the ERM, what is the threshold of divergence, and what is its significance? In what sense is the threshold of divergence smaller for the mark than for other ERM currencies, and what is the significance of this fact?

11. On May 13, 1991, the Spanish peseta was 6.06 percent above its bilateral par value with the French franc, and the peseta's divergence indicator was 80. The divergence indicator of the franc was −56. Under the rules of the ERM, what obligations, if any, did the central banks of Spain and France have under these circumstances?

12. What determines the quantities of Ecus held by members of the EMS?

13. The Ecu's use in financial transactions has become so large that the Ecu has become one of the world's major currencies. What explains this growth? Why is it that some holders of financial assets prefer to hold assets denominated in Ecus rather than marks?

14. Among the negative things that have been said about the EMS and its ERM are the claims that interest rate volatility has increased among EMS members and that some members have had to maintain such high interest rates that their economies have suffered. How can these criticisms be answered?

15. As a general proposition, small LDCs tend to peg their currencies to a national currency or a currency composite, while most larger LDCs have floating exchange rates with varying degrees of government control. How do you explain this difference?

16. From the end of 1984 through the end of 1990, the total international reserve assets of developed countries, excluding gold and measured in SDRs, increased by over 83 percent. With this as background, answer these questions:

    a. On what economic grounds can it be argued that the growth was excessive?

    b. Although the growth of the developed countries' reserve asset holdings strengthens their ability to support their currencies, it can be argued that it reduces the incentive of these countries to prevent their currencies from depreciating. Explain.

CHAPTER 4

The Measurement of
International Trade
and Investment

■

Both economic policymaking and financial management depend heavily on the collection and interpretation of data. In the realm of international finance, one of the most heavily used data sources is an accounting statement known as the **balance of payments (BOP),** which records the economic transactions between the residents and government of a particular country and the residents and governments of the rest of the world during a certain period of time, usually a year. For governments, the BOP provides valuable information for the conduct of economic policy. For firms and individuals, it provides clues about expectations for such matters as the volume of different types of trade and capital flows, the movement of exchange rates, and the probable course of economic policy. Like other accounting statements, however, the BOP provides useful information only if it is thoroughly understood and soundly interpreted.

This chapter gives much emphasis to explaining and interpreting the BOP of the United States, focusing on the technical aspects of the U.S. BOP's construction and interpretation. While it touches on the macroeconomic implications of the BOP, these implications are explored more fully in later chapters, particularly Chapters 9 through 11. An appendix to this chapter presents the BOP format used by the IMF for its member nations; this format differs in important respects from that used by the U.S. Department of Commerce for the United States.

During the past few years, as attention has been drawn to the growing dependence of the United States on capital inflows from the rest of the world and its emergence as a net debtor nation, another international accounting statement has begun to rival the BOP for people's attention. This statement, known generally as the **balance of international indebtedness (BII),** estimates the reciprocal claims between a nation and the rest of the world as of a specific date. In recognition of the BII's growing importance, a section of this chapter is devoted to it, explaining the nature of the BII and addressing the problems of its interpretation.

The Balance of Payments: An Overview

In order to understand the BOP as a technical accounting statement, it is necessary to be familiar with the nature of the transactions that it records, the accounting principles it employs, and the manner in which its accounts are classified. These matters are addressed in this section of the chapter. The points developed here apply generally to BOP accounting and are not limited to the particular case of the United States.

The Nature of BOP Transactions

Since the BOP records economic transactions between the residents and government of a particular country and the residents and governments of the rest of the world, it is important to understand what BOP transactions are. This requires, first, an understanding of the concept of residency for BOP purposes. Second, it requires examining the nature of the transactions themselves.

The Concept of Residency In BOP accounting, an individual may be a resident of one country and a citizen of another. Similarly, a firm may be resident in a country other than the country in which its headquarters is located. Taking individuals first, when citizens of a country reside abroad long enough, roughly 18 months currently, they are considered to be foreign residents for BOP purposes. This means that their transactions with other residents of the countries in which they reside ordinarily do not have BOP effects. For example, a U.S. citizen who resides in Switzerland long enough to be classified by the U.S. government as a foreign resident is considered to be a Swiss resident for BOP purposes; payments made by that person to other Swiss residents do not affect the BOPs of either Switzerland or the United States. This is true even if the payments are in dollars, since the dollars would already have been considered as foreign-held from the U.S. perspective and domestically owned from the Swiss perspective.

Not every citizen who resides abroad is considered to be a foreign resident for BOP purposes. Employees of the U.S. government who are stationed abroad are considered to be U.S. residents no matter how long they have lived outside the United States. Also, if a foreign "diplomat" were to purchase classified defense documents from a U.S. resident with access to them, the transaction should, in principle, be recorded in the U.S. BOP, even if the purchaser had resided in the United States for many years. Since the transaction would be illegal, however, it would probably not actually be recorded.

As a general rule, subsidiaries of foreign corporations are considered to be residents of the countries in which they operate, even if they are owned entirely by their parent companies. Transactions of the parents with such subsidiaries have BOP effects, while transactions of the subsidiaries with firms and individuals who reside in the same countries where the subsidiaries operate normally do not have BOP effects.

The treatment of overseas branches is less uniform than that of subsidiaries. In general, the foreign branches of domestic corporations are considered to be foreign residents if their operations are not temporary and their "centers of interest" are in foreign countries. Particularly notable is that branches of banks are generally treated as residents of the countries in which they are located. Thus, transactions between the offices of U.S. banks in the United States and foreign branches of those banks are generally shown as BOP transactions by the United States and the countries in which the branches are located. Similarly, if a U.S. branch of a foreign bank borrows from its home office, the transaction is generally recorded in BOP statements.

Transactions between a country's residents and international agencies such as the World Bank are considered to be BOP transactions, even if the headquarters of the agency is located in the same country as a resident with whom it has a transaction. The United Nations, the IMF, and the World Bank are all headquartered in the United States, but transactions between them and U.S. residents are recorded in the U.S. BOP. If, for example, U.S. philatelists buy mint U.N. stamps at the U.N. post office in New York City, they are considered to be importing merchandise.

Pinning Down the Transaction Concept   Once the concept of residency is clear, it becomes a simple matter in the vast majority of cases to determine if a transaction should be included in the BOP. In a few cases, however, items that may not fit the standard concept of a transaction are counted as BOP transactions.

Most BOP transactions involve current or future money flows, but there are some exceptions to this general rule. In particular, much international trade takes the form of barter. To the extent that this is the case, a nation's exports are offset by imports of equivalent value rather than by financial flows. Also, when corporations increase their investments in foreign subsidiaries by shipping them equipment without requiring payment, the merchandise trade account of the BOP is affected, but there is no offsetting flow of money.

Both of these cases are clearly economic transactions since they involve exchanges of equivalent values. In some BOP items known as **unilateral transfers,** however, parties give up goods, services, or money without receiving any quid pro quo. Such transfers include government grants to other countries, pension and social security payments to citizens or former residents residing abroad, and various types of private remittances and gifts. While it would be simpler to use the word *gift* instead of the relatively cumbersome term *unilateral transfers,* gifts are voluntary, while unilateral transfers may not be. A pension payment is a contractual obligation, not a gift. Moreover, unilateral transfers include such items as expropriations without full compensation and losses arising from unfavorable outcomes in courts of law. Since not all unilateral transfers are voluntary, the term seems appropriate.

Some "transactions" are recorded in the BOP without any actual transfer of goods, services, or assets. Suppose, for example, that a Brazilian subsidiary of a U.S. firm has profits that the parent could claim, but instead allows the subsidiary to retain them. Since the profits are not remitted to the parent, no actual transaction occurs. Nevertheless, it is the general practice to present reinvested earnings of subsidiaries in the BOP as if they were remitted to the parents and returned to the subsidiaries.

While reinvested earnings are the most important example of a BOP entry in which no international financial flow occurs, they are not the only example. The BOP statements of the United States record transfers of dollars from foreign corporations and banks to foreign governments, and vice versa, even if the total liabilities of U.S. banks to foreigners do not change. Also, until 1988, any time goods were imported into the United States in American-owned ships, the U.S. BOP showed the payments to the carriers as exports of services. This was done to offset the inclusion of freight charges in the value of U.S. imports. Furthermore, in the BOP statements of the IMF (but not in those of the United States, as prepared by the Department of Commerce), gold transactions between the U.S. government and U.S. residents are recorded as BOP transactions, even though no international transaction has occurred.

Debits and Credits

Like other accounting statements, the BOP conforms to the principles of double-entry bookkeeping. This means that every international transaction should produce debit and credit entries of equal magnitude. Because it is impossible to record all BOP transactions as they occur, however, it is necessary to estimate each BOP account separately, i.e., without making offsetting debit or credit entries in one or more other accounts. Because each account is estimated separately, and because there are enormous opportunities for error in compiling a statement as comprehensive as the BOP, it is extremely unlikely that the sum of all the debits will equal the sum of all the credits. The resulting imbalance between debits and credits gives rise to the statistical discrepancy problem, which is examined later in this chapter.

Because the BOP is a double-entry accounting statement, it is easier to understand if one is thoroughly familiar with accounting principles. Because the BOP differs so much from other accounting statements, however, people who are familiar with other statements often have difficulty in fully understanding the BOP. On the other hand, while the BOP's many nuances challenge even those who know accounting, the basic rules of BOP accounting are simple enough that those without prior training in accounting should be able to readily comprehend most of the BOP's fundamental features.

In double-entry bookkeeping, a debit entry occurs when any of the following is recognized on the books: an increase in the amount of an asset, a reduction in the amount of a liability, a reduction in equity, or a negative income flow (an expense). Correspondingly, a credit entry results when a change in any of these items in the opposite direction is recognized on the books. From this it follows that, once the accounts affected by particular transactions are identified, it should be easy to interpret entries to those accounts.

For individuals who lack confidence in their ability to analyze a BOP using the conventional accounting framework, an alternative framework may be helpful which, properly used, yields the same results. This alternative framework rests on the rule that *debits record what is received, while credits record what is given up.* If, for example, the United States imports automobiles, the merchandise import account of the U.S. BOP is debited; if U.S. residents acquire ownership rights in foreign companies, there is a debit to an account that reflects an increase in U.S. foreign investment. Conversely, merchandise exports are BOP credits, and when foreigners acquire shares of stock in U.S. companies from U.S. residents, an appropriate capital flow account is credited.

This rule (debit what you receive and credit what you give up) is usually easy to apply, but there are cases in which its application offers a bit of a challenge. Noteworthy in this regard are income from financial services and unilateral transfers. Consider, for example, a foreign corporation's payment of interest on bonds held by U.S. residents by drawing on dollars held in a U.S. bank. It is easy to see that a debit should record the receipt of the dollars, but what the United States has given up in return is not so obvious. The credit-what-you-give-up rule is applied here by reasoning that, in buying bonds issued by a foreign corporation. U.S. residents gave up the services of the money (capital) with which they purchased the bonds. While this application of the rule may seem strange initially, it accords with economists' concept of opportunity cost. Thus, just as a nation gives up the benefits of goods when it exports them, so also does it give up the benefits of capital when it elects to use its financial resources to acquire claims on foreigners.

Unilateral transfers cause a problem with applying the debit-what-you-receive rule because countries making such transfers do not receive anything tangible in return. If, for example, U.S. private charities contribute $50 million for African famine relief, the donors receive the gratitude of the beneficiaries and the satisfaction of having saved lives. The United States may receive some political benefit, but a tangible money value cannot be assigned to any benefits received by the United States.

Some confusion about BOP entries arises from the standard procedure of substituting minus signs for the word *debit* and plus signs for the word *credit*. It is only natural to assume that minus and plus mean, respectively, decrease and increase, but what is natural is likely to be wrong in the context of the BOP. Minus and plus signs in the BOP mean, respectively, debit and credit, *and nothing more*. Indeed, in most cases, *both* signs indicate a positive value in the mathematical sense, and a plus sign can indicate a decrease.

The Classification of BOP Accounts

Most fundamentally, BOP accounts are classified as either current accounts or capital accounts. **Current accounts** represent income flows, including unilateral transfers. **Capital accounts** represent asset flows. Among the capital accounts, a subcategory known as **official reserve accounts** is often set apart and treated as a third major account category. The official reserve accounts record changes in governments' holdings of international reserve assets.

Most current accounts reflect *real* income flows, that is, they record flows of goods and services. Exports of goods and services are current account credits, and imports of goods and services are current account debits. Unilateral transfers do not represent flows of goods and services. To the extent that they are associated with exports of goods and services to foreign beneficiaries, entries to the unilateral transfer accounts should be regarded as offsets to current account export transactions that prevent overstatements of income earned. To the extent that unilateral transfers take the form of money or other assets, they represent reductions in a nation's claims on its own or other countries' wealth. In either case, they can be viewed as negative income.

For the most part, it is easy to understand the treatment of current account items. Aside from unilateral transfers, students' chief problem in handling current account items is remembering that income derived from capital, most notably interest and dividends, is *always* considered to be current account. On the other hand, the capital flows that generate the income are always included in the capital accounts.

The capital accounts record the net changes in nations' claims on foreigners and in foreigners' claims on them. For the most part they are financial rather than real and consist of such things as bank deposits, shares of stock, bank loans, and interest-earning securities. In some cases, such as the acquisition of real estate, they involve exchanges of claims on real or tangible property. When foreigners acquire U.S. real estate, for example, a credit should appear in the U.S. BOP recording an increase in foreigners' claims on the United States.

A capital inflow into the United States is a *credit* entry in its BOP and can mean either a decrease in U.S. claims on foreigners (a decrease in U.S. holdings of foreign assets) or an increase in foreign claims on the United States (an increase in foreign holdings of U.S. assets, i.e., an increase in U.S. liabilities to foreigners).

The terms **capital inflow** and **capital outflow** are commonly used in referring to capital account transactions. A capital inflow into the United States is a **credit** entry in its BOP and means either a decrease in U.S. claims on foreigners or an increase in foreign claims on the United States. A capital outflow is a **debit** entry in the U.S. BOP and means either an increase in claims on foreigners or a decrease in foreign claims on the United States.

Another common distinction in the capital account section of the BOP is that between direct and portfolio investment. **Direct foreign investment** (**DFI**) carries with it control, or at least a substantial managerial voice. The Department of Commerce classifies foreign investment as direct when a single physical person, company, or group of affiliated companies holds an equity interest of 10 percent or more, based on book value, in an enterprise classified as a foreign resident. **Portfolio investment** provides no managerial voice. Most such investment is in debt obligations, but some consists of stock holdings. Portfolio stock investors exercise no individual influence over companies' dividend policies, however. Sometimes the term *portfolio investment* is confined to holdings of long-term assets, but the term is also used to include holdings of short-term assets.

The official reserve accounts reflect net changes in governments' international reserve assets. For the United States, they record changes in the U.S. governments' holdings of such assets and changes in foreign governments' holdings of liquid, dollar-denominated claims. In interpreting the U.S. BOP, it is important to remember that dollars held by foreign governments are official reserve assets of those governments.

When the current accounts, capital accounts, and official reserve accounts are totaled, debits never equal credits. Since double-entry bookkeeping requires equality of total debits and credits, this is forced by inserting an account, known in the United States as the **statistical discrepancy (SD),** whose function is to equate overall debits and credits. Formerly, this balancing account was called **errors and omissions (E&O)** in the U.S. BOP, and this term is still widely employed in BOP statements and literature. Apparently, however, when the Department of Commerce revised the reporting of the U.S. BOP in 1976, it decided that the public confession of error was not politic. Most of the omissions that cause the E&O account to be necessary undoubtedly consist of unrecorded short-term capital flows and trade flows, some of which are illegal. An analysis of the SD account in the U.S. BOP appears later in the chapter.

Since the emergence of SDRs, beginning in 1970, another account that has occasionally been used to force equality between debits and credits is **allocations of special drawing rights.** When the IMF allocates SDRs to its members, their amounts are debited to an official reserve account known as *special drawing rights* and equal amounts are simultaneously entered as credits to allocations of special drawing rights. In BOP accounting theory, this latter account can be viewed as either a unilateral transfer received or a contingent liability incurred. Viewing it as a liability is acceptable since a nation's SDRs would be eliminated in the unlikely event that it should either cease to be an IMF member or refuse to accept SDRs, or in the event of a general agreement among IMF members to discontinue SDRs.

Interpreting the BOP

In this section, our focus shifts from the BOP's structure to its interpretation. Much of our attention will be directed toward interpreting the BOP of the United States as presented by the Department of Commerce, but much of the analysis applies as well to the interpretation of the BOPs of other countries.

U.S. International Transactions in 1988, 1989, and 1990

Exhibit 4.1 presents a summary of the U.S. BOPs for 1988, 1989, and 1990 as published in the *Federal Reserve Bulletin* using data provided by the Bureau of Economic Analysis of the Department of Commerce. Exhibit 4.2 presents detail on current account transactions for the same years using data published in the *Survey of Current Business,* a publication of the Department of Commerce. In both exhibits, the amounts given are in billions of dollars, and the debit items are identified with a minus sign. Note that Exhibit 4.1 is titled U.S. International Transactions, not U.S. Balance of Payments. This follows Commerce Department practice, which virtually always refers to the U.S. BOP in this manner.

| E X H I B I T | 4.1 | *U.S. International Transactions: 1988, 1989, and 1990 (Billions of Dollars)*

Item Credits or Debits (−)	1988	1989	1990ᴾ
Balance on current account	−128.9	−110.0	−99.3
Merchandise trade balance	−127.0	−114.9	−108.7
Merchandise exports	320.3	360.5	389.3
Merchandise imports	−447.3	−475.3	−498.0
Military transactions, net	−5.5	−6.3	−6.4
Investment income, net	1.6	−0.9	7.5
Other service transactions, net	17.0	26.8	29.3
Remittances, pensions, and other transfers	−4.3	−3.8	−4.1
U.S. government grants	−10.7	−11.0	−17.0
Change in U.S. government assets, other than official reserve assets	3.0	1.2	3.0
Change in U.S. official reserve assets	−3.9	−25.3	−2.2
Gold	0.0	0.0	0.0
Special drawing rights	0.1	−0.5	−0.2
Reserve position in International Monetary Fund	1.0	0.5	0.7
Foreign currencies	−5.1	−25.2	−2.7
Change in U.S. private assets abroad	−83.2	−103.0	−62.1
Bank-reported claims	−56.3	−50.7	0.8
Nonbank-reported claimsᵃ	−2.8	1.4	0.3
U.S. purchase of foreign securities	−7.8	−21.9	−26.8
U.S. direct investments abroad	−16.2	−31.7	−36.4
Change in foreign official assets in the United States	39.5	8.8	30.8
U.S. Treasury securities	41.7	0.3	28.7
Other U.S. government obligations	1.3	1.4	0.7
Other U.S. government liabilitiesᵇ	−0.7	0.3	1.5
Other U.S. liabilities reported by U.S. banks	−0.3	4.9	1.5
Other foreign official assetsᶜ	−2.5	1.8	−1.6
Change in foreign private assets in the United States	181.9	205.8	56.8
U.S. bank-reported liabilities	70.2	61.2	19.8
U.S. nonbank-reported liabilitiesᵃ	6.7	2.9	6.0
Foreign private purchases of U.S. Treasury securities	20.2	30.0	1.1
Foreign purchases of other U.S. securities	26.4	39.6	4.1
Foreign direct investments in the United States	58.4	72.2	25.7
Allocation of SDRs	0.0	0.0	0.0
Statistical discrepancy	−8.4	22.4	73.0

ᴾPreliminary.

ᵃThe figure for 1990 includes only the first three quarters of the year.

ᵇPrimarily associated with military sales contracts and other transactions arranged with or through foreign official agencies.

ᶜConsist of investments in U.S. corporate stocks and in debt securities of private corporations and state and local governments

Source: *Federal Reserve Bulletin*, May 1991, p. A54.

Each account classified as a unilateral transfer, a capital flow, or an official reserve account is customarily shown on a net basis, i.e., after offsetting debits against credits. With the exception of unilateral transfers, current account items are often shown on a gross basis because their gross amounts represent real income flows. Note, however, that with the exceptions of merchandise exports and merchandise imports, current account items are shown on a net basis in Exhibit 4.1. In Exhibit 4.2, however, exports and imports of goods, services, and investment income are all shown on a gross basis.

Perhaps the most eye-catching thing about Exhibits 4.1 and 4.2 is the merchandise trade deficit (debit balance), whose smallest amount, $108.7 billion, was recorded in 1990. This deficit was offset to a considerable extent by surpluses (credit balances) in service transactions, and to a lesser extent (in 1988 and 1990) by small surpluses in investment income. These surpluses, were, however, completely or partly offset by debit balances in unilateral transfers (the last two current account items in Exhibit 4.1) and military transactions. Overall, therefore, there were **current account deficits** whose

| EXHIBIT | 4.2 | *U.S. Current Account Transactions: 1988, 1989, and 1990 (Billions of Dollars)*

Item Credits or Debits (−)	1988	1989	1990P
Exports of goods, services, and income	533.4	603.2	648.7
Merchandise, adjusted, excluding military[a]	320.3	360.5	389.3
Services[b]	103.1	115.2	130.6
Transfers under U.S. military sales agency contracts	9.5	8.3	10.2
Travel	28.9	34.4	39.3
Passenger fares	8.8	10.1	11.9
Other transportation	18.9	20.4	22.0
Royalties and license fees	10.9	11.8	14.8
Other private services	25.4	29.5	31.8
U.S. government miscellaneous services	0.7	0.6	0.7
Income receipts on U.S. assets abroad	110.0	127.5	128.8
Direct investment receipts	49.8	53.6	54.1
Of which, reinvested earnings	12.6	22.4	21.7
Other private receipts	53.5	68.4	64.8
Interest	52.3	67.3	63.1
Dividends	1.2	1.1	1.7
U.S. government receipts	6.7	5.5	9.9
Imports of goods, services, and income	−647.3	−698.5	−727.0
Merchandise, adjusted, excluding military[a]	−447.3	−475.3	−498.0
Services[b]	−91.5	−94.7	−107.7
Direct defense expenditure	−15.0	−14.7	−16.6
Travel	−33.1	−35.0	−38.4
Passenger fares	−7.9	−8.5	−9.5
Other transportation	−19.7	−20.8	−23.5
Royalties and license fees	−2.1	−2.2	−2.7
Other private services	−11.8	−11.5	−14.8
U.S. government miscellaneous services	−2.0	−2.0	−2.2
Income payments on foreign assets in the United States	−108.4	−128.4	−121.3
Direct investment payments	−16.7	−14.0	−4.8
Of which, reinvested earnings	−6.6	0.1	9.9
Other private payments	−61.5	−78.5	−79.1
Interest	−55.7	−71.9	−71.6
Dividends	−5.8	−6.6	−7.5
U.S. government payments	−30.2	−36.0	−37.5

(continued)

| E X H I B I T | 4.2 | *continued*

Item Credits or Debits (−)	1988	1989	1990ᴾ
Unilateral transfers, net	−15.0	−14.7	−21.1
U.S. government grants[c]	−10.7	−11.0	−17.0
U.S. government pensions and other transfers	−2.5	−2.4	−2.9
Private remittances and other transfers	−1.8	−1.3	−1.2
Balance on merchandise trade	−127.0	−114.9	−108.7
Balance on services	11.5	20.5	22.9
Balance on investment income	1.6	−0.9	7.5
Balance on goods, services, and income	−113.9	−95.3	−78.2
Balance on current account[d]	−128.9	−110.0	−99.3

[P]Preliminary.

[a]Excludes military sales and purchases of the U.S. military. The adjustments are of small magnitude and are made to bring census data into line with balance of payments requirements.

[b]Includes some goods, mainly military equipment and supplies and fuels purchased by airlines and steamship operators.

[c]Includes transfers of goods and services under U.S. military grant programs.

[d]This balance is a close approximation to the item "net foreign investment" that appears in the national income and product accounts of the United States. Conceptually, the two measures are the same, but there are certain technical differences in how they are obtained. For example, since U.S. territories and Puerto Rico are considered to be part of the United States for BOP purposes, but are not included with the United States in the national income and product accounts, a difference between the two measures results.

Sources: Christopher Bach, "U.S. International Transactions, Fourth Quarter and Year 1990," *Survey of Current Business*, March 1991, pp. 44, 45, and 50; and Robert E. Nicholson, Jr., "U.S. International Transactions, First Quarter 1989," *Survey of Current Business*, June 1990, pp. 76–77.

amounts approximated those of the merchandise trade deficits. The biggest difference between the two occurred in 1990, when the merchandise trade deficit exceeded the current account deficit by $9.4 billion.

During the 1980s, the BOP of the United States characteristically exhibited large current account and merchandise trade deficits, which reached record levels of $162.3 billion and $159.5 billion, respectively, in 1987.[1] These large and persistent deficits have attracted a great deal of attention. Again and again, politicians, media representatives, and even some economists have stated that they are economically undesirable and must be greatly reduced. Others have cautioned, however, that the deficits are not necessarily permanent and that some of the measures recommended for their removal are likely to do more harm than good. The matter of the cause or causes of these deficits is touched on a little later in the chapter and explored more fully in later chapters.

Ignoring the statistical discrepancy and any SDR allocation, *a current account deficit must always be offset by net capital inflows,* some of which may

---

[1]Robert E. Nicholson, Jr., "U.S. International Transactions, First Quarter 1989," *Survey of Current Business,* June 1990, pp. 76–77.

be official reserve assets. To illustrate this point, note that Exhibit 4.1 has three capital account and two official reserve account categories, and that their combined totals offset the balance on current account except as indicated by the SD account. Also note, however, that the SD account had a credit balance of $73.0 billion in 1990. A balance of this magnitude in SD is unprecedented. It points to a serious deficiency in the collection of BOP data and merits an effort on our part to understand its meaning. Accordingly, we shall consider its possible causes a little later in the chapter.

The two primary capital account categories in Exhibit 4.1 are change in U.S. private assets abroad and change in foreign private assets in the United States. It is highly significant that each category showed large net increases in each of the three years surveyed. In 1988 and 1989, the net capital inflows from increases in foreign private claims on the United States ($181.9 billion and $205.8 billion, respectively) greatly exceeded the net capital outflows from increases in U.S. private claims on foreigners ($83.2 billion and $103.0 billion, respectively). In 1990, however, the increase in U.S. private claims on foreigners ($62.1 billion) exceeded the increase in foreign private claims on the United States ($56.8 billion). It is likely, however, that 1990's SD of $73.0 billion occurred in large part because of unrecorded private capital inflows into the United States, and that even in 1990, therefore, foreigners increased their private claims on the United States by more than the United States increased its private claims on foreigners.

The remaining capital account category in Exhibit 4.1, change in U.S. government assets, other than official reserve assets, basically reflects new loans to foreign governments less repayments of previous loans. The credit balances in this item for each of the three years indicate that loan repayments and, as in the case of Egypt in 1990, cancellations exceeded new loans. While the credit balances to this item indicate that the U.S. government was not expanding its foreign aid in the form of loans, Exhibits 4.1 and 4.2 indicate that its foreign aid in the form of grants ranged from a low of $10.7 billion in 1988 to a high of $17.0 billion in 1990.[2]

The official reserve account categories of Exhibit 4.1 indicate that in each of the three years, the U.S. government increased its holdings of official or international reserve assets, and foreign governments increased their official reserve holdings of dollars. Most of the increase in the U.S. government's official reserves occurred in 1989, when its net purchases of foreign currencies were $25.2 billion. Foreign governments increased their official reserve holdings of dollars by only $8.8 billion in 1989, but in 1988 and 1990, the increases were $39.5 billion and $30.8 billion, respectively. Note that most of

[2]In the fourth quarter of 1990, the U.S. government relieved the government of Egypt of its obligation to repay $7.1 billion in principal and interest to the U.S. government. This entire amount was recorded as a unilateral transfer. The offsetting entries were credits of $5.9 billion to U.S. government assets, other than official reserve assets (see Exhibit 4.1) and $2.1 billion to U.S. government receipts of income (see Exhibit 4.2). The U.S. BOP for 1990 thus credited the U.S. government with the receipt of payments that did not occur. See Christopher L. Bach, "U.S. International Transactions, Fourth Quarter and Year 1990," *Survey of Current Business*, March 1991, p. 36.

the increase in foreign governments' reserve holdings went into U.S. Treasury securities. In similar fashion, though this is not indicated in Exhibit 4.1, most of the buildup in the U.S. government's official reserve assets went into liquid claims on foreign governments.

Interpreting the Current Account Deficit   The prevailing popular view about the relationship between the current account deficit of the United States and its accompanying net capital inflow is that the deficit causes the inflow. In this view, the United States has a fundamental tendency to incur a merchandise trade deficit because of such factors as its low saving rate, public sector budgetary deficits, and relatively open trade policy. In order to finance the deficit, it is argued, the United States must keep its interest rates relatively high and allow foreigners to acquire U.S. assets subject to few restrictions. The proponents of this view have often criticized the growing dependence on foreign capital, referring to it with such terms as the "selling of America," and they have tended to argue that the situation is inherently unstable since the capital inflows required to finance the trade deficit cannot be expected to continue indefinitely. Events in 1990, when the capital inflow diminished sharply in response to relatively lower U.S. interest rates and worsening conditions in the U.S. economy, and the dollar's exchange value plummeted by an average of 15 percent against other leading currencies, can easily be fitted to this scenario.

Buttressing the contention that the merchandise trade deficit is unsustainable at present levels is the fact that, as foreign investment in the United States rises relative to U.S. investment abroad, the balance on investment income tends to shift against the United States. Historically, the United States has tended to have a large surplus in this balance. From 1980 through 1984, the balance showed surpluses that ranged from $31.3 billion in 1981 to $23.4 billion in 1984.[3] In the three years included in Exhibit 4.2, however, the figures for this balance were $1.6 billion in 1988, −$0.9 billion in 1989, and $7.5 billion in 1990. The surplus in 1990 can be attributed to the effects of a recession and does not indicate the reversal of the trend. It appears, therefore, that the investment income surplus has fundamentally evaporated, thereby placing added pressure on the United States to reduce its merchandise trade deficit.

Historically, large current account deficits have generally been associated with weakening (overvalued) currencies, and in some periods in recent years, the dollar has definitely seemed to move downward under the pressure of current account deficits. On the other hand, the dollar has sometimes risen despite the deficits. From 1981 through 1984, for example, the current account went from a surplus of $6.9 billion in 1981 to a deficit of $99.0 billion in 1984,[4] yet the dollar's exchange value swung sharply upward. In most of 1988

---

[3]Nicholson, *op cit.*
[4]*Ibid.*

and 1989, the dollar moved upward against most leading currencies, and it has also been strong in 1991. Its frequent strength implies that caution is advisable before concluding that the current account deficits must inevitably weaken the dollar.

A strong case can be made for the proposition that the causal connection between the merchandise trade deficit and the accompanying capital inflows has often been the reverse of what is generally assumed. Capital inflows may tend to cause a merchandise trade deficit instead of the other way around. Those who support this idea claim that the United States and its dollar are, for several reasons, the favorite country and currency of foreign investors. Savings tend to flow toward the best combination of rates of return and safety. Since, so the argument goes, the United States supplies this combination in the judgment of many investors, the advance of international financial integration and the accompanying erosion of barriers to international capital flows have induced massive capital inflows into the United States. As capital flows in, the dollar's exchange value rises, leading to adjustments in international trade in which U.S. exports tend to decline relative to U.S. imports.

Whether the line of causation runs from the trade deficit to the capital inflows or from the capital inflows to the trade deficit, or whether the two lines of causation are so enmeshed that it is difficult to say with confidence which is dominant, we know that the dollar's ability to avoid a decline in exchange value hinges on the continuation of capital inflows. Since capital inflows exhibit much year-to-year variability, the current structure of the U.S. BOP implies that exchange rates between the dollar and other leading currencies are likely to continue the unstable pattern of behavior they have exhibited since 1973.

Finally, it is worthy of note to recall that the merchandise trade deficit has shown a decided tendency to diminish since 1987. If this trend continues, and if the United States continues to be a recipient of net capital inflows, the implication is that the capital inflows will increasingly be used to finance an investment income deficit rather than a merchandise trade deficit.

Discerning Exchange Rate Trends from the BOP To a large extent, we study BOPs in order to gain insight into the future. As guides to the future, BOPs are, likely other sources of information, imperfect. The future is influenced by random events, and it is hazardous to predict it on the basis of current trends. Nevertheless, it is undoubtedly true that a nation's BOP contains information that is helpful in understanding what the future is likely to bring.

Because the merchandise trade and current account balances may be fallible indicators of a currency's future performance, seasoned BOP analysts look elsewhere to discern exchange rate trends. Official reserve transactions; private capital flows, particularly those that are short-term; and even the SD account may yield valuable clues about what lies ahead. Thus, if a nation's BOP reveals a large increase in its official reserves, a sizable increase in private short-term capital inflows, a small increase or even a decrease in private short-term capital outflows, and an unusually large credit entry to the SD account, you can be sure that its currency was tending to strengthen during the period covered. This does not necessarily mean that it will continue to strengthen, but the presumption of strengthening is justified unless there have been, or probably will be, fundamental changes in the factors governing trade and capital flows.

In a "normal" year, the U.S. government has a modest increase (debit) in its official reserves, while other governments collectively have a somewhat larger increase (credit) in their holdings of dollar assets. There are two reasons for this pattern: (1) governments need to increase their reserves over time, and (2) increases in foreign governments' demand for dollar reserves usually exceed increases in the U.S. government's demand for official reserve assets. When this pattern does not hold, a valid inference about the trend of the dollar can often be made on the basis of the variance from it. For example, in 1990, there was a small increase ($2.2 billion) in the U.S. government's official reserve assets and a much larger increase ($30.8 billion) in foreign government's official reserve holdings of dollars. The large gap between the two figures suggests that the dollar was tending to fall in value and that foreign governments bought dollars to prevent it from falling further. In fact, the dollar did decline substantially for the year as a whole.

Changes in official reserve holdings are, however, a fallible guide to exchange rate behavior. This is brought out by what happened in 1988 and 1989. In 1988, the U.S. government's reserves increased modestly (by $3.9 billion), while foreign governments' holdings of dollar assets increased by a large amount ($39.5 billion). The resemblance to 1990 is obvious, but while the dollar declined substantially in 1990, it rose modestly in 1988. In 1989, the U.S. government's official reserves increased by $25.3 billion, while foreign governments' holdings of dollars rose by only $8.8 billion. Normally, this pattern would indicate a strengthening of the dollar. In fact, however, the dollar finished the year about where it started.

The fallibility of changes in official reserve holdings as an indicator of exchange rate behavior is rooted in the fact that central banks' forex operations are motivated by other factors than the desire to maintain exchange rates at their *existing* levels. These operations may be motivated by a desire to *change* exchange rates, and in some cases, they are determined by consider-ations of domestic monetary policy. For example, if a government other than that of the United States wants to expand the domestic money supply, its central bank may elect to accomplish this by buying dollars, even though this action tends to alter exchange rates.

In 1988, foreign governments were large net buyers of dollars because of considerations of domestic monetary policy and because they were not averse to a rise in the dollar. In 1989, the dollar actually tended to rise during much of the year. The U.S. government attempted to restrain the rise by buying foreign currencies, and when the dollar reversed its upward movement, the government actually gave it a downward push by continuing to buy foreign currencies, though in reduced amounts.

Because changes in official reserves are a flawed (but useful) indicator of exchange rate behavior, it is logical to pay close attention to the behavior of private capital flows to obtain a better idea of where exchange rates may be headed. The development of sophisticated hedging techniques has allowed international investors to diminish the exchange risk, but exchange rate expectations continue to exert great influence on capital flows. Everything else the same, for example, capital inflows into the United States tend to decrease when the expectation is that the dollar's exchange value will decline. The sharp decline that occurred in the growth of foreign private assets in the United States in 1990 (to $56.8 billion from $205.8 billion in 1989) can be attributed in large part to lower relative U.S. interest rates and worsening prospects for the U.S. economy, but it also reflected the expectation that the dollar's exchange value would tend to fall. As this example indicates, however, exchange rate expectations are only one factor affecting capital flows, and not necessarily the dominant one.

The Statistical Discrepancy (SD) Account

Formerly largely ignored, the SD account has blossomed into an important topic. This has especially been the case since the announcement that the SD for 1990 had a credit balance of $73.0 billion. In the past, the fluctuations in this account have sometimes been dismissed as being caused primarily by random variations in unrecorded transactions and/or changes in recording procedures. For some time, however, it has been clear to many observers that the size and sign (plus or minus) of the SD are not due primarily to these factors, but are related *systematically* to variations in trade flow, capital flows, and exchange rate expectations.

The Underground Economy Hypothesis   Because people tend to associate the SD with illegal activity (the underground economy), it is often assumed that illegal drug traffic and the earnings of undocumented aliens must be the dominant factors affecting this account. It is difficult to see, however, how these factors can explain a *credit* balance in the SD account, and with the exception of 1988, a credit balance is what the United States has had in every year since 1977.[5] When illegal drugs are smuggled into the United States, the failure to record an import means that a *debit* has been omitted from the BOP. A debit to SD occurs if all or some of the financial transactions spun off the drug business result in a net recorded BOP credit. If, as is likely, some of the profits from drug dealing result, after appropriate laundering, in claims by foreigners on U.S. banks, the drug trade causes *debits* to the SD account.[6]

The earnings of undocumented workers also probably tend to cause debits to the SD account. In principle, payments to these workers should be recorded as imports of services; because they are not, BOP deficits are understated. Some of these workers' earnings leak from the U.S. economy when the workers either

---

[5] *Ibid.*

[6] If American or foreign drug merchants deposit dollar earnings in foreign banks, there will tend to be a credit to the private liabilities to foreigners reported by U.S. banks. The same result tends to occur if the earnings of foreigners are deposited directly into U.S. banks.

remit funds to relatives in their home countries or return home (usually to Mexico) carrying dollars with them. Since many of the exported dollars ultimately wind up being owned by foreign banks, who use them to obtain dollar deposits in U.S. banks, credit entries in the U.S. BOP record the recapture of the dollars. Since the credits are not offset by recorded debits, the net effect of the undocumented workers is to tend to produce a debit to the SD account.

Plausible though these factors may be, they cannot explain the persistent credits in the SD account. We must, therefore, consider what the credit-causing factors may be. Since the SD records the unrecordable, any analysis of it must be tentative. We can, nevertheless, make some plausible guesses about some of these factors.

Variations in Merchandise Trade   One factor that clearly influences the SD account is how merchandise imports change relative to merchandise exports. The key to understanding this point is to recognize that the BOP entries that offset entries to the merchandise trade accounts tend to lag behind these merchandise trade account entries in being recorded. The movement of goods across international boundaries tends to appear in the BOP as it occurs, but the credit arrangements worked out for importers may not be registered simultaneously in BOP data. When payment is made for the goods, it is likely to be recorded in the banking data of the BOP, but the fact that payment often followed the importation of the goods means that the SD account is affected by variations in trade volume, particularly when exports rise relative to imports, or vice versa. If exports rise relative to imports, the payment lag tends to cause a debit to SD; if imports rise relative to exports, the SD account tends to receive a credit.

The payment lag effect probably explains, at least in part, why the SD account recorded a debit entry of $8.4 billion in 1988. In 1988, merchandise exports increased by the extraordinary figure of $70.0 billion of 1987, but merchandise imports increased by only $37.5 billion.[7] The payment lag effect should have tended to produce a debit to the SD account in 1988, and, in fact, there actually was such a debit. In 1989 and 1990, however, merchandise exports also grew faster than merchandise imports, but the SD account had credit balances in both years. Since the amounts by which the growth of merchandise exports exceeded the growth of merchandise imports in 1989 and 1990 were much smaller than the 1988 amount, it is doubtful that the payment lag should have tended to cause SD debits in 1989 and 1990. What remains to be explained, however, are the magnitudes of the shifts toward the credit side in 1989 and, especially, in 1990.

Overstatement of the Current Account Deficit   The persistent tendency since 1977 for the SD account to have a credit balance suggests persistent

---

[7]Nicholson, *op cit.*

overstatement of the current account deficit, persistent understatement of net capital inflows, or both. The both explanation seems likely, but it is also likely that most of the credit balance results from the understatement of net capital inflows.

As far as the persistent overstatement of the current account deficit is concerned, there are two strong reasons for believing that it occurs: the understatement of merchandise exports and the understatement of investment income. It is unclear which source of understatement is the more serious, but either of them tends to cause a credit to the SD account.

Like most governments, the government of the United States is better at recording imports than at recording exports. One consequence of this fact is that world trade statistics indicate that the world as a whole has a persistent merchandise trade deficit, which is, of course, impossible. One reason for the understatement of U.S. merchandise exports is that exporters undervalue exports in order to reduce the import duties applied to them. Another reason for it is that in some cases, goods are exported illegally into the importing countries. For example, imports from the United States that are technically illegal under Mexican law have long constituted a major portion of Mexico's imports. Some of these sales are recorded as exports in U.S. trade statistics, but many sales to Mexican residents along the border are probably not so recorded.

The understatement of U.S. investment income occurs because there is understatement of U.S. investment in foreign countries. In some cases, the flow of foreign investment income into the United States is estimated by applying current yields and interest rates to the estimated value of U.S. foreign investment, and since the investment is understated, the income flow is also understated.[8]

Understatement of Net Capital Inflows   The most important explanation for the persistent credit to the SD account is probably that capital inflows into the United States are understated. This problem has long been present, but it has grown more serious as the volume of capital inflows has increased and financial innovations have produced and expanded investment techniques whose effects are difficult to measure. Between 1960 and 1979, the SD was sometimes a credit and sometimes a debit and averaged only 0.8 percent of the total volume of dollar flows required to finance current account transactions. Between 1980 and 1989, the SD had a credit balance in every year but 1988 and averaged 2.0 percent of current account transactions. In 1990, the SD equalled 5.2 percent of current account transactions.[9] Unrecorded net capital inflows apparently accounted for most of this increase.

An example of the role of financial innovations in affecting the SD account is provided by the growing tendency for U.S.-issued securities to be distributed

---

[8]Bach, *op cit.*, p. 35.
[9]*Ibid.*

through private placements, i.e., sales of securities to a small number of investors that bypass organized exchanges. In such sales, the transfers of dollars from foreigners to the sellers of the securities tend to be recorded as debits to U.S. bank-reported liabilities, but the U.S. liabilities for the securities often go unrecorded. The net effect, therefore, is a credit to the SD account.

Similar in its effect on the SD account is the growth of international borrowing that bypasses banks and does not involve the issuance of securities. When, for example, U.S. firms borrow from foreign subsidiaries and other nonbank credit sources without issuing securities, the flows of funds through the international banking system are likely to be picked up in the BOP, but the borrowing of the funds is likely to be missed. A credit to the SD account tends to occur, therefore, when the outstanding amount of such borrowing increases.

It is widely agreed that a major contributor to the credit balance in the SD account is the underreporting of direct investment by foreigners in the United States. Some of the missed investment is in real estate, and some takes the form of purchases of shares of stock. Also, no doubt, there is unrecorded DFI by American investors, but it is probable that its amount is much smaller than that of unrecorded DFI by foreigners. Again because the cash flows through banks tend to be picked up in the BOP, a credit to the SD account tends to occur.

Finally, there is the influence of the growing world demand for U.S. paper currency, which has wide use in underground economic activity throughout the world and is popular as an openly used medium of exchange in countries that lack public confidence in the local currency, such as the Soviet Union. To the extent that the currency acquisitions are effected through banks, debits tend to occur to U.S. bank-reported liabilities and U.S. bank-reported claims. What goes unrecorded are the increased foreign holdings of U.S. paper money, which technically should be recorded in the BOP as foreign private claims against the U.S. government. Once more, a credit to SD tends to result.

The Role of Exchange Rates   Assume that a U.S. firm enters into an arrangement with a foreign firm known as a currency swap, in which the U.S. firm turns over $5 million to the foreign firm in exchange for DM 8.4 million and a commitment to reverse the exchange at the same exchange rate (DM 1.68/$) in 2 years. Also assume that at the time the swap is arranged, the market exchange rate is also DM 1.68/$. Assuming that the market exchange rate is used for BOP conversion, and also assuming that the transaction's effects are recorded in the BOP, there would be a debit of $5 million for the acquisition of marks and an offsetting credit of $5 million to record the foreign acquisition of dollars (a U.S. liability). Now assume that 2 years later, when the exchange is reversed, the market exchange rate is DM 1.50/$. The U.S. BOP should then receive a credit of $5.6 million to record the giving up of DM 8.4 million and a debit of $5.0 million to record the receipt of dollars. In other words, the SD account would receive a debit of $0.6 million because of the rise in the mark's value.

From this example we see that exchange rate changes have an impact on the SD account when they cause exchanges of currencies to occur at different rates from those used for BOP conversion. A fall in the dollar's exchange value tends to produce an SD debit in such cases, while a rise in the dollar's value tends to produce an SD credit.

It is not only realized exchange rate changes that affect the SD account, but also *expected* exchange rate changes. For example, U.S. firms are more likely to borrow in foreign currencies and foreign purchases of U.S. assets are more likely to occur when the dollar is expected to rise than when it is expected to fall. When the dollar is expected to rise, some buyers of U.S. goods who have to pay in dollars are likely to accelerate payment, thereby tending to reduce the average time elapsing between the exporting of goods and the payment for them. It seems reasonable to assume, therefore, that a sizable increase in the credit to SD signifies a bullish outlook for the dollar and that a shift in the SD account toward the debit side signifies a bearish outlook. Casual empiricism suggests that a sharp increase in the SD credit often coincides with either a strengthening dollar or the expectation that the dollar is going to strengthen. Unfortunately for this observation, most of the monumental SD credit of 1990 occurred when the dollar was growing decidedly weaker.

The disquieting effect of the SD of 1990 will certainly lead to a major effort to improve the collection and reporting of BOP data. Until improvements have been made, however, SD watching will be a popular activity for exchange rate forecasters and others who are trying to detect trends in the U.S. and world economies.

BOP Deficits and Surpluses

Exchange rates tend to change, as other prices do, when gaps develop between supply and demand at the existing price levels. It follows that if the BOP can be interpreted so as to identify such gaps, it should be possible to discern exchange rate trends. It must be recognized, however, that government interference with market forces can obscure the meaning of BOP data. If, for example, a government is maintaining an overvalued currency by employing exchange controls, the underlying or potential demand for foreign exchange will exceed what would be indicated by the BOP alone. It is necessary, therefore, to combine an understanding of the BOP with knowledge of institutional conditions that the BOP does not reveal.

In attempting to discern the directional tendencies of exchange rates and the probable course of government policy, economists have long relied on the concepts of BOP deficits and surpluses, which correspond to the aforementioned gaps between supply and demand. Specifically, a **BOP deficit** exists when the quantity of foreign exchange demanded at the existing level of exchange rates exceeds the quantity supplied. A **BOP surplus** exists when the quantity of foreign exchange supplied at the existing level of exchange rates exceeds the quantity demanded. According to these definitions, BOP deficits and surpluses are disequilibrium conditions and can be eliminated if exchange rates are allowed to move to their equilibrium levels.

Since 1973, less attention has been given to the measurement of BOP deficits and surpluses than in earlier days. Indeed, since 1976, the Department of Commerce has refrained from publishing estimates of deficits and surpluses.

In part, its reluctance to make such estimates stems from the belief that BOP deficits and surpluses have much less significance than they had when exchange rates were fixed. This reluctance has also been based, however, on the belief that such imbalances cannot be accurately and unambiguously measured. Some observers label Commerce's position a "copout." Exchange rates are often prevented by government action from finding their market levels, so BOP deficits and surpluses do exist. While it is probably true that they cannot be measured unambiguously, neither can GNP and many other variables that governments attempt to measure.

Measuring BOP Deficits and Surpluses   Since total debits must always equal total credits in the BOP, the idea of a BOP deficit or surplus may initially seem a little strange. As a simple analogy with personal finance should make clear, however, the accounting requirement of overall equality of debits and credits does not mean that total payments to foreigners must necessarily equal total receipts from them. If individuals were to maintain full double-entry records of their payments and receipts, they would find that their total debits and credits would always be equal, yet most of us are all too familiar with personal financial deficits! Such a deficit occurs when a person's expenditures run ahead of his or her income, with the consequence that it is necessary to finance the resulting expenditure–income gap by resorting to borrowing, dissaving, or receiving gifts and/or government transfer payments. Similarly, a nation can experience a BOP deficit if attaining a given level of international payments requires it to borrow, draw down its international reserves, or actively solicit unilateral transfers. In either case, a deficit exists to the extent that financing in excess of income is necessary.

When Keynesian theory was in its heyday, especially during the 1960s and early 1970s, BOP analysts made much of the difficult distinction between autonomous and accommodating transactions. **Autonomous transactions** are considered to be largely independent of the BOP itself. For the most part, they are income-motivated transactions for which the use of the forex market is incidental to the process of obtaining income. **Accommodating transactions** are, in some sense, caused by the autonomous transactions. Viewed broadly, accommodating transactions include all transactions that finance autonomous transactions. More narrowly, accommodating transactions represent the conscious response of governments to nations' international payments positions.

Even today, it is common to draw a line separating the autonomous accounts of the BOP from the accommodating accounts, placing the latter below the former. A BOP deficit is said to exist when there is a net debit balance in the autonomous accounts and a net credit balance in the accommodating accounts. Exhibit 4.3 presents a schematic classification of BOP accounts showing three different measures of BOP deficits and surpluses based on the distinction between autonomous and accommodating accounts. The measures are the basic balance, the net liquidity balance, and the official reserve transactions (ORT) balance.

| E X H I B I T | 4.3 | *Alternative Measures of BOP Deficits and Surpluses*

Account Classifications	Measure of BOP Deficits or Surpluses
Merchandise trade Services Investment income Unilateral transfers Long-term capital flows	Measure 1: Basic Balance
Private, nonliquid, short-term capital flows Errors and omissions (statistical discrepancy)	Measure 2: Net Liquidity Balance
Private, liquid, short-term capital flows	Measure 3: Official Reserve Transactions Balance

The basic balance concept treats all current account items and long-term capital flows as autonomous ("above the line") and all other items as accommodating. Its proponents have argued that factors of some permanence dominate trade flows and long-term capital flows, while official reserve transactions (ORT) and short-term capital flows are either clearly accommodating in nature or else are influenced by speculative considerations and other factors that render them undependable as guides to an economy's tendencies.

The net liquidity balance concept moves private, nonliquid, short-term capital flows and errors and omissions above the line, thus classifying them as autonomous accounts. Nonliquid, short-term capital flows consist primarily of bank loans and corporate receivables. Errors and omissions consist mainly of unrecorded trade flows and capital flows that are not of liquid, short-term capital. Logically, therefore, E&O should be grouped with other similar accounts. The net liquidity balance concept views *liquid,* short-term capital flows as being accommodating because transactions involving items above the line generally occur in conjunction with liquid, short-term capital flows, i.e., exchanges of bank deposits or short-term securities. This concept views the ORT as accommodating on the assumption that most such transactions are motivated by the desire to stabilize exchange rates and are, therefore, responses to nations' payments positions rather than causes of them.

Both of these concepts have severe limitations. The line between short-term capital flows and long-term capital flows cannot be drawn with precision. Neither is there a clear-cut distinction between short-term capital flows that are liquid and short-term capital flows that are not. Moreover, private, liquid, short-term capital flows may be autonomous in nature. When, for example, foreign firms react to relatively attractive U.S. short-term interest rates by purchasing U.S. Treasury bills, the resulting increase in U.S. liabilities is autonomous because it is income-motivated and undertaken for its own sake. Similarly, when foreign firms use part of their cash inflows to acquire larger dollar balances for working capital purposes, it is arguable that the resulting increase in liquid, short-term capital claims held by foreigners is autonomous, because it rests fundamentally on the desire for economic gain.

The **official reserve transactions balance** moves private, liquid, short-term capital flows above the line, leaving the ORT as the only account category classified as accommodating. Since a BOP deficit or surplus is defined as a gap between the supply of and demand for foreign exchange, and since governments commonly use official reserve transactions to finance deficits or absorb surpluses, the ORT balance appears to mesh with the view that accommodating transactions reflect the conscious response of governments to nations' international payments positions.[10] Furthermore, the ORT balance is used as the measure of BOP deficits and surpluses in the influential monetary theory of exchange rate determination because changes in this balance tend to have an impact on money supplies.

There is, however, a major problem with the view that changes in official reserves are accommodating. The quantity of reserves that a government holds depends on other factors than the status of the BOP. If, for example, a government adds to its holdings of dollars because it desires more reserves, not because it wants to prevent the dollar from declining in value, one could argue that the acquisition of dollars is autonomous since it is independent of the current status of the BOP and is motivated by the desire to strengthen the national economy, i.e., it is income-motivated.

From this brief analysis it follows that it is difficult, and perhaps impossible, to measure a BOP deficit or surplus unambiguously. Moreover, while each of the three measures examined can be challenged when exchange rates are fixed, they are even more problematic when exchange rates are flexible. If, for example, the chosen measure shows a BOP deficit for a period of time when the national currency rose in exchange value, as is quite possible (witness the United States in 1988), the significance of the measure is obviously questionable.

The Continuing Relevance of BOP Deficits and Surpluses   At this point, it must be tempting to conclude, as the Department of Commerce has done, that since the different measures of BOP deficits and surpluses are ambiguous, there is no point in calculating them. In the judgment of this writer, such a conclusion is wrong. As difficult as it is to measure BOP imbalances, this does

---

[10]Before 1976, the Department of Commerce used a variation of the ORT balance known as the *official settlements balance*. In this variation, changes in accounts other than official reserves were classified as accommodating when they occurred at government initiative in response to BOP considerations. When, for example, the West German government was induced to accelerate certain payments due to the U.S. government in order to reduce pressure on the dollar, the ensuing credit to an account indicating changes in the nonreserve assets of the U.S. government was considered to be accommodating and was, therefore, included with the official settlements balance in arriving at a measure of the BOP deficit or surplus. In current practice, the terms *official reserve transactions balance* and *official settlements balance* are used interchangeably.

not invalidate the *concept* of them. Like other prices, exchange rates tend to change in reaction to gaps between supply and demand. Such gaps arise when the quantity of foreign exchange that is autonomously demanded exceeds the quantity that is autonomously supplied. Successfully forecasting exchange rates depends, whether or not it is consciously realized, on the ability to determine the relative strengths of autonomous demand and autonomous supply. While it may be difficult to measure BOP deficits and surpluses, it is still operationally desirable to have some idea of their magnitudes.

Of the three measures of BOP deficits and surpluses that have been mentioned, the ORT balance is generally viewed as being the best. It is necessary to remember, however, that it is a flawed measure. Before predicting the future of a currency on the basis of the ORT balance, one must always watch for indications that this measure might give misleading indications of a country's balance in accommodating transactions.

The Mutual Determination of BOP Entries

By this time, it should be abundantly clear that the BOP is a complex statement whose interpretation requires careful judgment. Fools walk in where angels fear to tread, however, and people who are not fools sometimes act on the basis of faulty inferences drawn from BOP data. Such faulty inferences frequently result from failure to understand or appreciate that BOP entries are mutually dependent, not only because of the nature of double-entry accounting, but also because of the process known by economists as "general equilibrium." Changes in particular BOP accounts lead to economic adjustments that affect other BOP accounts. The complexity of these adjustments can make it difficult to predict them exactly in particular instances, but it is dangerous to ignore them. They are frequently ignored, nevertheless, because of a lack of economic knowledge, an almost universal tendency to oversimplify the dynamics of economic adjustment, and the temptation to allow political considerations to override economic evidence.

Economic policymakers commonly single out one or more offending items in a nation's BOP for corrective action without giving due consideration to the secondary effects of these actions. In the United States, for example, the large merchandise trade deficits of recent years have spurred claims of massive job losses because of imports, and strident demands are commonly heard for protection from "unfair" foreign competition. Less attention has been given to the possibility that the massive capital inflows that have accompanied the trade deficits have stimulated employment opportunities, thereby helping to explain the fact that, while the merchandise trade deficit was rising, the U.S. unemployment rate was falling.

During the 1960s, the United States was perceived to have a chronic BOP deficit. The government adopted various policy measures designed to effect marginal changes in certain BOP accounts that were identified as major contributors to the BOP problem. In the final analysis, these measures were mere palliatives that could not overcome basic economic trends. Much more effective would have been a policy of general macroeconomic restraint.

One of the most common and most pernicious errors in interpreting the BOP is to assume that when DFI leads to profit remittances from a country that exceed the amount of new DFI flowing into it, this necessarily implies downward pressure on the exchange value of the national currency. In reality, the BOP effects of DFI can never be determined solely by examining the accounts with which DFI is specifically associated. DFI generally contributes to the expansion of the host country's exports, and some of it substitutes for imports. Furthermore, to the extent that it increases a country's real rate of economic growth, general macroeconomic adjustments tend to occur that tend, as we shall see in Chapter 10, to lead to a BOP surplus. It would be going much too far, however, to assert that DFI always, or even usually, tends to provide the host country with a merchandise trade surplus; it makes more sense to assert that it does so, however, than to base a judgment solely upon a comparison of investment flows with profit remittances. Those who extol DFI for its allegedly positive effects on the host country's BOP may claim too much, but at least they recognize that the accounts of the BOP are mutually determined.

The Balance of International Indebtedness (BII)

The BOP records income flows and net changes in financial claims during a certain period of time. Suppose, however, that we want information on the total value of DFI in the United States, the total quantity of claims on foreigners held by U.S. banks, or the total amount of a government's official reserves. We cannot obtain such information from the BOP. By accumulating BOP data for a number of years, we might approximate such information, but our estimate would be incomplete if some years were excluded. Moreover, there would be the problem of accounting for valuation changes caused by changes in exchange rates and the prices of assets. While some BOPs, including those compiled by the IMF, incorporate some valuation changes, it would be contrary to the general design of the BOP to adjust fully for valuation changes since the BOP is supposed to measure flows, not stocks.

Many governments prepare a statement, known generally as the **balance of international indebtedness (BII)**, which presents estimates of the reciprocal claims between their nations and the rest of the world as of a specific date. The Department of Commerce publishes a version of the BII that it prefers to call **the international investment position of the United States.** Exhibit 4.4 presents a slightly modified version of this statement at yearend for 1988 and 1989 as published in the June 1990 issue of the *Survey of Current Business.* The 1989 figures are preliminary.

The International Investment Position of the United States

From World War I until the 1980s, the United States was classified as a net creditor nation, i.e., a nation whose claims on foreigners exceeded foreigners' claims on it. It was, in fact, the leading creditor nation during this period. In 1982, however, a slight decrease occurred in the official estimate of its net

| E X H I B I T | 4.4 | *U.S. Assets Abroad and Foreign Assets in the United States: Amounts Outstanding at Yearend, 1988 and 1989 (Billions of Dollars)*

Type of Investment	Type of Valuation	1988	1989[p]
U.S. assets abroad			
U.S. official reserve assets	Current[g]	47.8	74.6
Gold[a]	Historical	11.1	11.1
Special drawing rights	Current	9.6	10.0
Reserve position in the IMF	Current	9.7	9.0
Foreign currencies	Current	17.4	44.6
U.S. government assets, other than official reserve assets	Historical	85.6	84.3
Loans and other long-term assets[b]	Historical	84.9	83.8
Foreign currency holdings and short-term assets[c]	Historical	0.7	0.5
U.S. private assets			
Direct investment	Historical	333.5	373.4
Foreign securities	Current	156.8	189.6
Bonds	Current	94.0	98.5
Corporate stocks	Current	62.7	91.1
Claims on unaffiliated foreigners reported by U.S. nonbanking concerns	Historical	33.9	32.5
Claims reported by U.S. banks, not included elsewhere	Historical	608.0	658.0
Foreign assets in the United States			
Foreign official assets in the United States	Current[g]	321.6	337.2
U.S. government securities[d]	Current	260.9	265.9
Other U.S. government liabilities[e]	Historical	14.8	15.1
Liabilities of U.S. banks, not included elsewhere	Historical	31.5	36.5
Other foreign official assets[f]	Current	14.4	19.7
Other foreign assets in the United States			
Direct investment	Historical	328.9	400.8
U.S. Treasury securities	Current	100.9	134.8
U.S. securities other than U.S. Treasury securities	Current	395.6	489.8
Corporate and other bonds	Current	194.6	229.6
Corporate stocks	Current	201.0	260.2
U.S. liabilities to unaffiliated foreigners reported by U.S. nonbanking concerns	Historical	36.0	38.9
U.S. liabilities reported by U.S. banks not included elsewhere	Historical	613.7	674.8

[p]Preliminary.

[a]Valued at $42.22 per ounce.

[b]Includes paid-in capital subscriptions to international financial institutions. Over 98 percent of the amounts listed were repayable in dollars.

[c]These claims are not classified as reserves because they are in inconvertible currencies.

[d]Some of these securities were not U.S. Treasury issues. Such securities comprised 3.1 percent of the total in 1988 and 3.6 percent of the total in 1989.

[e]Primarily U.S. government liabilities associated with military sales contracts and other transactions arranged with or through foreign official agencies.

[f]Consist of investments in U.S. corporate stocks and in debt securities of private corporations and state and local governments.

[g]There is some use of historical valuation for the items in this group.

Source: Russell B. Scholl, "International Investment Position: Component Detail for 1989," *Survey of Current Business,* June 1990, p. 59.

creditor position, and this development was followed by a rapid shift toward net debtor status. In 1985, the United States became officially classified as a **net debtor nation.** Since then, the amount of its net indebtedness has increased when the reciprocal claims between the United States and the rest of the world are totaled *using the measuring techniques that have been employed in the past.* This change in status of the United States has generated intense political controversy and focused the nation's attention, as never before, on the subject of its reciprocal claims against other nations.

For some time, it has been clear to informed observers that the measurement of the net investment status of the United States has been grossly inaccurate and that its creditor position has been understated relative to its debtor position. This did not seem to matter much until the data showed the United States to have become a net debtor nation. Since 1985, however, the outcry about the distortion in the Commerce Department's estimates of the net investment position of the United States has induced the department, effective with the data for 1989, to avoid publishing an estimate of that position. Those who are determined to have such an estimate can derive it very easily from Commerce data. If they do so, however, they are ignoring sound warnings from the Commerce Department and are, in effect, mixing apples and oranges.

Turning to Exhibit 4.4, one can readily see that total U.S. assets abroad and total foreign assets in the United States can be estimated by adding their components. Doing so produces estimates for the net debtor position of the United States of $531.1 billion in 1988 and $663.9 billion in 1989. These estimates are obtained, however, by adding valuations that are partly current and partly historical. Since historical valuations of assets and liabilities often differ markedly from current or market valuations, the mixing of the two inevitably leads to faulty estimates of current values. This fact has not deterred some individuals from appearing to believe that the estimates are reliable enough to base public policy on them.

Highlights of the U.S. Investment Position   One of the most striking things about Exhibit 4.4 is the enormous volume of reciprocal banking claims. At the end of 1989, U.S. banks reported claims on foreigners of $658.0 billion, an increase of $49.9 billion in one year, and they also reported liabilities to foreigners, including liabilities to foreign governments, of $711.3 billion, an increase of $66.0 billion. This relative prominence of banking claims is fairly new. For many years, the foreign claims of U.S. banks were less than U.S. portfolio investment in foreign securities, and as recently as 1980, they were less than the recorded value of U.S. DFI.[11] The growth of U.S. banks' reciprocal foreign claims reflects the general expansion of international banking and the establishment, beginning late in 1981, of International Banking Facilities (IBFs). By setting up IBFs, whose features are explained in

[11]Russell B. Scholl, "International Investment Position: Component Details for 1989," *Survey of Current Business,* June 1990, p. 59.

Chapter 13, banks operating in the United States can engage in operations that were previously denied to them.

Exhibit 4.4 indicates that at the end of 1989, the volume of foreign official assets in the United States ($337.2 billion) far exceeded the volume of U.S. official reserve assets ($74.6 billion). Note, however, that the U.S. government continues to value its gold holdings at $42.22 per ounce. Most ($265.9 billion) of the foreign official claims against the United States were in the form of U.S. government securities.

While DFI and portfolio investment by foreigners in the United States have tended to grow more rapidly in recent years than DFI and portfolio investment by the United States, the United States has steadily increased both types of foreign investment. In 1989, for example, U.S. DFI increased by $39.9 billion, while U.S. portfolio holdings of foreign securities increased by $32.8 billion. Simultaneously, foreigners' DFI in the United States grew by $72.0 billion, and foreigners' private portfolio holdings of U.S. securities grew by $128.2 billion. Note that U.S. DFI greatly exceeds U.S. portfolio investment in Exhibit 4.4, and that foreigners' portfolio investment greatly exceeds their DFI.

Recall that the material on the BOP presented earlier in the chapter indicates that the growth of foreign investment in the United States slowed dramatically in 1990, but that it was greater than officially recognized because some of it went unrecorded. It seems certain that much of the decline occurred because of a recession in the United States and because U.S. interest rates declined relative to interest rates in other prominent countries. It remains to be seen whether the decline will prove temporary.

The Geographic Distribution and Origins of DFI   Exhibit 4.4 does not provide data on the geographic distribution of U.S. investment or on the geographic origins of foreign investment in the United States, but the *Survey* articles on the U.S. international investment position provide such data for DFI. At the end of 1989, approximately 75 percent of total DFI by the United States was shown to be in developed countries. Canada held the number-one position ($66.9 billion), followed by the United Kingdom ($60.8 billion), Germany ($23.1 billion), Switzerland ($20.0 billion), and Japan ($19.3 billion). DFI in Latin America and the Caribbean was estimated at $61.4 billion, but well over $20 billion of this amount was in tax-haven countries, of which Bermuda ($17.8 billion) was, by far, the most prominent.[12]

The United Kingdom, not Japan, leads all other countries in the recorded amounts of DFI by foreigners in the United States.[13] The figure credited to British investors at the end of 1989 was $119.1 billion. Second was Japan ($69.7 billion), and third was the Netherlands ($60.5 billion). Also prominent were Canada ($31.5 billion), Germany ($28.2 billion), and Switzerland ($19.3

---

[12]*Loc. cit.*, p. 61.

[13]A British-born colleague of the author has humorously suggested that the growth of British ownership of U.S. firms constitutes the recolonization of America.

billion). Over $17 billion of foreign DFI in the United States was credited to Western Hemisphere tax havens, the most important being the Netherlands Antilles ($10.6 billion).[14]

Data Problems with the U.S. International Investment Position

Of the various problems involved in interpreting the data on the international investment position of the United States, the most serious are those associated with interpreting the data on DFI. In the first place, some DFI has not been recorded. In the second place, and probably the cause of even more distortion, the recording of DFI using historical valuations tends to cause such investment to be understated in terms of current market values.

Valuation on a historical basis means, as a general principle, that DFI valuations are book values. While the market value of an enterprise can fall below its book value, the opposite is more likely to be the case. The average excess of market value over book value tends to increase as a function of time. Because DFI by the United States generally has greater age than DFI in the United States, the former is understated relative to the latter.

Some idea of the distortion resulting from valuing DFI on the basis of book values can be obtained by comparing Exhibits 4.2 and 4.4. The U.S. BOP for 1989 (Exhibit 4.2) indicates that the United States derived $53.6 billion in income from DFI, while foreigners derived only $14.0 billion in income from their direct investments in the United States. Exhibit 4.4 indicates, however, that at the end of 1989, DFI by foreigners in the United States was valued at $400.8 billion, while DFI by the United States was valued at $373.4 billion. While the possibility exists that 1989 was a relatively good year for American investors and a relatively bad year for their foreign counterparts, the fact is that the DFI income gap in 1989 was typical.

One possible interpretation of these figures is that foreigners are inferior investors by comparison with Americans. A more plausible interpretation is that foreigners are less concerned with short-run profits. But a far *more* plausible interpretation is that the value of U.S. DFI is greatly understated relative to the value of DFI in the United States. There is a tendency for the market values of stocks to be strongly influenced by current earnings, and even if it is true that foreigners have a longer-run investment outlook than Americans do, it is difficult to believe that they are content with receiving rates of return on their American stock holdings that are several times less than those received by their American counterparts. It seems likely, therefore, that Exhibit 4.4 understates the market value of U.S. DFI by hundreds of billions of dollars.

It should be noted, however, that the book values assigned to DFI estimates are not always original values. If, for example, a U.S. firms sells a foreign subsidiary to another U.S. firm for an amount that exceeds the subsidiary's book value, the sale establishes a new and higher book value.

---

[14]Scholl, *op. cit.*, p. 64.

Incidentally, the fact that DFI is recorded on a net equity basis, not an asset-liability basis, means that it is understated relative to bank assets and liabilities. If the DFI of the United States were shown in terms of total assets controlled, its amount would exceed the total claims of U.S. banks on foreigners. Correspondingly, of course, U.S. liabilities to foreigners would increase.

There are various other data problems with the international investment position of the United States, including the underrecording of investments in real estate and the overstatement of the value of U.S. banks' portfolio claims against LDC governments. From the analysis provided, however, it seems safe to conclude that if, in fact, the United States is a net debtor nation, the extent of its net indebtedness is much smaller than is widely assumed. This conclusion receives support from the fact that, as Exhibit 4.1 indicates, in the years 1988 through 1990 the income derived by the United States from foreign investment, including portfolio investment, approximately equalled the investment income paid to foreigners. Moreover, it should be recalled, there appears to be substantial understatement of the income derived by the United States from direct investment. Nevertheless, if the recent trends in investment flows continue, a day will arrive when the fact of net indebtedness is beyond dispute.

Summary

The BOP is a flow statement that records a country's transactions with the rest of the world. It follows double-entry bookkeeping principles and is divided into two main parts: the current accounts, which record income flows, and the capital accounts, which record flows of claims. The official reserve accounts are a capital account subcategory that records changes in official reserve assets, including claims of foreign governments that those governments treat as official reserve assets. Since the total debits and credits of a BOP must be equal, any net balance in the current accounts tends to be offset by an opposite net balance in the capital accounts. Any net imbalance between the current accounts and the capital accounts is counterbalanced by the statistical discrepancy or errors and omissions account.

For some years, the U.S. BOP has characteristically exhibited a large current account deficit offset by a large net capital inflow. Opinions differ as to whether the net capital inflow has been caused by the current account deficit or the deficit has been caused by the capital inflow. The truth probably lies between the extremes.

A growing problem in the interpretation and use of data on the U.S. BOP is the growing relative size of the entries to the SD account, which tends to show a persistent credit balance. The chief contributors to the credit balance appear to be the overstatement of the current account deficit and the understatement of net capital inflows. An increase in the SD credit entry often seems to signify a strengthening dollar, but there have been exceptions to this rule.

A BOP deficit or surplus occurs when the quantity of foreign exchange that is autonomously demanded differs from the quantity that is autonomously supplied. Measuring a BOP deficit or surplus accurately ranges from difficult to impossible. The official reserve transactions balance is, however, widely regarded as the best approximate measure.

Data on the reciprocal claims between the United States and the rest of the world indicate that foreign claims on the United States are growing more rapidly than U.S. claims on foreigners. Whether or not the United States is, as often claimed, a net debtor nation is unclear, primarily because U.S. direct foreign investment is greatly understated. It will certainly become a net debtor nation if the present trend continues.

References

Bach, Christopher L. "U.S. International Transactions, Fourth Quarter and Year 1990." *Survey of Current Business,* March 1990, pp. 34–68.

Bernstein, Edward M. "The United States as an International Debtor Country." *The Brookings Review,* Fall 1985, pp. 28–36.

Carvounis, Chris C. *The United States Trade Deficit of the 1980s.* Westport, Conn.: Quorum Books, 1987.

Eisner, Robert, and Paul J. Peiper. "The World's Greatest Debtor Nation?" *The North American Review of Economics and Finance.*

Heyne, Paul. "Do Trade Deficits Matter?" *Cato Journal,* Winter 1983–84, pp. 705–716.

International Monetary Fund. *Annual Report.* Washington, D.C., annual.

——. *Balance of Payments Manual.* 4th ed. Washington, D.C., 1977.

——. *Balance of Payments Statistics.* An annual with supplementary issues.

——. *International Financial Statistics.* Monthly publication.

Nicholson, Robert E., Jr. "U.S. International Transactions, First Quarter 1989." *Survey of Current Business,* June 1990, pp. 66–109.

Ott, Mack. "Have U.S. Exports Been Larger Than Reported?" *Federal Reserve Bank of St. Louis Review,* September–October 1988, pp. 3–23.

Scholl, Russell B. "The International Investment Position: Component Detail for 1989." *Survey of Current Business,* June 1990, pp. 54–65.

Stekler, Lois. "U.S. International Transactions in 1990." *Federal Reserve Bulletin,* May 1991, pp. 287–296.

Survey of Current Business. Various issues dealing with direct foreign investment.

Questions

1. Most BOP entries result from value-for-value exchanges of goods, services, or assets for current or future money payments. What are the leading examples of BOP entries that do *not* involve (a) a value-for-value exchange, (b) an actual international flow of goods, services, or assets, or (c) a current or future international flow of money?
2. Why are unilateral transfers and the income flows associated with foreign investment classified as current account items?
3. What are capital inflows and outflows? Which are debited, and which are credited? Why? Now consider the following example. A U.S. firm borrows $250 million by selling an issue of Eurobonds to foreign buyers, who pay for the bonds with dollars they obtain from banks in their countries. In the U.S. BOP, what is the capital inflow, and what is the capital outflow?

4. What items go into the official reserve transactions (ORT) section of the U.S. BOP? In a normal year, what do you expect to find in the ORT section in terms of overall debits and credits? Why? Does an unusually large increase in the U.S. government's official reserve assets necessarily mean that the dollar was tending to strengthen during the time the increase occurred? Explain.

5. Assume that you are in the business of forecasting foreign exchange rates and that you read a statement by a prominent economist that during the next year, the current account deficit of the United States will probably increase. No other information is provided. Are you justified in concluding, assuming that you believe the economist is right, that the exchange value of the dollar will probably fall? Explain.

6. Explain why and how a growth in U.S. merchandise exports relative to merchandise imports will tend to affect the SD account.

7. For 1989, the SD account had a credit balance of $22.4 billion. In 1990, the SD credit rose to $73.0 billion. During the year 1990, merchandise exports were recorded as increasing by $28.8 billion of 1989, while merchandise imports were recorded as increasing by $22.7 billion. The exchange value of the dollar against other leading currencies declined substantially during the year. What is a plausible explanation of this large increase in the credit entry to SD?

8. What is the basis for reasoning that a sharp increase in the amount of the SD credit in the U.S. BOP may indicate the expectation of a strengthening dollar?

9. Define what is meant by a BOP deficit, and explain what are the problems involved in using the ORT balance as the measure of a BOP deficit.

10. Judging from the recently published statements of the international investment position of the United States, in what major respects does the pattern of U.S. private investment in foreign countries differ from the pattern of foreign private investment in the United States?

11. What is the basis for arguing that U.S. investment in foreign countries is so understated relative to foreign investment in the United States that it is not entirely clear that the United States is, in fact, a net debtor nation?

12. Explain in what sense the statements of the international investment position of the United States overstate the importance of international banking relative to that of DFI.

| APPENDIX | 4.1 |

Exercises in BOP Accounting

The following examples are designed to improve your understanding of BOP accounting, in general, and the U.S. BOP, in particular. For each example, indicate which accounts should be credited, which should be debited, and by what amounts. Use account titles from Exhibits 4.1 and 4.2. Show the capital account, official reserve account, and unilateral transfer account items on a net basis.

Case 1   Assume that a U.S. firm imports $20 million worth of video recorders from South Korea under an agreement that allows the importer 30 days' credit after the equipment is unloaded at a U.S. port. Payment is made on schedule to the exporter's bank in South Korea. Assume that when the exporter receives this payment (in dollars), the firm converts the dollars into Korean won at its bank and the bank sells the dollars to a Japanese bank in exchange for yen. Show the final effects of these transactions on the U.S. BOP.

Case 2   Assume that Purehex, a U.S. firm, has a Brazilian subsidiary, Purobras, in which it holds a 50 percent equity. During the year, Purobras has after-tax profits in cruzeiros equal to $8 million at the end-of-the-year exchange rate. Purehex reaches an agreement with Purobras that requires the latter to remit $1.5 million at the end of the year. The rest of Purehex's share of the profits, equivalent to $2.5 million, are reinvested in Purobras. During the year, Purobras makes the following additional payments to Purehex, all in dollars: for license fees and royalties, $800,000; for legal and technical services, $400,000; and for imports of equipment from the United States, $1.8 million. All of these payments are from dollar deposits in U.S. banks which are purchased in the forex market from a Brazilian bank. Show the effects of these transactions on the U.S. BOP.

Case 3   Assume that Pilut Corporation, a Dutch firm, has a U.S. subsidiary, Petalco, in which it increases its investment by $40 million. Of this sum, $5 million consists of equipment shipped to Petalco from the Netherlands. A 4-year loan of $10 million from the London branch of a U.S. bank finances part of the investment, while the remaining $25 million is financed by selling 10-year, dollar-denominated Eurobonds to investors outside the United States. The $35 million raised by borrowing is all spent in the United States and winds up as deposits of U.S. residents in U.S. banks. Assuming that all of this occurs during a calendar year, show the effects of these transactions on the U.S. BOP for that year.

Case 4   Assume that a certain Central American country that maintains friendly relations with the United States experiences a severe earthquake that is accompanied by a massive tidal wave. The U.S. government responds by providing the country with $30 million in food, medical supplies, and other material assistance. In addition, the U.S. government gives the country's government $20 million in cash for the maintenance of essential imports. Meanwhile, private groups in the United States, consisting mainly of church-related organizations, provide the country's residents with $12 million in goods and services. A wealthy South American philanthropist, impressed by the performance of the church groups, donates $3 million worth of securities to them, of which $2 million consist of stocks in the U.S. companies and $1 million consists of U.S. Treasury securities. The church groups decide to hold onto the securities until they need cash for additional charitable projects in Latin America. Show the effects of these transactions on the U.S. BOP.

Case 5   Suppose that the members of the EMS decide to intervene in the forex market to moderate a decline in the exchange value of their currencies against the dollar. In doing so, they spend $620 million of their forex reserves, liquidating U.S. Treasury securities to obtain the money. They also arrange a swap with the Fed allowing them to obtain $1,200 million as needed. In addition, they turn over $100 million in SDRs to the Fed in exchange for dollars. Subsequently, the European central banks draw on their swap agreement to obtain $460 million, giving the Fed an equivalent amount of their currencies in exchange. The total amount of dollar sales by the European central banks is $620 million, of which $140 million is used to buy local currencies from U.S. banks and $480 million is used to buy local currencies from European banks. Keeping in mind that swap agreements have no BOP effects until they are exercised, show the effects of these transactions on the U.S. BOP.

| A P P E N D I X | *4.2* |

The BOP Statements of the IMF

The BOPs published by the Department of Commerce differ considerably from those published by agencies of other governments and international organizations. Among the most widely used BOP statements are those published by the IMF in *Balance of Payments Statistics* and *International Financial Statistics*. The wealth of detail provided by the first of these publications makes it a rich resource for BOP analysts.

This appendix focuses on the BOPs of Mexico for 1988 and 1989 as published in *Balance of Payments Statistics*. Mexico was chosen because of its importance to the United States and because it provides an excellent illustration of the BOP of a major LDC confronted with severe international financial problems which is attempting to restructure its economy.

From 1954 until 1976, the government of Mexico (GOM) successfully pegged the peso to the dollar at Ps 12.50/$. The peso became increasingly overvalued, however, and on August 31, 1976, the GOM was forced to allow the peso to float. From around the beginning of 1977 until the spring of 1982, the GOM relied on Mexico's growing prominence as a petroleum exporter to keep the peso fairly stable, but it again became overvalued. There was massive capital flight from Mexico in 1982, and the government exhausted its forex reserves in a futile effort to support the peso. The end to this effort came in August 1982, when the GOM announced that it could no longer service its debts to foreign banks and simultaneously allowed the peso to float. Even then,

| E X H I B I T | 4.5 | *The Balance of Payments of Mexico:*
1988 and 1989 (Millions of U.S. dollars)

Classification	1988	1989
A. Current account, excluding group F	−2,443	−5,447
Merchandise exports, f.o.b.	20,566	22,765
Merchandise imports, f.o.b.	−18,898	−23,410
Trade balance	1,668	−645
Other goods, services, and income: credit	11,441	13,135
Travel	4,000	4,795
Other	7,441	8,340
Other goods, services, and income: debit	−16,119	−18,609
Travel	−3,202	−4,247
Investment income	−9,769	−10,663
Other	−3,148	−3,699
Total: goods, services, and income	−3,010	−6,119
Private unrequited transfers	397	516
Official unrequited transfers	170	156
B. Direct investment and other long-term capital, excluding groups F through H	−5,192	763
Direct investment	635	1,852
Portfolio investment	−880	61
Other long-term capital		
Resident official sector	−3,490	−94
Deposit money banks	2,211	528
Other sectors	−3,668	−1,584
Total, groups A plus B	−7,635	−4,684
C. Other short-term capital, excluding groups F through H	−678	225
Resident official sector	6	−3
Deposit money banks	92	−485
Other sectors	−776	713

however, the GOM could not bring itself to allow the peso to find its market equilibrium value, and it resorted to exchange controls and other measures, most notably the nationalization of the banking system, which were motivated primarily or in part by the desire to limit the peso's decline.

Some idea of the lack of success of the Mexican government's policies from 1982 to 1986 is conveyed by the fact that the conversion rate between the peso and the dollar used in *Balance of Payments Statistics* went from Ps 56.4/$ in 1982 to Ps 611.4/$ in 1986. Meanwhile, capital flight continued, DFI in Mexico stagnated, and the merchandise trade surplus declined sharply after 1983. With its economy suffering from a vicious combination of hyperinflation, negative economic growth, and worsening employment conditions, and with the country's political stability beginning to be called into question, the GOM finally roused itself to undertake the task of fundamentally restructuring the economy. Essentially, this restructuring has involved moving from a centrally directed economy pursuing the mirage of economic independence to

Classification	1988	1989
D. Net Errors and Omissions	−2,840	4,250
Total, Groups A through D	−11,153	209
E. Counterpart Items	−151	−57
Monetization/demonetization of gold	20	−33
Allocation/cancellation of SDRs		
Valuation changes in reserves	−171	−24
Total, Groups A through E	−11,304	−267
F. Exceptional financing	4,515	389
Debt/equity swaps	1,959	389
Debt/bond swaps	2,556	
Rescheduled debt	—	—
Other loans for balance of payments support	—	—
Total, groups A through F	−6,789	122
G. Liabilities constituting foreign authorities' reserves		
H. Total change in reserves	6,789	−122
Monetary gold	−38	642
SDRs	312	11
Reserve position in the Fund		
Foreign exchange assets	6,873	−1,061
Other claims		
Credit from the Fund-administered resources	−358	286
Conversion rates: Mexican pesos per U.S. dollar	2,273.1	2,461.5

Source: IMF, *Balance of Payments Statistics, 1990: Yearbook, Part 1*, p. 441.

an open economy in which market forces have a much greater role than they have been permitted to play in the past.

In 1986, the Mexican BOP began changing in ways that indicated an improvement in the economy's international performance. Further improvement was registered in 1987. Some of the indicators of improvement included a rise in DFI in Mexico, a shift of the E&O account from a debit balance (indicating capital flight) to a credit balance, a shift in the current account balance from being negative to being positive, and a large increase (in 1987) in the government's official reserves. The economy remained severely troubled, however, as is shown by the continued rapid depreciation of the peso, whose IMF conversion rate was Ps 1,378.2/$ in 1987.

Exhibit 4.5 indicates that in 1988, Mexico's international financial position took a turn for the worse. The balance on current account, which had been a positive $3,968 million in 1987, went to a negative $2,443 million in 1988. DFI, though still positive in 1988 (by $635 million), fell well below the

1987 figure $(1,796 million), and the balance in portfolio investment went from a negative $397 million in 1987 to a negative $880 million in 1988. The E&O entry for 1988 was negative $2,840 million, as compared to positive $2,605 million in 1987. Official reserves, which increased by $5,684 million in 1987, decreased by $6,789 million in 1988. There was also bad news on the inflation front, as is indicated by the fact that the IMF's conversion rate for the peso went from Ps 1,378.2/$ in 1987 to Ps 2,273.1/$ in 1988.

Properly interpreted, however, the BOP for 1988 was not all bad news. The negative shift in the current account balance reflected an increase in merchandise imports which, in turn, reflected the consequences of government initiatives to open the economy. While the current account deficit raised questions about Mexico's ability to finance the structural readjustment process, the GOM took important steps toward improving the country's international credit standing by negotiating debt swaps with foreign creditors and repaying substantial amounts of its obligations to foreign banks.

The GOM's debt swaps in 1988 appear explicitly as credit entries (increases in liabilities) in group F. These entries were offset by debits to the residential official sector and other sectors accounts of group B, which were considered to be debt payments. The resident official account sector means the GOM proper, and the other sectors accounts of groups B and C refer to private firms and state enterprises. By swapping outstanding debts on a heavily discounted basis for equity interests in Mexican firms and collateralized bonds, the GOM eliminated a significant part of its obligations to foreign banks. The total amount of the canceled debt does not appear in the BOP, but the fact that the GOM arranged debt swaps valued at $4,515 million *after* the canceled debt had been discounted indicates that this amount was much greater than $4,515 million.

In 1989, the current account deficit increased to $5,447 million, reflecting the continued rapid growth of merchandise imports. In most other respects, however, the BOP for 1989 indicated improvements in Mexico's condition by comparison with 1988. The credit to DFI ($1,852 million) was much larger than in 1988, and the balance in portfolio investment shifted from being strongly negative to being slightly positive. The E&O account recorded a positive balance of $4,250 million in 1989, thereby providing strong evidence of the repatriation of capital. While the volume of debt swaps diminished greatly in 1989, the hemorrhage of official reserves was stopped. The improvement in the BOP owed much to the fact that after a lengthy and divisive presidential election in 1988, the winner of that contest moved decisively at the beginning of 1989 to accelerate the restructuring of the economy. Note that the peso's conversion rate averaged Ps 2,461.5/$ in 1989. This represented the smallest percentage decline in the peso's exchange value since 1981.

Although there are numerous differences between the IMF's format and that of the Commerce Department, perhaps the most striking difference between the two is the IMF's use of a category known as *counterpart items,* which appears in Exhibit 4.5 as group E. Three such items are shown: monetization/demonetization of gold, allocation/cancellation of SDRs, and valuation changes in reserves. The BOPs of the Commerce Department record any new SDR allocations, but they have no equivalent to the other two items appearing in group E.

The monetization/demonetization of gold account is affected when a government transacts in gold with its own residents. In 1988, the GOM was a net buyer of gold domestically. Since its purchases resulted in a $20 million debit to the monetary gold account of group H, an equal debit was made to the monetization/demonetization of gold account of group E. In 1989, the GOM was a large net seller of gold ($642 million). Since $33 million of these sales were net sales to domestic buyers, the monetization/demonetization account was debited $33 million.

More important than domestic transactions in gold were valuation changes in the GOM's forex reserves. The entries to valuation changes in reserves in group E of -171 million in 1988 and -24 million in 1989 mean that the GOM had credit entries (decreases) of the same amounts in the official reserve accounts of group H because of valuation changes. The details provided in *Balance of Payments Statistics* indicate that in 1988, the GOM lost $414 million on its holdings of SDRs. Partly offsetting these losses was a gain of $275 million on its obligations to the IMF as a result of a reduction in the dollar value of the liabilities. In 1989, the GOM lost $91 million on its foreign currency holdings and $11 million on its holdings of SDRs, but it gained $78 million on its liabilities to the IMF.[15]

---

[15]IMF, *Balance of Payments Statistics, 1990: Yearbook, Part 1*, p. 445.

The Foreign Exchange Market

■

CHAPTER 5

An Overview of the Foreign Exchange Market

■

Much of the subject matter of international finance deals with the consequences of differences in nations' economic policies, political arrangements, and institutional practices. Above all, however, what sets international finance apart from other fields of study is its preoccupation with actual or potential international exchanges of monetary units, known as *currencies*, whose prices in terms of each other, known as *exchange rates*, are subject to change.

Generally, international transactions, like domestic transactions, require money flows at some point. In international transactions, however, money flows often require the use of currencies other than the national currencies of the parties to the transactions. If such transactions are to occur, some mechanism must exist for converting currencies into other currencies to accommodate the currency preferences of the parties involved. This mechanism is the *foreign exchange market*, which encompasses all transactions involving the exchange of different monetary units for each other.

The forex market is worldwide in scope and, when the trading of currencies is unrestricted, extremely competitive. Its activities tend to be concentrated in major financial centers, most importantly London, Tokyo, and New York. Somewhat behind these centers in transaction volume, two others have transaction volumes large enough to place them in a "big five" of forex market centers: Frankfurt and Zurich. Numerous other cities can be regarded as major forex market centers, as well. These centers are in constant contact with each other, and the communications network that connects them performs so efficiently that when the business hours of different centers overlap, an exchange rate change in one center has an almost immediate impact on forex trading in other centers.

Because of the geographic extent of the forex market, the complexity and diversity of its transactions and products, and the large number of its participants, estimating its size is difficult. Clearly, however, it is the world's largest market in terms of transactions volume, and it is growing rapidly. A study conducted in April 1989 by the Federal Reserve Bank of New York estimated the *daily* volume of forex transactions in the United States at $129 billion after adjustments to eliminate double counting.[1] This was an increase of 120 percent over the estimate of a similar study in March 1986! Most agree that the volume of forex trading in the United Kingdom somewhat exceeds that of the United States. The total volume of forex trading in Japan is probably about the same as that of the United States. A conservative estimate of total daily forex trading in these three countries as of 1989 would be $425 billion, and for the world as a whole, the total figure considerably exceeds even this staggering sum.

In most forex transactions, both the buyer and the seller of a currency are money center banks, i.e., banks whose operations are heavily oriented toward the specialized activities of leading financial centers. Most of the remaining forex transactions have a money center bank as one party. Overwhelmingly, the currency exchanges effected by money-center banks produce present or future exchanges of bank deposits. Exchanges of paper money, including traveler's checks, are such a small part of the forex market's activity that they are often ignored in surveys of the market's operations.

Most currency trading is in the currencies of high-income nations whose governments impose few restrictions on currency trades. In a large majority of forex transactions, the U.S. dollar is one of the currencies involved. In general, the currencies of the LDCs and the nations of eastern Europe are not heavily used in international transactions because of their limited convertibility and other factors.

Although currency trading is severely restricted in much of the world, the characteristics of money assure that governments cannot completely control international exchanges of their currencies. Given sufficient incentive and even slight opportunity, the residents of countries with severe restrictions on currency trading find ways to acquire bank deposits and other assets in other countries and to obtain paper money denominated in currencies other than their own. Thus, even nations with comprehensive exchange controls are partly integrated into the forex market. The inevitable consequences of restricting forex transactions include the diversion of human energy from productive activities into financial endeavors and the diversion of employment opportunities from the domestic economy to foreign economies. From the perspectives of many governments, however, these costs are necessary.

Market Participants

Based on their motives for participation, the participants in the forex market can be divided into six groups. First, some parties participate as part of commercial, financial, or other transactions they undertake for reasons that are largely independent of the forex market's existence. Most such transactions are

---

[1]Federal Reserve Bank of New York, "Summary of Results of U.S. Foreign Exchange Market Survey Conducted in April 1989," unpublished report, 1989, p. 1.

incidental to either international trade or investment. For this reason, it is convenient to designate this group as traders and investors, even though some participants so classified are neither. This group's transactions result in commitments to make or receive payments in foreign currencies, and the need of this group for currency conversion that supplies the *raison d'être* for the forex market's existence. Second and third are the dealers and brokers, whose operations are linked to each other, but whose identity and functions are separate. They make profits by meeting the conversion needs of the other participants. Fourth are the *arbitrageurs,* who profit from market imperfections. Fifth are the *speculators,* who seek to gain on the basis of their presumably superior exchange rate expectations. Sixth are those participants, primarily *central banks,* who seek to influence exchange rates.

Traders and Investors

This group of participants can be divided into two main subgroups: exporters and importers of goods and services, and parties who either supply or demand foreign exchange for reasons connected with international investment. Some of those who are included in the second subgroup are not investors buying assets or receiving payments associated with international investment, but sellers of assets or parties (generally debtors) who have to make payments classified as interest, dividends, amortization, fees, or royalties. Also included among the traders and investors are those parties whose participation in the forex market results from **unilateral transfers,** the international equivalent of domestic transfer payments.

As was noted earlier, the need of traders and investors for currency conversion supplies the forex market's basic justification for existence. Nevertheless, the members of this group participate in a minority of forex transactions. In large part, this is because the banks that accommodate their conversion needs rely heavily on interbank transactions to manage their overall forex positions. A growing number of nonfinancial multinational firms have, however, developed sufficient expertise in forex trading to manage their forex positions with considerable independence from dealer banks. The total volume of the forex transactions of such firms consequently considerably exceeds the volume of forex transactions required to meet their basic need for conversion.

Dealers and Brokers

Forex dealers derive income by buying currencies at lower prices than the prices at which they sell currencies. Forex brokers bring buyers and sellers into contact with each other on a commission basis. Money-center commercial banks are the leading forex dealers. Their forex dealings are supplemented by those of commercial banks headquartered in other cities (often called "regional" banks), investment banks, and nonbank dealers. The last group consists of generally small-scale operators trading in bank notes and traveler's checks. Forex brokers are generally specialized brokerage houses, but in some cases, notably the currency futures and options markets, they may be well-known commercial banks and investment firms.

Dealers' operations are divided into the *wholesale* (or, somewhat less accurately, interbank) and *retail* levels of operation. At the wholesale level, dealers alter their currency inventories by transacting on a large scale, typically for more than $3 million per transaction, with other dealers, multinational companies, central banks, and anyone else who is willing and able to trade on such a large scale. At this level, the spreads between buying or "bid" prices and selling or "ask" prices are ordinarily very small. This reflects the intense competition among dealers, their expertise in exchange risk management, and the low transaction costs on large-scale exchanges. At the retail level, dealers cater to the needs of customers wishing to buy or sell foreign exchange on a small scale. The bid-ask spread in retail transactions is much wider than that in wholesale transactions, but is still typically well below 1 percent of transaction value. In volume terms, the forex market is dominated by wholesale transactions, some of which are with traders and investors. Such transactions probably account for close to 90 percent of the total value of forex transactions involving actual cash flows.

Commercial Banks and Investment Banks   Large money-center commercial banks constitute the backbone of the forex market because they serve as **marketmakers,** i.e., they simultaneously quote bid and ask prices, standing ready to trade (for extremely short time periods) at the quoted prices. Since their purchases seldom exactly equal their sales of particular currencies, they experience, at least temporarily, variations in their inventories of foreign currencies. These variations expose them to the exchange risk. While they sometimes deliberately bear this risk, thereby acting as speculators, they generally prefer to keep their forex exposure as low as they can without unduly restricting their operations.

Investment banks are financial institutions whose most basic activity is to help business firms and governments bring new issues of securities to market. They engage in numerous other activities, including secondary trading in the securities that they brought to market for their clients. Since 1933, the Glass-Steagall Banking Act has required the separation of commercial banking from investment banking within the United States, with the result, among other things, that investment banks are prohibited from acting as depository institutions domestically. Correspondingly, commercial banks are prohibited from engaging in the securities business domestically. In most other nations, no such separation of commercial banking from investment banking exists. Since the restrictions imposed by Glass-Steagall are not fully operative abroad, U.S. investment banking firms can engage in deposit banking outside the United States, and commercial banks are allowed, within limits, to participate in the securities business in other countries.

Increasingly, U.S. investment banks are availing themselves of the opportunity to engage in deposit banking abroad. The basic reason for doing so is that a complementary relationship often exists between investment banking and currency exchanges. If, for example, an investment bank is marketing a Eurobond issue or arranging a currency swap, it is convenient to be able to deal in the currencies involved. While investment banks have attained some importance as forex dealers, they play a limited role as marketmakers and are generally inferior to money-center commercial banks in currency-trading expertise and the scope of their forex dealings.

The Euromoney Surveys of Forex Dealers   Exhibit 5.1 on pages 130 and 131 presents the rankings of the world's top 20 forex dealers in 1989, 1990, and 1991 as determined by *Euromoney* from surveys conducted in those years. The respondents included banks, large nonbank corporations, and institutional investors from the United Kingdom, Continental Europe, North America, and the Pacific Rim.[2] *Euromoney* does not publish extensive information of the methodology of these surveys, and it is clear that their results are not necessarily definitive. Nevertheless, those results undoubtedly provide at least a rough indicator of dealers' true rankings among large-scale users of their services.

One thing that is immediately obvious from Exhibit 5.1 is the preeminence of forex dealers whose headquarters are in English-speaking countries. Of the 31 banks listed, 10 are from the United States, 5 are British, 1 is Canadian, and 4 are Australian. Of the top ten banks in 1991, 9 were either British or American. Only two of the banks listed are Japanese, and only one is German. Two of the banks listed, Goldman Sachs and Morgan Stanley, are U.S. investment banks.

To some extent, no doubt, the preeminence of U.S. and British banks in these lists reflects bias in the sample, but it also reflects the fact that, historically, banks from these countries have operated relatively free from government restrictions on forex transactions. Particularly for U.S. banks, the relative absence of restrictions on forex trading has been an essential ingredient in developing the capacity for innovation and change that has been the key to maintaining their market positions.

Another thing that is obvious from the *Euromoney* surveys is that the forex market is fiercely competitive. While Citicorp and Barclays have maintained a firm hold on the number-one and number-two positions, respectively, for several years, the rankings of other banks have shown great fluidity. Incidentally, the *Euromoney* survey for 1990 indicated that the top 21 banks in that year accounted for only 42.9 percent of the respondents' total forex turnover.[3] Obviously, there must have been many other banks besides these 21 that were competing strongly on the dealers' side of the market.

---

[2]The 1990 survey encompassed 320 banks, 176 major corporations, and 60 institutional investors. They were weighted on the basis of their estimated forex turnover, though how this turnover was determined is not explained. On a turnover basis, the geographic distribution of the respondents was as follows: United Kingdom, 22 percent; Continental Europe, 24 percent; North America, 26 percent; Far East, 25 percent; and other, 3 percent. "Citi Shows Its Staying Power," *Euromoney,* May 1990, p. 121.

[3]*Ibid,* p. 117. Even so, however, the *Euromoney* figures for 1989 and earlier years indicate some tendency for the total market share of the top 20 banks to increase. Furthermore, many knowledgeable observers believe that because of the growing complexity and scale of the operations of forex dealers, some tendency toward increased concentration of forex dealership is likely.

The slippage in the 1991 rankings shown by two U.S. banks, Chemical and Chase Manhattan, can be attributed primarily to the downgrading of their credit ratings. This fact highlights the importance of having a high credit rating for a bank that aspires to maintain a high position among the elite institutions of forex dealing. Some observers have suggested that other U.S. banks may be adversely affected by a lowering of their credit ratings and that this fact, in conjunction with a slowing of the pace of financial innovation, is creating opportunities for non-U.S. banks to gain market share.[4]

Forex Brokers   Forex brokers exist because they lower dealers' costs, reduce their risks, and provide anonymity. These services are so valuable that in New York, for example, most forex transactions between local banks and a high percentage of other forex transactions are brokered. For their services, brokers receive commissions, typically 0.01 percent of the transaction amounts in interbank trades. The payment of commissions is generally split between the trading parties.

Because it is standard brokers' practice to keep the identities of the parties they represent confidential until deals are sealed, the use of a broker tends to prevent either party from being influenced by the identity of the other. By relying on brokers, banks can often reduce the cost of gathering information and enlarge their customer base. Individual brokerage firms often specialize in particular currencies, and their knowledge about the currencies is likely to exceed what most banks could acquire without considerable expense. Finally, and very significantly, by relying on brokers, banks can avoid being saddled with positions they regard as undesirable. When banks serve as marketmakers instead of working through brokers, they must either buy or sell particular currencies at the discretion of their customers. This means that they sometimes have to buy when they prefer to sell or vice versa. By using brokers, however, banks can take only those positions that they want to take.

Arbitrageurs

Arbitrageurs make gains by discovering price discrepancies that allow them to buy cheap and sell dear. As traditionally viewed, arbitrage is virtually riskless. At present, however, it is common to broaden the concept of arbitrage to encompass situations in which parties accept some risk in the course of attempting to gain from perceived differences in risk-adjusted rates of return. This survey of forex market participants takes the traditional view of arbitrage.

If arbitrageurs are not considered to be risk takers, they stand in sharp contrast to speculators, who seek to profit from risky transactions. In the forex market, both groups can be distinguished from the traders and investors group by the fact that their actions are fundamentally responses to the market's existence and not causes of its existence. In a word, they are opportunists. They are distinguished from dealers and brokers in that they act on their own initiatives, not in response to the initiatives of others.

---

[4]Simon Brady, "American Banks' Last Stand," *Euromoney,* May 1991, pp. 81–86.

| EXHIBIT | 5.1 | Customers' Favorite Banks as Ranked by Euromoney: 1989–1991

Rank				
1991	1990	1989	Bank	Home Country
1	1	1	Citicorp	United States
2	2	2	Barclays	United Kingdom
3	8	6	JP Morgan	United States
4	4	7	NatWest (National Westminster)	United Kingdom
5	17–18	—	Union Bank of Switzerland	Switzerland
6	7	8	Lloyds	United Kingdom
7	3	4	Chemical	United States
8	10	18	Bank of America	United States
9	9	15	Midland	United Kingdom
10	14–15	—	First Chicago	United States
11	5	5	Royal Bank of Canada	Canada
12	—	—	Hongkong Bank	Hong Kong
13	17–18	16	Goldman Sachs	United States
14	6	3	Chase Manhattan	United States
15	16	—	SE Banken (Skandinaviska Enskilda Banken)	Sweden
16	12	—	Deutsche	Germany
17	—	13	Bankers Trust	United States

At least three distinctly different arbitrage processes are directly linked to exchange rates. **Currency arbitrage** arises from opportunities to buy currencies more cheaply than they can be sold. When forex transactions are allowed to occur freely, the opportunities for currency arbitrage tend to be very brief and accessible only to dealer banks. **Interest arbitrage** arises from disequilibria between two exchange rate variables and two interest rate variables. Interest arbitrage is often conducted by dealer banks, but other parties frequently have access to it. Interest arbitrage leads to a condition known as interest rate parity that constitutes one of the cornerstones of international financial theory and practice. **Commodity arbitrage** arises when the exchange rate between two currencies allows a good or asset to be bought more cheaply in one country than another after allowance for the cost of transferring the good or asset's ownership or possession.

Currency arbitrage is considered later in this chapter. Interest arbitrage is examined in Chapter 6 and elsewhere. Commodity arbitrage receives less emphasis in this book, but the reader should note that it often arises when exchange rates are not allowed to reach their equilibrium levels.

Rank				
1991	1990	1989	Bank	Home Country
18	20–21	—	Société Genéralé	France
19	—	—	Swiss Bank Corporation	Switzerland
20	—	—	Morgan Stanley	United States
—	12–13	—	Crédit Suisse	Switzerland
—	12–13	9	Westpac	Australia
—	14–15	—	Amro (Amsterdam-Rotterdam Bank)	Netherlands
—	19	—	ABN Bank (Algemene Bank Nederland)	Netherlands
—	20–21	14	Dai-Ichi Kangyo	Japan
—	—	10	National Australia	Australia
—	—	11	Bank of Tokyo	Japan
—	—	12	Commonwealth Bank of Australia	Australia
—	—	17	Standard Chartered	United Kingdom
—	—	19	Security Pacific	United States
—	—	20	ANZ (Australia and New Zealand Bank)	Australia

Sources: Julian Lewis, "Room at the Top, But Not for Sitting Tenants," *Euromoney*, May 1989, p. 79; "Citi Shows Its Staying Power," *Euromoney*, May 1990, p. 117; and "All Change in Foreign Exchange," *Euromoney*, May 1991, p. 91.

Speculators

There are two meanings of the term *speculation* in the world of international finance. In the broader sense, it means to accept an open (unhedged) position denominated in foreign currency. To accept either a net asset or a net liability position denominated in foreign currency can be viewed as a speculative act. In the narrower sense, speculation occurs when someone transacts in foreign exchange primarily or entirely because of an anticipated but uncertain gain as a result of an exchange rate change.

Usually references to "forex speculation" intend the narrower meaning, and it is this sense of the term that must be employed in a functional classification of forex market participants. With the exception of arbitrageurs and brokers, however, the normal operations of forex market participants often lead them to accept open positions in foreign currencies, making them speculators in the broader sense of the term. While it may be correct to call most market participants speculators, doing so blurs the meaningful distinction between the participants who are motivated primarily to gain from exchange rate changes and those for whom forex gains or losses are not the primary reason for their participation.

It is often difficult to distinguish even narrowly defined speculation from other activity. Suppose, for example, that a bank buys more French francs than it sells in the course of accommodating its customers. It is logical to argue that the bank's long position in francs is incidental to its status as a forex dealer. If, however, the bank accepts the long position in francs primarily because it anticipates a rise in the franc's exchange value, it is clearly speculating. In practice, it is difficult to distinguish one case from the other.

A similar problem arises when investors buy bonds denominated in foreign currencies. Assume, for example, that a U.S. investment firm purchases yen bonds with 10 years to maturity and that the yen yield on the bonds is lower than the yield on dollar bonds with the same maturity and, except for the exchange rate factor, comparable risk characteristics. Clearly, the firm buys the bonds in the anticipation that over time, the exchange value of the yen will rise. It is speculating. If accused of speculating, however, the firm's representatives would probably argue that the decision to buy the bonds was part of a diversified investment strategy that had (during a carefully selected period) permitted the firm to outperform most of its rivals in terms of providing a high rate of return with reasonable stability of earnings. The fact remains, nevertheless, that the firm stands to lose if the expected appreciation of the yen fails to materialize.

In general, investors in equities are probably less influenced by exchange rate considerations than investors in debt instruments. Nevertheless, since exchange rate changes affect the home currency values of equity investments, often by large amounts, exchange rate considerations affect such investments. Assume, for example, that there is a high probability of a short-term rise in both the dollar and the U.S. stock market. Foreign investors seeking quick capital gains can be expected to jump at the prospect of simultaneous gains from both exchange rate changes and rising stock prices, and foreign investors who are considering longer-term equity investments in the United States may well decide that now is the time. On the other hand, equity investment in export-oriented U.S. firms may be discouraged by the prospect of a rising dollar if the upward trend seems likely to persist, since this implies that U.S. exports will be less competitive in world markets.

International trade is influenced by exchange rate expectations less strongly than international investment, but it is by no means free of speculative elements. When, for example, a Japanese exporter that customarily accepts payment in dollars expects the dollar to decline in the near future, the firm has an incentive to encourage its customers to accelerate payment. Conversely, a Japanese firm that customarily pays for imports in dollars has an incentive to defer payment for imports when the dollar is expected to decline.

Viewed in its broader sense, forex speculation is a zero-sum game, i.e., total gains equal total losses. In the narrow sense of forex speculation, however, a question arises as to whether or not speculators gain at the expense of other market participants. Financial theorists have often argued that, in the absence of government intervention producing net losses for taxpayers, it is unlikely that narrow-sense speculators can persistently gain as a group by more than enough to compensate them for the costs and risks they accept. Since, however, governments frequently do intervene in the forex market, often incurring losses, it is arguable that narrow-sense speculators do make net profits. In any event, narrow-sense speculation is a prominent feature of the forex market's operations, and this implies that many forex market participants believe they are better-informed than other participants.

Central Banks

Finally, some forex market participants attempt to influence exchange rates by their participation. Conceivably, market manipulation could be undertaken by private parties, perhaps acting in collusion. The volume of forex trading is so huge, however, and the number of large-scale participants is so great that individual transactions as large as $100 million may have no discernible influence on exchange rate quotations in the larger market centers.[5] Ordinarily, this type of action is restricted to central banks. Since such central bank action is generally motivated by considerations other than the desire to make a profit, it is preferable to refer to it as "intervention" rather than "manipulation."

Both political and economic considerations move governments to intervene in the forex market. Politically, they intervene in response to domestic pressures. Economically, they intervene because they regard the market determination of exchange rates as a flawed process. In practice, it is difficult to ascertain the relative importance of political and economic factors when intervention occurs because normative economic judgments are influenced by political considerations and also because politically motivated intervention is invariably accompanied by economic rationalizations, which may or may not be plausible.

Government intervention may be designed either to stabilize an exchange rate or to move it to a new level. In either case, if a currency's exchange value is lower than desired, intervention requires the purchase of the currency with foreign currency. If the exchange value of a currency is higher than desired, intervention requires the sale of the currency. Whether intended to strengthen or weaken a currency, intervention may be conducted solely by the government of the country whose currency is the object of intervention (the home country)

---

[5]Conceivably, an exchange rate forecaster with an exceptional track record could exert some influence on exchange rates, but it is rare for a single forecaster to be held in such high esteem. Another possibility is that a dealer, or (more likely) two or more dealers acting in concert, might be able, probably after circulating an appropriate rumor, to start a snowball effect with strategically placed transactions. Such an effort at market manipulation is most likely to succeed if launched when trading volume is low, as when several trading centers are celebrating a holiday or when the leading centers are closed for the night.

or by one or more other governments, with or without the participation of the home country government.

In general, it is easier for a government to lower its currency's exchange value (or keep it from rising) than to raise its exchange value (or keep it from falling). If a government wants to lower the exchange value of its currency, it can easily have its central bank supply the currency to the forex market. If, therefore, a government is determined to lower the exchange value of its currency, it can certainly succeed! Sometimes, however, a country whose currency's exchange value is higher than its government desires has strong political resistance to inflation. Since intervention by its central bank to lower the currency's exchange value would tend to expand the national money supply, intervention may not be feasible, even if there is official agreement that a lower exchange value is desirable.

If a government wants to increase the exchange value of its currency, the success of intervention hinges on its ability to supply foreign exchange to the market and on the degree to which other governments cooperate with it. The government's ability to supply foreign exchange to the market depends, of course, on its holdings of reserve assets and its ability to borrow such assets.

The U.S. dollar is generally chosen as the **intervention currency**, i.e., the currency that is bought or sold to influence exchange rates. There are, however, cases in which one or more other currencies are used. If, for example, a central bank wants to influence the exchange rate between its currency and the dollar and desires to disguise its intervention, it might trade in a third currency and depend on exchange arbitrage to affect the exchange rate between its currency and the dollar. Also, there are cases in which the purpose of intervention is not to affect a currency's exchange rate with the dollar, but with a third currency. As the yen's importance has increased, greater significance has been attached to its exchange rates with various European currencies, with the result that intervention to affect yen exchange rates with such currencies has become more common.

Forex Rates

Fundamental to an understanding of the forex market is familiarity with the different types of exchange rates and the measurement of exchange rate changes. These matters are more complicated than they may appear initially because each exchange rate can be expressed in two ways, each being the reciprocal of the other. When people encounter an exchange rate in the form of an unfamiliar reciprocal, this causes, at best, a small inconvenience and, at worst, a financial loss or a deduction of points on an examination.

Another complication is that, while it is convenient to think of *the* exchange rate between two currencies, at any given time there are usually several different exchange rates between freely traded currencies. Dealers' ask prices differ from their bid prices, and the prices quoted by individual dealers vary according to transaction size and other factors. The quotations of different dealers may vary, at least temporarily, from each other. The exchange rates applied to spot transfers of bank demand deposits differ significantly from those applied to exchanges of bank notes and traveler's checks, and the exchange rates applicable to contracts for future delivery differ from those applicable to spot exchanges, in which delivery normally occurs after 2 business days. Black-market exchange rates materialize when governments impose controls on forex transactions, and such rates may differ greatly from the exchange rates that are officially recognized. Fortunately, because the different exchange rates between two currencies are linked together and tend to rise and fall in concert, the convenience gained by referring to "the" exchange rate does not entail much cost.

The Quoting of Exchange Rates

There are three aspects of dealers' exchange rate quotations which, in the judgment of the author, should be stressed at the outset of our examination of exchange rates. These are the distinction between direct and indirect quotations, the use of the U.S. dollar as the forex market's numeraire, and the nature of exchange rate points. Other aspects of exchange rate quotations will be considered later in this and other chapters.

Direct and Indirect Quotations   The currency whose value is unity in an exchange rate quotation is said to be quoted on the **direct basis,** while the other currency is said to be quoted on the **indirect basis.** For example, if a dealer offers to buy French francs (FF) at the rate of FF 6.0750 per dollar, the dollar is quoted directly and the franc indirectly. If this rate were stated in its reciprocal form, $0.1646 per franc, the franc would be quoted directly and the dollar indirectly. Alternatively, a dealer quoting FF 6.0750 per dollar could be said to be quoting on **European terms,** while a dealer quoting $0.1646 per franc could be said to be quoting on **American terms.** In other words, "European terms" means that the dollar is quoted directly, while "American terms" means that the other currency is quoted directly.

Because of the need for uniformity in interbank quotations, and because dealers outside the United States quote most currencies against the dollar on European terms, the interbank quotations of U.S. dealers are also generally on European terms. There are exceptions to this rule, however. Most notably, U.S. dealers habitually quote the British pound, the Irish punt, and the Ecu directly. They quote the pound and the punt directly because London dealers have long quoted these currencies indirectly against the dollar,[6] and they quote the Ecu directly because that is the way the Ecu is generally quoted.

While most U.S. interbank quotations price foreign currencies indirectly, direct quotations are common in other situations. If, for example, a customer prefers having the dollar quoted directly against other currencies, the dealer will quote in that manner. In addition, at the organized exchanges that trade forex futures and options in the United States, foreign currencies are always quoted against the dollar on the direct basis.

---

[6]London dealers developed this practice when the pound sterling was the world's dominant currency. Their motive for doing so was to save their customers the trouble of calculating exchange rates against the pound sterling, which was, in those days, a nondecimal currency.

The U.S. Dollar as the Dealers' Numeraire   The U.S. dollar has long served as the unofficial numeraire of the forex market. What this means in this particular context is that dealers have generally preferred to quote all currencies other than the dollar against the dollar rather than against each other. For example, a party wishing to effect a wholesale exchange of Canadian dollars for marks has normally had to engage in two forex transactions: a purchase of U.S. dollars with Canadian dollars, and a purchase of marks with U.S. dollars.

The basic explanation for the practice of using the dollar as the numeraire has been twofold: (1) the dollar has been the world's dominant currency, and (2) this practice simplifies life for forex dealers. For example, if a dealer trading 16 currencies were audacious enough to quote each currency against each other currency, a minimum of 120 exchange rate quotations would be required.[7] By quoting each of the 15 other currencies against only the U.S. dollar, however, this number would be reduced to 15. Obviously, it is simpler to offer 15 quotations than 120. Moreover, a dealer bank offering 120 quotations would have to be constantly concerned about the danger of setting up profitable exchange arbitrage opportunities for other dealers.

Despite this rationale for using the dollar as the forex market's numeraire, currency trading without the use of quotations against the dollar has expanded noticeably in the past few years. Such trading is known as cross trading. Its growing popularity is a direct result of the decline in the dollar's preeminence among the world's currencies. Later in the chapter, we shall examine the possible arbitrage implications of cross trading.

Exchange Rate Points   In their dealings with each other, dealers and brokers use a highly refined form of communication that saves valuable time. Interbank quotations are commonly given in *points,* which are the absolute numerical values, ignoring decimals, that are relevant to exchange rate quotations. A single point has an absolute value of one in the last digit of an exchange rate quotation. Because dealers' quotations are often carried to the fourth decimal point, the numerical value of a point is often 0.0001, i.e., one ten-thousandth. This value can, however, be more or less, depending on the currencies involved. If, for example, the exchange rate between the Italian lira (Lit) and the dollar is quoted at Lit 1311.51 per dollar, 1 point equals one one-hundredth of a lira, not one ten-thousandth.

In quoting exchange rates over the telephone, traders tend to include only the numbers that they regard as essential. For example, rather than state the bid and ask prices of the dollar in terms of marks as DM1.6895 per dollar and DM1.6905 per dollar, respectively, a trader might simply quote the bid-ask rates as "895-905" on the assumption that the listener would already know the first two digits of each quotation. The party quoting these rates would also probably indicate in condensed form, saying, for example, "three by three," the quantity of dollars to be traded at these rates (to indicate $3 million to be

---

[7]The applicable formula here can be expressed as $N = n(n - 1)/2$, where N is the number of quotations, and n is the number of currencies. The division by 2 is made on the assumption that an individual exchange rate will be quoted either directly or indirectly, but not both.

either bought or sold). When dealers' spot quotations flash across video screens in the trading rooms of dealer banks and other firms, the bid price (shown first) is usually stated with all the numbers included, but the only numbers appearing for the ask price are normally those that differ from the bid price. Thus, DM1.6895-905 would be the standard form for the mark/dollar quotation given above. The absolute difference between the two prices indicates a 10-point spread.

In dealing with customers who are not totally versed in trader jargon, forex dealers allow more time for conversation and even depart from the practice that is customary in the United States of quoting foreign currencies indirectly. In keeping with the old adage that "time is money," however, a customer who consumes much of a trader's time is likely to pay for the privilege.

Because of exchange rate volatility, when an offer is made, whether directly or through a broker, it must be accepted almost immediately if it is to stand. There is usually no time to call around to other dealers hunting for a better offer. For this reason, forex traders stay closely to their video screens. They also endeavor, as best they can, to ascertain which direction exchange rates are moving at the moment.

Spot and Forward Exchange Rates

Exchange rate quotations vary systematically as a function of the time between the date on which an agreement to exchange currencies is reached and the date, known as the **value** or **delivery date,** on which the exchange actually occurs. **Spot exchange rates** apply to transfers of bank demand deposits occurring within 2 business days after the reaching of an agreement to exchange currencies. **Forward exchange rates** apply to transfers of demand deposits with value dates 3 or more business days in the future. In interbank trading, dealers customarily quote forward rates with value dates that are multiples of 30 days from the value dates for spot transactions. Particularly popular are forward rates for periods of 30, 60, 90, and 180 days. Forward contracts can have any value date that is mutually agreeable to the contracting parties, however, and for a suitable price, a dealer will gladly provide a forward contract with a value date that is not a 30-days multiple. Forward contracts with maturities of less than 30 days are extremely common in interbank trading. At the other end of the time scale, forwards with 1 year maturities are common, and maturities of up to several years may be available. **Futures exchange rates** are very similar to forward rates, but have some differences. For example, futures rates are quoted with fewer maturities than forwards.

While most forex transactions are spot exchanges, forward and futures transactions are commonplace. In addition, forex options became popular during the 1980s. Such an option confers the right to buy or sell a currency at the current spot rate or at a forward or futures rate.

Exhibit 5.2 presents New York interbank (wholesale) selling prices for 52 currencies in exchanges with the U.S. dollar at 3 p.m. Eastern time on Monday, June 10, 1991, and Friday, June 7, 1991, as submitted by Bankers Trust Company to *The Wall Street Journal*. The minimum transaction amount at the

EXCHANGE RATES

Monday, June 10, 1991

The New York foreign exchange selling rates below apply to trading among banks in amounts of $1 million and more, as quoted at 3 p.m. Eastern time by Bankers Trust Co.and other sources. Retail transactions provide fewer units of foreign currency per dollar.

Country	U.S. $ equiv. Mon.	U.S. $ equiv. Fri.	Currency per U.S. $ Mon.	Currency per U.S. $ Fri.
Argentina (Austral) ...	.0001010	.0001008	9900.01	9925.00
Australia (Dollar)	.7530	.7517	1.3280	1.3303
Austria (Schilling)	.08035	.08019	12.44	12.47
Bahrain (Dinar)	2.6522	2.6522	.3771	.3771
Belgium (Franc)				
Commercial rate	.02750	.02743	36.37	36.45
Brazil (Cruzeiro)	.00355	.00357	281.49	280.38
Britain (Pound)	1.6700	1.6700	.5988	.5988
30-Day Forward	1.6627	1.6626	.6014	.6015
90-Day Forward	1.6501	1.6491	.6060	.6064
180-Day Forward	1.6352	1.6332	.6115	.6123
Canada (Dollar)	.8737	.8711	1.1445	1.1480
30-Day Forward	.8718	.8692	1.1470	1.1505
90-Day Forward	.8683	.8655	1.1517	1.1554
180-Day Forward	.8635	.8604	1.1581	1.1623
Chile (Peso)	.002832	.003004	353.09	332.89
China (Renmimbi)	.186916	.188324	5.3500	5.3100
Colombia (Peso)	.001738	.001750	575.25	571.35
Denmark (Krone)	.1472	.1470	6.7916	6.8017
Ecuador (Sucre)				
Floating rate	.000966	.000966	1035.51	1035.00
Finland (Markka)	.23973	.23929	4.1713	4.1790
France (Franc)	.16703	.16667	5.9870	6.0000
30-Day Forward	.16653	.16617	6.0050	6.0178
90-Day Forward	.16561	.16529	6.0382	6.0500
180-Day Forward	.16450	.16419	6.0790	6.0905
Germany (Mark)	.5658	.5645	1.7675	1.7715
30-Day Forward	.5645	.5632	1.7715	1.7756
90-Day Forward	.5618	.5605	1.7800	1.7840
180-Day Forward	.5585	.5571	1.7906	1.7950
Greece (Drachma)	.005185	.005161	192.85	193.75
Hong Kong (Dollar) ...	.12940	.12928	7.7280	7.7350
India (Rupee)	.04762	.04766	21.00	20.98
Indonesia (Rupiah)	.0005165	.0005144	1936.03	1944.00
Ireland (Punt)	1.5140	1.5115	.6605	.6616
Israel (Shekel)	.4268	.4248	2.3430	2.3542
Italy (Lira)	.0007625	.0007622	1311.51	1312.01
Japan (Yen)	.007060	.007125	141.65	140.35
30-Day Forward	.007050	.007115	141.85	140.54
90-Day Forward	.007033	.007099	142.19	140.86
180-Day Forward	.007018	.007083	142.49	141.18
Jordan (Dinar)	1.4684	1.4684	.6810	.6810
Kuwait (Dinar)	z	z	z	z
Lebanon (Pound)	.001091	.001091	917.00	917.00
Malaysia (Ringgit) .	.3599	.3611	2.7785	2.7690
Malta (Lira)	2.9586	3.0628	.3380	.3265
Mexico (Peso)				
Floating rate	.0003317	.0003322	3015.00	3010.00
Netherland (Guilder) .	.5020	.5013	1.9920	1.9950
New Zealand (Dollar)	.5765	.5800	1.7346	1.7241
Norway (Krone)	.1451	.1448	6.8932	6.9053
Pakistan (Rupee)	.0420	.0422	23.82	23.67
Peru (New Sol)	1.2231	1.2381	.82	.81
Philippines (Peso)	.03697	.03697	27.05	27.05
Portugal (Escudo)	.006538	.006585	152.96	151.86
Saudi Arabia (Riyal) ..	.26663	.26663	3.7505	3.7505
Singapore (Dollar)	.5610	.5629	1.7825	1.7765
South Africa (Rand)				
Commercial rate	.3512	.3515	2.8473	2.8448
Financial rate	.3030	.3012	3.3000	3.3200
South Korea (Won) ...	.0013805	.0013806	724.35	724.30
Spain (Peseta)	.009153	.009137	109.25	109.45
Sweden (Krona)	.1575	.1571	6.3489	6.3650
Switzerland (Franc) ..	.6623	.6583	1.5100	1.5190
30-Day Forward	.6612	.6573	1.5124	1.5214
90-Day Forward	.6593	.6553	1.5168	1.5260
180-Day Forward	.6569	.6529	1.5222	1.5317
Taiwan (Dollar)	.036792	.037202	27.18	26.88
Thailand (Baht)	.03880	.03900	25.77	25.64
Turkey (Lira)	.0002418	.0002434	4135.02	4109.00
United Arab (Dirham) .	.2723	.2724	3.6725	3.6715
Uruguay (New Peso)				
Financial	.000518	.000518	1930.00	1930.00
Venezuela (Bolivar)				
Floating rate	.01847	.01836	54.15	54.47
SDR	1.32142	1.32866	.75676	.75264
ECU	1.16193	1.17136	....	....

Special Drawing Rights (SDR) are based on exchange rates for the U.S., German, British, French and Japanese currencies. Source: International Monetary Fund.

European Currency Unit (ECU) is based on a basket of community currencies. Source: European Community Commission.

z-Not quoted.

quoted rates was $1 million. The currencies quoted include the SDR and the Ecu. Most of the exchange rates shown are spot rates, but there are forward rates for six currencies: the British pound, the Canadian dollar, the French franc, the German mark, the Japanese yen, and the Swiss franc.

Note that in every instance in which a forward rate is quoted in Exhibit 5.2, the forward rate is lower in terms of dollars than the corresponding spot rate. It is not always true, however, that forward prices are lower in terms of dollars than spot prices. As is explained in Chapter 6, divergences of forward rates from spot rates are determined primarily by differences in nations' short-term interest rates. The reason that the forward rates of Exhibit 5.2 are below the spot rates is that short-term U.S. interest rates in June 1991 were lower than short-term interest rates in the other six countries. Historically, this was an unusual situation.

Although Exhibit 5.2 presents forward rates for only six currencies, banks regularly quote forward rates for a number of other currencies, almost all of them being currencies of high-income countries. The primary requirements for interbank forward trading in a currency are that the home country's government allow such trading and that the volume of trading be sufficient to provide the necessary market depth—thin trading allows large price fluctuations, with the result that banks either refuse to quote forward rates or insist on such large bid-ask spreads that potential customers are discouraged. The currencies of most LDCs fail to satisfy one or both of these requirements. In some cases, however, LDC governments allow forward transactions at controlled rates.

A comparison of the exchange rates of June 10, 1991 with those of the previous trading day, June 7, 1991, indicates that while many rates changed, some did not. The currencies with the greatest day-to-day changes tend to be those of high-income countries, whose governments typically allow currency trading to occur largely free of exchange controls. Most LDC governments, on the other hand, impose exchange controls that restrict or eliminate day-to-day fluctuations. Periodically, however, the currencies of most LDCs are allowed to depreciate abruptly by relatively large amounts. There has been some tendency for the LDCs whose currencies are included in *The Wall Street Journal's* daily trading summary to be allowed greater daily fluctuations.

For several currencies listed in Exhibit 5.2, the existence of exchange controls can be inferred from such terms as *floating rate, commercial rate,* and *financial rate.* The currencies of eastern Europe, all of Africa except South Africa, and such Middle Eastern nations as Iraq and Iran are absent from Exhibit 5.2 because trading in their currencies is subject to comprehensive exchange controls. We shall briefly examine the use of exchange controls toward the end of this chapter.

Exchange Rate Changes

When an exchange rate changes, the fact that it can be expressed as either of two reciprocals means that a little care has to be exercised in determining the percentage of change for each currency. Suppose, for example, that the market exchange value of a certain currency goes from 20 units per dollar to 30 units per dollar. It is easy to see that the dollar has risen by 50 percent against this currency, but this does not mean that the value of the other currency has fallen by 50 percent! The decline in the other currency's value in this case is, instead, 33⅓ percent. This value can be readily determined by applying the following rule:

(a) If a currency is priced directly, the percentage change in its value is:

$$\frac{\text{Ending rate} - \text{Beginning rate}}{\text{Beginning rate}} \times 100$$

(b) If a currency is priced indirectly, the percentage change in its value is:

$$\frac{\text{Beginning rate} - \text{Ending rate}}{\text{Ending rate}} \times 100$$

Since the other currency in this case is priced indirectly, alternative (b) applies: $100(20 - 30)/30 = -33⅓$ percent. It would be possible to obtain this result by converting the exchange rates to the direct basis and using alternative (a), but doing so would be wasteful of time. Moreover, the formula given in alternative (b) can readily be adapted to other percentage calculations, such as the percentage by which a forward rate differs from the corresponding spot rate when both rates are indirect.[8] In short, if you lack familiarity with alternative (b), you need to develop it. One way to do so is to practice with some of the exchange rates in Exhibit 5.2.

The Bank Note Exchange Rate

Spot and forward exchanges lead to transfers of bank demand deposits. When forex transactions involve the use of paper money, including traveler's checks,

---

[8] A given percentage difference can be expressed as follows:

$$\%\Delta = \frac{a_2 - a_1}{a_1} \times 100,$$

where $\%\Delta$ is the percentage difference, a_1 is the base or original quantity, and a_2 is the other quantity. If the reciprocal of a_1 is b_1, and the reciprocal of a_2 is b_2, the above formula can be rewritten as follows:

$$\%\Delta = \frac{1/b_2 - 1/b_1}{1/b_1} \times 100.$$

Simplification then results in the following alternative formula:

$$\%\Delta = \frac{b_1 - b_2}{b_2} \times 100.$$

Therefore:

$$\frac{a_2 - a_1}{a_1} = \frac{b_1 - b_2}{b_2} \text{ and } \frac{b_2 - b_1}{b_1} = \frac{a_1 - a_2}{a_2}$$

The text's alternative (b) must therefore give the same result as alternative (a).

the applicable exchange rate is known as the **bank note exchange rate.** This rate is ordinarily considerably less favorable for dealers' customers than the spot rate because the bid-ask spread is much wider in bank note transactions than in spot transactions. The wider spread reflects the costs and risks of dealing in foreign bank notes. A dealer firm earns no interest on its inventory of foreign bank notes, transactions at the bank note exchange rate are usually relatively small, the cost of transporting bank notes is high relative to the cost of transferring the ownership of deposits, and the risk of loss due to theft and other causes is higher in the handling of bank notes than in the handling of bank deposits.

While much of the demand for foreign bank notes arises from legitimate causes, including foreign travel, some of that demand is associated with tax evasion and other illegal activity. Frequently, a demand for foreign bank notes arises when domestic residents want to speculate against their national currencies and cannot use bank deposits to do so because of exchange controls. The supply of foreign bank notes comes in part from travelers and in part from forex dealers and other parties who cater to the demand for foreign bank notes. Gaps between supply and demand are eliminated by exchange rate adjustments and, as is explained in Appendix 5.1, arbitrage between the spot and bank note markets.

Cross Rates of Exchange

An exchange rate between two currencies that is derived from the exchange rates of those currencies with a third currency is known as a *cross rate of exchange*. A cross rate can be obtained by multiplying two exchange rates by each other so as to eliminate a third currency that is common to both rates. The most common use of cross rate calculations is to determine the exchange rate between currencies that are quoted against the U.S. dollar, but not against each other.

Assume that a Canadian investment fund with holdings of mark bonds receives a large quantity of marks that it wants to convert into Canadian dollars (C$). Dealers customarily quote the Canadian dollar and the mark against the U.S. dollar rather than against each other. Therefore, when the firm contacts a dealer, it receives quotations for buying U.S. dollars with marks and Canadian dollars with U.S. dollars. Assuming that the mark/U.S. dollar rate quoted is DM1.7150 and that the Canadian dollar/U.S. dollar rate quoted is C$1.1720, the cross rate for converting marks into Canadian dollars is C$0.6834 per mark, as is shown by the following calculation:

$$\frac{\$}{DM1.7150} \times \frac{C\$1.1720}{\$} = C\$0.6834/mark$$

An obvious disadvantage of buying marks in this way is that the investment fund is on the paying end of two bid-ask spreads instead of one. While this firm might possibly be able to negotiate lower than average spreads by packaging both exchanges into a single deal, it could happen that one of these exchange rates is less favorable for the fund than what could be obtained

| E X H I B I T | 5.3 | *Key Currency Cross Rates: June 11, 1991*

Key Currency Cross Rates Late New York Trading June 11, 1991

	Dollar	Pound	SFranc	Guilder	Yen	Lira	D-Mark	FFranc	CdnDlr
Canada	1.1443	1.8955	.75472	.57249	.00810	.00087	.64486	.19019	....
France	6.0165	9.966	3.9681	3.0101	.04259	.00456	3.3905	....	5.2578
Germany	1.7745	2.9395	1.1704	.88778	.01256	.00135	....	.29494	1.5507
Italy	1319.0	2184.9	869.94	659.90	9.338	....	743.31	219.23	1152.7
Japan	141.25	233.98	93.161	70.667	....	.10709	79.690	23.477	123.44
Netherlands	1.9988	3.3110	1.3183	....	.01415	.00152	1.1264	.33222	1.7467
Switzerland	1.5162	2.5116	....	.75856	.01073	.00115	.85444	.25201	.3250
U.K.	.60368	....	.39815	.30202	.00427	.00046	.34020	.10034	.52756
U.S.	....	1.6565	.65954	.50030	.00708	.00076	.56354	.16621	.87360

Source: Telerate

Source: *The Wall Street Journal,* June 12, 1991, p. C12.

from another dealer. Moreover, for both the dealer and the customer, there are small accounting and other costs associated with working through the U.S. dollar in order to exchange Canadian dollars for marks. Given the forex market's competitiveness, therefore, it stands to reason that if the volume of Canadian dollar-mark exchanges becomes large enough, some dealers will try to increase their volume by offering to exchange these currencies directly against each other.

The volume of currency exchanges that bypass the U.S. dollar has, in fact, substantially increased since around 1986. One prominent brokerage firm has stated that such trading accounted for 9 percent of total forex trading in 1988, as compared to 3 percent in 1986.[9] Further evidence of the growth of this so-called "cross trading" is the fact that futures trading has recently moved into it. The use of the term cross trading to refer to such exchanges is misleading since the U.S. dollar is not used in them.

The most popular cross trades have been between the mark and the yen, but others have developed rapidly. Particularly popular are cross trades involving either the yen or the mark and another prominent currency. If the trend toward greater cross trading continues, as seems probable, a point will be reached where the use of the term cross trading to refer to exchanges in which only two currencies are directly involved will, no doubt, be discontinued. Even so, however, the concept of a cross rate as defined earlier will be important because of the ever-present possibility of exchange arbitrage.

Exhibit 5.3 shows how *The Wall Street Journal* reports cross rates among eight leading currencies. Note that there is nothing to indicate there that these

---

[9]Butler, Harlow, and Ueda Ltd. "Background to the Cross Currencies Market" (Sponsored statement), *Euromoney*, May 1990, p. 129.

rates are cross rates as defined earlier. They are called cross rates because they are not confined to rates against the U.S. dollar. Note, too, that in this table, each exchange rate also appears in its reciprocal form.

Some Spot Market Fundamentals

The ability of the forex market to handle transactions worth billions of dollars daily rests on its low transaction costs and its highly efficient communications system, which allows currency trades to be quickly arranged and settled. In this part of the chapter, we shall examine the institutional arrangements that allow the forex market to operate so efficiently.

Bid–Ask Spreads in Spot Exchanges

The volume of transactions in the forex market is huge because, in part, the prevailing bid–ask spreads in exchanges between leading currencies are ordinarily quite small. The low spreads allow market participants to implement sophisticated risk-management strategies that require numerous forex transactions. Low spreads are also a boon for speculators, and they have an important impact on trade and investment by making firms more willing to make or receive payments denominated in foreign currencies.

The width of bid–ask spreads in forex transactions depends fundamentally on transaction costs and risks. Implicit in this statement is the assumption that market conditions are so competitive that gains cannot be realized through the time-dishonored practice of restricting supply and raising price. While this assumption is valid when applied to the great majority of forex trading between freely convertible currencies, there are many exchange control countries in which governments set bid and ask prices for foreign exchange at levels that assure some monopoly profits for authorized dealers (who are frequently government-owned banks) in their own countries. In such cases, governments commonly restrict not only forex transactions, but also transfers of deposits in domestic currencies between residents and foreigners.

In trading between freely convertible currencies, the size and frequency of transactions are major factors affecting the costs and risks that underlie the bid–ask spreads. Transaction size obviously has a great effect on transaction cost per unit of currency traded, while the frequency of exchanges (the turnover rate) affects both transaction costs and risks. A high turnover rate obviously reduces risks since there is less time for something unforeseen to occur. Moreover, a high turnover rate spreads the fixed costs of currency dealing over a larger volume of transactions and permits a given volume of business to be effected with a smaller inventory of foreign currencies, lowering the opportunity cost of committing funds to forex dealing.

Exhibit 5.4 presents interbank spot quotations including bid-ask spreads. These quotations are taken from the June 8/June 9, 1991 issue of the *Financial Times*. They are for wholesale trading toward the close of trading on Friday, June 7, 1991. Two sets of quotations are shown. The first lists exchange rates between the U.S. dollar and 17 currencies, while the second lists exchange rates

| E X H I B I T | 5.4 | *Closing Interbank Spot Quotations in London: June 7, 1991*

Country or Currency	Currency Units per Dollar[a]	Currency Units per Pound
United States and United Kingdom	1.6710-1.6720	1.6710-1.6720
Ireland	1.5120-1.5130	1.1035-1.1045
Canada	1.1465-1.1475	1.9160-1.9170
Netherlands	1.9935-1.9945	3.3275-3.3375
Belgium	36.30-36.40	60.70-60.80
Denmark	6.7925-6.7975	11.3535-11.3625
Germany	1.7710-1.7720	2.9575-2.9625
Portugal	153.65-153.75	256.50-257.50
Spain	109.30-109.40	182.45-182.75
Italy	1311.75-1312.75	2192.50-2193.50
Norway	6.8950-6.9000	11.5250-11.5350
France	5.9950-6.0000	10.0200-10.0300
Sweden	6.3550-6.3600	10.6225-10.6325
Japan	140.25-140.35	234.00-235.00
Austria	12.4300-12.4400	20.82-20.85
Switzerland	1.5175-1.5185	2.5325-2.5425
Ecu	1.1630-1.1640	1.4360-1.4370

[a]The Ecu and the currencies of the United Kingdom and Ireland are in dollars per currency unit.

Source: *Financial Times,* June 8–9, 1991, p. 11.

for the same currencies with the pound sterling.[10] In both columns, the bid prices (for dollars or pounds) are listed first and the ask prices second.

Since the exchange rate applicable to a particular transaction depends on the size of the transaction and other factors peculiar to it, the spreads shown in Exhibit 5.4 should be regarded as approximations. Subject to this

---

[10]Perhaps the reader has wondered why the British pound is frequently called the "pound sterling." This practice, which serves to distinguish the British monetary unit from other monetary units called "pounds," stems from the Middle Ages, when a monetary pound was equivalent to a physical pound of silver of a degree of fineness known as "sterling." Incidentally, from the fact that a pound of sterling silver has a monetary value today that far exceeds the monetary value of a British pound, one can deduce something about the extent of inflation in the United Kingdom since the Middle Ages. Even so, Britain has had less inflation than most other European nations.

limitation, it is clear that the bid-ask spreads in interbank transactions are typically small relative to the exchange rates on which they are based. In a number of instances in Exhibit 5.4, the indicated spreads are only 10 points, which means they are a very small percentage of the corresponding exchange rates.

In measuring the width of bid-ask spreads, it is standard practice to divide the amount of the spread by the **middle exchange rate,** which is the average of the bid and ask prices. For example, in the case of the mark/dollar quotation in Exhibit 5.4, the width of the spread is 0.06 percent, i.e., 0.0010/1.7715. With this spread, a dealer who bought and sold $4 million worth of marks at the prices of Exhibit 5.4 would have realized a gross gain of DM 4,000, against which would have been charged the transaction costs, including the broker's commission, if any.

While a spread of 0.06 percent may seem very small, spreads may be as narrow as 0.02 percent in very large transactions when exchange rates are relatively calm. On the other hand, when exchange rates are volatile, or when the currencies involved are not heavily traded, spreads may be considerably wider than those of Exhibit 5.4. The latter point can be readily verified by checking any issue of the *Financial Times,* which prints quotations for a number of less traded currencies in a table headed "other currencies" on the same page as the currencies included in Exhibit 5.4. On June 7, 1991, for example, the spot quotation between the Mexican peso and the U.S. dollar shown in the other currencies table was Ps 3011.00–3014.00 per dollar, which indicates a spread of 0.10 percent.

The narrow spreads with which dealers must be satisfied when trading the leading currencies may seem to imply that, in the absence of gains from favorable exchange rate movements, the profits derived from spot dealing are normally small. Narrow spreads can be very profitable, however, if turnover rates are high and losses from unfavorable exchange rate movements are few. If, for example, a dealer were to average a daily net gain of only 0.10 percent of the capital invested in spot trading for a period of 1 year, this would provide an annual rate of return on that capital of approximately 25 percent.

While narrow spreads may suffice to provide attractive profits, some trading losses are inevitable. Accepting an open position in a currency, particularly overnight, is always risky, but to avoid such positions would unduly restrict banks' operations and add substantial hedging costs. To reduce the risk of loss, dealers limit the positions their traders may take in different currencies and adjust their quotations and spreads to prevent these limits from being exceeded more than temporarily. By widening their spreads when exchange rates are unusually volatile, they reduce the probability of losses, although at the cost of a possible loss of trading volume. Ever-alert to exchange rate trends, traders attempt to position themselves favorably with their trading limits, comforting themselves in the knowledge that if they forecast exchange rates a little more accurately than their competitors, that should suffice to guarantee themselves substantial performance bonuses.

Settlement Dates and Procedures

In spot interbank transactions, the settlement or value date is customarily 2 business days after the transaction date, but in the United States, exchanges of Canadian dollars and Mexican pesos against U.S. dollars are cutomarily settled after 1 business day. Same-day settlement can be arranged, for a price. Value dates vary more in transactions between dealers and nondealer customers than in wholesale trades.

The lags between transaction dates and value dates are designed to allow sufficient time for the necessary communications and clearing procedures that will permit each party to a transaction to receive its funds on the same day the other party receives funds from it. The 1-day settlement in exchanges between the U.S. dollar and either the Canadian dollar or the Mexican peso stems from the use of U.S. banks to effect the exchanges and the similarity of time zones among the three countries.

The huge volume of forex transactions and the need for fast and cost-efficient clearing and settlement have led to the development of computerized systems for international transfers of funds. Although these systems are expensive in an absolute sense, their cost per dollar traded is very low in interbank transactions. Among these computerized systems, the best-known in the United States are the Clearing House Interbank Payments System (CHIPS) and the Society for Worldwide Interbank Financial Telecommunications (SWIFT).

CHIPS and Other Clearing Systems   Operated by the New York Clearing House Association in cooperation with the Fed, CHIPS processes interbank transfers of dollars in international transactions, including not only forex transactions, but also Eurocurrency and other transactions affecting the interbank ownership of dollar accounts. Its approximately 140 participants include New York banks and other U.S. banks, but most of them are foreign banks with U.S. branches or subsidiaries. CHIPS processes the vast majority of international transfers of dollar deposits. As of 1989, it was handling an average of more than $840 billion of such transfers per day.[11]

Most CHIPS participants are nonsettling participants, but about 20 of the U.S. participants are settling participants. Each nonsettling participant clears its transactions through a particular settling participant during the business day, and by 6 p.m., nonsettling participants receive either credits or debits to their clearing accounts, depending on whether they have, respectively, positive or negative clearing balances. The settling participants then settle accounts with each other through the New York Clearing House, acting as the agent of the Federal Reserve Bank of New York. All participants must maintain adequate collateral to guarantee settlement. The transfers and the ensuing

---

[11]Eugene Sarver, *The Eurocurrency Market Handbook,* 2d ed. (New York: New York Institute of Finance, 1990), p. 337.

settlements are processed through computers which have been instructed to conform to the norms for deposit transfers, such as transfer after 2 business days for most spot transactions.

As far as U.S. banks outside New York City are concerned, interbank transfers of dollars in forex transactions are processed through the Fed's regular clearing system or through clearing arrangements developed independently by commercial banks. The efficiency of these systems allows them to maintain the 2- (or 1-) business day norm for settling spot exchanges.

Leading financial centers in other countries also have automated clearing systems that maintain the 2-business day norm. Thus, on the same business day on which the ownership of dollar deposits is transferred in the United States, a corresponding change occurs in the ownership of deposits denominated in the currency against which the dollars are exchanged.

SWIFT and Other Message Transfer Systems   National clearing systems (and the Ecu clearing system maintained by the BIS) provide an efficient mechanism for bank transfers of demand deposits linked to forex transactions. However, 2-day settlement for spot exchanges requires not only an efficient clearing mechanism, but also a fast and cost-effective system for the international transmission of instructions regarding deposit transfers. There are a number of such message transfer systems, of which SWIFT is the largest and best-known.

SWIFT is a private nonprofit corporation headquartered near Brussels that is owned and operated by its more than 2,000 members, most of whom are banks. It maintains message switching centers in the Netherlands and Virginia which are linked to autonomous regional processing centers throughout the globe. With the installation, in 1990, of a modular network system known as SWIFT II, it has a virtually unlimited capacity in terms of the number of messages transmitted. The messages transmitted pertain not only to forex transactions, but also to payment confirmations, transactions in securities, the documentation of international trade, and various other matters of chiefly financial interest. The cost of sending a standard message through SWIFT averages approximately $0.50.[12]

Although SWIFT is the most widely used international message transfer system, it is by no means the only one. A number of leading banks have developed their own electronic message systems for distributing information among clients and affiliates. Of particular importance in forex trading is the Money 2000 Service developed by Reuters, which furnishes current information on exchange rates and allows traders to negotiate with each other. It is Reuters which is providing the hardware and software to be used for the GLOBEX trading system being developed by the Chicago Mercantile Exchange. This system will allow the 24-hour trading of currency futures and options on a worldwide basis.

---

[12]*Ibid*, p. 341. Note, however, that this a marginal cost. Substantial fees are charged to join SWIFT and maintain a membership.

Currency Arbitrage

Currency arbitrage occurs when a price discrepancy exists in the forex market that permits a gain to be made by a party working against the bid–ask spread. When currencies are freely traded, opportunities for currency arbitrage tend to be of very brief duration. Also, because such opportunities are most likely to occur when the bid–ask spread is narrow, they are almost always confined to interbank transactions. When currency trading is restricted, however, currency arbitrage is sometimes carried out by nondealers.

Two-Point Currency Arbitrage

In the simplest and most common currency arbitrage technique, two-point or locational arbitrage, there are two currencies, a price discrepancy great enough to provide a gain, and arbitrageurs who can respond to the discrepancy. The following illustrative example assumes that the price discrepancy exists in different countries. It is possible, however, for two-point arbitrage to occur in a single country.

Assume that the following interbank spot exchange rates are being quoted by a New York dealer and a London dealer:

	Bid ($/£)	Ask ($/£)
New York	1.6285	1.6295
London	1.6305	1.6315

A glance at these figures indicates that the pound is relatively cheap in New York and that the price discrepancy is great enough that the New York ask price for the pound is below the London bid price. This means, assuming that the price difference is great enough to cover an arbitrageur's transaction costs, that pounds should be bought in New York and sold in London. Buying them at $1.6295 and selling them at $1.6305 gives a gain of $0.0010 (10 points) on each pound bought and sold. On a turnover of $3 million this indicates a gross profit of $3,000. This may seem small, but obtaining it would require only a few minutes' work with little risk or cost.[13] Alternatively, it could be reasoned that since the pound is relatively cheap in New York, the dollar is relatively cheap in London. The indicated transactions are, therefore, to buy dollars in London and sell them in New York. The transactions are thus the same as before, and while their sequence could be reversed, it would not have to be.

If exchange arbitrage were riskless and involved no other cost than the bid–ask spread, then, theoretically, the New York ask price for pounds would

---

[13]If the trader's salary and the cost of transmitting messages are considered to be fixed, then the marginal cost of the two transactions would approach zero. On the other hand, since conducting arbitrage would reduce the time allocated to other activities, there would be a small opportunity cost. In any event, the cost of exchange arbitrage is substantially less than the cost of normal currency trading since the time involved is short and the amount of information to be processed is small. The risk is also small, but a small risk exists because of the time elapsing between transactions.

be brought into equality with the London bid price, but the London bid price could still exceed the New York bid price by the bid–ask spread. This difference would tend to be eliminated, however, by competition between the two centers. Buyers of pounds (sellers of dollars) would tend to look to New York, and sellers of pounds (buyers of dollars) would tend to look to London. The resulting pressure on dealers' positions would then tend to squeeze the price discrepancy between the two centers. A very small difference in quotations might still exist because of transaction costs.

Triangular Currency Arbitrage

Opportunities for currency arbitrage can arise if two currencies are quoted against each other at a rate that differs from their cross rate. Because three currencies are involved in such cases, the process of profiting from the opportunities provided is known as **three-point** or **triangular arbitrage.** This type of arbitrage was formerly common, but for many years it receded in importance because dealers customarily quoted currencies against the dollar rather than against each other. As was pointed out earlier, however, the quoting of so-called "cross rates" in which the dollar is absent has recently gained in importance. For this reason, triangular arbitrage has also gained in importance.

How triangular arbitrage works is illustrated by the following example, in which the currencies are the dollar, the mark, and the yen. Assume that in New York, the dollar is trading against the mark at DM 1.6895-905 and against the yen at ¥145.40-50. Also assume that a London dealer is offering to trade yen against marks at ¥ 85.75-84 per mark. A London trader, seeing an opportunity for triangular arbitrage, calculates the mark/dollar cross rate that gives the dollar cost of buying marks by buying yen first by making the following calculation:

$$\frac{¥145.40}{\$} \times \frac{DM}{¥85.84} = DM1.6938/dollar.$$

This calculation indicates that if marks are purchased with dollars obtained by first buying yen, the quantity of marks obtained is DM1.6938/dollar. This is far better than the rate of DM1.6895/dollar if marks are purchased directly with dollars. The difference between the two rates, 43 points, is somewhat greater than one would expect to find in practice and would certainly indicate that triangular arbitrage would be profitable. Ignoring the arbitrageur's transaction costs, and keeping in mind that the arbitrageur must always work against the bid–ask spread, the gain per dollar of funds committed can be calculated as follows:

$$\$1 \times \frac{¥145.40}{\$} \times \frac{DM}{¥85.84} \times \frac{\$}{DM1.6905} = \$1.001981.$$

This result indicates that an arbitrageur operating with, for example, $3 million would gain $5,943, ignoring transaction costs, assuming that he or she would be able to use all available funds in each of the three transactions.

Since the transaction costs would be much smaller than this gain, certainly no more than a few hundred dollars, arbitrage would definitely be profitable. The arbitrageur would probably begin the process by exchanging yen for marks before the yen/mark quotation could be adjusted. On the negative side is the fact that interbank transactions normally trade in even millions of currency units. For this reason, engaging in triangular arbitrage would have some slight net effect on the arbitrageur's currency positions. The process of determining the net gain is thus not quite as simple as the above calculation implies.

While the exchange rate difference of 43 points in this example may be larger than what one would normally hope to find, the yen/mark quotation of this example, ¥ 85.75–84/mark, is only slightly different from a quotation that would prevent arbitrage. Given the quotations of DM1.6895–905/dollar and ¥ 145.40–50/dollar, the yen/mark middle exchange rate that would exactly equal the yen/mark cross rate calculated from the middle exchange rates of these two quotations is ¥ 86.065/mark. This rate differs from the middle exchange rate of the quotation ¥ 85.75–84/mark by only 0.3 percent. The lesson is that a dealer who chooses to quote the yen against the mark, as some dealers are now doing, must be very careful about those quotations.

Suppose the trader in this example had initially chosen to calculate the yen/dollar cross rate resulting from buying yen by first buying marks:

$$\frac{DM1.6895}{\$} \times \frac{¥85.75}{DM} = ¥144.87/dollar$$

This cross rate indicates that if yen are acquired by first buying marks, fewer yen per dollar are obtained than if yen are purchased directly with dollars at the exchange rate of ¥145.40. Clearly, there is no arbitrage gain by buying marks first, but the difference between the cross rate and the rate of ¥145.40 is large enough (53 points) to suggest the possibility of arbitrage by first buying *yen*. The calculation of the yen/dollar cross rate thus leads to the same conclusion as the calculation of the mark/dollar cross rate—a gain in dollars can be made by using dollars to buy yen and yen to buy marks.

Opportunities for triangular arbitrage sometimes arise involving currencies that are subject to rigid exchange controls. When a government sets the rates at which its currency can be exchanged against other currencies, chances for triangular arbitrage tend to arise unless these rates are constantly adjusted to maintain cross rates that are consistent with the rates that the government sets. Assume, for example, that the government of an exchange control country allows its currency to be exchanged against dollars and yen at fixed rates and that the dollar falls substantially against the yen. If the controlled rates against these currencies are not adjusted, a party with access to currency transactions at the controlled rates can gain by buying yen at the controlled rate, selling the yen for dollars in some other country, and selling the dollars at the controlled rate. The government of the country would, no doubt, attempt to prevent this from happening, but experience has demonstrated that it is difficult to make exchange controls fully effective.

| E X H I B I T | 5.5 | *Restrictions Associated with Exchange Controls*

1. Requiring permits to buy foreign exchange from importers wanting to pay in foreign currency
2. Allowing some imports to occur only through barter arrangements or if payment is made in domestic currency
3. Requiring importers or other purchasers of foreign exchange to make advance deposits in domestic currency on which little or no interest is paid
4. Prohibiting or restricting domestic exchanges of national paper money goods, or services for foreign paper money
5. Using different exchange rates for different categories of imports and capital outflows
6. Using different exchange rates for different categories of exports and capital inflows
7. Requiring the surrender to the government or government-controlled banks of all or portions of forex receipts from exports and/or foreign investments at exchange rates set by the government
8. Limiting the quantity of domestic currency that can be taken or shipped out of the country by domestic residents
9. Taxing purchases of foreign exchange
10. Restricting residents' purchases of foreign exchange for investment purposes
11. Restricting transfers of domestic bank deposits between domestic and foreign residents and between domestic and foreign banks
12. Restricting borrowings by foreigners from domestic banks
13. Restricting the amounts borrowed abroad by domestic firms and government agencies and enterprises and the interest payments on such borrowings
14. Restricting foreign currency remittances by subsidiaries of foreign corporations for dividend payments and other purposes
15. Restricting the domestic sale of securities issued by foreign firms and governments

Exchange Controls

Exchange controls range from mild restrictions on one or more types of transactions to comprehensive efforts to control the supply of foreign exchange and its allocation among users. Exhibit 5.5 lists some of the types of restrictions on forex transactions that qualify as exchange controls.

Comprehensive exchange control systems generally arise when governments try to maintain exchange values for their currencies that are higher than what would otherwise prevail. In such cases, the controlled currency is said to be *overvalued*. When a currency is overvalued at the controlled exchange rate (or rates), the quantity of foreign exchange demanded exceeds the quantity supplied, which puts pressure on the national government to restrain or reduce demand. Furthermore, since the holders of foreign exchange will be able to gain if they can sell it at a price that exceeds the controlled price, measures must be taken either to remove the temptation (through penalties) or to reduce the opportunity to respond to it. Accordingly, the governments of exchange control countries often attempt to control the supply of foreign exchange and to allocate that supply according to criteria that they regard as appropriate.

A single-rate exchange control system imposes a fixed exchange rate between the national currency and any foreign currency against which it can legally be exchanged. If the system is comprehensive, recipients of foreign exchange are required to sell it to the government (or designated banks) at a price which, except for the bid–ask spread, is the same as that at which foreign exchange is sold to authorized users. A **multiple-rate exchange control system** sets more than one price at which foreign exchange can legally be bought and sold. The price in a particular instance depends on whether the government wants to encourage or discourage the activity involved. Thus, favored imports are allowed to purchase foreign exchange at low prices, while those parties who want foreign exchange for other purposes either pay dearly or are excluded altogether from legal access to it.

The Economic Effects of Exchange Controls

Even with vigorous enforcement of comprehensive exchange controls, it is difficult to prevent some transactions from occurring at unauthorized exchange rates. Would-be buyers of foreign exchange who are not favored by the controls may enter into the illegal or black market, in which the price paid for foreign exchange is higher than the price (or prices) set by the government. Illegal purchases of foreign currency can sometimes be made by purchasing bank notes from foreign visitors, but most illegal acquisitions are accomplished by other means. Local currency can be mailed abroad. The ownership of bank deposits denominated in local currency can be transferred to foreigners or domestic residents who have access to foreign bank accounts. Exporters can attempt to underinvoice goods and deposit the difference between the invoice price and the actual price in foreign banks. Importers can attempt to overinvoice purchases with the same end in mind.

Such technically illegal transactions are sometimes arranged by making donations to the favorite charities of government officials, for whom exchange controls are sometimes important sources of supplementary income. To the extent that exchange controls are evaded, the black market is invigorated and the controls are undermined. Foreigners are often willing to participate in this market, especially when (as is often the case) their participation does not violate their own nations' laws.

Currency arbitrage can occur despite the existence of exchange controls if foreign exchange can be purchased at an official price and sold at the black market price. Suppose, for example, that a firm in an exchange control country is allowed to buy dollars at an official rate of 20 local currency (LC) units per dollar for authorized imports and that it succeeds in overinvoicing a purchase and placing the extra dollars in a foreign bank account. If the firm is able to sell the dollars to a domestic resident at, say LC30/dollar, it effectively gains a gross arbitrage profit of 50 percent.

Economists tend to be extremely critical of comprehensive exchange control systems. Their opposition is based in large part on the distorting effects of exchange controls on international trade and the allocation of resources, but it also reflects the beliefs that exchange controls tend to fail in the long run and exert a corrupting influence on those who administer them and those who are subject to them. Nevertheless, when a country faces the situation known as

capital flight, in which its residents seek to transfer their wealth to foreign assets on a large scale, exchange controls may be essential to restrain capital outflows. On the other hand, it is difficult to find any convincing economic rationale for using comprehensive exchange controls on international trade.

Floating Rate Exchange Controls: The Case of South Africa

Since 1973, exchange controls have tended to be less rigid than they were before that time. In a number of countries, governments have adopted policies of frequently adjusting pegged exchange rates to limit the extent to which their currencies are overvalued, or even to eliminate the overvaluation altogether. In some cases, governments have adopted systems with no officially fixed exchange rate with the dollar, but two floating rates based on different categories of transactions. South Africa provides an outstanding example of this type of exchange rate system.

The South African exchange rate system developed during the middle of the 1980s in response to the country's growing political problems and a threatened liquidation of foreign holdings of South African assets, a process known as **divestment.** Facing wholesale capital flight, the South African government divided forex transactions into two categories: commercial and financial. The transactions in each category were to occur at a floating rate applicable only to transactions in that category. In short order, the exchange value of the South African rand became a good deal lower in financial transactions than in commercial transactions. The more extensively the holders of South African assets liquidated them in order to acquire other assets, the wider the gap between the commercial and financial rands became. As the financial rand cheapened, the purchase of South African assets became more appealing for potential foreign investors who were willing to resist the political pressure, if any, to avoid investing in a country where racial discrimination against the majority of its residents was official policy.

In general, the forex transactions associated with international trade are less variable in volume than those associated with capital flows. This means that when a country has separate commercial and financial exchange rates, the commercial rate tends to be more stable than the financial rate. International trade is thus insulated from exchange rate fluctuations based on variations in capital flows. Moreover, when, as in the case of South Africa, foreign exchange costs substantially more at the financial rate than at the commercial rate, imports are not only more stable in price, but also cheaper than they would be with a single exchange rate.

The gap between the financial and commercial exchange rates of the South African rand (R) provides a rough indicator of the world's assessment of political and economic conditions in South Africa. Consider, for example, that on January 18, 1990, the financial and commercial rands stood, respectively, at R 3.4211 and R 2.5589 per dollar.[14] Exhibit 5.2 indicates that on June 10,

---

[14]*The Wall Street Journal,* January 19, 1990, p. C11.

1991, these rates were R 3.3000 for the financial rand and R 2.8473 for the commercial rand. The gap between the two rates thus diminished from R 0.8622 to R 0.4527. The reduction in the gap suggests a consensus on the part of the financial community that the South African investment climate had improved in the interim.

Belgium long used a similar system, though one with a much smaller gap between the financial and commercial rates, in order to minimize fluctuations in capital flows and provide greater exchange rate stability for trade flows. The Belgian government abandoned this system in 1990, however, evidently because it tended to reduce the magnitude of capital flows as well as their instability.

Numerous countries use mild exchange controls to reduce forex speculation and prevent undesired transactions. Even countries whose currencies are considered to be freely convertible regulate or prohibit some forex transactions because they are politically undesirable or likely to be linked to criminal activity. Overall, forex controls are extensive and important enough that the IMF publishes an *Annual Report on Exchange Arrangements and Exchange Restrictions,* a thick volume which provides great detail (and little analysis) about exchange controls on a country-by-country basis.

Summary

Although the basic reason for the forex market's existence is to accommodate the need of participants in international trade and investment to convert currencies, most of the market's transactions are between banks. Money-center banks serve as marketmakers and use forex transactions to manage the risks that arise from their commitments as dealers. Arbitrage, speculation, and central bank intervention are among the factors that have a major influence on the forex market.

Most forex transactions are spot exchanges, for which the value or delivery dates are normally 2 business days after the agreements to exchange. The value dates for forward transactions are 3 or more business days after the agreements to exchange. Competition and the possibility of currency arbitrage tend to keep the currency quotations of dealers in line with each other, but small differences in the rates quoted by dealers still occur.

In interbank trading, both U.S. and other dealers generally quote the U.S. dollar against other currencies on the direct basis. While dealers generally prefer to quote a currency against the U.S. dollar rather than against another currency, there is a growing practice, known as cross trading, of quoting currencies against each other without quoting them against the dollar. This has rekindled interest in the process of triangular currency arbitrage.

Restrictions imposed by governments on forex transactions are called exchange controls. Most countries have extensive exchange controls, but the currencies of high-income countries are generally freely tradable. While the use of exchange controls can be criticized in terms of economic efficiency, such controls are often the most feasible way to deter undesired capital outflows.

References

Andrews, Michael D. "Recent Trends in the U.S. Foreign Exchange Market." *Federal Reserve Bank of New York Quarterly Review,* Summer 1984, pp. 38–47.

Chrystal, K. Alec. "A Guide to Foreign Exchange Markets." *Federal Reserve Bank of St. Louis Review.* March 1984, pp. 5–18.

Coninx, R. *Foreign Exchange Dealer's Handbook.* Homewood, Ill.: Dow Jones–Irwin, 1986.

Federal Reserve Bank of New York. "Summary of Results of U.S. Foreign Exchange Market Survey Conducted in April 1989." Unpublished report, 1989.

Financial Times. Daily newspaper.

"Foreign Exchange Review." *Euromoney,* May 1991, pp. 79–102.

Gregory, Ian, and Philip Moore. "Foreign Exchange Dealing." *Corporate Finance,* October 1986, pp. 33–46.

International Monetary Fund. *Annual Report of Exchange Arrangements and Exchange Restrictions.* New York: IMF, annual.

Lee, Peter. "The Corporate Dealer Is the Star." *Euromoney,* May 1988, pp. 66–74.

Lewis, Julian. "Room at the Top, But Not for Sitting Tenants." *Euromoney,* May 1989.

Riehl, Heinz, and Rita M. Rodriguez. *Foreign Exchange and Money Markets.* New York: McGraw-Hill, 1983.

Sarver, Eugene. *The Eurocurrency Market Handbook.* 2d ed. New York: New York Institute of Finance, 1990.

Tygier, Claude. *Basic Handbook of Foreign Exchange.* London: Euromoney Publications, 1983.

"The Ups and Downs of Forex." *Euromoney,* May 1990, pp. 115–168.

The Wall Street Journal. Daily newspaper.

Winder, Robert. "Be Big—and Bright." *Euromoney,* May 1986, pp. 184–202.

Questions

1. Explain the role of forex brokers.
2. Explain the two senses in which the word *speculation* applies to the forex market.
3. As a general proposition, why is it easier for central banks to use market intervention to prevent the exchange values of their currencies from rising than to prevent them from falling? Why is it that, nevertheless, central banks often have difficulty in preventing the exchange values of their currencies from rising?
4. What factors govern the width of dealers' spreads in spot forex trading?
5. Forex dealers commonly quote forex rates in points. What are points?
6. Explain precisely what is the difference between a spot exchange and a forward exchange in the forex market.
7. What is CHIPS, and how does it differ from SWIFT?
8. With regard to currency arbitrage:
   a. Why are opportunities for it largely confined to forex dealers, and when would this not be the case?
   b. Is it correct to say that currency arbitrage assures the uniformity of exchange rates when currencies are freely traded? Explain.
   c. What is wrong with saying that currency arbitrage is riskless?

9. Explain how South Africa's dual floating rate exchange control system works.

10. Assume that there is a certain country named Vegetaria whose monetary unit is the gourd (Gd), and that the Vegetarian government uses comprehensive exchange controls. At present, the government requires the gourd to be exchanged against the dollar and the yen at the rates of Gd 420/$ and Gd 3.20/¥. Also assume that the market exchange rate between the yen and the dollar is ¥ 140/$. What are the implications of this situation for Vegetaria's forex transactions?

Problems

1. Using the data in Exhibit 5.3, determine by what percentage each of the following currencies' spot rates rose or fell in terms of the U.S. dollar from June 7, 1991, to June 10, 1991: the Japanese yen (¥), the Canadian dollar (C$), and the Irish punt (Ir £). Calculate these percentages using exchange rates the way they are normally quoted in interbank trading. Give the answers in percentages that are equivalent to 4 decimal points.

2. Early in June 1986, the Mexican peso went from around Ps600/dollar to around Ps730/dollar. By what percentage did the peso depreciate?

3. Assume that a New York forex dealer finds a New York bank is quoting the Italian lira (Lit) against the U.S. dollar at Lit1,259.00–1,259.50 and that a bank in London is quoting Lit1,260.00–1,260.50. Also assume that the trader has $3 million available for arbitrage and estimates the transaction cost of two-point arbitrage at 0.015 percent of $3 million. Is there a profitable opportunity for arbitrage here? Explain.

4. Assume that a forex trader working for a U.S. bank's Singapore branch finds that banks in Sydney are offering to trade Australian dollars for U.S. dollars at A$1.2590–600/dollar and Australian dollars for yen at ¥ 115.40–55/Australian dollar. Also assume that the trader can exchange between the U.S. dollar and yen in Singapore at ¥ 146.30–42/dollar.

   a. Determine the Australian dollar/U.S. dollar and ¥/U.S. dollar cross rates at which the trader can buy Australian dollars and yen, respectively, with U.S. dollars.

   b. Assuming that the trader starts and finishes with U.S. dollars, is there a profitable triangular arbitrage opportunity here? Explain, ignoring transaction costs.

| A P P E N D I X | 5.1 |

Bank Note Arbitrage

Trading in bank notes, like trading in spot foreign exchange, is subject to exchange arbitrage. Because the spreads in bank note trading are much wider than those in spot trading, however, it is unlikely that the bid price in one location will rise above the ask price in another. Nevertheless, arbitrage occurs in the bank note market because of the linkages between spot and bank note trading.

Assume that in all forex trading centers, the interbank spot rates between the U.S. dollar and the French franc are FF6.0200–25/dollar. Also assume that the wholesale franc/dollar rates for bank notes that are quoted in both New York and Paris are bid FF5.920/dollar and ask FF6.125/dollar and that the cost, including implicit interest, of shipping bank notes from New York to Paris or vice versa and disposing of them are $0.0012/franc and $0.0072/dollar.

Given this information, a New York bank note dealer could exchange $2 million for FF12,040,000 at the spot rate, convert the resulting deposit into franc notes, and ship the notes to New York. Ideally, the dealer would obtain commitments from one or more banks handling franc notes to buy them at or close to FF5.920/dollar prior to shipping them. At the price of FF5.920/dollar, the dealer would be able to exchange the FF12,040,000 for $2,033,784, for a gross gain of $33,784. From this would be deducted the transaction costs of FF12,040,000 × $0.0012/franc = $14,448, arriving at a net gain of $19,336. Simultaneously, a bank note dealer (perhaps the same one) could gain by shipping dollar bank notes to Paris. If $2 million in bank notes were shipped to Paris, they could presumably be sold for as much as FF12,250,000. At the spot rate of FF6.0225/dollar, the FF12,250,000 could be exchanged for $2,034,039. From the gross gain of $34,039 would be deducted the transaction cost of $2 million × $0.0072/franc = $14,400 to arrive at a net gain of $19,639.

The arbitrage process would lead to price adjustments that would tend to eliminate the profitability of further arbitrage. The increased supply of franc notes in New York would tend to lower the price there, i.e., the dollar bid price of FF5.920/dollar would rise, and the increased supply of dollar notes in Paris would tend to lower their price there, leading to a downward adjustment in the dollar ask price of FF6.125/dollar. Bank note dealers in Paris would feel competitive pressure to match the price change in New York, and New York dealers would feel pressure to match the price change in Paris. Otherwise, travelers would buy their francs in New York and their dollars in Paris.

Even if the bank note spread were not as wide initially as in this example, a New York bank note dealer would have an incentive to import franc notes if their ask price in New York exceeded the ask price for spot francs by enough to cover the cost of transporting and disposing of franc notes. Thus, if franc notes can be sold in New York at FF5.920/dollar, spot francs can be purchased for FF6.0200/dollar, and the cost of shipping and disposing of franc notes is $0.0012/franc, the dealer will profit by transporting franc notes whether or not the bank note spread is wide enough to justify shipping dollar notes to Paris. From this it can be seen that bank note arbitrage is a function of three variables: the bank note exchange rate, the spot rate, and the cost of transporting and disposing of bank notes.

The Forward Market and Interest Rate Parity

■

While spot transactions form the backbone of the forex market, much of the market's activity revolves around arrangements that fix the rates at which *future* exchanges of currencies will occur. The forward contract holds the leading position among these future-oriented arrangements, but alternatives to it have attained enough prominence so that they now compete vigorously with it for allotments of space in surveys of the forex market. This chapter examines the forward market and the associated relationship known as **interest rate parity (IRP).** Chapter 7 examines the forex futures market, and Chapter 8 deals with forex options. Chapter 16 examines currency swaps, which are closely related to forward contracts. In addition, Chapter 7 examines money market operations that are combined with spot transactions to achieve the same objectives as forward contracts.

An Overview of the Forward Market

The fundamental reason for the forward market's existence is to provide an efficient means for hedging the exchange risk, which is the risk of loss (or gain) due to unforeseen exchange rate changes. As a hedging tool, the forward contract has had its greatest use in offsetting the exchange risk on short-term commitments whose amounts are known in advance. While they are heavily relied upon for this purpose by parties classified as traders or investors, most forward contracts result from the risk management operations of banks and are, therefore, interbank transactions.

While the speculative use of forward contracts occurs, it is far less important than hedging. The banks that make the forward market generally avoid entering into speculative forward contracts with customers, and the fact that forwards typically require commitments for more than a million dollars precludes many potential speculators from considering them. The large size of forward contracts and banks' reluctance to accommodate speculators largely explain the emergence of the market in forex futures.[1]

Although banks generally show reluctance to support forward speculation by their customers, they cannot totally avoid it themselves and sometimes actively engage in it. On the whole, however, banks regard forward speculation as dangerous. Accordingly, they set tight limits on the unhedged forward positions that their traders can accept.

Other motives for entering into forward contracts include arbitrage and market intervention. Currency arbitrage operates in the forward market much like it does in the spot market, and, as we shall see, interest arbitrage exerts great influence on the forward market. Central banks sometimes enter into forward contracts in recognition of the fact that it is difficult to influence spot rates without also influencing forward rates.

Types of Forward Contracts

The traditional forward contract is an **outright agreement,** i.e., a transaction providing for an unconditional, one-time exchange of currencies. Outright forwards are typically arranged by banks with nonbank customers who wish to hedge forex exposures. No cash flows occur between the contracting parties before the contact's maturity, but the nonbank party may be required to maintain a minimum deposit balance with the dealer bank or put up some other form of collateral. The maintenance of a minimum deposit balance need not entail an interest cost unless the amount of the required deposit exceeds the cash balance a customer would otherwise have maintained. The nonbank party continues earning interest on any collateral used that is in interest-earning form. The bid-ask spread in forward transactions is wider than in spot transactions, but the difference in spreads is usually not great when the currencies involved are widely traded and the forward contract has a standard maturity.

Today, most forward contracts are swap agreements, in which two parties agree to exchange specific amounts of currencies on a certain date and to reverse the exchange on a later date, usually at an exchange rate that differs from that of the first exchange. In most forward swaps, one of the exchanges is a spot transaction, in which case the swap is a spot-forward swap. Also

---

[1]The development of the International Monetary Market (IMM) of Chicago, the first and still the foremost exchange trading forex futures, owes much to the frustration experienced by famed economist Milton Friedman when he was denied access to the forward market by Chicago banks late in 1967. Friedman wanted to speculate against the pound sterling, which he (correctly) anticipated would soon be devalued substantially. After being turned down, despite his tender of ample margin for a contract of up to $300,000, Friedman became a vigorous advocate of a forex futures market. See Alan C. Shapiro, *Multinational Financial Management*, 3d. ed. (Boston: Allyn & Bacon, 1989), p. 131. Friedman's role in bringing this market into existence is readily acknowledged by the IMM.

common, however, are **forward-forward swaps,** in which a forward exchange
is reversed by another forward exchange with a later maturity.

While some forward swaps are between banks and nonbank customers,
most are interbank. The popularity of forward swaps arises from their
usefulness in managing the exchange risk. Thus, when a bank finds that
providing outright forwards to its customers has resulted in an undesired forex
exposure, it can use one or more forward swaps to reduce or rearrange its
exposure. Most forward swaps originate, however, for other reasons than to
reduce the risks of outright forwards. Later in the chapter, we shall take a
detailed look at the uses of forward swaps and the role that they play in the
management of banks' forex exposure.

Exhibit 6.1 presents a summary of average daily forex transactions in the
United States for the month of April 1989 as estimated by the Federal Reserve
Bank of New York. It conveys some idea of the magnitude of forward
transactions and their distribution between swaps and outrights. For comparison, Exhibit 6.1 includes data on three other forex categories: spot, option,
and futures transactions. The New York Fed's survey included 127 banks, 14
nonbank financial institutions, and 13 forex brokers. The figures have been
adjusted to avoid counting transactions between banks twice. For the nonbank
financial institutions, the figures have been adjusted to avoid double counting
of transactions between nonbanking institutions and banks and between pairs
of nonbanking institutions. Transactions between surveyed banks and nonbank financial institutions have been assigned to the latter category. The
transactions effected through brokers are also included in the data for bank
and nonbank transactions, so brokered transactions should not be added to the
other two types in order to obtain the total volume of forex transactions,
which was $128.9 billion per day. Incidentally, the figure of $56.9 billion for
brokers means that 44.1 percent of the total forex transactions went through
brokers.

Although the figures presented in Exhibit 6.1 do not distinguish between
spot–forward and forward–forward swaps, it is clear that the volume of spot
transactions greatly exceeds that of forward transactions, for even if all of the
swap transactions are allocated to the forward transactions, spot transactions
still account for a substantial majority of all forex transactions. The New York
Fed's survey does not provide sufficient detail about the swaps to permit
differentiation between forward and spot exchanges, but it is certain that the
forward component of swaps is very large. Included with the swaps are
currency swaps, whose nature is examined in Chapter 16. For now, let it suffice
to note that currency swaps can be viewed as being equivalent to or similar to
long-dated forwards.

It is noteworthy that forex brokers play a large role in arranging both spot
and swap transactions. On the other hand, their role in arranging outright
forwards is very minor. Only 4.2 percent of the forex transactions of banks
were outright forwards, and while outright forwards were relatively more
important for nonbank financial institutions, they still accounted for only 8.3
percent of the total forex transactions of those institutions.

| E X H I B I T | 6.1 | *U.S. Foreign Exchange Market Survey, April 1989: Distribution of Foreign Exchange Trading by Types of Institutions and Transactions*

Type of Institution	Net Daily Turnover (in Billions of Dollars)[a]	Percentage Distribution by Transaction Type				
		Spot	Swap	Forward	Option	Futures
Banks	$110.5	63.9%	27.0%	4.2%	4.3%	0.7%
Nonbank financial institutions	18.4	55.7	15.1	8.3	14.9	6.0
Brokers	56.9	54.1	42.3	0.3	3.3	n.a.[b]

[a]For banks, the net daily turnover figure has been adjusted to avoid double counting of the same transactions reported by participating banks. For nonbanks, the figure has been adjusted to avoid double counting of the same transactions if reported by participating banks or non-banks. The net daily turnover figure of $56.9 billion for brokers is also incorporated into the net daily turnover figures for banks and nonbanks.

[b]Not reported.

Source: Federal Reserve Bank of New York, "Summary of Results of U.S. Foreign Exchange Market Survey Conducted in April 1989," unpublished report, 1989, pp. 1, 4–5, and 9.

It can be argued that Exhibit 6.1 exaggerates somewhat the importance of option and futures contracts because few of these contracts result in actual deliveries of foreign exchange. By contrast, most forward contracts do result in delivery.

The Duration of Forward Contracts

Recall from Chapter 5 that in interbank trading, forward rates are customarily quoted in multiples of 30 days. Since the financial year is generally 360 days in length, it is convenient, and basically accurate, to regard these standard time periods as being equivalent to 1 month, 2 months, etc. As was noted in Chapter 5, forward contracts with value dates less than 30 days after the agreements are common in interbank trading. Beyond 30 days, forward contracts for time periods that are not 30-day multiples can generally be arranged without great difficulty.

The value date for a forward contract is based on the value date of the corresponding spot contract. For example, a forward contract with a 1-month (30-day) maturity is settled 1 month from the spot value date for a transaction occurring on the same day, provided that the resulting date is a business day. If it is not a business day, the value date is *advanced* to the nearest prior business day, unless advancing it would move it into another month, in which case the value date is moved backward to the next business day. One other settlement rule states that is the value date of a spot contract is the last business day of a month, then the settlement date for a forward contract stated in whole months must also be on the last business day of the corresponding month.

Prospective bank customers commonly want forward contracts with value dates that do not coincide with the whole-month format. Assume, for example, that a U.S. investment firm holds yen-denominated bonds that mature in 139 days and that the firm's management believes that the yen may decline against the dollar during the next few days and remain lower until after the bonds mature. The management would therefore like to have a forward contract that allows it to exchange yen for dollars in 139 days. A shorter contract would not suffice to provide complete protection against the exchange risk, while a contract for more than 139 days would saddle the firm with the problem of managing yen-denominated funds during the resulting time gap.

A bank would probably be willing to enter into a forward contract for 139 days, that is, to purchase yen 139 days forward, as long as it would receive an exchange rate that compensated it for its transaction costs and any additional risks it incurred. Since these costs and risks would probably not be great, it can be presumed that a bank would be willing to offer an appropriate forward contract at a price that would be acceptable to the firm.

How can we be sure that the additional costs and risks would not be great? For one thing, a bank providing the desired forward contract would probably be able to hedge the exchange risk it incurred. After entering into a contract to buy yen 139 days forward, a bank could, for example, enter into a forward swap with another bank in which it would buy yen spot and sell them forward 5 or even 6 months. At virtually the same time, the bank could sell yen spot, thereby avoiding taking a position in spot yen. For reasons that are explained later in the chapter, the forward sale portion of the swap would largely neutralize the risk arising from the purchase of yen 139 days forward. Moreover, the bank could probably arrange a bridge swap later to take care of the gap between 139 days and the end of either 5 or 6 months, thereby eliminating most of the remaining risk.

A very small risk for the accommodating bank would be that of default by either the investment firm or the bank with which it subsequently swapped. To protect itself, the bank could require the investment firm to provide collateral or to maintain a sizable minimum balance with it. Defensive action to protect against default by the other bank would probably be unnecessary, but if it should be deemed desirable, the first bank might arrange things so that its obligations to the other bank would exceed that bank's obligations to it. In any event, the transfer of yen to the other bank under the terms of the swap would be contingent upon its receiving dollars at the same time.

Although the bank providing the 139-day forward contract would incur additional transaction costs because of its hedging transactions and because it might have to manage funds during the time gap between maturities, these costs would be reflected in the forward rate charged to the customer. Accordingly, the investment firm could probably obtain a slightly more favorable forward rate by waiting to enter into a forward contract until the maturity date of the bonds coincided with the value date of a 4-month forward contract.

Additional flexibility in forward maturities is provided by the use of **forward option contracts,** which allow customers to choose any date within specified limits, generally 10 days from the contract's maturity date, as the date for settling the contract. Such a contract is particularly desirable when a customer does not know the exact date on which a foreign currency payment or receipt will occur. Thus, if a firm is obligated to make a payment in a foreign currency 30 days after receiving imported goods, it might be well-advised to use a forward option contract if there is doubt about the date on which the goods will be received. In return for providing this flexibility, the accommodating bank receives a favorable exchange rate, which is usually the more desirable of the forward rates for the beginning and ending dates of the period of the option.

While there is a sizable business in long-dated forwards (2 to 5 years), the volume of short-term forwards is many times greater. Part of the explanation for this fact is that short-term hedging has received greater emphasis than long-term hedging, part of it is that the market in long-dated forwards lacks the liquidity of the market in short-term forwards, and part of it is that alternative techniques for medium and long-term hedging have lessened the need for long-dated forwards. Particularly important among these alternative techniques are financial swaps, the subject of Chapter 16. Another example of an alternative to long-dated forwards is the dual currency bond, examined in Chapter 14, which essentially amounts to a long-dated forward contract.

Forward Exchange Rate Quotations

Forward exchange rates are quoted in two different ways. An **outright forward rate** simply states a forward rate in the familiar form of the amount of one currency per unit of another currency. A **swap rate** is the absolute difference, in basis points, between a forward rate and its corresponding spot rate.

Assume that an interested party receives a two-way quotation from a bank for 30-day yen in the form "134.36−50." This indicates that the bank stands ready to sell yen at ¥134.36/dollars and to buy them at ¥134.50/dollars. Both quotations are outright, though the yen ask price for dollars states only those digits that are necessary to indicate the bid−ask spread. Now assume that the same bank quotes spot yen at ¥135.85−95/dollars. Based on this information, the swap rates for 30-day yen can be determined to be 49−45, i.e., the absolute differences in points between the outright forward rates and their corresponding spot rates.

Banks customarily quote forward rates as swap rates in interbank trading. Minus and plus signs are often ignored, and those who work with swap rates are expected to know at a glance whether these rates should be added to or subtracted from their corresponding spot rates in order to derive outright rates. Determining whether to add or subtract swap rates is a simple process when you keep in mind that the bid-ask spread widens as the time period lengthens. Thus, in the yen example given here, the swap rates are subtracted from the corresponding spot rates to derive the outright forward rates. From this example, we can derive a simple rule: if the first swap rate exceeds the second swap rate, subtract both rates from the spot rates to get the outright forward rates; and if the first swap rate is less than the second swap rate, add both rates to get the outright forward rates.

Exhibit 6.2 presents hypothetical forward exchange rate quotations in both swap rate and outright form. In part (a), the 1-month, 3-months, and 6-months forward rates between the U.S. dollar and four other currencies are shown as swap rates. One currency, the pound sterling, is quoted directly in terms of the U.S. dollar, while the other three are quoted indirectly in terms of the U.S. dollar. For each forward maturity in each currency, two numbers appear. The first is the absolute difference in points between the forward and spot bid prices, while the second is the absolute difference in points between the spot and forward ask prices. Following the explanation given in the last paragraph, the swap rates are deducted from the corresponding spot rates for the pound and the yen in order to obtain the outright forward rates. For the Canadian dollar, however, the swap rates are added to the corresponding spot rates in order to obtain the outright forward rates. In the case of the mark, the 1-month swap rates are deducted from the spot rates, while the 3-months and 6-months swap rates are added to the spot rates.

When a currency's forward price exceeds its spot price, it is said to be at a **forward premium;** when the forward price is less than the spot price, a currency is said to be at a **forward discount.** In those exceptional cases in which a forward rate equals the corresponding spot rate (as in the mark bid price for dollars 3 months forward in Exhibit 6.2), the forward rate is said to be *flat.* In Exhibit 6.2, the pound and the Canadian dollar are discounted in all forward maturities, the yen is at a premium in all forward maturities, and the mark is at a premium 1 month forward and a discount 6 months forward.

That some forward rates are premiums and others are discounts is explained primarily by differences in nations' interest rates. When a country's interest rates are higher than those of the United States, its currency tends to be at a forward discount in terms of the dollar, and when a country's interest rates are lower than those of the United States, its currency tends to be at a forward premium. As is shown later in the chapter, the explanation for this pattern is found in IRP.

At any given point in time, a pronounced tendency exists for the interest rate differentials between countries to exhibit a high degree of uniformity among different interest rate periods. If, for example, Canadian interest rates on a certain type of security are 3 percent higher (on an annual basis) than U.S. interest rates on similar securities for 1 month maturities, it is likely that the interest differential for the same type of security with 3 months to maturity will also be close to 3 percent.

If the interest rate differential is indeed uniform across time periods, it is said to exhibit linearity. It is generally assumed that linearity holds approximately for the time periods of the most frequently used forward maturities. The linearity assumption means that forward swap rates tend to vary directly and proportionately with the length of the forward period. Note, however, that the linearity exhibited in Exhibit 6.2, whose figures approximate actual exchange rates early in 1990, is not perfect.

| E X H I B I T | 6.2 | *The Quoting of Forward Exchange Rates*

(a) Forward Swap Rates

Exchange Rate	Spot	1 Month	3 Months	6 Months
$/£	1.6440-50	99-97	278-275	536-530
DM/$	1.7140-50	4-2	0-3	13-19
C$/$	1.1720-30	40-43	105-109	175-181
¥/$	145.80-90	22-20	48-45	136-130

(b) Outright Forward Rates

Exchange Rate	Spot	1 Month	3 Months	6 Months
$/£	1.6440-50	1.6341-53	1.6162-75	1.5904-20
DM/$	1.7140-50	1.7136-48	1.7140-53	1.7153-69
C$/$	1.7120-30	1.1760-73	1.1825-39	1.1895-911
¥/$	145.80-90	145.58-70	145.32-45	144.44-60

Exchange rate symbols: $ = U.S. dollar, £ = pound sterling, DM = German mark, C$ = Canadian dollar, and ¥ = Japanese yen.

Forward Hedging

Defined broadly, **hedging** means to reduce risk by acting to offset it. In international finance, the term applies to numerous types of action to offset the various risks encountered, but it is hedging to reduce the exchange risk that has captured the most attention. Applied to the exchange risk, hedging means to alter the composition of assets and liabilities so as to fully or partially offset an existing or potential exposure to the exchange risk.

The Traditional Role of Forward Hedging

Recall that it was stated earlier that as a hedging tool, the forward contract has had its greatest use in offsetting the exchange risk on short-term commitments whose amounts are known in advance. Examples of such commitments are a U.S. firm's obligation to pay in marks 30 days after receiving goods it has agreed to import, a Spanish firm's semiannual interest payment on a dollar-denominated Euroloan, and a U.S. institutional investor's anticipated receipts of interest and amortization payments in yen at the end of the next quarter. These examples illustrate what is known as **transaction exposure**, which is the *net* amount of *existing* commitments to make or receive outlays in foreign currency. Such commitments need not be short-term, but the short-term hedging of transaction exposure has been the primary concern of parties that hedge with forwards.

It should be recognized, however, that short-term forward contracts are used to hedge medium-term and even long-term transaction exposure. Consider, for example, the case of a Swedish firm with an outstanding 3-year, floating-rate Eurodollar loan on which it pays interest every 6 months. Assume that when this loan begins, the firm enters into a 6-month forward contract to sell Swedish krona for dollars. The amount of dollars purchased will not necessarily equal the amount of the loan principal plus 6 months' interest since the firm will want to take into account its other transaction exposure in dollars. It may well be, for example, that the forward contract will be substantially less than the loan principal plus interest because the firm is to be a net recipient of dollars from other transactions.

If the dollar rises during the next 6 months, the firm gains from the forward contract by selling the dollars it buys, less those that are needed to pay the interest due, at the current spot rate. This gain is offset by a loss from an increase in the krona amount of the loan. If the dollar falls during the next 6 months, the firm has a negative cash flow from the forward contract, but it gains from the decline in the krona amount of the loan. Whether the dollar rises or falls, the firm enters into a new 6-month contract to buy dollars at the maturity of the first contract. This second contract will probably not be for the same dollar amount as the first one since the interest rate will probably have changed and the firm's overall transaction exposure in dollars will probably also have changed.

Choosing a forward contract to hedge transaction exposure rather than an alternative depends on cost considerations and other factors, such as the certainty of the anticipated expenditure or receipt and the hedger's view of exchange rate probabilities. If, for example, a U.S. firm has an outstanding offer to sell goods for a specified quantity of pounds sterling which may or may not be accepted, it might well prefer to hedge with an option rather than a forward contract. Once entered into, a forward contract cannot be canceled unless both parties consent to cancellation, and while it would be possible to nullify an outstanding forward position by, for example, entering into a forward contract that reverses it, this involves another transaction.

As far as exchange rate probabilities are concerned, it is important to remember that while hedging with forwards prevents losses, it also prevents gains. If, for example, a firm sells marks forward because it is going to be receiving marks in the near future and wants protection against a decline in the mark, it forgoes the opportunity to gain from a rise in the mark. If the firm's management believes that the mark will rise substantially during the relevant time period, it could protect against a decline in the mark by entering into an option contract that guarantees a minimum price for marks. The option would, however, preserve the chance to gain from a rise in the mark.

While situations arise in which the forward contract is not the best alternative for hedging transaction exposure, there are many cases in which it *is* the best alternative. Forwards are simple, and they are generally both low-cost and low-risk. It seems probable, therefore, that they will continue to have a prominent role in the hedging of transaction exposure.

An important principle in hedging transaction exposure is that it should be done on the basis of a party's overall transaction exposure, not parts of it. If, for example, a U.S. firm is going to be paying DM 5 million in 90 days on outstanding debts while simultaneously receiving DM 8 million from exports, it makes no sense to enter into a forward contract to buy DM 5 million and another forward contract to sell DM 8 million. If these are the only mark flows to worry about, it can fully hedge its mark exposure by selling DM 3 million forward. Moreover, if the firm has transaction commitments in other ERM currencies which mature in 90 days or thereabouts, it might do well to include those commitments with its mark commitments in order to arrive at the amount to be hedged.

Other Types of Forex Exposure

Hedging on the basis of short-term transaction exposure is not the only feasible rationale for forward hedging. Indeed, one of the leading challenges for international financial theory and research is how to properly expand the use of forward hedging beyond its transaction exposure base. In a book devoted primarily to international financial markets rather than international financial management, however, some aspects of exchange risk hedging must be regarded as peripheral. This is the case with the matter of choosing among exposure concepts. Nevertheless, this matter merits some of our attention because of the influence that these concepts have on the hedging instruments used in international financial markets.

Translation or Accounting Exposure   **Translation** or **accounting exposure** is the net *book value* of assets and liabilities denominated in foreign currency. If, for example, a US. firm has a Canadian subsidiary, a decline in the Canadian dollar's exchange value would probably diminish the book value of the parent's investment in the subsidiary, thereby causing the parent to experience a translation loss. This loss would not necessarily equate to a loss of U.S. dollar earnings. Thus, if the subsidiary produces inputs for the parent's manufacturing operations in the United States, a lowering of the U.S. dollar cost of the parent's imports could lead to an increase in its U.S. dollar earnings. Nevertheless, to the extent that investors and others consider translation losses to be meaningful—and abundant evidence exists that they often consider them to be so—the parent has an incentive to hedge its translation exposure.

Transaction exposure overlaps translation exposure to the extent that existing commitments to make or receive outlays in foreign currency are recorded on the books. In important respects, however, the two exposures do not overlap. The transaction exposure of a U.S. firm from its investment in a Canadian subsidiary, for example, can be construed as including the transaction exposure of the subsidiary and the subsidiary's transaction commitments in Canadian dollars, but it does not include all the items on the subsidiary's balance sheet. An example would be the subsidiary's investment in capital equipment. Furthermore, there are transaction exposure items, such as scheduled future interest payments on bonds denominated in foreign currency, that do not appear on balance sheets and are, therefore, excluded from translation exposure. Translation exposure thus differs substantially from transaction exposure. This means that to the extent that translation exposure influences hedging, the use of forward contracts is likely to be affected.

The Forward Hedging of Translation Exposure In order to gain a better understanding of the implications of hedging on the basis of translation exposure, consider the following example. Assume that Zitimax, a U.S. multinational firm, calculates that its translation exposure in ERM currencies is the equivalent of DM 40 million on the net asset side, i.e., its exposed assets exceed its exposed liabilities by that amount. The spot rate and the 6-month forward rate between the mark and the dollar are both currently DM 1.80 per dollar. At the moment, therefore, the dollar amount of Zitimax's translation exposure in ERM currencies is $22.2+ million (the + indicates a repeating number). Zitimax's hedging strategy is to use forward transactions to reduce by half any translation loss caused by a decline in the mark during the next 6 months. Assuming that Zitimax's book assets and liabilities denominated in foreign currencies remain unchanged and that they are translated into dollars at the currently existing spot exchange rates,[2] Zitimax can implement its strategy by selling DM 20 million 6 months forward. The forward sale would create a transaction exposure liability, but this liability would probably not appear on Zitimax's balance sheet.

Assume that Zitimax makes the forward sale and that the spot mark declines by 10 percent to DM 2.00 per dollar at the end of 6 months. By buying spot marks at this rate, Zitimax gains $1.1+ million, thereby offsetting half the translation loss of $2.2+ million. If the spot mark had risen, it would have had a loss on the forward sale equal to half the translation gain. Either way, since the gain or loss on the forward sale would affect Zitimax's balance sheet through its effect on realized income, the forward sale would partly offset the balance sheet effect of the translation loss or gain.

Complicating matters is the fact that translation gains and losses generally do not have income tax effects for U.S. firms, while gains and losses on forward transactions do have such effects. It is conceivable, therefore, that Zitimax might want to assign the forward sale to a subsidiary located in a country with a more lenient tax treatment of income derived from forex operations.

As this example demonstrates, using forward transactions to hedge translation exposure increases transaction exposure and the attendant cash flows unless the transactions undertaken offset other transactions. Whether or not the resulting effect on the balance sheet justifies this transaction exposure effect is open to question because translation losses and gains do not necessarily signify corresponding changes in either current or potential earnings. Thus, as was suggested in the case of the U.S. firm with a Canadian subsidiary, a translation loss may be followed by an increase in the parent's U.S. dollar earnings. It is difficult to justify the expense and time involved in hedging a "loss" that signals a future gain on the ground that investors and other pay excessive attention to accounting statements.

---

[2]The second of these assumptions does not necessarily hold in the United States for all balance sheet assets and liabilities denominated in foreign currencies. For a good overview of the U.S. system of accounting for translation exposure, see *ibid.*, Chapter 8.

Economic Exposure Just as the hedging of translation exposure may run counter to changes in potential earnings, so also may the hedging of transaction exposure. Assume, for example, that Schnorkel Corporation, a U.S. manufacturer of high-tech equipment, estimates that a lasting 10 percent depreciation of the dollar against the Ecu will lead to an increase of $30 million in its net annual earnings. At the moment, however, Schnorkel has a net liability transaction exposure in ERM currencies of $4 million. If Schnorkel only uses forwards to hedge transaction exposure, it will buy forward Ecus, marks, or some other ERM currency since that will permit it to avoid a transaction loss if the dollar depreciates. Since such a loss would signal an improvement in Schnorkel's earnings prospects, however, it is not evident that it should be buying an ERM currency forward. Much more logical would be to *sell* one or more ERM currencies forward to protect itself against an *appreciation* of the dollar.

We have now come to the domain of **economic exposure**, which is the extent to which the present value of a firm, an asset, or a liability may be affected by exchange rate changes. Increasingly, this is the exposure concept that is being regarded as the most appropriate guide to exchange risk hedging. Unfortunately, it is also the exposure concept that is most difficult to measure, and it suffers the disadvantage relative to the other two exposure concepts of being relatively long-term in nature.

Economic exposure overlaps transaction exposure to the extent that the value of a firm, an asset, or a liability may be affected by the outcome of existing transaction commitments in foreign currencies. It is much more inclusive than transaction exposure, however. This is true, in part, because present value often depends on the expected outcomes of commitments that have not yet been made. For example, the present value effect on a U.S. firm of an appreciation in the dollar is likely to depend more on what the firm is expected to do after it occurs than on what the firm did before then. Economic exposure likewise differs from translation exposure because it depends on the future, while translation exposure reflects what has happened in the past.

Economic exposure also differs from both transaction and translation exposure in that a firm may be economically exposed to exchange rate changes even if it has neither assets nor liabilities denominated in foreign currency. Thus, any U.S. firm whose profitability is influenced by the appreciation or depreciation of the dollar has an economic exposure problem even if its managers have a firm policy of conducting all their business in U.S. currency and have never entertained the idea of hedging the exchange risk. Without any doubt, there are many such firms.

The principle of basing hedging on economic exposure has great merit, but its acceptance has been impeded by skepticism regarding its feasibility. The present value effect of a given exchange rate change may not be known with a high degree of confidence. That being the case, some argue, it is better to hedge on the basis of what *is* known. Against this position, one can argue that there are numerous situations in which economic exposure can be estimated with enough confidence to warrant basing hedging on it.

The shortcomings of hedging on the basis of either transaction exposure or translation exposure are clear enough so that the idea of giving economic exposure a stronger role in hedging is gaining force. What the outcome of this emphasis will be for the forward market is unclear, but it does not necessarily mean that the volume of forward hedging will diminish. As the understanding of economic exposure increases and its extent becomes more fully appreciated, the volume of forward hedging may tend to increase.

Forward Covering versus Forward Hedging

A minor semantic problem in discussions of exchange risk hedging is the choice of terminology for actions taken to avoid the exchange risk. *Hedging* this risk means to obtain an asset or to incur a liability denominated in foreign currency in order to fully or partially offset an existing foreign currency exposure. *Covering* means to generate a foreign currency cash flow in order to offset a commitment to make or receive a cash flow denominated in the same or an equivalent currency. Using a forward contract to eliminate transaction exposure is covering since the forward contract offsets an existing cash flow commitment. It is also hedging since it involves offsetting a previously existing asset or liability with a newly acquired liability or asset. When a firm uses a forward contract to hedge either translation exposure or economic exposure, however, this action is not covering unless it also offsets a transaction exposure.

Interest Rate Parity (IRP)

Covering transaction exposure with forward contracts presumes the existence of an equilibrium condition known as *interest rate parity* (IRP). In this condition, an interest rate differential between two countries is offset by the forward premium or discount so that a forward contract cannot be used to make a gain based on the interest rate differential. For example, if short-term interest rates in Canada exceed those in the United States, IRP means that the forward Canadian dollar will tend to be at a discount sufficient to prevent arbitrageurs from shifting funds from the United States to Canada and then using the forward market to lock in gains based on the difference in interest rates. From this it can be seen that IRP depends on four variables: interest rates in two countries and the spot and forward exchange rates between their currencies.

The Equal Returns Formulation of IRP

If IRP holds, an investor's rate of return from a domestic asset will tend to equal the rate of return from a covered foreign investment in a comparable asset. Similarly, the cost of borrowing domestically will tend to equal the cost of covered borrowing in a foreign currency. If transaction costs were zero, all relevant information were known, there were no barriers to financial transactions, and there were no differences in risk internationally, the equality between domestic and covered foreign interest rates would be exact. Such a condition is expressed by the following equation, which is the equal returns formulation of exact IRP:

$$1 + r_{a,0}^t\left(\frac{t}{360}\right) = \frac{1}{S_0}\left[1 + r_{b,0}^t\left(\frac{t}{360}\right)\right]F_0^t \qquad (6-1)$$

where $r_{a,0}^t$ is the annual interest rate in Country A on date 0 for an asset to be held t days; t/360 is the fraction of a 360-day year represented by t days; S_0 is the spot exchange rate on date 0, expressed as units of A's currency per unit of Country B's currency; $r_{b,0}^t$ is the annual interest rate in Country B on date 0 for an asset held t days which is comparable to the Country A asset; and F_0^t is the forward rate on date 0 for a period of t days, also expressed as the price of a unit of B's currency in terms of A's currency. B's currency is thus stated directly in both exchange rates.

Equation 6–1 indicates that the rate of return in A's currency is the same whether an investor buys an A-currency asset or makes a fully covered investment in a B-currency asset. In other words, if an investor exchanges A's currency for B's currency at the spot rate of day 0, invests the funds in a B-currency asset, and sells forward for t days the amount of B's currency to be accumulated, the amount of A's currency realized is the same as if the investor simply buys an A-currency asset on day 0 and holds it for t days.

Equation 6–1 uses a 360-day year because that is the length of the financial year in most international financial operations. In some cases, however, such as the United Kingdom, a 365-day year generally prevails. Equation 6–1 can readily be modified to accommodate this longer year by simply substituting 365 for 360 where appropriate.

Here is an example illustrating the use of Equation 6–1. Assume that the spot exchange rate between the Dutch guilder (Fl) and the U.S. dollar is Fl 1.9940 per dollar and that the 90-day forward rate is Fl 2.0090 per dollar. Also assume that the relevant interest rate in the United States is 6.25 percent and that a 360-day year applies to interest rates in both countries. Let the Netherlands be Country A and the United States be Country B. Solving for the interest rate in the Netherlands ($r_{a,0}^t$) that will cause exact IRP to hold produces a figure of 9.31 percent (rounded upward from 9.306 percent). You should verify this for yourself.

Other Exact IRP Formulations

By rearranging the terms of Equation 6–1, the IRP condition can be stated in whatever form best suits the circumstances. Thus, since forex dealers commonly base their forward quotations on the assumptions that IRP holds, it is convenient for them to employ a formulation of IRP that expresses the forward rate as a function of the other three IRP variables. This formulation can be expressed as follows:

$$F_0^t = S_0 \frac{1 + r_{a,0}^t\left(\frac{t}{360}\right)}{1 + r_{b,0}^t\left(\frac{t}{360}\right)} \qquad (6-2)$$

By basing forward rates on this equation, banks can protect themselves from providing arbitrage opportunities for other banks. Such opportunities may nevertheless arise, however, when banks' spot exchange rate and/or interest rate quotations differ. Note that Equation 6−2 ignores bid−ask spreads. It is desirable, therefore, to view the exchange rates and interest rates in the equation as being middle exchange rates and interest rates.

Another formulation of exact IRP involves the use of a swap rate. In this formulation, Equation 6−2 is modified by shifting S_0 to the left side and subtracting the denominator of each side from the numerator. After simplification, the following equation results:

$$\frac{F_0^t - S_0}{S_0} = \frac{r_{a,0}^t \left(\frac{t}{360}\right) - r_{b,0}^t \left(\frac{t}{360}\right)}{1 + r_{b,0}^t \left(\frac{t}{360}\right)} \qquad (6-3)$$

In Equation 6−3, $F_0^t - S_0$ is a swap rate. Multiplying the left side of the equation by 100 gives the percentage of the forward premium or discount. Note, however, that this premium or discount is not annualized unless the time period is 360 days. The right side of Equation 6−3 gives the interest rate differential between Countries A and B. Multiplying that side of the equation by 100 gives the percentage (not percentage points) by which Country A's interest rate differs from Country B's interest rate, but note that the interest rates are not annualized. If, for example, A's annual interest rate is 8 percent, B's annual interest rate is 6 percent, and the time period is 180 days, A's 180-day interest rate exceeds B's 180-day interest rate by 0.97 percent, not 1 percentage point.

Equation 6−3 can be refined to state both the forward premium or discount and the interest rate differential on an annualized basis. This is accomplished by multiplying each side of the equation by 360/t. This refined version of Equation 6−3 can be written as follows:

$$\frac{F_0^t - S_0}{S_0} \left(\frac{360}{t}\right) = \frac{r_{a,0}^t - r_{b,0}^t}{1 + r_{b,0}^t \left(\frac{t}{360}\right)} \qquad (6-4)$$

Equation 6−4 is preferable to Equation 6−3 because interest rates are customarily stated on an annual basis, as are forward premiums and discounts.

Equation 6−4 is of particular interest to forex dealers and other parties with offsetting forex commitments that have different maturities. It is evident from Equation 6−4 that changes in the interest rate differential must lead to adjustments in the corresponding swap rates. As is explained later in the chapter, banks attempt to position themselves to gain from these adjustments or at least not be harmed by them.

In all of the IRP formulations that have been presented, the exchange rates have priced B's currency directly. If B's currency is priced indirectly (units of B's currency per unit of A's currency), that fact must be taken into account.

One way to handle cases where B's currency is priced indirectly is to convert the exchange rates into direct rates by dividing them into 1.

This takes a little time and is unnecessary, however. Moreover, when it is customary to state B's currency indirectly, it is inadvisable to change the exchange rate to the direct form because it may be necessary to convert it back into the indirect form. Assume, for example, that you are confronted with an exam problem that requires you to use Equation 6−2 to calculate a forward rate for the Dutch guilder (Fl) that is consistent with exact IRP. The exchange rate between the guilder and the dollar is customarily stated in guilders per dollar (Fl/dollar). If you take a spot rate in this form, change it to the dollars/guilder form, and plug this reciprocal into Equation 6−2, the forward rate that emerges will also be in the dollars/guilder form, and you will then have to divide by 1 again to get the forward rate into its standard form. Meanwhile, some of your classmates will be working on the next question.

One solution in the guilder example is to switch the country labels so that the United States is Country B and the Netherlands is Country A. The spot rate can then be inserted into Equation 6−2 in its customary Fl/dollar form, and the forward rate that then emerges is also in its customary form. In similar fashion, the other equations that have been presented can be adapted to the switching of country labels.

It is unnecessary, however, to switch country labels in order to deal efficiently with exchange rates expressed as the quantity of B's currency per unit of A's currency. If B's currency is stated in this indirect way, the spot and forward rates can be incorporated into Equations 6−1 through 6−4 by simply substituting $1/S_0^*$ for S_0 and $1/F_0^{*t}$ for F_0^t while leaving the country labels intact, where S_0^* and F_0^{*t} are, respectively, the spot and forward rates in B's currency per unit of A's currency that correspond to S_0 and F_0^t. When these substitutions are made, the following equations can be derived from, respectively, Equations 6−1, 6−2, and 6−4:

$$1 + r_{a,0}^t \left(\frac{t}{360}\right) = S_0^* \left[1 + r_{b,0}^t\left(\frac{t}{360}\right)\right] \frac{1}{F_0^{*t}} \tag{6-5}$$

$$F_0^{*t} = S_0^* \frac{1 + r_{b,0}^t \left(\frac{t}{360}\right)}{1 + r_{a,0}^t \left(\frac{t}{360}\right)} \tag{6-6}$$

$$\frac{S_0^* - F_0^{*t}}{F_0^{*t}}\left(\frac{360}{t}\right) = \frac{r_{a,0}^t - r_{b,0}^t}{1 + r_{b,0}^t \left(\frac{t}{360}\right)} \tag{6-7}$$

Note that Equation 6−7 should be paired with Equation 6−4, not with Equation 6−3.

If the United States is generally taken to be Country A, this second set of equations will be applicable most of the time. The reason is that exchange rates are generally expressed in other currency units per dollar.

Interest Arbitrage

Since IRP involves equilibrium among four variables, it follows that a divergence of any of the four from that condition can provide an opportunity for an almost riskless gain. The process of realizing such a gain is known as **covered interest arbitrage.** It is in that freest of free markets, the Eurocurrency market, that the influence of interest arbitrage is greatest, but its influence is also felt in other markets where transactions occur freely and forward currency contracts are used.

Interest Arbitrage Simplified

Interest arbitrage occurs when the interest rate differential between two countries differs from the corresponding forward premium or discount on the exchange rate between their currencies. More precisely, if Equations 6–4 and 6–7 do not hold, an opportunity for interest arbitrage exists if the necessary transactions are available and the difference between the forward premium or discount and the interest rate differential is great enough to cover the transaction costs of arbitrage.

One can more easily discover interest arbitrage opportunities by using formulas that are slightly less complicated than either Equation 6–4 or Equation 6–7, converted into inequalities. This simplified method, which is based on the concept of inexact IRP, employs either of the following formulations:

$$\frac{F_0^t - S_0}{S_0}\left(\frac{360}{t}\right) \neq r_{a,0}^t - r_{b,0}^t \tag{6-8}$$

and

$$\frac{S_0^* - F_0^{*t}}{F_0^{*t}}\left(\frac{360}{t}\right) \neq r_{a,0}^t - r_{b,0}^t \tag{6-9}$$

Aside from the fact that these two formulas are inequalities and not equations, they differ from Equations 6–4 and 6–7 in their omission of the expression $1 + r_{b,0}^t (t/360)$ as the right-side denominator. This omission means, of course, that the interest rate differential of Inequalities 6–8 and 6–9 is not the same as that of Equations 6–4 and 6–7. This is why the former are called "inexact" formulations. Normally, however, the Country B interest rate is low enough and the time period is short enough that the distortion involved in Inequalities 6–8 and 6–9 is not great enough to warrant using a more exact formulation. Nevertheless, it is advisable to remember that the interest rate differentials found by Inequalities 6–8 and 6–9 are always at least a little larger than the exact measurements given by Equations 6–4 and 6–7.

The following example illustrates the use of the inexact method for detecting interest arbitrage opportunities. Assume that the relevant interest rates are 8.62 percent in the United States and 7.24 percent in the Netherlands, both rates being stated on an annual basis. Also assume that the relevant exchange rates are a spot rate of Fl1.8920/dollars and a 60-day forward rate of Fl1.8850/dollars, a difference of 70 points. An experienced practitioner would probably recognize an opportunity for interest arbitrage simply with a glance at these figures. For most of the rest of us, however, it is necessary to use a mathematical formula to reach correct conclusions. In this case, we can use Inequality 6–9 to determine that the forward premium on the guilder is 2.23 percent and that the interest rate differential (with the United States as Country A) is 1.38 percentage points (you should gain practice by verifying this for yourself).

The gap between the forward premium and the interest rate differential is large enough in this case to indicate that interest arbitrage should be profitable. The procedure is as follows: (1) If necessary to obtain sufficient dollars, borrow them at 8.62 percent. (2) Buy spot guilders at Fl 1.8920 per dollar. (3) Obtain a guilder-denominated asset yielding 7.24 percent that either matures in 60 days or can be liquidated easily at that time. (4) Sell forward 60 days at Fl 1.8850 per dollar the quantity of guilders that will be available in 60 days. Since the gain on the currency exchanges (2.33 percent) substantially exceeds the loss from the interest differential (1.38 percentage points), a gain can be realized by following this procedure. Calculations based on this information reveal that if a sum of $5 million were fully utilized for interest arbitrage at a dollar interest cost of 8.62 percent, the gain achieved would exceed what could be earned in dollars invested at 8.62 percent by $7,292. This would far exceed the transaction cost of obtaining the gain.

Equations 6–4 and 6–7 would give an interest rate differential of 1.36 percent instead of 1.38 percentage points. Needless to say, the simpler, inexact of Inequality 6–9 does not seriously bias the calculation of interest arbitrage's profitability. Using this method is, therefore, preferable.

The Neutral Band

In practice, the feasibility of interest arbitrage is limited by exchange rate and interest rate spreads, by the arbitrageur's transaction costs, and (usually to a small extent) by risk. Even though one arbitrage transaction is a spot exchange and another is a forward exchange, there is still a spread to be overcome between bid and ask exchange rates. Similarly, there is an interest rate spread to be overcome, even though the interest rates involved are in different currencies. That the arbitrageur incurs transaction costs that are not incorporated into the spreads is self-evident.

Risk becomes a major consideration in interest arbitrage when an asset acquired in the arbitrage process is potentially illiquid or otherwise risky, when the soundness of the bank providing the covering forward contract is in question, or when there is more than a remote possibility that a government will prevent or impede the on-time completion of the process. Among the countries and currencies which are usually involved in interest arbitrage, however, these risks are likely to be negligible. Nevertheless, because the credit ratings of some leading banks have recently been downgraded, the risk factor is receiving more attention than was formerly the case.

Because of these factors, IRP need not hold exactly to prevent interest arbitrage. There is a range of possible combinations of forward premiums or discounts and interest rate differentials on either side of exact IRP combinations within which IRP *effectively* holds. This range is known as the **IRP neutral band.** Within this band, either the forward premium or discount or the interest differential can change without leading to interest arbitrage.

Exhibit 6.3 portrays the IRP neutral band. The vertical axis plots the interest rate differential between Countries A and B, while the horizontal axis plots the forward premium or discount. The interest rate differential is expressed in exact form as in Equations 6–4 and 6–7, while the forward premium or discount is expressed on an annualized basis. Sloping upward from left to right, parallel lines represent the outer limits of effective IRP after spreads and other relevant factors are taken into account. The other relevant factors include transaction costs, risks, and the time period involved. Any combination of a forward premium or discount and an interest differential that lies inside the parallel lines (the neutral band) represents effective IRP, while any such combination that lies outside the parallel lines represents a chance for interest arbitrage. From this it follows that, on some occasions, a small change in an interest rate or an exchange rate may induce interest arbitrage, while on other occasions, a much larger change may fail to bring interest arbitrage about.

With reference to Exhibit 6.3, assume that Country A's interest rate initially exceeds that of Country B by enough that the interest differential equals 1.0 percent. Also assume that the forward premium on B's currency equals 1.0 percent. With this combination, represented by Point x, IRP holds exactly. Now assume that the interest rate differential declines to 0.8 percent because A's interest rate falls relative to B's interest rate. Assuming that the forward premium remains 1.0 percent, this new combination, represented by Point y, still lies inside the band. Finally, assume that the interest rate differential declines further to 0.6 percent, the forward premium remaining at 1.0 percent. This new combination, indicated by Point z, lies outside the band, so interest arbitrage now becomes feasible.

Rephrasing what was stated at the outset, the width of the neutral band depends on the width of the exchange rate and interest rate spreads, the transaction costs of the arbitrageur, and whatever risks there may be. It also depends, though this may not be immediately obvious, on the time period involved. In general, the chance for interest arbitrage increases with the length of the time period. The basic reason this is true is that the costs of arbitrage and the relevant spreads do not increase proportionately as the time period increases, while the money amount of the gain from arbitrage *does* tend to increase proportionately with the time period.

To see why the opportunity for interest arbitrage increases as the time period lengthens, recall the guilder–dollar example presented earlier in which the premium on 60-day forward guilders is 2.23 percent and the interest rate

| EXHIBIT | 6.3 | *The IRP Neutral Band*

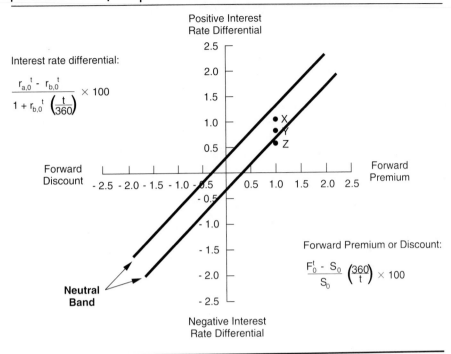

Positive Interest
Rate Differential

Interest rate differential:

$$\frac{r_{a,0}^t - r_{b,0}^t}{1 + r_{b,0}^t \left(\frac{t}{360}\right)} \times 100$$

Forward Discount   Forward Premium

Neutral Band

Negative Interest
Rate Differential

Forward Premium or Discount:

$$\frac{F_0^t - S_0}{S_0} \left(\frac{360}{t}\right) \times 100$$

differential, measured exactly, is 1.36 percent. Assume that linearity holds with respect to both the forward premium and the interest rate differential, i.e., they are the same on an annual basis, whatever the time period. Also assume that the exchange rates and interest rates given are middle rates. Whether or not interest arbitrage is profitable now depends on the spreads as well as the arbitrageur's transaction costs, and we cannot say that arbitrage will be profitable without knowing the spreads. If the linearity assumption holds, however, and if the dollar amounts of the spreads and the arbitrageur's transaction costs do not increase in proportion to increases in the relevant time period, we *can* say that arbitrage is more likely to be profitable if the time period is, say, 180 days than if it is 60 days. The reason we can say this is that the dollar amount realized from employing a given sum to take advantage of the difference between 2.23 percent and 1.36 percent increases directly and proportionately with increases in the time period.

In the real world, middle exchange rates and interest rates do not exhibit perfect linearity, but they generally come close enough that the linearity assumption is reasonable, at least for the time periods that are relevant to most forward contracts. On the other hand, neither arbitrageurs' transaction costs nor (normally) spreads increase in proportion to increases in the time period. The conclusion that follows is that the chance for interest arbitrage increases as the time period increases. A gap between the forward premium or discount and the interest differential like that of the guilder–dollar example will not induce interest arbitrage if the time period is a few days, but as the time period lengthens, a point is reached at which the same gap *does* induce interest arbitrage.

Muddying the waters a bit is the risk factor. In general, the risks associated with financial activity increase more than proportionately with increases in time periods, which explains why long-term interest rates are generally higher than short-term interest rates. To some extent, no doubt, this risk factor tends to cause the neutral band to widen as a function of time. For the generally short-term time periods applicable to interest arbitrage, however, the risks are normally small. For this reason, the risk factor does not normally invalidate the rule that interest arbitrage opportunities increase with increases in the time period.

The Impact of Interest Arbitrage on Financial Markets

In the highly competitive environment in which most forward trading occurs, interest arbitrage opportunities tend to be brief. Therefore, the forex market's practitioners generally operate under the assumption that, at any given moment, IRP effectively holds. Thus, a forex trader who wants to make two-way forward quotations that will approximately balance purchases and sales is likely to quote forward rates based on Equations 6–2 and 6–6 or their inexact cousins.

If interest arbitrage opportunities tend to be brief, then it is relevant to ask whether or not the phenomenon of interest arbitrage is important. The answer to the question is clearly yes. In the first place, even if interest arbitrage never occurred, its absence would mean that the forex market's participants were working to avoid it; arbitrage would then be important because of its role in enforcing IRP. In the second place, interest arbitrage opportunities do arise, and frequently enough that many of the forex market's participants are constantly on the lookout for them.

In understanding how interest arbitrage works in practice, it is necessary to distinguish two forms of it which will be designated here as *complete interest arbitrage* and *partial interest arbitrage.* **Complete interest arbitrage** is a four-step process in which the arbitrageur borrows in one currency, buys another currency spot, buys an asset or lends with the other currency, and sells the other currency forward to lock in a gain. In **partial interest arbitrage,** a forward contract is used to lock in a gain as in complete interest arbitrage, but the arbitrage process involves either the acquisition or the use of funds, not both. Partial arbitrage thus entails one less transaction than complete arbitrage.

Recall again the guilder–dollar example presented in connection with the explanation of the inexact method for discerning interest arbitrage opportunities. Assume this time, however, that the dollar borrowing rate of 8.62 percent is higher than the rate that the arbitrageur can earn on dollars at his/her disposal. In the earlier example, if the arbitrageur begins the operation by borrowing dollars at 8.62 percent, the operation has four steps and is complete interest arbitrage. If, however, the arbitrageur already has the necessary funds and does not have to borrow them, the operation is an example of partial interest arbitrage. Partial arbitrage involves an interest opportunity cost, but since this cost would be less than 8.62 percent, the gain would be larger than that from complete arbitrage. This implies that partial arbitrage may be profitable when complete arbitrage is not.

Partial interest arbitrage can also omit the lending or investing step. Assume, for example, that a U.S. multinational firm desires to make expenditures in guilders on which it anticipates a rate of return as high as 10 percent. The guilders are to be obtained by borrowing. Assume that the 7.24 percent guilder interest rate used earlier is the yield rate on a guilder-denominated security or time deposit, not the rate at which the firm can borrow. The borrowing rate, let's assume, is somewhat higher, say 7.42 percent. Clearly, the firm is justified in borrowing, but should it borrow *guilders?* Assuming the 8.62 percent dollar borrowing rate still applies, the answer is no. The firm should borrow *dollars,* convert them into guilders at the spot rate, and buy dollars forward, thereby locking in an effective reduction in the cost of borrowing guilders. This case, too, is one of partial interest arbitrage. Three steps are involved in the arbitrage process here—borrowing, selling spot, and buying forward. Omitted from the *arbitrage* process (but not from the operation as a whole) is the use of the borrowed funds.

The most ideal conditions for interest arbitrage exist when the costs and risks of arbitrage operations are low, access to the forex market and to different money markets is unrestricted, and both interest rates and exchange rates fluctuate freely. Because these conditions exist more completely in the Eurocurrency market than elsewhere, the Eurocurrency market is the setting for much interest arbitrage activity.

Interest Arbitrage and the Eurocurrency Market   As was pointed out in Chapter 2, bank deposits denominated in currencies other than the national currencies of the banks in which they are held are called *Eurocurrency deposits.* This term encompasses all such foreign currency-denominated deposits, whether or not they are held in European banks. In referring to a specific Eurocurrency, it is customary to precede the currency's name with the prefix *Euro.* Thus, U.S. dollar-denominated deposits in London or Singapore are "Eurodollars," while yen-denominated deposits in the same cities are "Euroyen."[3]

The banks that participate in the Eurocurrency market are, of course, called *Eurobanks.* They lend in the same currencies as those in which they have deposit liabilities. When a Euroloan is made, the borrower receives a demand deposit in the country in whose currency the loan is denominated, and the loan

---

[3]In order to distinguish the far eastern part of the Eurocurrency market from the rest of it, it is common to refer to the far eastern component as the *Asia* currency market and to substitute *Asia* or *Asian* for *Euro* in referring to these operations. The Asia currency market is thoroughly integrated into the Eurocurrency market and can be regarded as a part of it.

is generally payable in the currency in which it is made. When a Eurocurrency time deposit matures, it is also payable in the currency in which it is denominated. Accordingly, Eurobanks maintain small reserves in the form of demand deposit balances in the currencies in which they have time deposit liabilities, and they make certain that they can quickly raise additional funds in those currencies as needed.

The lending and deposit operations of Eurobanks are carried out in part with nonbank customers, but most of these operations are interbank transactions. Banks seeking safe and highly liquid investment media often place funds into Eurocurrency deposits, and banks needing additional funds can readily obtain them by getting Euroloans from other banks. The spread between interbank Eurodeposit and Euroloan rates is smaller than the deposit and loan spreads of domestic banking markets, but it is usually somewhat wider than the bid–ask spreads in interbank forward transactions.

The U.S. dollar is by far the most important Eurocurrency, but Eurocurrency loans and deposits are readily available in numerous European currencies (including the Ecu), the yen, the Australian dollar, and the Canadian dollar. Because the Eurocurrency market offers a wide choice among currencies, a high degree of freedom, maturity dates for loans and deposits that match the standard maturities of interbank forward contracts, and few risks, it provides an almost ideal environment for carrying out interest arbitrage. Accordingly, the IRP neutral band applicable to Eurocurrency market operations tends to be narrow.

To illustrate this point, a study by Otani and Tiwari that measured the width of the neutral band in transactions between Eurodollars and Euroyen in London found the average width of the band to be 0.146 percent when measured for 3-month time periods on the basis of quarterly interest rates.[4] With reference to Exhibit 6.3, which uses annual interest rates, this would be equivalent to a band of 0.58 percent, which is about the same as the width of the neutral band shown there. The Otani and Tiwari study employed the concept of partial interest arbitrage.

The neutral band tends to be narrower for transactions occurring entirely within the Eurocurrency market than for transactions between domestic money markets because the relevant spreads and transaction costs tend to be smaller in the Eurocurrency market. Moreover, whereas government-imposed restrictions can affect the ability to conduct arbitrage between domestic money markets, there are virtually no such restrictions to contend with in the Eurocurrency market.

We must consider, however, the matter of risk. Recall the earlier statement that the width of the neutral band is affected, though usually to a small extent,

---

[4]Ichiro Otani and Siddharth Tiwari, "Capital Controls and Interest Rate Parity: The Japanese Experience," *IMF Staff Papers,* November 1981, pp. 793–815. Reprinted in Donald R. Lessard, ed., *International Financial Management: Theory and Applications,* 2d ed. (New York: John Wiley & Sons, 1985), pp. 197–210.

by the risk factor. It is arguable that, because Eurobanking is less regulated than domestic banking, it is also riskier. Thus, governments are under less obligation to bail out troubled banks when their problems arise from their Eurobanking operations rather than from strictly domestic origins. For this reason, it cannot be stated with total confidence that the IRP neutral band is invariably narrower in the Eurocurrency market than in all other situations. On the other hand, most transactions in the Eurocurrency market are made by banks that are very highly rated, and very few Eurobanks have failed to fulfill any Eurocurrency market commitments.

In general, the political risk associated with Eurobanking is both small and homogeneous among assets and financial centers. The risk is small because there is little likelihood that a financial center's government would interfere with the realization of a locked-in arbitrage gain. It is homogeneous because center countries differ little in their probabilities of government interference. Moreover, all of the transactions associated with interest arbitrage may occur in the same center. Since there is little likelihood that a center country government will take action affecting loans or deposits in any foreign currency, there is little reason to expect the political risk in a center country to vary as a function of the currencies in which loans and deposits are denominated.

Outside the Eurocurrency market, the situation is somewhat different. Suppose, for example, that an arbitrageur were to discover a discrepancy between U.S. and Canadian interest rates that warranted obtaining a Canadian dollar time deposit in a bank in Canada. Every aspect of the arbitrage process is then subject to the jurisdiction of either the U.S. government or the Canadian government. In the parallel case where arbitrage occurs between Eurodollars and Euro-Canadian dollars in London, only the transfers of bank deposits associated with the spot exchange and the forward exchange at its maturity are subject to the control of the U.S. and Canadian governments. It follows, therefore, that the political risk is more diverse outside the Eurocurrency market than within it. In any event, political risk is ordinarily not a major factor in interest arbitrage, whether it occurs within the Eurocurrency market or outside it.

Interest Arbitrage between Markets Without question, much of the interest arbitrage that occurs is between the Eurocurrency market and domestic money markets. The basic reason for this is that there is sufficient market segmentation that interest rates in a particular currency are not brought into intermarket equality. Typically, Eurocurrency deposit rates are a little higher than domestic deposit rates, while Eurocurrency loan rates are a little lower. These differences in interest rates allow for profitable arbitrage between the Eurocurrency market and domestic money markets. If the lending rate in the U.S. domestic money market is higher than the Eurodollar lending rate by a wide enough margin, a bank (foreign or U.S.) with lending offices in the United States may find it profitable to borrow in a currency other than the U.S. dollar in the Eurocurrency market, sell that currency for dollars in a spot exchange, lend the dollars in the domestic money market, and cover by buying the borrowed currency forward.

It is also possible for interest arbitrage to occur between domestic money markets. If, for example, the differential between interest rates on U.S. Treasury bills and commercial paper and their Canadian equivalents departs sufficiently from the forward discount on the Canadian dollar, there will be arbitrage between markets.

Forward Swaps

The popularity of forward swaps rests fundamentally on their usefulness in reducing and otherwise managing the exchange risk. This usefulness rests on their flexibility and the built-in protection that IRP provides against the exchange risk. The built-in protection results from the fact that, when a currency changes in exchange value, spot and forward rates tend to adjust in the same direction so as to maintain IRP.

Assume, for example, that a bank swaps with another bank so that the first bank buys marks spot and sells them forward in equal amounts. If the mark's exchange value subsequently declines, the bank will experience an opportunity loss from its purchase of spot marks, but if IRP holds, it will have an offsetting gain from its forward sale. The swap format will thus protect the bank against the exchange risk.

As will be shown, a single swap provides imperfect protection against the exchange risk. The residual risk can be eliminated, however, with one or more additional swaps. Moreover, as we shall see, to the extent that a party is willing to bear the risks associated with swaps, they can be used to arrange forward maturities that are in line with the party's expectations.

The Uses of Forward Swaps

Our examination of interest arbitrage has shed some light on how forward swaps can be used to lower the exchange risk. In covered interest arbitrage, the arbitrageur locks in a gain by combining a spot exchange with a forward exchange. Using a swap for these two exchanges is standard procedure. A swap does not provide 100 percent cover, however. This is because the amounts of at least one of the currencies are the same in both parts of a swap. With a swap, however, the arbitrageur should be able to reduce the bid−ask spread by comparison with relying on outright transactions, and the arbitrageur also saves time.

Forward swaps are also used to roll over existing foreign currency exposures to maturities that are deemed more desirable. Assume, for example, that a firm has an asset that will provide a receipt of marks in 2 business days. If its financial managers believe that the spot mark will rise during the following month, or if the firm must make a mark outlay in a month, it might want to enter into a swap in which it sells marks spot and buys them 1 month forward. The effect is the same as if the firm arranged two separate exchanges, but by combining these exchanges into a swap, it saves time and probably obtains more favorable exchange rates. Suppose that the receipt of marks is to occur in a month rather than in 2 business days, but either the mark is expected to rise subsequently or a mark payment is scheduled to occur in, say, 3 months. The firm might then want to consider a forward–forward swap in which it agrees to sell marks in a month and to buy them in 3 months.

Even without any rollover of an existing position, a forward swap may be chosen over an outright forward transaction because arranging a swap generally consumes less time. Because exchange rates are volatile, and because a spot exchange can often be arranged more quickly than an outright forward, a firm wanting a particular forward position may elect to combine a spot exchange with a swap. Suppose, for example, that a firm wants to buy yen 2 months forward, but fears that by the time it can arrange an outright forward purchase, the yen will have moved upward. Its best course of action would probably be to buy yen spot and then, as quickly as possible, arrange a swap in which it would sell yen spot and buy them 2 months forward. If the yen's price were to rise before the swap were arranged, what the firm lost from the increase in the forward rate would be approximately offset by what it gained from the increase in the spot rate. This procedure may involve greater transaction costs than an outright forward contract, but the exchange risk protection gained may more than justify the additional cost.

Another important use of forward swaps is to manage the risks associated with **swap positions,** i.e., situations in which forex purchases match sales in amount, but not in maturity. Such positions need not arise from swaps, but the result is the same as if they had.

The Risks of Swap Positions

Earlier, it was indicated that a forward swap provides built-in protection against the exchange risk, but that this protection is imperfect. We now consider why the protection is imperfect. The simple answer to this question is that it is imperfect because swap rates vary, thereby subjecting the holders of swap positions to a type of exchange rate risk known as the swap rate risk. This risk is small, however, relative to the sums involved.

Here is an illustration of the swap rate risk. Assume that on day 1 of a 90-day period, Colossal Bank enters into a forward–forward swap involving exchanges of Swiss francs for U.S. dollars. Colossal agrees to buy 5 million Swiss francs 30 days forward at SF 1.5374 per dollar and to sell 5 million Swiss francs 90 days forward at SF 1.5422. The spot exchange rate on day 1 is SF 1.5345. The 30-day swap rate $(S^* - F^{*t}_0)$ is thus minus 29 points, and the 90-day swap rate is minus 77 points.

Now assume that 30 days later, the spot rate has moved to SF 1.5604 and that the 60-day forward rate is SF 1.5628, i.e., a difference of 24 points. Colossal Bank now enters into a spot-forward swap that is designed to offset the earlier swap. Specifically, Colossal sells 5 million Swiss francs spot in order to offset its earlier 30-day forward purchase, and it buys 5 million Swiss francs 60 days forward in order to offset its earlier 90-day forward sale.

Ignoring any other forex transactions by Colossal Bank, the results of these two swaps can be summarized as follows:

	Points	Dollars
Results on day 30		
Day 30 spot sale at SF 1.5604		$3,204,307
Day 1 30-day forward purchase at SF 1.5374		3,252,244
Loss	(230)	($ 47,937)
Results on day 90		
Day 1 90-day forward sale at SF 1.5422		$3,242,122
Day 30 60-day forward purchase at SF 1.5628		3,199,286
Gain	206	$ 42,736
Net loss	(24)	($ 5,201)

Colossal has had a net cash flow loss from the two swaps of $5,201. Furthermore, since it had a realized loss of $47,937 on day 30, it has incurred an interest opportunity loss. Given the sums involved, the losses are small, but they are sufficient to demonstrate that holding swap positions involves risk.

The key to understanding why a net loss occurs in this case is to look at the swap rates. On day 1, Colossal bought Swiss francs 30 days forward at a swap rate of 29 points and sold them 90 days forward at a swap rate of 77 points. The difference between the swap rates was 48 points. Since the forward Swiss franc was trading at a discount, these 48 points constituted a built-in loss that, had swap rates remained unchanged, Colossal would have recovered by entering into the second swap. By the time of the second swap, however, the 60-day swap rate was 24 points, which was half the gap between the 30-day and 90-day forward rates that existed on day 1. As a result, Colossal had a net loss of 24 points.

If the 60-day forward rate had been SF 1.5652 on day 30 instead of SF 1.5628, i.e., if the swap rate had been minus 48 points, there would have been no loss in terms of points. The dollar gain on day 90 would then have been $47,642 instead of $42,736, and the net loss would have been reduced to only $295 plus the opportunity interest cost on the realized loss occurring on day 30. A loss this small is negligible.

Components of the Swap Rate Risk   By considering the implications of the IRP equations and the neutral band, we can readily see the origins of the swap rate risk. From Equations 6–4 and 6–7 we can see that swap rates ($F_0^t - S_0$ or $S^* - F^*{}_0^t$) are determined by (1) the interest rate differential ($r_{a,0}^t - r_{b,0}^t$), (2) the values of the spot and forward rates, (3) the interest rate in Country B, and (4) the amount of time. Moreover, since IRP does not necessarily hold exactly, a swap rate can vary independently of the right side of these equations within limits determined by the neutral band.

In practice, large variations in swap rates are most likely to occur because of changes in the interest rate differential. If changes in this differential can be predicted, then swap rate changes can also be predicted. For this reason, predicting the change in the interest rate differential and the approximate time of the change are the keys to success in managing the swap rate risk.

Swap Rate Speculation   The swap rate risk is small enough so that ignoring it is arguably a defensible policy. On the other hand, it is arguable that when a bank does many millions of dollars' worth of forward transactions daily, the absolute amount of the gains or losses from swap rate variations may be large enough to warrant action to reduce the possible losses, provided that such action is both effective and low-cost.

There is evidence that, in fact, banks adapt their swap positions to their swap rate expectations.[5] To the extent that they do so, they engage in swap rate speculation. It is reasonable to assume that banks engage in such speculation because of its low cost, the small risk involved, and the fact that their other operations take their interest rate expectations into account.

The key question in swap rate speculation is how do you arrange a swap to gain from an expected change in swap rates? You can answer this question by applying the old rule of buying cheap and selling dear. This means that for time periods *after* a swap rate change is expected to occur, you should be a net buyer when swap rates are expected to increase and a net seller when they are expected to decrease, relying primarily on interest rate forecasts to decide which way swap rates are likely to move. In applying this rule, it is important to note, you need to take into account whether swap rates have a positive or negative value.

Applying this rule to the Swiss franc–U.S. dollar case presented earlier, we can surmise that the swap rate change there, which was mathematically positive, probably occurred because Swiss interest rates fell relative to U.S. interest rates. Such an interest rate change would have reduced the forward discount on the Swiss franc, i.e., it would have tended to increase swap rates. Colossal Bank had a loss because the first swap it entered into committed it to sell Swiss francs at a swap rate (minus 77 points) which was destined to increase. Had this first swap been reversed, Colossal Bank would have been positioned to gain from the subsequent rise in swap rates.

Summary

Most forward transactions are interbank swaps that combine spot exchanges with reversing forward exchanges or forward exchanges with other forward exchanges with different maturities. An outright forward contract provides for a single exchange of currencies. In interbank trading, forward contracts are generally traded with 30-day maturity intervals, but forward contracts for less

---

[5]See Arvind Mahajan and Dileep Mehta, "Strong Form Efficiency of the Foreign Exchange Market and Bank Positions," *Journal of Financial Research*, Fall 1984, pp. 197–205; and, by the same authors, "Swaps, Expectations, and Exchange Rates," *Journal of Banking and Finance*, March 1986, pp. 7–20.

than 30 days are also common. Some forwards have maturities exceeding a year, but it is essentially correct to view forward contracts as short-term financial instruments.

The primary use of forward contracts is for hedging, and forward hedging has been mainly concerned with the component of the exchange risk known as transaction exposure. There is some use of forward contracts to hedge translation or accounting exposure, but this practice is vulnerable to the criticism that translation exposure is not a sound basis for hedging the exchange risk. The soundest basis for hedging the exchange risk is the concept of economic exposure, but economic exposure is often difficult to quantify. As the understanding and measurement of economic exposure improves, this concept is certain to have more influence on forward hedging.

According to the condition known as IRP, interest-rate differentials between countries tend to be offset by the forward premiums or discounts between their currencies. A discrepancy between an interest-rate differential and the corresponding forward premium or discount will lead to interest arbitrage if it falls outside the neutral band, within which IRP effectively holds. The width of the neutral band is a function of the interest rate and exchange rate trading spreads, the arbitrageur's transaction costs, the (normally small) risks involved, and time. Complete interest arbitrage is a four-step process involving both borrowing and either lending or investing. Partial interest arbitrage is a three-step process in which either the borrowing or the lending-investing step is omitted.

The popularity of forward swaps rests on their flexibility as a tool of risk management. They can be used to effect interest arbitrage, to roll over existing forex positions to more desirable maturities, and to achieve desired forward positions more quickly than would be possible with outright forward contracts. They are also used to manage the risks of swap positions, which are forex positions in which purchases and sales are matched as to amount but not as to maturity. The main risk involved in holding a swap position is that a change in the interest-rate differential between countries will alter the swap rate, which is the difference between a forward rate and the corresponding spot rate. The swap rate risk is normally small, however, and certainly much smaller than the risk of holding an open forward position.

References

Andrews, Michael D. "Recent Trends in the U.S. Foreign Exchange Market." Federal Reserve Bank of New York *Quarterly Review*, Summer 1984, pp. 38–47.

Bahmani-Oskooee, Mohsen, and Satya P. Das. "Transaction Costs and the Interest Parity Theorem." *Journal of Political Economy*, August 1985, pp. 793–799.

Cornell, Bradford W. "Determinants of the Bid–Ask Spread on Forward Exchange Contracts under Floating Exchange Rates." *Journal of International Business Studies*, Fall 1978, pp. 33–41.

Deardorff, Alan. "One-Way Arbitrage and Its Implications for Foreign Exchange Markets." *Journal of Political Economy*, April 1979, pp. 351–364.

Federal Reserve Bank of New York. "Summary of Results of U.S. Foreign Exchange Market Survey Conducted in April 1989." 1989.

Frenkel, Jacob A., and Richard M. Levich. "Covered Interest Arbitrage: Unexploited Profits?" *Journal of Political Economy*, April 1975, pp. 325–338.

_____. "Transaction Costs and Interest Arbitrage: Tranquil versus Turbulent Periods." *Journal of Political Economy*, November–December 1977, pp. 1,209–1,226.

Grabbe, J. Orlin. *International Financial Markets*. New York: Elsevier, 1986, Chapter 4.

Mahajan, Arvind, and Dileep Mehta. "Strong Form Efficiency of the Foreign Exchange Market and Bank Positions." *Journal of Financial Research*, Fall 1984, pp. 197–205.

_____. "Swaps, Expectations, and Exchange Rates." *Journal of Banking and Finance*, March 1986, pp. 7–20.

Otani, Ichiro, and Siddharth Tiwari. "Capital Controls and Interest Rate Parity: The Japanese Experience." *IMF Staff Papers*, November 1981, pp. 793–815. Reprinted in Donald R. Lessard, ed. *International Financial Management: Theory and Applications*, 2d ed. New York: John Wiley & Sons, 1985, pp. 197–210.

Riehl, Heinz, and Rita M. Rodriguez. *Foreign Exchange and Money Markets*. New York: McGraw-Hill, 1983.

Shapiro, Alan C. *Multinational Financial Management*. 3d ed. Boston: Allyn & Bacon, 1989, Chapters 8 through 11.

Tygier, Claude. *Basic Handbook of Foreign Exchange*. London: Euromoney Publications, 1983, Chapters 8 and 9.

Questions

1. What is a forward option contract?
2. Summarize the rules for determining the value date for a 30-day forward contract.
3. Give examples that show (a) how transaction exposure can overlap translation exposure and (b) how transaction exposure can differ from translation exposure.
4. Explain how the concept of economic exposure differs from that of transaction exposure.
5. Provide an example that illustrates a case where the forward hedging of the exchange risk is not also the forward covering of the exchange risk.
6. What determines whether a particular currency has a forward premium or a forward discount in terms of the U.S. dollar?
7. What is the nature of the bias in the inexact method for determining when an opportunity for interest arbitrage exists? Under what circumstances is this bias greatest?
8. Assuming that there is a uniform (linear) short-term interest rate differential between two currencies, why is it that the chances for interest arbitrage tend to increase as the time period lengthens?
9. What are the characteristics of the Eurocurrency market that make it an especially appropriate vehicle for the conduct of interest arbitrage?
10. Explain why it is that most forward contracts are swaps.
11. What is a forward swap position? What are the possible causes of the swap rate risk associated with holding such a position?

Problems

1. Assume that a firm requests an outright forward contract from AAA Bank with a value date 78 days hence that will obligate AAA Bank to sell marks forward for that period. If AAA agrees to the exchange, how could it use a spot–forward swap with a 90-day maturity to minimize the exchange risk involved in providing the customer with the desired contract?

2. Assume that AAA Bank offers the following two-way mark/dollar quotations:

0.61005

Spot	1 Month	3 Months	6 Months
1.6472–82	30–28	80–74	182–170

1.6442-1.6454   *1.6392-1.6408*

What is the outright bid price for marks (the ask price for dollars) 3 months forward? What are the outright ask prices for marks 1 and 6 months forward? On an annualized basis, what are the forward premiums on the mark in these three quotations?

3. Assuming that there are no transaction costs or other factors to prevent IRP from holding exactly, that the spot and 90-day forward rates for the pound sterling are, respectively, $1.5760/pound and $1.5605/pound, and that the relevant dollar interest rate is 8.72 percent on an annual basis, what is the comparable interest rate in the United Kingdom if IRP holds exactly? (Hint: Remember that the United Kingdom has a 365-day financial year.)

4. Assume that a New York forex dealer is quoting the spot Dutch guilder at Fl2.0680–92 for interbank trades. Also assume that the Euroguilder interbank deposit and loan rates with 30-day maturities are 5.625 percent and 5.750 percent, respectively. The 30-day Eurodollar deposit and loan rates are, respectively, 9.6875 percent and 9.8125 percent. The dealer wants to make a two-way quotation for guilders 30 days forward that is consistent with IRP. Using middle exchange rates and interest rates and assuming a 16-point spread, what will be the dealer's 30-day two-way quotation based on the calculation of exact IRP?

5. Purehex Corporation, a U.S.-based firm with extensive foreign operations, wants to borrow $5 million for 60 days. It can borrow the desired funds in the Eurodollar market at an annual interest rate of 9.60 percent. Alternatively, it can borrow Euroguilders at 5.80 percent or Euro-French francs at 8.60 percent. The spot rates at which it can sell guilders and francs for dollars are, respectively Fl2.0010/dollar and FF6.0255/dollar, and the 60-day forward rates at which it can buy guilders and francs are, respectively, Fl1.9885/dollar and FF6.0180/dollar. Ignoring transaction costs, in which currency should Purehex borrow and why?

6. Assume that you work for the London branch of a U.S. bank and are allowed to conduct interest arbitrage operations through forward swaps in which the quantity of dollars in each part of the swap is $5 million. The relevant mark/dollar exchange rates at which you can arrange a 90-day swap are currently 1.7021 spot and 1.7002 90 days forward. Eurocur-

rency interest rates for 90 days (on an annual basis) include the following: for dollars, 8.50 percent on deposits and 8.625 percent on loans, and for marks, 8.375 percent on deposits and 8.50 percent on loans. What is the premium or discount on the forward mark? Ignoring transaction costs, is complete interest arbitrage feasible? Explain.

7. Assume that a forex trader is under orders to avoid taking a net overall position in marks, but is allowed to accept swap positions, i.e., positions in which overall forex purchases and sales are equal as to amount, but different as to maturity. Also assume that the trader's bank is forecasting that within 60 days, Eurodollar interest rates will rise relative to Euromark interest rates and that this change will persist for at least a year. Assuming that swaps are available in which the bank sells marks 2 months forward and buys them 1 year forward, or vice versa, what should the trader do to act on the basis of the bank's interest rate forecast?

8. Now assume that to the information in Question 7, we add that the Euromark deposit rate is 6.625 percent for all maturities from 60 days to 360 days, the Eurodollar deposit rate is 8.500 percent for the same maturities, the current spot rate is DM1.6350/dollar, and the 60-day and 360-day rates applicable to forward–forward swaps are, respectively, DM1.6300/dollar and DM1.6067/dollar. Also assume that the quantity of dollars that can be committed to each side of a swap is $5 million. Based on this information, answer the following questions:

   a. Assuming the trader makes the appropriate swap today and that on Day 60 the Eurodollar deposit rate is 8.8250 percent for all relevant maturities, while the mark deposit rate is 6.600 percent for all relevant maturities, what will be the approximate realized gain, ignoring transaction costs, if the spot rate remains unchanged, IRP holds, and the trader makes the appropriate swap on Day 60?

   b. What will be the trader's approximate gain if the spot rate existing on Day 60 is DM1.6130/dollar and everything else is as in Part a?

CHAPTER 7

The Money Market Alternative and the Currency Futures Market

■

Among the alternatives to the forward market are forex (currency) futures, forex (currency) options, currency swaps, and the combination of spot exchanges with appropriate money market transactions. For convenience, the last of these alternatives is generally called the money market alternative. This chapter examines the money market and futures alternatives. Chapter 8 examines currency options, and Chapter 16 examines currency swaps. Because the money market alternative is comparatively uncomplicated, the bulk of this chapter deals with currency futures.

The abundance of alternatives to the forward market points to the fact that forward contracts fall short of perfection in some situations. There are many currencies for which forward contracts are unavailable, and in the currencies for which they are available, small-scale hedgers and speculators generally lack access to them. They often have less than the desired flexibility and lack liquidity.

Like forward contracts, the alternatives examined in this chapter and Chapter 8 are primarily short term in nature. It should be kept in mind, however, that alternative techniques for short-term exchange risk management exist other than those examined in these two chapters. For example, a multinational firm with financial operations in a number of currencies may employ a technique known as **netting,** in which it offsets the foreign currency positions of its various operating units against each other to minimize the volume of forex transactions required to satisfactorily manage the exchange risk.

The Money Market Alternative

Whether for hedging or speculation, a viable alternative to the forward market is often found by combining a money market transaction with a spot forex transaction. Suppose, for example, that a U.S. firm is to receive a specific quantity of Canadian dollars in 30 days and that the firm wishes to hedge the exchange risk. Rather than sell Canadian dollars forward, the firm could arrange a 30-day loan in Canadian dollars whose amount equals the present value of its future receipt, buy U.S. dollars spot, and pay the loan with the Canadian dollars received 30 days later. Similarly, if someone without an existing position in Canadian dollars wishes to speculate that the Canadian dollar will decline, that person could borrow Canadian dollars, convert the loan proceeds into U.S. dollars at the spot rate, and plan on paying the loan at maturity by buying Canadian dollars at the then current (and presumably lower) spot rate.

When an obligation exists to make a future payment in a foreign currency, the exchange risk can be hedged by calculating the present value of the obligation, borrowing the equivalent amount in domestic currency, buying the foreign currency spot, and holding an interest-earning asset until the payment date. Similarly, if someone wishes to speculate that a certain currency will rise against the dollar, that person could borrow dollars, purchase the currency spot, and invest the funds for the life of the loan in the expectation of buying dollars spot at a lower future price.

Money Market Hedging

There is a pronounced tendency for money market hedging and forward hedging to yield similar outcomes. Indeed, if IRP always held exactly, transaction size were infinitely divisible, there were no transaction costs or risks, and the relevant interest rates for the two hedging techniques were the same, the outcomes would be identical. In practice, however, such perfect conditions do not hold, with the practical consequence that one technique is likely to be preferable to the other in a given case. The markets for the leading currencies, however, match these conditions closely enough that the superiority of one technique over the other is likely to be slight, though still significant.

A moment's reflection should indicate why money market hedging and forward hedging tend to provide similar outcomes. Assuming that IRP effectively holds and that the interest rates in money market hedging are about the same as those relevant to IRP, the two techniques tend to yield similar outcomes because they both depend on interest rates in two countries and the spot exchange rate between their currencies.

In reality, IRP does not usually hold exactly, and the interest rates applicable to IRP are not necessarily applicable to money market hedging. This means that the outcomes of the two techniques may differ significantly. Moreover, when the relevant interest rates are not identical, it is likely that forward hedging will be slightly preferable unless access to a relevant national money market is restricted in a way that favors money market hedging. Forward hedging requires fewer transactions, which means that it is simpler and often cheaper in terms of transaction costs. Nevertheless, situations arise in which money market hedging is preferable, even though forward hedging is readily available.

AAA Bank and Pilut Corporation   Assume that two U.S. firms stand to lose from existing exposures in Dutch guilders if the guilder's exchange value rises during the next 60 days. One, AAA Bank, is short Fl8 million in forward contracts with 60 days to maturity. The other, Pilut Corporation, is a multinational firm with a Euroguilder loan maturing in 60 days that requires the payment of Fl8 million at maturity. Assume that IRP effectively holds and that AAA Bank has ready access to interbank exchange rates and money market interest rates that are relevant to interest arbitrage and, therefore, to IRP. Assume also, however, that while Pilut Corporation has access to exchange rates that are very close to those available to AAA Bank and can obtain a rate of return on short-term guilder-denominated assets that matches what AAA Bank can obtain, Pilut has to pay a significantly higher interest rate on a short-term dollar loan than does AAA Bank.

Each firm can effect a money market hedge by borrowing dollars for 60 days, purchasing guilders spot, and investing in a guilder-denominated asset. Each could effect a forward hedge by an outright purchase of guilders or by a swap combining a forward purchase of guilders with a spot sale. If a swap is used, the spot sale can be offset by a virtually simultaneous spot purchase.

In this situation, it is likely that both firms would prefer the forward hedge. Its superiority would be particularly pronounced for Pilut since it would be charged a higher interest rate than AAA Bank on a short-term borrowing. Even the bank would probably prefer the forward hedge, however, because it would be simpler and involve lower transaction costs. Whereas the money market hedge requires three transactions, a forward hedge with an outright purchase of guilders requires one. A forward hedge combining a forward swap with a spot purchase of guilders would require three currency exchanges, but the bid-ask spreads involved would probably be less than the spreads involved in the money market hedge. In addition, the forward hedge avoids the commitment of funds to a guilder-denominated asset that the money market hedge entails.

Choosing the Money Market Hedge   Despite the apparent advantages of forward hedging, situations can easily arise in which money market hedging is preferable. Suppose, for example, that either AAA Bank or Pilut Corporation has dollar balances available with which they can effect a money market hedge without borrowing. The money market hedge might then be preferable because the opportunity cost (in dollars) of acquiring a guilder-denominated asset could be less than the explicit interest cost of borrowing dollars plus the transaction costs associated with borrowing.

Another situation favoring the money market hedge arises when market segmentation allows selected borrowers to have access to credit at below-market interest rates. Such market segmentation commonly results from government subsidy programs. If, for example, a French manufacturing firm qualifies for government-sponsored credits at artificially low interest rates, it might well decide to use money market hedging rather than forward hedging in protecting itself against the exchange risk associated with fuel imports denominated in dollars.

Money market hedging is also likely to be preferable when a hedging party can obtain a higher rate of return than what is generally available on short-term assets. Suppose, for example, that Pilut Corporation can generate a higher rate of return from the internal use of guilders than it can obtain from a short-term investment in a guilder-denominated asset. The money market hedge might then be clearly superior to a forward contract in hedging its Euroguilder loan.

Occasionally, when the forex market becomes unusually volatile, the risks involved in forex dealing cause dealer banks to protect themselves by widening the bid–ask spreads in forward trading. For example, a bid–ask spread that is normally about 16 points may suddenly expand to 50 points. When this happens money market hedging is likely to become decidedly preferable to forward hedging. Finally, there are many currencies in which forward contracts are unavailable. Needless to say, using the money market hedge may be very appealing in such cases.

Money Market Speculation

In money market speculation, a speculator makes a spot exchange in anticipation of a change in the spot rate, possibly after first borrowing the funds used for the spot exchange. If a currency is expected to depreciate, a speculator may borrow it and sell it spot in anticipation of buying the currency back at a lower price. If a currency is expected to appreciate, a speculator may buy it spot and hold it in interest-earning form in anticipation of a rise in its value.

For the same reasons that were advanced in connection with money market hedging, forward speculation is generally slightly preferable to money market hedging, assuming that there is no government interference in the relevant markets. Also for the same reasons, however, there are situations where money market speculation is preferable.

Money market speculation is particularly likely when there are no good alternatives available. Forward speculation is often ruled out either because no forward market exists or because access to forward transactions is closed to would-be speculators by bank practice or government policy. If neither futures nor option contracts are available, money market speculation may be chosen simply because it can be chosen.

Governments with weakening currencies often attempt to prevent speculation against their currencies by combining credit controls with exchange controls. It is difficult to suppress such speculation, however, because money is the most fungible (substitutable) of assets. Numerous ingenious techniques have been developed for getting around such controls, with the consequence that making them highly effective may be impossible or excessively costly to the economy. Assume, for example, that a company (either domestic or foreign) operating in Brazil wishes to shift funds from cruzeiros to dollars in anticipation of a rapid depreciation of the cruzeiro, but that the Brazilian government requires banks to refrain from lending to finance currency speculation. If the firm already has enough cruzeiros for its working capital needs, but has a line of credit with a domestic bank that allows it to routinely borrow to finance normal operations, it may request a working capital loan with the real purpose of financing the speculative purchase of dollars. If the Brazilian government uses exchange controls to prevent such purchases, the firm may attempt to circumvent the controls by such techniques as overinvoicing imports or turning cruzeiros over to a Brazilian subsidiary of a foreign firm in exchange for a dollar deposit supplied by the subsidiary's parent company.

Speculating by Buying a Depreciating Currency   It may be tempting to assume that money market speculation always entails the spot sale of a currency one expects to depreciate, but this is not necessarily the case. Suppose the expected rate of return available in a country whose currency is expected to depreciate exceeds the interest rate in another country by more than enough to offset the expected depreciation. Money market speculation then leads to the spot *purchase* of the currency that is expected to depreciate. If, for example, the cruzeiro interest rate is high enough, a speculator may purchase cruzeiros spot even if the cruzeiro is expected to depreciate by a large percentage.

The condition governing money market speculation can be expressed as follows:

$$1 + r_{a,0}^t \left(\frac{t}{360}\right) \neq \frac{1}{S_0}\left[1 + r_{b,0}^t \left(\frac{t}{360}\right)\right] E_0^t \qquad (7-1)$$

Aside from the inequality sign in this condition, the only difference between it and Equation 6–1 is that E_0^t has been substituted for F_0^t. The term E_0^t stands for the expected spot rate on Date t as of Date 0. Both exchange rates in Inequality 7–1 are expressed as units of Country A's currency per unit of Country B's currency. If the exchange rates are expressed as units of B's currency per unit of A's currency, S_0^* can be substituted for $1/S_0$ and $1/E_0^{*t}$ can be substituted for E_0^t so as to arrive at the following condition:

$$1 + r_{a,0}^t \left(\frac{t}{360}\right) \neq S_0^* \left[1 + r_{b,0}^t \left(\frac{t}{360}\right)\right] \frac{1}{E_0^{*t}} \qquad (7-2)$$

If either of the inequalities holds in a given case, money market speculation will be feasible if the inequality is large enough to more than offset transaction costs. If the left side of the inequality exceeds the right side, for example, a speculator may want to purchase A's currency spot in order to acquire an asset denominated in that currency. The reverse sequence is indicated if the right side exceeds the left side.

Money market speculation often involves the spot sale of a currency that is expected to depreciate. Assuming that B's currency is expected to depreciate, Inequalities 7–1 and 7–2 indicate that speculation against B's currency will occur if B's interest rate (or expected rate of return) is too low to offset the expected depreciation. Sometimes, the belief that a country's interest rate level is too low to offset an expected depreciation of its currency is not widespread enough to cause heavy speculation against its currency. On other occasions, however, this belief is general and stems from government interference with domestic interest rates designed to keep them below their equilibrium levels. This suggests that if the government of a country with a depreciating currency wants to discourage speculation against its currency, it should allow domestic interest rates to find their market levels. Governments often shrink from taking such a simple step, however, because of political considerations; for a long time, "protecting" the general public against high interest rates has been good politics and, on the whole, bad economics.

Money Market Speculation Compared to Bond Investment   Money market speculation is, as the term implies, a short-term phenomenon. The term is not usually applied to transactions in medium-term and long-term interest-bearing securities, whose purchasers are generally classified as investors rather than speculators. A little reflection indicates, however, that when investors hold unhedged foreign-currency-denominated bonds, the investment outcome depends on the same variables as those in Inequalities 7−1 and 7−2. If, for example, a Japanese investor holds unhedged dollar bonds, the investment outcome is inferior to an investment in yen bonds if the dollar's yen value declines beyond a certain point. Clearly, therefore, the investor is betting on the exchange rate in much the same manner as a money market speculator. Given the short-term volatility of exchange rates, money market speculation is, generally speaking, more heavily influenced by exchange rate expectations than are investments in bonds denominated in foreign currencies, but this does not mean that the two actions are fundamentally different in nature.

The Basics of Foreign Exchange Futures

Since its inception in 1972, the forex futures market has become a major feature of the forex landscape. The market's growth has been based on the continuing volatility of exchange rates and the fact that futures contracts offer, for some market participants, important advantages over forward contracts. These advantages have to do with speculation, liquidity, and transaction size.

There is a basic similarity between forward contracts and futures contracts in that the contracting parties of both arrangements agree to future exchanges of currencies and set applicable exchange rates in advance. There are also, however, fundamental differences between them. Most fundamentally, futures contracts are traded on organized exchanges using a highly standardized format, while forward contracts are informal arrangements that vary according to the wishes of the contracting parties.

Exhibit 7.1 provides a comparison of forward contracts with currency futures contracts. The points stressed there are explained in the material that follows.

It is likely that, as commercial banks continue expanding the sources of their earnings, they will increasingly be willing to provide forward contracts with relatively small face values. To date, however, the financial commitments

| EXHIBIT | 7.1 | *Comparison of Forward and Futures Contracts for Exchanges of Currencies*

Feature	Forward Contracts	Futures Contracts
Type of contract	An informal arrangement between a forex dealer and a customer. The terms are highly flexible.	Standardized according to the specifications of the futures exchange.
Maturity	The contracting parties may choose any maturity desired, but maturities are commonly in multiples of 30 days.	There are only a few maturity dates.
Contract size	Generally large, averaging more than one million dollars per contract.	Small enough so that the futures market is accessible to small-scale forex market participants.
Security arrangements	Banks' forward customers must often maintain minimum deposit balances.	All traders must maintain margin deposits that are small percentages of contract face values.
Cash flows	No cash flows occur until delivery.	Daily settlement results in cash payments to some parties and additions to margin deposits by others.
Final settlement	Over 90 percent of forward contracts are settled by delivery.	Less than 2 percent of currency futures contracts are settled through delivery. Normally, they are settled through contract reversal.
Default risk	Since there is no daily settlement, substantial loss can occur if a party defaults. For this reason, banks need high credit ratings in order to	Daily settlement assures that the default risk is small in magnitude. All contracts cleared by the exchange are guaranteed by the clearinghouse. Some

involved in forward contracts have been so large that many parties are precluded from using them. Moreover, although the pressure to increase earnings is causing banks to modify their reluctance to provide customers with speculative forward contracts, such contracts continue to be used primarily for hedging. Futures contracts, by contrast, are designed with speculators in mind, and they have much smaller face values than forward contracts. These facts, along with the highly standardized nature of futures contracts and other features, provide the currency futures market with a high degree of liquidity that makes it feasible to speculate on almost any scale after posting margins that are very small relative to contract face value.

Feature	Forward Contracts	Futures Contracts
	maintain strong positions as forward dealers.	default risk exists between brokers and their customers.
Quotations and prices	Dealers quote prices with bid–ask spreads. Small price discrepancies may exist among dealers. Against the U.S. dollar, currencies are generally quoted on European terms.	Traders quote bid–ask spreads on the exchange floor, but a single price exists at any moment. Against the U.S. dollar, currencies are generally quoted on American terms.
Variety of currencies	Forward contracts are available in all the currencies of developed countries and in some currencies of LDCs.	Offerings are limited to a small number of currencies.
Price certainty	The exchange rate is locked in for the duration of the contract.	The exchange rate effectively paid or received fluctuates slightly according to the basis spread.
Commissions	Determined by the bid–ask spreads obtained by dealers.	Floor traders and brokers pay commissions and fees as required by the exchange. Brokers charge explicit commissions to customers. Commissions and fees are paid on a round-turn basis.
Regulation	Self-regulation prevails, subject to government restrictions.	U.S. exchanges are regulated by the CFTC. Exchanges maintain detailed regulations for their members.

While currency futures are particularly appealing to speculators, they can also be used for hedging. They are especially popular for small-scale hedging, but even parties with access to the forward market often hedge with futures.

Trading Arrangements

All futures contracts are traded on organized exchanges. Within limits established by regulation, a futures exchange is controlled and operated by its membership. Exchange memberships are held by individuals, who may be either agents of firms, including commercial banks, or traders for their own accounts. Because a single membership entitles its holder to no more floor trading privileges than other members enjoy, a firm that wishes to expand its operations beyond a certain point must acquire additional memberships. Exchange memberships are limited in number and they can be sold. Members can also lease their trading rights, and when an exchange is trying to build volume in a particular contract, it may license nonmembers to trade it. Brokerage firms may be authorized to have representatives on the floor who are not exchange members, but all trades are effected through members, lessees, or licensed nonmembers.

In the United States, the trading of currency futures works through an "open outcry" system that relies on hand signals and shouts. In this system, an offer to trade must be public; that is, it must be made openly to all interested parties at a location on the exchange floor, known as the *pit,* which has been assigned a particular futures contract. All trades are processed through an *exchange clearinghouse,* whose basic functions are to confirm trades and guarantee the fulfillment of contracts. The clearinghouse guarantees fulfillment by interposing itself between the parties to a trade so that it is technically a party to every contract. If one of the parties to a trade defaults, the clearinghouse must fulfill the commitment to the other party (the *counterparty*).

The clearinghouse protects itself by requiring all trades to be formally arranged through **clearing members,** who are exchange members that have met certain requirements imposed by the clearinghouse to protect itself against default. Thus, if one of the parties to a trade is not a clearing member, that party must arrange (for a fee) to have a clearing member act for it in formalizing the agreement with the clearinghouse. Clearing members post margins with the clearinghouse, and if they are acting on behalf of other parties, they require those parties to maintain margins with them. If such a party is, in turn, representing others who do not trade on the exchange floor, it requires them to post margin with it. A given transaction can, therefore, produce a chain of three margin deposits. The clearinghouse's obligation to guarantee performance extends only to clearing members and not to their customers.

Outside the United States, much of the trading of currency futures is conducted electronically, meaning that it is completely computerized. Traders enter their offers into an exchange's computer system, a computer matches offers to buy with offers to sell, and all of the details associated with confirming trades and adjusting the accounts of the trading parties are computer processed. In such a system, any trader with a computer linkage to one of the system's computer terminals can trade futures without being physically present at the exchange. Open outcry trading can thus be eliminated.

The substitution of fully electronic trading for the open outcry system has been strongly resisted in the United States. Nevertheless, the Chicago Mercantile Exchange (CME) has developed an electronic trading system, known as GLOBEX, which is currently (summer of 1991) in the process of implementation. Other U.S. futures exchanges will participate in this system. When GLOBEX is fully operational, its uses will include the after-hours trading of currency futures. No plans are being made to replace the open outcry trading system in use during standard trading hours, but the desirability of retaining this system has become an important topic for public debate.

The Participants

The people who trade on the floor of a futures exchange either trade for their own accounts or serve as brokers for parties who lack floor trading privileges. Those who trade for their own accounts, or **floor traders,** are, for the most part, speculators, most of whom operate with very short time horizons. Some represent banks or other firms that use the futures market to complement their forward operations or, in the case of banks, for arbitrage between the forward and futures markets. **Floor brokers** are generally representatives of investment firms that act on behalf of customers on a commission basis.

In terms of volume, the forward market is much larger than the currency futures market. Nevertheless, the fact that the futures market is accessible to parties of widely varying financial capacities and motivations means that it exhibits a greater diversity of participants than does the forward market.

Contract Characteristics

Although forward contracts offer great flexibility in terms of maturity and contract amount, they lack the liquidity that an ideal speculative medium should have and that some hedgers desire. A party to a forward contract cannot sell it to realize a gain or avoid a loss. If a party desires to cancel a forward contract, it can enter into another such contract that reverses the earlier one, but such a reversal does not liquidate the earlier contract unless both contracts are with the same party and that party agrees to liquidation.

Futures contracts offer greater liquidity because the clearinghouse stands ready to enter into reversing contracts whenever willing traders can be found to take the other side of proposed reversing transactions. When a contract is reversed, both contracts are cancelled and a cash settlement is made for any difference in their face values. The vast majority of currency futures contracts are liquidated through reversal rather than through cash settlement (delivery) at maturity. Only about 1.5 percent of all currency futures contracts traded in the United States result in delivery. By contrast, the vast majority of forward contracts, probably more than 90 percent, are carried to maturity.[1]

Currency futures contracts are always for a standard amount of a currency, such as DM125,000, and anyone wanting to trade in larger amounts must enter into additional contracts for this standard amount. The standard amount feature slightly limits the usefulness of futures contracts for hedging, but it is essential to market liquidity. Moreover, achieving a satisfactory hedge does not necessarily require an exact match between a futures position and a foreign currency exposure.

---

[1]Robert W. Kolb, *Understanding Futures Markets,* 3d. ed. (Miami: Kolb Publishing, 1991), pp. 16 and 501. The 1.5 percent figure comes from the *Annual Report* of the Commodity Futures Trading Commission and is for the period October 1, 1988, through September 30, 1988.

While forward contracts can have any maturities that the contracting parties desire, futures contracts offer only a few maturities. At present, the value dates of most currency futures contracts are the third Wednesdays of March, June, September, or December, and relatively few of these contracts have initial lives of more than 6 months. These limited maturities do not necessarily prevent the use of futures contracts for hedging. Someone who wants a hedge targeted for a date that does not coincide with a futures contract value date can enter into an appropriate number of contracts with a maturity that extends beyond the desired date. The hedger can then liquidate those contracts by the desired date.

Prices and Daily Settlement

At any given moment, there are numerous, slightly different forward rates between freely traded currencies for contracts of the same maturity. The informality of the forward market permits divergences based on bid–ask spreads, transaction volume, differences in information, and other factors. At a futures exchange, however, a single price exists at any given moment. Brokers obtain compensation for their services by charging commissions rather than by simultaneously buying and selling foreign exchange at slightly different prices. Floor traders quote two-way prices that incorporate bid–ask spreads, thereby serving as marketmakers, but at any given time, there is only one price at which trading actually occurs. That price is decided by matching the highest bid against the lowest offer so that trading occurs when they coincide.

Because the forward and futures markets have roughly comparable transaction costs on trades of comparable size, and because arbitrage between the markets occurs if their prices differ significantly, there is close correlation between forward and futures exchange rates. Since the volume of forward transactions exceeds that of futures transactions, forward rates are fundamentally more important than futures rates in overall exchange rate determination. Nevertheless, because a single futures rate is in effect at any given time, and that rate is readily available to the public, the futures market provides a convenient benchmark from which to make forward quotations. Indeed, some banks use the futures market for **price discovery,** i.e., they quote forward rates after taking into account the latest futures rates and their assessments of conditions on the exchange floor.

It is often assumed that forex speculation contributes to exchange rate instability, and it is arguable that allowing forward rates to be influenced by futures rates adds to that instability. As is explained in Chapter 11, however, it is by no means clear that the net effect of speculation on exchange rates is destabilizing. Moreover, the fact that futures rates are affected by many small-scale traders means that they are insulated to some degree from the distorting effects of large individual transactions. If, for example, a large sale of mark futures lowers the mark's price below the level that is considered sustainable, speculative floor traders will immediately buy marks, exerting upward pressure on the mark's price. In any event, it is an institutional fact that the futures market is generally considered to be an efficient indicator of market opinion.

Determining Gains and Losses While the applicable exchange rate in a forward contract is fixed for the life of the contract, the applicable exchange rate in a futures contract is the current futures rate. In those relatively few cases where a futures contract is carried to maturity, the rate at which delivery occurs equals or is very close to the then-current spot rate. Since the futures rate is constantly changing, the rate at which a contract is settled is almost certain to differ from its initial rate. As the rate changes, the resulting differences become realized gains or losses through a process known as **daily settlement** or **marking-to-market.** At the end of each trading day, the change in a contract's face value from the previous trading day's closing (settlement) price is determined. Clearing members with gains receive cash from the clearinghouse, while clearing members with losses post additional margins unless their previously posted margins are deemed sufficient. The clearing members, in turn, distribute gains to winning customers and obtain additional margins from customers whose margin deposits have fallen below the allowable minimum.

The overall gain or loss from a futures contract is, ignoring transaction costs and interest, the difference between the initial exchange rate and the rate in effect when the contract is closed out. The net gain or loss from a forward contract when, as is normally the case, it is held until maturity, again ignoring transaction costs and any interest factor, is the difference between the forward rate and the spot rate at maturity. If a futures transaction and a forward transaction are identical as to amount, maturity, and initial exchange rate, and if both are carried to maturity, they will produce identical gains or losses, ignoring transaction costs and interest. Because of marking-to-market on futures contracts, however, an interest factor prevents the results of identical forward and futures transactions from being quite the same.

Can Futures and Forward Exchange Rates Differ? A currency futures contract amounts to a standing commitment to place a series of daily bets. This commitment can be eliminated on any trading day by contract reversal, at which point the gain or loss from the previous day's settlement price is determined and the bettor receives any gain plus what remains of the margin deposit. There is an interest opportunity cost associated with net losses arising from daily settlement, and such a cost may be associated with the posting of margins.[2] Because daily settlement means that the margins traders must maintain are very small relative to contract face values, the interest opportunity cost of posting margins is also normally very small.

Since the cash flows resulting from forward contracts are normally deferred until delivery, it may seem that forwards do not entail any interest cost. In reality, however, there may be an interest cost involved in holding a

---

[2]In the United States, it is customary to permit all or most of the initial margin to be deposited in U.S. Treasury bills or, in some cases, other interest-earning securities. Interest accrues to the depositor's account unless the margin deposit is lost through daily resettlement. Subsequent margin calls must be met in cash, though the later substitution of Treasury bills is permissible.

forward contract. If a bank requires a forward customer to maintain a minimum deposit balance that exceeds what the customer would otherwise hold with it, an interest opportunity cost exists to the extent that any interest received from the excess deposit is less than the interest that could have been earned with those funds. In effect, this excess deposit balance is a margin deposit. Moreover, it is a margin deposit that is likely to be a good deal larger than the margin initially deposited on a futures contract since a forward contract is unlikely to provide for additional margin deposits should the relevant exchange rate move against a dealer bank's customer.

Any interest cost of maintaining excess deposit balances under the terms of forward contracts exists whether the customer gains or loses from daily exchange rate movements. With forex futures, however, the interest cost falls much more heavily upon losers than upon winners. Indeed, when a futures contract provides a positive cash flow, the interest attributable to this flow normally exceeds the interest cost, if any, associated with temporary losses and the posting of margin.

Largely because of the interest factor, a question has arisen as to whether or not futures and forward exchange rates can differ without giving rise to arbitrage that eliminates the price differences. It has also been suggested that because of transaction costs and differences in risk, forward exchange rates may differ from futures exchange rates without inducing arbitrage. Banks with relatively low credit ratings, for instance, have to offer relatively attractive forward rates in order to avoid losing business to futures brokers, who are backed by clearinghouse guarantees. Nevertheless, it is the interest factor that has captured the most attention as a source of possible differences between forward and futures exchange rates.

It has been shown mathematically that futures prices should tend to diverge from forward prices as a function of the covariance between futures prices and interest rates.[3] Fortunately, why this should be true can be explained using fairly simple economic reasoning that avoids mathematical complications. This reasoning suggests that the futures price of a currency should tend to exceed its forward price *if* changes in the exchange value of that currency tend to be positively correlated with changes in the interest rate differential between the two relevant countries. If, however, a negative correlation exists between the exchange rate and the interest rate differential, the futures price of the currency should tend to be less than the forward price.

These relationships are illustrated as follows. Assume that U.S. interest rates tend to rise relative to Japanese interest rates when the exchange value of

---

[3]See the December 1981 issue of the *Journal of Financial Economics,* which contains three articles comparing forward prices with futures prices: John C. Cox, Jonathan E. Ingersoll, Jr., and Stephen A. Ross, "The Relation between Forward Prices and Futures Prices," pp. 321–346; Robert A. Jarrow and George S. Oldfield, "Forward Contracts and Futures Contracts," pp. 373–382; and Scott F. Richard and M. Sundaresan, "A Continuous Time Equilibrium Model of Forward Prices and Futures Prices in a Multigood Economy," pp. 347–371. Also see George E. Morgan, "Forward and Futures Pricing of Treasury Bills," *Journal of Banking and Finance,* December 1981, pp. 483–496.

the yen rises against the U.S. dollar and to fall relative to Japanese interest rates when the yen's exchange value declines. When the yen rises, the holders of long (buying) positions in yen futures have positive cash flows, which they can invest, and if U.S. interest rates increase when the yen's exchange value increases, the gain from holding a long position is thereby augmented.[4] When the yen's exchange value decreases, the holders of long positions in yen futures have negative cash flows, but if U.S. interest rates simultaneously decrease, the interest cost of financing the cash flows is less than if U.S. interest rates had remained stable.

From this analysis, it follows that whether the yen futures exchange rate rises or falls, the holder of a long position in yen futures is better off when U.S. interest rates are positively correlated with the futures exchange rate than when they are not. If there is a negative correlation between the yen futures rate and U.S. interest rates, the holder of a long position in yen futures is worse off than in the positive correlation case whether the yen's exchange value rises or falls. Since the cash flows associated with futures contracts do not occur with forward contracts, a positive correlation between U.S. interest rates and the futures exchange rate implies that the futures rate should be higher than the forward rate. A negative correlation implies, however, that the futures rate should be less than the forward rate.

While economic theory thus holds out the possibility that futures and forward exchange rates may tend to diverge in a way that is not arbitrageable, forward and futures exchange rates seem to remain close enough together in practice to suggest that any differences between them are normally insignificant.[5] Furthermore, when differences between them do arise, they tend to be speedily removed by arbitrage. Nevertheless, the divergence of forward and futures exchange rates remains a theoretical possibility.

Regulation

Whereas forward transactions in the leading financial centers are essentially unregulated, futures transactions are extensively regulated by government agencies and private associations. The regulations encompass contract terms, trading procedures, and the standards of conduct that exchange members and other market participants are expected to observe.

In the United States, futures exchanges are regulated by the Commodity Futures Trading Commission (CFTC), an agency established by Congress in

---

[4]Note that U.S. interest rates can rise *relative* to Japanese interest rates if Japanese interest rates decline while U.S. interest rates remain the same. The text assumes that the increase in the interest rate differential occurs because of an increase in the U.S. interest rate because that case is easier to analyze. Even if the interest rate differential were to increase because of a decline in yen interest rates, however, that would not alter the conclusions reached in the next paragraph.

[5]Bradford Cornell and Marc R. Reinganum, "Forward and Futures Prices: Evidence from the Foreign Exchange Markets," *The Journal of Finance*, December 1981, pp. 1035–1045; and Hun Y. Park and Andrew H. Chen, "Differences between Futures and Forward Prices: A Further Investigation of the Marking-to-Market Effects," *Journal of Futures Markets*, Spring 1985, pp. 77–88.

1974. The establishment of a new futures exchange requires CFTC approval, as do offers of new contracts by existing exchanges or substantive changes in existing contracts. In deciding whether to allow a requested extension of futures offerings, the CFTC follows the principle that it must serve an economic purpose. What constitutes such a purpose is, of course, arguable, but to allow speculation is not, in itself, a sufficient reason to grant approval. If, however, it can be shown that a proposed extension of offerings will improve competitive conditions and provide additional hedging opportunities, approval is likely, even if most of the resulting trading would be speculative. The CFTC recognizes that speculation can provide market liquidity and competitiveness and thereby facilitates hedging and the acquisition of price information, but it remains concerned about speculative excesses and the possibility of unscrupulous behavior.

Until 1985, the CFTC set maximum limits for daily price fluctuations in currency futures trading in an attempt to reduce exchange rate volatility. This practice was abandoned when it became evident that sharp swings in forward rates rendered it counterproductive, but it illustrates the CFTC's underlying concern with the dangers of unrestrained trading.

Because of beliefs that the CFTC was overextended and that self-regulation is appropriate for many aspects of futures trading, a private association of futures traders, the National Futures Association (NFA), has been given responsibility for implementing regulations applying to such trading. The CFTC retains overall supervisory authority and monitors the NFA's work, and it retains the power to approve or deny requests for new futures contracts or for significant changes in existing contracts.

Each futures exchange establishes detailed rules and procedures to be followed by the users of its facilities and makes violators of these rules and procedures subject to fines, sanctions, and/or expulsion. These rules and procedures are designed to accomplish such purposes as assuring the financial integrity of exchange members, preventing unfair competition, and protecting an exchange's reputation for treating the general public fairly. In addition, some control over the behavior of futures traders is exercised through *broker associations* or *broker groups*. These associations exist primarily to facilitate cooperation in such matters as carrying out large trades and to protect customers from default,[6] but they also provide some control over the trading practices of association members.

Outside the United States, a pattern of self-regulation prevails. It is likely to be the case, however, that if the volume of currency futures trading outside the United States increases substantially, the pressure for outside regulation will increase.

The Sting of 1989   In January 1989, the financial community of the United States was rocked by the revelation that the FBI had been conducting an extensive sting operation in the futures trading pits of the Chicago Mercantile

---

[6]The capital of the members of a broker group is generally available to cover defaults by individual members.

Exchange (CME) and the Chicago Board of Trade (CBOT). Included within the scope of this operation were the yen and Swiss franc pits of the International Monetary Market (IMM), the division of the CME that trades currency futures. The sting resulted from suspicions that some brokers were defrauding customers and that some trading gains were not being reported as taxable income. It produced indictments against 47 traders and 1 clerk.[7]

The results of the sting have been mixed. Thirty-six of the accused either plead guilty without being brought to trial or were convicted in court. A court trial for 12 accused yen traders resulted in the acquittal of 2 and a mistrial for the other 10. In general, the offenses indicated by the guilty pleas or convictions were relatively minor in terms of the amounts of money involved. Particularly in the cases of the yen traders, a serious problem for the government prosecutors was that the complexity of the trading practices involved made it difficult for jurors to evaluate the government's charges. In any event, the government generally failed to prove the existence of large-scale fraud, and public confidence in the integrity of futures traders does not seem to have been seriously damaged. It is noteworthy, however, that U.S. futures exchanges, particularly those in Chicago, have substantially reformed their trading practices and the monitoring of them so as to reduce the likelihood that their customers will be cheated by brokers. For example, the CME has placed severe restrictions on personal trading among members of the same broker associations.[8]

Dual Trading   By its very nature, the open outcry system leaves brokers' customers dependent on brokers' integrity and the effectiveness of exchange self-regulation. When brokers are allowed to trade both for themselves and their customers, a practice known as **dual trading,** the temptation exists for a dishonest broker, perhaps in league with another such person, to cheat customers.

Suppose, for example, that a customer places an order with a broker to buy yen futures at the current price. In dual trading, the broker could buy yen at a favorable price and then, assuming the yen moves upward, arrange a phony transaction with a conspirator in which the yen are allegedly purchased at a higher price. The customer would then be charged the higher price, and the conspirators would pocket the difference between the two prices. Among the steps taken by the CME to discourage such practices are camera surveillance of trading pits and the requirement that trades be recorded almost immediately after being agreed to, as well as the limits on trading among members of the same broker associations previously alluded to.

The same basic result can be achieved without an accomplice, however, by resorting to *front running,* which occurs when a dual trader executes a transaction for his or her own account while holding a customer's order that is awaiting execution. Dual traders are supposed to execute customers' orders

[7]Susan Abbott, "How FBI's Sting Has Changed Pit Life," *Futures*, June 1991, pp. 46–49.
[8]*Ibid.*

first. Suppose, however, that a dual trader senses the yen is going to move upward and buys yen for his own account while holding an order to buy yen for a customer. If the yen rises, he could use contract reversal to make a gain and execute the customer's order at the higher price. If the yen falls, he could use contract reversal to offset his purchase and buy yen at the lower price while charging the customer the higher price. Presumably, the faster recording of trades should help curb front running. So should the more severe disciplinary measures that the CME has adopted for violating trading rules.

Because dual trading can lead to abuses, some effort has been made to curtail its use in futures trading. The practice has its staunch defenders, however. The chief argument in its defense is that it helps promote market liquidity. It is also argued that most brokers who are authorized to engage in dual trading either concentrate on trading for their own accounts or fulfilling customers' orders and do not mix the two activities. Nevertheless, enough of a cloud has developed over the practice to assure that dual traders are not as unregulated as they were before 1989.

Currency Futures Exchanges and Contracts

The history of currency futures goes back only to 1972 when the CME established a separate division, the International Monetary Market (IMM), for the explicit purpose of trading them. Chicago had long been the world's leading center for trading commodity futures, and while it had not been a leading forex center, the similarity between futures trading in commodities and futures trading in currencies and the city's well-developed banking facilities with forex expertise made it a natural location for trading currency futures.

During the first few years of its existence, the IMM conducted its currency futures business on a modest, but generally expanding scale. Early in the 1980s, increased exchange rate volatility and the IMM's demonstration of the feasibility of a market in currency futures led to both an expansion of the IMM's trading volume and the establishment of new currency futures exchanges, beginning in 1982 with the London International Financial Futures Exchange (LIFFE). The trading of currency futures soon spread to other financial centers, while in Chicago, the MidAmerica Commodity Exchange (MCE), an affiliate of the long-established CBOT, began competing on the IMM's home turf by offering a line of currency futures contracts. The IMM continues to hold a dominant position, however, and it remains to be seen if the other exchanges can capture a large share of the market from it.

Currently Offered Currency Futures Contracts

Exhibit 7.2 on pages 208 and 209 summarizes the available contracts in currency futures on a worldwide basis as of the fall of 1990. Of the 35 contracts listed there, all but 4 contracts offered by Brazilian exchanges are either priced in U.S. dollars or contracts on the U.S. dollar priced in other currencies. The most important contracts, those offered by the IMM, are all for fixed amounts of currencies priced in dollars. Only 4 of the 35 contracts listed are for fixed amounts of dollars priced in other currencies.

The rapid expansion of currency futures trading has encouraged the offering of new contracts, but the mortality rate among futures contracts has been high. In the fall of 1989, for example, *Futures* listed 42 currency futures contracts. The most important dropouts during the following year were the 5 contracts of the LIFFE, which suspended the trading of currency futures after an 8-year effort. During this same period, however, the first Japanese currency futures contract made its appearance, the dollar/yen contract offered by the Tokyo International Financial Futures Exchange (TIFFE).

Since the fall of 1990, by far the most important development in terms of new offerings of currency futures contracts has been the emergence of cross-rate contracts offered by U.S. exchanges. In May 1991, the CME launched futures trading in 6 such contracts: mark/pound, yen/pound, Swiss franc/pound, yen/mark, yen/Swiss franc, and Swiss franc/mark. These contracts are valued and settled in U.S. dollars, and each has a minimum contract value fluctuation of $25, which is approximately twice that on the IMM's other currency futures contracts.[9]

The IMM's entry into cross-rate futures trading is being challenged by a new exchange, the Twin Cities Board of Trade (TCBT) of Minneapolis. As of midsummer 1991, the TCBT had received CFTC approval for a pound/mark contract and was awaiting approval of yen/mark and Swiss franc/mark contracts. While the cross-rate contracts of the IMM are settled in dollars, those of the TCBT are to be settled in marks.

The International Monetary Market (IMM)

The IMM dominates trading in currency futures, and most of the currency futures contracts traded by other exchanges are modeled on its offerings. The IMM has capitalized on its head start in currency futures to achieve advantages in financial expertise and liquidity that are difficult for other exchanges to overcome. The currency futures contracts that the IMM has used to achieve its dominating position feature a fixed quantity of a foreign currency that is exchangeable for a variable quantity of U.S. dollars. At present, the IMM trades six such contracts, which are stated in yen, marks, Canadian dollars, pounds sterling, Swiss francs, and Australian dollars. In addition, as was noted earlier, the IMM has recently introduced a line of cross-rate futures contracts between currencies other than the U.S. dollar that are, nevertheless, valued and settled in U.S. dollars. In the past, the IMM has traded contracts between the U.S. dollar and the Mexican peso, the Dutch guilder, the Ecu, and the French franc, but these contracts have been discontinued.

All of the IMM's contracts between the U.S. dollar and another currency have as their delivery dates the third Wednesdays of March, June, September, or December. The new cross-rate contracts follow the same quarterly maturity cycle, but their delivery dates are six days earlier than the third Wednesdays of

---

[9]Jon Stein, "Exchanges Cross Swords on Cross Rates," *Futures*, June 1991, p. 52.

EXHIBIT | 7.2 | Currency Futures Contracts in 1990

Currency	Exchange[a]	Contract Amount	Minimum Fluctuation[b]	Contract Months	Trading Hours (Local Time)
Australian dollar	IMM	A$100,000	$0.0001/A$ = $10	Mar./June/Sep./Dec.	7:20–2:00
	PBOT	A$50,000	$0.0001/A$ = $5	Mar./June/Sep./Dec. plus near 2 months	6:00 p.m.– 2:30 p.m. next day[c]
	SFE	A$100,000	$0.0001/A$ = $10	Mar./June/Sep./Dec. out to 6 months ahead	8:30–4:30
British pound	IMM	£62,500	$0.0002/£ = $12.50	Mar./June/Sep./Dec.	7:20–2:00
	MCE	£12,500	$0.0002/£ = $2.50	Mar./June/Sep./Dec.	7:20–2:15
	PBOT	£62,500	$0.0001/£ = $6.25	Mar./June/Sep./Dec. plus near 2 months	6:00 p.m.– 2:30 p.m. next day[c]
	SIMEX[d]	£62,500	$0.0002/£ = $12.50	Mar./June/Sep./Dec.	8:25–5:15
Canadian dollar	IMM	C$100,000	$0.0001/C$ = $10	Mar./June/Sep./Dec.	7:20–2:00
	MCE	C$50,000	$0.0001/C$ = $5	Mar./June/Sep./Dec.	7:20–2:15
	PBOT	C$100,000	$0.0001/C$ = $10	Mar./June/Sep./Dec. plus near 2 months	4:30–2:30
Ecu	FINEX	Ecu100,000	$0.0001/Ecu = $10	Mar./June/Sep./Dec.	8:00–1:00
	PBOT	Ecu125,000	$0.0001/Ecu = $12.50	Mar./June/Sep./Dec. plus near 2 months	4:30–2:30
French franc	PBOT	FF500,000	$0.00002/FF = $10	Mar./June/Sep./Dec. plus near 2 months	4:30–2:30
German mark	IMM	DM125,000	$0.0001/DM = $12.50	Mar./June/Sep./Dec.	7:20–2:00
	MCE	DM62,500	$0.0001/DM = $6.25	Mar./June/Sep./Dec.	7:20–2:15 5:00–8:30[e]
	PBOT	DM125,000	$0.0001/DM = $12.50	Mar./June/Sep./Dec. plus near 2 months	6:00 p.m.– 2:30 p.m. next day[c]
	BBF	DM10,000	Cr$0.01/DM = Cr100	All months	10:30–4:30
	BM&F	DM10,000	Cr$0.005/DM = Cr50	All months	10:30–4:30
	SIMEX[d]	DM125,000	$0.0001/DM = $12.50	Mar./June/Sep./Dec.	8:20–5:10

Currency	Exchange	Contract Size	Tick Value	Contract Months	Trading Hours
Japanese yen	IMM	¥12,500,000	$0.000001/¥ = $12.50	Mar./June/Sep./Dec.	7:20–2:00
	MCE	¥6,250,000	$0.000001/¥ = $6.25	Mar./June/Sep./Dec.	7:20–2:15 5:00–8:30[e]
	PBOT	¥12,500,000	$0.000001/¥ = $12.50	Mar./June/Sep./Dec.	6:00 p.m.– 2:30 p.m. next day[c]
	BBF	¥1,000,000	Cr0.0001/¥ = Cr100	All months	10:30–4:30
	BM&F	¥1,000,000	Cr0.00005/¥ = Cr50	All months	10:30–4:30
	TIFFE	¥12,500,000	$0.000001/¥ = $12.50	Mar./June/Sep./Dec.	9:00–noon 1:30–3:30
	SIMEX[d]	¥12,500,000	$0.000001/¥ = $12.50	Mar./June/Sep./Dec.	8:15–5:05
New Zealand dollar	NZFOE	NZ$100,000	$0.0001/NZ$ = $10	All months	8:15–4:45
Swiss franc	IMM	SF125,000	$0.0001/SF = $12.50	Mar./June/Sep./Dec.	7:20–2:00
	MCE	SF62,500	$0.0001/SF = $6.25	Mar./June/Sep./Dec.	7:20–2:15
	PBOT	SF125,000	$0.0001/SF = $12.50	Mar./June/Sep./Dec.	6:00 p.m.– 2:30 p.m. next day[c]
U.S. dollar	BBF	$5,000	Cr0.01/$ = Cr50	All months	10:30–4:30
	BM&F	$5,000	Cr0.01/$ = Cr50	All months	10:30–4:30
	NZFOE	$50,000	NZ$0.0001/$ = NZ$5	All months	8:15–4:45
	OM	$50,000	SEK0.0001/$ = SEK5	Mar./June/Sep./Dec.	9:30–4:00
U.S. dollar	FINEX	$500 x index	0.01 (1 basis point) = $5	Mar./June/Sep./Dec.	8:20–3:00

[a]BBF—Bolsa Brasileira de Futuros (Brazilian Futures Exchange), Rio de Janeiro; BM&F—Bolsa Mercantil & de Futuros, Sao Paulo; FINEX—Financial Instrument Exchange, New York; IMM—International Monetary Market, Chicago; MCE—MidAmerica Commodity Exchange, Chicago; NZFOE—New Zealand Futures & Options Exchange Ltd., Auckland; OM—Stockholm Options Market; PBOT—Philadelphia Board of Trade; SFE—Sydney Futures Exchange Ltd., SIMEX—Singapore International Monetary Exchange; and TIFFE—Tokyo International Financial Futures Exchange.

[b]This equals the minimum "tick" or change in a futures exchange rate, multiplied by the face amount of the corresponding contract.

[c]Eastern Standard Time. For Eastern Daylight Time, the trading hours are 7:00 p.m. through 2:30 p.m. the next day. The trading week begins on Sunday.

[d]The currency futures contracts of the SIMEX are linked to those of the IMM; i.e., the contracts are interchangeable.

[e]The 5:00 p.m. to 8:30 p.m. trading session is for Central Standard Time. For Central Daylight Time, the hours of this session are 6:00 p.m. to 9:30 p.m.

Sources: Federal Reserve Bank of New York, *The Chicago Mercantile Exchange*, New York: Federal Reserve Bank of New York, 1989, pp. 35 and 37; and *Futures*, "1991 Reference Guide to Futures/Options Markets," 1990, pp. 60–81.

the delivery months. Trading in a contract ends two business days before delivery, which means that if a contract has not been cancelled through reversal by the last trading day, delivery must occur two business days later. Few contracts result in delivery, however, and trading often becomes frantic on or immediately before the last trading day as traders maneuver to close out positions as advantageously as possible.

The Reporting of IMM Currency Futures Trading   The trading volume in seven currency futures contracts is large enough so that *The Wall Street Journal* regularly publishes detailed summaries of daily transactions in the most heavily traded maturities. The seven are the IMM's contracts that trade the U.S. dollar against yen, marks, Canadian dollars, pounds sterling, Swiss francs, and Australian dollars and the dollar index futures contract of the Financial Instrument Exchange (FINEX), a division of the New York Cotton Exchange (CTN). Exhibit 7.3 reproduces the *Journal's* summary of trading in these seven contracts on Friday, July 19, 1991.

With reference to Exhibit 7.3, consider the data on trading in the September 1991 contract for the mark. The mark is traded in contracts of DM125,000, and the applicable exchange rates are in dollars per mark. Thus, when trading in the September 1991 contract opened on July 19, 1991, the initial rate at which marks exchanged was $0.5667 per mark. During the day, the highest rate reached was $0.5702, while the lowest was $0.5651. The settlement price announced at the end of trading was $0.5701. This price was probably the last price at which trading occurred, but it could have been chosen because it was judged by the committee charged with setting settlement prices to be the most representative price at the end of the day. The settlement price of $0.5701 represented an increase of 91 points ($0.0091) over the previous day's settlement price. The lifetime columns indicate the highest ($0.6810) and lowest ($0.5401) prices reached since the initiation of trading in the September 1991 contract. The figure of 63,707 for open interest in the September contract shows the total number of *pairs* of contracts outstanding at the close of trading. There were 63,707 contracts to buy and an equal number to sell.

The figures at the bottom of the mark section of Exhibit 7.3 indicate that the volume of contract pairs in all mark contracts that was traded on July 19, 1991 was estimated at 47,132. The figures also indicate that 53,794 contract pairs were traded on the preceding day, that the total open interest for all maturities at the close of trading on July 19 was 65,699 contract pairs, and that this last figure was a decrease of 1,586 from Thursday, July 18, 1991. By adding the three numbers in the mark open interest column and deducting the resulting figure of 65,693 from the total open interest of 65,699, it can be determined that only 6 outstanding contract pairs had a June 1992 maturity. Clearly, trading in mark futures was heavily oriented toward the nearest maturity (September 1991) and dropped off sharply as the contract maturity lengthened.

Note that the settlement price for the March 1992 mark contract ($0.5623) was higher on July 19 than the highest price ($0.5610) at which that

| E X H I B I T | 7.3 | *Trading in Currency Futures: Friday, July 19, 1991*

	Open	High	Low	Settle	Change	Lifetime High	Low	Open Interest
JAPAN YEN (IMM)—12.5 million yen; $ per yen (.00)							
Sept	.7292	.7320	.7281	.7318	+.0064	.7995	.7003	54,774
Dec	.7269	.7300	.7263	.7300	+.0064	.7770	.6997	3,979
Mr92	.7293	.7293	.7293	.7297	+.0064	.7540	.7000	1,315
June	....	....		.7299	+.0064	.7220	.7015	1,510
Est vol 20,009; vol Thur 29,911; open int 61,578, −1,838.							
DEUTSCHEMARK (IMM)—125,000 marks; $ per mark							
Sept	.5667	.5702	.5651	.5701	+.0091	.6810	.5401	63,707
Dec	.5630	.5662	.5612	.5659	+.0089	.6670	.5365	1,866
Mr92	.5590	.5610	.5590	.5623	+.0086	.5840	.5353	120
Est vol 47,132; vol Thur 53,794; open int 65,699, −1,586.							
CANADIAN DOLLAR (IMM)—100,000 dlrs.; $ per Can $							
Sept	.8625	.8626	.8563	.8567	−.0038	.8718	.7985	21,065
Dec	.8571	.8571	.8512	.8514	−.0042	.8670	.8175	1,072
Mr92	.8520	.8520	.8465	.8470	−.0046	.8630	.8253	1,631
June	.8476	.8476	.8420	.8426	−.0050	.8585	.8330	117
Est vol 12,330; vol Thur 11,678; open int 23,887, −786.							
BRITISH POUND (IMM)—62,500 pds.; $ per pound							
Sept	1.6674	1.6824	1.6640	1.6818	+.0286	1.9360	1.5824	25,001
Dec	1.6490	1.6670	1.6460	1.6642	+.0280	1.7900	1.5670	1,478
Mr92	1.6400	1.6510	1.6400	1.6508	+.0276	1.6510	1.5560	144
Est vol 23,566; vol Thur 16,470; open int 26,623, −1,398.							
SWISS FRANC (IMM)—125,000 francs; $ per franc							
Sept	.6540	.6604	.6528	.6602	+.0127	.8055	.6254	33,934
Dec	.6506	.6582	.6502	.6578	+.0127	.8090	.6235	830
Est vol 23,630; vol Thur 24,852; open int 34,846, −2,235.							
AUSTRALIAN DOLLAR (IMM)—100,000 dlrs.; $ per A.$.							
Sept	.7717	.7740	.7714	.7738	+.0068	.7740	.7415	1,436
Est vol 278; vol Thur 574; open int 1,438, +1.							
U.S. DOLLAR INDEX (FINEX)—500 times USDX							
Sept	94.56	94.75	94.08	94.09	−1.26	98.23	83.17	5,383
Dec	95.42	95.53	94.88	94.93	−1.28	98.96	92.05	746
Mr92	....	....		96.71	− .28	98.45	97.27	456
Est vol 3,000; vol Thur 4,610; open int 6,587,+1,255.							
The index: High 94.10; Low 93.45; Close 93.46 − 1.22							

contract traded during the day. This means that the settlement committee decided that the price of $0.5623 more accurately reflected the mark's March 1992 value than the last price at which the contract actually traded.

Exhibit 7.2 showed that the minimum permitted price variation *(tick)* in an IMM mark futures contract is $0.0001 per mark, and that such a variation means a change of $12.50 in the face value of a mark contract. Since the September mark rose by 91 points ($0.0091) on July 19, 1991, a party holding one contract to buy September marks (a long position) from the end of trading on Thursday, July 18 through the end of trading on Friday, July 19 had a positive cash flow of $1,137.50. A party holding a contract to sell September marks (a short position) had a negative cash flow of the same amount.

The Wall Street Journal's summaries for the five other IMM currency futures contracts are interpreted in the same way as the mark contract. Note, however, that IMM yen futures prices are stated in dollars per 100 yen. The change of plus 64 points in the September yen contract on July 19, 1991, thus indicates that the face value of a yen contract increased by $800 from the previous trading day.

The IMM's yen and mark contracts generally have the highest trading volumes, but trading also tends to be heavy in the Swiss franc, pound sterling, and Canadian dollar contracts. The trading volume of the Australian dollar contract has always been smaller than that of the other five contracts, but interest in this contract was much smaller than in 1991 than it had been a year or two earlier.

The IMM's Cross-Rate Futures Contracts   As was noted earlier, the IMM has initiated trading in six currency cross-rate futures contracts. As of midsummer 1991, two of these contracts were being traded in sufficient volume so that *The Wall Street Journal* was publishing short trading summaries for them. These were the yen/mark contract and the mark/pound contract.

The IMM's yen/mark contract has a face value equal to U.S.$125,000 times the yen/mark exchange rate expressed as 100 yen per mark. The mark/pound contract has a face value equal to U.S.$50,000 times the mark/pound exchange rate. As of the close of trading on July 19, 1991, the outstanding open interests in the two contracts were only 340 contract pairs for the yen/mark contract and 161 contract pairs for the mark/pound contract.

The IMM Currency Futures Trading Process[10]   Trading in IMM currency futures begins at 7:20 a.m. Chicago time and closes at 2:00 p.m. except on the final trading day, when trading closes after about two hours. The 7:20 starting time allows IMM trading to begin before the end of the European business day, but a key factor in the choice of this time was the fact that many important U.S. economic statistics are released by the government at 7:30 a.m. Chicago time. Because the price fluctuations occurring immediately after the release of these figures can be large, the CME imposes opening price fluctuation limits on the days when important statistics are released. These limits are 400 points for the pound, 100 points for the Canadian dollar, and 150 points each for the yen, mark, Swiss franc, and Australian dollar. The limits apply for only a few minutes. After 7:35 a.m. on the days when limits are imposed, prices are free to fluctuate without limits.

---

[10]The material in this and the next subsection is based primarily on Federal Reserve Bank of New York, *The Chicago Mercantile Exchange* (New York: Federal Reserve Bank of New York, 1989).

When agreements to trade are reached, they must be processed by CME clearing members. Such members fall into two categories: Class A and Class B. Only Class A clearing members process trades for floor traders and floor brokers who are not representatives of clearing member firms. Class B clearing members are solely concerned with arbitraging for their own accounts between the IMM and commercial banks. Commercial banks cannot be Class B clearing members. Class A clearing members are firms that hold at least two memberships in each of the CME's three trading divisions.[11] These divisions are the CME proper, which is primarily concerned with trading agricultural futures, the IMM, and the Index and Option Market (IOM), whose activities include the trading of options on IMM currency futures contracts. In addition, Class A clearing members must meet certain financial requirements established by the CME Clearinghouse (also known as the Clearing Division) for the purpose of guaranteeing the ability of clearing members to meet their obligations with the clearinghouse.

If one of the parties to a trade is not affiliated with a Class A clearing member, that party must use a Class A clearing member to process the trade with the clearinghouse. Based on information received from clearing members, the clearinghouse confirms and accepts trades, at which point it technically becomes a party to each side of the transaction. The acceptance process is completed at night, well after the day's trading has ended. Around 3:00 a.m. the next day, the clearinghouse contacts designated banks with which clearing members maintain accounts and advises them about the funds that the clearinghouse is to pay into or receive from those accounts. These settlement banks process the information provided by the clearinghouse and, during the next business day, adjust the accounts they hold for clearing members and the clearinghouse to reflect the results of the previous day's trading. A transaction is thus settled on the next trading day after agreement is reached. There are, of course, margin calls associated with the trading process, which are discussed in the next subsection.

Brokerage fees charged for handling IMM currency futures trades are collected on a **round-turn** basis, which means that they are paid when a contract is closed out through reversal or delivery. Floor traders are charged very low fees when they effect round turns in a single day. The low fees encourage a large volume of trading and, therefore, high liquidity. For parties relying on the services of floor brokers for their trades, the round turn fees are much higher, some floor brokers charging their customers more than $30 per contract per round turn.

Much of the IMM's currency futures trading is performed by a class of professional speculators known as **locals,** who typically execute many round

---

[11]This minimum memberships requirement applies to clearing member firms that have relatively few branch offices and affiliated brokers. The larger clearing member firms are required either to hold one or more additional exchange memberships or to satisfy additional financial requirements designed to guarantee their performance of contracts. Ibid., p. 51.

turns per day. Included among them are **scalpers,** who open and close contracts in a few minutes in the hope of profiting from exchange rate movements of one or two ticks. **Day traders** are locals with longer time horizons who nevertheless execute their round turns within a day. Relatively few locals go to bed at night with open positions. Those who do so are known as **position traders.**

The extensive participation by locals gives the IMM a huge liquidity advantage over other exchanges, and this advantage encourages other parties to trade there. Nonlocals know that positions at the IMM are quickly opened and quickly closed at prices that are very close to those prevailing when trading decisions are made.

When an IMM futures position is reversed, the associated contracts are cancelled and settlement is made based on the difference in contract face values and the amount of margin on deposit. When a contract is carried to delivery, the delivery process begins on the morning of the last trading day (normally a Monday). Using information received from customers, each clearing member informs the clearinghouse of the banks and account numbers from which or to which transfers of dollars and foreign currencies are to be made. At about the same time, the designated banks are notified of the transfers that are to occur. The transfers are actually made on the following Wednesday. Margin deposits are not released until delivery has been confirmed.

IMM Margin Requirements   The IMM has established four categories of margin requirements for the users of its currency futures trading facilities. Clearing members post original margin and, possibly, **settlement margin** with the clearinghouse. In turn, clearing members are required to collect **initial margin** and, possibly, **maintenance margin** from the parties they represent. In addition, floor brokers who are not acting for clearing members are expected to obtain margin deposits from their customers that are at least equal to the margins that they must post with clearing members.

Original margin is posted by clearing members on the morning of the next trading day after an agreement to trade has been made. It may be in cash, U.S. Treasury securities, or a letter of credit that satisfies IMM guidelines.[12] At about the same time, clearing members collect initial margins from their customers. Both of these margins are designed in principle to cover any loss in a position that could occur with an unusually large 1-day variation in the relevant exchange rates. Roughly speaking, the initial margin equals about 3 percent of the face value of a customer's position, but its specific amount is a function of the contract currency. Thus, the initial margin for a Canadian dollar contract is less than those for other contracts because its price normally varies less than the prices of the other traded currencies. Initial margin may be in the same form as original margin, but in addition, it may be in securities

---

[12]Acceptable letters of credit must be issued by approved banks for the specific purpose of guaranteeing commitments arising from trading at the IMM or the IOM.

listed on the New York or American Stock Exchanges or in gold warehouse receipts.[13]

Settlement margin, also known as **variation margin,** restores clearing members' margin accounts to their required levels after position losses. It is calculated twice per trading day, once in the early afternoon after the cessation of trading and once at night after the day's trades have been confirmed. In the afternoon (intraday) calculation, margin calls are made on clearing members whose positions show losses of $1 million or more from the previous day. Upon request, clearing members gaining $1 million or more from their previous day's positions receive 90 percent of their gains.

In the nighttime (end-of-session) calculation, settlement margins are determined on the basis of the cash flows associated with the daily resettlement process. As part of that process, the banks that are used for settlement purposes are notified of position changes arising from the day's trading, and transfers are effected from losers to gainers after the beginning of the next day's trading. Losers are required to restore their margin accounts prior to the beginning of trading on the next day. All gains are paid in cash and all payments of settlement margin are also in cash, but the clearing members who have to pay settlement margin are allowed to substitute Treasury securities for cash during the next trading day to avoid any loss of interest earnings on their margin deposits.

The operating rules of the CME permit it to call for emergency payments of settlement margin in currency futures trading. Thus, if particularly violent exchange rate variations were to occur with the result that the regular intraday margin calls should prove inadequate for restoring some clearing members' margin accounts to safe levels, the president of the CME could require additional settlement margin. In such an extraordinary margin call, the deposit of U.S. Treasury securities rather than cash would be acceptable.

Maintenance margin protects clearing members in much the same way that settlement margin protects the clearinghouse. A clearing member is not required, however, to call for maintenance margin from a customer unless that customer's margin deposit should fall below a certain level, in which case the clearing member is required to obtain enough additional margin to restore the customer's deposit to its initial level.

The New York Cotton Exchange (CTN)

The explosive growth of currency futures and options markets has led not only to the establishment of new exchanges, but also to the development of new offerings by existing exchanges. In the currency futures market, the most successful new offerings since the early 1980s have been registered by the long-established CTN, with its dollar index and Ecu contracts, and by the

---

[13]Equities are accepted at no more than 70 percent of market value, and gold warehouse receipts are accepted at no more than 50 percent of market value.

IMM with its Australian dollar futures contract. The CTN's dollar index and Ecu contracts are offered by its futures and options division, known as the Financial Instrument Exchange (FINEX), which was established in 1985.

The dollar index used by the FINEX is closely tied to the trade-weighted dollar index calculated by the Federal Reserve System. The Fed's index is a weighted average of the indexes of 10 currencies, 8 of which are European.[14] All 10 currency indexes are referenced to March 1973. The weights assigned to individual currencies are based on the corresponding countries' relative participation in world trade during the years 1972 to 1976.[15] Using a sample of spot bid quotations from New York banks, the Fed calculates its index daily and disseminates it weekly. The FINEX's index employs identical weights and the same base period, but it is calculated continuously on a 24-hour basis using a larger sample of exchange rate quotations. On the FINEX's floor, the index is updated every 30 seconds.

The dollar index futures contract has the usual March, June, September, and December maturities, but since it is based on an index rather than a specific currency, no delivery occurs at maturity. Instead, final settlement of balances takes place. The face value of the contract is $500 times the value of the index, and the tick is 0.01, which means that the minimum change in contract face value is $5. An increase in the index indicates a rise in the dollar's value, in which case the gainers are the parties who have purchased the contract. Correspondingly, gains are realized by sellers of the contract when the index declines.

According to Exhibit 7.3, the FINEX's dollar index closed at 93.46 on July 19, 1991. Because the dollar was at a forward premium against the currencies in the index during the summer of 1991, the dollar index contracts were trading at higher prices than the index, which is based on spot rates. On July 19, 1991, for example, the settlement prices for September 1991, December 1991, and March 1992 were, respectively, 94.09, 94.93, and 96.71. These prices, incidentally, represented decreases of 126, 128, and 28 points, respectively, from the previous day's settlement prices. This means that those parties that were long in either contract experienced negative cash flows of $630, $640, and $140, respectively, while those parties with short positions experienced positive cash flows of the same amounts.

Because the dollar index is generally less volatile than a specific exchange rate, speculation in dollar index contracts is less risky than speculation in a

---

[14]As of 1991, the 10 currencies, with percentage weights in parentheses, were as follows: mark (20.8), yen (13.6), French franc (13.1), pound sterling (11.9), Canadian dollar (9.1), lira (9.0), guilder (8.3), Belgian franc (6.4), Swedish krona (4.2), and Swiss franc (3.6). Because of its heavy orientation toward European currencies and the relatively low weight assigned to the yen, the accuracy of the index as a measure of the dollar's overall performance is questionable, but the index is still considered by many to be a reasonably good measure of the dollar's overall performance against the world's most heavily traded currencies.

[15]Specifically, the weight for each of the ten countries is the 1972–1976 average world trade of that country divided by the average world trade of all ten.

particular currency. Moreover, it sometimes happens that the dollar value of a currency moves in the opposite direction from the index, in which case a speculator who has correctly anticipated the general direction of the dollar's movement could still lose by betting on a currency instead of the dollar index.

The dollar index futures contract has considerable appeal as a hedging instrument for firms with a forex exposure that is distributed among a number of currencies. A U.S. firm with a portfolio of securities denominated in yen, Canadian dollars, and several European currencies distributed so that no single currency dominates could protect itself against an appreciation of the dollar by buying dollar index futures. Conversely, a firm with maturing payments obligations that are similarly distributed could hedge by going short in dollar index futures.

The Ecu futures contract offered by the FINEX differs from the dollar index contract in that the Ecu is a currency rather than an index. The appeal of the two contracts is similar, however, because the Ecu's composite currency mix overlaps that of the dollar index. The mark, the French franc, the pound sterling, the lira, the guilder, and the Belgian franc are common to both. While their weights differ, the overall similarity of currency composition is close enough that variations in the index tend to be mirrored by variations in the Ecu. There are, however, sufficient differences in currency composition and weights so that variations in the Ecu and the index are not perfectly correlated.

Ecu futures contracts appeal to some speculators, and they are useful for both hedging and price discovery. In hedging, they are particularly attractive to parties holding positions denominated either in Ecus, several European currencies, or a particular EMS currency for which futures contracts are unavailable.

At present, the volume of trading in Ecu futures is not large enough for *The Wall Street Journal* to publish a daily trading summary. In the past, however, the *Journal* has sometimes published abbreviated summaries for trading in the FINEX's Ecu futures contract. There would seem to be an excellent chance that trading in this contract will grow in the near future.

Other Currency Futures Exchanges

As is evident from Exhibit 7.1, various other exchanges trade currency futures. They include the MidAmerica Commodity Exchange (MCE) of Chicago, the Philadelphia Board of Trade (PBOT), the Singapore International Monetary Exchange (SIMEX), the Tokyo International Financial Futures Exchange (TIFFE), and exchanges in Rio de Janeiro, Sao Paulo, Stockholm, Sydney, and Auckland.

The Singapore International Monetary Exchange (SIMEX) The SIMEX trades contracts in yen, marks, and pounds sterling that are priced in dollars and are identical to the contracts in those currencies traded at the IMM. A mutual offset system in effect with the IMM permits contracts opened at one exchange to be closed out at the other. This means, for example, that if a party with an open position at one exchange finds it advisable to close out that position after trading at the exchange has ceased, the necessary transaction can be effected at the other exchange. Clearing members of the two exchanges maintain margin accounts with New York banks to facilitate mutual offset transactions, and the two exchanges maintain a Mutual Offset Settlement Account with a New York bank to record transfers between them. The margin accounts and the Mutual Offset Settlement Account are adjusted daily after the close of business at each exchange.

To date, the operation of the mutual offset system has not generated as much business at the SIMEX as had been hoped, but the business volume has been sufficient to keep the system in operation since 1984. Interest in all types of futures trading is on the increase outside the United States, and this fact gives the SIMEX good reason to stay in the currency futures business.

Other Currency Futures Exchanges Outside the United States   Interest in futures trading is on the rise in Europe, as is evident from the growing number of European exchanges engaged in trading various types of futures products. Such exchanges now exist in Denmark, Finland, France, Germany, Ireland, the Netherlands, Spain, Sweden, Switzerland, and the United Kingdom. With the recent decision by the LIFFE to suspend the trading of currency futures, however, the only currency futures contract being traded in Europe is the Swedish krona/dollar contract of the Stockholm Options Market. This situation is likely to change as Europeans become more familiar with futures trading. Inhibiting the development of currency futures trading in Europe are the dominant position achieved by the IMM and the belief that the GLOBEX trading system being promoted by the CME will achieve the objective of allowing the IMM to trade currency futures on a 24-hour basis.

The most promising challenge to the IMM's dominance from an exchange located outside the United States is likely to come from the TIFFE, which has been in operation only since June 30, 1989. The Japanese have taken a very cautious approach to the trading of new financial products and generally embark upon such trading only when the probability of success seems very high. The yen/dollar futures contract is one of only three futures contracts being traded by the TIFFE, the other two being a three-month Euroyen interest rate futures contract and a similar three-month Eurodollar contract.

Other Currency Futures Exchanges in the United States   In the United States, both the MCE and the PBOT trade currency futures contracts. The MCE is affiliated with the Chicago Board of Trade, the world's largest commodity futures exchange. Its currency futures contracts are scaled-down versions of IMM contracts, for example, their face values are generally one-half those of IMM contracts. The MCE's pound sterling contract is for only £12,500, only one-fifth the amount of the IMM contract in sterling. The MCE generates sufficient activity to justify an abbreviated summary of trading in its pound, mark, Swiss franc, and yen contracts in *The Wall Street Journal,* but its total trading volume remains small and has not shown much tendency to grow.

The PBOT is a subsidiary of the Philadelphia Stock Exchange (PHLX) and was established in 1986 to complement the PHLX's highly successful forex options trading. The PBOT's currency futures offerings are quite extensive and include all of the currencies traded at the IMM plus the Ecu and the French franc. The face values of the PBOT's contracts are the same as those of the IMM, and the PBOT offers the same maturities as the IMM, plus the nearest 2 months. In order to improve its competitive position, the PBOT has added nighttime trading for some contracts, and it opens trading well before the IMM begins its trading day. Nevertheless, the PBOT has not yet become a significant factor in the currency futures market.

Hedging with Forex Futures

While the appeal of currency futures for speculation is obvious, hedging is a different matter. Because currency futures contracts are standardized, their maturities are limited, and they require daily settlement, their usefulness for hedging may initially seem quite limited. In reality, however, currency futures are a good hedging medium, as the following example illustrates.

Hedging the Swiss Franc

Assume that an American travel agency sponsoring European tours recorded the following experience during a recent summer. In June, it estimated that it would need to acquire SF450,000 around August 15 in order to meet its projected expenditures in Swiss francs during the following month. Accordingly, on June 20, it went long four IMM Swiss franc September contracts of SF125,000 each at the exchange rate of $0.5424/franc. Although the firm could have purchased spot francs on the same date at $0.5412, it chose to hedge with futures in order to avoid having to handle francs prior to August 15. On August 15, the firm liquidated its four contracts by going short four September contracts at $0.6029. Simultaneously, it purchased SF450,000 spot at $0.6021. Ignoring transaction costs and any interest factor, the results of these transactions are summarized in the following table, which indicates that the firm effectively acquired the needed Swiss francs at an exchange rate of $0.5349/franc.

Spot purchase of SF450,000 on August 15 at $0.6021/franc	$270,945
Less: cash flow gain from futures transactions	
Sale of SF500,000 on August 15 at $0.6029/franc	
Purchase of SF500,000 on June 20 at $0.5424/franc	
Cash flow gain: ($0.0605/franc) × SF500,000	30,250
Total cost of purchasing SF450,000 with a futures hedge	$240,695
Cost per Swiss franc = $240,695/SF450,000 = $0.5349/franc	

The hedge proved highly successful. Although the spot franc rose by more than 11 percent, the gain from the long futures position was so large that the exchange rate at which spot francs were effectively acquired in August was lower than the June 20 spot rate of $0.5412. Moreover, since most of the cash flow gain undoubtedly occurred before August 15, it can be presumed that the firm had the opportunity to earn enough interest to offset its transaction costs, including round-turn commissions.

The results of the hedge would have been rather different had the franc declined instead of rising. Suppose, for example, that on August 15, the spot franc was $0.4882 and that the futures contracts were reversed at $0.4890. The results would then have been as follows:

Spot purchase of SF450,000 on August 15 at $0.4882/franc	$219,690
Plus: cash flow loss from futures transactions	
Sale of SF500,000 on August 15 at $0.4890/franc	
Purchase of SF500,000 on June 20 at $0.5424/franc	
Cash flow loss: ($0.0534/franc) × SF500,000	26,700
Total cost of purchasing SF450,000 with a futures hedge	$246,390
Cost per Swiss franc = $246,390/SF450,000 = $0.5475/franc	

Not only is the cost per franc higher in the second case, but also there would be an interest cost associated with the negative cash flows resulting from holding a long position in franc futures. Moreover, by hedging with futures, the firm would have lost the opportunity to benefit from the spot franc's decline. With either a forward hedge or a money market hedge, the cost of francs could have been locked in on June 20, and the negative cash flow from holding a long futures position could have been avoided. With these alternatives, however, the opportunity to benefit from the spot franc's decline would still have been lost.

The difference in results between this second case and the first case is primarily due to the difference between the face value of the futures contracts and the amount of spot purchase of August 15. It may be tempting to conclude from this that a futures hedge is likely to be inferior to a forward hedge since a forward contract can be for any amount that is mutually agreeable. In practice, however, the banks that deal in forwards offer their most attractive forward rates on transactions in which they buy or sell currencies in even millions of units. Thus, our travel agency might not have had quick and easy access to a forward contract for SF450,000, and even if it had had such access, the exchange rate would probably not have been as favorable as the futures rate.

Basis

The literature on futures markets makes much of **basis,** which is the cash or spot price of a good, currency, financial instrument, or index minus the corresponding futures price. In other words, basis corresponds to the forward swap rate of Chapter 6. Just as banks often manage swap positions in their forward operations to reflect their swap rate expectations, so also do some traders in currency futures attempt to profit from changes in basis. Such traders are known as *spreaders,* and their efforts to profit from anticipated changes in basis are often called *spread trading.* Except for the fact that daily settlement in futures trading produces cash flows that do not occur in forward trading, the material of Chapter 6 on swap rate speculation applies equally well to basis speculation in currency futures. In both cases, successful speculation hinges primarily on the ability to forecast changes in the interest rate differential.

The outcome of a futures hedge depends to some degree on what happen. to the basis. If the basis changes, the hedger gains or loses relative to the original spot rate, depending on the direction of change and on whether the hedger holds a long or short futures position. If, however, the futures rate changes one-for-one with the underlying spot rate, so that the basis remains the same, *and* the face value of the futures hedge equals the amount of the exposure being hedged, the futures hedger effectively receives or pays the spot rate in existence on the date the hedge began.

Assume that in the Swiss franc hedging example the amount to be hedged had been SF500,000 and that the basis had remained at the June 20 level of −12 points no matter what happened to the spot rate by August 15. In that case, whether the spot rate on August 15 had been $0.6021, $0.4882, or any other figure, the effective exchange rate paid for the francs would have been $0.5412/franc, i.e., the same price as the June 20 spot rate. Such an outcome is sometimes called a *perfect hedge*. Even in that case, however, the pattern of cash flows during the lives of the contracts and, therefore, the true outcome, would have depended on daily variations in futures rates.

Normally, the basis amount (whether positive or negative) tends to diminish as a futures contract approaches maturity. This follows from the fact that on the maturity date, the futures exchange rate merges into the spot exchange rate. Thus, in the Swiss franc example, if the amount hedged had been SF500,000 instead of SF450,000, and if the futures contracts had been carried to delivery, the basis would have risen to zero, and the price effectively paid for the Swiss francs would have been $0.5424/franc, irrespective of where the spot franc actually stood on the maturity date. Similarly, if the hedged amount had been SF500,000 and the basis amount had decreased steadily, so that, for example, it had been −5 points on August 15, the hedging firm would have effectively paid $0.5419/franc had it liquidated its futures contracts on that date.

In practice, just as forward swap rates can vary substantially, so also can the basis of futures trading. In both cases, the variations primarily reflect changes in the interest rate differential and departures from exact IRP within the confines of the neutral band. And just as the swap rate risk of forward trading is normally small, so is the basis risk of trading in currency futures. Incidentally, ignoring the cash flow element, a forward contract that is liquidated or effectively reversed before maturity is subject to the swap rate risk in the same manner as a futures contract is subject to the *basis risk*.

Summary

One alternative to the forward market is to combine an appropriate money market transaction with a spot transaction. In general, the forward market offers a slight advantage over this money market alternative in terms of simplicity and transaction costs, but situations arise in which the money market alternative is better.

The money market-spot exchange technique is used for either hedging or speculation in currencies for which forward contracts are not available. This technique has often been used to speculate against depreciating currencies when governments have attempted to maintain domestic interest rates below their equilibrium levels. When interest rates are free to fluctuate, however, the fact that a currency is expected to depreciate does not necessarily lead to money market speculation that is predominantly against it.

Forward and futures contracts have important similarities, but they also have important differences. Most fundamentally, forward contracts are informal agreements, while futures contracts are traded on organized exchanges. One of the most important consequences of this basic difference is that futures contracts are marked to market daily, thereby leading to cash flows that are absent from forward contracts. Most forward contracts are carried to maturity, but the vast majority of currency futures contracts are closed out before maturity by contract reversal.

Theoretically, forward and futures exchange rates can differ slightly without inducing arbitrage. In practice, however, they seem to differ little, and the price differences that do emerge tend to be speedily arbitraged away.

Trading in currency futures is dominated by the IMM, which has a great advantage over other exchanges in liquidity. Besides the IMM, only the FINEX, with its dollar index contract, has succeeded in developing a currency futures contract with major status. The IMM has recently begun cross-rate trading in currency futures, and the GLOBEX trading system being developed by the CME will allow the IMM to trade currency futures on a 24-hour basis.

Hedging with currency futures is more complicated than hedging with forwards, but currency futures are an effective hedging instrument. The difficulty of exactly matching the amounts to be hedged with the face values of standardized futures contracts can be a problem in small-scale hedging with futures, but small-scale hedging may not be feasible with forward contracts. Some variability in the results of hedging with currency futures occurs because of the basis risk, which is analogous to the swap rate risk with forward contracts. Just as some forward market participants speculate on swap rates, some futures traders speculate on basis movements.

References

Abbott, Susan. "How FBI's Sting Has Changed Pit Life." *Futures*, June 1991, pp. 46–49.

Ahmadi, Hamid Z., Peter A. Sharp, and Carl H. Walther. "The Effectiveness of Futures and Options in Hedging Currency Risk." *Advances in Futures and Options Research 1*, Part B, 1986, pp. 171–191.

Chance, Don M. *An Introduction to Options and Futures*. Chicago: The Dryden Press, 1989. Chapters 7 and 12.

Cornell, Bradford and Marc. R. Reinganum. "Forward and Futures Prices: Evidence from the Foreign Exchange Markets." *Journal of Finance*, December 1981, pp. 1035–1045.

Cox, John C., Jonathan E. Ingersoll, Jr., and Stephen A. Ross. "The Relation between Forward Prices and Futures

Prices." *Journal of Financial Economics,* December 1981, pp. 321–346.

Euromoney. "Futures and Options." Supplement to October 1986 issue.

_____. "Futures and Options." Supplement to October 1987 issue.

Federal Reserve Bank of New York. *The Chicago Mercantile Exchange.* New York: Federal Reserve Bank of New York, 1989.

Futures. "1991 Reference Guide to Futures/Options Markets," 1990, pp. 60–81.

Grabbe, J. Orlin. *International Financial Markets.* New York: Elsevier, 1986. Chapter 5.

Jarrow, Robert A. and George S. Oldfield. "Forward Contracts and Futures Contracts." *Journal of Financial Economics,* December 1981, pp. 373–382.

Kolb, Robert W. *Understanding Futures Markets.* 3d. ed. Glenview, IL: Kolb Publishing Company, 1991. Chapters 1–3 and 11.

Morgan, George E. "Forward and Futures Pricing of Treasury Bills." *Journal of Banking and Finance,* December 1981, pp. 483–496.

Park, Hun Y. and Andrew H. Chen. "Differences between Futures and Forward Prices: A Further Investigation of the Marking-to-Market Effects." *Journal of Futures Markets,* Spring 1985, pp. 77–88.

Richard, Scott F. and M. Sundaresan. "A Continuous Time Equilibrium Model of Forward Prices and Futures Prices in a Multigood Economy." *Journal of Financial Economics,* December 1981, pp. 347–371.

Schwarz, Edward W., Joanne M. Hill, and Thomas Schneeweis. *Financial Futures: Fundamentals, Strategies, and Applications.* New York: McGraw Hill, 1984. Chapters 13 and 17.

Silber, William L. "Marketmaker Behavior in an Auction Market: An Analysis of Scalpers in Futures Markets." *Journal of Finance,* September 1984, pp. 937–953.

Solnik, Bruno. *International Investments.* 2d. ed. Reading, Mass.: Addison-Wesley, 1991. Chapter 8.

Teweles, Richard J. and Frank J. Jones. *The Futures Game: Who Wins? Who Loses? Why?* New York: McGraw-Hill, 1987. Chapters 9 and 21.

The Wall Street Journal.

Questions

1. Why is it that, as a general proposition, hedging with forward contracts is slightly preferable to money market hedging? Under what circumstances is money market hedging likely to be preferable?
2. If, in fact, money market speculation often involves speculating against currencies that are expected to depreciate, what does that tell you about monetary policy in the countries with the depreciating currencies?
3. Although the volume of forward trading far exceeds that of currency futures trading, futures prices have considerable influence on forward prices. Why? Does the fact that the currency futures market has a large speculative component mean that forward rates are therefore less stable than they would otherwise be?
4. Under what circumstances should either a speculator or a hedger consider using dollar index futures or Ecu futures instead of futures contracts denominated in national currencies?
5. Why is the IMM the dominant exchange in currency futures?
6. Distinguish between the functions of the exchange clearinghouse and clearing members in currency futures trading.

7. Compare the merits of forwards and futures in hedging the exchange risk.
8. Explain how currency futures trading is regulated in the United States.
9. Explain what each of the following parties do in IMM currency futures trading: Class A clearing members, Class B clearing members, floor brokers, locals, scalpers, day traders, and position traders.
10. Explain the nature of original margin, settlement margin, initial margin, and maintenance margin in IMM currency futures trading.
11. How does the currency futures market's concept of basis differ from the forward market's concept of the swap rate? Ordinarily, how does basis change as a futures contract nears maturity, and what could prevent the normal change from occurring?
12. What is meant by a "perfect" futures hedge, and why is it that such a hedge is not, in fact, "perfect"?

Problems

1. Purehex, a U.S.-based firm, has a partial interest in an Italian company, Nailati Corporation, from which it expects to receive dividends of Lit1.5 billion in 30 days. Purehex wants to hedge this expected inflow so as to lock in its dollar amount. One alternative is to sell the lire forward 30 days at Lit1,376/dollar. Alternatively, it can borrow lire in the Eurocurrency market at 12.75 percent for 30 days and sell the borrowed funds at the spot rate of Lit1,371.50/dollar. Purehex estimates that it can generate a 10.25 percent rate of return with the borrowed funds. Which alternative should Purehex choose?

2. Assume that at the moment, the spot rate between the Argentine peso (Ps) and the dollar is Ps 1.16/dollar. A wealthy Argentine with funds in liquid short-term dollar assets anticipates that in 90 days the spot rate will be Ps 1.20/dollar. He can borrow pesos for 90 days at an annual rate of 22 percent, and the interest rate that he can obtain on a highly liquid, low-risk peso asset is 19 percent. If he leaves his funds in dollars, he can obtain an annual interest rate of 6.8 percent. Given this information, should this investor (1) borrow pesos and convert to dollars, (2) liquidate some or all of his dollar assets and convert to pesos, or (3) maintain the present distribution of assets between dollars and pesos?

3. Assume that on February 26, 1990 (see Exhibit 7.3) you were long one March contract each in marks, pounds, Swiss francs, and Australian dollars and short one contract each in yen and Canadian dollars. What would you have gained or lost on each contract? Also, assume you were short two March dollar index contracts. What would you have gained or lost on them?

4. Assume that High Roller Investments, a firm that specializes in handling pension funds for local governments, was slated to collect DM450,000 in interest at the end of December 1987. In early November 1987 the firm decided to hedge a possible decline in the mark by entering into the minimum number of IMM March futures contracts that would fully cover this mark exposure. The exchange rate at which the contracts were opened

was $0.6032/DM, and the spot rate was $0.5967/DM. On December 28, 1987, High Roller liquidated its futures position by entering into reversing contracts at $0.6306. Simultaneously, it sold DM 450,000 spot at $0.6255.

a. Based on this information, and assuming a commission charge of $28 per contract per round turn, what was the net dollar amount realized by High Roller, and what was the exchange rate it effectively received?
b. Why was this firm's hedge not a "perfect" hedge?
c. What would have been the exchange rate effectively received by High Roller if the December 28 spot rate had been $0.5824 and the futures rate at which liquidation occurred had been $0.5875? How does this result compare with that of Part a and why?

Foreign Exchange Options

■

Even in the dynamic world of international finance, the sudden emergence of forex options to great prominence stands out as a singular phenomenon. The awareness of this instrument's potential can be traced back to at least 1978, when such options were introduced by the newly established European Options Exchange (EOE) of Amsterdam. Most of the EOE's business focused on its options on European stocks, and the Amsterdam exchange had little success with currency options.

By 1982, however, increasing exchange rate volatility had made the forex market highly receptive to new techniques of exchange risk management. Beginning with the Montreal Exchange in that year, a number of exchanges have come forth with currency option products. The key that opened the currency options door was the immediately successful introduction of options on spot foreign exchange by the PHLX late in 1982. This achievement spurred the CME in 1984 to introduce a line of option contracts on its already popular forex futures contracts. Today, exchange trading in currency options is dominated by the PHLX and the CME, but it is likely that, in time, other exchanges will gain larger shares of this rapidly evolving market.

Even before 1978, banks sometimes provided currency options for valued customers, but it was the success of the PHLX that awakened them and their investment firm competitors to these options' potential. Known as *over-the-counter (OTC) options*, the volume of such informally written currency options exceeds that of exchange-traded currency options. OTC currency options are sometimes modeled on exchange-traded options, but they are often tailor made to meet customers' special needs. The relationship of OTC currency options to exchange-traded currency options is thus analogous to that of forward contracts to currency futures contracts.

It is difficult to determine just how significant currency options are for the forex market as a whole. The difficulty arises in part from the lack of adequate data on OTC options, and in part from the fact that since most currency options are never exercised, their total face value far exceeds the actual cash flows generated by them. It is clear, however, that they have attained great importance. They can be used for both hedging and speculation and are particularly useful for locking in existing positions that are regarded as desirable.

Currency Option Fundamentals

A currency option confers on its buyer the right either to buy or to sell a specified amount of a currency at a set price known as the **strike price.** An option that gives the right to buy is known as a **call,** while one that gives the right to sell is known as a **put.** Depending on the contract terms, an option may be exercisable on any date during a specified period, or it may be exercisable only on the final or **expiration date** of the period covered by the option contract. In return for guaranteeing the exercise of an option at its strike price, the option seller, or writer, charges a **premium,** which the buyer usually pays up front. Under favorable circumstances, the buyer may choose to exercise it. Alternatively, the buyer may be allowed to sell it. If the option expires without being exercised, the buyer receives no compensation for the premium paid. The situation of an option buyer is thus analogous to that of a buyer of insurance, while the situation of an option writer is analogous to that of a seller of insurance.

If an option can be exercised on any date during its lifetime, it is called an **American-style option,** but if it can be exercised only on its expiration date, it is called a **European-style option.** Currency options are also classified according to whether they are **options on spot** or **options on futures.** Beyond these categories, they are divided into various subcategories, most of which are varieties of OTC options that differ in one or more respects from the standard exchange-traded options that must be, because of limitations on the scope of this book, our primary concern. These customized currency options can contain such features as combinations of puts and calls into individual units, combinations of forward contracts with options, and handling option premiums so that payment is deferred or does not appear explicitly as such on the books of the buyer. Clearly, currency options are a complex subject. Fortunately, the general principles that govern their use are fairly easy to comprehend.

Exchange-traded currency options are overwhelmingly of the American type, while OTC currency options are generally of the European type. Since most of the former are traded on U.S. exchanges, while many of the currency options sold outside the United States are OTC options of the European type, the American–European distinction is not totally without geographical foundation. The foundation is weak, however, because European exchanges trade American-style options, there is some trading of European-style options at the PHLX, and OTC options sold in the United States are generally of the European type.

Whereas each purchase is matched against a sale in futures markets, option markets do not require the matching of puts and calls, nor are option buyers commonly required to post margins. On the other hand, the writers of exchange-traded options *are* required to post margins, and the writers of OTC options may be required to post them when they write options through banks or investment firms acting as brokers.

Like futures positions, the positions taken with options can be eliminated through contract reversal. Thus, the buyer of an option can cancel or offset it by writing an equivalent option, while an option writer can cancel or offset an option by buying an equivalent option. Note, however, that the buyer of a call does not eliminate the position by buying a put, nor does the writer of a call offset it by writing a put. If the buyer of a call buys a put, the call remains in effect, but the buyer is now out the cost of two premiums and will realize a net gain only if the relevant exchange rate changes in either direction by more than enough to cover the total premium cost. If the writer of a call also writes a put, the risk from the put is added to that from the call.

The Pricing of Currency Options

The most technically challenging aspect of currency options is setting their prices or premiums. Since even small exchange rate changes can have significant effects on the profitability of writing options, it has been necessary to develop option pricing models that are elaborate enough to be accurate and that can be fed into computers along with appropriate data to rapidly adjust premiums in accordance with the latest exchange rate movements. The detailed study of option pricing models lies beyond the scope of this book, but this chapter's appendix examines the currency option version of the Black-Scholes option pricing model, which is widely used in the actual pricing of currency options.

Fortunately, the factors that must be taken into account in formulating a model for the pricing of currency options are fairly easy to understand. The most important of these factors are the strike price, the interest rate differential between the countries whose currencies are included in the relevant exchange rate, the time to expiration, the exchange rate's expected volatility, and whether an option is American or European style.

The Role of the Strike Price   The premium or price for calls increases as the strike price decreases, and the premium or price for puts increases as the strike price increases. For both puts and calls, the difference between the strike price and the relevant market or *underlying* exchange rate of a currency option helps to establish an option's minimum price. If a currency option's price should ever fall below this minimum, an arbitrage opportunity would result.

Ignoring commissions, exchange rate spreads, and any other factors that limit arbitrage opportunities, the price of an American-style currency call option cannot be less than the amount, if any, by which the underlying exchange rate exceeds the strike price. If, for example, you buy an American-style call option on spot Canadian dollars with a strike price of $0.85 per Canadian dollar when the spot exchange rate is $0.86, you can be sure that the option's price will be at least $0.01 per Canadian dollar. Otherwise, you could arbitrage by immediately exercising the option and selling the Canadian dollars acquired at the spot rate of $0.86. If, however, the option had a strike price of $0.86 or more, the minimum value of the option would be zero.

In similar fashion, and employing the same assumptions, the price of an American-style put option on a currency cannot be less than the amount, if any, by which the strike price exceeds the underlying exchange rate. If, for example, you buy an American-style put option on spot Canadian dollars with a strike price of $0.87 per Canadian dollar when the spot exchange rate is $0.86, an option price of less than $0.01 per Canadian dollar would allow you to arbitrage by buying Canadian dollars spot and immediately exercising the option. If, however, the option had a strike price of $0.86 or less, the minimum value of the option would be zero.

In reality, the minimum prices for American-style currency options are likely to be somewhat higher than indicated in the examples given. Why this is so becomes evident a little later when we examine the roles of the interest rate differential and time to expiration in determining the price of a currency option.

Determining the minimum prices for European-style currency options requires more than a simple comparison of the strike price with the exercise price. Suppose, for example, that you can buy a European call option on spot Canadian dollars with a strike price of $0.85 per Canadian dollar at a price of less than $0.01 per Canadian dollar when the spot exchange rate is $0.86. Since the option is European style, you cannot arbitrage by immediately exercising it and selling Canadian dollars spot. Nevertheless, you might be able to conduct interest arbitrage by treating the option as a long forward contract and selling Canadian dollars spot. Complicating matters is the fact that the forward Canadian dollar generally exchanges at a discount because Canadian interest rates are generally higher than U.S. interest rates. This implies that the minimum price for the option in this case should be less than $0.01 per Canadian dollar.

Relying on the usual assumptions, the minimum price for a European-style currency call option on spot can be stated as follows:[1]

$$C_E(S,T,E) \geq Max[0, S(1 + b)^{-T} - E(1 + a)^{-T}]. \qquad (8-1)$$

C_E means a European call on a spot currency, S is the underlying spot rate, T is the time to expiration, E is the strike or exercise price, a is the risk-free interest rate in Country A, and b is the risk-free interest rate in Country B. The exchange rates are in units of A's currency per unit of B's currency. Equation 8−1 should be read as indicating that a European call currency option with given strike price, time to expiration, and underlying spot rate has a minimum price that exceeds zero if the spot rate discounted at Country B's interest rate exceeds the strike price discounted at Country A's interest rate.

The corresponding formulation for the minimum price of a European currency put option on spot can be stated as follows:

$$P_E(S,T,E) \geq Max[0, E(1 + a)^{-T} - S(1 + b)^{-T}]. \qquad (8-2)$$

Equation 8−2 indicates that a European put currency option with given strike price, time to expiration, and underlying spot price has a minimum price that

---

[1]This formulation and formulation 8−2 are based on Don M. Chance, *An Introduction to Options and Futures* (Chicago: The Dryden Press, 1989), pp. 479−480.

exceeds zero if the strike price discounted at Country A's interest rate exceeds the spot rate discounted at Country B's interest rate.

Assume that the underlying spot rate is $0.86 per Canadian dollar, that the interest rates are 6.4 percent in the United States and 8.0 percent in Canada, that the strike price for a European call on Canadian dollars is $0.85, and that the time to expiration is 90 days. By assigning a value of 0.25 to T and using $0.85, 6.4 percent, $0.86, and 8.0 percent, respectively, for E, a, S, and b, Equation 8−1 gives $0.0067 per Canadian dollar as the call's minimum price. By substituting a strike price of $0.87 on a European put for the call's strike price of $0.85 and otherwise using the same values, Equation 8−2 gives $0.0130 per Canadian dollar as the put's minimum price. It can also be determined that if the U.S. interest rate were 8.0 percent and the Canadian interest rate were 6.4 percent, and everything else remained the same, the call's minimum price would be $0.0130, while the put's minimum price would be $0.0067.

Since an American currency option can be exercised before expiration, and since the early exercise privilege is presumably worth something, it may seem strange that a European currency option can have a minimum price that exceeds the minimum price of a corresponding American option. In reality, however, the minimum price of an American currency option must always at least equal that of a comparable European option. The apparent contradiction displayed in the examples used will be resolved in the material that follows.

The Role of the Interest Rate Differential   Some indication of the role of the interest rate differential in determining a currency option's price was provided by the examples used to illustrate the determination of the minimum price for a European currency option. It was shown that a European call option on Canadian dollars has a higher price when the U.S. interest rate exceeds the Canadian interest rate than when the interest rate differential is reversed. Similarly, it was shown that a European put option on Canadian dollars has a higher price when the Canadian interest rate exceeds the U.S. interest rate than when the interest rate differential is reversed.

The influence of the interest rate differential on the prices of currency options extends to American options as well as to European options, with the result that the minimum prices of the former may exceed the differences between strike prices and underlying exchange rates. The higher the U.S. interest rate relative to the foreign interest rate, the higher is the price of an American call option on the foreign currency, and the lower is the price of an American put option on the foreign currency.

The logic behind the influence of the interest rate differential on a currency option's price can be understood by comparing the purchase of a currency option with the alternative of a spot transaction. With a call option on a foreign currency whose premium is priced in U.S. dollars, the option buyer avoids the U.S. dollar interest cost of a spot purchase and sacrifices the interest that could have been earned in the foreign currency. From this it follows that the price of a call option will increase as the U.S. dollar interest rate increases relative to the foreign currency interest rate. The situation is reversed in the purchase of a put option on a foreign currency. In buying a put, the buyer avoids the cost in terms of the foreign currency and sacrifices the interest that could have been earned in U.S. dollars. From this it follows that the price of a put option will *decrease* as the U.S. dollar interest rate increases relative to the foreign currency interest rate.

The analysis presented here holds equally for American-style and European-style currency options. This means that the interest rate differential that determines the minimum price of a European-style currency option may also influence the minimum price of an American-style currency option. Equations 8–1 and 8–2 are thus applicable to the pricing of American-style currency options to the extent that is necessary to prevent their prices from ever falling below the prices of comparable European currency options.

Since the interest rate differential is subject to constant changes, the price of an option varies because of interest rate changes as well as because of changes in the underlying exchange rate. Changes in the underlying exchange rate are likely to be of greater significance than changes in the interest rate differential, but the latter are also important.

The Role of Time to Expiration   Obviously, a mathematical relationship exists between the influence on a currency option's price of the interest rate differential and the influence of time to expiration. The longer the time to expiration, the greater is the influence of the interest rate differential. A large interest rate differential has little effect on the price of a currency option that is about to expire, but a much smaller differential may have an important effect on the price of a currency option with a relatively distant expiration date.

The influence on a currency option's price of time to expiration is not, however, primarily explained by the existing interest rate differential. More significant is the probability of a favorable change in the underlying exchange rate—the longer the time to expiration, the greater the probability of a favorable change. Also relevant is the probability of a favorable change in the interest rate differential. Changes in the underlying exchange rate or in the interest rate differential may also, of course, have a negative effect on a currency option's price, but the holder of such an option can always realize or lock in a gain that has been achieved. It is a general rule, therefore, that a currency option's price increases as the time to expiration increases. The increase in price is not, however, proportional to the increase in time.

The Role of Expected Volatility   Exchange rate volatility is the most difficult to quantify of the factors involved in determining the prices or premiums of currency options. Barring perfect clairvoyance by exchange rate forecasters, there is no way to precisely measure the future volatility of exchange rates. Lacking clairvoyance, option traders employ two volatility measures to help them set appropriate prices. One is **historical volatility,** in which data on past exchange rates are analyzed to derive the standard deviation of past volatility.

Assuming that the immediate future will replicate the past, probability theory can then be applied to estimate the prices that would adequately compensate option writers for assuming the exchange risk. The other measure is **implied volatility,** in which information on current option prices and exchange rates is combined with information on the other factors involved in determining option prices and plugged into an option pricing model to estimate the volatility implied by existing prices. If the implied volatility of these estimates exceeds what a potential option writer feels is warranted, then the writing of options should be undertaken. If, however, the implied volatility is less than expected volatility, the writing of options should be avoided.

Since the writers of currency options accept the risk that the actual volatility of exchange rates will prove greater than expected, that portion of a currency option's price that reflects expected volatility must incorporate a risk premium. It should be noted, however, that the writers of currency options can lay off the risk involved. For example, the writer of a large OTC put on marks can eliminate most of the risk by buying exchange-traded puts with a lower strike price and, therefore, a smaller premium cost. The writer might then lose all or part of its net premium income should the mark decline, but it would be protected against a large decline in the mark.

Since option writers can reduce or even eliminate the risks entailed in writing currency options, the statement that expected volatility must incorporate a risk premium should be modified. It is a little more accurate to say that expected volatility incorporates into a currency option's price an amount that compensates the option writer for either accepting the risk or incurring the costs involved in offsetting it.

In-the-Money, Intrinsic Value, and Time Value Whenever the relevant underlying exchange rate is above the strike price of a call or below the strike price of a put, a currency option is said to be **in-the-money.** Being in-the-money does not necessarily mean that the exercise of the option would be profitable, if permissible, for the difference between the strike price and the underlying exchange rate may be too small to permit the recovery of the full option premium.

Because of the early exercise feature of American options, the concept of being in-the-money is more applicable to them than to European options. As we have seen, a European currency option is not necessarily worth a difference between the strike price and the underlying exchange rate that is favorable from the buyer's perspective. An American currency option, however, is always worth at least the amount, if any, by which it is in-the-money. Even for European options, however, the concept of being in-the-money is relevant, for the potential gain embodied in an in-the-money European currency option can be protected through appropriate action.

The **intrinsic value** of an option is the amount, if any, by which it is in-the-money. The **time value** of an option is the amount by which the price of an option exceeds its intrinsic value. An option's time value is, of course, a function of time to expiration and falls to zero on the expiration date. We have seen, however, that the time value of a currency option depends not only upon the time to expiration, but also upon the size of the interest rate differential, the probability of a favorable movement in the underlying exchange rate, and even the probability of a favorable change in the interest rate differential.

The relationship between the price of an American-style option and the underlying price of the asset on which it is based is illustrated in Exhibit 8.1. The straight line that originates along the asset price axis represents the option's intrinsic value, while the curved line above it represents the option's total value. The vertical distance between the two lines is the time value. The intrinsic value graphs as a straight line because when the underlying price is above the call strike price or below the put strike price, a linear relationship exists between the intrinsic value and variations in the underlying price. The time value is greatest when the underlying price is at or near its strike price, which reflects the high probability that the underlying price will move to an exercisable level. As the underlying price falls farther below the strike price for calls or rises farther above the underlying price for puts, the probability of exercise diminishes and the time value therefore decreases, falling ultimately to zero. As the intrinsic value increases, the probability of additional gains decreases and the time value again diminishes.

Although Exhibit 8.1 may convey the impression that a single time value holds for each intrinsic value, a particular intrinsic value may be associated with various time values, depending on the time to expiration and the other

| E X H I B I T | 8.1 | *The Relationship between Value and Underlying Asset Price for an American Option*

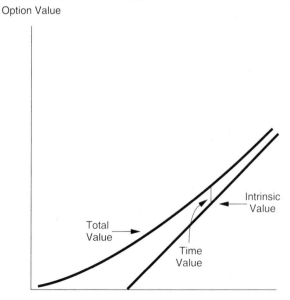

Option Value

Total Value

Time Value

Intrinsic Value

Underlying Asset Price
(Increasing for Calls, Decreasing for Puts)

variables that determine time value. As the time to expiration diminishes, for example, the total value curve shifts downward, and if price volatility increases, this curve shifts upward.

The Early Exercise of American-Style Currency Options   The fact that American-style options generally command somewhat higher prices than European-style options of otherwise comparable characteristics indicates that the right of early exercise has value. Nevertheless, it is generally inadvisable to exercise an American option before its expiration date because its time value is lost if it is exercised early. Since American options are generally exchange traded and, therefore, readily salable, the time values embodied in their prices can generally be realized before expiration by simply selling them. One can infer, however, that the possibility must exist for advantageous early exercise. Otherwise, there would be no reason for American options to command higher prices than European options.

The early exercise of an American currency option is likely to occur under two conditions. First, the option must be deeply in-the-money. Second, the interest differential $(a - b)$ must be sufficiently negative for a call or positive for a put to more than compensate for the loss of time value as a consequence of early exercise.

As Exhibit 8.1 indicates, when an option is deeply in-the-money, it is likely to have a relatively small time value. If the interest rate in Country B sufficiently exceeds the interest rate in Country A and the time to expiration is sufficiently low, the holder of an American call option on spot will gain enough in terms of interest to warrant the early exercise of the option and the consequent loss of time value. Similarly, if Country A's interest rate sufficiently exceeds Country B's interest rate and the time to expiration is sufficiently long, the holder of an American put option on spot will gain by exercising the option early.

Does this analysis apply equally well to American currency options on futures? As will be shown, the answer is yes.

Options on Spot and Options on Futures   For European currency options, an option on spot should have the same price as an otherwise identical option on futures if the expiration date of the underlying futures contract on which the option on futures is based is the same as the expiration date of the option. This price equality condition follows from the fact that the futures exchange rate merges into the spot rate at maturity. Since European currency options on futures are not traded at exchanges, however, the practical relevance of this equality condition is small.

For American currency options, options on spot and options on futures with identical strike prices rarely have the same market prices since futures exchange rates ordinarily differ from spot exchange rates. Moreover, since the difference between a spot rate and a corresponding futures rate (the basis) fluctuates, there are corresponding fluctuations in the prices of currency options on futures relative to the prices of currency options on spot. In general, these prices move closer to equality as the time to expiration diminishes because of the convergence of spot and futures exchange rates.

The preceding analysis of the pricing of American currency options was oriented primarily toward options on spot. Fortunately, the analysis of the pricing of American currency options on futures differs little from the analysis of the pricing of American currency options on spot. A notable difference, however, lies in the related area of early exercise.

Recall that it was indicated earlier that the early exercise of an American currency option requires two conditions: the option must be deeply in-the-money, and the interest rate differential must be large enough in the option holder's favor to more than offset the loss of time value from early exercise. These two conditions apply equally to options on spot and to options on futures, but they apply in different ways. For example, if an American call on spot is deeply in-the-money and the interest rate in Country B sufficiently exceeds the interest rate in Country A for a long enough time period, it pays the option holder to exercise and use the resulting proceeds to buy a B currency asset. If the option held is an American call on futures, early exercise is still likely to be desirable. The incentive for early exercise, however, is not interest earnings so much as the opportunity to buy currency futures at a discount in terms of basis points that is certain to evaporate by the maturity date of the underlying futures contract or contracts.

One other aspect of the early exercise of American currency options on futures is worth noting. When you buy an American currency option on futures, you pay the option premium up front. If you exercise the option, you enter into a futures contract with the option writer at the futures rate existing at the time of exercise, receiving a cash flow equal to the option's intrinsic value. By exercising early, you accelerate the recovery of the premium and obtain a cash flow gain, both of which could conceivably be lost if you refrain from early exercise. By contrast, if you exercise an American currency option on spot early, you have to make a cash outlay equal to the face value of the option contract.

The Uses of Currency Options: An Overview

Exchange-traded currency options, particularly options on futures, are more often used speculatively than are OTC options, but both types of options are used for both hedging and speculation. For either purpose, their attractiveness lies in the fact that, for a price, they avoid an adverse outcome while retaining the opportunity to gain from a favorable exchange rate movement. The decision to hedge or speculate by buying a currency option depends, of course, on the cost of doing so relative to the cost of the alternatives, but it also depends upon the option buyer's exchange rate outlook. Also relevant is the fact that the option format is admirably suited for locking in desired positions. This latter aspect of options is often referred to as their ability to provide *portfolio insurance*.

To understand currency options, it is as necessary to understand the motivations of option writers as it is to understand the motivations of option buyers. In the aggregate, the writers' motivations are considerably more complicated than the desire to generate income by acting as an insurer.

Hedging and Speculation   As a general proposition, choosing options over alternative hedging or speculative instruments is most appealing when there is a better than even chance of a favorable exchange rate change, but a considerable chance of an unfavorable change. Consider, for example, a U.S. firm that is obligated to make a known yen payment in a few weeks and wants protection against an increase in the spot yen's price. Assume that the probability of a decline in the spot yen is believed to exceed 50 percent but that a good chance remains the yen will rise. In this situation, hedging with a call option or options is likely to be better than, for example, a forward purchase because calls preserve the possibility of gaining from a decline in the yen while simultaneously guarding against a rise. A forward purchase would protect against a rise in the yen but forgo the chance to gain from a decline. If, however, the chance of a decline is regarded as slight, it would be better to buy yen forward and avoid the premium outlay.

Similarly, if a speculator wants to bet that the yen will fall, but feels that there is a considerable (but less than 50–50) chance of a rise, buying exchange-traded puts may be more appealing than, say, going short in futures. Moreover, because option purchases effectively limit losses to the premium outlay, they tend to be the choice among speculators who habitually fret about the outcomes of their bets and don't want to be bothered with reversing futures contracts when they have bet wrongly. On the other hand, if the chance of a sizable increase in the yen is regarded as small, it may be advisable to go short in futures and avoid the premium cost. In the final analysis, however, a speculator's decision about using currency options is likely to depend as much on his or her familiarity with them as on other factors.

In hedging, a factor of considerable importance affecting the use of currency options is the possibility that a foreign currency receipt or outlay being hedged may not occur. If, for example, a firm may have to make an outlay in Swiss francs during the next few months but there is a good chance that it may not, hedging with one or more calls is probably better than taking a long forward or futures position since these alternatives entail the risk of a realized net loss if the Swiss franc were to decline and the outlay does not occur. Moreover, by writing a call or calls the firm can recover all or part of its premium outlay in the event that the outlay does not occur.

Locking in Positions with Currency Options   A particularly appealing feature of buying currency options is the ease with which they can be used to safeguard an existing portfolio. Consider, for example, the following case. A U.S. pension fund specializes in bond investments and holds sizable amounts of foreign-currency bonds in its portfolio. Several years earlier, the fund purchased yen bonds in anticipation of an appreciation of the yen that would more than compensate for the relatively low yen interest rate existing at the time. Subsequently, let's assume the yen appreciated, and the fund's management now wants to lock in the gain without closing the door to further gains if, as expected, the yen continues its long-term upward trend. Also assume that the firm does not want to sell the bonds.

By going short in futures, the fund can guard against a short-term decline in the yen at the cost of forgoing a gain if the yen rises while it holds the futures contracts. By buying exchange-traded puts, however, the fund can guard against yen depreciation while preserving the possibility of gaining from appreciation. If the probability of short-term appreciation is less than 50–50, the correct decision might well be to purchase the puts.

Assume, however, that the fund's management decides the probability of a short-term decline in the yen is so high that it need not protect itself against a rise. Accordingly, it elects to go short in yen futures. Now assume that the yen does indeed decline but that the decline appears to be temporary. At this point, the fund's management might be well advised to rely on currency options to lock in its overall position.

One alternative would now be to buy yen *calls* for the duration of the outstanding futures contracts. The futures contracts would continue to provide protection against any further decline in the yen, and the calls would offset any loss on the futures contracts if the yen were to move upward. Since the fund would also have a portfolio gain should the yen rise, it would once more be positioned to gain overall from yen appreciation.

Alternatively, the short futures position could be liquidated through contract reversal, and protection against a decline in the yen could be provided by purchasing yen *puts*. The choice between puts and calls would depend on premium costs and the amount of the cash flow that could be obtained by closing out the futures position.

As this example shows, currency options are a flexible tool for insuring a portfolio. The primary drawback to their use for this purpose is their cost, which can be considerable if the option buyer seeks to completely eliminate the exchange risk. In practice, many portfolio managers accept some exchange risk when buying currency options. They use them in a manner analogous to the use of insurance policies with sizable deductions, i.e., the cost of buying currency options can be lowered by accepting some risk and electing strike prices that provide less protection but offer lower-cost premiums. In addition, many buyers of currency options also write them, for while the writing of options involves accepting risk, it provides premium income to offset premium payments. Moreover, the writing of options can be used to provide some protection against the exchange risk.

Writing Currency Options Like insurance companies, writers of options underwrite others' risk in the belief that the premiums they receive will be large enough to cover total losses and still provide adequate rewards. Both commercial banks and investment firms write large volumes of currency options. For banks, the appeal of writing currency options lies largely in the fact that options have less impact on their capital requirements than do deposit liabilities. The earnings from premiums and commissions have generally made the writing of currency options profitable, and since the resulting exposures can easily be hedged, it is hardly surprising that financial firms have enthusiastically spread the currency options gospel.

The writing of currency options is not limited to banks and investment firms. As noted earlier, some buyers of currency options also write them to earn premium income because option writing can be used to a limited extent for hedging. Indeed, some nonfinancial firms prefer to write currency options rather than buy them.

To see how the writing of currency options can be used for hedging, consider the case where a U.S. firm anticipates periodic cash receipts in a convertible foreign currency. The firm could protect the dollar value of these anticipated inflows by buying puts but that would entail premium outlays. Alternatively, it could partially hedge by writing calls in the foreign currency. In doing so, it would forgo potential gains from rises in the currency's price above the strike price, but the premium income would provide some compensation for either a rise in the currency's price above the strike price or a decline in the currency's price. Rather than rely solely on buying puts or writing calls, the firm might do some of both. Its premium income would then help defray the cost of the puts, and its protection against a decline in the currency's price would be greater than if it relied solely on writing calls.

Exchange-Traded Currency Options, OTC Options, and Currency Warrants

Like currency futures contracts, exchange-traded currency options come in standardized amounts with only a few expiration dates. They are generally American style and freely tradeable. The maximum life of an exchange-traded currency option is little more than a year, and most of these options have lives that fall well short of a year. They are not available in all freely traded currencies. Their liquidity and relatively small face value make them a popular speculative medium, but they are readily used for hedging. Thus, banks and investment firms that write OTC currency options rely heavily on exchange-traded currency options to hedge their positions.

OTC options can be modeled on exchange-traded options, but their primary appeal lies in what they offer that exchange-traded options do not. An OTC option is likely to have a much larger face value than an exchange option, its life can be for any period of time that is mutually acceptable to the contracting parties, and it can be on a currency on which exchange options do not exist. On average, OTC currency options have longer lives than exchange-traded currency options. They are generally of the European type and are frequently incorporated into hedging packages that contain multiple options, forward contracts, or other arrangements.

OTC currency options frequently take forms that are unavailable at exchanges. Illustrative of the point is the **compound option**, which is an option on an option. Suppose, for example, that a U.S. building contractor bids on a Canadian project that will require sizable short-term outlays in Canadian dollars if its bid is accepted. The firm might be well advised to buy a (relatively low-priced) compound option conferring the right to buy a call option on spot Canadian dollars. The strike price and the amount of the call premium would be specified in the compound option contract.

A promising recent development in the currency options field is the emergence of **currency warrants**, which are tradable currency options with small face values that typically have longer times to expiration than other currency options. Currency warrants are often offered with new bond issues. The warrants can be detached from the bonds and sold separately. Alternatively, currency warrants may be issued independently of any bond issue, in which case they are known as *naked warrants*. Legally they are considered to be a type of security. Accordingly, they can be traded at exchanges other than those that trade currency options.

Currency warrants began attracting attention early in 1987 when some European issuers of dollar-denominated Eurobonds, wishing to capitalize on growing market sentiment that the dollar's exchange value might rise, offered to attach them to bonds. The warrants were calls on the dollar with strike prices in marks or Swiss francs. Typically, they carried face values of $500 and were sold at substantial premiums. Their buyers tended to be speculators and institutional investors seeking medium-term alternatives to conventional currency options.

The issuers of the warrants were able to hedge by buying dollar-denominated, exchange-traded puts on marks or Swiss francs. Because the premiums paid by the issuers were much less than those they received from the warrants (which were also, in effect, puts on marks or Swiss francs), the issuers stood to make sizable profits, barring problems in hedging during the interval between the expiration dates of the exchange-traded puts and the expiration dates of the warrants. The liquidity and small face values of the warrants help explain how their issuers were able to charge high premiums, but the dominant factor in their appeal was their relatively long time to expiration.[2]

In April 1991, Merrill Lynch attracted much attention by offering three million American-style naked put warrants on marks at the American Stock Exchange. The warrants had a face value of 85 marks each, an effective strike price of $0.5882 per mark, and a September 1992 expiration. They were speedily sold at an issue price of $3.30 each, and even though an investor buying them at this price and holding them until the expiration date required an 8.6 percent appreciation of the mark just to break even, their market price rose to $4 each within three days after they were issued.[3]

Prospects for the development of currency warrants into a financial instrument of considerable importance seem excellent. Their relatively high cost severely restricts their appeal to parties with large-scale international financial operations, but for many smaller-scale participants in such operations, they may prove to be useful. It has been suggested, for example, that relatively small-scale U.S. investors in foreign stocks, whose numbers are growing rapidly, may find currency warrants to be a better medium than currency futures or option contracts for hedging against declines in the currencies in which their foreign stockholdings are denominated. Moreover, it is to be expected that the premiums on currency warrants will tend to decline as the use of the instrument expands.

---

[2]"Warranting a Loss on the Roundabout?" *Euromoney*, March 1987, pp. 15–16.

[3]"Merrill Scores with New Currency Warrants, but a Dollar Downturn Would Scare Investors," *The Wall Street Journal*, April 22, 1991, p. C2.

A Closer Look at the Use of Currency Options

The preceding discussion has provided an overview of the nature of currency options, the factors involved in determining their prices, and their uses. We shall now take a closer look at specific features. An in-depth examination of the technical aspects of using currency options would, however, require the writing of another book. Therefore, the ensuing examination of the use of currency options is highly selective.

Synthetic Options

Recall the example where a U.S. pension fund holding yen bonds hedges against a decline in the yen by going short in yen futures and subsequently, after the yen declines, has a choice between combining its futures position with the purchase of yen calls or closing out the futures position and buying yen puts. As this example makes clear, the combination of a short futures (or forward) position with the purchase of a call is equivalent to buying a put. Accordingly, this combination can be called a **synthetic put.** In similar fashion, the combination of a long futures/forward position with the purchase of a put can be called a **synthetic call.**

There are two situations where the concept of a synthetic currency option is particularly relevant. First, in making the original decision to buy or write a currency option, the buyer or writer normally can choose between an actual option and its synthetic equivalent. Thus, a prospective buyer of a put may choose instead to combine the purchase of a call with a futures or forward sale, and a prospective writer of a put may choose instead to combine the writing of a call with a futures or forward purchase. Second, once a desired portfolio position has been achieved, the concept of synthetic options becomes relevant to the insuring of the portfolio. We shall examine each of these situations in turn.

The Original Buying or Writing Decision   Assume that a U.S. firm must make sizable outlays in European currencies in about 90 days, primarily in marks, and that its management anticipates that the mark will rise. Also assume that the 90-day forward mark is currently at DM1.8518 per dollar, equivalent to $0.5400 per mark. Finally, assume a premium of $0.0150 per mark currently exists on either a put or a call American-style option on an IMM mark futures contract with a strike price of $0.5400 per mark and an expiration of 105 days (the most convenient expiration date).

Given this information, and ignoring the commission charges on futures contracts, the combination of buying equal face value amounts of futures contracts and put options is the exact equivalent of buying call options with the same face value. In parallel fashion, the combination of selling equal face value amounts of futures contracts and put options is the exact equivalent of selling call options of equal face value. These equivalencies are illustrated in the payoff graphs of Exhibit 8.2.

| E X H I B I T | 8.2 | *Synthetic Currency Options*

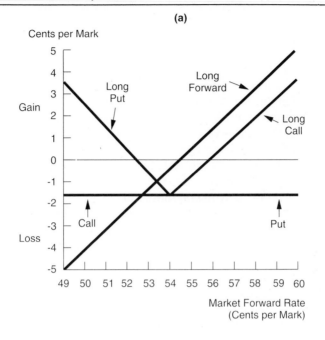

(a)

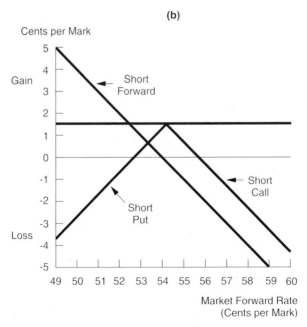

(b)

Panel (a) of Exhibit 8.2 demonstrates the equivalency to the buying of a call of the combination of buying of a put and holding a long forward or futures position. Note that the purchase of a put is designated as a *long put* and that the purchase of a call is designated as a *long call*. Note also that if the payoffs of the long put and the long futures are added vertically, the net result coincides exactly with the payoff of the long call. The long put-long futures combination is, therefore, a synthetic long call.

Panel (b) of Exhibit 8.2 demonstrates the equivalency to the writing of a call of the combination of writing a put and holding a short forward or futures position. Note that the writing of a put is designated as a *short put* and that the writing of a call is designated as a *short call*. Note also that if the payoffs of the short put and the short futures are added vertically, the net result coincides exactly with the payoff of the short call. The short put-short futures combination is, therefore, a synthetic short call.

Intuitively, it would seem that it would ordinarily be preferable to use the "plain vanilla" approach of simply buying or writing actual calls since buying or writing synthetic calls would entail accepting the additional costs of entering into forward or futures contracts. Nevertheless, it is conceivable that situations could arise in which the use of the synthetic option approach is desirable. Suppose, for example, that most buyers of currency options want to hedge against a rise in the dollar and therefore buy puts on other currencies. The resulting increase in the demand for puts could cause their premiums to rise sufficiently to tip the scales in favor of buying synthetic puts, i.e., long calls combined with short forwards or futures.

Arbitrage possibilities emerge when sufficient discrepancies develop between the prices of options and their synthetic alternatives. Thus, if actual puts on foreign currencies become overpriced relative to synthetic puts, it becomes possible to arbitrage by buying synthetic puts and writing actual puts.

Put–Call Parity   Relevant to discussions of synthetic options is the relationship known as **put–call parity**. Applied to European currency options on spot, this relationship can be expressed as follows:[4]

$$C_E(S,T,E) = P_E(S,T,E) + S(1 + b)^{-T} - E(1 + a)^{-T}. \qquad (8-3)$$

C_E and P_E stand for, respectively, the price of a European call and the price of a European put on a currency, S is the underlying spot rate, T is the time to expiration for both options, E is the strike price for both options, a is the risk-free interest rate in Country A, and b is the risk-free interest rate in Country B. The exchange rates are expressed in units of A's currency per unit of B's currency. Equation 8–3 indicates that a European call currency option on spot differs in price from a European put currency option on spot with the same strike price and time to expiration by the amount by which the

---

[4]This formulation is based on Chance, p. 481.

underlying spot rate, discounted at Country B's interest rate, differs from the exercise or strike price, discounted at Country A's interest rate.

For American currency options, whether on spot or futures, the calculation of put–call parity is complicated by the possibility of early exercise. We need not consider the complications here in order to grasp the significance of put-call parity for American-style currency options: a synthetic American option differs in price from its actual counterpart by an amount that reflects both the difference between the options' strike price and the underlying exchange rate and the interest rate differential between the countries.

Synthetic Currency Options as Portfolio Insurance Returning to our mark hedging example, assume that the U.S. firm elects to hedge its anticipated outlays in marks by buying exchange-traded calls on mark futures with a time to expiration of 105 days. Also assume that the expectation of a rise in the mark proves correct and that after 30 days, the underlying mark futures exchange rate has moved to $0.5800 per mark. Assume further that there are strong indications that the German government will act to prevent any significant additional rise in the mark by lowering interest rates. Sixty days remain until the firm has to buy foreign currencies. If the mark declines, it stands to lose on the calls, but this loss will be offset by what it gains from buying marks at a lower price if the decline persists. Ideally, the firm's management would like to avoid the loss on the calls while retaining the chance to gain from the mark's expected decline.

Among the alternatives that the firm could consider is to convert the calls into synthetic puts by going short the appropriate number of futures contracts at $0.5800 per mark while holding onto the calls. The resulting payoff graph is shown as Exhibit 8.3. It indicates that by going short in futures, the firm assures itself it will retain the gain of $0.0250 per mark it has accumulated on the calls (a gain of $0.0400 per mark relative to the underlying price minus the premium cost of $0.0150 per mark) while acquiring the opportunity to gain from the anticipated decline in the mark. In effect, by going short in futures, the firm obtains puts with a strike price of $0.5400 per mark and a negative premium of $0.2500 per mark. Moreover, it would now be positioned to gain doubly from the anticipated decline in the mark since it would be able to buy spot marks in 60 days at a more favorable price should the mark decline. In other words, if the mark now declines, the firm gains in both a cash flow sense and an opportunity cost sense.

Note, however, that if the firm follows the suggested strategy, it gives up protection against a rise in the spot mark above the current futures rate of $0.5800 per mark. To protect against a rise in the mark, it could consider giving up some of its accumulated gain by buying mark calls with a strike price of $0.5800 per mark or higher.

In this example, it has been assumed that the firm initially hedged with American-style calls on IMM futures. Because of the possibilities of early exercise or selling the calls, other strategies could have been pursued than the one indicated. For example, on day 30, the firm could sell the calls and buy puts. Had the firm initially hedged by buying a European-style OTC call on

| E X H I B I T | 8.3 | *A Synthetic Put as Portfolio Insurance*

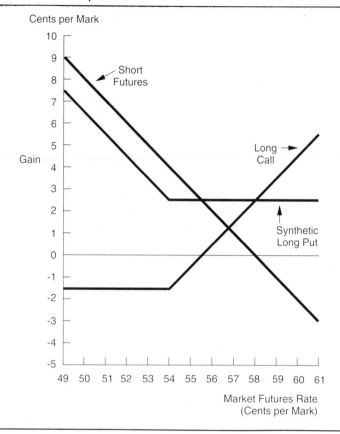

Cents per Mark

spot, it would have had fewer alternatives available on day 30, but it could still have followed the strategy suggested here—going short in futures (or with a forward) and, possibly, protecting itself against a rise in the mark by buying a call option or options with a higher strike price.

Further Complications

The examples of currency option use presented are relatively simple by comparison with others that could have been used. It was assumed, for example, that a firm bought currency options with a strike price that matched the current forward rate. It was also implicitly assumed that a firm wanting to protect itself against an increase in the mark's exchange value would buy call options whose face value would equal the amount of its anticipated future purchase of spot marks. In reality, an option buyer selects from an extensive menu of strike prices, and the face values of the options purchased may differ considerably from the amount of the buyer's forex exposure. Moreover, as was suggested earlier, the writing of options can be combined with their purchase to provide a hedge that costs little or even turns a profit. The choice among the myriad of alternatives depends on exchange rate expectations, the current structure of option premiums, how much risk an option user is willing to accept, and the skill of the user or the user's financial advisor in handling complicated financial operations.

Reducing the Cost of Using Currency Options   To keep down the cost of buying currency options many buyers are content to live with some risk. Accordingly, they buy options with strike prices that allow some loss but still provide protection against large losses. For example, in the case where a U.S. firm anticipates a sizable outlay on European currencies in 90 days and the 90-day forward mark is currently $0.54 per mark, the firm's managers might conclude they can live with a rise in the mark to, say $0.56, but want protection against a rise above that level. Calls with a strike price of $0.56 would, of course, cost considerably less than calls with a strike price of $0.54.

Another strategy often followed is to combine the buying and writing of currency options to target a net premium outlay of zero. For example, in the mark hedging example, the firm's managers could decide at the outset to simultaneously buy calls and write puts in equal face value amounts with a strike price of $0.54 per mark, thereby offsetting the premium outlay for the calls with the premium income from the puts. The payoff graph applicable to this case is shown as Exhibit 8.4, from which it is obvious that this particular combination amounts to a *synthetic long forward/futures position*. It would, of

| E X H I B I T | 8.4 | *A Synthetic Forward/Futures Position*

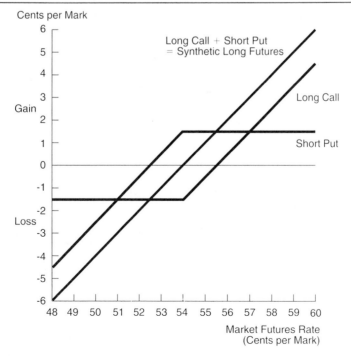

course, be simpler to buy either a long forward or the appropriate number of long futures contracts, but circumstances may sometimes favor using the synthetic alternative. It is always possible, for example, that a slightly more favorable exchange rate can be obtained with a synthetic forward/futures position than with an actual forward/futures transaction. As in similar situations, arbitrage possibilities tend to limit the price discrepancies that develop between actual and synthetic forwards and futures.

An advantage of relying on synthetic forwards and futures, as opposed to relying on actuals, is that the transactions required to create the synthetics may be entered into at different times. Recall, for example, the case where the pension fund holding yen bonds is concerned that the yen's exchange value might decline. One alternative for the fund would be to buy yen puts and subsequently recover all or most of the premium cost by writing yen calls of equal face value. The net effect of these transactions would be to establish a synthetic short forward/futures position, whose creation presumably would be timed so as to conform more perfectly with evolving market conditions and the fund's changing expectations than buying into a short forward/futures position at the outset.

Other Uses of Currency Options   For potential users, currency options offer a wide variety of combinations with various degrees of cost and risk.

Suppose, for example, that some speculators believe exchange rate volatility is likely to be greater than is implied by the existing structure of option premiums, but they are unsure which way a particular exchange rate will move, or they feel that it will oscillate first in one direction and then the other. One strategy used in such a situation is to buy options in a combination known as a **straddle,** which consists of equal amounts of puts and calls with the same strike price and time to expiration. Straddles can be sold as well as bought, and option writers who feel that the exchange rate volatility implied by the current premium structure is excessive may choose to speculate by doing so. Similar to a straddle is a *strangle,* which consists of equal amounts of puts or calls either purchased or sold with the same expiration date but different strike prices.

There is no compelling reason why a speculator who anticipates high exchange rate volatility will necessarily expect the volatility to be symmetrical. If, for example, a speculator expects high volatility on both sides of the mark/dollar exchange rate but believes that the trend for the mark will be downward, he or she may purchase more mark puts than calls. Similarly, there is no compelling reason why an option writer must match puts and calls.

Many users of currency options engage in **spread trading,** which, in the context of options, means they both buy and sell either puts or calls with different strike prices and/or different expiration dates. As in other cases of spread trading, such as speculating on futures basis points, successful spread trading in options offers relatively small profits under circumstances of limited risk. Consider, for example, the case of a writer of calls on marks with a relatively low strike price who wants to limit the loss if the mark moves sharply upward. One way to do so would be to buy an equal face value amount of calls with the same expiration date and a higher strike price. If the mark subsequently moves downward, the writer pockets the difference in premium costs. Depending on the width of the spread and the premiums, any loss from a rise in the mark will be nil or limited. Such an alignment is called a *bear spread* since the writer gains if the mark declines. It represents but one of numerous spread configurations.

It is obvious that the ways in which currency options can be combined with each other and with other instruments are numerous, being limited only by the imaginations, experience, and predilections of their users. The outlook for continued growth in the use of this instrument seems very bullish.

Currency Option Exchanges

Exhibit 8.5 summarizes the currency option contracts offered worldwide on exchanges as of 1990, excluding offerings of currency warrants. Of the 23 entries there, 15 are for exchanges in the United States. In terms of trading volume, the U.S. exchanges are far more dominant than this approximately two-to-one ratio would seem to imply. Moreover, 7 of the 8 listings for the PHLX actually represent two listings each since in those cases, the PHLX offers both American-style and European-style contracts.[5]

Exhibit 8.5 indicates that exchange-traded currency options can be either options on spot or options on futures. The PHLX dominates trading in the former, while the IMM dominates trading in the latter. In terms of the total face value of contracts traded, the IMM is ahead of the PHLX, but in terms of the total value of contracts outstanding (open interest) carried from day-to-day, the PHLX tends to have the edge. For example, according to *The Wall Street Journal,* at the end of trading on August 30, 1991, the PHLX had a total open interest of 994,544 currency option contracts, while the comparable figure for the IMM at the end of trading on August 29, 1991, was 447,004 such contracts.[6] Since IMM currency option contracts have face values that are twice those of PHLX contracts, it would appear, however, that the lead of the PHLX in terms of total contract face value was probably small. The reason for the difference between trading volume and open interest is that the IMM is more of a speculators' market than the PHLX and has a much larger volume of one-day trades.

Among the other exchanges offering currency options, only one is located in the United States. This exchange, the FINEX, offers an option on its dollar index futures contract. Outside the United States, currency options are traded at exchanges in Amsterdam, Stockholm, Singapore, Auckland, and Sydney.

---

[5]Originally, the PHLX offered only American-style currency options. In August 1987, however, the Chicago Board Options Exchange gave up on a 2-year experiment with trading European-style currency options and transferred its outstanding contracts of that type to the PHLX, which then developed its own European-style currency option contracts. The European-style contracts account for only a small part of the PHLX's total volume of business in currency options, generally less than 5 percent.

[6]*The Wall Street Journal,* September 3, 1991, p. C13.

| E X H I B I T | 8.5 | *Currency Option Contracts in 1990*

Currency	Exchange[a]	Contract Amount	Minimum Fluctuation[b]	Contract Months	Trading Hours (Local Time)
			Options on Spot		
Australian dollar	PHLX[c]	A$50,000	$0.0001/A$ = $5	Mar./June/Sep./ Dec. plus near 2 months	6:00 p.m.– 2:30 p.m. next day[d]
British pound	PHLX[c]	£31,250	$0.0001/£ = $3.125	Mar./June/Sep./ Dec. plus near 2 months	6:00 p.m.– 2:30 p.m. next day[d]
	EOE	£10,000	Fl 0.05/£ = Fl 500	Mar./June/Sep./ Dec.	10:00–4:30
Canadian dollar	PHLX[c]	C$50,000	$0.0001/C$ = $5	Mar./June/Sep./ Dec. plus near 2 months	4:30 a.m.– 2:30 p.m.
Ecu	PHLX[c]	Ecu62,500	$0.0001/Ecu = $6.25	Mar./June/Sep./ Dec. plus near 2 months	4:30 a.m.– 2:30 p.m.
French franc	PHLX[c]	FF250,000	$0.00002/FF = $5	Mar./June/Sep./ Dec. plus near 2 months	4:30 a.m.– 2:30 p.m.
German mark	PHLX[c]	DM62,500	$0.0001/DM = $6.25	Mar./June/Sep./ Dec. plus near 2 months	6:00 p.m.– 2:30 p.m. next day[d]
Japanese yen	PHLX[c]	¥6,250,000	$0.000001/¥ = $6.25	Mar./June/Sep./ Dec. plus near 2 months	6:00 p.m.– 2:30 p.m. next day[d]
Swiss franc	PHLX[c]	SF62,500	$0.0001/SF = $6.25	Mar./June/Sep./ Dec. plus near 2 months	6:00 p.m.– 2:30 p.m. next day[d]
U.S. dollar	EOE	$10,000	Fl 0.05/$ = Fl 500	Mar./June/Sep./ Dec.	10:00–4:30
	EOE	$100,000 (jumbo)	Fl 0.01/$ = Fl 1,000	Mar./June/Sep./ Dec.	9:45–4:30
	OM	$50,000	SEK 0.0001/$ = SEK 5	Mar./June/Sep./ Dec.	9:30–4:00
			Options on Futures		
Australian dollar	IMM	A$100,000	$0.0001/A$ = $10	Jan./Mar./Apr./June/ July/Sep./Oct./Dec. and spot month	7:20–2:00
	SFE	A$100,000	$0.0001/A$ = $10	Mar./June/Sep./Dec. out to 6 months ahead	8:30–4:30

Currency	Exchange[a]	Contract Amount	Minimum Fluctuation[b]	Contract Months	Trading Hours (Local Time)
British pound	IMM	£62,500	$0.0002/£ = $12.50	Jan./Mar./Apr./June/ July/Sep./Oct./Dec. and spot month	7:20–2:00
Canadian dollar	IMM	C$100,000	$0.0001/C$ = $10	Jan./Mar./Apr./June/ July/Sep./Oct./Dec. and spot month	7:20–2:00
German mark	IMM	DM125,000	$0.0001/DM = $12.50	Jan./Mar./Apr./June/ July/Sep./Oct./Dec. and spot month	7:20–2:00
	SIMEX[e]	DM125,000	$0.0001/DM = $12.50	Mar./June/Sep./Dec. and spot month	8:20–5:10
Japanese yen	IMM	¥12,500,000	$0.000001/¥ = $12.50	Jan./Mar./Apr./June/ July/Sep./Oct./Dec. and spot month	7:20–2:00
	SIMEX[e]	=Y12,500,000	$0.000001/¥ = $12.50	Mar./June/Sep./Dec. and spot month	8:15–5:05
New Zealand dollar	NZFOE	NZ$100,000	$0.0001/NZ$	All months	8:15–4:45
Swiss franc	IMM	SF125,000	$0.0001/SF = $12.50	Jan./Mar./Apr./June/ July/Sep./Oct./Dec. and spot month	7:20–2:00
U.S. dollar index	FINEX	$500 x index	$0.01 = $5	Mar./June/Sep./Dec.	8:20–3:00

[a]EOE—European Options Exchange (Amsterdam); FINEX—Financial Instrument Exchange (New York); IMM—International Monetary Market (Chicago); NZFOE—New Zealand Futures & Options Exchange (Auckland); OM—Stockholm Options Market; PHLX—Philadelphia Stock Exchange; SFE—Sydney Futures Exchange; and SIMEX—Singapore International Monetary Exchange.

[b]This is the minimum permitted "tick," or change in an option's underlying exchange rate multiplied by the face amount of the corresponding contract.

[c]With the exception of the Ecu contract, which is only available American style, all PHLX currency option contracts can be either American or European style.

[d]Eastern Standard Time. For Eastern Daylight Time, the trading hours are 7:00 p.m. through 2:30 p.m. the next day. The trading week begins on Sunday.

[e]The currency option contracts of the SIMEX are linked to those of the IMM; i.e., the contracts are interchangeable.

Sources: Federal Reserve Bank of New York, *The Chicago Mercantile Exchange,* New York: Federal Reserve Bank of New York, 1989, pp. 35 and 37; Federal Reserve Bank of New York, *Trading of Foreign Currency Options and Futures in Philadelphia,* Federal Reserve Bank of New York, 1989, pp. 5–7; and *Futures,* "1991 Reference Guide to Futures/Options Markets," 1990, pp. 60–81.

As of the summer of 1991, plans were being implemented at both the IMM and the PHLX for the introduction of cross-rate trading in currency option contracts. Each exchange had received approval for several such contracts. In addition, it is worthy of note that currency warrants are now traded on U.S. stock exchanges, including both the New York Stock Exchange and the American Stock Exchange.

PHLX Currency Options

The PHLX offers both American-style and European-style options on spot foreign exchange in seven different currencies and an American-style option on spot Ecus. The contract amounts are half those of IMM futures and option contracts. For example, while the IMM's mark futures contract is for DM125,000, the PHLX option on marks has a face value of DM62,500. Up to six different expiration dates are available per contract at any given time: in March, June, September, December, and the nearest 2 months other than these "quarter" months. In late April, for example, the possible expiration dates are in May, June, July, September, and December of the current year and March of the following year. The final settlement or delivery date for exercised options is the third Wednesday of the expiration month, and trading in all contracts stops on the Friday before the final delivery date. American-style options may be exercised on any business day prior to the last trading day and also on the Saturday (known as the *expiry Saturday*) after the last trading day. The exercise date for European options is the expiry Saturday. Delivery on an option exercised before the last trading day occurs on the fourth following business day, and delivery on an option exercised on the expiry Saturday occurs on the final delivery date, the third Wednesday of the expiration month. Approximately 25 to 30 percent of all PHLX currency options are exercised at expiration, and another 5 percent are exercised prior to expiration.[7]

Spurred by its intense competition with the IMM and its desire to attract business from writing OTC options in the Far East and Europe, the PHLX has greatly extended its trading hours for currency options, which originally ran only from 8 a.m. to 2:30 p.m. In September 1987, it introduced a 4-hour night trading session, for 5 currencies, and in January 1989, it moved the opening time for trading currency options to 4:30 a.m. At present, trading is continuous for the 5 leading currencies from 6 p.m., beginning on Sunday, to 2:30 p.m. the next day.

Participants and Trading Procedures PHLX memberships are held by individuals who are affiliated with either partnerships or corporations. Single proprietors may not become members. Neither may individuals who are directly employed by commercial banks, but some PHLX members are employed by commercial banking subsidiaries. In 1988, there were 505

---

[7]Federal Reserve Bank of New York, *Trading in Philadelphia*, p. 25.

members of the PHLX representing 290 firms. Of these 290 firms, 160 had member representatives certified to participate in the trading of PHLX currency options. In addition, 44 firms were represented on the trading floor by nonmember participants, who have the same trading privileges as members, but are not assured of permanent access to the trading floor.[8]

The parties that trade PHLX currency options fall into three categories: *specialists, registered options traders,* and *floor brokers.* **Specialists** act as marketmakers, determine the order in which options are traded, and execute orders entrusted to them by other parties. **Registered option traders (ROTs)** may trade either for the accounts of the firms they represent or broker orders from other parties on the exchange floor and the general public. In trading for their firms' accounts, they may act as marketmakers. **Floor brokers** execute orders for other parties on the exchange floor and the general public. They may not trade for their own accounts.

The fundamental responsibility of specialists is to guide trading at the locations (posts) where options on particular currencies are sold. For each trading session at each location, there is a single firm that provides the specialist or specialists. As of September 1991, Salomon Brothers provided all of the specialists for the night-time trading session (6 p.m. to 4:30 a.m.). For the daytime trading session, the specialist firms were Mitsui T & B for the Australian dollar and the Ecu, Tague Securities for the pound sterling and the yen, Canadian Dollar Options, Ltd. for the Canadian dollar, Timber Hill for the French franc, Société Générale Options, NA for the mark, and S.B.C. Derivatives, Inc. for the Swiss franc.

Subject to guidelines set by the PHLX, a specialist determines the order of rotation in which different contract variations are traded. At any given moment, trading is in either puts or calls (but not both) with a particular expiration date. The specialist is responsible for determining that all executable trades in a particular contract are made before moving on to another contract. As a marketmaker, the specialist is obligated to keep trading moving continuously by offering at all times to buy or sell with a suitable spread between the offers. Normally, specialists are content with narrow spreads because it is in their interest to stimulate trading. Sometimes the marketmaking aspect of a specialist's work leads to losses because of adverse price trends, but losses can be limited through appropriate hedging transactions involving interbank forex transactions, trading in futures, or trading in other options (including options in different currencies). On the whole, specialists derive considerable profits from the bid–ask spread, from taking favorable positions, and from commissions earned by executing orders accepted from other participants.

A specialist must avoid trading for his or her firm's own account except as is necessary in marketmaking. A specialist's firm is permitted to have other floor participants trade for its account in the specialist's designated currency,

---

[8]*Ibid.,* p. 8.

but a "Chinese wall" is supposed to separate them from the specialist, i.e., the specialist is to avoid exchanges of information or other forms of cooperation with other representatives of his or her firm. A specialist is, however, allowed to serve as an ROT or a floor broker to trade options on currencies other than the currency of specialization.

While ROTs may trade for their firms' accounts, they are subject to a rule that, during any given trading session, they may not both trade for their firms' accounts and serve as floor brokers. They are also obligated to serve as marketmakers as is necessary to keep trade flowing smoothly, but they do not serve as marketmakers when acting as floor brokers. In order to retain their classifications, at least half of their transactions during a quarter must be for their firms' accounts.

Trading Rounds   Exhibit 8.6 reproduces the summary of trading in PHLX currency options for Friday, August 30th that appeared in *The Wall Street Journal*. It records the last trading round in the afternoon and gives, at the bottom, the total trading volume during the day and the total open interest at the end of the day for all currency options combined. It shows exchanges of 3,008 calls and 13,149 puts, and total open interest of 501,758 calls and 492,786 puts for a total of 994,544 contracts. The figures for total exchanges during the day include the night session of the previous day.

In each trading round, options are priced on the basis of the underlying price, which is the current spot rate. A series of strike prices corresponds to each underlying price. The strike price intervals are typically $0.01 per currency unit, but when strike prices are close to the underlying price, a strike price interval of $0.005 may be used. When the underlying price changes by a certain minimum amount (a "tick"), a new round of trading begins with a new series of strike prices. As is shown in Exhibit 8.5, the changes in contract face value per tick are $6.25 for the Ecu, the yen, the Swiss franc, and the mark; $5 for the Australian dollar, the Canadian dollar, and the French franc; and $3.125 for the pound sterling. The variations in underlying prices that constitute ticks are $0.0001 per Australian dollar, pound sterling, Canadian dollar, Ecu, Swiss franc, and mark; $0.0002 per 10 French francs; and $0.0001 per 100 yen.

Exhibit 8.6 shows the premiums paid on transactions consummated in the last trading round. Thus, at least one put American-style option on the pound with an October expiration date was sold with a premium of $0.0161 per pound, which amounts to a total premium cost of $503.125 per contract.

Clearing, Margins, and Delivery   Trading on the PHLX floor is on the open outcry basis. When two parties agree to a trade, they prepare an order ticket, a copy of which is given to an exchange employee, who enters the information into the PHLX's computer system. The computer then prepares a trade report, copies of which are distributed to representatives of the **clearing member firms** who process the trade with the clearinghouse for PHLX transactions, the Options Clearing Corporation (OCC) of Chicago. The clearing members include information about the trade in data they transmit to the OCC. Between

| E X H I B I T | 8.6 | *Currency Option Trading at the PHLX: August 30, 1991*

Option & Underlying	Strike Price	Calls—Last			Puts—Last		
		Sep	Oct	Dec	Sep	Oct	Dec
50,000 Australian Dollars-cents per unit.							
ADollr	77	r	r	r	0.08	r	r
78.47	78	0.65	r	r	0.24	0.72	r
78.47	79	0.18	r	r	r	r	r
31,250 British Pounds-European Style.							
BPound	162½	r	r	r	r	0.90	r
31,250 British Pounds-cents per unit.							
BPound	162½	r	r	r	r	1.00	r
168.39	165	r	r	r	0.48	1.61	3.98
168.39	167½	1.30	r	r	1.50	2.73	r
168.39	170	0.65	r	r	r	r	r
168.39	175	r	r	1.50	r	r	r
50,000 Canadian Dollars-cents per unit.							
CDollr	87½	0.18	0.25	r	r	0.42	r
62,500 German Marks-European Style.							
DMark	58	0.20	r	r	r	r	r
57.34	58½	0.10	r	s	r	r	s
62,500 German Marks-cents per unit.							
DMark	53	4.21	r	r	r	r	0.33
57.34	55½	r	r	s	r	0.37	s
57.34	56	r	r	r	r	0.51	1.20
57.34	57	0.57	r	r	0.49	1.00	1.51
57.34	57½	0.33	r	s	r	r	s
57.34	58	0.21	0.51	0.95	r	1.37	2.14
57.34	58½	0.16	r	s	r	r	s
57.34	59	0.06	0.28	0.62	r	r	r
57.34	59½	r	0.18	s	r	r	s
57.34	61½	r	0.06	s	r	r	s
57.34	64	r	r	r	6.75	r	r
6,250,000 Japanese Yen-100ths of a cent per unit.							
JYen	73	0.39	r	r	0.39	r	r
62,500 Swiss Francs-European Style.							
SFranc	64	r	r	r	r	0.60	r
65.61	66	0.33	r	r	r	r	r
65.61	66½	r	0.58	s	r	r	s
62,500 Swiss Francs-cents per unit.							
SFranc	66	r	0.82	r	r	r	r
65.61	67	r	0.51	s	r	r	s
65.61	68	0.07	r	r	r	r	r
65.61	70	r	r	0.33	r	r	r
Total Call Vol	3,008				Call Open int		501,758
Total Put Vol	13,149				Put Open int		492,786

r—not traded; = s—no option offered.
Source: *The Wall Street Journal*, September 3, 1991, p. C13.

4:30 p.m. and 5 p.m. of each trading day, data on the transactions for that day and for the night session of the previous day are sent via computer to the OCC. By 9 a.m. the following day, the OCC instructs the designated bank of the clearing member that represents the option buyer to debit a special account of the clearing member for payment of the option premium, and by 10 a.m. these funds are transferred to the OCC's account with the bank. By 11 a.m., the premium amount is credited to the designated bank account of the clearing member who represents the option writer. By 10 a.m., meanwhile, the option writer's clearing member representative must deposit with its bank whatever margin the OCC requires. By 1 p.m., the option or options are officially issued by the OCC, and the OCC has completed the process of technically becoming a party to each transaction, thereby guaranteeing contract fulfillment.

The OCC clears and settles options traded on five U.S. exchanges and in the electronically operated market known as the National Association of Securities Dealers Automated Quotations (NASDAQ) system, but the PHLX is the only one of these six entities that trades currency options.[9] The OCC is owned in equal shares by these entities. Its headquarters is in Chicago, but it has branch offices in several other cities, including Philadelphia. Its clearing members are registered brokers and dealers and foreign securities firms that meet its financial and other requirements. The flows of money and other assets in connection with premium payments, margin deposits, liquidated positions, and currency deliveries all occur through clearing members acting for themselves or as agents for other firms that conduct business on the PHLX floor.

The margins required by the OCC from clearing members who are on the writing side of currency options are determined through a complicated procedure that employs an options pricing model and takes into account a clearing member's overall portfolio of outstanding option writing commit-ments. Basically, the OCC protects itself against a worse-case scenario. The margin deposits maintained by clearing members are adjusted daily, and a margin call may be issued during a trading day if exchange rates are unusually volatile. The margins posted may be in the form of interest-earning collateral acceptable to the OCC, and margin credit is allowed for premium income left on deposit in designated bank accounts.

Just as the OCC requires margin deposits from clearing members, clearing members require margin deposits from their customers. In fact, they must do so under PHLX rules, which specify the margins that must be maintained by all customers for whom options are written on the exchange floor. The PHLX determines its margin requirements with a different procedure from that used by the OCC, but it likewise embraces the principle that margin deposits should be risk-based. This means, for example, that if an option writer has also purchased options, the required margin may be reduced in some instances.

---

[9]Besides the PHLX and the NASDAQ, the exchanges are the American Stock Exchange, the Chicago Board Options Exchange, the New York Stock Exchange, and the Pacific Stock Exchange.

Customers can satisfy margin requirements with deposits of cash, any kind of securities, or letters of credit from approved banks. For each customer, the required margin is calculated when an option is written and at the end of each trading day. While customers are not automatically required to post additional margin equal to any increases in the prices of options they have written, they are subject to *some* additional margin calls when those prices increase unless they have offsetting gains on purchased options for which allowances are made in setting margin requirements.

When an option buyer notifies the appropriate clearing member of an intention to exercise one or more options he or she holds, the clearing member includes an exercise notification in the information that it transmits daily to the OCC. The OCC then randomly assigns an exercise notice to one or more clearing members with matching writing commitments. The clearing member selected to make delivery is allowed credit against the delivery obligation for any receipts it will have because of delivery on exercised options. A clearing member with a settlement obligation in either dollars or a foreign currency has an obligation to make the necessary arrangements to notify the OCC of the availability of funds 2 business days before the settlement date. As was previously noted, in most cases, the settlement date is the third Wednesday of the expiration month.

Regulation In the United States, government responsibility for regulating the trading of currency options is divided between the CFTC, which regulates futures exchanges, and the SEC, which regulates stock exchanges. Since the trading of currency options at the PHLX evolved from its trading in stock options, which had developed under the SEC's auspices, the SEC was assigned the responsibility for regulating the PHLX's currency options. Similarly, when the CME (IMM) and the CTN (FINEX) desired to initiate the trading of options on their currency futures, it seemed appropriate to assign the regulatory authority over them to the CFTC. The resulting regulatory structure, though logical, has led to a certain element of political tension that would not have existed had a single agency been given regulatory authority over all trading in currency futures. It has also probably meant that regulations have been less stringent than they would have been had a single agency been placed in control.

The SEC provides the general guidelines under which PHLX currency options are traded and approves new contract offerings and important modifications to existing contracts. Within the general limits established by the SEC, trading is regulated by the PHLX's Board of Governors, consisting of at least 28 members, most of whom represent firms trading on the PHLX floor. The board appoints various committees to deal with such matters as setting and enforcing trading rules, admitting new members, evaluating the PHLX's performance, monitoring compliance with SEC and PHLX rules, arbitrating disputes, and imposing penalties for rules violations. The board has a chairman, two vice-chairmen, and a president, who serves as its chief executive officer.

IMM Currency Options

Although it is customary to identify the currency options traded at the CME with its IMM division, these options are actually traded at the CME's Index and Option Market (IOM) division, which handles stock index futures, lumber futures, and options on futures, including options on the currency futures contracts traded at the IMM. The IOM has been in existence since 1976, though it did not receive its present name until 1982. In the following account of currency options trading at the CME, the customary practice of identifying them with the IMM rather than the IOM will be generally followed.

As is shown in Exhibit 8.5, as of 1990, the IMM was supporting trading in options on six currency futures contracts. The contract months available are January, March, April, June, July, September, October, December, and the spot month, which is the nearest month that is not one of the other eight contract months. In late April, for example, the spot month would be May, while in late May, it would be August. For all six currencies, therefore, options may be traded with expiration dates during the following three months. In addition, as of the summer of 1991, the IMM began trading three cross-rate currency option contracts on its new line of cross-rate currency futures contracts. In each of these three new contracts, the mark is one of the currencies.

If an IMM currency option is exercised, the exercising party receives a futures contract that expires in March, June, September, or December. Accordingly, a currency option that expires in a month other than one of the quarter months is actually on a futures contract that expires in one of these four months. For example, a put on Swiss francs with a January expiration date gives the buyer the right to go short one *March* futures contract by exercising the option on or before its expiration date. The expiration date for IMM currency options is two Fridays before the third Wednesday of the expiration month, and the last trading day is the day before expiration. The last trading day for IMM currency futures contracts is the second business day before the third Wednesday of the expiration month. That day is, of course, normally a Monday. Both buyers and sellers of currency options may freely trade their holdings until the last trading day, and when an option is exercised, an option writer is randomly selected to assume the other side of the resulting futures position.

Participants and Trading Procedures   The trading of IMM currency options closely resembles the trading of IMM futures described in Chapter 7. Trading is on the open outcry basis. It begins at 7:20 a.m. and closes at 2 p.m. When two parties agree to a trade, the trade is processed by clearing members. When the trade is validated by the CME clearinghouse, the clearinghouse assumes the role of counterparty on each side of the transaction, thereby guaranteeing performance.

The trading of IMM currency options is limited to individuals with memberships in at least one of the CME's three trading divisions along with persons with temporary trading privileges. There are three CME membership categories: CME, IMM, and IOM. CME members may trade in any contract traded by any of the three divisions; IMM members may trade in contracts traded by the IMM and the IOM; and IOM members are restricted to trading at the IOM. As of 1989, the number of CME memberships was limited to 625, while the numbers of IMM and IOM memberships were limited, respectively, to 812 and 1,287.[10] Temporary floor trading privileges are allowed to nonmembers who have been issued *trading permits,* which are valid for one year and nontransferable. Recently, however, the only currency options traded by the holders of trading permits have been those in Australian and Canadian dollars, provided that the holders of the permits are acting for their own accounts.[11] Note that Exhibit 8.7 does not show the decimals applying to the strike prices.

While trading at the PHLX relies on specialists, the trading of currency options at the IMM is directed by officers of the exchange. The underlying prices on which IMM currency option premiums are based are the current futures prices at the IMM. The ticks and corresponding changes in contract face values for IMM currency options are shown in Exhibit 8.5. When the underlying futures rate for an option contract changes by one or more ticks, a new series of option strike prices goes into effect, and the premiums are adjusted accordingly.

Trading Data   Exhibit 8.7 reproduces the summary of trading in IMM currency options for Friday, August 30, 1991, which appeared in *The Wall Street Journal.* It shows put and call premiums with combinations of six strike prices and three possible expiration dates for each of five currencies. Excluded from Exhibit 8.7 is trading in the Australian dollar option, whose volume was too small to be listed in the *Journal's* main summary. The premiums shown in Exhibit 8.7 applied to the last transactions of the day.

By including the open interest of 2,059 contracts in Australian dollars, it can be determined that the total open interest in all listed IMM currency option contracts at the end of trading on Thursday, August 29, 1991, was 447,004 contracts. As was pointed out earlier, the IMM evidently ranked somewhat behind the PHLX on this date in terms of open interest. Note, however, that it can be determined from Exhibit 8.7 that on August 30, 1991, the volume of currency option contracts traded at the IMM was 21,999, and that on the previous day, the trading volume was 40,446 (there being no trading in Australian dollar options on either day). Exhibit 8.6 indicates that the total trading volume at the PHLX on August 30, 1991 was 16,157. Since IMM contracts have twice the face value of PHLX contracts, these figures support the point made earlier that the IMM leads the PHLX in terms of daily trading volume.

[10]Federal Reserve Bank of New York, *The Chicago Mercantile Exchange* (New York: Federal Reserve Bank of New York, 1989), p. 45.

[11]*Ibid.,* p. 50.

| E X H I B I T | 8.7 | *Currency Option Trading at the IMM: August 30, 1991*

Strike Price	Calls — Settle			Puts — Settle		
	Sep-c	Oct-c	Nov-c	Sep-p	Oct-p	Nov-p
JAPANESE YEN 12,500,000 yen; cents per 100 yen						
7200	1.09	1.15	....	0.04	0.36	....
7250	0.65	0.83	....	0.10	0.54	....
7300	0.30	0.58	0.93	0.25	0.79	1.14
7350	0.13	0.41	0.73	0.58	....	....
7400	0.06	0.28	0.57	1.01	....	....
7450	0.03	0.19	0.43	1.48	....	....

Est. vol. 3,767, Thur vol. 3,071 calls, 1,348 puts
Open interest Thur 55,288 calls, 54,775 puts

DEUTSCHEMARK 125,000 marks; cents per mark						
5600	1.25	1.22	....	0.07	0.55	0.91
5650	0.83	0.93	1.29	0.15	0.76	1.12
5700	0.47	0.70	1.06	0.29	1.03	1.38
5750	0.25	0.51	0.86	0.57	1.34	....
5800	0.11	0.37	0.70	0.93	1.69	....
5850	0.06	0.27	0.55	1.38	....	....

Est. vol. 14,748, Thur vol. 14,330 calls, 14,596 puts
Open interest Thur 118,009 calls, 122,497 puts

CANADIAN DOLLAR 100,000 Can.$; cents per Can.$						
8650	1.00	0.54	0.69	.0000	0.15	0.29
8700	0.53	0.25	....	0.02	0.35	....
8750	0.11	0.11	0.23	0.11	....	....
8800	0.01	....	....	0.51	....	....
8850	....	....	....	....	....	....
8900	....	....	....	....	....	....

Est. vol. 705, Thur vol. 130 calls, 229 puts
Open interest Thur 10,895 calls, 12,940 puts

Clearing, Margins, and Delivery   The clearing process for IMM currency options is essentially the same as that for IMM futures. Individuals who trade on the IOM floor submit records of their transactions for a day's session to the clearing members who represent them, and the clearing members submit the information to the clearinghouse. The clearinghouse matches and confirms trades, finishing between 9 and 10 p.m., and then determines the margin and settlement obligations of clearing members as a result of the day's transactions. Around 3 a.m. the following day, the clearinghouse contacts the four Chicago banks used by the CME for clearing and settlement purposes and notifies them of the amounts it should receive from and pay to individual clearing members. The settlement banks confirm the amounts involved, and the clearinghouse proceeds on the assumption that payments owed to it will be credited to its account later in the day. Assuming no hitch develops, option contracts are officially opened on the day after they are negotiated.

Strike Price	Calls—Settle			Puts—Settle		
	Sep-c	Oct-c	Nov-c	Sep-p	Oct-p	Nov-p

BRITISH POUND 62,500 pounds; cents per pound

1625	5.26	4.36	....	0.04	1.18	2.10
1650	2.92	2.78	3.84	0.22	2.12	3.14
1675	1.20	1.64	2.68	0.98	3.46	....
1700	0.32	0.92	1.82	2.60	5.22	....
1725	0.06	0.48	1.18	4.84	....	....
1750	0.004	0.24	....	7.30	....	....

Est. vol. 870, Thur vol. 444 calls, 1,706 puts
Open interest Thur 15,824 calls, 14,842 puts

SWISS FRANC 125,000 francs; cents per franc

6450	1.06	1.30	....	0.13	0.74	....
6500	0.68	1.00	1.42	0.25	0.96	1.36
6550	0.39	0.78	1.20	0.46	1.23	1.63
6600	0.20	0.59	0.98	0.77	1.53	....
6650	0.09	0.44	....	1.16	....	2.24
6700	0.05	0.33	0.67	1.62	2.24	....

Est. vol. 1,909, Thur vol. 2,815 calls, 1,777 puts
Open interest Thur 18,736 calls, 21,139 puts

Settlement Prices for IMM Futures Contracts, August 30, 1991

Yen		British pound	
Sept	$.7305 per 100 yen	Sept	$1.6770
Dec	.7279 per 100 yen	Dec	1.6570
Mark		Swiss franc	
Sept	$.5718	Sept	.6543
Dec	.5667	Dec	.6506
Canadian dollar			
Sept	$.8750		
Dec	.8690		

Source: *The Wall Street Journal*, September 3, 1991, p. C13.

The margin requirements for option writers imposed by the CME are substantially different from those for futures contracts, and considerably more complicated. Adding to the complications is the fact that a clearing member's holdings of IMM futures are taken into account in determining its margin requirements on options. The premiums received by option writers are assigned to their margin accounts. At the end of each trading day, a clearing member's margin requirement is determined by taking into account its options portfolio and a risk factor based on the estimated volatility of option premiums and the margins required on the underlying futures contracts. Margin credit is given equal to the option premiums on long positions, while margin charges are made equal to the option premiums on short positions. The resulting margin figures are adjusted on the basis of the risk factor and portfolio considerations, including a clearing member's position in futures. If, for example, a clearing member has written calls, but is also a net buyer of futures in the same currency, the margin requirement for the calls is reduced. As a general principle, the margin deposits of clearing members must be sufficient to cover losses for a day of greater than normal exchange rate variations.

The CME also has margin requirements for floor traders who have written options through clearing member firms and for the customers of floor traders for whom options have been written. These margin requirements are also portfolio-based, but they are considerably less complicated than the margin requirements for clearing members. Brokers are permitted to require more margin from their customers than the CME requires them to collect.

When an IMM currency option is exercised, the exercise notice is passed to the clearinghouse by 7 p.m. of the same day. A clearing member with a matching outstanding option writing commitment is randomly selected to take the other side of the resulting futures contract. On the next business day, the option positions are cancelled and the futures positions are substituted for them. Subsequently during that day, the cash flow due is determined on the basis of the difference between the futures price and the exercised option's strike price. Assuming that neither party elects to close out its futures position before the end of the day's trading, the futures settlement price at the close of the day decides the cash flow.

Other Exchanges

To date, the trading of currency options at exchanges other than the PHLX and the IMM has generally been small. Outside the United States, the development of exchange trading in currency options has been inhibited by the dominance of the U.S. exchanges and the ready availability of OTC options that mirror the characteristics of exchange-traded options. The greatest success by a non-U.S. exchange recorded to date has been by the SIMEX, whose options on yen and marks are traded on a mutual offset basis with the IMM. It may well turn out to be the case that as foreign exchanges tie in to the GLOBEX trading system being developed by the CME, some of these exchanges will become much more active in the trading of currency options than they have been to date.

Inside the United States, the FINEX has had considerable success with its option on its dollar index futures contract. The volume of trading in this option contract has recently soared. On August 29, 1991, for example, the estimated volume of trading in this contract was 1,491 calls and 2,243 puts, and the total open interest was 17,926 calls and 18,600 puts.[12] These figures demonstrate that this option has attained major status.

---

[12]The Wall Street Journal, September 3, 1991, p. C13.

Summary

Currency options are traded either on organized exchanges or over the counter. Exchange trading is dominated by the PHLX, which trades options on spot, and the IMM, which trades options on futures. Exchange-traded options are usually American style (exercisable before their expiration dates),while OTC options are usually European style (exercisable only on their expiration dates.

Central to the use of currency options is the setting of their premiums or prices. The most important of the factors that determine currency options' prices are the strike price, the interest rate differential between the countries whose currencies are included in the relevant exchange rate, the time to expiration, the exchange rate's expected volatility, and whether an option is American or European style.

A currency option's value can be separated into two components: intrinsic value and time value. For American options, intrinsic value is the amount by which an option is in-the-money, which is the amount that could be obtained from early exercise. For European options, it is the in-the-money amount that can be insured through appropriate action. An American currency option's time value is lost if it is exercised early, but if such an option is deeply in-the-money and the interest rate differential is sufficiently favorable, early exercise may be desirable.

The choice between buying currency options or relying on alternatives depends on the cost of option premiums relative to expected exchange-rate volatility. The option alternative is most appealing when there is a good chance of a favorable exchange rate movement, but a considerable (though lesser) chance of an unfavorable movement. A particularly appealing feature of currency options is the ease with which they can be used to safeguard or insure unrealized portfolio gains. Frequently, currency options are combined with forwards, futures, or even other options in order to insure such gains.

The primary deterrent to the use of currency options is their cost. The cost of using them is often reduced by buying options with less favorable strike prices or by combining the writing of options with the buying of them. The writing of currency options is thus not just a matter of earning income by betting that exchange rate volatility will be less than many option buyers fear, but is often an integral part of overall hedging strategy.

The relationship between OTC currency options and exchange-traded currency options resembles that between forwards and futures. OTC options offer greater flexibility and less liquidity. Both can be viewed as short-term instruments. Currency warrants, which are, in effect, tradable currency options with relatively long maturities and small face values, can be used for medium-term hedging and speculation and are developing into a promising instrument. The cost of buying currency warrants is, however, high.

The daily trading volume of the IMM exceeds that of the PHLX, but the PHLX tends to have edge in terms of the total face of value of currency options carried as open interest. The PHLX relies on a specialist system and has a very long trading day that allows it to capture business from around the globe. The

IMM has a much shorter trading day, but it has a mutal offset system with SIMEX and is in the process of integrating exchanges in other countries into its GLOBEX trading system. To date, the only currency option exchange besides the PHLX or the IMM which has been able to generate a large trading volume in a currency option contract is the FINEX, which has recently enjoyed great success with the option on its dollar index futures contract.

References

Abuaf, Niso. "Foreign Exchange Options: The Leading Hedge." *Midland Corporate Financial Journal,* Summer 1987, pp. 51–58.

Adams, Paul D., and Steve B. Wyatt. "Biases in Option Prices: Evidence from the Foreign Currency Option Market." *Journal of Banking and Finance,* December 1987, pp. 549–562.

Ahmadi, Hamid Z., Peter A. Sharp, and Carl H. Walther. "The Effectiveness of Futures and Options in Hedging Currency Risk." *Advances in Futures and Options Research 1,* Part B, 1986, pp. 171–191.

Biger, Nahum, and John Hull. "The Valuation of Currency Options." *Financial Management,* Spring 1983, pp. 24–28.

Bodurtha, James N., Jr., and George R. Courtadon. "Efficiency Tests of the Foreign Currency Options Market." *Journal of Finance,* March 1986, pp. 151–162.

_____. "Tests of an American Option Pricing Model on the Foreign Currency Options Market." *Journal of Financial and Quantitative Analysis,* June 1987, pp. 153–167.

Brady, Simon. "The Options Explosion." *Euromoney.* Supplement to the April 1989 issue, pp. 48–53.

Chance, Don M. *An Introduction to Options and Futures.* Chicago: The Dryden Press, 1989, Chapter 12.

Euromoney. "Futures and Options." Supplement to the October 1986 issue.

_____. "Futures and Options." Supplement to the October 1987 issue.

Federal Reserve Bank of New York. *The Chicago Mercantile Exchange.* New York: Federal Reserve Bank of New York, 1989.

_____. *An Overview of the Operations of the Options Clearing Corporation.* New York: Federal Reserve Bank of New York, 1989.

_____. *Trading of Foreign Currency Options and Futures in Philadelphia.* New York: Federal Reserve Bank of New York, 1989.

Gadkari, Vilas. "Relative Pricing of Currency Options: A Tutorial." *Advances in Futures and Options Research 1,* Part A, 1986, pp. 227–245.

Garman, Mark B., and Steven W. Kohlhagen, "Foreign Currency Option Values," *Journal of International Money and Finance,* December 1983, pp. 231–237.

Giddy, Ian H. "The Foreign Exchange Option as a Hedging Tool." *Midland Corporate Finance Journal,* Fall 1983, pp. 32–42.

Grabbe, J. Orlin. "The Pricing of Call and Put Options on Foreign Exchange," *Journal of International Money and Finance,* December 1983, pp. 239–253.

_____. *International Financial Markets.* New York: Elsevier, 1986, Chapter 6.

Ogden, Joseph P., and Alan L. Tucker. "The Relative Valuation of American Currency Spot and Futures Options: Theory and Empirical Tests." *Journal of Financial and Quantitative Analysis,* December 1988, pp. 351–368.

Peterson, David R., and Alan L. Tucker. "Implied Spot Rates as Predictors of Currency Returns: A Note." *Journal of Finance,* March 1988, pp. 247–258.

Scott, Elton, and Alan L. Tucker. "Predicting Currency Return Volatility." *Journal of Banking and Finance*, December 1989, pp. 839–851.

Shastri, Kuldeep, and Kishore Tandon. "Valuation of American Options on Foreign Currency." *Journal of Banking and Finance*, June 1987, pp. 245–269.

Solnik, Bruno. *International Investments*, 2d. ed. Reading, Mass: Addison-Wesley, 1991, Chapter 9.

Tucker, Alan T. "Empirical Tests of the Efficiency of the Currency Option Market." *Journal of Financial Research*, Winter 1985, pp. 275–285.

_____. "Foreign Exchange Option Prices as Predictors of Equilibrium Forward Exchange Rates." *Journal of International Money and Finance*, September 1987, pp. 283–294.

Tucker, Alan T., Jeff Madura, and Thomas C. Chiang, *International Financial Markets*. St. Paul: West Publishing, 1991, Chapters 14 and 15.

The Wall Street Journal.

Warren, Geoffrey. "Quick Brown Fox Breaks Forward Over Lazy Scout." *Euromoney*, May 1987, pp. 245–258.

Whaley, Robert E. "Valuation of American Futures Options: Theory and Tests." *Journal of Finance*, March 1986, pp. 127–150.

Questions

1. Assume that U.S. interest rates rise relative to interest rates in Germany. Everything else remaining the same, how will this tend to affect the premiums on puts and calls on the mark? Why?
2. Explain the meanings of the terms *in-the-money, intrinsic value,* and *time value.*
3. Why is a currency option likely to have some time value even when it is out-of-the-money? When is its time value likely to be greatest?
4. What are the circumstances that are most favorable for the early exercise of an American currency option? How does the gain derived from the early exercise of an option on spot differ from that derived from the early exercise of an option on futures?
5. Assume that you are an officer for a pension fund that holds a portfolio of British stocks. Recently, anticipating a downward swing in the pound sterling and not wanting to sell the stocks, you purchased a European put option on the pound. Subsequently, the pound declined below the option's strike price. There are still two months to go until the option's expiration, and you don't think the pound is likely to decline any more. What action could you now take to protect most of the gain you are showing on the option?
6. What are currency warrants, and what are their attractions to both the buyers and writers of them?
7. Suppose that the spot Swiss franc is currently at SF 1.6000 per dollar, equivalent to $0.6250 per franc, and that U.S. short-term interest rates currently average about 2 percentage points below Swiss franc interest rates. Should you expect the premium on a PHLX call option on the franc with a strike price of $0.6250 to equal, exceed, or be less than the premium on a PHLX option on the franc with the same strike price? Explain.

8. What is a synthetic put? What are two different situations in which it might be desirable to use one?
9. How would you go about constructing a synthetic short forward with European options with a net premium outlay of close to zero?
10. How do PHLX currency option contracts differ from IMM currency option contracts with respect to: (a) face values, (b) expiration dates, and (c) delivery on exercised options?
11. What does a PHLX specialist do, and how does his/her work differ from that of a registered option trader (ROT)?
12. Who are the parties who are permitted to trade currency options at the CME's Index and Option Market division?
13. Explain why the current futures price for a currency is the underlying price for up to three different IMM currency option contracts.

Problems

1. Assume that High Roller (HR) Investments manages pension funds for a certain prominent local government. HR is allowed to place up to 10 percent of these funds in bonds denominated in foreign currencies, and it has bought the maximum amount of such bonds that it is permitted to buy. Most of them are denominated in Swiss francs. HR expects a short-term rise of the dollar against the franc and wants both to retain the bonds and protect their dollar value.

   Assume that the spot Swiss franc is currently $0.6756 per franc and that franc futures with 98 days to expiration are priced at $0.6712 per franc. IMM puts on Swiss franc futures that expire in the same month as the futures contracts can be purchased with a strike price of $0.6700 at a premium of $0.0160 per franc. HR estimates that during the next 98 days, the spot franc could go as low as $0.61 or as high as $0.70, and that the most probable value in 98 days is about $0.65.

   Given a choice between hedging by either going short in Swiss franc futures with 98 days to expiration or buying the puts with a strike price of $0.6700, which alternative is better? Show on a graph the outcome with either alternative over the range of possible exchange rates. Ignore commission costs.

2. Now assume that HR is uneasy about relying on plain vanilla futures contracts in the situation described in problem 1 and will go with either the put options with a strike price of $0.6700 or synthetic options. For the synthetic options alternative, it is considering the purchase of IMM calls on Swiss francs that expire in the same month as the underlying futures contracts, have a strike price of $0.6800, and a premium of $1.20 per franc. Show both of these alternatives and make a recommendation. Ignore commission costs.

3. A popular use of OTC options is to arrange what is known as a *range forward,* in which a party combines the writing and buying of options with a bank counterparty so as to minimize or eliminate the premium outlay

while receiving a guarantee that the price it pays or receives for foreign exchange will fall within predetermined limits.

Consider the following example. A firm that is going to receive a large sum of marks in 90 days agrees to a range forward in which it buys a European put on spot marks with a strike price of $0.5700 per mark and writes an equal face value European call on spot marks with a strike price of $0.6300. Both options have 90 days to expiration, and no premium payment is made. If, in 90 days, the spot mark is at or above $0.6300, the bank counterparty exercises its option and buys the marks at $0.6300, and if the spot mark is at or below $0.5700, the bank counterparty buys the marks at $0.5700. At any exchange rate between these limits, the bank buys the marks at the current spot rate. At present, the forward rate is $0.6010. Show this arrangement on a payoff graph and briefly suggest why the firm might prefer it to a simple forward sale at $0.6010.

| A P P E N D I X | 8.1 |

The Black-Scholes Currency Option Pricing Model*

The best-known formulation for pricing currency options is derived from a 1973 article by MIT professors Fischer Black and Myron Scholes.[13] The original Black-Scholes model was for pricing European-style calls on non-dividend-paying stocks, but the model proved readily adaptable to other European-style options. It was extended to currency options in 1983 in articles by Mark Garman and Steven Kohlhagen[14] and by J. Orlin Grabbe.[15]

For European calls on currencies, the Black-Scholes model can be expressed as follows:

$$C_E = Se^{-bT}N(d_1) - Ee^{-aT}N(d_2) \qquad (8-4)$$

where C_E is the price of a European call option on a spot currency, S is the current spot rate in units of Country A's currency per unit of Country B's

*Written by John S. Evans and D. K. Malhotra. The authors are indebted to Robert E. Brooks of the University of Alabama for his helpful comments pertaining to this appendix.

[13]Fischer Black and Myron Scholes, "The Pricing of Options and Corporate Liabilities," *Journal of Political Economy,* May-June 1973, pp. 637–659.

[14]Mark B. Garman and Steven W. Kohlhagen, "Foreign Currency Option Values," *Journal of International Money and Finance,* December 1983, pp. 231–237.

[15]J. Orlin Grabbe, "The Pricing of Call and Put Options on Foreign Exchange," *Journal of International Money and Finance,* December 1983, pp. 239–253.

currency, E is the exercise or strike price expressed in the same way, T is the time to expiration in years, a is the continuously compounded risk-free interest rate in Country A, b is the continuously compounded risk-free interest rate in Country B, e is the number 2.71828 (the base for natural logarithms), and $N(d_1)$ and $N(d_2)$ are the appropriate values of the standard normal probability distribution function.

The values e^{-bT} and e^{-aT} are used to obtain discounted values for S and E. The discounting of S and E is necessary because the buyer of a European call option forgoes the interest that could be earned by buying B's currency spot and avoids the interest cost in A's currency that would be incurred if the option were exercised immediately.

The high esteem in which the Black-Scholes model is held stems from the elegant way in which it derives the probability functions $N(d_1)$ and $N(d_2)$. It would be beyond the intended scope of this book to explain in detail how these functions are derived. Nevertheless, it is appropriate to look at their components and provide some commentary about them.

The terms d_1 and d_2 are defined as follows:

$$d_1 = \frac{\ln(S/E) + [a - b + (\sigma^2/2)]}{\sigma\sqrt{T}}$$
$$d_2 = d_1 - \sigma\sqrt{T}$$

where ln means natural logarithm, σ is the annualized standard deviation of percentage changes in the natural logarithm of the spot rate, and σ^2 is the variance of these percentage changes. The other terms are the same as in Equation 8–4. It is assumed that the standard deviation and, therefore, the variance remain constant during the option's lifetime.

The values obtained for d_1 and d_2 can be used with a standard normal probabilities table to obtain the values for $N(d_1)$ and $N(d_2)$. The values for $N(d_1)$ and $N(d_2)$ are then plugged into Equation 8–4, and the option's price is calculated. Among option traders, it is standard practice to use computers that have been programmed to calculate currency option prices using the Black-Scholes model. There are various option computer programs available that can be readily adapted to currency options.[16]

Equation 8–4 indicates that the price of a European call option on a currency depends on the strike price relative to the underlying spot exchange rate, the risk-free interest rate in the two countries, the time to expiration, and the standard deviation of changes in the underlying spot rate. It employs the following assumptions: interest rates remain constant, lending and borrowing

---

[16]One way for the reader to acquire such a program is to buy Robert W. Kolb's *Options: An Introduction* (Miami: Kolb Publishing Company, 1991). The buyers of this paperback receive the software for running an option pricing program. The software contains a module for pricing options on a stock with continuous dividends that can be adapted to pricing currency options. The Fall 1988 issue of the *Journal of Financial Education* (Boca Raton, Fla.: Florida Atlantic University) contains two examples of computer programs that can be adapted to pricing currency options.

interest rates are the same, there are no taxes or transaction costs, exchange rate variations are lognormally distributed, and the standard deviation (and, therefore, the variance) remain constant during the option's lifetime. Notwithstanding the restrictiveness of these assumptions, it is generally agreed that the Black-Scholes model provides a good approximation of what prices on European options should be.

With a lognormal distribution, the percentage variations in the natural logarithm of the relevant variable—the spot exchange rate in this case—take the form of a normal distribution. If spot rate variations are lognormally distributed, this means that the values for the spot rate (as opposed to the percentage variations in the natural logarithm of the spot rate) are not normally distributed, but are skewed to the right, as indicated in Exhibit 8.8. In practical terms, if exchange rate variations are lognormally distributed, there is a greater probability of large variations than if exchange rates themselves varied normally. The lognormal assumption of the Black-Scholes model allows the model, however, to incorporate the statistical convenience of the normal curve.

European-style put options can readily be priced with the Black-Scholes model. Since a call option on B's currency is, in effect, a put option on A's currency, a call on A's currency can be priced by reversing the country labels of Equation 8–4. Alternatively, the put-call parity formula of Equation 8–3 can be used to derive a formulation for pricing puts without altering the country labels.

The Black-Scholes model for pricing European options can be used for pricing either options on spot or options on futures since the futures exchange rate merges into the spot rate at maturity. Since exchanges do not trade European options on currency futures, however, this fact is of limited significance. When applied to American-style options, the Black-Scholes model results in underpricing since it rules out early exercise. Accordingly, the traders of American options on currencies who rely on Black-Scholes must make upward price adjustments from the prices given by the model.

The accuracy of the Black-Scholes currency option pricing model is open to some question because the model's restrictive assumptions do not necessarily hold in practice. Interest rates and exchange rate volatility may change abruptly, but the Black-Scholes model assumes they are constant. Lending and borrowing interest rates are not identical, there are transaction costs, and there may be tax considerations. There is doubt that exchange rate variations are actually lognormally distributed. Understandably, therefore, there are ongoing efforts to improve on the Black-Scholes model, and there is some evidence of success with these efforts.[17]

Despite its shortcomings, the Black-Scholes model will probably continue to be widely used for pricing currency options, in part because of inertia and

---

[17]For a summary of recent efforts to improve on the Black-Scholes currency option pricing model, see Alan L. Tucker, Jeff Madura, and Thomas C. Chiang, *International Financial Markets* (St. Paul: West Publishing, 1991), pp. 303–306.

| E X H I B I T | 8.8 | *Lognormal and Normal Exchange Rate Distributions*

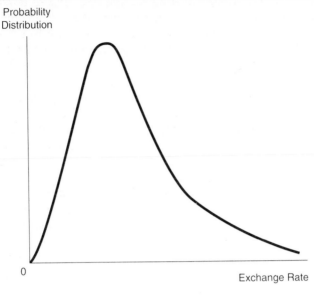

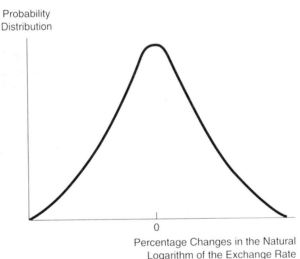

in part because of its relative simplicity. While there is some evidence that it can lead to mispricing, it does not appear that the mispricing has been serious enough to give rise to significant profits from arbitrage based on mispricing. For example, if Black-Scholes pricing leads to the underpricing of calls on sterling, the possibility emerges of arbitrage by buying calls and selling pound futures. It appears, however, that there have been relatively few cases in which the profits from such arbitrage opportunities have been large enough to offset the transaction costs of arbitraging.[18] In conclusion, it appears that the Black-Scholes currency pricing model provides good results and that no alternative has yet appeared that is, in the minds of most observers, clearly superior.

---

[18]Chance, *op. cit.*, pp. 508–511.

Exchange Rate Theory and Policy

■

| C H A P T E R | *9* |
Exchange Rate Determination and Forecasting

| C H A P T E R | *10* |
Exchange Rate Theory

| C H A P T E R | *11* |
Portfolio Theory, Speculation, and Exchange Rate Policy

Exchange Rate Determination
and Forecasting

■

Because of the enormous importance attached to exchange rates, they are among the most studied of economic phenomena. Even so, their determination remains something of a mystery. The forecasters with the most impressive records are frequently wrong by substantial margins. While it is arguable that their errors are derived from the impossibility of foreseeing all of the events that exert a major influence on exchange rates, there have been numerous instances in which poor forecasting results could not be convincingly explained by unforeseeable events. At the beginning of 1984, for example, forecasters uniformly predicted that the dollar would decline against other major currencies, but the dollar proceeded to rise throughout the year, although in other respects the general performance of the world economy did not radically depart from forecasts. The clear implication is that the forecasters erred in setting up their theoretical models, which suggests that the mechanics of exchange rate determination are imperfectly understood.

In large part, the lack of understanding of exchange rate determination stems from complications caused by the tremendous increase in the international mobility of capital due to improvements in telecommunications and generally looser restrictions on international financial transactions. Economic theory long regarded exchange rate determination as being dominated by flows of goods and services, but economists have been forced to revise their thinking about exchange rates to recognize that, with the increased international mobility of capital, the forex market often behaves like a volatile stock market.

While much remains to be learned about exchange rates, much is also understood about them. It is dangerous, therefore, to assume that ignorance reigns so supreme that one guess is as good as another. Exchange rate forecasters have often been wrong, but they have also scored impressive successes. Furthermore, when theories of exchange rate determination are matched against the historical record, it seems evident that they have much explanatory power. It is essential, therefore, to understand these theories if the process of exchange rate determination is to be made comprehensible.

While there are enormous differences between various theories of exchange rate determination, there is a common core of analysis that appears in much of the theoretical work on the subject. This common core is built on four key relationships:

1. *Purchasing power parity (PPP),* which links spot exchange rates to nations' price levels
2. *The international Fisher effect (IFE),* which links exchange rates to nations' nominal interest rate levels
3. *Interest rate parity (IRP),* which links spot exchange rates, forward exchange rates, and nominal interest rates
4. *The expected exchange rate,* which links exchange rate expectations to the forward rate.

The bulk of this chapter is devoted to examining these four relationships. In addition, we shall be looking in this chapter at exchange rate forecasting and the question of whether or not the forex market is efficient. It is shown that the four key relationships leave much of the short-term behavior of exchange rates unexplained and that exchange rate forecasting services have apparently had some success in outperforming them as guides to short-term exchange rate behavior.

Purchasing Power Parity (PPP)

A cornerstone of theories of exchange rate determination has long been the idea that exchange rates are greatly affected by nations' price levels, especially in the long run. Since approximately 1920, this idea has been labeled **purchasing power parity (PPP)**.[1] While sometimes called a theory, PPP is more accurately labeled a relationship. This is because PPP does not, in itself, tell us how exchange rates and price levels are causally related. All it does is indicate that exchange rates and price levels tend to be related in a certain way. It does not indicate which determines which.

A basic distinction to understand is that between absolute PPP and relative PPP. In *absolute PPP,* the exchange rate is obtained by dividing the local currency price of a good in one country by its local currency price in another country or, alternatively, by dividing the local currency cost of a collection of goods in one country by the local currency cost of the same "market basket" in the other country. In *relative PPP,* a *change* in an exchange rate matches a change in the two nations' relative price levels. It is relative PPP that primarily interests economic theorists, but we shall first take a quick glance at absolute PPP in order to see why reliance on relative PPP is necessary.

---

[1]This term was popularized by the Swedish economist Gustav Cassel, who developed an analysis of the relationship between price levels and equilibrium exchange rates during and after World War I which was designed to guide governments in setting exchange rate parities during the postwar period. See, in particular, Cassel's "The Present Situation of the Foreign Exchanges," *Economic Journal,* March 1916, pp. 62–65; and "Abnormal Deviations in International Exchanges," *Economic Journal,* December 1918, pp. 413–415.

Absolute PPP

In absolute PPP, the exchange rate enforces the **law of one price,** which holds that after allowance for transportation costs and other impediments to the movement of goods and services, individual goods and services tend to sell for the same price everywhere. If, for example, a certain type of cheese sells for 21 Danish krone (Dkr) per pound in Denmark and $3.50 per pound in the United States, the absolute PPP exchange rate between the krone and the dollar should be Dkr6/dollar, ignoring transportation costs, tariffs, or other complications.

In reality, international trade between Denmark and the United States in cheese is affected by transportation costs and trade barriers, and cheese buyers perceive qualitative differences between Danish and U.S. cheese. This means that the krone/dollar exchange rate could vary considerably from Dkr6/dollar without necessarily inducing commodity arbitrage based on the law of one price. Furthermore, since many goods and services change hands in international trade, and since they differ greatly in terms of transportation costs and the other factors relevant to the absolute PPP exchange rate, it is difficult, if at all possible, to determine this rate exactly by comparing the local currency prices of goods and services. Attempts have been made, without notable success, to determine absolute PPP exchange rates by comparing the local currency costs of a representative market basket of goods and services. If this approach is at all applicable, however, it can only be used when countries have similar economic structures, including consumption patterns, for only then could a single market basket apply to both countries. Fortunately, the availability of relative PPP as an alternative means that the attempt to devise such a common market basket should be unnecessary.

The Traditional Version of Relative PPP

Assuming that the law of one price tends to hold, an exchange rate tends toward an equilibrium based on it. Transportation costs and other obstacles to international trade prevent the law from working perfectly and affect the value of the equilibrium exchange rate, but if goods, services, and currencies can be freely traded, even the existence of import duties does not prevent the law from operating. At the equilibrium exchange rate, the quantity of foreign exchange autonomously demanded tends to equal the quantity autonomously supplied so that there is neither a deficit nor a surplus in the BOP. If the two countries experience a change in their relative price levels, the law of one price tends to bring about a new equilibrium exchange rate that is consistent with the new price levels.

This line of reasoning implies that the tortuous and dubious process of relying on absolute PPP to calculate exchange rates that reflect the operation of the law of one price may be unnecessary. If the equilibrium exchange rate of an earlier time period can be identified, and if changes in relative price levels since that time can be correctly measured, it is a simple matter to calculate an exchange rate that approximates what the corresponding absolute PPP exchange rate would be if it could be calculated directly. An exchange rate that is calculated in the recommended manner is said to be based on the concept of *relative PPP*.

One form in which relative PPP can be expressed is as follows:

$$e_t = e_0 \times \frac{P_{a,0}^t}{P_{b,0}^t} \qquad (9-1)$$

where e_t is the PPP exchange rate at time t, expressed in units of country A's currency per unit of Country B's currency; e_0 is the equilibrium exchange rate at the intitial time 0, expressed in the same manner; $P_{a,0}^t$ is the price index of Country A at time t based on time 0; and $P_{b,0}^t$ is the price index of Country B at time t based on time 0. The reader should recall that this same formulation was used in Chapter 3.

Assume that at the time designated as 0, the exchange rate between the French franc and the German mark was in equilibrium at FF3.2000/mark and that at the present time (t), the French price index is at 125 percent, while the German price index is at 112.5 percent. From this information, and if France is designated as A, it can be determined that the PPP exchange rate at Time t is FF3.5556/mark.

If the actual exchange rate is also FF3.5556/mark, individual goods will tend to retain the same relative position in each country as they had originally. Suppose, for example, that in Period 0, France was importing a good from Germany costing DM10,000 or FF32,000. If this good's mark price rose to DM11,250, matching the general inflation rate in Germany, the franc price of the good would rise to FF40,000, an increase of 25 percent in francs. The good would thus have the same relative price in both Germany and France that it had originally.

An alternative way for deriving the relative PPP exchange rate is as follows:

$$\Delta e_0^t = \frac{\Delta P_{a,0}^t - \Delta P_{b,0}^t}{1 + \Delta P_{b,0}^t} \qquad (9-2)$$

where Δe_0^t is the change in the equilibrium exchange rate from Time 0 to Time t; $\Delta P_{a,0}^t$ is the change in the price index of Country A during the same time span; and $\Delta P_{b,0}^t$ is the corresponding change in Country B's price index.

Applying this equation to the franc–mark example gives the following result:

$$\Delta e_0^t = (0.25 - 0.125)/(1 + 0.125) = 0.1111 \text{ or } 11.11 \text{ percent}$$

Multiplying the original exchange rate of FF3.200/mark by 1.1111 then gives FF 3.5556/mark as the PPP exchange rate at Time t, the same rate as is obtained with Equation 9-1.

The exchange rate e_t is an equilibrium rate if (1) e_0 was an equilibrium rate (2) changes in the equilibrium rate are perfectly correlated with changes in relative price levels, and (3) the price indexes chosen are perfect measures of the price level changes in Countries A and B. If any of these three conditions is not met, e_t will not be an equilibrium rate, though it will, of course, be close to the equilibrium rate if departures from these three conditions are not very large.

Since the validity of using relative PPP to indicate the equilibrium exchange rate depends on the extent to which the enumerated conditions are satisfied, we turn now to the examination of those conditions.

Choosing a Base Period Exchange Rate   While the selection of a base period equilibrium exchange rate is always somewhat arbitrary, it is not necessarily impossible. One can generally find periods in which exchange rates were arguably at or near their equilibrium levels by looking for periods when exchange rates were either relatively stable or else close to their long-run moving averages. When one wants to select as a base period a time when the actual exchange rate was clearly not at equilibrium, it is often possible using long-term trend lines to designate a rate that did not actually exist as representing the base period equilibrium exchange rate.

Some economists have argued that, because the variables that determine exchange rates are constantly changing, it is conceptually wrong to envision such a thing as an equilibrium exchange rate. A particularly forceful expression of this point of view was made by Joan Robinson, who wrote: "The notion of *the* equilibrium exchange rate is a chimera. The rate of exchange, the rate of interest, the level of effective demand, and the level of money wages react upon each other like the balls in Marshall's bowl, and no one is determined unless all the rest are given."[2] Since the variables singled out by Robinson as determinants of the exchange rate are always changing, it would seem to follow that any exchange rate designated as the long-run equilibrium rate during a particular time period is suspect and that any calculation of a relative PPP exchange rate must therefore also be suspect.

In deference to Joan Robinson, it should be conceded that any exchange rate chosen to serve as the base period rate in a PPP calculation can be challenged. On the other hand, if, as seems to be the case, changes in relative price levels are the dominant influence on long-run exchange rates, it hardly seems rational to abandon PPP because of the difficulty of identifying a base period equilibrium exchange rate that would satisfy Robinson's conception of an equilibrium exchange rate. When an exchange rate is tentatively selected as an equilibrium rate, one should check whether or not adjustments should be made for factors other than relative price levels that might have influenced the

---

[2]Joan Robinson, "The Foreign Exchanges," in *Essays on the Theory of Employment* (New York: Macmillan, 1937), p. 208. Reprinted in Howard S. Ellis and Lloyd A. Metzler, eds. *Readings in the Theory of International Trade* (Homewood, Ill: Richard D. Irwin, 1949).

exchange rate during the time period in question. If no such factors seem to have played significant roles, this rate should be accepted as the equilibrium rate.

The concept of a long-run equilibrium exchange rate is the obverse of the concept of fundamental disequilibrium employed by the IMF. If a fundamental disequilibrium exists when a nation tends to have a persistent payments imbalance at the existing level of exchange rates, the absence of such a tendency would seem to imply the existence of the opposite of disequilibrium, namely equilibrium. Consequently, if fundamental disequilibrium is an operational concept, then the concept of long-run equilibrium exchange rates is also an operational concept.

Changes in Relative Price Levels   If the exchange rate e_t is to be accepted as an equilibrium rate, changes in the equilibrium exchange rate should correlate closely with changes in relative price levels. It is universally agreed that such a correlation is more likely to be found in the long run than in the short run because of the influence on short run exchange rates of factors other than relative price levels. These factors include changes in the pattern of capital flows, changes in the market conditions affecting individual goods that are important in international trade, central bank intervention in the forex market, and speculation. By comparison with relative price levels, each of these factors exerts more influence over exchange rates in the short run than in the long run. They can, with some reservations, be likened to a wallet in the pocket of a cruise ship passenger who jogs from bow to stern. If the ship is moving slowly southward, the wallet's net movement may temporarily be northward. In time, however, the wallet will, like the rest of the ship's contents, follow a southward course.

It is frequently held that forex speculation can be destabilizing in the sense that it can cause exchange rates to move away from their long-run equilibrium levels. Since history records numerous instances in which speculative excesses caused losses for most of the speculators, it would be foolish to deny the possibility that a speculative bubble could carry an exchange rate away from its correct level on the basis of relative PPP. Indeed, in Chapter 11, material will be presented indicating that short-term exchange rates commonly diverge from long-term trend lines. In the long run, however, deviations of exchange rates from their equilibrium levels tend to be corrected, which means that if relative price levels are indeed the fundamental force behind exchange rate trends, their influence must eventually dominate.

The influence of central bank intervention on exchange rates, like that of speculation, tends to be short term. At any given time, intervention may cause an exchange rate to differ from what it would otherwise be. In the long run, however, central bank intervention cannot, by itself, impose exchange rates that are at odds with macroeconomic fundamentals. A central bank that persists in trying to maintain an overvalued currency without pursuing an appropriately restrictive monetary policy will eventually exhaust its intervention assets, and a central bank that tries to maintain an undervalued currency without allowing inflation to increase is ultimately likely to abandon this policy as its forex reserves multiply and upward pressure on domestic interest rates increases.[3]

Changes in market conditions affecting goods of major importance in international trade generally have more exchange rate significance in the short run than in the long run, but it is conceivable that they could exert a permanent impact on exchange rates. Suppose, for example, that a country suddenly emerges as a major exporter of petroleum at a time when petroleum prices are moving upward, as Mexico did in 1976. Everything else remaining the same, the exchange value of this country's currency will tend to rise independently of what happens to relative price levels. If the change in the structure of its foreign trade is permanent, the exchange rate effect will also tend to be permanent.

This does not necessarily mean, however, that the long-run exchange value of the country's currency will depart from PPP. To the contrary, the law of one price suggests that adjustments will tend to bring the prices of other goods and services into line with PPP. In other words, PPP allows for the possibility that relative price levels may adjust to the exchange rate, as well as the possibility that the exchange rate adjusts to relative price levels.

International capital flows are another factor, along with relative price levels, that influences exchange rates. As far as short-term exchange rate behavior is concerned, it is universally conceded that capital flows affect exchange rates independently of price levels and that their ability to exert such influence has increased with the growth of capital mobility. Whether or not the enhanced mobility of capital exerts sufficient influence to cause exchange rates to depart significantly from PPP in the long run is more debatable, for the long run allows sufficient time for the allocation of resources to adjust to changed price relationships in accordance with the law of one price.

Capital tends to flow internationally in response to differences in actual and expected real rates of interest and real rates of return. In the short run, capital inflows tend to cause the appreciation of the currency of a country whose risk-adjusted real interest rate and real rate of return on equity investments are relatively high, with the result that actual exchange rates depart from PPP rates. In the long run, however, differences in real interest rates and real rates of return tend to be eliminated, or at least reduced. Moreover, relative price levels tend to adjust to changes in exchange rates brought about by capital flows. Thus, if the exchange value of a nation's currency rises because of capital inflows, this puts downward pressure on the domestic prices of exportable goods and import substitutes. Because of substitution among goods and resources, this downward pressure extends to goods and services that do not enter into international trade. Then, too, to the extent that cheaper imports of raw materials and capital goods contribute to lower domestic production costs, the nation's relative price level tends to fall. In other nations, there will tend to be corresponding inflationary pressures. In

---

[3]The more forex reserves a central bank accumulates, the greater will be the capital loss that occurs when the undervaluation of the national currency is corrected. Upward pressure on domestic interest rates results if the central bank neutralizes the effect on domestic bank reserves of its purchases of foreign exchange by selling government securities in the open market.

the long run, therefore, exchange rate changes caused by capital flows tend to produce adjustments in relative price levels that are consistent with PPP.

At this point, it may appear that economic theory rules out the possibility that exchange rates can vary substantially from PPP in the long run. If that were indeed the case, there would be a problem in reconciling theory with reality, for as was pointed out in Chapter 3, real exchange rates have often shown substantial long-term variability since 1973. This means that over periods of quite a few years, actual exchange rates have departed widely from PPP.

There are several possible explanations of the long-term variability of real exchange rates that do not require discarding PPP as a factor in the long-run determination of exchange rates. First, the base period exchange rate used in calculating a PPP rate may be faulty. Second, the actual exchange rate existing at time t may be heavily influenced by one or more factors that cause short-run deviations from PPP. Third, during the time period encompassed in a PPP calculation, transportation costs or other impediments to international trade may have changed. For example, if a nation shifts its trade policy away from protectionism, the exchange value of its currency may tend to fall independently of changes in relative price levels. A similar result would tend to occur if a nation shifted the composition of its imports toward goods with relatively low transportation costs. Fourth, the price indexes chosen may be faulty.

In this context, recall Joan Robinson's statement that an equilibrium exchange rate is a chimera, i.e., an imaginary creature. It must be conceded that the determinants of exchange rates are constantly changing, which means that time may be insufficient for an exchange rate to reach its long-run equilibrium position with *given* determinants. As long as the short-run influences on exchange rates do not cause actual exchange rates to fall persistently on one side or the other of PPP rates, PPP calculations may still yield results that correspond closely to actual exchange rates. If, however, the short-run factors operate primarily in one direction, actual exchange rates may differ significantly from PPP rates, even over overall time periods of a decade or more in length.

Assume that the United States passes through a period of two decades in which, on several occasions, its expected real rates of return rise well above those in other countries. On each of these occasions, the exchange value of the dollar will tend to rise above what would be expected on the basis of PPP. Adjustments would then tend to align actual exchange rates with PPP. Still, it is conceivable that the actual exchange rate would differ substantially from the PPP rate for most, if not all, of the two decades because of the influence of new short-run disturbances.

We are forced to conclude from this analysis that, while exchange rates are heavily influenced by nations' relative price levels, especially in the long run, relative PPP should not be regarded as an infallible guide to what exchange rates should be, even after the passage of substantial periods of time.

The Choice of Price Indexes   An important issue regarding the choice of price indexes for deriving PPP exchange rates is whether the indexes should be confined, as much as is feasible, to **tradables,** which are that part of a nation's output that can either compete against imports or be exportable at existing exchange rates. **Nontradables** are goods and services that ordinarily do not enter into international trade because of transportation costs, perishability, or other factors. Since only tradables enter directly into the determination of exchange rates, it is sometimes argued that the price indexes used in PPP calculations should be confined to them.

In practice, it is difficult to confine the price indexes used to tradables because indexes of tradables are not readily available and are not easily constructed. Such readily available indexes as the consumer price index (CPI), the wholesale price index (WPI),[4] and the GNP implicit price deflator are not confined to tradables. Among these readily available indexes, the WPI is often favored in PPP calculations because it contains a relatively large tradables component.

If the relative prices of tradables and nontradables were constant, there would be no reason to distinguish between them in PPP calculations. Their relative prices do not remain constant, however. Generally, the prices of nontradables have tended to rise relative to the prices of tradables, primarily because nontradables generally contain more personal services than tradables and are, therefore, less susceptible to productivity improvements.

In practice, it is difficult to draw the line between tradables and nontradables because the ability of goods and services to enter into international trade depends upon exchange rates. For example, as the exchange value of the U.S. dollar decreases, some goods and services that were not previously exportable by the United States become so, and some goods that were previously subject to competition from imports are relieved of that competition. So far as tradability is concerned, goods and services comprise a continuum, so that any classification of them into tradables and nontradables is somewhat arbitrary. For those who insist on constructing tradable goods indexes for PPP calculations, it should be a source of concern that the resulting PPP exchange rates indicate which goods should have been included in their indexes!

Another reason for doubting the wisdom of distinguishing between tradables and nontradables is that it is possible to construct situations in which price indexes that include both more accurately indicate equilibrium exchange rates than price indexes that are confined to tradables. Suppose, for example, that in Japan, land previously reserved for farming becomes available for home construction. As a result, Japan experiences a boom in home building. As the boom proceeds, resources are shifted into industries that produce nontradables, such as the production of cement, and away from the production of exportables. Although exporters experience some upward pressure on their costs because of reduced supplies of resources, they hold the line on prices in an attempt to maintain market shares. Imports of lumber, copper, and other raw materials increase, but let's assume that they are mostly supplied under long-term contracts that prevent significant price increases. In this situation, the exchange value of the yen should tend to decline but a price index confined to tradables might not indicate this. On the other hand, a price index with a large nontradables component might well indicate that the yen should decline.

Nevertheless, a presumption exists among many analysts that PPP calculations should employ indexes with large components of tradables. Because of this presumption, the use of WPIs is widely favored over the use of CPIs or implicit price deflators. Lending support to this presumption is the fact that cases can be presented in which WPIs were better indicators of what exchange rates should have been.

A spectacular instance in which the use of WPIs proved superior is the yen/dollar exchange rate from 1963 to 1972. During these years, the U.S. CPI rose by less than the Japanese CPI, but the U.S. WPI rose by more than the Japanese WPI. CPI-based estimates of PPP exchange rates thus indicated a growing overvaluation of the yen, while WPI-based estimates indicated a growing undervaluation. The WPI's superiority was demonstrated conclusively in December 1971, when the Smithsonian Agreement resulted in a substantial increase in the yen's dollar value.[5]

An authoritative voice in the matter of choosing indexes for PPP calculations is that of the IMF, which now calculates real effective exchange rate indexes for 17 industrial countries. As was pointed out in Chapter 3, real exchange rates can be derived by multiplying actual exchange rates by $P_{b,0}^t/P_{a,0}^t$. Since Equation 9-1 uses the same price indexes (in inverted form) to calculate PPP exchange rates, it follows that the IMF's method for calculating real effective exchange rates can be used to calculate PPP exchange rates.

The indexes favored by the IMM for calculating real effective exchange rates are of relative normative unit labor costs in manufacturing. These indexes are obtained by dividing indexes of actual hourly compensation per worker in manufacturing by five-year moving averages of output per man-hour. Moving averages minimize the influence of cyclical fluctuations in economic activity. The IMF contends that these indexes are freer from distortions and comparability problems than such alternatives as WPIs and CPIs.[6] The indexes used by the IMF are not confined to tradables, but manufactured goods tend to have relatively large tradable components.

Since the different indexes that can be used for PPP calculations often differ substantially from each other, the choice of indexes is an important matter. We should remain open to the possibility, therefore, that long-term departures of actual exchange rates from PPP may reflect, in part, short-comings in the price indexes used.

---

[5]Alan C. Shapiro, *Multinational Financial Management* (Boston: Allyn and Bacon, 1983), pp. 45–46.

[6]See any recent issue of *International Financial Statistics,* particularly the introduction and the general tables on real effective exchange rates.

The Efficient Markets Version of Relative PPP

One implication of the traditional or historical version of relative PPP is that long-term departures of actual exchange rates from PPP rates may indicate that the actual rates are not long-run equilibrium rates. Logically, the existence of a discrepancy between an actual exchange rate and its corresponding long-run equilibrium rate should trigger corrective speculation, for whether or not equilibrium is actually achieved, prices tend to move toward equilibrium levels. If the corrective speculation does not occur, that implies that the observed discrepancy does not indicate disequilibrium or that the forex market somehow fails to respond logically.

This raises the issue of whether or not the forex market is efficient. An **efficient market** is one with many participants in which access to information about market conditions is distributed widely enough that new information is immediately incorporated into prices. In such a market, an individual participant cannot rationally expect to find unexploited profit opportunities unless he or she possesses knowledge that is superior to that possessed by other participants.

There are three classes of market efficiency. In **weak-form efficiency**, current prices fully reflect all historical information relevant to price determination. As a result, no one should be able to obtain supranormal profits by analyzing past price behavior. In **semistrong efficiency**, current prices fully reflect all information that is publicly available, but insiders in firms or government agencies who have first access to key information may conceivably profit (though perhaps illegally) from the possession of superior information. In **strong-form efficiency**, there is no inside information.

A diversity of opinion exists as to whether or not the forex market is efficient. If it is, however, it is generally believed that it is efficient in the weak-form sense. Even that degree of efficiency would be sufficient, however, to prevent the realization of supranormal profits from perceiving discrepancies between actual and equilibrium exchange rates. If the forex market is weak-form efficient, existing exchange rates represent the market's best judgment as to what equilibrium exchange rates actually are. Furthermore, if existing exchange rates can be regarded as equilibrium rates, they can be used as the base period rates in forecasts that incorporate the effects of expected changes in relative price levels. The idea that existing exchange rates can be so used is called the *efficient markets version of relative PPP.*

The traditional version of relative PPP is often used to estimate what a *current* exchange rate should be on the basis of historical data. In the efficient markets version, the objective is to estimate what a *future* exchange rate should be based on expectations about relative price levels. Both versions can be used in forecasting, but they can obviously lead to very different forecasts.

Assume that the spot exchange rate between the Belgian franc and the dollar is currently BF38.40/dollar. Also assume that the expected inflation rates for the next year are, respectively, 3.2 percent for the United States and 4.8 percent for Belgium. Equation 9–1 can then be pressed into the service of the efficient markets version as follows: e_t (the expected exchange rate) =

$(1.048/1.032) \times$ BF38.40/dollar $=$ BF 39.00/dollar. Thus, if the inflation rate in Belgium is expected to exceed that of the United States by 1.6 percentage points, one can anticipate that the Belgian franc price of the dollar will also rise by approximately 1.6 percent.

Since various factors other than relative price levels can influence exchanges rates in the short run, it can hardly be expected that the efficient markets version of relative PPP will result in accurate forecasts. If the forex market is efficient, however, it should produce *unbiased forecasts,* forecasts in which variations from actual exchange rates are likely to be as great on one side as on the other. In an efficient forex market, at least one of the weak-form efficient class, everything that could be known by the majority of market participants would be incorporated into forecasts, which means that expectations about capital flows, central bank intervention, and other relevant factors would be reflected in existing exchange rates. Unforeseen events could cause market exchange rates to vary substantially from expected PPP rates, but those events would be *random,* i.e., as likely to push exchange rates in one direction as the other. If the events that cause variations from expected PPP rates are random, then over sufficient time, the variations should average out.

More than a decade ago, Richard Roll tested the efficient markets version of relative PPP by examining data for more than 20 countries for a 20-year period in order to determine whether the data supported the efficient markets version. He found that it is *future* inflation that affects exchange rates, not past inflation, as measured by the traditional version. He concluded that the efficient markets version thus appears to hold, and for short periods of time as well as longer ones.[7] His findings have received some support from other studies, but strong resistance continues to the idea that the efficient markets version of relative PPP is valid. Whether or not it is valid, it is clear that price level changes account for only a small part of short-term variations in exchange rates. For this reason, even if the efficient markets version is valid, betting on it is highly risky.

The International Fisher Effect (IFE)

The efficient markets version of relative PPP calls attention to the possibility that exchange rates may be predictably affected by price level expectations. But how does one determine what such expectations are? A possible answer to this question is provided by the **international Fisher effect (IFE),** which is rooted in the belief that nominal interest rates reflect expected inflation rates.

Over 60 years ago, Irving Fisher forcefully argued that within a country, the nominal interest rate tends to approximately equal the real interest rate plus the expected inflation rate. Both theoretical considerations and empirical

---

[7]Richard Roll, "Violations of Purchasing Power Parity and Their Implications for Efficient International Commodity Markets," in Marshall Sarnat and George P. Szego, eds., *International Trade and Finance,* vol. I (Cambridge, Mass.: Ballinger, 1979).

research had convinced him that changes in price level expectations cause a compensatory adjustment in the nominal interest rate and that the rapidity of the adjustment depends on the completeness of the information possessed by the participants in financial markets.[8] The proposition that the nominal interest rate varies directly with the expected inflation rate, known as the *Fisher effect,* has subsequently been incorporated into the theory of exchange rate determination. Applied internationally, it metamorphoses into the IFE, which indicates that nominal interest rates are unbiased indicators of future exchange rates.

A country's nominal interest rate is customarily defined as the risk-free interest rate paid on a virtually costless loan. A Treasury bill rate or its local equivalent is customarily used as a measure of the nominal interest rate. "Risk-free" in this context refers to risks other than inflation.

In an expectational sense, a country's real interest rate is its nominal interest rate adjusted for the expected annual inflation rate. It can be viewed as the real amount by which a lender expects the value of the funds lent to increase on an annual basis. For a firm using its own funds, it can be viewed as the expected real cost of doing so. In a realized sense, the real interest rate is the nominal interest rate adjusted for the actual inflation rate.

Although it is often asserted that an increase in a country's interest rates tends to increase the exchange value of its currency by inducing capital inflows, the IFE indicates that a rise in a country's nominal interest rate relative to the nominal interest rates of other countries signals that the exchange value of the country's currency is expected to *fall.* Note, however, that it is not the increase in the nominal interest rate that causes this result, but the increase in the country's expected inflation rate. The IFE implies that if the nominal interest rate did not increase by enough to maintain the real interest rate, the exchange value of the country's currency would tend to decline even farther.

Deriving the IFE

The IFE is derived by combining the (domestic) Fisher effect with the efficient markets version of relative PPP. Underlying the IFE is the assumption that the law of one price tends to equalize real interest rates internationally because of the arbitrage among assets that would otherwise occur.

The Fisher effect is commonly presented in the following form:

$$1 + n_p = (1 + r_p)(1 + i_p) \qquad (9-3)$$

where n_p, r_p, and i_p are, respectively, the nominal interest rate, the real interest rate, and the expected inflation rate, each stated on an annual basis, for the number of periods (usually years) p. Written in this form, however, Equation 9–3 has a possible ambiguity in the interpretation of p. The ambiguity has to do with whether or not n, r, and i are compounded at the end of each period.

---

[8]Irving Fisher, *The Theory of Interest* (New York: Augustus M. Kelley, 1965), Chapters II and XIX, especially pp. 438–442. Reprinted from the 1930 version published by Macmillan.

The simplest solution to the compounding problem is to assume no compounding, but this solution leads to serious distortion as the values of r, i, and p increase. To see why this is the case, compare the results obtained with the no compounding assumption with those obtained on the assumption of annual compounding when p equals 2 years and the values of r and i are, respectively, 4 percent and 6 percent. If we assume no compounding, the values of r_p and i_p become, respectively, 8 percent and 12 percent, and when we solve for n, we get 10.48 percent. If, however, we assume annual compounding, the values of $1 + r_p$ and $1 + i_p$ become, respectively, 1.0816 and 1.1236, i.e., $(1.04)^2$ and $(1.06)^2$, and when we solve for n, we get 10.24 percent, i.e., $(1.0816)(1.1236)/(1 + n)^2$.

Because of the distortion that results when there is no compounding, it is recommended that Equation 9–3 be interpreted so as to require the annual compounding of n, r, and i. It would, of course, be possible to compound on some other basis, such as quarterly, but it is the author's belief that the compounding period need not be shortened in order to provide adequate results. This means, for example, that if p equals 6 months and r and i equal, respectively, 4 percent and 6 percent, then r_p and i_p equal, respectively, 2 percent and 3 percent.

As long as the time period is short and neither the real interest rate nor the expected inflation rate is high, the Fisher effect can be stated approximately as follows:

$$n_p = r_p + i_p \qquad\qquad (9\text{–}4)$$

In this very inexact but simple form, the nominal interest rate exceeds the real interest rate by the expected inflation rate. Thus, if p equals 1 year, r equals 4 percent, and i equals 6 percent, then n equals 10 percent. By comparison, Equation 9–3 results in a value of 10.24 percent for n. The results achieved with Equation 9–4 are obviously inaccurate but Equation 9–4 is often used, nevertheless, because of its appealing simplicity.

Now assume that the law of one price assures a uniform real interest rate internationally. With this assumed equality, the following equation can be derived from Equation 9–3:

$$\frac{1 + n_{a,p}}{1 + i_{a,p}} = \frac{1 + n_{b,p}}{1 + i_{b,p}} \qquad\qquad (9\text{–}5)$$

where $n_{a,p}$ and $i_{a,p}$ are, respectively, the nominal interest rate and the expected inflation rate in Country A, and $n_{b,p}$ and $i_{b,p}$ are, respectively, the nominal interest rate and the expected inflation rate in Country B.

By rearranging Equation 9–5, we can obtain the following equation:

$$\frac{1 + n_{a,p}}{1 + n_{b,p}} = \frac{1 + i_{a,p}}{1 + i_{b,p}} \qquad\qquad (9\text{–}6)$$

The nominal interest rates of Countries A and B thus differ by an amount that is a function of the countries' differences in expected inflation rates.

The next step is to incorporate PPP. If we substitute the p of Equation 9−6 for the t of Equation 9−1 (the number of years for the specific date t) and assign to the base period price indexes of Equation 9−1 the numerical value of 1, we can substitute $1 + i_{a,p}$ and $1 + i_{b,p}$, respectively, into Equation 9−1 for $P_{a,0}^t$ and $P_{b,0}^t$. Equation 9−1 can then be rewritten as follows:

$$\frac{e_p}{e_0} = \frac{1 + i_{a,p}}{1 + i_{b,p}} \qquad (9-7)$$

The expected exchange rate (e_p), stated in units of A's currency per unit of B's currency, is a function of the expected relative inflation rates of A and B. Equation 9−7 is thus an alternative formulation of the efficient markets version of relative PPP.

The final step in the derivation of the IFE is to substitute from Equation 9−6 into Equation 9−7 to obtain the following equation:

$$\frac{e_p}{e_0} = \frac{1 + n_{a,p}}{1 + n_{b,p}} \qquad (9-8)$$

The expected exchange rate is thus shown to be a function of the two countries' nominal interest rates. If Country A's nominal interest rate exceeds that of Country B, A's currency will be expected to depreciate; if Country A's nominal interest rate is lower than Country B's, A's currency will be expected to appreciate.

Assume that the Norwegian krone (NOK)/dollar spot rate is currently NOK 6.7872 per dollar, that the yield on six-month U.S. Treasury bills is 5.82 percent, and that the yield on equivalent Norwegian government securities is 8.02 percent. From Equation 9−8 (let Norway be Country A), it can be determined that the IFE predicts a spot rate in six months of NOK 6.8597 per dollar.

Now consider a longer-range example. Let the yield on U.S. government securities with exactly two years to maturity be 6.42 percent and the yield on equivalent Norwegian government securities be 8.88 percent. Using the same spot rate as in the first example and assuming annual compounding, the IFE predicts a spot rate in two years of NOK 7.1046 per dollar.

As an approximation that is useful when nominal interest rates are relatively low and the time period is relatively short, the IFE can be stated as follows:

$$n_{a,p} - n_{b,p} = \frac{e_p - e_0}{e_0} \qquad (9-9)$$

The expected percentage change in the exchange rate approximately equals the absolute difference in nominal interest rates. Thus, if the six-month Norwegian interest rate exceeds the six-month U.S. interest rate by 2.20 percentage points on an annual basis, the dollar should rise against the krone by about 1.1 percent in six months.

Skepticism about the predictive value of the IFE is evident when, for example, the Federal Reserve moves to raise short-term interest rates. When that happens, many observers are usually reluctant to conclude that the expected value of the dollar has declined. On the other hand, the dollar does not invariably move upward when U.S. interest rates rise, for it is well understood that rising interest rates sometimes signal an increase in the expected inflation rate. Skepticism about the IFE thus appears to be tempered by the realization that it may, at times, be valid.

Three major obstacles block the general acceptance of the IFE's validity. First, while capital flows limit international differences in real interest rates, doubt exists that these rates tend toward equality. Second, even if real interest rates tend toward equality, considerable time may elapse before equality is achieved. Third, the difference between the nominal interest rate and the real interest rate may not equal the inflation premium.

In *The Wealth of Nations,* which was published in 1776, Adam Smith called attention to merchants' preference for keeping their capital at home, where it was subject to close control and could be employed in familiar surroundings, including the laws on which merchants might have to rely. As a result of this preference, Smith indicated, a merchant might be satisfied with somewhat lower profits if he could avoid internationalizing his operations.[9] In modern terms, his analysis implies the existence of a natural bias against investing abroad. This, in turn, implies that there may be lasting differences in nations' real interest rates. Notwithstanding the tremendous advances that have been made in international financial integration and investment analysis, it may be that home-country bias continues to allow such differences to exist.[10]

Following Smith's reasoning, one would expect the most pronounced tendency toward real interest rate equality internationally to exist among countries with stable and uniform laws and financial practices. The Eurocurrency market provides an almost ideal environment for achieving real interest rate equality, and it is hardly surprising that believers in this equality have looked to that market for evidence that real interest rate differences tend to be arbitraged away. Smith's reasoning implies, however, that as the homogeneity of financial markets diminishes, the likelihood of real interest rate inequality increases. Thus, it could be the case that real interest rate equality occurs in the

---

[9]Adam Smith, *An Inquiry into the Nature and Causes of the Wealth of Nations,* Modern Library Edition (New York: Random House, 1937), p. 421.

[10]Accordingly, Donald R. Lessard argues that "investors who overcome the traditional resistance to international investment should be able to expect a significantly superior risk-adjusted performance than investors who restrict themselves to their home markets." See his "Principles of International Portfolio Selection" in Donald R. Lessard, ed., *International Financial Management: Theory and Application,* 2d ed. (New York: John Wiley & Sons, 1985), p. 29. Reprinted from Abraham George and Ian Giddy, eds., *International Finance Handbook* (New York: John Wiley & Sons, 1983).

Eurocurrency market but fails to be completely realized in other financial markets in the same countries.

A serious problem confronting those who would like to settle the real interest rate equalization controversy is that it is difficult to determine what expected real interest rates are because it is difficult to determine what expected inflation rates are. That realized real interest rates often differ substantially among countries is not in dispute, but the real interest rate equality assumed in the IFE is the equality of *expected* real interest rates.

It is true that economic forecasts include expected inflation rates and that it is possible to compose a consensus forecast from them, but doubt remains as to the degree to which a consensus forecast accurately reflects expectations. What weights should be assigned to the different forecasts, and to what extent do the forecasts mirror the expectations of those who actually make international financial decisions?

The yields on assets other than "risk-free" government securities include risk premiums and recompense for the costs incurred in lending and investing, and the yield spreads between these assets and government securities fluctuate. IFE enthusiasts try to work around these problems by confining the concept of the nominal interest rate to government securities, particularly short-term government securities. Even such supposed risk-free assets carry some risk, however, and this risk varies from country to country. For example, it is always possible that a government may increase the taxation of the income derived from holding its securities or offer tax advantages to the holders of some issues that are not extended to the holders of other issues.

As for yield spreads, assume that the U.S. Treasury borrows short-term in an unusually large amount. This tends to diminish the yield spread between those securities and other assets, including Eurodollars, but does this mean that the expected inflation rate in the United States has increased and that the dollar should tend to depreciate? An alternative, and more plausible, interpretation is that the real interest rate on short-term Treasuries has risen relative to the real interest rates on other assets and that the exchange value of the dollar may temporarily rise as investors shift from other assets into short-term Treasuries.

Ideally, real interest rate estimates for the purpose of exchange rate forecasting should be calculated on after-tax bases. Unfortunately, the complexities of international taxation make it difficult to calculate real interest rates in this way. The tax factor thus represents one more obstacle to verifying the IFE's assumption of international real interest rate equality.

The foregoing analysis shows that the IFE is a flawed forecasting tool. This does not mean, however, that it should be tossed on the junk heap. Exchange rate forecasting is a difficult art, and a flawed tool with *some* predictive value should still be used. The IFE does have predictive value, for there can be no doubt that nominal interest rate differences result largely from inflation premiums and that exchange rates do tend to respond, at least in the long run, to differences in inflation rates. Before using the IFE for forecasting purposes, however, it is always advisable to attempt to determine whether an interest rate change is real or only nominal.

Interest Rate Parity

The third key relationship in the theory of exchange rate determination is IRP, which was examined in detail in Chapter 6. The operation of IRP, like that of the IFE, depends on nominal interest rates, but whereas the IFE is concerned with the direction of movement of a single exchange rate (usually the spot rate), IRP is concerned with the relationship between the spot rate and a corresponding forward rate. The IFE is used to predict how an existing spot rate should change, while IRP is used to determine the correct premium or discount on a current forward rate.

According to IRP, a forward rate is related to the corresponding spot rate so as to offset any difference in nominal interest rates. If nominal interest rates are higher in Country A than in Country B, the forward rate for B's currency should be at a premium sufficient to prevent interest arbitrage. When the nominal interest rates are stated on an annualized basis and the exchange rates are stated as quantities of A's currency per unit of B's currency, the equilibrium condition for IRP can be expressed as follows:

$$\frac{F_0^t - S_0}{S_0} \left(\frac{360}{t}\right) = \frac{r_{a,0}^t - r_{b,0}^t}{1 + r_{b,0}\left(\frac{t}{360}\right)} \qquad (9-10)$$

The meaning of these terms is the same as in Chapter 6.

| E X H I B I T | 9.1 | *The Relationship between the IFE and IRP*

The IFE rests on two fundamental assumptions: real interest rates are uniform internationally, and nominal interest rates differ from real interest rates by amounts that reflect inflation premiums. The formula given in the text for the exact IFE is:

$$\frac{e_p}{e_0} = \frac{1 + n_{a,p}}{1 + n_{b,p}}$$

One formula given in the text for exact IRP is:

$$\frac{F_0^t - S_0}{S_0} \left(\frac{360}{t}\right) = \frac{r_{a,0}^t - r_{b,0}^t}{1 + r_{b,0}^t\left(\frac{t}{360}\right)}$$

Now assume that Germany is Country A and the United States is Country B.

Case 1
Given that:
the German interest rate on a 90-day risk-free asset $(r_{a,0}^t)$ = 7.66%
the U.S. interest rate on a 90-day risk-free asset $(r_{b,0}^t)$ = 6.44%
the current spot exchange rate (S_0) = DM 1.6850/dollar
the current 90-day forward rate exchange rate (F_0^t) = DM 1.6901/dollar

(continued)

| E X H I B I T | 9.1 | *continued*

From the IFE formula, it can be determined that the expected spot rate in 90 days is

$$e_p = 1.6850 \ \frac{1 + .0766 \left(\frac{1}{4}\right)}{1 + .0644 \left(\frac{1}{4}\right)} = 1.6901$$

which equals the current 90-day forward rate. This means that IRP holds exactly.

Case 2

Now assume that the expected inflation rate of the United States declines, with the result that $r_{b,0}^t$ declines to 6.20%. The expected real interest rates in both countries remain the same, and Germany's expected inflation rate remains the same. Assuming that the spot rate is still DM 1.6850/dollar, the expected spot rate in 90 days becomes

$$e_p = 1.6850 \ \frac{1 + .0766 \left(\frac{1}{4}\right)}{1 + .0620 \left(\frac{1}{4}\right)} = 1.6911$$

The expected spot rate in 90 days thus increases by 10 points to reflect the lower expected inflation rate in the United States and the consequent decline in the U.S. nominal interest rate.

Given the assumptions underlying this case, the current spot rate will remain DM 1.6850/dollar. This can be confirmed by letting DM 1.6911/dollar be the value for F_0^t in the IRP equation (the expected spot rate equals the forward rate) and solving for S_0. Under these assumptions, therefore, a change in a nominal interest rate changes the expected spot rate and the forward rate, but not the current spot rate. The current spot rate changes in response to a nominal interest rate change only if there is also a real interest rate change or the change in the nominal interest rate is not entirely due to a change in the expected inflation rate.

As was pointed out in Chapter 6, when capital is allowed to flow freely, IRP asserts itself so strongly that interest arbitrage opportunities tend to be very short-lived. IRP may not hold exactly because of transaction costs and risks, but deviations from exact IRP are normally small. Thus, whereas both relative PPP and the IFE have shaky foundations, the IRP relationship is built on solid ground.

The role of IRP in exchange rate determination is limited, but important. It assures that forward rates are consistent with nominal interest rates. This means, in turn, that forward rates coincide closely with the IFE's expected future spot rates.

The Expected Exchange Rate (EER)

The fourth and last key relationship included in the common core of exchange rate theory is what will be called the **expected exchange rate (EER)**, which links exchange rate expectations to the forward rate. Ignoring the other three relationships, it is logical to assume that the EER tends to equal the forward rate since, if it did not, speculation should align the forward rate with expectations. Because these other relationships influence forward rates, however, we cannot ignore them. A question therefore arises as to whether or not the forward rates resulting from the interaction of these relationships are consistent with the EER.

The Unbiased Predictor Controversy

Because of IRP, forward exchange rates tend to differ from current spot exchange rates in accordance with differences in nominal interest rates. If the resulting forward rates are to be viewed as expected future spot rates, it needs to be shown that forward rates are unbiased predictors of future spot rates. Determining whether or not forward rates are unbiased predictors involves studying historical data to ascertain whether the differences between forward rates and realized spot rates appear to be random. The differences will appear to be random if variations of forward rates on one side of the realized spot rates offset variations on the other side so that any remaining differences are statistically insignificant. If the differences are statistically insignificant, forward rates can be viewed as unbiased predictors of future spot rates.

If forward rates are unbiased predictors of future spot rates, this has important implications for international financial management, for it implies that money and resources invested in exchange rate forecasting are wasted. Avoiding such costs would free the services of talented individuals for other, more socially productive pursuits, and firms could limit their outlays for exchange rate forecasts to purchases of *The Wall Street Journal,* the *Financial Times,* and other publications listing the latest forward rates.

During the 1970s, when the world's experience with floating exchange rates had been rather limited, the prevailing view among financial researchers was that the evidence generally supported the unbiased predictor hypothesis.[11] This view was reinforced when, late in 1978, *Euromoney* published an article by Stephen Goodman with the attention-grabbing title "No Better than the Toss of a Coin," which suggested that forward rates were probably a better

[11]See Bradford Cornell, "Spot Rates, Forward Rates, and Market Efficiency," *Journal of Financial Economics,* August 1977, pp. 55–65; Ian H. Giddy and Gunter Dufey, "The Random Behavior of Flexible Exchange Rates," *Journal of International Business Studies,* Spring 1975, pp. 1–32; Stephen W. Kohlhagen, "The Performance of the Foreign Exchange Markets: 1971–1974," *Journal of International Business Studies,* Fall 1975, pp. 33–39; and Richard M. Levich, "Tests of Forecasting Models and Market Efficiency in the International Money Market," in J. A. Frenkel and H. G. Johnson, eds., *The Economics of Exchange Rates* (Reading, Mass.: Addison Wesley, 1979).

predictor of future spot rates than professional forecasts.[12] Specifically, Goodman found that during the first 6 months of 1978, forward rates outperformed all available forecasts, and that forecasts based on econometric models had produced particularly dismal results. As his article's title implies, Goodman found that during this particular time period, a forecast had no better than a 50 percent chance of beating the forward rate.

Although Goodman did not test the unbiased predictor hypothesis, he provided support for it. If the forward rate is an unbiased predictor, and if the EER incorporates what is known about future spot rates, then one should not expect forecasts predicting substantial differences of future spot rates from current forward rates to be more accurate than forward rates over time periods long enough to constitute a fair test.

During the 1980s, both theoretical and empirical work led to increased questioning of the unbiased predictor hypothesis. A consensus seems to be building that the forward rate is probably not an unbiased predictor after all. Nevertheless, the predictive power of forward rates is generally regarded as good enough that PPP, the IFE, and IRP continue to be important to exchange rate determination.

Forward Rate Bias

There are two major obstacles to accepting the unbiased predictor hypothesis. One is the fact that exchange rate forecasting is a thriving business in which firms charge corporate clients thousands of dollars per year for advisory services that provide forecasts for periods ranging from a few minutes to 10 years. If the forward rate is an unbiased predictor, then why are highly efficient, profit-oriented corporations willing to pay generously for worthless information? The second obstacle is the fact that academic opinion has increasingly swung toward accepting the proposition that the forward rate may be a biased predictor.

Deflating the Forecasts Particularly among academics, but also among practitioners, some skeptics question the usefulness of exchange rate forecasts and argue that buying forecasts is a waste of money or, at best, a purchase of information that returns just enough to cover its cost. Some of the skeptics appear to view the forward rate as an unbiased predictor, or close to being one, while others concede that there may be some forward bias, though not enough to conclude that the forex market is inefficient.

A possible explanation of the willingness of corporate clients to buy exchange rate forecasts is **bureaucratic hedging.** Just as individuals are often well-advised to seek a second medical opinion before risking major surgery, it can be argued that firms are also well-advised to seek advice from others besides their own forex specialists before taking forex positions that have important financial implications. If wrong decisions are made anyway, purchased forecasts may have value as scapegoats, i.e., the people who made the decisions can argue that they were backed by the best technical advice that money could buy. The bureaucratic hedging hypothesis implies that, viewed objectively, buying forecasts may be a waste of money, but one that helps to preserve the positions of those charged with making decisions.

It has also been argued that forecasters who truly possessed superior information would seek to exploit it by speculating for their own accounts rather than being satisfied with the much smaller gains from selling their information to others. Typically, however, forecasting services derive most of their income by selling advice, not by following it. They often defend this practice by arguing that if they made speculation the primary object of their actions, they might become emotionally involved with currency trading and lose objectivity. Needless to say, skeptics tend to find this line of argument self-serving and unconvincing.

Another argument that downplays the importance of forecasts is the contention that any forecasters who succeeded in demonstrating superior forecasting ability would give others the incentive to acquire the same information as they possessed. As a result, given the highly competitive nature of the forex market, any advantage would be temporary. Superior forecasters might earn enough to cover the costs of acquiring and assimilating information, but they could not be expected to earn superior profits for more than brief time periods. Normally, the best that could be expected from buying a forecast is that it would just cover its cost.

It is noteworthy that this last argument allows for the forward rate being a biased indicator of the future spot rate. If forecasters outperform the forward rate, then the forward rate is not the expected future spot rate for those with the best information. If the forward rate is not the expected spot rate in this sense, then the EER is apparently in conflict with the other key relationships examined in this chapter. Why, then, are forex dealers willing to enter into forward contracts that require them to trade at rates which, though consistent with IRP, are not expected to prevail? The answer has to be that they will be willing to do so if the income generated compensates them for accepting additional risk and the costs involved in managing it.

In Defense of the Forecasters   Neither of the first two arguments that question the value of exchange rate forecasts is particularly strong. Bureaucratic hedging undoubtedly exists, but it seems inadequate to explain the popularity of forecasting services. These services attract clients by offering impressively packaged evidence on how profits could have been made in the past by following their advice. While such evidence should be heavily discounted, it cannot be totally dismissed.

Also, while it is true that the services derive most of their income by selling forecasts, they do put some of their money where their mouths are. Some of the leading services commit part of their capital to betting on their own forecasts, and some obtain part of their income by charging clients on a share-of-the-profits basis rather than flat fees. If the forecasting firms seem reluctant to commit the bulk of their capital to forex speculation for their own accounts, this can readily be ascribed to the riskiness of such speculation. Forecasting services tend to be relatively small, highly specialized enterprises, or departments of large banks. Individual firms have strong desires to avoid **gambler's ruin,** a losing streak that exhausts a speculator's capital before it can be broken. The banks that run forecasting services are better able to overcome gambler's ruin because of their large capital bases, but they tend to be very risk-averse.

The third argument downplaying the significance of forecasts, that superior forecasting performance is likely to be temporary, is more difficult to meet. At least, though, it recognizes that speculating on the basis of forecasts may be profitable. It is certainly true that the profitability of forecasting services has attracted new entrants into the industry and forced established firms to improve their offerings. It is also true that some corporate managers have concluded that their firms have developed sufficient forecasting expertise that they need not rely on the forecasting services. In addition, some forecasting services have broadened the scope of their operations to include managing clients' forex positions and offering participation in **currency funds,** in which the services use clients' money, and possibly some of their own, for forex speculation. These developments are consistent with what one would expect in a highly competitive industry in which above-normal profits have been earned in the recent past, and they suggest that such profits are unlikely to be permanent. These developments are also consistent with the existence of a market in which the forward rate is a biased predictor of the future spot rate.

Given the emphasis in academic circles on empirical statistical research, one might think that many academics would have investigated the profitability of exchange rate forecasts. There are, however, severe obstacles to such research, namely the technical difficulty of measuring speculative profitability over a substantial time period and acquisition of the necessary data. Nevertheless, some statistical studies of forecasting profitability since the publication of Goodman's 1978 *Euromoney* article have indicated that speculation on the basis of forecasts may be profitable.

Some of the most interesting empirical work on exchange rate forecasting has been carried out by Richard Levich, a researcher with close ties to forex professionals. Levich's best-known study of exchange rate forecasts covered the period January 1977 through December 1980 and led him to conclude that, in some cases, speculators could have profited by using forecasts to bet against the forward rate.[13] Nevertheless, Levich also found the forward rate to

---

[13]Richard M. Levich, "Evaluating the Performance of the Forecasters," in Richard Ensor, ed., *The Management of Foreign Exchange Risk,* 2d ed. (London: Euromoney Publications, 1982), pp. 121–134. Reprinted in Donald R. Lessard, ed., *International Financial Management: Theory and Application,* 2d ed. (New York: John Wiley & Sons, 1985), pp. 218–233.

be more accurate than all but one of the 13 forecasting services he examined, and that one exception was a service that had begun operating in 1980.

An obvious question is how it is possible to profit by using exchange rate forecasts that are less accurate than the forward rate. Levich answered that a number of forecasting services were on the correct side of the difference between the forward rate and the subsequently realized spot rate a good deal more than 50 percent of the time. As a result, a speculator who consistently bet against the forward rate using these forecasts would have profited. Levich suggests that such a record can hardly be ascribed to chance and justifies the conclusion that the services demonstrated forecasting expertise.

The following example illustrates the nature of Levich's findings. Assume that the 90-day Swiss franc is currently at SF1.5343/dollar, that the spot franc is SF1.5495/dollar, and that forecasting service X predicts that the spot rate will be SF1.5500/dollar in 90 days. Now assume that 90 days later, the spot franc has moved to SF1.5365/dollar. The forward rate will have proved more accurate than the forecast because the error of the former (22 points) is much less than the error of the latter (135 points). Nevertheless, because the forecast predicted that the value of the spot franc in 90 days would be less than what was indicated by the forward rate, a speculator would have gained if, acting on X's forecast, he or she had contracted to sell francs forward at SF1.5343/dollar. Admittedly, this example ignores the bid–ask spread and transaction costs, but this does not invalidate the point that, in the sense specified by Levich, the forecast beat the forward rate.

If forecasts can outperform the forward rate in the sense indicated by Levich, this is particularly important for speculators and firms interested in making all-or-nothing hedging decisions. On the other hand, if accuracy is what matters, Levich's study indicates that the forward rate is the better guide. Consider, for example, the case of an investment firm holding shares of stock in a Swiss company that it plans to sell within 90 days. The timing of the sale would probably hinge on the firm's expectation about the spot franc. If the firm goes by the forecast of service X, it might decide to sell immediately. On the other hand, if it relies on the forward rate, it would probably defer the sale for a while. In this case, the forward rate would prove to be the better guide.

As Levich acknowledges, his testing procedure was not entirely fair to the forecasting services. He assumed, in effect, that a user of a service would bet, in equal amounts, on every one of a number of dates and hold the bets until the forward maturity dates. In reality, a speculator using a forecasting service would probably not bet that way. Typically, a service feels more strongly about some of its forecasts than others and tailors its advice accordingly. Moreover, services do not necessarily recommend holding given forward positions until maturity. These facts suggest that perhaps the best way to test the performance of the services is to carefully examine the profitability of following their advice. Unfortunately, obtaining the necessary data for a satisfactory test along these lines is not a simple task. Interestingly, Stephen Goodman conducted a profitability study based on the recommendations of technical forecasting services during the same period as that surveyed by Levich. Goodman concluded that, his 1978 article notwithstanding, the services had demonstrated forecasting expertise.[14]

From the evidence presented, it seems plausible to conclude that forward rates do sometimes exhibit bias and that the future spot rates expected by the best-informed observers may differ significantly from forward rates. On average, however, the bias that sometimes exists in forward rates is not so great as to warrant ignoring their predictive value.

Bias and Efficiency   If speculators can bet against the forward rate and win, the forward rate is not an unbiased predictor of the future spot rate. If bias exists, this suggests to some that the forex market may be inefficient. It is not necessarily true, however, that forward bias indicates market inefficiency. Forward bias may simply reflect a premium that just covers the cost of acquiring superior information and the risk involved in acting on it. If this is the case, it does not follow that the forex market is necessarily inefficient. The payments made to forecasters may just suffice to compensate them for the use of specialized facilities that allow them to process information at a lower cost than what their clients would have to spend to collect and analyze it on their own. If entry into the forecasting industry is easy, which it certainly appears to be, then competition among the forecasters should tend to eliminate any extra-normal profits derived from forecasting expertise. As far as the earnings of the speculators are concerned, they can be construed as a premium received in compensation for the risk and costs involved in speculation, a premium which, under competitive conditions, should not be a long-term source of above-normal profits.

If forward rates are often biased, this leads to an important question: Why hasn't the bias been more evident in empirical studies? A number of studies, especially older ones, have indicated that the forward rate is an unbiased predictor of the future spot rate. Even those studies that suggest the presence of bias do not generally find it to be large. The explanation for these results is probably threefold. First, empirical studies of forward bias generally cover fairly lengthy periods since otherwise, their validity might be impaired by the selection of unrepresentative time periods. Second, any bias may not be consistent in one direction. If, for example, bias sometimes causes the expected price of the mark to exceed its forward price, at other times the expected price of the mark may be less than its forward price. As a result, a study that is not confined to a short time period may find little bias, if any. Third, the bias, if any, must normally be small.

That any bias should normally be small follows from the nature of the process that keeps the EER and the forward rate in equilibrium. This process can be illustrated as follows. Suppose that the forecasters with the best information perceive that the expected spot price of the mark exceeds its

---

[14]Stephen H. Goodman, "Evaluating the Performance of the Technical Analysts," in Boris Antl and Richard Ensor, eds., *The Management of Foreign Exchange Risk* (London: Euromoney Publications, 1982).

forward price. Accordingly, they buy forward marks, causing the forward price of the mark to tend to rise. The banks that sell forward marks to accommodate the speculators engage in hedging operations in which they become net buyers of spot marks to offset their forward sales. In this manner, the spot mark tends to be pulled upward by the speculative purchases of forward marks. Since even the best-informed speculators will have some differences of opinion about the exact size of the initial gap between the EER and the forward rate, some speculators will refrain from buying forward marks as the price rises. At some point, everything else remaining the same, an equilibrium will be reached between the EER and the forward rate so that any remaining gap between them just suffices to provide the necessary speculative premium.

Since the adjustment process described here allows for the possibility that persons with superior knowledge may enjoy speculative gains, it may seem to support the proposition that the forex market is inefficient. The efficient market concept allows, however, for the possibility that some market participants may be less risk-averse than others and will speculate only if a premium exists that suffices to compensate them for their costs and the acceptance of risk.

A possible objection to this analysis is that banks may refuse to accommodate speculators. If, however, the speculators include corporate clients with sufficient forex risk-management capabilities, it is unlikely that banks will turn them away. Furthermore, would-be speculators who lack access to the forward market can always use futures and exchange-traded options.

An Overview of Foreign Exchange Forecasting

Since it appears that the forex market may have participants with genuine forecasting expertise, it is worth a little of our time to look at forex rate forecasting techniques. Before doing so, however, it is advisable to review what has been presented about exchange rate determination up to this point, for this may help us discern something about where forecasters' opportunities for improvement lie.

Fitting the Pieces Together

Exhibit 9.2 consists of a diagram that portrays the interaction among the key relationships that have been the primary concern of this chapter and also indicates how these relationships impact upon current spot and forward exchange rates. The key relationships (both versions of PPP, the IFE, IRP, and the EER) are shown as rectangles, and the current spot and forward rates are shown as triangles. Shown in circles are the factors that influence the key relationships: the base period exchange rate, historical relative inflation rates, the expected real interest rate, nominal interest rates, expected inflation rates, and a catchall other factors category that includes the influence on the EER of such things as central bank intervention and speculation.

| E X H I B I T | 9.2 | *Parity Relationships and the Determination of Exchange Rates*

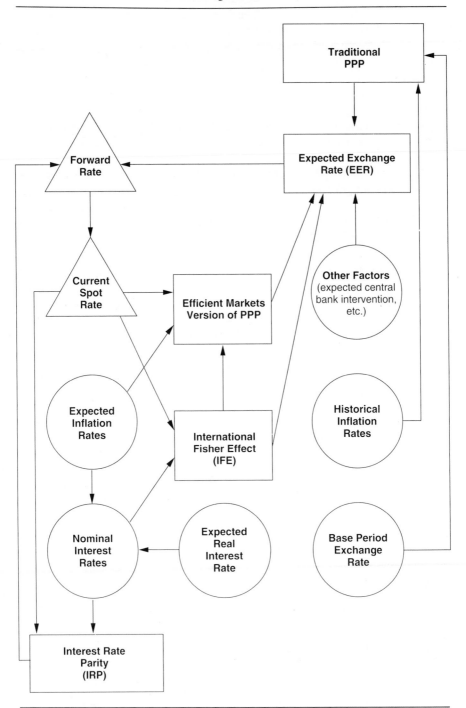

Exhibit 9.2 indicates that the efficient markets version of relative PPP is influenced by expected inflation rates and the current spot rate. Since nominal interest rates tend to incorporate differences in expected inflation rates, the efficient markets version is also shown to be influenced by the IFE. Because differences in nominal interest rates may not be due entirely to differences in expected inflation rates, nominal interest rates and expected inflation rates are shown separately in Exhibit 9.2 to allow for the possibility that they will have somewhat different effects on the EER. If nominal interest rate differences are viewed as being solely due to differences in expected inflation rates, it is not necessary to incorporate the efficient markets version of PPP; the IFE can be shown as directly affecting the EER rather than as working through the efficient markets version.

Exhibit 9.2 indicates that the forward rate is determined by IRP and the EER. The spot rate influences the forward rate through IRP. If the EER diverges sufficiently from the forward rate, it will have an impact on the forward rate, and, through the hedging process and IRP, the forward rate will have an impact on the current spot rate. The spot rate, in turn, operates through the efficient markets version and the IFE to affect the EER. The forward rate and the EER are thus mutually determining so that any difference between them is normally small.

The current spot rate is likely to differ from the historical PPP rate, primarily because of factors operating in the short run. It is conceivable that traditional PPP may sometimes have an impact on the current spot rate, so Exhibit 9.2 allows for this possibility. Any such impact is normally small, however, if the EER is viewed as being short term.

The central tasks of forecasters with a short-term focus are to predict inflation rates and to correctly assess the influence of the other factors that operate on exchange rates in the short run. These other factors, such as central bank intervention and differences in existing and expected real interest rates, generally have more short-term influence on capital flows than on trade flows. For this reason, short-term forecasters are primarily concerned with capital flows. In the final analysis, their success depends largely on the validity of the proposition that the influence of the other factors is not completely random, but can be discerned, in part, from analyzing available information.

A Note on the Forecasting Services

In general, exchange rate forecasts can be classified into two types: those that rely primarily on economic fundamentals and those that are based on what is called *technical analysis*. A brief account of each type follows.

Economic Fundamentalists In exchange rate forecasting based on *economic fundamentals,* exchange rate theory is applied to identify and weight the variables that influence exchange rates. Analysts who use this technique very commonly develop **econometric models,** which range from very complex models involving many variables to simple models that rely on a small number of key variables. At the opposite extreme from elaborate econometric models, in *judgmental forecasting,* forecasters rely on their skills, experience, and feelings in arriving at their conclusions.

It is tempting to assume that more complex models give better results, but this is not necessarily true. The explanation for this is twofold. In the first place, a complex model that weights variables incorrectly is likely to produce worse results than a simple model that correctly weights its variables. In the second place, complex models are at a disadvantage in terms of timeliness. Suppose, for example, that a complex model assigns a major weight to reported quarterly GNP estimates. Since such data are available only after considerable time lags, there is a danger that such a model will give an inaccurate forecast if the trend in a nation's output has changed since the last reported figures were released. Despite these problems, however, a complex model that incorporates all the information contained in a simple model should outperform the simple model if it can be properly adjusted for timeliness.

In practice, the short-term performance of forecasts based on economic fundamentals has been disappointing by comparison with the performance of technical forecasts. The short-term behavior of exchange rates is evidently greatly influenced by factors that are difficult to incorporate into models that rely on economic fundamentals. As the time period lengthens, however, the balance tends to swing toward econometric and judgmental forecasting.

Technical Analysis for Forecasting In exchange rate forecasting based on **technical analysis,** economic theory takes a back seat to the statistical analysis of past exchange rate behavior. The technical analyst operates on the assumption that past patterns of price behavior tend to be repeated. He or she therefore seeks, from the study of exchange rate data, one or more situations that have occurred previously that seem to correspond to the existing situation. If, for example, a technical analyst finds that a short-term moving average of the yen/dollar exchange rate has never been more than a certain percentage below the long-term moving average, he or she is likely to predict an increase in the yen value of the dollar when the current short-term average falls below the long-term average by that percentage.

Academic specialists have traditionally been skeptical of technical analysis, but their skepticism has been tempered somewhat by the fact that the technical analysts have recorded some impressive results in short-term forecasting. This success may well indicate that the different participants in the forex market tend to behave over time in approximately the same way in response to similar market conditions. When, for example, a given exchange rate moves a certain distance in one direction during a specified time period, central bankers and other market participants may become psychologically conditioned to reverse the directional swing. In any event, however, the technical analyst is less concerned with understanding *why* market participants behave as they do than with understanding *how* they behave in response to given stimuli.

Like econometric forecasts, technical forecasts tend to be highly computerized. The two approaches differ radically, however, in their choice of data to feed into computers. Whereas econometric models invariably assign great weight to PPP and the determinants of interest rates, technical models emphasize data on exchange rates. The exchange rate data included are not necessarily restricted to a particular exchange rate that the model is designed to predict, since what happens to one exchange rate is influenced by what happens to other exchange rates.

While technical analysis dominates short-term exchange rate forecasting, its usefulness diminishes rapidly as the time period lengthens. A technical forecast is designed to analyze a situation as of a given point in time. As time advances and new data are assimilated, a revised technical forecast is likely to differ substantially from its immediate predecessor. In effect, technical forecasts are designed to ascertain variations around trends. By contrast, forecasts based on economic fundamentals are designed to pick up the trends. The longer the time period, the more dominant the influence of trends becomes. Understandably, therefore, as the time period lengthens, forecasters tend to switch from reliance on technical analysis to reliance on economic fundamentals. This explains why some forecasting services advertise that their techniques combine technical and econometric models.

Summary

There is a common core of exchange-rate theory that emphasizes four key relationships: PPP, the IFE, IRP, and the EER. Because absolute PPP is not considered to be operational, relative PPP is generally used.

An important distinction exists between traditional or historical relative PPP and the efficient markets version of relative PPP. In traditional relative PPP, historical price level variations are referenced to a base period exchange rate to determine the exchange rate that should exist currently or that should have existed in the past on the assumption of a perfect negative correlation between exchange rate changes and changes in relative price levels. The efficient markets version discards the concept of a historical base period exchange rate and takes existing exchange rates to be equilibrium rates. From expectations of future price level changes, it then ascertains expected exchange rates.

During relatively short time periods, market exchange rates may vary substantially from relative PPP rates because of capital flows and other factors. Relative PPP is generally believed to be a better guide to long-term exchange rates than to short-term exchange rates, but nominal exchange rates and, therefore, real exchange rates, frequently depart substantially from relative PPP rates during relatively long time periods. Evidently, there is much more to exchange rate determination than variations in relative price levels.

According to the IFE, nations' nominal interest rates are a function of expected inflation rates and should, therefore, be unbiased indicators of future spot exchange rates. Empirical evidence provides considerable support for the idea that countries with relatively high nominal interest rates tend to have depreciating currencies, but there are major obstacles to accepting the IFE as an unbiased predictor. It may be that the tendency toward expected real interest rate uniformity internationally is incomplete, and it is difficult to distinguish nominal interest rate differences based on expectations of inflation from nominal interest rate differences caused by other factors. IRP assures the consistency of forward rates with the IFE, with the result that forward rates correspond to the IFE's expected future spot rates (the EERs).

While there is reason to believe that the current forward rate should be the EER, empirical evidence points to the possibility of some forward rate bias that allows successful speculation. Successful speculation based on a difference between the EER and the forward rate does not necessarily mean, however, that the forex market is inefficient. The demonstrated success of technical forecasts may be temporary and may simply represent a premium that just suffices to cover the cost of acquiring and using superior information.

References

Cassel, Gustav. "The Present Situation of the Foreign Exchanges." *Economic Journal*, March 1916, pp. 62–65.

———. "Abnormal Deviations in International Exchanges." *Economic Journal*, December 1918, pp. 413–415.

Chiang, Thomas C. "Empirical Analysis on the Predictions of Future Spot Rates." *Journal of Financial Research*, June 1986, pp. 153–162.

Cornell, Bradford. "Spot Rates, Forward Rates, and Market Efficiency." *Journal of Financial Economics*, August 1977, pp. 55–65.

Cumby, Robert E., and John Huizinga. "The Predictability of Real Exchange Rate Changes in the Short and Long Run." NBER *Working Paper* No. 3468, 1990.

Cumby, Robert E., and Maurice Obstfeld. "A Note on Exchange-Rate Expectations: A Test of the Fisher Hypothesis." *Journal of Finance*, June 1981, pp. 697–703. Reprinted in Donald R. Lessard, ed. *International Financial Management: Theory and Application*, 2d ed. New York: John Wiley & Sons, 1985, pp. 211–217.

———. "The Forward Rate as a Predictor of the Future Spot Rate — A Stochastic Approach." *Journal of Money, Credit, and Banking*, May 1988, pp. 212–232.

Frankel, Jeffrey A., and Kenneth Froot, "Exchange Rate Forecasting Techniques, Survey Data, and Implications for the Foreign Exchange Market. NBER *Working Paper* No. 3470, 1990.

Giddy, Ian H., and Gunter Dufey. "The Random Behavior of Flexible Exchange Rates." *Journal of International Business Studies*, Spring 1975, pp. 1–32.

Goodman, Stephen H. "No Better than the Toss of a Coin." *Euromoney*, December 1978, pp. 75–85.

———. "Evaluating the Performance of the Technical Analysts." In Boris Antl and Richard Ensor, eds. *The Management of the Foreign Exchange Risk*. London: Euromoney Publications, 1982.

Jaycobs, Richard. "Profit Is Hard to Measure." *Euromoney*, August 1987, pp. 121–124.

Lessard, Donald R. "Principles of International Portfolio Selection." In Abraham George and Ian H. Giddy, eds. *International Finance Handbook*. New York: John Wiley & Sons, 1983. Reprinted in Donald R. Lessard, ed. *International Financial Management: Theory and Application*, 2d ed. New York: John Wiley & Sons, 1985, pp. 16–30.

Levich, Richard M. "Tests of Forecasting Models and Market Efficiency in the International Money Market." In J. A. Frenkel and H. G. Johnson, eds. *The Economics of Exchange Rates*. Reading, Mass.: Addison Wesley, 1979.

———. "Evaluating the Performance of the Forecasters." In Richard Ensor, ed. *The Management of the Foreign Exchange Risk*, 2d ed. London: Euromoney Publications, 1982, pp. 121–134. Reprinted in Donald R. Lessard, ed. *International Financial Management: Theory and Application*, 2d ed. New York: John Wiley & Sons, 1985, pp. 218–233.

Mishkin, Frederic S. "Are Real Interest Rates Equal Across Countries? An Empirical Investigation of International Parity Relationships" *Journal of Finance*, December 1984, pp. 1345–1357.

Officer, Lawrence H. *Purchasing Power Parity and Exchange Rates: Theory, Evidence, and Relevance*. Greenwich, Conn.: Jai Press, 1982.

Pitman, Joanna. "Unsettled Outlook for Forecasters." *Euromoney*, August 1988, pp. 99–108.

Roll, Richard. "Violations of Purchasing Power Parity and Their Implications for Efficient International Commodity Markets." In Marshall Sarnat and George P. Szego, eds. *International Trade and Finance*. Vol. I. Cambridge, Mass.: Ballinger, 1979.

Shapiro, Alan C. "What Does Purchasing Power Parity Mean?" *Journal of International Money and Finance*, June 1983, pp. 295–318. Reprinted in Donald R. Lessard, ed. *International Financial Management: Theory and Application*, 2d ed. New York: John Wiley & Sons, 1985, pp. 236–259.

Solnik, Bruno. *International Investments*. 2d ed. Reading, Mass.: Addison-Wesley, 1991, Chapters 1 and 3.

Williamson, John. "Measures of Exchange Rate Variability." In *The Exchange Rate System*. Washington, D.C.: Institute for International Economics, 1983. Reprinted in Donald R. Lessard, ed. *International Financial Management: Theory and Application*, 2d ed. New York: John Wiley & Sons, 1985, pp. 260–283.

Questions

1. Why is it better to classify PPP as a relationship than a theory?
2. If you wanted to use absolute PPP to determine the proper exchange rate between, for example, the dollar and the Italian lira, how might you go about it? Why might two different people trying to calculate an absolute PPP exchange rate come up with substantially different results?
3. If an exchange rate calculated on the basis of traditional relative PPP is to be an equilibrium exchange rate, what three conditions must be satisfied?
4. Joan Robinson argued that the equilibrium exchange rate is indeterminate. Does this mean that relative PPP cannot be used to calculate a valid exchange rate? Explain.
5. Traditional relative PPP is generally more useful as a guide to what exchange rates should be after lengthy time periods than after short time periods. Explain why, being careful to take into account the role of capital flows and changes in the market conditions affecting goods of major importance in international trade.
6. Fully evaluate the contention that traditional relative PPP is a poor guide to exchange rate determination since it ignores the influence on exchange rates of capital flows.
7. Explain why, over long time periods, and even if base period exchange rates are equilibrium rates and price indexes are correctly chosen, market exchange rates can differ substantially from traditional PPP exchange rates.

8. Fully evaluate the contention that the price indexes used for PPP calculations should be indexes of tradables.

9. How does the efficient markets version of relative PPP differ from the traditional version?

10. Should an increase in the nominal interest rate in the United States be interpreted to mean that the dollar is likely to strengthen or to weaken?

11. In what respect, if any, does the efficient markets version of relative PPP differ from the IFE?

12. What are the reasons for questioning the proposition that the IFE is an unbiased predictor of future spot rates?

13. Assume that the nominal interest rate in the United Kingdom declines relative to the nominal interest rate in the United States, with the result that the discount on the forward pound declines through the operation of IRP. Can we conclude from this information that the spot pound should increase? Explain.

14. It is sometimes argued that if forecasting services truly possessed forecasting expertise, they would profit by speculating themselves rather than selling information to others. Instead, it is claimed, they avoid risking their own money. Evaluate this argument.

15. Even if forward rates are, on average, more accurate predictors of future spot rates than exchange rate forecasting services, speculators may still manage to gain by relying on forecasts. Explain.

16. What is meant by forward rate bias? Why is it that the existence of forward bias does not necessarily mean that the forex market is inefficient?

17. If forward rates are biased, why hasn't this bias been more evident in empirical studies? Related to this question, explain why forward bias should normally be small if the forex market is efficient.

18. Technical analysis is apparently superior to relying on economic fundamentals in short-term exchange rate forecasting. Why?

Problems

1. Assume that in Year 1, the market exchange rate between the Mexican peso and the dollar averaged Ps2,500 per dollar. You believe that the peso was slightly undervalued at that time because of interest rate controls used by the Mexican government. Accordingly, you decide that the correct or equilibrium value of the peso in Year 1 was Ps2,400 per dollar. Now assume that in year 5, the market exchange rate is averaging Ps3,620 per dollar. Using Year 1 as the base year, the Mexican CPI currently stands at 175.4 percent, while the U.S. CPI based on Year 1 stands at 126.8. You estimate, however, that the Mexican CPI understates the cumulative inflation since Year 1 by about 12 percent (based on Year 1) because of government controls on the prices of goods included in the CPI market basket. What is the relative PPP exchange rate in Year 5? What is the real exchange rate in Year 5 referenced to Year 1?

2. Assume that the spot guilder/dollar exchange rate is currently F1.8960 per dollar, that 60-day U.S. Treasury bills are currently yielding 5.82 percent

on a bond-equivalent (annual yield) basis, and that the interest rate on comparable Dutch securities is 6.48 percent. The 60-day forward rate is currently F1.8981 per dollar. Now assume that the interest rate on the Dutch securities abruptly rises to 6.72 percent, everything else remaining the same. According to the IFE, what was the predicted spot exchange rate in 60 days before the interest rate change, and what is this rate after the change?

3. Assume that the spot guilder/dollar exchange rate is currently F1.8960 per dollar, that U.S. Treasury securities with three years to maturity are currently yielding 6.68 percent on an annual yield basis, and that the interest rate on comparable Dutch securities is 7.44 percent. Assuming annual compounding, what is the predicted spot exchange rate in three years if IFE holds exactly?

Exchange Rate Theories

■

Chapter 9 examined four parity relationships that are relevant to exchange rate determination and briefly considered other factors that influence exchange rates. It did not, however, give much consideration to what lies behind these relationships and other factors.

While variations in price levels and interest rates were pinpointed as having great importance in the determination of exchange rates, Chapter 9 provided no analysis of the causes of such variations. While speculation and central bank intervention were identified as being among the other factors that influence exchange rates, neither was examined very deeply. It was pointed out that both have more significance in the short run than in the long run, and it was suggested that forecasting expertise might permit the making of speculative gains. Chapter 9 virtually ignored the important question of whether or not speculation can have a destabilizing effect on exchange rates in the short run, however, and the related question of whether or not central bank intervention enhances exchange rate stability.

The purpose of this chapter is to survey several of the leading theories of the determination of exchange rates and BOP equilibrium. The theories selected come under the headings of the Keynesian theory, with its associated absorption approach, the elasticities approach, the monetary theory, and the latest candidate for major status among such theories, the equilibrium theory. Chapter 11 completes our examination of exchange rates by examining the portfolio balance theory and considering the role of speculators and central banks in the exchange rate determination process.

The Keynesian Theory

For more than 50 years, macroeconomic theory and policy have been greatly influenced by the ideas of John Maynard Keynes, whose *General Theory* affected macroeconomics like no other work before or since.[1] The Keynesian

---

[1]John Maynard Keynes, *The General Theory of Employment, Interest, and Money* (New York: Harcourt, Brace, and World, 1936).

models that subsequently became standard fare for students of economics gave primary emphasis to fiscal policy and relegated the study of money and the conduct of monetary policy to secondary importance. Because the *General Theory* was written when the author was preoccupied with promoting recovery from the Great Depression, the book had little relevance for economic growth. As far as international economics is concerned, one should recall that at the time the book was published, both economic theory and policy employed the assumption that exchange rates were, or should be, fixed. Over subsequent decades, the Keynesian theory has been expanded to incorporate economic growth, monetary dynamics, and exchange rate flexibility, but the Keynesian theory of today still looks much like the design of its architect.

With the passage of time, the use of the Keynesian theory to explain exchange rates has diminished because of progress in the development of other approaches. Elements of the theory are, nevertheless, worth including here because they have had lasting influence. Specifically, we shall examine three such elements: the marginal propensity to import, the relationship between interest rates and capital flows, and the absorption approach, the last of which was grafted onto the Keynesian theory in the 1950s.

The Marginal Propensity to Import

The following analysis assumes that the reader has enough familiarity with the basic Keynesian open economy model that it is unnecessary to review that model in detail. Our starting point is the observation that in the Keynesian theory, a nation's economy tends to reach an equilibrium level of output–income that is determined by its aggregate demand function (AD) defined as total planned spending on newly produced goods and services at various possible price levels. AD has four components: consumption (C), domestic investment (I), government spending for goods and services (G), and exports (X). Imports (M) are excluded from AD because they are not part of a nation's flow of output and income. Nevertheless, it is common to write the AD equation as $AD = C + I + G + X - M$, which is the same way that the equation for GNP is commonly written (the difference between the two equations being that AD deals with planned magnitudes while GNP deals with actual magnitudes). Imports are subtracted in the GNP equation because they are actually included in the figures for C, I, G, and even X and must, therefore, be eliminated in order to avoid double counting. The material that follows assumes that C, I, G, and X do not include imports. Therefore, the AD equation is simply $AD = C + I + G + X$.

In equilibrium, AD equals national output (O). Since total spending for goods and services must always equal the total income generated from their production (Y), $O = Y$. The income included in Y is allocated in four different ways: consumption, saving (S), taxes and other payments to government (T), and imports. Customarily, the government revenues that fund transfer payments are subtracted from T to arrive at net taxes (T_n). S, T_n, and M are conventionally called *leakages* because they are not, in themselves, expenditures on domestically produced goods. On the spending, or *injections,* side of the O = Y equation, I, G, and X are the counterparts to S, T_n, and M. In equilibrium, I + G + X equals S + T_n + M in an expectational sense, but I + G + X is *always* equal to S + T_n + M in a realized sense because any imbalance between planned leakages and planned injections is offset by unplanned changes in business inventories, which are included in I.

The three injections are generally considered to be virtually autonomous with respect to changes in a nation's output–income level. By contrast, the leakages are all considered to be determined primarily by income and to vary directly with it. Since M is a function of Y, while X is considered to be basically autonomous with respect to Y, M rises relative to X as Y increases. This means that increases in GNP tend to cause a nation to have a trade deficit. If other nations simultaneously experience GNP growth, a nation tends to have an increase in its exports, but if its growth in GNP is relatively rapid, M tends to rise relative to X.

The trade balance effect of an increase in GNP depends, in part, on a nation's **marginal propensity to import (mpm)**, which is the ratio between a change in imports and the accompanying change in income, i.e., $\Delta M/\Delta Y$. The larger the mpm, the larger the increase in M associated with a given change in Y. On the other hand, the larger the mpm, the smaller the change in Y. This is because the expenditure multiplier tends to diminish in size as the mpm increases.

Recall that in its simplest formulation, the *Keynesian expenditure multiplier* equals $1/(1 - \text{mpc})$, where mpc is the *marginal propensity to consume,* i.e., C/ Y. Since imports represent a leakage from the income stream, the value of the mpc and, therefore, the value of the multiplier both become smaller as the value of the mpm increases.

The following example illustrates the role of the mpm in determining a nation's trade balance. Assume that there is a country named Vegetaria whose exports initially equal its imports and whose mpc and mpm are, respectively, 60 percent and 15 percent. Also assume that Vegetaria is initially at its equilibrium output–income level but that changes in planned spending cause AD to rise initially by 20 billion gourds, the gourd being the Vegetarian monetary unit. Since the expenditure multiplier in this case has a value of 2.5, Vegetaria's equilibrium income level will increase by 50 billion gourds. Given the mpm of 15 percent, M will increase by 7.5 billion gourds. Assuming that X remains unchanged, 7.5 billion gourds will also be the trade deficit caused by the increase in income.

An increase in a country's imports tends to increase income in other countries, and this increase in income tends to have a feedback effect, known as the **foreign repercussions effect,** on the first country's exports. The foreign repercussions effect serves, however, only to reduce a trade deficit caused by the expansion of a country's income, not to eliminate it.[2] It follows that unless

---

[2]The fundamental reason that a trade deficit is not eliminated by foreign repercussions is that any income change transmitted abroad must be smaller than the income change that produced the deficit.

capital flows somehow adjust automatically to offset a trade deficit, the currencies of countries that experience relatively rapid income growth will tend to depreciate against other currencies unless the income growth is caused primarily by the expansion of exports.

Interest Rates and Capital Flows

If relatively rapid income growth tends to produce a trade deficit that is not totally removed by subsequent trade flow adjustments, can this be the end of the story? If Vegetaria is content to allow its currency to continue to depreciate as long as its relatively rapid income growth continues, then evidently the tale has been told, since the continuous depreciation of its currency would tend to prevent trade deficits from actually being realized. If, however, the Vegetarian government, like most governments, chooses to limit the depreciation of its currency, there is still something to be said. If the Vegetarian gourd is not to be left hanging in disequilibrium, either some adjustment must eliminate the trade deficit or else something must happen to produce a net capital inflow that can be sustained indefinitely.

According to the Keynesian theory, if currencies are not allowed to fluctuate freely, then trade imbalances will tend to have monetary effects. These monetary effects, in turn, bring about real interest rate changes that tend to produce a stable equilibrium in which current account deficits or surpluses are fully offset, respectively, by net capital inflows or outflows.

Keynesian Payments Equilibrium Let us return to Vegetaria, which is assumed to have a trade deficit as a consequence of its relatively rapid economic growth and the Vegetarian government's policy of limiting the gourd's depreciation. When the Vegetarian central bank intervenes in the forex market to support the gourd, it buys gourds with foreign exchange, and it collects the gourds due to it by reducing commercial banks' accounts with it. In other words, the central bank's intervention reduces the reserves of Vegetarian banks, which tends to produce a multiplied decline in the Vegetarian money supply.

The resulting decline in the money supply could be prevented if the central bank would neutralize the decline in reserves through appropriate monetary action, but let us assume that it refrains from neutralization in order to accelerate the adjustment process. The combination of tight money and rapid income growth tend to boost the real interest rate level, and the rise in the real interest rate level tends to pull in capital from abroad. In due course, Vegetaria achieves an equilibrium in its BOP in which its current account deficit is offset by a net capital inflow occurring in response to its relatively high interest rate.

Assuming that the Vegetarian economy is large enough to have a significant impact on other countries, the adjustment process may be accelerated by changes occurring in the rest of the world. Other countries would tend to experience some income growth because of the income expansion in Vegetaria, and this would tend to produce a foreign repercussions effect on Vegetaria's exports. In addition, other countries would tend to experience some monetary expansion as a consequence of central bank intervention to restrain the tendency of their currencies to rise against the gourd. The monetary expansion would tend to lower their real interest rates and to accelerate the flow of capital into Vegetaria.

Exhibit 10.1 illustrates, in simplified fashion, the achievement of BOP equilibrium according to the Keynesian theory when exchange rates are not allowed to fluctuate freely. The vertical axis measures the nominal domestic interest rate (r), which is also a real interest rate as long as the price level remains unchanged. The horizontal axis measures both current account and capital account balances. The segment of the horizontal axis to the right of the origin measures current account deficits and net capital inflows, while the segment to the left of the origin measures current account surpluses and net capital outflows.

The TT lines are functions that relate the current account balance to r. They slope downward from left to right because as r declines, domestic investment increases, income rises, and imports increase, thereby tending to cause a current account deficit. A TT line reflects the assumption that the income level is given except for changes caused by variations in r. If, for example, income falls for some reason other than a rise in r, the relevant TT line shifts to the left because of the resulting fall in imports relative to exports. At any given level of r, therefore, there will be a larger current account surplus or a smaller current account deficit than before.

While Exhibit 10.1 assumes a given domestic price level, it can be adapted to a change in the price level. If, for example, the price level rises, the TT function shifts rightward reflecting a movement toward a negative current account balance.

Line KK plots the balance on capital account. It slopes upward from left to right because as r rises, more capital flows in or less capital flows out. If the price level rises, KK shifts upward because investors require a higher r (which now becomes a nominal interest rate) to provide the same net capital flow as before.

Because interest rate changes in the rest of the world could affect both trade and capital flows, it is convenient to assume that interest rates in foreign countries are fixed. This simplifies the analysis without altering its basic character.[3]

Originally, there is an equilibrium in which T_1T_1 intersects K at the interest rate E. As a result, the current and capital account balances are both zero. An autonomous decline in exports occurs, with the result that the TT line shifts to the right, throwing the current account into a deficit. This deficit leads to a decline in the money supply, an increase in r, and a net capital inflow in response to the increase in r. Assuming that the central bank undertakes no

---

[3]Interest rate changes in the rest of the world are incorporated into the analysis in Lloyd A. Metzler, "The Process of International Adjustment under Conditions of Full Employment: A Keynesian View," in Richard E. Caves and Harry G. Johnson, eds., *Readings in International Economics* (Homewood, Ill.: Richard D. Irwin, 1968).

| E X H I B I T | 10.1 | *Keynesian BOP Adjustment with Exchange Rate Rigidity*

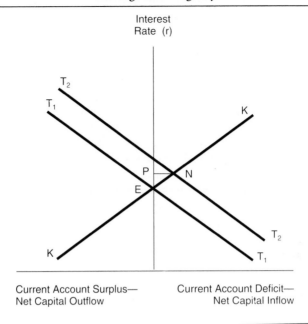

Interest
Rate (r)

T_2

T_1

K

P N

E

T_2

K

T_1

Current Account Surplus—
Net Capital Outflow

Current Account Deficit—
Net Capital Inflow

neutralization of changes in bank reserves, the money supply continues to fall and the interest rate to rise until KK intersects the stabilized TT function, T_2T_2, at N. In the new equilibrium indicated by N, there is a current account deficit and a net capital inflow, both of which equal PN, i.e., this equilibrium requires no official reserve financing of the current account deficit. Note that the new equilibrium interest rate of P exceeds the original interest rate of E.

T_2T_2 is the current account function after the income adjustments associated with the expenditure multiplier. Immediately after the autonomous fall in exports that brought about a disequilibrium, the TT line would have shifted to the right of T_2T_2. The adjustment process can thus be viewed as a large initial rightward shift in the TT function followed by a continuing shift to the left until it stabilizes with T_2T_2. The capital account function, KK, remains in place because, given the assumption of a stable price level, the r axis is a scale of real interest rates.

If the assumption of a given price level in the home country is dropped and the price level is allowed to fall when both the money supply and the income level decline, the stabilized TT function will be to the left of T_2T_2. In that event, however, the capital account function would also shift, moving downward and to the right, because with a falling price level, a given value for r would represent a higher real interest rate. The decline in the price level would tend to reduce the downward pressure on the exchange value of the country's currency because it would tend to diminish the size of the trade deficit and stimulate capital inflows.

Implications of the Adjustment Process   In Keynesian theory, the restoration of BOP equilibrium after an initial disturbance involves the interaction of trade and capital flows in response to changes in income, interest rates, price levels, and exchange rates. Income variations, operating through trade balances, tend to have an important exchange rate impact, but to the extent that price levels and interest rates are flexible, the exchange rate impacts of changes in income tend to be reduced. The sensitivity of capital flows to interest rate changes is also important, for to the extent that capital flows respond to interest rates, the exchange rate impact of income variations is moderated.

Note that the Keynesian theory implies that real interest rates do not tend to uniformity internationally, for otherwise the equilibrium that is portrayed in Exhibit 10.1 could not be stable. A country with a current account deficit could hardly rely on interest rate adjustments to achieve BOP stability if it were unable to maintain a real interest differential between itself and the rest of the world. In any event, the Keynesian equilibrium should be regarded as being short-term in nature because of doubts about the permanence of a real interest rate differential.

Absorption

While Keynesian theory is adaptable to a framework in which the dominant factors affecting exchange rates are variations in price levels and interest rates, it is its emphasis on the role of variations in income that has most distinguished it from other theories and produced the greatest controversy. In the form in which the Keynesian theory is usually presented, which is a short-run model employing highly restrictive assumptions, it can be sharply criticized because it seems to be at variance with reality.

Because of the Keynesian theory, many people have long believed that a nation's trade balance tends to vary inversely with its rate of growth in real income. Accordingly, in both textbooks and the financial press, one frequently encounters the idea that a recession in the United States tends to strengthen the dollar because of a reduced U.S. demand for imports and that a boom tends to have the opposite effect. In fact, however, this apparently plausible pattern of correlation may not hold. Part of the explanation as to why it may not hold is provided by examining the connection between real income growth and **absorption,** which is defined as total domestic expenditure on goods and services, including imports.

Exchange Rates and Economic Growth   The application of the absorption concept to the analysis of payments adjustment and exchange rate determination is generally credited to Sidney Alexander of the IMF.[4] By using an

---

[4]Sidney Alexander, "Devaluation versus Import Restriction as an Instrument for Improving Foreign Exchange Balance," *IMF Staff Papers*, April 1951, pp. 279–296; "Effects of Devaluation on a Trade Balance," *IMF Staff Papers*, April 1952, pp. 263–278; and "Effects of Devaluation: A Simplified Synthesis of Elasticities and Absorption Approaches," *American Economic Review*, March 1959, pp. 22–42.

absorption framework, it is possible using relatively simple analysis to extend the Keynesian theory so that it deals more satisfactorily with the international dynamics of economic growth. In this framework, the growth process does not necessarily tend to cause a trade deficit in a rapidly growing economy, nor does a recession necessarily tend to cause a trade surplus.

The standard absorption equation is as follows:

$$A = C + I + G + M \qquad (10\text{--}1)$$

A is absorption, and the other letters have the meanings that were given to them earlier. Note, however, that C, I, and G are all assumed to be net of imports.

The absorption equation differs slightly from the equation for national output, which is:

$$0 = C + I + G + X \qquad (10\text{--}2)$$

Whereas absorption includes imports and excludes exports, the output equation does the reverse. Again, C, I, and G are all assumed to be net of imports.

Subtracting Equation 10–2 from Equation 10–1 gives us the following equation:

$$A - 0 = M - X \qquad (10\text{--}3)$$

In other words, if a nation has a trade deficit, its absorption exceeds its output. It follows from this that elimination of a trade deficit requires that output rise relative to absorption. This means that although the mpm tends to increase imports when income increases, it is not necessarily true that the growth of output–income tends to cause a trade deficit and a depreciation of the national currency.

The absorption approach indicates that as long as output rises faster than absorption, a nation does not have to orient its growth toward the export sector of its economy in order to improve its trade balance and boost its currency. If all of the increase in output is absorbed domestically, and the growth in total absorption is less than the increase in output, domestic expenditures are switched from imports to domestic goods, causing an improvement in the trade balance. In such a case, import substitution swamps the tendency of increases in income to generate additional imports. It is also possible, however, that much of the increase in output may be exported, in which case import substitution need not occur in order to achieve an improvement in the trade balance.

The absorption approach provides a simple and clearcut explanation of why it is the case that countries with relatively high rates of economic growth often tend to have appreciating currencies. It is necessary to remember, however, that economic growth does not, in itself, assure an appreciating currency. It is always possible that a country with rapid economic growth may have even more rapid growth in its absorption, in which case its currency will tend to depreciate unless a deterioration in its trade balance is offset by simultaneous capital inflows.

If a nation with a trade deficit problem cannot generate much expansion of output, correcting the deficit requires that absorption be reduced. One way to reduce it is to curtail imports with trade and/or payments restrictions while simultaneously acting to restrain the growth of domestic spending. These measures can be accompanied by measures that directly promote import substitution in production. Another way to reduce absorption is to decrease its domestic components, particularly C and G, to free resources for the expansion of exports. As a general proposition, the second of these alternatives is probably the sounder economically, but it is usually politically difficult to reduce absorption in this way. Accordingly, it is hardly surprising that countries with low rates of economic growth often have depreciating currencies.

The absorption approach also helps us to see why a country in a recession need not necessarily experience an improvement in its trade balance that tends to boost the exchange value of its currency. If output drops more rapidly than absorption, the trade balance worsens. It is distinctly possible, therefore, that if a country enters into a recession and its government takes steps to increase domestic spending, it will experience a worsening of its trade balance, not an improvement.

Implementing the Absorption Approach   The absorption approach is obviously not a complete theory of payments adjustment and exchange rate determination since, among other things, it leaves out capital flows and does not, in itself, explain how payments equilibrium is achieved. It does, however, identify how to avoid trade balance problems, and it can be combined with other elements of Keynesian theory to construct a program for dealing with such problems.

Recall that it was pointed out earlier that in a realized sense, it is always true that $I + G + X = S + T_n + M$. Given this, it follows that if a nation has a trade deficit, i.e., if M exceeds X, then $I + G$ must exceed $S + T_n$. Thus, a trade deficit can be reduced by increasing $S + T_n$ relative to $I + G$, and a trade deficit *cannot* be reduced by restricting M without a simultaneous reduction in $I + G$, or an increase in $S + T_n$, or both.

Since most governments try to avoid discouraging domestic investment because of its connection with economic growth, and since almost all of the world's central governments run annual budget deficits, the most promising lines of attack for reducing a trade deficit are generally considered to be the following: (1) expanding exports, (2) reducing the rate of growth in G, particularly when this can be done without harm to economic growth, (3) increasing S, and (4) increasing T_n, perhaps in part by slowing the growth of transfer payments. Note that options 3 and 4 tend to slow the growth of consumption. In addition, it is always possible to attack a trade deficit problem directly by restricting imports, but such a strategy tends to provoke international ill will and retaliation. Furthermore, the restriction of imports is generally considered to be economically inefficient.

It should now be evident why the emergence of a persistent U.S. trade deficit has led to a general insistence among economists that the U.S. government should reduce its budget deficits and actively promote domestic saving. It should also be clear why the dollar's forex value tends to rise with news of progress on the budget deficit and saving fronts and to fall when the news indicates the opposite.

The Elasticities Approach

Even before Keynesian theory, economists had begun to analyze the payments adjustment–exchange rate determination process by examining the factors that affect the elasticities of supply and demand that appear to be relevant to that process. Appropriately, the method of analysis that they developed along these lines is known as the **elasticities approach.** The elasticities that are central to this approach are those of the demand for and the supply of foreign exchange, but because each of these functions is derived from the demand and supply functions of the goods and assets that enter into international trade and investment, the elasticities approach tends toward considerable complexity. Given that complexity, there follows a highly simplified presentation of this approach.

The Desirability of High Elasticities

Exhibit 10.2 provides a simple supply and demand framework for illustrating the possible relevance of elasticities in exchange rate determination. Using the U.S. dollar to stand for all foreign currencies, the exchange rate chosen is that between the Philippine peso (₱) and the U.S. dollar. Two different cases are illustrated, but each features a disturbance to equilibrium caused by a 50 percent increase in the Philippine demand for foreign exchange over that demanded at the original equilibrium exchange rate of ₱24/dollar. In Panel a, both demand and supply are relatively elastic, while in Panel b, both functions are relatively inelastic. Because of the differences in elasticities, the exchange rate change required to restore equilibrium in Panel b is much greater than in Panel a. In Panel a, the equilibrium exchange rate rises to only ₱29/dollar, while in Panel b, it rises to ₱40/dollar. Evidently, therefore, what happens to exchange rates depends greatly on the elasticities of supply and demand in the forex market.

As far as trade in goods and services is concerned, the demand for foreign exchange is derived from the domestic demand for imports, while the supply of foreign exchange is derived from foreign demand for a country's exports. Each of these demands is part of a larger demand. The demand for imports is part of a larger demand for importables, some of which are domestically produced, while the foreign demand for a country's exports is part of a demand for exportables, some of which are produced in foreign countries. A further complication is that a nation's demand for imports and the demand of foreigners for its exports are influenced by supply conditions. Thus, the

| E X H I B I T | 10.2 | *Elasticities and Exchange Rates*

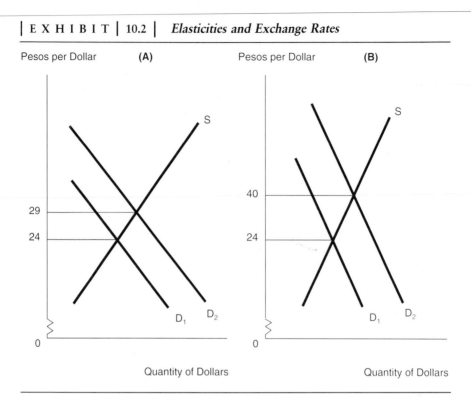

demand for imports is influenced by the availability of domestically produced import substitutes, while foreign demand for a nation's exports is influenced by the supply of competing goods produced in other countries.

In general, greater elasticities of the various supply and demand functions that are relevant to international trade means greater elasticities of supply and demand in the forex market. Nations differ greatly in terms of the relevant elasticities, which implies that exchange rates are more variable for some countries than for others. The factors that tend to cause high elasticities include the ability to rapidly expand or contract the production of exportables, having exports and imports for which world demand is elastic, and the ability to alter the nation's trade volume without having a large impact on the world prices of the traded goods and services.

The Perverse Elasticities Case

The claim has often been advanced, particularly with respect to LDCs, that because the relevant supply and demand elasticities are low, the exchange rate adjustments required to maintain equilibrium are large and even uncertain. Since large exchange rate changes and exchange rate uncertainty are economically disruptive, low elasticities have been used to rationalize extensive government interference with market forces, including the use of exchange controls.

It has also been claimed that the elasticities affecting the forex supply curve may be so low that this curve is negatively sloped over the relevant range of exchange rates. This happens, it is claimed, if the world demand for a country's exports is inelastic, for in such a case, the country's forex earnings from exports decline with declines in the forex prices of its exports, i.e., with increases in forex rates. With such **perverse elasticities,** the standard remedy for a trade deficit of reducing the national currency's exchange value may fail completely. Indeed, it is conceivable that, rather than allowing the national currency to depreciate, the country's government should raise its exchange value.

Exhibit 10.3 illustrates the perverse elasticities case. The supply curve for foreign exchange bends backward over the upper range of peso/dollar exchange rates, and the demand curve for foreign exchange slopes steeply enough that at exchange rate E, it crosses the supply curve from above. Assuming that the existing exchange rate is N, it would be a mistake for the Philippine government to allow market forces to determine the exchange rate, for in that case, the price of the dollar would rise further (or even explode), leading, no doubt, to economic collapse. Equality between the quantity supplied and the quantity demanded could be achieved by lowering the exchange rate to E. Much better, however, would be a reduction in the price of the dollar to X, for the equilibrium reached at that level would tend to be a stable one.

| E X H I B I T | 10.3 | *Perverse Elasticities in the Forex Market*

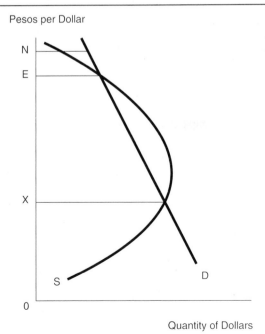

Pesos per Dollar

Quantity of Dollars

We can see that the supply curve of foreign exchange can·slope backward at relatively high exchange rates since the demand for individual goods tends to become less elastic as their prices fall. When a nation's currency depreciates, the forex prices of its exports tend to decline, and it is conceivable that if the depreciation proceeds far enough, the overall demand for its exports could become inelastic, causing the forex supply curve to bend backward if we ignore capital flows. It does not necessarily follow, however, that perverse elasticities are a realistic possibility.

There is good reason to believe that foreign demand for a country's exports is normally elastic and that perverse elasticities should be regarded as an intellectual curiosity with little real-world applicability. Even though world demand for many goods is inelastic over the price ranges that are likely to prevail, the demand for the exports of individual nations may be elastic. Thus, while world demand for sugar is undoubtedly inelastic, the demand for Philippine sugar is probably elastic. Moreover, as a nation's currency depreciates, it becomes feasible to export goods that were previously too high-priced to be exportable. Nevertheless, perverse elasticities have often been used as a rationale for market interference with the determination of exchange rates.

The Marshall–Lerner Condition

Additional ammunition against the perverse elasticities case is provided by a famous proposition known as the **Marshall–Lerner (ML) condition,** which states that a country with a trade deficit can reduce the deficit through a depreciation of its currency if the sum of the elasticity of its demand for imports and the foreign elasticity of demand for its exports has an absolute value greater than 1. If either its imports or its exports have less than perfect elasticity of supply, some improvement in the trade balance may occur even if the sum of the demand elasticities is less than 1.[5]

The elasticity requirements of the ML condition are so easily satisfied that it must be presumed that a trade deficit will ordinarily tend to be diminished by a depreciation of a nation's currency, *provided that the demand and supply curves in the forex market remain the same.* This presumption is strengthened by the fact that demand elasticity tends to increase over time as buyers adjust to price changes.

The ML condition applies to changes in nations' relative price levels as well as to changes in the exchange rates of their currencies. If, for example, a nation with a trade deficit attempts to eliminate it by lowering its price level relative to other countries, its success depends, everything else remaining the same, on its ability to satisfy the ML condition. If a nation with a depreciating currency experiences higher inflation than other countries, it loses the benefit

---

[5]This proposition is named after Alfred Marshall, who supplied the basic geometrical analysis, and Abba P. Lerner, who provided a refined algebraic analysis based on the assumption of perfect supply elasticities. Because additional refinements were made by Joan Robinson, it is sometimes called the Marshall–Lerner–Robinson condition. In any event, it deals only with the current account part of a nation's BOP.

of ML to the extent that its inflation offsets the depreciation of its currency since the ML condition operates with respect to both exchange rate and price level changes.

The J Curve

In the financial press, and occasionally on TV news programs, references are made to the *J* **curve,** usually in connection with a statement that a decline in the dollar's exchange value has been followed by deterioration of the U.S. trade balance that is expected to be reversed in due course. This *J* curve effect of an exchange rate change is by far the best-known manifestation of the elasticities approach.

The *J* curve materializes on a graph plotting the country's trade balance on the vertical axis and time on the horizontal axis following a depreciation of the country's currency. Exhibit 10.4 illustrates a hypothetical *J* curve that emerges following a depreciation of the dollar. The U.S. merchandise trade balance is portrayed initially as being negative at the rate of about $10 billion per quarter and tending to grow larger. In the fourth quarter of Year I, following a substantial depreciation of the dollar (not shown), the trade deficit increases sharply until bottoming out at around $30 billion per quarter at the beginning of Year II.

After that, however, the response of the elasticities takes over, with the result that, by the second quarter of Year III, the trade deficit has almost been

| E X H I B I T | 10.4 | *A Hypothetical J Curve*

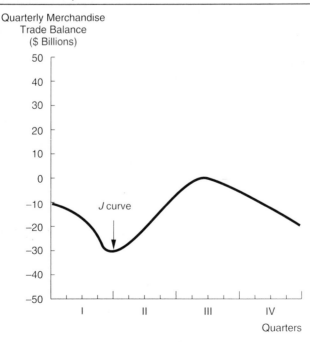

eliminated. The trend toward a negative trade balance then reasserts itself, perhaps because of the influence of U.S. inflation, and the deficit grows larger through the end of Year IV. The improvement in the trade balance thus proves temporary, though it is conceivable in other scenarios that it might be permanent. The *J* curve looks like an elongated, "lazy" *J* that is steeply tilted on its side.

The Problems with the Elasticities Approach

The elasticities approach has long held considerable fascination for economists, no doubt in large part because of its extensive use of the popular methodology of comparative statics, which involves going from one equilibrium position to another on the assumption that the relevant supply and demand functions are unaffected by the adjustment process. This methodology is appropriate in cases of partial equilibrium, but currency devaluation—depreciation is a general equilibrium phenomenon that tends to cause shifts in the functions that partial equilibrium analysis assumes to remain unchanged.

If exports rise and imports fall with devaluation, AD will rise in the devaluing country, causing an increase in the demand for imports and possibly causing a decline in the growth of exports. Devaluation also gives rise to upward pressure on domestic prices from the cost side, for the local currency prices of imports tend to rise, and so do the prices of the resources used to produce both exportables and import substitutes. The combination of higher AD and cost-generated price increases leads to pressure on the government to expand the money supply, which also tends to expand if the trade balance improves. If monetary expansion is allowed to occur (and it usually is in such cases), the entire elasticities apparatus may have to be junked since the demand for foreign exchange will continue to rise and its supply to fall as long as the monetary expansion continues. In short, the devaluing country may arrive at the same basic trade balance problem that it had originally, but with a higher price level and a less valuable currency.

The comparative statics methodology of the elasticities approach assumes stable expectations when an exchange rate changes. Unless this assumption is made, the supply and demand functions that affect the trade balance become subject to revision. The lack of realism in this assumption sharply limits the usefulness of the elasticities approach with respect to trade flows, but this lack is even more serious with respect to capital flows, which are typically disregarded in elasticities analysis. It seems proper to conclude therefore that while the elasticities approach sheds a little light on exchange rate determination, one must look elsewhere for fuller illumination.

The Monetary Theory

In the material that has been examined so far, payments imbalances and exchange rate changes have been treated largely as functions of income changes, the allocation of income and output among consumption and the various leakages and injections, and the elasticities of supply and demand that affect international trade. Money has been allowed a role, but it has been kept largely in the background. By contrast, monetarism thrusts money into the limelight, admitting the other relevant phenomena onto the stage only as necessary to explain the achievement of equilibrium between money supply and money demand. Monetarists believe that this is appropriate since, after all, exchange rates are a monetary phenomenon. Moreover, the monetarists argue, when exchange rate determination is viewed as a monetary phenomenon, it is easy to fit expectations and capital flows into the scene, whereas in alternative approaches, these actors are barely recognized.

Money Supply and Money Demand

The monetary approach seeks to explain macroeconomics in terms of the interplay between money supply (Ms) and money demand (Md). Since both Ms and Md are stocks, this approach can be viewed as a theory of stock adjustment. By contrast, the Keynesian theory and the elasticities approach are concerned with flows. In explaining exchange rate determination, the fact that the monetary theory works with stocks gives it a marked advantage over flow-based theories. This is largely because the monetary theory readily incorporates capital flows into its explanation of how payments equilibrium is achieved, whereas flow-based theories either disregard capital flows or else incorporate them in such a way as to leave doubt about the stability of the equilibrium achieved.

Money demand depends on such factors as the price level, real income, the prices of assets that compete with money as a store of value and the risks of holding such assets, the current interest rate, the expected interest rate, the expected inflation rate, and institutional factors such as credit availability and the frequency with which employees are paid. Money supply depends primarily on central bank policy, although institutional factors, such as the public's preference between holding currency or checking accounts, also have some role.

Money demand is commonly expressed in the form of equation Md = kPY, in which k is the fraction of nominal income (GNP) that the public wants to hold in the form of money, P is the GNP deflator, and Y is real GNP. Note that the money demand equation indicates that Md varies *directly* with k, P, and Y. Historically, monetarists have tended to regard k as stable, but they now generally recognize that this assumption is not realistic, particularly in the short run, because k is affected somewhat by changes in interest rates and expectations. If, for example, the prevailing expectation about nominal interest rates in a country shifts from expecting stability to expecting an increase, k tends to increase because of the expectation that the prices of assets other than money will fall and because of the prospect obtaining higher yields on assets later by waiting to buy them.

In the conduct of monetary policy, it is primarily the money supply that concerns the monetarists. This is because the Ms is something that government can control, at least within narrow limits. By achieving stability in the Ms and its rate of growth, the monetary authorities can contribute to stability in expectations and, therefore, stability in both k and Md. Because the public's preference between holding currency and holding checking accounts is largely beyond the control of monetary authorities, monetarists generally recommend that these authorities concentrate on controlling the monetary base (B), which equals the reserves of banks (deposits with the central bank and vault cash) plus currency in circulation.

Following the tradition of classical economics, monetarists tend to hold that government cannot manipulate the real interest rate through monetary policy except for short periods of time, if then. In the monetarist view, if a government attempts to lower the real interest rate by expanding the money supply, the Fisher effect is likely to come into play and raise the nominal interest rate by enough to prevent the expected real interest rate from declining. Once international financial flows are admitted into the picture, the attempt to manipulate the real interest rate becomes even more futile because of the operation of the IFE. If a central bank should actually succeed in temporarily lowering the real interest rate of its country, capital outflows from that country would tend to move this rate back upward. Note that the belief that real interest rates tend toward equality internationally requires the monetarists to regard foreign assets as perfect substitutes for domestic assets.

Monetary equilibrium requires that Md equal Ms. A change in either Md or Ms from its equilibrium level leads to adjustments that tend to restore this equality. If Ms is held constant during the adjustment process, the burden of adjustment falls entirely on Md. Theoretically, variations in Ms could be used to accelerate the process of adjusting to variations in Md, but monetarists shy away from advocating that central banks use their power to affect Ms in that way. They recognize that economic growth requires some increase in Ms over time in order to avoid the deflationary pressure that economic growth would otherwise produce, but they hold that Ms should be increased at a steady rate. Their advocacy of steady growth in the money supply stems from their belief that rules should be favored over discretion in the conduct of economic policy.

The Official Reserve Transactions Balance and the Money Supply

When the monetary approach is extended to encompass international financial flows, the official reserve transactions (ORT) balance of the BOP takes on special significance because this balance can affect B, the monetary base. In general, a deficit (net debit balance) in the ORT tends to reduce B, while a surplus (net credit balance) tends to increase B. It cannot be said, however, that an ORT deficit or surplus always changes B by an equal magnitude because the effect on B depends on how the deficit or surplus is financed. If, for example, the United States has an ORT deficit that is financed by Federal Reserve purchases of dollars with foreign currencies, B decreases because banks lose reserves from the clearing process when they buy foreign currencies from the Fed. On the other hand, if the deficit is financed by the purchase of dollars by foreign central banks, B does not necessarily change.

The statement that B does not necessarily change when foreign central banks buy dollars requires an explanation. When foreign central banks buy dollars, they normally deposit the dollars with the Fed. This means that the reserves of the banks that sell the dollars are decreased, just as they are when banks sell dollars to the Fed in exchange for foreign currencies. Foreign central banks are not normally content to hold dollars in nonearning form, however, and generally use newly acquired dollar deposits with the Fed to buy earning assets, such as Treasury bills. When that happens, the banks recover the reserves they lost when they sold dollars to the foreign central banks. If, therefore, foreign central banks use all of the dollars they obtain to purchase dollar-denominated earning assets, they cause no net decrease in banks' reserves.

When central bank intervention in the forex market involves the sale of dollars for foreign currencies, the situation is reversed. Any forex purchases by the Fed increase banks' reserves, while any purchases of foreign currencies by foreign central banks normally have little impact on banks' reserves because the purchases are effectively financed, for the most part, by liquidating interest-earning dollar assets rather than by simply drawing down dollar deposit balances with the Fed.

The Fed may choose, and it generally does, to neutralize or sterilize the effects on banks' reserves of its forex transactions with offsetting open market sales or purchases of Treasury securities. Usually, however, the monetary theory is presented with the assumption that no neutralization occurs. If neutralization does not occur, Ms fluctuates, subject to the limitations that have been noted, as fluctuations occur in the ORT balance. In the monetary theory, the fluctuations in Ms accelerate the process of attaining equilibrium in the BOP. If neutralization occurs, however, Ms is not permitted to fluctuate according to the status of the ORT balance, which means that the attainment of BOP equilibrium is slowed. In that case, it is up to Md to provide the adjustments necessary to equalize Md and Ms while simultaneously providing BOP equilibrium.

The Monetary Theory and Exchange Rate Determination

We turn now to the application of the monetary theory to exchange rate determination. The starting point is the observation that the monetary theory integrates exchange rate determination with the process of achieving equilibrium between Md and Ms. This means that exchange rates are greatly influenced by the demand for a nation's currency relative to the supply of it.

In broad outline, the monetarist version of the process of achieving BOP equilibrium is simple. Consider, for example, the case where an increase in real output (Y) leads to an increase in Md that disrupts a previously existing equilibrium between Md and Ms. If the monetary authorities hold Ms constant, the public have to satisfy their demand for larger cash balances by reducing the rate at which they purchase goods and services and by selling noncash assets. Some of the goods they don't buy will be imports, and some of the assets they sell will be denominated in foreign currencies. The demand for foreign exchange on current account will thus decline, while the supply of foreign exchange on capital account will increase. Both of these events tend to increase the exchange value of the country's currency. The monetary theory, like the absorption approach, thus indicates that a rise in real output tends, if everything else stays the same, to increase the exchange value of a nation's currency. Indeed, the monetary theory suggests this relationship even more emphatically because it includes capital flows.

If the central bank of the home country intervenes to slow the appreciation of the national currency, the country will tend to have an ORT surplus that tends to increase B. Since an increase in B leads to an increase in Ms, the achievement of BOP equilibrium will not have to rely entirely on reductions in imports and the country's holdings of foreign assets unless the central bank neutralizes the effect on B of the ORT surplus.

In similar fashion, it can be shown that a decrease in the national money supply also tends to cause a currency to appreciate. Of course, any decrease in Md or increase in Ms will tend to reduce the exchange value of a country's currency.

A Simple Monetary Model of Exchange Rate Determination   Exchange rate determination depends not only on the home country's experience with respect to Md and Ms, but also on what is happening in the rest of the world. For this reason, it is desirable, even in the construction of a simple monetary model, to account for money demand and money supply in at least one other country. In addition, the construction of a simple monetary model requires certain common assumptions: (1) PPP always holds, (2) real output is at its full-employment or "natural" level in both countries, and (3) money demand is not affected by interest rates. All of these assumptions can be challenged, particularly the last one, but let's ignore this complication for the moment.

Monetary equilibrium requires that Md equal Ms. Since Md = kPY, then in equilibrium, Ms = Md = kPY. Now let's assume that Md and Ms are money demand and money supply, respectively, in the United States, and that Md* and Ms* are money demand and money supply in another country, say Germany, which represents the rest of the world. The condition for monetary equilibrium in Germany is Ms* = Md* = k*P* Y*.

Now allow Ms to increase in the United States. Assuming that Y is given and that k is constant (which is plausible if we ignore interest rate changes), P rises in proportion to the increase in Ms. Since PPP holds, the dollar tends to depreciate relative to the mark to offset the increase in P. Since the law of one price is presumed to hold by virtue of the PPP assumption, the exchange rate, e, serves to equate P and P*. In an absolute sense, PPP is expressed as P = eP*; if P rises, e (in dollars per mark) must rise by the same proportion if P* is to remain unchanged.

Since each country's price level depends on its money demand and money supply, changes in e can be related to changes in Md, Ms, Md*, and Ms*.

Thus, Ms* = k*P*Y* and Ms = kPY can be combined so that Ms*/Ms = k*P*Y*/kPY. Substituting the PPP relationship (P = eP*) into this equation then yields:

$$e = \frac{Ms}{Ms^*} \frac{k^* Y^*}{kY} \qquad (10-5)$$

From this it can be seen that if the supply of dollars rises relative to the supply of marks, the mark will appreciate. Similarly, if money demand in either country changes relative to money demand in the other country because of a change in k, k*, Y, or Y*, this change will have exchange rate implications. If, for example, Y increases over time more rapidly than Y*, the mark will tend to depreciate, everything else remaining the same. The country with the faster rate of economic growth thus tends to have an appreciating currency unless there are offsetting changes in the money supplies and the k values.

Expectations and Changes in Interest Rates   From Equation 10–5, it follows that if k and k* are constants, then exchange rate changes can be predicted by incorporating data on expected money supplies and real output. But, of course, k and k* are not real-world constants, especially in the short run. Moreover, short-term exchange rates are more volatile in the real world than can be explained by variations in the actual values of the components of Equation 10–5. If the monetary theory is to be of much use in short-term exchange rate forecasting, therefore, it has to deal with the variability of k and k*, and it has to explain the observed exchange rate variability in a manner that is consistent with Equation 10–5.

Somewhat reluctantly, monetarists have been forced to acknowledge that k is a short-term variable. That done, the key question for them is whether or not k can be shown to vary in a way that is predictably linked to variations in the money supply, for if k is, in fact, linked to Ms in a predictable fashion, monetary policy and exchange rate determination can still be based on changes in money supplies. On the other hand, if k varies independently of money supplies, the usefulness of the monetary theory for both monetary policy and the explanation of exchange rate determination is severely restricted.

In the monetarists' view, variations in k are compatible with the monetary theory because they are caused primarily by changes in actual and expected interest rates which, in turn, are based on changes in actual and expected money supplies. Specifically, k tends to vary inversely with changes in actual interest rates and directly with changes in expected interest rates. Holding everything else the same, as the actual interest rate increases, the cost of holding money increases, with the result that the percentage of nominal income (PY) held in the form of money decreases, i.e., k decreases. If, however, people come to expect that the interest rate level will rise in the near future, it makes sense for them to increase cash holdings temporarily rather than hold assets whose yields are soon likely to rise and whose prices are soon likely to fall because of an increase in interest rates. If interest rates are expected to rise, it is most likely to be because of an expected increase in Ms that leads, via the Fisher effect, to the incorporation of an inflation premium into the interest rate structure.

Monetarists attribute the observed short-term volatility of exchange rates to changes in expectations about the variables in Equation 10–5, and to a large extent, they attribute these changes to uncertainty about governments' economic policies, particularly their monetary policies. This volatility cannot be completely eliminated as long as exchange rates are allowed to fluctuate, but the monetarists believe that it can be greatly reduced if governments follow clear and consistent policies, and above all, if they increase national money supplies at steady, almost constant rates. Exchange rate variations would then diminish both because of greater interest rate certainty and because of greater stability in the other factors that influence money demand, such as changes in expectations regarding inflation and the growth of real output.

Problems with the Monetary Theory   In important respects, the monetary theory offers advantages over the other approaches that have been examined in explaining the determination of exchange rates. In particular, by focusing attention on money supply and money demand, it smoothly integrates capital flows into the exchange rate determination process, and it recognizes that exchange rates are, after all, a monetary phenomenon. Nevertheless, there are problems with the monetary theory, most notably its questionable usefulness in explaining short-term exchange rate behavior.

The monetary theory rests firmly on PPP and the IFE, and, as was pointed out in Chapter 9, questions can be raised about these concepts, particularly about their short-term significance. Exchange rates often vary greatly from those suggested by PPP in the short run, and there are solid reasons for doubting that the IFE assumption of real interest rate equality holds in the short run. Moreover, the short-term variability of k may be partly explainable in terms of other factors than interest rates.

A serious technical problem for the monetary theory is the measurement of money supplies. Because of the ambiguity involved in distinguishing between what money is and what it is not, different measures of the money stock are used, most notably M1, which corresponds closely with the concept of money as a medium of exchange, and M2, which consists of M1 plus some highly liquid earning assets, such as savings deposits, that are not normally used in making payments. The growth rates of M1 and M2 can diverge considerably from each other as wealth holders shift back and forth between interest-earning liquid assets included in M2 and assets that are included only in M1. In addition to the problem of divergent growth rates, there is the problem of making international comparisons of money supplies. This problem results from the fact that nations have differences among them in the assets included in their measures of M1 and M2. An additional measurement problem arises from errors in official estimates of the money stock, particularly when those estimates are preliminary in nature.

Because of the difficulties in measuring and comparing money stocks, some monetary analysts prefer to work with estimates of the monetary base. The problem with this is that the multiplier relationship between B and any measure of the money stock is variable since it depends on such factors as variations in currency in circulation, variations in banks' holdings of excess reserves, and the reserve ratios that banks must maintain with respect to different types of monetary liabilities. For these reasons, it is difficult to predict precisely the effect on any measure of the money stock of a given change in B.

The monetary approach to exchange rate determination has been much acclaimed and is generally viewed as superior to the approaches that were examined earlier. It obviously suffers from major problems, however, and these problems are particularly relevant to the prediction of short-term exchange rate variations. Understandably, therefore, there has been a keen interest in developing more realistic models of exchange rate determination that might have more short-term usefulness than the monetary theory.

The Equilibrium Theory

Either explicitly or implicitly, most exchange rate theories incorporate the idea that exchange rate changes alter nations' international competitiveness. For example, the J curve of the elasticities approach rests on the belief that a depreciation of a nation's currency improves its trade balance after an initial worsening of that balance. In theories that incorporate the belief that PPP tends to hold in the long run, the implication exists that deviations of exchange rates from historical PPP will ultimately be reversed. When exchange rates exhibit such deviations, they are, therefore, regarded as *disequilibrium exchange rates* that cannot be expected to persist unless governments act, as in the gold standard, to force their national economies to adjust to existing exchange rates.

When a currency is regarded as "overvalued" or "undervalued," this implies that its exchange rates with other currencies are in disequilibrium, and if exchange rates are in disequilibrium, governments can readily justify efforts to limit deviations of exchange rates from their presumed equilibrium levels and to nudge exchange rates toward those levels. In a world where currencies are considered to be overvalued or undervalued, therefore, governments virtually have a duty to intervene frequently in the forex market and to conduct monetary policy so as to influence exchange rates. The belief that exchange rates are commonly in disequilibrium thus supports the view that government should play an active role in exchange rate management.

Especially since the 1970s, many prominent economists have attacked the proposition that government should maintain an activist stance in the conduct of macroeconomic policy. The attacks on policy activism were initially spearheaded by monetarists. Increasingly, however, attention has been drawn to attacks on policy activism from economists identified with the *new classical school*, such as Thomas Sargent, Robert Lucas, and Robert Barro. Whereas the monetarists have focused their attacks through the lenses of money supply and money demand, the new classical economists have found the basis for their attacks on policy activism in the real phenomena that underlie monetary aggregates.

In the realm of exchange rate theory, an important development related to the rise of the new classical school has been the emergence of the **equilibrium** theory of exchange rates, whose most effective spokesman has been Alan Stockman.[6] The equilibrium theory fits neatly into a growing body of literature that stresses the efficacy of free markets, and since it has emerged at a time when belief in free markets is in the ascendancy, it is likely that it will exercise considerable influence.

Central Features of the Equilibrium Theory

The equilibrium theory holds that the real exchange rates established among freely traded currencies tend to persist as long as the various supply and demand factors that underlie those rates remain unchanged. This means that even if the real exchange rates that currently exist differ substantially from the real exchange rates of the past, there is no reason to expect the differences to be reversed by the operation of market forces. Historical PPP is thus irrelevant to exchange rate determination since it rests on the assumption that a long-run tendency exists for real exchange rates to be maintained at the levels of an earlier period.

According to the equilibrium theory, nominal or market exchange rates adjust as they must to maintain current real exchange rates at levels that are consistent with the underlying factors that determine them. Real exchange rates are not altered simply by altering nominal exchange rates. This means that attempts by governments to alter real exchange rates through market intervention and the conduct of monetary policy are likely to fail. If, for example, a government raises the nominal exchange value of its national currency by reducing the country's relative inflation rate, it is unlikely that the real exchange value of the currency will also increase.

Much of the body of exchange rate theory rests on the assumption that the nominal or market prices of goods, services, and even assets adjust sluggishly to changes in nominal exchange rates. If this assumption is correct, nominal exchange rate changes are, initially, real exchange rate changes. In the equilibrium theory, however, nominal exchange rates change so as to maintain real exchange rates or reflect changes in real exchange rates, but changes in nominal exchange rates do not cause changes in real exchange rates. There is, therefore, no need for the nominal prices of goods, services, and assets to adjust to changes in nominal exchange rates. Adjustments in nominal exchange rates and the nominal prices of goods, services, and assets occur simultaneously, and one type of adjustment should not be viewed as the cause of the other.

Since the equilibrium theory holds that nominal exchange rates change in response to real exchange rate changes, it follows that if we are to understand nominal exchange rate changes, we must understand real exchange rate changes. In general terms, we can state that real exchange rates depend on underlying supply and demand conditions and the impact of government policies on these conditions. The central challenge for equilibrium theorists is

---

[6]Alan C. Stockman, "The Equilibrium Approach to Exchange Rates," *Economic Review*, Federal Reserve Bank of Richmond, March/April 1987, pp. 12–30.

to show how the specific factors that influence real exchange rates operate. Meeting this challenge is fraught with difficulty. Illustrative of this point is the fact that Stockman indicates that while real exchange rates are influenced by money demand, patterns of money demand differ across countries.[7] He also indicates that the exchange rate effects of variations in trade balances and real output cannot be known without understanding the underlying causes of these variations.[8] There is much that remains to be learned about such matters.

Questions about the Equilibrium Theory

The equilibrium approach to exchange rates shows sufficient promise so that we can anticipate considerable future research to pin down the main causes of real exchange rate variations and determine the magnitude and duration of their influence. There is no denying that a strong correlation often exists between nominal and real exchange rate changes, and the equilibrium approach provides a plausible explanation of this correlation. Questions remain, however, about the approach's validity.

In his 1987 article, Stockman points out one problem by noting that real exchange rate variability has been much greater with floating exchange rates than with pegged exchange rates.[9] This fact suggests to some that nominal exchange rates exercise considerable influence over real exchange rates when exchange rates float and that the equilibrium theory is, therefore, wrong. Stockman concedes that nominal exchange rates may not be totally without influence on real exchange rates, but he also indicates that when governments peg exchange rates, they may use restrictions on international transactions and other measures that have the effect of forcing real exchange rates to conform to pegged nominal exchange rates. If government policies are not identical under pegged and floating exchange rates, one should not expect real exchange rates to be the same irrespective of the exchange rate system chosen.[10]

In a 1988 paper, Stockman suggests that when exchange rates are pegged, variations in governments' reserve holdings influence their policies in ways that tend to stabilize real exchange rates. When governments lose reserves, they tend to resort to restrictions on international trade and capital flows that have the effect of limiting real exchange rate fluctuations. Moreover, the expectation that such restrictions will be employed contributes to real exchange rate stability. This is because the expectation of policy actions that will affect the relevant variables in the future affects those variables currently.[11]

---

[7]*Ibid.*, pp. 19–20.

[8]*Ibid.*, pp. 22–29.

[9]*Ibid.*, p. 29.

[10]*Ibid.*

[11]Alan C. Stockman, "Real Exchange Rate Variability under Pegged and Floating Nominal Exchange Rate Systems: An Equilibrium Theory," in Karl Brunner and Bennett T. McCallum, eds., *Money, Cycles, and Exchange Rates: Essays in Honor of Allan T. Meltzer*, Carnegie-Rochester Conference Series on Public Policy, Vol. 29 (Amsterdam: North Holland, 1988), pp. 259–294.

Alan Shapiro has suggested that a problem with the equilibrium theory is that it disregards the fact that money has value as an asset. If money has such value because of its liquidity and its usefulness as a store of value, and if the asset value of money fluctuates more with floating exchange rates than with fixed exchange rates, that could explain, in part, why real exchange rate fluctuations are greater with floating exchange rates.[12] If, for example, the asset value of dollar balances increases relative to the asset values of other currencies, the demand for dollar balances increases, thereby tending to increase both the real and nominal exchange values of the dollar. Shapiro's point does not necessarily invalidate the equilibrium theory's contention that nominal exchange rates result from rather than cause real exchange rate changes, but it does suggest, in seeming contradiction of the equilibrium theory, that monetary policy exerts an important influence upon real exchange rates

Finally, some economists continue to believe that historical PPP is relevant to the determination of exchange rates among freely traded currencies. For example, Robert Cumby and John Huizinga have found empirical support for the proposition that exchange rates that are overvalued or undervalued in terms of PPP tend to change so as to correct the overvaluation or undervaluation.[13] Whereas Stockman regards real exchange rate changes as tending to be permanent in the sense that their reversal cannot be rationally predicted on the basis of current information, Cumby and Huizinga suggest that there is considerable predictability to real exchange rate changes. It is difficult to see how such diametrically opposed positions can be reconciled.

It is obvious that enormous disagreement exists among leading economists about the determination of exchange rates, and it will be interesting to see what future developments bring. There is hardly an area of economics that is more relevant in terms of real world significance. It is literally true that billions of dollars are riding on the outcome of economists' efforts.

Summary

This chapter has examined some leading theories of exchange rate determination. Some of the ideas presented in it are dated, but all of these theories continue to influence people's beliefs about exchange rates.

The Keynesian theory holds that exchange rates tend to respond to real income changes so that countries with relatively rapid growth in real income tend to experience trade deficits and depreciating currencies. Real interest rate changes contribute to exchange rate equilibrium by bringing about capital flows that offset current account imbalances. The highly restrictive assumptions of the theory and its lack of a long run render its usefulness questionable.

[12]Alan C. Shapiro, *Multinational Financial Management*, 3d ed. (Boston: Allyn and Bacon, 1989), p. 57

[13]Robert E. Cumby and John Huizinga, "The Predictability of Real Exchange Rate Changes in the Short and Long Run," NBER Working Paper No. 3468, 1990.

The absorption approach adds a dynamic dimension to the Keynesian theory. Absorption measures a nation's use of goods and services, including imports. If absorption exceeds output, a trade deficit occurs, with a resulting tendency toward the depreciation of the national currency. If output exceeds absorption, the national currency tends to appreciate. In contradiction to the static version of the Keynesian theory, therefore, the absorption approach allows economic growth to be a cause of currency appreciation. The ability of economic growth to raise a currency's value increases if absorption is restrained through measures that increase saving or reduce budget deficits.

The elasticities approach focuses on the various supply and demand elasticities that influence the demand for and supply of foreign exchange. In general, higher elasticities allow smaller exchange rate changes to achieve BOP equilibrium. The Marshall-Lerner condition suggests that the elasticity of demand for imports and the elasticity of foreign demand for a country's exports need not be very high if a currency depreciation is to reduce a nation's trade deficit. In practice, any improvement in a nation's trade balance achieved by currency depreciation may prove short-lived because of shifts in the relevant supply and demand curves. A serious problem with the elasticities approach is the difficulty of integrating capital flows into it.

The monetary theory smoothly incorporates capital flows into its explanation of payments adjustment and exchange rate determination. A currency tends to appreciate if the demand for it increases relative to its supply and to depreciate if the opposite occurs. Economic growth tends to cause a nation's currency to appreciate because it increases the demand for its currency. The monetary theory rests firmly on relative PPP and the IFE, and this fact raises doubts about its usefulness. The theory has more usefulness in explaining the determination of exchange rates in the long run than in the short run.

The equilibrium theory minimizes the role of money in exchange rate determination and emphasizes the real factors that affect exchange rates. According to this theory, nominal exchange rates adjust in response to changes in real exchange rates and exercise little influence on real exchange rates. Government action that focuses on managing nominal exchange rates rather than real exchange rates is, therefore, misguided. One problem for this theory is that money exercises some influence on real exchange rates because it has value as an asset. Another problem is that some economists insist that historical PPP is relevant to the long-run determination of real exchange rates. If these economists are correct, then real exchange rate changes tend to be temporary rather than the permanent changes favored by the equilibrium theory.

References

Adler, Michael, and Bruce Lehman. "Deviations from Purchasing Power Parity in the Long Run." *Journal of Finance,* December 1983, pp. 1471–1487.

Cumby, Robert E., and John Huizinga. "The Predictability of Real Exchange Rate Changes in the Short and Long Run." NBER Working Paper No. 3468, 1990.

———, and Maurice Obstfeld. "International Interest Rate and Price Level Linkages under Flexible Exchange Rates." In J. F. O. Bilson and R. C. Marston, eds. *Exchange Rate Theory and Practice*. Chicago: University of Chicago Press, 1984, pp. 121–151.

Dernberg, Thomas F. *Global Macroeconomics*. New York: Harper & Row, 1989.

Dornbusch, Rudiger. "Expectations and Exchange Rate Dynamics." *Journal of Political Economy*, December 1976, pp. 1161–1176.

———. *Open Economy Macroeconomics*. New York: Basic Books, 1980.

———. "Equilibrium and Disequilibrium Exchange Rates." *Zeitschrift fur Wirtschafts und Sozialwissenschaften*, no. 6., 1982, pp. 573–599. Reprinted in Donald R. Lessard, ed. *International Financial Management: Theory and Application*, 2d ed. New York: John Wiley & Sons, 1985, pp. 151–172.

Flood, Robert P. "Explanations of Exchange Rate Volatility and Other Empirical Regularities in Some Popular Models of the Foreign Exchange Market." In Karl Brunner and Allan H. Meltzer, eds. *The Costs and Consequences of Inflation*. Carnegie-Rochester Conference Series on Public Policy, Vol. 15. Amsterdam: North-Holland, 1981, pp. 219–249.

Frenkel, Jacob A., T. Gylfason, and J. F. Helliwell. "A Synthesis of Monetary and Keynesian Approaches to Short-Run Balance of Payments Theories." *Economic Journal*, September 1980, pp. 582–592.

Frenkel, Jacob A., and Harry G. Johnson. *The Monetary Approach to the Balance of Payments*. London: Allen & Unwin, 1976.

———, eds. *The Economics of Exchange Rates: Selected Readings*. Reading, Mass.: Addison-Wesley, 1978.

Hafer, R. W. "Does Dollar Depreciation Cause Inflation?" Federal Reserve Bank of St. Louis *Review*, July–August 1989, pp. 16–28.

Huizinga, John. "An Empirical Investigation of the Long-Run Behavior of Real Exchange Rates." In Karl Brunner and Allan H. Meltzer, eds. *Empirical Studies of Velocity, Real Exchange Rates, Unemployment, and Employment*. Carnegie-Rochester Conference Series on Public Policy, Vol. 27, Amsterdam: North-Holland, 1987, pp. 149–214.

Johnson, Harry G. "The Monetary Approach to the Balance of Payments: A Nontechnical Guide." *Journal of International Economics*, August 1977, pp. 251–268.

Meese, Richard, and Kenneth Rogoff. "Was It Real? The Exchange Rate-Interest Differential over the Modern Floating-Rate Period." *Journal of Finance*, September 1988, pp. 933–948.

Mussa, Michael. "Nominal Exchange Rate Regimes and the Behavior of Real Exchange Rates." In Karl Brunner and Allan H. Meltzer, eds. *Real Business Cycles, Real Exchange Rates, and Actual Policies*. Carnegie-Rochester Conference Series on Public Policy, Vol. 25, Amsterdam: North-Holland, 1987, pp. 117–214.

Metzler, Lloyd A. "The Process of International Adjustment under Conditions of Full Employment: A Keynesian View." In Richard E. Caves and Harry G. Johnson, eds. *Readings in International Economics*. Homewood, Ill.: Richard D. Irwin, 1968.

Obstfeld, Maurice, and Alan C. Stockman. "Exchange Rate Dynamics." In Ronald W. Jones and Peter B. Kenen, eds. *Handbook of International Economics*, Vol. II. Amsterdam: North-Holland, 1984, pp. 917–977.

Stockman, Alan C. "The Equilibrium Approach to Exchange Rates." Federal Reserve Bank of Richmond *Economic Review*, March/April 1987, pp. 12–30.

———. "Real Exchange Rate Variability under Pegged and Floating Nominal Exchange Rate Systems: An Equilibrium Theory." In Karl Brunner and Bennett T. McCallum, eds. *Money, Cycles, and Exchange Rates: Essays in Honor of*

Allan T. Meltzer. Carnegie-Rochester Conference Series on Public Policy, Vol. 29. Amsterdam: North-Holland, 1988, pp. 259–294.

Yeager, Leland. *International Monetary Relations: Theory, History, and Policy,* 2d ed. New York: Harper & Row, 1976.

Questions

1. Assume that the U.S. mpc and mpm are, respectively, 60 percent and 12 percent and that Japan's mpc and mpm are, respectively, 50 percent and 16 percent. Now assume that each country has an initial increase in AD of $10 billion due to changes in planned C, I, and/or G. Ignoring foreign repercussions, which country will, according to the Keynesian theory, experience the larger increase in imports?

2. Explain, according to the Keynesian theory, how a country that develops a current account deficit tends to reach an equilibrium in its BOP that stabilizes the exchange value of its currency. What role does price level flexibility play in the adjustment process?

3. Whereas the Keynesian theory indicates that real income growth tends to cause a country to have a current account deficit and a weakening currency, the absorption approach implies that real income growth tends to cause a current account surplus and a strengthening currency. How can this radical difference in the theories be explained?

4. Why is it that an increase in a government's budget deficit tends to cause a current account deficit? Under what circumstances will an increase in a budget deficit tend not to cause a current account deficit?

5. Assume that two countries with current account deficits are lowering the exchange values of their currencies. One, Valhallistan, is a high-income country with an economy oriented toward manufacturing and services. Valhallistan has great flexibility in production. The other country, Bovinaria, is a low-income country whose economy is oriented toward the production of agricultural products and raw materials. Bovinaria's manufacturing industries operate behind a steep protectionist wall and depend heavily on government subsidies to finance needed imports of capital goods. Assuming that the current account deficits of both countries are about the same percentage of their exports, explain why Bovinaria will probably have to have the greater currency depreciation in order to eliminate its current account deficit. Why might a depreciation of Bovinaria's currency fail to improve its current account balance?

6. Explain why it is that even a country like Bovinaria in question 5 can probably reduce its current account deficit by depreciating its currency, provided that it avoids an acceleration in the rate of growth of its money supply.

7. Explain what is the J curve. What are the reasons for doubting that the J curve actually exists when currencies are freely traded, and why is it that the trade balance improvement implied by the J curve may not be very great in practice?

8. According to the monetary theory, how are capital flows involved in the attainment of BOP equilibrium? How does the role of capital flows in the monetary theory differ from their role in the Keynesian theory?

9. According to the monetary theory, how does each of the following tend to affect the exchange value of a nation's currency?

   a. A rise in domestic real income
   b. A rise in the domestic price level
   c. An increase in the nation's expected inflation rate
   d. An increase in the nation's nominal interest rate
   e. An increase in the nation's expected nominal interest rate

10. Assume that the dollar's exchange value is falling and that both foreign central banks and the Fed intervene in the forex market to support the dollar. Assume that both the Fed and the foreign central banks fully neutralize the effects of intervention on domestic money supplies. According to the monetary theory, if the dollar's exchange value is to be stabilized without intervention, what needs to happen, and how might it occur?

11. Explain why it is widely believed that the monetary theory has limited usefulness in explaining short-term exchange rate behavior.

12. What is the basis for the equilibrium theory's criticism of using the terms overvalued and undervalued to refer to the exchange values of freely traded currencies?

13. Why does the fact that real exchange rate variations tend to be greater with floating exchange rates than with pegged exchange rates pose a problem for the equilibrium theory? Does this difference in behavior necessarily mean that we must reject the equilibrium theory's contention that nominal exchange rate changes do not cause real exchange rate changes? Explain.

Portfolio Theory, Speculation, and Exchange Rate Policy

■

The last two chapters have examined the parity relationships that affect exchange rates, the nature of exchange rate forecasting, and some of the leading theories of exchange rate determination. This chapter extends the coverage of exchange rate theory by bringing in the portfolio balance approach and examining the influence on exchange rates of speculation. In addition, it discusses the role of central bank intervention in the forex market and the motivation behind government actions to stabilize exchange rates. The chapter closes with a brief commentary on how the international monetary system may tend to evolve in the near future.

Portfolio Balance

The increasing importance of international transactions in assets has induced economic theorists to give greater attention to the role of such transactions in the determination of exchange rates. Accordingly, elements of financial theory concerned with the management of investment portfolios have been pressed into service to help explain exchange rates. The resulting body of theory, known as the **asset management** or **portfolio balance approach,** resembles the monetary approach because it looks at stocks as well as flows, but it also has important differences from monetarism. Most fundamentally, the portfolio balance approach to exchange rates rejects the notions of perfect international substitutability among interest-bearing assets and the attainment of a uniform real interest rate among nations.

The portfolio balance approach rests on the belief that exchange rates between freely traded currencies are influenced more by capital flows than by trade flows, at least during short time periods. When financial markets are highly integrated internationally, the volume of international capital flows often far exceeds that of international transactions in goods and services. Moreover, as the *J* curve reminds us, it may be that trade flows respond to exchange rate changes only after a considerable lag. By contrast, small changes in such factors as real interest rates, risk perceptions, inflation rates, and taxes often lead quickly to large changes in capital flows. It stands to reason, therefore, that exchange rate changes are frequently dominated by capital flows, particularly in the short run.

The following material on the portfolio balance approach to exchange rates is a highly condensed summary of a complex body of analysis. It makes no attempt to develop a comprehensive portfolio balance model that fully integrates current account flows into the analysis, for to do so would require going beyond the intended scope of this book. Sufficient detail is provided, however, to allow readers to understand the main outlines of this important body of theory and to appreciate why it is highly regarded.

Portfolio Choice and Foreign Assets

In the monetary theory, an increase in the expected real interest rate of Country A above that of Country B tends to generate a flow of capital from B to A until the interest rate differential disappears. In portfolio theory, this event would also tend to trigger a flow of capital from B to A, but because of the imperfect substitutability of assets internationally, real interest rate equalization need not occur. It need not occur because investments differ in their risk characteristics and because investors differ in their willingness to bear risk and manage it.

Generally, capital flows internationally from countries in which it is relatively abundant to countries in which it is relatively scarce. This does not mean, however, that the prevailing pattern of international capital flows is from wealthy countries to poor ones. Low-income countries often lack the requisites for attracting large capital inflows. These requisites might include the availability of complementary resources such as abundant skilled labor and efficient transportation and communication networks, and a comparative absence of impediments to business that unduly raise costs, magnify risks, and limit access to markets. Because the necessary requisites for attracting foreign investment exist more abundantly in wealthy countries than in poor ones, most international flows of capital go to wealthy countries in which capital is relatively scarce compared with other wealthy countries.

In reality, the directional flow of capital is two way. The countries that tend to be net recipients of capital flows, including both wealthy countries and LDCs, also tend to have substantial capital outflows. At times, such countries even become net exporters of capital. It seems to many observers that portfolio theory is the most promising route to follow, which could explain this pattern.

The Risk–Return Tradeoff   In making portfolio choices, investors have to evaluate the tradeoffs between risk and return. At one end of the asset scale is money, which offers little, if any, return and, except for the inflation risk, the maximum degree of safety. At the other end are assets that promise very high rates of return, but these assets are extremely risky.

Most investors are believed to be **risk averse,** i.e., they desire to avoid risk, but will accept it if the expected gain from doing so is large enough to overcome their risk aversion. Risk-averse investors seek to diversify their assets

| E X H I B I T | 11.1 | *The Optimal Investment Portfolio*

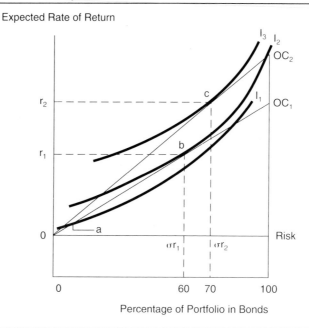

to obtain the optimal combination between risk and return; they avoid putting all of their investment eggs into one basket. An increase in expected rates of return induces them to put more of their portfolios into relatively risky assets, as does a general reduction in risk.

Exhibit 11.1 illustrates the general nature of the risk–return tradeoff for risk-averse investors.[1] It illustrates the case of an investor who can choose among various combinations of a riskless asset (money) that provides no return and interest-earning assets (bonds) that offer positive expected returns that vary directly with risk. The line OC_1 represents the investor's original perception of the tradeoff between risk and return. It is called an **opportunity locus** and it shows the investor's range of choice between money and bonds assuming a constant tradeoff rate exists between risk and return.

The exhibit has two horizontal scales. The upper one measures the risk associated with various investment portfolios and the lower one shows the percentage distribution of investment portfolios between bonds and money. The curves I_1, I_2, and I_3 represent a family of **portfolio indifference curves,** each of which indicates the various combinations of risk and return that provide equal investor utility. Because risk and return are imperfect substitutes, the curves' shapes indicate that it takes progressively larger increases in the expected rate of return to induce the investor to accept equal increments in risk.

---

[1]Exhibit 11.1 is based on an analysis that appears in Thomas F. Dernburg, *Global Macroeconomics* (New York: Harper & Row, 1989), pp. 299–302.

When the applicable opportunity locus is OC_1, the investor could settle for the risk−return combination represented by Point a, which gives both a low expected rate of return and a small amount of risk. This combination is not optimal, however, for it gets the investor only to I_1, whereas by accepting additional risk, he/she can move to Point b, which touches the higher indifference curve I_2. At Point b, the expected rate of return is r_1, and 60 percent of the portfolio is held in bonds.

Now assume that there is a general increase in the expected rate of return on bonds. As a result, the investor's opportunity locus shifts from OC_1 to OC_2, and the investor substitutes bonds for money in his/her portfolio to reach Point c on indifference curve I_3. As a result, the percentage of the total portfolio invested in bonds rises from 60 to 70 percent.

The measure of risk in Exhibit 11.1 is σr, which is the standard deviation of possible gains or losses associated with particular expected rates of return. For example, when the investor is at Point b on I_2, the expected rate of return is r_1, and the standard deviation of that expected rate of return is σr_1. When the investor is at Point c on I_3, the expected rate of return is r_2, and the corresponding standard deviation is σr_2. That σr_2 has a higher value than σr_1 simply reflects the fact that as risk increases, so does its accompanying standard deviation. Note that a reduction in risk tends to shift the opportunity locus upward since it means that a given σr will be associated with a higher expected rate of return.

Variance and Covariance   One of the central principles of portfolio theory is that, within limits, risk can be reduced relative to expected rates of return through portfolio diversification. For example, an investor who is interested in using a given sum of money for the purchase of one or both of two assets which he/she views as being equally risky generally faces less risk in buying some of both assets than in spending all of the money for one or the other. If the expected rates of return from the assets are equal, the reduction in risk obtained through portfolio diversification therefore means that, on a risk-adjusted basis, diversification improves an investor's prospects, i.e., the same expected rate of return with less risk means a higher expected rate of return after deducting a risk premium.

The ability to increase risk-adjusted rates of return through diversification rests on the fact that variations in the yields of different assets are unlikely to be perfectly correlated. The yields on bonds vary considerably over time from the yields on stocks, and within each of these asset categories, particularly for stocks, the yields of individual securities vary significantly. There is a cyclical pattern to the yields of assets, but individual assets differ greatly in the degree to which their yields correspond to the moving average of yields on other assets in their category.

Exhibit 11.2 illustrates how portfolio diversification can reduce risk without giving up return. It also introduces two of the common statistical measures of risk, variance and covariance. **Variance** is defined as the average of squared deviations from the mean and can be expressed mathematically as

$$V = E(R^2) - [E(R)]^2$$

| E X H I B I T | 11.2 | *Variance and Covariance*

Possible Outcomes	Rates of Return (R)			Squared Rates of Return			
	Security X	Security Y	50–50 Port-folio (P)	X	Y	P	$R_x \times R_y$
1	−0.12	0.0	−0.06	0.0144	0.0000	0.0036	0.0000
2	0.0	−0.12	−0.06	0.0000	0.0144	0.0036	0.0000
3	0.12	0.36	0.24	0.0144	0.1296	0.0576	0.0432
4	0.36	0.12	0.24	0.1296	0.0144	0.0576	0.0432
Sum	0.36	0.36	0.36	0.1584	0.1584	0.1224	0.0864
Expected value (E)	0.09	0.09	0.09	0.0396	0.0396	0.0306	0.0216

Variance and Covariance

$V = E(R^2) - [E(R)]^2$

V of X $= 0.0396 - 0.09^2 = 0.0315$
V of Y $= 0.0396 - 0.09^2 = 0.0315$
V of P $= 0.0306 - 0.09^2 = 0.0225$

$Cov(R_1, R_2) = E(R_1)(R_2) - E(R_1)E(R_2)$

$Cov(R_x, R_y) = 0.0216 - (0.09)(0.09)$
$= 0.0135$

where V is variance, $E(R^2)$ is the expected value (the average) of the squared deviations from a base value, and $[E(R)]^2$ is the square of the average expected deviation from the base value.

Covariance is a measure of the correlation between two variables. Applied to securities, it can be written as:

$$Cov(R_1, R_2) = E(R_1)(R_2) - E(R_1)E(R_2)$$

where $Cov(R_1, R_2)$ is the covariance between two securities, $E(R_1)(R_2)$ is the expected value of the possible returns on Security R_1 times the possible returns on Security R_2, and $E(R_1)E(R_2)$ is the value of the expected return on Security R_1 times the expected return on Security R_2.

Exhibit 11.2 identifies four possible outcomes in terms of rates of return for each of two securities, X and Y. Each outcome is considered equally probable. For each security, the outcomes range from a negative 12 percent to a positive 36 percent, and the average or expected rate of return for each security is 9 percent. The two securities also have the same variance, 0.0315.

Although X and Y have identical expected rates of return and variances, the correlation between their rates of return is not perfect. With Outcome 1, for example, X yields a negative 12 percent, while Y yields 0 percent. Consequently, an investor who chooses some of X and some of Y can reduce the variance of his/her investment by comparison with the alternative of choosing only one of them. By investing equally in the two securities to obtain Portfolio P, the variance can be reduced to 0.0225, a reduction of 28.6 percent relative to the variance of either X or Y. Even though P gives a substantial reduction in variance, it does not reduce the expected rate of return, which remains 9 percent. Clearly, therefore, the selection of P is superior to buying only X or Y for the risk-averse investor.

The calculation of the covariance between X and Y results in a positive value of 0.0135. The fact that the covariance between X and Y is positive indicates that some of their variance is joint, i.e., that their rates of return tend to vary in the same direction. On the other hand, since the value of the covariance is much less than that of the variance of either X or Y (0.0315), it is evident that their rates of return vary somewhat independently. If the value of the covariance were zero, this would mean that X and Y would have statistically independent expected rates of return; if the covariance were negative, this would indicate a negative correlation between their expected rates of return. From this follows the conclusion that a smaller covariance gives a larger reduction in variance by portfolio diversification. Thus, if the returns of securities X and Y in Exhibit 11.2 were so correlated that the outcomes for X of −0.12, 0, 0.12, and 0.36 coincided, respectively, with the Y outcomes of 0.36, 0.12, 0, and −0.12, it can be determined that the covariance between X and Y would become −0.0297, while the variance of P would decline to 0.0009, i.e., portfolio variance would almost be eliminated.

Systematic and Unsystematic Risk   If the risk-adjusted rate of return can be increased by buying two securities instead of one, this suggests that further improvements can be obtained by buying three securities instead of two, four instead of three, etc. Rather quickly, however, portfolio diversification tends to exhaust the possibilities for further gains, particularly, of course, if the assets added to the portfolio are chosen on the basis of low covariances relative to the rest of the portfolio. Eventually, therefore, the investor comes to the point where portfolio risk can no longer be reduced through diversification. In such a case, the remaining risk is said to be **systematic risk** because it is common to all assets. The risk that can be eliminated through portfolio diversification is said to be **unsystematic risk,** i.e., it is the risk that is not common to all assets.

Systematic risk is explained in large part by general economic fluctuations (business cycles), which tend to affect the yields of all assets, even those with countercyclical yield patterns. While it is true that assets with countercyclical yield patterns tend to have negative covariances when paired with "normal" assets, this feature tends to cause their prices to be bid up during downward fluctuations in the economy, bringing their risk-adjusted yields into line with those of other assets. Suppose, for example, that Workwell Company specializes in finding employment for business executives and highly skilled workers, and that Workwell's profits are negatively correlated with the business cycle, i.e., it earns its largest profits when the economy is in a recession. Up to a point, it might be true that portfolio gains could be made by buying Workwell stock. Ultimately, however, portfolio diversifiers would tend to push up the price of the stock until any diversification gains would be negated by the stock's low yield in terms of dividends and capital gains.

Diversification through Foreign Investment   Historically, the segmentation of financial markets on the basis of national boundaries and the bias of domestic residents against foreign investments have contributed to the development of opportunities for portfolio gains through the acquisition of foreign assets. While there have been instances of spectacular failure in foreign investments, ranging from the Mississippi Bubble of the early 1700s to the foreign debt crisis of the 1980s, there can be little doubt that, on the whole, investment opportunities abroad have been underexploited by comparison with domestic opportunities. In the past three decades, foreign investment has grown rapidly, and the long-standing debate over its merits has been resolved largely in its favor. Correspondingly, governments have made progress in reducing the barriers imposed on foreign investment by law, administrative practice, language, and custom. The result has been a dynamic situation in which existing foreign investment opportunities are rapidly exploited and new ones are constantly arising.

The rapid growth in foreign investment that has been occurring recently reflects relatively high expected rates of return and the diversification gains that such investment makes possible. The diversification gains arise from imperfect correlations between the systematic risks of different countries. Thus, when one country has a recession, other countries may experience recessions of greater or lesser severity or even avoid serious economic downturns. In effect, there is a *world* systematic risk that is less than the systematic risk of any single nation.

As Donald Lessard has shown, systematic risk tends to be lower in the United States than in other countries.[2] The most plausible explanation for this is the large size and industrial diversity of the U.S. economy, but it is also true that the United States has a more stable political environment than most other countries. Because systematic risk is lower in the United States than elsewhere, the diversification motive provides a very potent attraction for foreign investment in the United States. Still, U.S. investors can reduce risk by investing in foreign assets, as well. Illustrating this point, Lessard has claimed that U.S. investors in stocks could reduce their portfolio risk by about one-third through international diversification of their stock holdings.

Complicating the matter of achieving diversification gains through foreign investment is the fact that many of the world's prominent corporations are multinational firms that derive major shares of their income from international operations. This raises the possibility of achieving diversification gains by investing in the securities of such firms. Conceivably, by correctly selecting the securities of multinational firms, an investor might achieve substantial diversification gains without owning foreign assets.

There is general agreement among those who are knowledgeable about foreign investment, however, that at least for U.S. investors, the securities of domestically based multinationals are very imperfect substitutes for the securities of foreign firms. This is because the operations of U.S. multinationals are heavily oriented toward the United States and also because the results of

---

[2]Donald R. Lessard, "Principles of International Portfolio Selection," in Abraham George and Ian H. Giddy, eds., *International Finance Handbook* (New York: John Wiley & Sons, 1983). Reprinted in Donald R. Lessard, ed., *International Financial Management: Theory and Application,* 2d ed. (New York: John Wiley & Sons, 1985), pp. 16–30.

their foreign operations are not necessarily closely correlated with the economic performance of the countries in which those operations occur. If, for example, a U.S. firm has a manufacturing operation in Brazil that produces primarily for export from Brazil, there is no reason to believe that the profitability of that operation will mirror the performance of the Brazilian economy.

It should be remembered that much foreign investment occurs simply because of higher expected rates of return, not because of the reduction in risk obtained through diversification. The diversification motive is important, however, and its relative importance has undoubtedly increased. This motive has obviously played a prominent role in bringing about the increased internationalization of stock markets that has occurred in the past few years. Also, there can be little doubt that this process of internationalizing stock ownership will continue.

It is sometimes assumed that the exchange risk casts doubt on the argument that risk-adjusted diversification gains can be attained through foreign investment. Certainly, this risk deters foreign investment, but it is easy to overrate its impact. As far as equity investment is concerned, PPP reminds us that changes in domestic price levels tend to at least partly offset exchange rate variations in the long run. This means that when a currency depreciates, there has been, on average, a corresponding increase in the prices of assets denominated in that currency. In other words, what foreign investors lose from exchange rate changes tends to be offset by changes in asset values. An increase in asset value may not fully compensate foreign investors for the exchange rate loss, but on the other hand, it may exceed that loss. In any event, it is simply wrong to assume that a currency depreciation signals a proportionate loss for foreign investors holding equity investments denominated in the depreciated currency.

As far as foreign investment in interest-yielding assets is concerned, the IFE reminds us that nominal interest rate differentials tend to compensate for exchange rate changes in the long run. The correlation between nominal interest rates and exchange rates is far from perfect, but it is sufficiently strong to eliminate much of the exchange risk. Moreover, hedging operations can be carried out when the exchange risk seems particularly threatening, and this can protect investments in both interest-yielding assets and equities. Finally, some protection against the exchange risk can be attained by diversifying the currency composition of foreign investments in both equities and interest-yielding assets.

Summing up, portfolio diversification provides a powerful motive for foreign investment, one that gives the residents of any country ample reason to consider such investment. Because systematic risk in the United States is relatively low, the diversification motive provides foreigners with a powerful incentive to acquire U.S. assets, yet it also provides U.S. investors with ample reason to acquire foreign assets. For both U.S. and foreign investors, the diversification motive provides a reason to hold assets denominated in a variety of currencies. Other factors besides diversification influence capital flows of course, including expected rates of return, the amounts of wealth at investors' disposal, and exchange rate expectations, but there can be little doubt that diversification belongs high on any list of the factors that determine these capital flows.

The Role of Wealth   Wealth plays a central role in portfolio theory because portfolio investment presupposes the existence of wealth. It increases with saving and capital gains, and it decreases with dissaving and capital losses. As an economy grows, wealth accumulates and investors tend to increase their holdings of all financial assets, including money and claims on foreigners. Generally, wealthier investors are more willing to accept risk than are less wealthy investors because they are better able to absorb losses. Accordingly, as per capita wealth increases, the proportion of wealth held in relatively risky assets tends to increase. Even in wealthy countries, however, a general increase in risk induces investors to shift their portfolios toward money and other low-risk, but relatively safe, assets. If an increase in risk coincides with a reduction in expected rates of return, as can happen in a recession, the shift in asset holdings to money and other relatively safe assets may become dramatic. The relative impact of a recession on holdings of foreign assets depends on how the risks and returns for those assets correlate with the risks and returns for domestic assets.

Historically, a country's accumulation of wealth has led to an increase in the proportion of wealth held in foreign assets. The trend toward internationalizing portfolios has gained momentum in recent years and can be expected to continue. This trend is being accompanied, however, by sharp fluctuations in the volume and geographical distribution of international capital flows that reflect the volatility of their determinants.

While increases in wealth generally tend to increase foreign asset holdings, much depends on how the increases in wealth occur. For example, a stock market boom in the United States simultaneously increases domestic wealth and induces U.S. investors to expand their holdings of domestic stocks. In itself, the increase in wealth tends to induce U.S. investors to acquire more foreign assets, but this wealth effect may be swamped by the substitution of U.S. assets for foreign assets as the boom proceeds. Thus, there is no a priori guarantee that an increase in wealth will always lead to a net increase in holdings of foreign assets.

Exchange Rate Implications of Portfolio Theory

Portfolio models of exchange rate determination portray exchange rates as being determined by the interaction of real income, interest rates, risk, price levels, and wealth. Realized and expected changes in these variables lead to portfolio adjustments as investors seek to reestablish the desired balance in their portfolios. To the extent that portfolio adjustments affect the demand for foreign assets, exchange rate changes tend to occur. Exchange rate changes, in turn, affect wealth and other variables that influence portfolio choices. For example, when portfolio adjustments lead foreigners to purchase U.S. assets, the dollar tends to appreciate. U.S. investors then experience capital losses on their foreign asset holdings, and foreigners experience capital gains on their holdings of U.S. assets. These capital gains and losses tend to lead to additional portfolio and exchange rate adjustments until equilibrium is reached.

The equilibrium that tends to be reached between portfolio holdings and exchange rates is, however, temporary. To the extent that real exchange rates change because of portfolio adjustments, real trade flows are affected with additional exchange rate effects. Moreover, because the acquisition of foreign assets sets up a return flow of income, exchange rates are affected as this flow occurs. Thus, if capital inflows into the United States can cause the dollar to appreciate, the subsequent return flow of income can cause it to depreciate. Meanwhile, portfolio adjustments are constantly occurring in response to changes in wealth and other factors that decide the allocation of asset holdings among nations. The incorporation of portfolio theory into the theory of exchange rate determination suggests, therefore, that exchange rates tend to be unstable if governments allow them to fluctuate.

The Exchange Rate Effects of Changes in Wealth While the portfolio approach recognizes that real income, interest rates, risk, and price levels play important roles in exchange rate determination, its emphasis on the role of changes in wealth gives it the greatest claim to uniqueness. Accordingly, much of the remaining material on the portfolio approach deals with the ways changes in wealth may influence exchange rates.

When an increase in a country's wealth leads to greater holdings of foreign assets, a depreciation of the national currency tends to occur. As has been noted, however, a substitution effect may be associated with an increase in wealth that outweighs the impact of the wealth effect on holdings of foreign assets. Moreover, while an increase in wealth tends to increase portfolio holdings of foreign assets, it also tends to increase portfolio holdings of money. In other words, an increase in wealth increases Md. Since the monetary approach indicates that an increase in Md tends to increase the exchange value of a nation's currency, how investors choose to allocate their portfolios among foreign assets and money has an important bearing on how changes in wealth affect exchange rates.

As wealth accumulates from saving, some of it is normally used to purchase foreign assets. This suggests that saving may tend to cause a nation's currency to depreciate, at least initially. Recall, however, that the absorption approach indicates that saving can have a positive effect on the current account balance of a nation's BOP and, thus, tends to strengthen its currency. Assuming that each additional amount of saving reduces absorption relative to output by an equal amount, the current account impact of saving should dominate the capital account impact as far as exchange rates are concerned. It is always possible, however, that a shift of the risk−return tradeoff in favor of foreign assets could lead to a surge of capital outflows financed out of past savings, and this could swamp the effect of current saving on the current account. The greater the accumulation of savings, the greater is the possibility that this will occur.

When wealth changes because of capital gains or losses resulting from interest rate changes, the exchange rate effects are even more difficult to sort out. When market interest rates decline in a country, there are corresponding capital gains on domestic assets that pay fixed amounts of interest. The increase in wealth tends to lead to purchases of foreign assets and larger holdings of domestic currency. Because reductions in market interest rates tend to lead to higher prices for domestic stocks, wealth may be shifted from foreign assets into domestic stocks in anticipation of capital gains. Moreover, if a decline in market interest rates leads to the expectation of lower real interest rates, real investment may increase, thereby stimulating economic growth and attracting capital from abroad. On one hand, it is conceivable that a reduction in market interest rates could affect capital flows to cause a nation's currency to appreciate. On the other hand, if a decline in interest rates coincides with a worsening of a country's economic outlook, the net shift in capital flows may be outward.

Another complication in the relationship between exchange rates and changes in wealth is that consumption spending and, therefore, personal saving, are affected by changes in wealth. A general rise in the prices of stocks and real estate increases households' ability to finance consumption expenditure. The more permanent an increase in wealth is perceived to be, the more likely it is that consumption will increase, and an increase in consumption tends to increase imports. Thus, the sharp decline in the dollar from March 1985 through the end of 1987 may have been due, in part, to the negative influence exerted on the personal saving rate by large increases in wealth that occurred before and during this period because of rising stock and real estate values. Recall that the United States' merchandise trade deficit soared to record levels during these years.

Finally, the exchange rate impact of changes in wealth is influenced by the extent to which changes in wealth are positively correlated among countries. If wealth rises or falls in different countries by approximately the same percentage, the exchange rate effects caused by portfolio adjustments will differ from those that result when levels of wealth vary independently.

Because cyclical fluctuations in economic activity tend to be positively correlated among countries to the extent that their economies are internationally integrated, there is also a pronounced tendency for fluctuations in wealth to be positively correlated internationally. For example, when the U.S. stock market is booming, it is generally the case that stock prices in other countries are also rising, although not necessarily to the same extent. On the other hand, there are times when stock price fluctuations are not closely correlated internationally. In 1990, for instance, the prices of Japanese stocks declined much more (about 40 percent) than stock prices in other leading countries. As a result, the yen was weaker in 1990 than it would have been had stock markets in other countries been equally weak.

Longer-Term Implications of Portfolio Balance The value of the portfolio balance approach to exchange rate determination lies largely in its ability to explain how one-time portfolio adjustments can exercise a short-term impact on exchange rates. As was noted earlier, however, portfolio adjustments that result in larger holdings of foreign assets produce income flows that tend to have longer-term exchange rate effects in the opposite direction. Moreover, if the increase in holdings of foreign assets should fail to be permanent, the exchange rate effects of the income flows will be reinforced by those resulting from the repatriation of capital.

The portfolio balance approach implies that if financial wealth does not grow over time in the rest of the world, it will be difficult for a country (such as the United States) to finance large and persistent current account deficits with capital inflows. By raising its real interest rate above real interest rates in other countries, a country could induce a one-time capital inflow that would soon generate a return flow of income to the investing countries. If financial wealth in other countries were to remain static, financing persistent current account deficits with capital inflows would require an ever-widening real interest rate gap between the deficit country and the rest of the world. Inevitably, such a course would prove excessively costly and provoke actions designed to reduce or eliminate the deficits. If, however, financial wealth grows sufficiently rapidly in the rest of the world, it is conceivable that by maintaining an approximately fixed real interest rate premium over other countries, a country could finance its current account deficits for a long time without having to take corrective action. The task of financing the deficits in this manner would be eased to the extent that the capital importing country could lower its level of systematic risk.

Incorporating the Unexpected   Underlying international financial flows are real economic phenomena of nations' rates of economic growth, expected real interest rates, and current account deficits and surpluses. This being the case, the portfolio approach's focus on financial flows does not eliminate the need to take real factors into account. What distinguishes the portfolio balance approach from other exchange rate theories in this respect is the great emphasis that the portfolio balance approach places on *unanticipated* developments. Prior to the arrival of such *news,* i.e., unanticipated events that alter expectations, investors will have arranged their portfolios to reflect previous information. When news arrives, investors immediately adjust their portfolios to reflect their revised expectations.

Suppose, for example, that investors are awaiting the release of data on the U.S. trade balance and inflation rate, and that the consensus among them is that the quarterly merchandise trade deficit will be $6.8 billion, while the quarterly GNP deflator is expected to indicate an annual inflation rate of 4.4 percent. Investment portfolios will have been adjusted on the basis of these estimates. Now assume that when the data arrive, they show a trade deficit of $5.4 billion and an annual inflation rate of 3.6 percent. The resulting portfolio adjustments will tend to strengthen the dollar. Similarly, assume that investors anticipate that the Bundesbank will not act to raise German interest rates in order to restrain inflation, but that the Bundesbank pulls a surprise by actually reducing the growth of the money supply. Portfolio adjustments will then occur that will tend to weaken the dollar against the deutschemark and other European currencies.

Conclusions on Portfolio Balance By now, it should be clear why the portfolio balance approach has had a profound impact on the thinking of exchange rate theorists. During short time periods and when the currencies involved are those of high-income countries, exchange rate movements are generally dominated by asset flows. The portfolio balance approach surpasses other theories in explaining why such flows occur and what their exchange rate effects are likely to be. As the time period lengthens, however, the exchange rate baton passes from asset markets to goods markets, and the economic fundamentals governing flows of goods and services attain greater exchange rate significance.

To better understand the implications of the portfolio balance approach for exchange rate determination, consider the following case, in which that approach is contrasted to the monetary approach, its chief rival in terms of comprehensiveness. Assume that a country's government adopts a more expansionary monetary policy than it had been following, with the result that its money supply expands relative to the money supplies of other countries. In the monetary approach, since Ms would now presumably exceed Md, the country's residents would attempt to rid themselves of the excess money by, among other things, importing more goods and buying more foreign assets. Fairly quickly, the adjustment process, reflecting the operation of the IFE, would boost the country's nominal interest rate level to tend to maintain real interest uniformity internationally. The interest rate adjustment would slow the capital outflow, but that outflow would continue as long as Ms continued to exceed Md. Perhaps with a lag after the increase in Ms, but perhaps almost immediately if the inflationary consequences of monetary expansion were fully anticipated, the country's price level would rise, causing a further decline in the exchange value of its currency in accordance with PPP. The expectation of persistent currency depreciation would influence speculation so that it would tend to smooth the process of adjusting from one exchange rate level to another.

In the portfolio balance approach, the expansionary monetary policy is also likely to cause a depreciation of the country's currency, but the depreciation process is likely to follow a convoluted path. The increase in Ms would probably tend to lower the country's real interest rate relative to the rest of the world, and this would stimulate portfolio adjustments involving the purchase of foreign assets. Moreover, since the expansion of the money supply would probably involve central bank purchases of government securities in the open market, there would be a reduction in the stock of domestic securities available to investors, which would augment the capital outflow caused by real interest rate changes. The capital outflow, which would probably be sudden, would tend to cause a rapid depreciation of the country's currency. Since adjustments in goods markets are viewed in portfolio balance theory as lagging behind adjustments in asset markets, the depreciation would tend to stimulate exports and discourage imports. The expansion of exports relative to imports would continue after the portfolio adjustments had occurred and would tend to cause an *appreciation* of the country's currency following the initial depreciation. The tendency toward appreciation might well be reinforced by an inflow of investment income in response to the portfolio adjustments. Eventually, however, the rise in the country's price level would assert itself and work through PPP to reverse the currency appreciation so as to send the currency once more on a downward path.

From this analysis it can be seen that the portfolio balance approach is consistent with the observed reality that exchange rates tend to fluctuate in convoluted fashion around their long-term trend lines. This does not mean, however, that a high degree of confidence can be placed in the ability of the portfolio balance approach to predict exchange rates. Some portfolio balance models may well have proved better than the toss of a coin, but exchange rates often change in ways that baffle portfolio theorists.

The Limitations of Exchange Rate Theories

When evaluating exchange rate theories, one should keep in mind that all of them have serious limitations that are, to some extent, inherent. Even if a particular theory correctly identifies the key factors that determine an exchange rate, a prediction based on it may turn out to be wrong because of the intrusion of unforeseeable events. It is desirable, however, to move beyond the generalization that the predictive capabilities of theories are impaired by unforeseeable events and to specify in greater depth the nature of the limitations to which they are subject.

A particularly careful analysis of the limitations of exchange rate theories has been provided by Rudiger Dornbusch of MIT.[3] According to Dornbusch, "*simple* structural models of exchange rate determination all fail to account for actual exchange rate behavior."[4] This implies that more complex models might yield more satisfactory results, but Dornbusch warns that formidable barriers impede the construction of such models. To start with, it is often difficult to know if the empirical failures of models are caused more by news than by the exclusion of factors that could have been anticipated.

Beyond that, Dornbusch discerns four major problems confronting those who would improve upon existing models. First, speculative "bubbles" occur in which exchange rates depart temporarily from their supposed fundamental levels. Second, current exchange rates are affected by expectations about influences on future exchange rates, most notably government policy. The problem of taking such expectations into account is compounded by the fact that government policy is influenced by the public's expectations about it. Third, "extraneous beliefs" about how exchange rates are determined that

---

[3]Rudiger Dornbusch, "Equilibrium and Disequilibrium Exchange Rates," in Donald R. Lessard, ed., *International Financial Management: Theory and Application*, 2d ed. (New York: John Wiley & Sons, 1985), pp. 151–172. Reprinted from *Zeitschrift fur Wirtschafts und Sozialwissenschaften*, no. 6, 1982, pp. 573–579.

[4]Ibid., p. 157.

arise from "fads, fashions, or misperceptions" may cause exchange rates to vary substantially from what they would be with a correct assessment of economic fundamentals. Fourth, U.S. macroeconomic policy and its resulting exchange rate impact have "spillover effects" on other countries that may affect their macroeconomic policies in ways that are difficult to foresee.

Dornbusch's analysis provides strong support for the position that exchange rates tend to be highly unstable and unpredictable. Under these circumstances, and given that exchange rate variations exert great influence over production and the international division of labor, a strong case exists for government action to reduce exchange rate instability. Before considering government's role in exchange rate policy, however, we shall explore the possibility that speculative bubbles are commonplace in the forex market.

Speculation and Foreign Exchange Rates

The belief has long existed that, in the absence of government intervention in the forex market, exchange rate fluctuations may be accentuated by **destabilizing speculation,** i.e., speculation that drives exchange rates farther from their underlying equilibrium positions than they would otherwise go. Behind the destabilizing speculation hypothesis lies the belief that a deviation of an exchange rate from its underlying value may give rise to the expectation of further changes in the same direction.

Exhibit 11.3 illustrates in simple fashion how an exchange rate might behave, depending on the nature of speculation. It assumes that the dollar/pound sterling exchange rate tends to decline over time as shown by the trend line. In the absence of speculation, or if speculation is neutral, the actual market path of the exchange rate will be the solid line labeled "Neutral Speculation," in which case the exchange rate oscillates around the trend line. If speculation is stabilizing, the fluctuations indicated by the solid line will be reduced, resulting in the exchange rate taking the path indicated by the dashed line labeled "Stabilizing Speculation." Finally, if speculation is destabilizing, the exchange rate path will be that indicated by the dotted line labeled "Destabilizing Speculation."

The Case for Stabilizing Speculation

Economists who believe strongly in the efficiency of free markets have difficulty accepting the idea that destabilizing exchange rate speculation may be common. They have argued that the existence of prolonged or frequent destabilizing speculation is implausible since it implies the continual misjudgment of market conditions and the persistence of error in the face of failure.

Even the skeptics about the possibility of persistent destabilizing speculation have recognized that the majority of market participants may misjudge an exchange rate trend, but they argue that destabilizing speculation is unlikely to persist since it is unprofitable for the mass of speculators. To make it profitable, it is argued, they must somehow be able to gain by buying a currency when its price is high and selling it when its price is low! Conceivably,

| E X H I B I T | 11.3 | *Stabilizing and Destabilizing Exchange Rate Speculation*

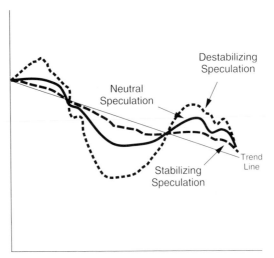

Exchange Rate ($/£)

Destabilizing Speculation

Neutral Speculation

Stabilizing Speculation

Trend Line

Time

the mass of speculators could profit from destabilizing speculation if nonspeculators were to mistake the current path of an exchange rate for its trend line. For example, if the price of the pound were to rise above the value indicated by its trend line and nonspeculators assumed that it would continue to rise, speculators might gain by buying it at a high price and selling it later to nonspeculators at an even higher price. It seems implausible, however, that the nonspeculators would be so much less knowledgeable than the speculators that they would persistently supply the latter with a means of livelihood, especially since many nonspeculators are multinational companies with high levels of forex market expertise.

It is arguable that, even if destabilizing speculation results in net losses for the mass of speculators, this does not rule out the possibility that it may occur frequently. Just as compulsive gamblers persist in losing money in casinos and on lottery tickets, so also there may be forex speculators who are similarly "hooked." Furthermore, just as the ranks of fallen gamblers are replenished by fresh recruits, it is also conceivable that the places of decapitalized forex speculators may be taken by other speculators who want to try their hand at a challenging game. There is, however, at least one vital difference between forex speculators and gamblers: gamblers generally act on their own account while most forex speculators must report their results to their superiors.

Another argument against the possibility of destabilizing speculation is that it is subject to increasing cost. Suppose, for example, that speculators drive the pound well above where it would otherwise be. To continue driving the pound up, they must commit more resources to the venture, but as the proportion of their assets committed to speculation rises, they will probably have to pay higher interest rates on borrowings and the opportunity cost of speculating with their own funds will probably increase. Moreover, the interest cost of speculation may increase further if the U.S. monetary authorities should tighten credit in order to prevent the dollar from declining further.[5]

If speculation is not generally destabilizing, then it must be either neutral or stabilizing. On logical grounds, it is plausible that it should be stabilizing since stabilizing speculation tends to be profitable for the mass of speculators. If, for example, the pound rises above its trend line and speculators react by selling pounds, their action has the effect of driving the pound downward, i.e., making it more stable. If the pound does indeed fall, the mass of speculators will profit.

Rational Speculative Bubbles

While the arguments against the likelihood of persistent destabilizing speculation are certainly plausible, their weight is diminished by the abundance of evidence that exchange rates often deviate substantially from their underlying or fundamental values. Do such deviations occur despite unfavorable odds or do they reflect a correct judgment by speculators that the odds favor the deviations? Increasingly, exchange rate theorists have endorsed the latter interpretation, with many now arguing that the forex market produces **rational bubbles** in which short-term (or even long-term) variations occur in exchange rates that cause **overshooting,** i.e., exchange rate movements away from expected long-term values.

The various overshooting models tend to have a common theme—that overshooting is related to the fact that exchange rates are influenced by both asset and goods markets. As the portfolio balance approach has emphasized, asset markets adjust more rapidly to changes in economic fundamentals than goods markets. When, for example, the United States simultaneously experiences changes in its real interest rate, its real GNP growth rate, and its inflation rate, capital flows respond more quickly to these events than flows of goods and services. Over relatively short time periods, the exchange rates that tend to result from capital flows may be quite different from those that will tend to prevail over longer time periods after current account flows have fully adapted to changes in the fundamentals, including exchange rates themselves. Under these circumstances, it could conceivably be rational to speculate on a short-term movement away from an exchange rate that is perceived to coincide with the long-term trend line, especially if speculators have a good idea as to approximately when a corrective adjustment is likely to occur. It may thus be a mistake to label the dotted line in Exhibit 11.3 "Destabilizing Speculation" since, in a world with great capital mobility, there is no reason to believe that market-determined exchange rates tend to adhere closely to their long-term

[5]A good formal elaboration of most of these points is found in Robert M. Stern, *The Balance of Payments* (Chicago: Aldine, 1973), Chapter 3.

trend lines in the absence of speculation. Indeed, it is conceivable that speculation is generally stabilizing around *short-term* trend lines and that the dotted line of Exhibit 11.3 would be even more erratic if this were not the case.

Whatever the verdict on forex speculation, the fact that market-determined exchange rates often exhibit instability raises the question of whether or not governments can improve matters by attempting to reduce that instability. Accordingly, we turn now to the consideration of this question.

Limiting Exchange Rate Flexibility

Prior to the advent of generalized floating in 1973, many economists championed the idea of highly flexible exchange rates. Among the arguments they advanced, the most powerful one was that flexible exchange rates would allow governments to exercise monetary autonomy with less damage to their nations' economies and those of other nations than if exchange rates were predominantly fixed. It was argued, for example, that if the United States needed monetary expansion to prevent a recession, exchange rate flexibility would permit it to expand its money supply without transmitting inflation to other countries. A relatively high U.S. inflation rate would tend to cause the dollar to depreciate to maintain the law of one price for goods and the existing pattern of real rates of return on assets. Some conceded that eliminating the **disciplinary effect** on monetary policy that results from having to eliminate BOP deficits when exchange rates are fixed might leave the door wide open for inflation in some countries. By and large, however, the advocates of flexible exchange rates believed that the inflation virus would be contained for the world as a whole.

Subsequent experience with flexible exchange rates lends support for the pendulum theory of history, in which wide swings in one direction are believed to be followed by wide swings in the opposite direction. Flexible exchange rates have proved far more volatile than their early proponents had predicted, and this has led to a renewed emphasis on the advantages of exchange rate stability. The pendulum is thus swinging once more toward fixed exchange rates, but it may be that it will be brought to a halt somewhere between the extremes of highly flexible and rigidly fixed exchange rates.

Among the arguments for a high degree of exchange rate stability, three will be briefly considered here. These are the optimum currency area case, the dependent economy case, and the proposition that governments should promote real exchange rate stability. In addition, some consideration will be given to the mechanisms for bringing about greater exchange rate stability.

Optimum Currency Areas

Many economists have suggested that governments' insistence on having uniform national monies indicates that there are limits to the desirability of exchange rate flexibility. If exchange rate flexibility is so desirable, they ask, then why don't governments permit each region within their respective boundaries to have its own currency? For that matter, why not allow each community, firm, or person to have its, his, or her own currency and to issue it to anyone who will accept it?

There is an obvious political dimension to national governments' insistence on domestic currency uniformity, but there are also economic reasons. As the United States discovered during the colorful era of wildcat banking in pre-Civil War days, a lack of currency uniformity impedes the flow of goods and services and discourages financial integration.[6] It is arguable that regional monetary autonomy might sometimes allow a region to achieve fuller use of its resources than is possible with a uniform national monetary system, but it is doubtful that any resulting gain would outweigh the loss from diminished national economic integration and regional specialization that such monetary autonomy would bring. Furthermore, the case for regional monetary autonomy is weakened to the extent that national governments assume responsibility for giving assistance to regions whose economies perform relatively poorly.

The desire for national monetary uniformity has led to the development of the concept of an **optimum currency area,** an area possibly larger than a single country for which currency uniformity promotes economic efficiency. In this context, currency uniformity exists when there is either a single currency or multiple currency units that are mutually convertible and always exchange for each other at permanently fixed rates.

The term *optimum currency area* was coined by Robert Mundell in a now-classic article that indicated that the key ingredient for such an area is a high degree of resource mobility.[7] Other writers have elaborated upon Mundell's work, of whom the most influential has been Ronald McKinnon, who has stressed the importance of economic openness among the countries constituting an optimum currency area.[8] From the work of Mundell, McKinnon, and others has emerged a broad consensus that a multiple-country optimum currency area has the following characteristics: (1) the member states are highly integrated economically, (2) they pursue closely coordinated economic policies, (3) they have similar resource endowments, and (4) their resources are flexible in the ways in which they can be used.

The groups of countries that presently constitute optimum currency areas are probably few in number, but no doubt numerous groups of countries have

---

[6]This period began with the presidential election of 1832, when the victory of Andrew Jackson over Henry Clay assured the demise of the second Bank of the United States. The bank's elimination, in combination with the adoption of "free banking" legislation soon afterward resulted in a banking system with a very large number of commercial banks, each of which issued dollar-denominated bank notes as circulating currency. The notes of different banks circulated at various rates of exchange in terms of the gold dollar, ranging from parity to zero. Where bank notes circulated at a discount, which was generally the case except in New England, the discount was a function of the cost and probability of their redemption into gold. In effect, the country had many different currency units, and because their rates of exchange in terms of each other were highly variable, it also had what amounted to an internal system of multiple currencies with flexible exchange rates.

[7]Robert A. Mundell, "A Theory of Optimum Currency Areas," *American Economic Review,* September 1961, pp. 657–665.

[8]Ronald I. McKinnon, "Optimum Currency Areas," *American Economic Review,* September 1963, pp. 717–725.

the potential for becoming optimum currency areas. Even where such potential exists, however, as it apparently does among the nations of the EMS, government reluctance to cede sovereignty over economic policy stands in the way of realizing this potential. While there may be few optimum currency areas at present, it stands to reason that as nations approach the enabling conditions, the pressure for exchange rate stability among their currencies grows. Even as matters currently stand, therefore, the optimum currency area concept justifies some degree of exchange rate stability.

Dependent Economies

Even if a country is not a hot prospect for inclusion in an optimum currency area, it may be in its interest to maintain a high degree of exchange rate stability with one or more currencies of particular importance to it. This is especially likely if the country in question is highly dependent on international trade and investment. Because relatively small countries tend to exhibit the greatest degree of economic dependence, they are particularly likely to find it in their interest to maintain some degree of exchange rate stability.

The policy autonomy supposedly provided by flexible exchange rates may prove completely illusory if exchange rate changes have disruptive effects on a nation's economy, and such effects are likely to occur in many countries should they allow exchange rates to fluctuate freely. Suppose, for example, that the government of a certain LDC launches an ambitious economic development program that requires fiscal and monetary expansion for its implementation. Suppose, also, that the government is prepared to allow the national currency to depreciate as needed to prevent BOP deficits. Also suppose that the country has little influence on the world prices of its imports and exports and that when its currency depreciates, the domestic prices of both promptly rise to compensate fully for the depreciation.

The inflation stemming from price increases in tradable goods will probably trigger demands for wage increases and government subsidies for both producers and consumers who are injured by rising prices for imports. The anticipation of inflation is likely to lead to wage and price increases for workers and firms that are not directly involved in international trade. The uncertainty resulting from inflation and questions about the government's response to it may engender capital flight, especially if the government attempts to prevent interest rates from rising to offset expected inflation. It may prove difficult for the government to borrow internationally in such circumstances, and foreign investment in the country may be deterred by investors' fear that the country's investment environment has become riskier. In short, the experience with exchange rate flexibility may prove extremely unsatisfactory.

If a country's economy is likely to be severely damaged by exchange rate instability, it makes sense for it to minimize the fluctuations between its currency and the currency upon which its dependence is greatest. If the country's dependence is not focused on a single currency, then it may be desirable to stabilize its currency against some kind of currency composite. In any event, it is clearly desirable for countries that fall into the dependent economy category that exchange rates among the leading currencies not be subject to wide fluctuations.

The Real Exchange Rate Problem

Recall that it was shown in Chapter 3 that the exchange rate flexibility that has existed since 1973 has been both real and nominal. If PPP held at all times, nominal exchange rates could change with differences in national inflation rates, but real exchange rates would be unaltered. Because PPP often does not hold, however, it is often the case that a nominal exchange rate change is also a real exchange rate change, even though the time period involved may be several years.

Many observers deem the high degree of real exchange rate variability existing today to be undesirable because they believe that its effects on international trade and investment have negative economic consequences. Concerning international trade, the argument runs as follows. When a nation's currency is overvalued, its exports shrink and its imports expand, causing unemployment and the shifting of resources into activities that are less economically desirable in the long run. When the overvaluation is corrected, resources tend to shift back into the industries from which they were driven earlier, but it may prove difficult to restore some of the lost production, particularly in industries where technology changes rapidly. As a result, a permanent economic loss may occur. Moreover, the back-and-forth shifting of resources in accordance with the capricious behavior of exchange rates imposes costs that would not arise if real exchange rates were more stable.

As far as international investment is concerned, it is argued that because large and sudden changes in real exchange rates can cause large losses for borrowers and investors, the existence of a high degree of real exchange rate flexibility substantially increases the risk associated with international capital flows, particularly those that are long term. As a result, the volume of these flows used to finance international trade and real international investment is less than it would be if real exchange rates were more stable. While the risk can be reduced through hedging and the currency diversification of assets and liabilities, these measures entail considerable cost.

While these arguments seem plausible, an argument exists for the proposition that it would be a mistake for governments to attempt to stabilize real exchange rates. If the equilibrium theory of exchange rates has much validity, then real exchange rate changes are largely a response to changes in economic fundamentals, such as the relative prices of tradable goods and risk-adjusted real interest rates. Governments' attempts to stabilize real exchange rates by operating on nominal exchange rates are likely to fail, but it is by operating on nominal exchange rates that the advocates of real exchange rate stability generally pin their hopes for success. More promising is the approach of promoting real exchange rate stability by using government policy to affect economic fundamentals, but there is a danger that this effort will interfere with the operation of market forces in ways that reduce economic efficiency. For example, if governments resort to on-again, off-again taxes and controls on international transactions in the name of real exchange rate stability, the negative effects of these measures may outweigh the alleged benefits because of the discouragement to such transactions.

The Role of Central Bank Intervention

If forex transactions are allowed to occur freely, but governments are charged, nevertheless, with the responsibility for limiting exchange rate fluctuations (real or nominal), then central banks must engage in market intervention if the desired degree of exchange rate stability is to be attained. Experience since 1973 has demonstrated, however, that central bank intervention is unlikely to be very successful unless it is consistent with governments' monetary policies. Otherwise, at some point intervention is likely to lose its ability to hold the line against speculation.

The Profitability of Central Bank Intervention   In line with reasoning presented earlier in the chapter, it can be contended that if monetary policy is fundamentally exchange-rate stabilizing, central bank intervention should be both stabilizing and profitable. This seems to follow from the fact that, since central banks are charged with the conduct of monetary policy (with varying degrees of autonomy from their central governments), they possess inside information about that policy. If, for example, the dollar rises higher than is consistent with central bankers' intentions and central bankers are prepared to act to move the dollar downward, it is arguable that central banks should profit from selling dollars in anticipation of buying them back after their price has fallen since, unlike ordinary speculators, they exercise direct control over some of the variables that influence the outcome on which they are betting.

The problem with this hypothesis of central banks as profitable speculators is that it is not clear that central banks profit from their currency intervention. Indeed, it has been convincingly argued by Dean Taylor that from 1973 to 1979 the central banks of the United States, Canada, and six western European nations experienced collective net losses of approximately \$12 billion from forex market intervention.[9] Taylor's study thus appears to support Milton Friedman's contention that central banks, which unlike private speculators do not risk their own money, are poor speculators.[10]

While Taylor's findings are a serious challenge to the hypothesis that central bank intervention tends to be stabilizing, there are reasons for questioning their relevance for the current state of affairs. First, central banks have altered their intervention strategies since the time covered by Taylor's study and are now able to plausibly claim that their currency interventions are often profitable. Second, there are problems involved in trying to determine the

---

[9]Dean Taylor, "Official Intervention in the Foreign Exchange Market, or, Bet against the Central Bank," *Journal of Political Economy*, April 1982, pp. 356 and 359–361.

[10]Milton Friedman, "The Case for Flexible Exchange Rates," in *Essays in Positive Economics* (Chicago: University of Chicago Press, 1953), p. 188.

profitability of central bank intervention to stabilize exchange rates. Third, even if intervention is unprofitable, this does not necessarily mean that it is destabilizing.

During the 1960s and 1970s, central banks often defended unrealistic exchange rates, with the result that they enriched speculators at the expense of taxpayers without achieving lasting exchange rate stability. This experience led many observers, most notably Reagan administration policymakers, to question the wisdom of exchange rate stabilization efforts. The steep descent of the dollar after February 1985 ultimately induced the U.S. government to change its position on intervention, and it is now common for the central banks of leading industrial countries to engage in coordinated intervention to hold exchange rates within broad limits.

Unambiguously determining the profitability of central banks' interventions is a challenge because the gains and losses from particular interventions are typically mingled with the results of their other foreign currency operations. If, for example, a central bank holding $16 billion in dollar assets at the beginning of an intervention period sells $200 million of them to prevent the dollar from rising against its currency, and the dollar, nevertheless, rises in value, the central bank will show a gain on its forex holdings even though it lost money in its intervention effort. Moreover. some of central banks' transactions in foreign currencies have other motivations than the desire to stabilize exchange rates. For example, if a foreign central bank buys dollars because it wants to increase its forex reserves, not because it wants to prevent its currency from rising against the dollar, its purchase of dollars should not be regarded as an act of stabilizing intervention.

The Federal Reserve regularly publishes quarterly reports of forex operations conducted by it and the U.S. Treasury in the *Federal Reserve Bulletin* and the Federal Reserve Bank of New York's *Quarterly Review*. These reports are highly informative, but they do not permit an easy determination of the profitability of particular intervention operations.

Exhibit 11.4 presents the profitability summary of Treasury and Federal Reserve forex operations for the quarter May 1, 1991 through July 1, 1991, that appeared in the October 1991 issue of the *Federal Reserve Bulletin*.[11] It indicates that the Fed had realized gains of $147.5 million from forex operations during the quarter, while the Treasury's Exchange Stabilization Fund (ESF) realized gains of $60.3 million from its own foreign currency operations. It also indicates that both the Fed and the ESF experienced valuation losses on their holdings of foreign currencies. At the end of the quarter, the Fed and the Treasury were showing $1,919.9 million and $321.4 million, respectively, in valuation gains on their forex holdings, but these figures were less by $396.4 million and $249.2 million, respectively, than at the beginning of the quarter. The valuation losses occurred because the dollar's exchange value rose slightly during the period.

---

[11]"Treasury and Federal Reserve Foreign Exchange Operations," *Federal Reserve Bulletin,* October 1991, pp. 784–788.

| E X H I B I T | 11.4 | *Net Profits on U.S. Treasury and Federal Reserve Foreign Exchange Operations, April 30, 1991 through July 31, 1991 (in millions of dollars)*

Period and Item	Federal Reserve	U.S. Treasury Exchange Stabilization Fund
Valuation profits on outstanding assets and liabilities as of April 30, 1991	2,316.3	570.6
April 30, 1991–July 31, 1991		
Realized	147.5	60.3
Valuation profits on outstanding assets and liabilities as of July 31, 1991	1,919.9	321.4

[1]Data are on a value-date basis.

Source: "Treasury and Federal Reserve Foreign Exchange Operations," *Federal Reserve Bulletin*, October 1991, p. 787.

The text of the accompanying quarterly report indicates that there were two interventions during the period, both of which were intended to resist the rise of the dollar against the mark. The total amount of dollars sold for marks in these interventions was only $150 million. The interventions were dwarfed by off-market market transactions in which the U.S. monetary authorities sold $8,548.5 million of foreign currencies for dollars. The off-market transactions were for the purpose of allowing the governments involved to effect a mutual reduction of their forex reserves, not for the purpose of stabilizing exchange rates. Most of the realized gains shown in Exhibit 11.4 obviously resulted from the off-market transactions, not from the interventions, although it may be that some of the currencies sold in off-market transactions were acquired through intervention activity.

Because the interventions occuring during this quarter involved the purchase of marks and the mark finished the quarter with a higher value than it had when they occurred, it can be presumed that the interventions were profitable. What is unclear, however, is the extent to which the valuation losses occurring during the quarter affected the profitability of earlier interventions. In any event, this example should help to give the reader a better understanding of the problems involved in determining the profitability of intervention activity by monetary authorities.

Even if central banks incur intervention losses, this does not prove that intervention failed to contribute to exchange rate stability. If, for example, a central bank buys dollars to restrain a decline in the dollar and the dollar declines anyway, the central bank's purchases may still have had a moderating effect, i.e., the dollar might have fallen farther in the absence of intervention.

Central Banks' Motivation   While governments can achieve complete exchange rate stability if they are willing to subordinate other policy objectives to that end, most governments are reluctant to assign the highest priority to achieving exchange rate stability. Accordingly, even if central bank intervention contributes to exchange rate stability, exchange rates will probably not remain indefinitely within targeted levels.

The three macroeconomic objectives that have generally received the highest priorities are avoiding excessive unemployment, avoiding excessive inflation, and achieving gains in real output. Because exchange rate stability generally receives a somewhat lower priority, any conflict between one or more of these three goals and the goal of stabilizing exchange rates is likely to be resolved to the detriment of exchange rate stability. If, for example, the United States is in a recession, the Federal Reserve is probably going to attempt to promote a recovery by expanding the money supply even if this tends to cause a decline in the dollar's exchange value.

There are factors at work, however, that are tending to induce central banks to assign a higher priority to exchange rate stability. This is obviously true in Europe, where central banks are trying to maintain stable exchange rates among European currencies, but it is also true for the world as a whole. One of these factors is the growing desire of governments to attract foreign capital to their countries. Another is that as the volume of governments' forex reserves has increased, the danger of losses from declines in the exchange values of the currencies in which those reserves are held has also increased. For example, if a central bank holds $20 billion in dollar assets, a 10 percent decline in the dollar's exchange value costs the national treasury dearly. To the extent that the desire to protect the value of its reserve holdings influences central banks' behavior, therefore, they might be reluctant to take or support actions that tend to lower the exchange value of a reserve asset currency.

It is often assumed that governments of countries with which the United States conducts most of its international trade are biased in favor of a high exchange value for the dollar because this makes it easier for their countries to have trade surpluses with the United States. When such a bias exists, it would appear to be reinforced by the desire of central banks to protect the value of their holdings of dollar assets. It makes little sense, however, to try to maintain the dollar at a level that cannot be sustained, and if U.S. trade deficits are not financed with autonomous capital inflows, the dollar's value must ultimately decline. If, however, foreign central banks try to sustain a high value for the dollar by promoting autonomous capital outflows to the United States, the funds involved are used for the immediate benefit of the U.S. economy, not their own. Moreover, a high value for the dollar means high prices for dollar-invoiced imports, especially oil, and this can be inflationary. Finally, countries with large dollar-denominated debts have good reason to oppose the propping up of the dollar. It is not necessarily true, therefore, that it is in the interest of foreign governments to try to keep the exchange value of the dollar at a high level.

While it cannot be denied that governments have often tried to manipulate exchange rates to the perceived advantage of their own particular countries, there seems to be a growing recognition that nations' best interests are served if exchange rates are relatively stable and sustainable. If central banks try to manipulate exchange rates, but are not in general agreement as to what they should be, their operations will be at cross purposes and are likely to accentuate exchange rate instability instead of reducing it. Because there is general agreement among central bankers that exchange rates are presently too unstable, and because the growing financial integration among nations is making it increasingly difficult for governments to conduct autonomous monetary policies, a strong incentive exists among governments to assign the objective of exchange rate stability a higher priority than it has received in the past.

Restricting Capital Flows

Inasmuch as exchange rate instability is largely traceable to the growth of capital flows, it is hardly surprising that an approach that has gained some support is that of restricting capital flows. Because the use of comprehensive exchange control systems to restrict capital flows has been discredited in high-income countries, however, those who favor the restriction of capital flows to help stabilize exchange rates have tended to package their proposals as tax measures.

An example of the taxation approach is James Tobin's recommendation of a worldwide tax of 1 percent on all spot exchanges of currencies.[12] Admittedly, this measure would impose an added burden on international trade, but in Tobin's view, its negative impact on short-term capital flows would more than compensate for this defect. Because the tax would be a function of transaction size, it would be more discouraging for short-term capital flows than for long-term ones.[13] Presumably, it would reduce exchange rate instability because of its impact on speculative short-term capital flows.

Another tax proposal is Rudiger Dornbusch's recommendation that nations protect themselves against exchange rate instability by imposing taxes to equalize real interest rates.[14] If, for example, the United States' real interest rate rises relative to the rest of the world, the U.S. government could avoid unwanted capital inflows and their effect on the dollar by subjecting them to a tax designed to eliminate the real interest gain from purchasing dollar assets. Like Tobin's proposal, Dornbusch's tax would impose a cost in terms of lost economic efficiency, but this would presumably be made up by a gain in exchange rate stability.

Such proposals are, no doubt, worthy subjects for economic journals, but they remind one why political decision makers sometimes state that "economics is too important to be left to economists." For the time being, at least, the

---

[12]James Tobin, "A Proposal for International Monetary Reform," *Eastern Economic Journal*, July/October 1978, pp. 153–159.

[13]This is because the money amount of a given differential in terms of annual rates of return increases as the time period involved grows longer. Thus, a 2 percent difference in long-term rates of return might still easily justify a capital flow, whereas the same differential on short-term rates of return might not. Note that if a capital flow involved two spot transactions, the tax rate would effectively be about 2 percent.

[14]Dornbusch, "Equilibrium and Disequilibrium," pp. 168–169.

political tide has turned against proposals calling for the fine-tuning of taxes in order to achieve second-best solutions. It is always possible, however, that the tide will turn in favor of restricting capital flows and that such proposals will be taken seriously.

A More Promising Approach—Monetary Cooperation

If capital flows are not to be curtailed, the key to achieving greater exchange rate stability is to better coordinate monetary policy among the world's leading financial powers. Thus, if the United States, Japan, and the jointly floating countries of Europe all expanded their money supplies at the same rate and refrained from using fiscal policy to offset their monetary actions, exchange rate stability would undoubtedly be increased. Understandably, therefore, the quest for greater exchange rate stability has resulted in greater emphasis on monetary cooperation, and one can anticipate a continued effort in this direction.

The adoption of a policy to expand money supplies at the same rate in leading countries would be too rigid, however, and would probably not be sufficient to ensure exchange rate uniformity. There is no assurance that national demands for money would also grow at a uniform rate. Suppose, for example, that the dominant financial powers are committed to expanding their money supplies at a uniform rate and that the United States experiences an investment boom that causes its interest rates to rise. The higher interest rates would induce capital inflows into the United States that would tend to increase the U.S. money supply and cause the dollar to appreciate. If the Federal Reserve authorities were to adhere to the policy of maintaining the prescribed growth rate of the money supply, they would sterilize the monetary effect of the capital inflows by selling securities in the open market. This action could, however, raise interest rates further and attract *more* capital inflows. Only by allowing the money supply to expand beyond the prescribed rate could the authorities hope to relieve the pressure on the dollar to appreciate. Thus, just as the rules of the gold standard game required different rates of monetary growth in order to maintain fixed exchange rates, so must the modern monetary system allow such differences if a high degree of exchange rate stability is to be attained.

A promising avenue for improving international monetary cooperation would be the adoption of rules governing the accumulation of international reserves. Under such rules, governments that accumulate reserves in amounts that are defined as excessive would be obligated to allow the appreciation of their currencies. The threat of capital losses on their reserve holdings would provide an incentive to slow the reserve accumulation.

It is likely that the trend toward greater currency diversification of governments' reserve holdings will continue. If so, this will further increase the pressure on governments to cooperate monetarily in order to avoid the problem of sudden shifts of reserve holdings among currencies.

To a great extent, the future of the international monetary system hinges on what happens in Europe after the implementation of the common market agreement in 1992. If, as many anticipate, the European nations ultimately adopt a common monetary unit as a medium of exchange, that unit will bid to replace the dollar as the world's leading currency. It is widely believed that Europe, North America, and much of eastern Asia will coalesce into three distinct monetary areas based on the Ecu, the dollar, and the yen, with each area exercising a high degree of monetary autonomy vis-a-vis the other two. Given the momentum of the process of international financial integration among economically developed countries, however, it is also conceivable that, at some point down the road, the world's most financially advanced countries may come to regard themselves as belonging to a gigantic optimum currency area. In this case, they will probably elect to eliminate the problem of exchange rate instability among their currencies for good.

Summary

The asset or portfolio balance theory assigns the dominant role in exchange rate determination to capital flows. Because different countries' assets exhibit different risk and return characteristics, the theory rejects the contention of the monetary theory that assets are perfectly substitutable internationally. Portfolio managers strive to allocate their asset holdings to maximize their risk-adjusted expected rates of return. Capital tends to flow toward countries with relatively high risk-adjusted rates of return, but portfolio managers differ in their evaluations of assets and their willingness to accept risk. Moreover, the systematic risks of different countries are imperfectly correlated, which means that investors in each country can realize diversification gains by investing in assets of other countries. One cannot expect, therefore, that the pattern of international capital flows should be unidirectional. Exchange rates tend to exhibit a high degree of short-term instability because the factors that determine the distribution of portfolio holdings among countries are constantly changing. Changes in flows of goods and services lag behind changes in capital flows.

Among the factors that the portfolio balance approach emphasizes as being important in the determination of exchange rates is its emphasis on the role of changes in wealth that most distinguishes it from other approaches. An increase in wealth tends to lead to greater holdings of foreign assets, but whether or not it tends to lead to a depreciation of the national currency depends on the particular circumstances under which it occurs. Moreover, a capital outflow that tends to cause a nation's currency to depreciate sets up a return flow of income, and possibly capital, that tends to have the opposite effect.

The proponents of the portfolio theory suggest that it is possible to have rational speculative bubbles in which short-term exchange rate movements deviate substantially from exchange rates' underlying or long-term values. So long as speculators can approximately time the turning points in short-term exchange rate movements away from underlying values, the collapse of a bubble need not lead to widespread losses.

While the participants in international financial operations have developed sophisticated and effective techniques for coping with exchange rate instability, good arguments exist for limiting exchange rate flexibility in some instances. Notwithstanding past failures, a case can be made for some central bank intervention. The optimum currency area concept suggests that there should be a high degree of exchange rate stability among some currencies, and relatively small countries often find it necessary to limit the flexibility of exchange rates against their currencies. Among financially powerful nations, however, a high degree of exchange rate stability is likely to be unattainable so long as they insist on monetary autonomy, but there are factors at work that are pressuring these nations to reduce the variability of exchange rates among their currencies.

References

Adler, Michael and Bernard Dumas. "Portfolio Choice and the Demand for Forward Exchange." *American Economic Review*, May 1976, pp. 332–339.

Batten, Dallas S. and Mack Ott. "What Can Central Banks Do about the Value of the Dollar?" Federal Reserve Bank of St. Louis, *Review*, May 1984, pp. 16–25.

Belongia, Michael T. "Prospects for International Policy Coordination: Some Lessons from the EMS." Federal Reserve Bank of St. Louis, *Review*, July–August 1988, pp. 19–29.

Bilson, John F. O. "Rational Expectations and the Exchange Rate." In Jacob A. Frenkel and Harry G. Johnson, eds. *The Economics of Exchange Rates: Selected Studies*. Reading, Mass.: Addison-Wesley, 1978, pp. 75–96.

Branson, William H. "Asset Markets and Relative Prices in Exchange-Rate Determination." *Sozialwissenschaftliche Annalen*, 1977, pp. 69–89.

Cooper, Richard. "Economic Interdependence and Coordination." In Ronald W. Jones and Peter B. Kenen, eds. *Handbook of International Economics*. Amsterdam: North-Holland, 1985, Chapter 23.

Dernburg, Thomas F. *Global Macroeconomics*. New York: Harper & Row, 1989, Chapters 11, 12, and 15.

Dornbusch, Rudiger. "Equilibrium and Disequilibrium Exchange Rates." In Donald R. Lessard, ed. *International Financial Management: Theory and Application*, 2d ed. New York: John Wiley & Sons, 1985, pp. 151–172. Reprinted from *Zeitschrift fur Wirtschafts und Sozialwissenschaften*, no. 6, 1982, pp. 573–599.

Feldstein, Martin. "The Case against Trying to Stabilize the Dollar." *American Economic Review: Papers and Proceedings*, May 1989, pp. 36–40.

Frankel, Jeffrey A. "Monetary and Portfolio-Balance Models of Exchange Rate Determination." In J. S. Bhandari and B. H. Putnam, eds. *Economic Interdependence and Flexible Exchange Rates*. Cambridge, Mass.: The MIT Press, 1983.

Frenkel, Jacob A. "The International Monetary System: Should It Be Reformed?" *American Economic Review: Papers and Proceedings*, May 1987, pp. 205–210.

_____. "Tests of Monetary and Portfolio Balance Models of Exchange Rate Determination." In John F. O. Bilson and Richard C. Marston, eds. *Exchange Rate Theory and Practice*. Chicago: The University of Chicago Press, 1984, pp. 239–259.

_____ and Michael L. Mussa. "Asset Markets, Exchange Rates, and the Balance of Payments." In Ronald W. Jones and Peter B. Kenen, eds. *Handbook of International Economics*, vol. II. Amsterdam: North-Holland, 1984, pp. 679–748.

Friedman, Milton. "The Case for Flexible Exchange Rates." In *Essays in Positive Economics*. Chicago: The University of Chicago Press, 1956

Kenen, Peter B. *The International Economy*, 2d ed. Englewood Cliffs, N.J.: Prentice-Hall, 1989, Chapters 18–20.

_____. "Exchange Rate Management: What Role for Intervention?" *American Economic Review: Papers and Proceedings*, May 1987, pp. 194–199.

Lessard, Donald R. "Principles of International Portfolio Selection." In Donald R. Lessard, ed. *International Financial Management: Theory and Application*, 2d ed. New York: John Wiley & Sons, 1985, pp. 16–30. Reprinted from Abraham George and Ian H. Giddy, eds. *International Financial Handbook*. New York: John Wiley & Sons, 1983.

Levich, Richard M. "Empirical Studies of Exchange Rates: Price Behavior, Rate Determination and Market Efficiency." In Ronald W. Jones and Peter B. Kenen, eds. *Handbook of International Economics*, vol. II, 1984, pp. 979–1040.

McKinnon, Ronald I. "Optimum Currency Areas." *American Economic Review*, September 1963, pp. 717–725.

_____. "Monetary and Exchange Rate Policies for International Financial Stability: A Proposal." *Journal of Economic Perspectives*, Winter 1988, pp. 83–103.

Mundell, Robert A. "A Theory of Optimum Currency Areas." *American Economic Review*, September 1961, pp. 657–665.

Obstfeld, Maurice. "Floating Exchange Rates: Experience and Prospects." *Brookings Papers on Economic Activity*, vol. 2, 1985, pp. 369–464.

Rivera-Batiz, Francisco L. and Luis Rivera-Batiz. *International Finance and Open Economy Macroeconomics*. New York: MacMillan, 1985, Chapters 15–17.

Sachs, Jeffrey. "The Uneasy Case for Greater Exchange Rate Coordination." *American Economic Review: Papers and Proceedings*, 1986.

Stern, Robert M. *The Balance of Payments*. Chicago: Aldine, 1973, Chapter 3.

Taylor, Dean. "Official Intervention in the Foreign Exchange Market, or, Bet against the Central Bank." *Journal of Political Economy*, April 1982, pp. 356–368.

Tobin, James. "A Proposal for International Monetary Reform." *Eastern Economic Journal*, July–October 1978, pp. 153–159.

Williamson, John. "The Case for Roughly Stabilizing the Real Value of the Dollar." *American Economic Review: Papers and Proceedings*, May 1989, pp. 41–45.

_____. "Exchange Rate Management: The Role of Target Zones." *American Economic Review: Papers and Proceedings*, May 1987, pp. 200–204.

Questions

1. How does the portfolio balance theory explain the fact that international capital flows are often two-way?
2. If a U.S. investor wants to avoid the forex risk and other problems associated with owning foreign assets and elects to achieve diversification gains by acquiring a portfolio of stocks issued by U.S. multinational companies, is this a fully satisfactory alternative to holding a portfolio of stocks in foreign companies? Explain.
3. Evaluate the argument that the diversification gains achieved from holding foreign assets are likely to be wiped out by the exchange risk.

4. If a country has a relatively high rate of growth in wealth because of the accumulation of savings, does portfolio theory indicate that the exchange value of its currency should tend to decline over time? Explain.

5. Portfolio theory suggests that market-determined exchange rates are likely to exhibit a good deal of instability. Why?

6. If common stock prices in the United States are expected to rise relative to common stock prices in other countries, how, according to the portfolio balance theory, should this tend to affect the exchange value of the dollar? Why? Would your answer change significantly if you knew that the expected rise in U.S. stock prices was due primarily to the expectation of falling U.S. interest rates?

7. Under the portfolio balance theory, what would be required for the United States to finance a current account deficit with net capital inflows for a period of more than a few years?

8. Explain the meaning of news and how news tends to affect exchange rates in the portfolio balance theory.

9. Assume that the United States adopts a tight money policy in order to restrain inflation. Compare the monetary and portfolio balance theories' versions of how this action would tend to affect the dollar's exchange value.

10. Evaluate the contention that if forex speculation is destabilizing, it must be unprofitable.

11. What, according to Rudiger Dornbusch, are the inherent limitations of exchange rate theories that prevent them from being fully adequate explanations of the determination of actual exchange rates?

12. What is exchange rate overshooting, and how does the portfolio balance theory account for it?

13. There is a broad consensus about the characteristics of multiple-country optimum currency areas. What are these characteristics?

14. In your judgment, does it make sense for the governments of the leading financial powers to adopt a strategy of stabilizing real exchange rates among their currencies?

15. Why is it that central banks' gains or losses from their forex operations cannot necessarily be used to measure the profitability of their market interventions to stabilize exchange rates? Can a case be made for intervention even if it isn't profitable for central banks?

16. Summarize the factors that are resulting in pressure on the central banks of leading countries to increase their cooperation with each other to achieve a higher degree of exchange rate stability.

CHAPTER 12

International Banking

■

Until now, the international financial market that has drawn most of our attention has been the forex market. In this chapter and Chapters 13 through 16, however, we shall examine other international financial markets, namely those that involve international banking, international transactions in securities, and financial swaps. This chapter is concerned primarily with aspects of international banking that can be labeled traditional banking activity, i.e., that are not normally included with the Eurocurrency market. Chapter 13 deals with Eurobanking, Chapter 14 deals with international markets in securities, Chapter 15 deals with the financing of international trade, and Chapter 16 examines the international use of financial swaps.

The Nature of International Financial Markets

Like their domestic counterparts, international financial markets transfer purchasing power from lenders and investors to parties who desire to acquire goods and assets that they expect to yield future benefits. The world's leading international financial centers are located, for the most part, in countries that have historically contained large reservoirs of savings that could be tapped by residents of other countries. International financial markets are, however, considerably more than a device for transferring funds from countries with abundant savings to countries with savings deficiencies. To a large degree, these markets are based on the existence of different monetary units and differences among nations' cultural and legal environments. Much international financial activity is, therefore, more of a response to such considerations as exposure management and the desire to avoid regulations and taxes than a response to the desire to shift funds to countries with savings deficiencies.

The Classification of Financial Markets

Financial markets effect exchanges of assets. The assets exchanged may be physical property (tangibles), but more often (particularly in international finance) they are paper claims (intangibles). **Primary financial markets** alter the total stock of assets through transactions in securities or through direct lending without issuing securities. **Secondary financial markets** trade previously existing assets. **Derivative financial markets,** of which the market in financial swaps is an outstanding example, involve the creation of financial assets that are based on other financial assets.

A common distinction separates money markets from capital markets. In **money markets,** the assets that are created or traded have relatively short maturities, typically a year or less. In **capital markets,** the assets created or traded either have maturities that exceed a year or, as in the case of perpetual bonds and most stocks, lack definite maturities.

While most of the material in this chapter and the next three chapters deals with primary transactions, some space is allocated to secondary transactions since they have attained considerable prominence. Secondary transactions are particularly important for securities and for some negotiable debt instruments, notably certificates of deposit and bankers' acceptances, that are not generally classified as securities. There is a symbiotic relationship between primary and secondary transactions in that a strong secondary market strengthens its primary counterpart and vice versa.

International financial markets fit into five main categories: the forex market, markets based on direct lending by financial institutions, markets in negotiable instruments of debt, markets in equity securities, and markets in internationally arranged financial swaps. Because the forex market has been examined in detail in earlier chapters, it is covered only incidentally in this chapter and the next four chapters.

International financial markets characteristically involve exchanges of assets between residents of different countries. Frequently, however, exchanges of assets between domestic residents have an international aspect. Such is the case, for example, when one foreign holder of securities issued by a U.S. company sells them to another foreign resident, or when a domestic firm borrows in local currency from a domestic bank in order to finance the purchase of imports. In another example, a **parallel loan,** firms that are resident in the same country negotiate a loan between them as part of a larger arrangement in which two (probably related) firms simultaneously work out an offsetting local currency loan in another country. Thus, one U.S. subsidiary in Argentina can lend Argentine pesos to another U.S. subsidiary in return for a simultaneous offsetting dollar loan from one parent company to the other.[1] Both loans are technically between residents of the same countries in which they occur, and yet they are clearly international in character. Clearly, therefore, the scopes of international financial markets are not confined to transactions that appear in nations' BOPs.

Euromarkets and Traditional Markets

In both direct international lending and international trading of securities, some operations are commonly labeled with the prefix *Euro-*. This designation identifies certain types of financial activity that take place outside the countries

---

[1] At the beginning of 1992, the new peso replaced the austral as the Argentine monetary unit. It was hoped that the name change would be of assistance in the continuing struggle against inflation.

in whose currencies they are denominated. The **Eurocurrency market** is concerned with deposit and lending operations conducted by banks in currencies other than those of the countries in which the banks operate. The **Eurobond market** features bonds that are issued and sold outside the countries in whose currencies they are denominated. **Euroequity markets** trade corporate stocks outside the home countries of the issuing corporations.

Paralleling the various Euromarkets, some financial operations without the *Euro-* prefix are, nevertheless, international in nature. If, for example, a U.S. bank lends dollars to a foreign firm, or a foreign government floats a dollar-denominated bond issue in the United States, these are clearly international financial arrangements, even though neither occurs in a Euro-market. These parallel arrangements can be distinguished from Euromarkets by referring to them as *traditional markets*.

While traditional international financial operations are denominated in the currency of the home country, they may take place to some extent outside that country. Suppose, for example, that a U.S. bank maintains representative offices abroad that do not conduct deposit and lending operations in the host countries, but rather assist banks' head offices in locating foreign customers. If one of these offices arranges a loan from the bank's head office to a host country borrower, the transaction would definitely be traditional in nature. Similarly, if a U.S. securities firm has an office abroad that arranges a purchase of dollar-denominated bonds issued in the United States, this would be a traditional market transaction.

The distinction between traditional markets and Euromarkets is not always easy to make. In practice, some borderline cases could be assigned to either classification. This is particularly the case when the same financial institution participates in both a traditional market and its Euromarket counterpart. Despite such cases, the distinction is fundamentally important and should be observed as accurately as is feasible.

The Scope of International Banking

Because international financial operations often require the services of commercial banks, the study of international financial markets necessarily entails the study of commercial banking's international dimensions. Commercial banks dominate forex dealing. They are predominant among financial institutions that engage in direct lending, i.e., lending that does not occur through the medium of securities. They are involved in the creation of negotiable certificates of deposit, bankers' acceptances, and commercial paper, none of which are usually classified as securities. They are increasingly prominent in the international aspects of markets in securities, not only because they lend money for purchases of securities, but also because they perform investment banking functions, borrow by issuing internationally traded securities of their own, and buy securities as investments. Included among the securities that they buy as investments are not only obligations issued by their own governments, but also securities issued by other governments and private corporations.

The Glass-Steagall Act of 1933 has long required depository institutions in the United States to limit their transactions in securities to the issues of domestic governments (except when acting as trustees). Internationally, however, U.S.-based commercial banks are permitted to engage in activities from which they are barred domestically. With the very important exception of Japan, the governments of other countries typically do not attempt to divorce commercial banking from the securities business to the extent that the government of the United States has done. Overall, therefore, the range of commercial banks' operations internationally is considerably broader than what is customarily identified with commercial banking in the United States.

In what is known as *investment banking*, financial firms assist governments, private corporations, and international organizations to raise funds by issuing securities. Specifically, the firms known as *investment banks* manage, underwrite, and serve as marketing agents for new security issues. As underwriters, they temporarily purchase securities from their issuers with the intention of reselling them for profit net of the underwriting fees that they receive. In international securities markets, investment banking is a highly competitive field that U.S. investment banking firms and (to a lesser degree) commercial banks share with foreign firms, most of which are commonly classified as commercial banks.

The operations of **merchant banks** further blur the lines between commercial and investment banking. Of largely British origin and historically associated with trade financing, these firms typically conduct deposit banking while simultaneously engaging in the types of operations with new security issues that are associated with investment banks. The deposit and direct lending operations of merchant banks are confined almost exclusively to their corporate and governmental clients. They have very limited retail commercial banking ties with the general public. Some merchant banks, like some investment banking firms and even some commercial banks, have attained prominence as investment managers for institutional investors, notably pension funds. Most merchant banks are British, some of them being subsidiaries of such giant commercial banks as Barclays and Lloyds. In some cases, however, notably Bankers Trust Company of New York and Mitsubishi Bank of Japan, the operations of non-British commercial banking firms closely resemble those of British merchant banks.

Supplementing the operations of commercial, investment, and merchant banks are those of various government agencies and international organizations that are, in the broad sense of the word, "banks." The IMF and the World Bank Group are foremost among these official institutions, but many others have considerable importance. With the exception of the IMF, which is concerned primarily with exchange rates and the overall payments positions of its members, these institutions can generally be divided into those that are primarily concerned with financing trade and those that are primarily concerned with financing economic development. In general, official banks that finance trade tend to be government-owned institutions designed to stimulate exports. Development banks are often jointly operated by various governments for the benefit of particular world regions, but also common are institutions, such as Nacional Financiera in Mexico, run by a single government. Official banking institutions are largely financed by public treasuries, but they also obtain funds from bank loans and issues of debt securities. In some cases, exemplified by the International Finance Corporation of the World Bank Group, they allow equity participation by private investors in ventures they sponsor.

The rest of this chapter deals with topics that fall largely within the scope of traditional international banking. Emphasis is given to commercial banks' lending and related activities, namely the use of bankers' acceptances and commercial paper. Also included are sections on the sovereign debt problem and the different forms of organization in international banking.

Direct International Lending By Commercial Banks

International financial markets are largely constructed around direct lending, an activity that has been dominated historically by commercial banks. Most direct international lending continues to take place in the offices of commercial banks, and commercial banks perform vital functions in the markets for negotiable money market instruments that provide borrowers with alternatives to direct bank loans.

The Evolution of Banks' International Lending

The history of direct international lending by commercial banks is almost as old as the history of banking itself. In late medieval times, not only did foreigners borrow from money lenders in northern Italy, Flanders, and elsewhere, but itinerant merchants also frequently lent to residents of the countries to which their journeys carried them. The loans were generally, but not always, for the purpose of financing the movement of goods. The most spectacular loans went to rulers striving to extend and consolidate their power. In terms of profitability, such "sovereign loans" had mixed results.

While banking practice has changed enormously over the centuries, some features of banks' international lending have remained broadly similar. Such lending tends to develop in the financial centers of countries that have accumulated relatively large pools of savings. As these countries expand their international trade, their banks tend to increase their financing of domestic firms' imports and exports, and as trading and manufacturing firms of domestic origin expand their operations abroad, domestic commercial banks tend to establish offices abroad to lend to these firms and to local firms that either have business ties to domestic firms or are otherwise engaged in international trade.

Although international banking has a long history, its most spectacular growth has occurred since the late 1950s. During the ensuing decades, banks' international lending has generally grown at a faster rate than their overall lending, and while the sovereign debt crisis of the 1980s has slowed the growth of their direct international lending and encouraged them to "securitize" their assets, the total volume of their outstanding international loans has continued to grow. Banks' international lending has expanded in response to several factors: (1) the historical tendency of banks to follow their clients abroad, (2) the expectation of obtaining higher interest rates after due allowance for the exchange risk and the cost of managing it, (3) gains from portfolio diversification, (4) the pursuit of defensive strategies of following rival banks abroad to avoid losses caused by failure to do so, and (5) encouragements from both home and host country governments.

For various reasons, but especially because of the short-term nature of most bank liabilities, banks have historically tended to make predominantly short-term loans, at least ostensibly. Over time, however, the average maturity of bank loans has lengthened, in part because of the realization that short-term loans with renewal privileges are often, in fact, medium- or even long-term loans. Making explicitly medium- or long-term loans removes much of the uncertainty about their durations. Other factors involved in the lengthening of loan maturities include the longer average maturity of banks' liabilities and improvements in banks' liquidity. While it is true that bank loans have shorter maturities, on average, than bonds, the maturities of these types of lending overlap a great deal. This has served to increase the competitiveness of bank financing with bond financing.

The Magnitude of Banks' International Operations

According to data compiled by the BIS, the total amount of the outstanding cross-border claims of "reporting" banks at the end of 1990 was $5,907.2 billion. To this figure is added $1,309.4 billion in local bank claims denominated in foreign currency to arrive at a figure of $7,216.6 billion for gross international bank assets. From this figure of $7,216.6 billion are deducted $3,866.6 billion in interbank claims to arrive at a total of $3,350.0 billion as the amount of international bank lending to nonbank borrowers.[2] The reporting banks include the banks of all countries that are significant sources of bank credit to other countries.[3] Because some of the claims included in the $3,350.0 billion figure consist of assets such as securities and forex holdings that were not necessarily acquired from loans, it is arguable that this figure overstates banks' direct lending to nonbank borrowers. On the other hand, direct international lending by banks in nonreporting countries is excluded from this figure.

Exhibit 12.1 presents data in billions of dollars on the international claims and liabilities of banks in the reporting countries. The vast majority of both claims and liabilities lie within the reporting area. Note, however, that of the $3,350.0 billion in estimated net international bank credit outstanding at the end of 1990, $718.6 billion was credit extended to borrowers in countries outside the reporting area. Of that $718.6 billion, $390.5 billion was credit

---

[2]Bank for International Settlements, 61st Annual Report, Basle: BIS. 1991, p. 121.

[3]Including in the reporting area are the Group of Ten, Switzerland, most of the rest of Europe exclusive of the former Soviet bloc, Hong Kong, Singapore, and such "offshore" banking centers as the Bahamas, the Caymans, the Netherlands Antilles, and Bahrain.

	Changes, Excluding Exchange Rate Effects[a]				Stocks at End of 1990
	1987	1988	1989	1990	
A = Claims on outside-area countries	11.6	13.5	−1.7	−17.0	718.6
On non-banks	2.7	−4.3	−11.5	−15.3	390.5
B = International claims on entities within the reporting area[b]	740.9	496.4	793.8	583.6	6,336.1
(1) Claims on non-banks	187.2	159.9	229.5	241.0	1,684.4
(2) Banks' own use of international inter-bank funds for domestic lending	108.9	85.6	167.2	133.6	785.1
(3) Interbank redepositing	444.8	250.9	397.1	209.0	3,866.6
C = Unallocated[c]	12.4	1.1	15.0	22.4	161.9
D = A + B + C = total gross international bank assets	764.8	510.9	807.1	589.0	7,216.6
E = D − B(3) = estimated net international bank credit	320.0	260.0	410.0	380.0	3,350.0
A = Liabilities to outside-area countries	48.7	41.5	57.6	69.4	656.3
To non-banks	12.0	21.1	27.8	20.2	252.6
B = International liabilities to entities within the reporting area[b]	725.6	460.8	720.1	525.9	6,177.6
(1) Liabilities to non-banks	71.0	66.3	159.7	111.3	1,044.7
(2) Banks' own supply of domestic funds to the international inter-bank market[d]	164.1	118.8	147.0	171.3	1,333.0
(3) Interbank redepositing	490.5	275.7	413.4	243.3	3,799.9
C = Unallocated[c]	36.2	33.3	45.7	28.0	316.0
D = A + B + C = total gross international bank liabilities	810.5	535.7	823.4	623.3	7,149.9

[a]Bank flows in currencies other than dollars have been converted into dollar amounts using end-of-quarter exchange rates.

[b]Includes banks in the Group of Ten plus Luxembourg, Austria, Denmark, Finland, Ireland, Norway, Spain, the Bahamas, Bahrain, the Cayman Islands, Hong Kong, the Netherlands Antilles, Singapore, and the branches of U.S. banks in Panama.

[c]Consist mainly of securities and reciprocal claims between reporting banks and international agencies.

[d]Including trustee funds channeled into the market via banks in Switzerland.

Source: Bank for International Settlements, *Sixty-First Annual Report,* Basle: BIS, 1991, pp. 121 and 124.

extended to nonbank borrowers. The decline that occurred in these credits in 1988, 1989, and 1990 is explained by debt write-offs and other actions to reduce banks' exposure to heavily indebted LDC borrowers in combination with the slow growth in new lending to these countries.

Notwithstanding the slow overall growth in claims on countries outside the reporting area that occurred from 1987 to 1990, the prevailing impression conveyed by Exhibit 12.1 is one of rapid growth in both claims and liabilities. The expansion in estimated net international bank credit is particularly noteworthy, and it is also noteworthy that gross international bank liabilities (mostly deposits) expanded more rapidly than gross international bank claims.

Exhibit 12.2 provides a breakdown by lending countries of reporting banks' gross external claims and gross foreign currency claims on local residents. Two sets of figures are presented here, one set showing total amounts outstanding at the end of 1990 and the other set showing the changes that occurred in 1989 and 1990. The amounts are in billions of dollars.

Among the noteworthy things about Exhibit 12.2 are the standout position of the United Kingdom, the impressive increases recorded by European countries and Japan, the comparative stagnation of international lending by U.S. banks, and the great importance of banks located in such small countries as Luxembourg, Hong Kong, Singapore, and the Bahamas. The term **offshore banking centers** is commonly applied to these countries even though Luxembourg has no sea coast. The importance of the offshore centers underscores the importance of the Eurocurrency market, of which they are a part. So does the fact that the United Kingdom holds the number one position among individual countries.

Some sense of the relative importance of traditional international banking and the Eurocurrency market is conveyed by Exhibit 12.2. Cross-border claims in domestic currency arise, for the most part, from traditional banking operations. Note, however, that the International Banking Facilities (IBFs) of the United States and the Japan offshore market, both of which have large external positions in domestic currency, can be regarded as extensions of the Eurocurrency market. External claims denominated in foreign currency can arise from either traditional banking or the Eurocurrency market, but generally come from the latter. Local positions in foreign currency are assigned to the Eurocurrency market. Clearly, the Eurocurrency market is much larger than the market in traditional international bank credit.

The relative stagnation of international lending by U.S. banks in 1989 and 1990 is probably a temporary phenomenon. It is explained primarily by the unusually slow expansion of bank credit in the United States during these years, particularly in 1990, and by U.S. banks writing off claims on LDC governments. Note that Exhibit 12.2 indicates that the external claims of the IBFs were somewhat larger at the end of 1990 than the other external claims of U.S. banks. Also note the absence of local positions in foreign currency on the part of the U.S. banks.

Exhibit 12.2 also indicates that, as of the end of 1990, the external claims of Japanese banks were second in volume only to those of banks located in the United Kingdom. Moreover, the local positions in foreign currency held by

| E X H I B I T | 12.2 | *External Claims and Local Foreign Currency Claims of Reporting Banks: Year-End 1990 and Changes in 1989 and 1990 (in Billions of U.S. Dollars)* |

| Positions of Banks in | Stocks at End of 1990 | | | Change 1989–1990[a] | | |
| | External Positions in | | Local Positions in Foreign Currency | External Positions in | | Local Positions in Foreign Currency |
	Domestic Currency	Foreign Currency		Domestic Currency	Foreign Currency	
United Kingdom	97.6	971.4	315.0	13.4	126.8	37.8
France	66.6	358.1	77.8	13.2	106.1	2.0
Germany	244.6	124.4	7.8	63.9	58.8	3.2
Luxembourg	4.9	291.1	50.3	1.1	76.8	10.5
Belgium	13.8	183.2	57.0	2.4	40.2	6.7
Netherlands	33.1	141.3	27.2	6.4	38.2	8.2
Switzerland	66.0	76.6	20.5	−9.3	6.6	3.9
Sweden	1.7	24.4	73.4	−0.3	9.1	38.3
Other European countries[b]	34.4	225.8	151.9	4.7	45.3	43.4
Total European countries	562.7	2,396.3	780.9	95.5	507.9	154.0
Japan: Offshore market	215.0	280.0	92.0	87.6	80.0	51.0
Other	202.8	252.8	406.3	5.3	52.2	19.8
United States: IBFs	251.3	51.5	0.0	−9.3	−6.9	0.0
Other	261.1	14.5	0.0	30.7	4.0	0.0
Asian Market centers[c]	6.8[d]	827.9[e]	. .	1.1[d]	232.9[e]	—
Other centers[f]	4.4[g]	580.0	30.2[g]	0.6[g]	83.2	6.4[g]
Total	1,504.1	4,403.0	1,309.4	211.5	953.3	231.2

[a]Excludes changes in the dollar value of claims because of exchange rate changes.
[b]Includes Austria, Denmark, Finland, Ireland, Italy, Norway, and Spain.
[c]Includes Hong Kong and Singapore.
[d]Hong Kong only.
[e]Includes Bahrain.
[f]Includes Canada, the Bahamas, the Cayman Islands, and the Netherlands Antilles
[g]Canada only.
Source: Bank for International Settlements, *Sixty-First Annual Report*, Basle:BIS, 1991, p. 127.

Japanese banks were larger enough than the comparable positions held by banks in the United Kingdom so that, overall, Japanese banks held the number one position in terms of gross international bank assets. Because many banks operating in the United Kingdom are foreign-owned, while banks operating in Japan are overwhelmingly Japanese-owned, a fair conclusion is that Japanese banks hold the number one position as sources of international lending.

Incidentally, the operations of the Japan offshore market as well as those of the IBFs of the United States are examined in Chapter 13.

In interpreting the data in Exhibit 12.2, keep in mind that location may differ from nationality. As already noted, many banks located in the United Kingdom are foreign-owned. Foreign ownership is even more prevalent in Luxembourg and in most of the countries included in the Asian market centers and other centers categories of Exhibit 12.2. Foreign-ownership is also an important feature of the U.S. banking scene.

Differences in the Internationalization of Nations' Banking Systems

Nations' banking systems differ enormously in their international orientations. Some small nations have developed into offshore financial centers that are so highly integrated into the Eurocurrency market that these nations can hardly be said to have banking systems of their own. Some economically powerful nations, most notably the United States and the United Kingdom, have open banking systems that allow a high degree of participation by foreigners as both bankers and customers. At the other extreme, many nations prohibit deposit banking by foreigners and severely limit foreign access to credit from domestic banks. In general, the banking systems of DCs are far more open than those of LDCs. DCs differ widely in their degrees of banking openness, and the banking systems of some third-world nations allow foreigners to conduct deposit banking, borrow from domestic banks, and even acquire controlling interests in domestic banking firms. The chief barriers to the internationalization of banking systems are protectionist financial policies, nondiscriminatory but severe restrictions on banking practices, and otherwise unpromising financial environments. These three barriers explain why most international banking occurs in the Eurocurrency market.

Governments that follow policies of banking protectionism claim that this diminishes foreign domination of their national economies, increases the availability of credit to domestic borrowers, and promotes exchange rate and monetary stability by reducing the volatility of capital flows. Banking protectionism is often accompanied by measures designed to allocate available savings according to desired economic and political criteria.

There are, however, serious problems with banking protectionism that are causing it to decline in many countries. It reduces the pressure on domestic banks to match their foreign counterparts in efficiency and service. To the extent that the policy works to keep domestic interest rates down, it discourages the placement of savings with domestic financial institutions and encourages their investment abroad. Also, while favored categories of borrowers may obtain credit domestically in generous amounts and on favorable terms, less favored borrowers may feel compelled to borrow abroad.

In countries whose banks have the capacity for foreign operations, domestic bankers naturally tend to seek protection from competition at home while striving for a free hand abroad. A major obstacle to this tactic is the practice of **reciprocity**, which means that if a particular country restricts the operations of foreign banks within its territory, other countries tend to restrict the operations of its banks within their territories. Reciprocity has prodded many governments, including the government of Japan, into modifying discriminatory banking practices. In other cases, however, including the notable case of Mexico, governments have been willing to sacrifice the benefits of financial openness on the protectionist altar.[4] There is, however, a decided tendency to modify banking protectionism.

Even if a government does not follow a clearly protectionist banking policy and allows the national currency to be freely traded in the forex market, the internationalization of the nation's banking system tends to be slowed if its banks must operate under more severe restrictions than banks in countries with roughly comparable conditions of risk and return. This fact is evident from the experiences of France and Germany, both of which allow foreign-owned banks to operate with little overt discrimination, have freely traded currencies, and have banks that are prominent direct international lenders. Both countries, however, have traditions of close regulation of banking. Their money and capital markets have consequently not developed as fully or as rapidly as those in some financially more liberal countries. While their banks have overcome their handicaps in part by setting up operations in foreign financial centers, their overall operations have been diminished in size and scope by the effects of the domestic restrictions to which they have been subject.

France, Germany, and the other members of the EMS have moved recently toward greater financial openness in attempting to fulfill their common market commitment for 1992. Outside the EMS, the general trend is also toward greater financial openness because of a growing belief that the costs of protectionist banking policy are greater than the benefits.

Direct International Lending in Traditional Markets

Although most of the direct international lending by banks is effected through the Eurocurrency market, a large volume of such lending can be classified as traditional. Such lending is particularly important in the United States, Japan, and Germany (see Exhibit 12.2), but it is also important in a number of other countries. International lending of this type is subject to the conventions of domestic lending. In the United States, for example, the prime

---

[4]While foreign banks are allowed representative offices in Mexico, it is a long-standing policy of the Mexican government to exclude them from deposit banking. Because Citibank had a deposit banking branch in Mexico City before the adoption of the Constitution of 1917 and its accompanying legislation, it has been allowed to continue the deposit operations of this branch, thereby constituting a single exception to the government's general prohibition. The deposit operations of this branch have been confined, however, to the building in which it was housed in 1917. It is likely that the Mexican government will modify its policy of banking protectionism in the near future.

interest rate is used as a benchmark loan rate for both international and domestic bank loans.[5] Whether loans are domestic or international in nature, U.S. banks often require business borrowers to maintain minimum amounts, known as **compensating balances,** on deposit. In Eurocurrency lending, however, the benchmark bank lending rate is customarily the LIBOR (London interbank offered rate), and no compensatory balances are required. Because compensating balances are required in the United States, but not in Eurocurrency lending, the prime rate and the LIBOR are not directly comparable.

The interest rate is, of course, a key factor in the choice between Eurocurrency borrowing and traditional borrowing. As explained in Chapter 13, this generally favors the Eurocurrency market. There are, however, situations that favor traditional borrowing. When, for example, a foreign firm wishes to cultivate a relationship with a particular local bank, it may be willing to borrow from that bank at a slightly higher interest rate than it would pay in the Eurocurrency market.

Traditional bank borrowing commonly finances international trade. A major reason for this is that governments commonly sponsor credit insurance programs to stimulate exports by protecting lending domestic banks and exporting firms from virtually all of the commercial and political risks associated with credit purchases of exports. Moreover, because the transactions in the Eurocurrency market tend to be large, relatively small-scale borrowers, including many firms involved in international trade, tend to rely on traditional financing sources. Traditional borrowing may also offer advantages in terms of convenience and familiarity.

While the Eurocurrency market and traditional banking markets are imperfect substitutes, they are close enough that traditional banking markets are greatly affected by developments in the Eurocurrency market. When the Eurocurrency market experiences a growth spurt, some of the growth comes at the expense of traditional banking. Although a nation's banks may avoid some loss of business if they have Eurobanking operations of sufficient size and depth, jobs and tax revenues may be lost if domestic banks migrate to offshore and other foreign financial centers. As a consequence, the growth of the Eurocurrency market tends to promote looser domestic banking regulations and practices and larger incentives to banks and their borrowers for using traditional banking channels.

---

[5]Conventionally, the prime rate is viewed as the short-term rate charged by U.S. banks to their best or "prime" business customers. For many years, this rate tended to be uniform among banks and to have a restraining effect on explicit interest rate competition among them. During the 1980s, however, increased competition in financial markets and greater interest rate volatility weakened the role of the prime rate. While U.S. banks still commonly use a prime rate as a benchmark loan rate, this rate is not always the same for all banks. Furthermore, whereas the prime rate was formerly the rate charged to the best business customers, highly rated borrowers can often borrow below the stated prime (or basis) rate. In part, the weakening of the prime rate's role has resulted from pressure exerted by the Eurocurrency market.

Bankers' Acceptances and Commercial Paper

While direct lending is the heart of commercial banking, banks' international operations extend to various other activities. As was noted earlier, commercial banks perform investment banking functions internationally. More characteristically associated with traditional commercial banking, however, are the subjects of this section: bankers' acceptances and commercial paper.

Bankers' Acceptances (BAs)

For centuries, exporters have employed a standard financial instrument known as a **bill of exchange** or **draft.** In the course of time, bills of exchange have evolved into a highly liquid, bank-guaranteed negotiable instrument known as the **banker's acceptance (BA).**

A bill of exchange is an order to pay addressed to a specific party that calls for payment of a specified sum on a specific or determinable date to a specified party. An ordinary check written on an individual's checking account is a bill of exchange, but the bills of exchange used in international trade differ in three respects from ordinary checks. First, the writer of a bill of exchange is technically the *drawer,* not the *writer.* Second, whereas writing an ordinary check leads to a disbursement from the writer's bank balance, drawing a bill of exchange commonly leads to an increase in the drawer's cash balances. Third, whereas a check is usually payable on presentation to the bank on which it is written, the bills of exchange used in international trade are commonly drawn to allow deferred payment.

While bills of exchange may be drawn on importers, they are often drawn, with prior approval, on commercial banks that charge fees for the use of their names and the services they provide. When a bill of exchange drawn on a bank provides for deferred payment, the drawer (or its bank) commonly sends it to the bank on which it is drawn (the *drawee*) to secure the bank's guarantee of payment, i.e., its *acceptance.* When the drawee bank accepts the bill by indicating its commitment to honor the bill at maturity, the bill becomes a BA.

Because BAs are highly standardized negotiable instruments that are guaranteed by banks with generally high credit ratings, they can readily be sold (*discounted*) to investors seeking high-quality, short-term uses for funds. Because of the dollar's prominent position as a vehicle currency, most of the world's acceptance financing is done through banks in the United States. BAs offer yields to investors that are very close to those on certificates of deposit and considerably higher than the yields on Treasury bills. On the borrowing side, BAs often allow importers and other users to obtain credit on better terms than would otherwise be possible.

A full account of the use of BAs would take us beyond the intended scope of this chapter. Some additional material on them is presented in Chapter 15, which deals with trade finance. Two additional aspects of BA financing are, however, covered in this chapter: their relationship to bank lending and a comparison of the cost of BA financing with the costs of financing with direct loans and commercial paper.

When a bank accepts a bill of exchange, it is not necessarily lending money, but it is lending its name by guaranteeing payment at maturity to the bill's holder. A BA is not only a means of guaranteeing payment, though, but also a device for obtaining credit on favorable terms. Who obtains credit and who provides it depend on the circumstances of particular cases. The credit recipient may be an importer, an exporter, or someone else, and the credit source is effectively the party that holds the BA.

The credit recipient is often a firm that acquires imported goods at about the same time that a bank accepts the corresponding bill of exchange. Typically, the importer applies the proceeds from the sale of the goods to make payment to the accepting bank on or before the bill's maturity. The party that effectively finances the importer is the BA's holder. Depending on the circumstances, this may be the exporter, the accepting bank, or a party (possibly another bank) that buys the accepted bill in the BA market. Since a BA can be discounted more than once, more than one holder can be a credit source.

While the holders of BAs are often commercial banks, especially the accepting banks, most BAs wind up in the hands of nonbank investors. In many cases, the credit provided is extended to a domestic borrower by a domestic holder and hence does not constitute international lending in the sense of a transaction between a resident and a nonresident. In many other cases, however, the lending process is unambiguously international in nature. Such is the case, for example, when the U.S. financial system uses BAs to lend to foreign importers or when U.S. banks accept bills drawn on them by foreign banks wishing to provide credit to their own customers.

Exhibit 12.3 presents data from the *Federal Reserve Bulletin* on outstanding dollar BAs in the United States from the end of 1985 through the end of 1990. It indicates that BAs are a financial instrument of modest importance. Their use has tended to decline in recent years because of the improvement of alternative trade financing techniques. Most BAs in the United States are held by investors other than banks, and many of them held in the United States were issued to finance the international trade of countries other than the United States.

While the volume of BA financing is modest, BAs are high-quality assets, as is borne out by the fact that the Fed holds some of them on account for foreign central banks.[6] They are almost as safe as Treasury bills, but offer higher yields.[7] In addition, they are highly liquid and available in widely varying amounts and maturities.

---

[6]Federal Reserve Banks formerly discounted BAs for member banks seeking additional reserves, but their use in this way has not been authorized since 1984.

[7]No loss of principal has been recorded on BAs since their introduction in the United States in 1914. See John H. Wood and Norma L. Wood, *Financial Markets* (Harcourt, Brace, Jovanovich, 1985), p. 204.

| E X H I B I T | 12.3 | *Bankers' Dollar Acceptances Outstanding in the United States: 1985–1990*[a, b]

	End-of-Year Figures in Billions of Dollars					
Holder	1985	1986	1987	1988	1989	1990
Accepting banks	$11.2	$13.4	$10.9	$ 9.1	$ 9.4	$ 9.0
Own bills	9.5	11.7	9.5	8.0	8.5	7.9
Bills bought	1.7	1.7	1.5	1.1	0.9	1.1
Held by Federal Reserve Banks for foreign correspondents	0.9	1.3	1.0	1.5	1.1	0.9
Others	56.3	50.2	58.7	56.1	52.5	44.8
Basis						
Imports into United States	$15.1	$14.7	$16.5	$15.0	$15.7	$13.1
Exports from United States	13.2	13.0	15.2	14.4	13.7	12.7
All other	40.1	37.3	38.9	37.2	33.6	29.0
Total	$68.4	$65.0	$70.6	$66.6	$63.0	$54.8

[a]Not seasonally adjusted.

[b]Data on bankers' acceptances are gathered from institutions whose acceptances total $100 million or more annually. The reporting group is revised every January. In January 1988, the group was reduced from 155 to 111 institutions. The current group, totaling approximately 100 institutions, accounts for more than 90 percent of total acceptances activity.

Source: *Federal Reserve Bulletin*, May 1989, p. A23 and December 1991, p. A22.

Commercial Paper (CP)

The use of commercial paper is an American technique that has recently spread to the Eurocurrency market and various national money markets. Although most CP issued in the United States is not directly associated with the financing of international trade, the U.S. market in CP has considerable international financial significance. Some CP issued in the United States is issued by foreign borrowers, and much of it is issued by U.S. multinational firms. Moreover, the domestic market in CP has a large impact on short-term borrowing decisions in markets with a more decidedly international flavor.

Commercial paper consists of unsecured, short-term notes that are sold, usually on a discount basis, either through dealers or directly to investors. Direct placement is used by large companies with excellent credit ratings and short-term borrowing needs that are large enough and persistent enough to justify developing their own placement facilities. Other CP issuers work through dealers, some of which are well-known investment banking firms. These "dealers" are more accurately brokers since they strive to avoid taking positions. Because the heterogeneity of CP works against the development of secondary trading, CP investors normally hold paper until maturity. Dealers make markets, however, by generally standing ready to buy, at substantial discounts, any CP they have placed that investors wish to sell before maturity.

The CP market is not as clearly an adjunct to traditional commercial banking as the BA market is because commercial banks in the United States have not been as active in the CP market as in the BA market. Nevertheless, commercial banks are vital to the CP market because CP issuers commonly support their paper by maintaining bank lines of credit that provide, upon the payment of fees, bank guarantees that their paper will be honored at maturity. Furthermore, spearheaded by Bankers Trust Company and supported by the Federal Reserve System, commercial banks have attempted to carve a niche for themselves as CP dealers. Rallying under the ancient banner of the Glass-Steagall Act, investment bankers have vigorously contested this intrusion, fearing, it has been suggested, "for the future of their summer homes" because of the enormous amounts of capital at the disposal of large commercial banks.[8] To date, U.S. courts have tended to side with the investment bankers, ruling that CP is a type of security and that commercial banks are, therefore, barred from dealing in it under the provisions of Glass-Steagall. The commercial banks contend that CP is not a security, but a form of loan paper. The ultimate outcome of this controversy hinges on the U.S. Supreme Court and what the legislative and executive branches of the U.S. government decide to do with the Glass-Steagall Act.

The CP market is much larger than the BA market. Moreover, while the BA market has generally declined in recent years, the volume of CP has expanded impressively, with the result that what was once a peculiarly American method of short-term financing has gained a foothold in other countries.

At the beginning of the 1980s, the average volume of CP outstanding in the United States was less than $150 billion. By the end of 1984, the volume had grown to $237.6 billion, and at the end of 1990, it stood at $566.7 billion. Exhibit 12.4 gives the *Federal Reserve Bulletin's* summary of CP financing in the United States at year's end from 1985 through 1990.

The rapid recent growth of CP financing appears to be due to four causes: (1) a shift from long-term to short-term financing in response to high interest rates, greater interest rate volatility, and, at times, a steep yield curve; (2) the aggressive promotion of CP financing by investment firms; (3) a reduction in the cost of CP financing relative to the costs of alternatives; and (4) a reduction in the risks of CP financing.

Historically, the discount rates for CP have been slightly higher than those for BAs because the risks of holding CP have been deemed slightly greater. CP lacks the secondary market that BAs have, and, historically, the accepting banks for BAs have had higher credit ratings, on average, than CP issuers. Moreover, in contrast to BAs' impeccable record, in a few instances, such as the Penn Central bankruptcy of 1970, defaults on CP have resulted in losses of principal.[9] On the other hand, the increased use of bank guarantees for CP issues and generally narrower gaps between the credit standings of commercial banks relative to those of leading nonbank corporations have narrowed the

---

[8]Nick Gilbert, "Bankers Trust Cliffhanger," *Euromoney,* April 1986, p. 13.

[9]Wood and Wood, *Financial Markets,* pp. 204 and 221. The same source indicates (on p. 204) that in legal distributions of assets, holders of BAs take precedence over banks' creditors because, in accepting bills of exchange, banks are legally viewed to be trustees rather than debtors.

| EXHIBIT | 12.4 | *Outstanding Commercial Paper in the United States: 1985–1990ᵃ (End-of-Year Figures in Billions of Dollars)*

Category	1985	1986	1987	1988	1989	1990
Financial companies						
Dealer-placed paperᵇ						
Total	$ 78.4	$101.7	$102.7	$159.8	$186.3	$219.0
Bank-related (not						
seasonally adjusted)ᶜ	1.6	2.3	1.4	1.2	n.a.	n.a.
Directly placed paperᵈ						
Total	135.3	151.9	174.3	194.9	212.6	201.9
Bank-related (not						
seasonally adjusted)ᶜ	44.8	40.9	43.2	43.2	n.a.	n.a.
Nonfinancial companies	85.0	77.7	81.9	103.8	131.1	145.9
All issuers	$298.8	$331.3	$359.0	$458.5	$530.1	$566.7

ᵃSeasonally adjusted unless otherwise noted.

ᵇIncludes all financial company paper sold by dealers in the open market.

ᶜBank-related series were discontinued in January 1989.

ᵈAs reported by financial companies that place their paper directly with investors.

Source: *Federal Reserve Bulletin,* May 1989, p. A23 and December 1991, p. A22.

yield gap between CP and BAs. In fact, directly placed CP now generally has yields that are slightly below those of BAs. At the end of September 1991, for example, 3-month directly placed CP was discounted, on average, at 5.33 percent on an annualized, 360-day year basis, compared with 5.38 percent for 3-month BAs. The comparable discount rate for 3-month dealer-placed CP averaged 5.57 percent, however.[10]

The Comparative Costs of Direct Loans, BAs, and CP

Exhibit 12.5 provides a hypothetical illustration of how to compare costs among three alternative methods of short-term borrowing: a direct bank loan, using a BA, and issuing CP. Two variations are presented for the direct loan approach, one in which the borrowing corporation is effectively required to increase its cash on deposit with the lending bank, and one in which such a compensating balance requirement, if any, has no effect on the amount of cash held on deposit in the lending bank.

While Exhibit 12.5 shows BA financing as the cheapest alternative, followed, in order, by direct loan financing without a compensating balance, CP financing, and finally the direct loan with a compensating balance effect, it should be kept in mind that the example given is for illustrative purposes only. Actual cases may depart substantially from the results presented here.

Assume that Purehex Corporation, located in Hockville, USA, desires to borrow $2 million for 3 months to finance imports of video recorder parts

---

[10]*Federal Reserve Bulletin,* December 1991, p. A23.

from South Korea. Purehex can borrow from Local Bank at the current prime rate of 8.50 percent without any compensating balance effect, i.e., any compensating balance required by the loan does not increase Purehex's deposit with Local beyond its normal level. As an alternative, assume that Purehex can borrow from Global Bank at 8.30 percent, 20 basis points below Local's prime rate, but a loan from Global would require a 20 percent compensating balance that would force it to raise its normal minimum deposit with Global above the current level of $200,000. The other alternatives available to Purehex are to draw a bill of exchange on Global that can be discounted after acceptance at 6.66 percent or to issue CP that can be discounted at 6.80 percent through a dealer.

At first sight, it may appear that Purehex can reject the direct loan route out of hand since it involves paying a much higher rate than the other alternatives. Two additional factors should, however, be taken into account. First, since both BA and CP financing are done on a discount basis, their costs in terms of simple interest are higher than 6.66 percent and 6.80 percent, respectively. Second, BA and CP financing both entail noninterest costs beyond those encountered in direct loan financing.

The simplest case, identified as 1a in Exhibit 12.5, is the direct loan without a compensating balance effect. From the information given, it can be determined that the cost of this alternative would be $42,500.

Next, Alternative 1b is a loan from Global Bank with a 20 percent compensating balance requirement that would require Purehex to raise its deposit with Global. Even though Global is willing to discount from the prime rate to lend at 8.30 percent, the compensating balance requirement results in an effective interest rate of 9.34 percent. Alternative 1b must therefore be rejected unless Purehex expects future benefits from expanding its relationship with Global Bank.

Alternative 2, BA financing, appears to offer the cheapest way to borrow the $2 million. With an effective interest rate of 7.81 percent, BA financing offers the lowest effective interest cost of the four alternatives. Realistically, however, other factors could tip the balance against BA financing. There might be additional costs associated with preparing and processing a BA, including the cost of providing the accepting bank with documentation about the imported goods. Also, in return for agreeing to accept a bill of exchange drawn on it, Global Bank might require Purehex to deposit sufficient funds to cover the BA several days before maturity.

Alternative 3, CP financing, appears to be considerably more expensive than BA financing, but without the credit rating fee of $6,000, and if there were no other costs to be considered than those shown in Exhibit 12.5, the CP alternative would be cheaper than BA financing. If Purehex had recently issued CP, or if it intended to issue a much larger quantity of CP than $2 million, the CP route might well be the most attractive of all.

Not only do CP issuers normally pay credit rating fees, but this fee would probably be a good deal larger than the $6,000 assumed in this example. Moreover, CP issuers commonly incur costs excluded from Exhibit 12.5 that, like the credit rating fee, do not vary proportionally with either the time period

| E X H I B I T | 12.5 | *Hypothetical Effective Interest Rates on Different Types of Short-Term Financing: Direct Bank Lending, Banker's Acceptance, and Commercial Paper*

Alternative Methods for Borrowing $2 Million for 90 Days	Charges (Expressed as annual Interest Rates)	
1a. *Direct Loan, No Compensating Balance Effect*		
Loan made at 8.50 percent prime rate	Prime interest rate	8.500%
	Adjustments	0.000
	Effective interest rate	8.500%
1b *Direct Loan with Compensating Balance Effect*		
8.50 percent prime rate	Prime interest rate	8.500%
Loan at discount of 0.20 percent from	Less discount	0.200
prime rate (loan rate of 8.30 percent)	Loan rate	8.300%
20 percent compensating balance required	Adjustment for	
Normal minimum balance of $200,000	compensating balance[a]	1.040
	Effective interest rate	9.340%

[a]Lex x be the sum that would have to be borrowed in order to obtain a net disposable amount of $2 million. With a 20 percent compensating balance and the assumption that a balance of $200,000 would be maintained in any event, the following equation results: x −(0.2x − $200,000) = $2,000,000. Solving for x yields $2,250,000 as the sum that would have to be borrowed. Since this exceeds $2 million by 12.5 percent, the effect on the amount of interest paid would be the same as if $2 million were borrowed at an interest rate equal to 8.30 percent plus an additional charge equal to 0.083 × 0.125, or 1.0375 percent. Rounding upward gives 1.04 percent.

[b]The formula for converting an annual discount rate to a simple annual interest rate can be written as:

$$\text{Simple annual interest rate} = \frac{\text{All-in discount rate}}{1-\left(\text{All-in rate} \times \dfrac{\text{Days financed}}{360}\right)} \times 100$$

Given an all-in discount rate of 7.66 percent, this formula indicates an interest rate of 7.81 percent when the financing period is 90 days. The interest rate thus exceeds the discount rate by 15 basis points (0.0015 percent).

[c]Using the same formula as in exhibit note b, it can be determined that an all-in discount rate of 6.925 percent converts to an interest rate of 7.047 percent when the financing period is 90 days.

[d]If an outlay is fixed with reference to the interest rate, the effective interest rate formula can be written as:

$$\frac{\text{Simple annual}}{\text{interest rate}} = \frac{\text{Interest charges + Fixed charges}}{\text{Borrowed funds}} \times \frac{360}{\text{Days financed}} \times 100$$

Applying this formula to the commercial paper data gives an effective interest rate that rounds to 8.75 percent. This indicates that the $6,000 credit rating fee is equivalent to a 1.2 percent interest charge.

Alternative Methods for Borrowing $2 Million for 90 Days	Charges (Expressed as annual Interest Rates)	
2 Banker's Acceptance		
6.66 percent annual discount rate	Discount rate	6.660%
1.00 percent acceptance commission, discount basis	Acceptance commission	1.000
	All-in discount rate	7.660%
	Adjustment for conversion to interest rate basis[b]	0.150
	Effective interest rate	7.810%
3 Commercial Paper		
6.80 percent annual discount rate	Discount rate	6.800%
0.125 percent dealer placement fee, discount basis	Dealer placement fee	0.125
0.50 percent bank standby commitment fee, simple interest basis	All-in discount rate	6.925%
$6,000 credit rating fee	Adjustment for conversion to interest rate basis[c]	0.122
	Effective interest rate of discounted costs, rounded	7.050%
	Commitment fee	0.500
	Adjustment for credit rating fee[d]	1.200
	Effective interest rate	8.750%

or the volume of CP issued. Issuers commonly pay fees, for example, to banks that keep the records and handle the redemption payments when CP matures.

Given the lump sums required for credit rating fees and some of the other costs of CP financing, the attractiveness of this alternative increases as the amount of the CP issue increases and its maturity lengthens. It is uncommon for CP to be issued with a maturity exceeding 9 months, however, because such issues must be registered with the SEC.[11] On the other hand, the average CP issue is larger than the average BA, and this fact reduces the significance of the lump sum costs associated with CP financing.

Since the direct borrowing alternative seems to carry relatively high interest charges, especially considering compensating balances, the question emerges as to why borrowers use it more heavily than the alternatives. The answer is largely that direct borrowing offers advantages in terms of flexibility and risk minimization. A loan can often be paid early or extended, but BA and CP commitments are locked in until maturity. BAs are generally used to finance

---

[11]R. Charles Moyer, James R. McGuigan, and William J. Kretlow, *Contemporary Financial Management*, 2d ed. (St. Paul: West, 1984), p. 673.

specific international trade transactions, not working capital needs. The CP alternative is largely confined to issuers with high credit ratings and short-term liquidity positions that inspire confidence in their ability to redeem CP at maturity. Moreover, the use of CP is questionable for borrowers who require assured access to credit for periods that exceed 9 months. The CP market is impersonal, highly competitive, and subject to sharp fluctuations in supply and demand. Borrowers who rely heavily upon it run the risk that sometimes it might not supply their short-term financial needs. The relationships established through direct borrowing are more personal, and when a borrower has built up a good working relationship with a particular bank, that bank will probably still supply credit on relatively attractive terms when money is tight. In short, the advantages of direct borrowing may more than compensate for its cost.

Alternative Organizational Formats for International Banking

In deciding how to arrange their international operations, commercial banks can copy various organizational forms. At one extreme, a bank can avoid setting up offices in foreign countries and rely on correspondent banks to handle any international business that it cannot conduct from its home country. At the other extreme, it can create a wholly owned foreign subsidiary that conducts full-service banking in its location. In between are other forms of organization, of which the branch and the representative office are the most important. The choice among alternatives depends on a bank's goals, the size and scope of its operations, and the financial environments in which it operates.

Correspondent Banking

A **correspondent banking** relationship exists when a bank uses the services of another bank with a separate corporate identity that is located in another city or country. Such a relationship is often reciprocal, i.e., each bank renders services for the other. The services include forex transactions, originating and processing bills of exchange and other documents related to international trade, handling payments and collections, providing credit information about potential borrowers, and providing loans and services to clients.

The chief advantage of relying on correspondents is that they provide low-cost access to international banking. With a given outlay, a bank can achieve greater geographic coverage in its operations with correspondents than by using another alternative. Furthermore, correspondents can often deal with local conditions more capably than a foreign bank with a more visible presence could.

The chief disadvantages of correspondent relationships are the lack of full control and the limited range and extent of services they offer. For example, a bank cannot force a foreign correspondent to make a local currency loan to a client. Furthermore, the limited range of correspondents' activities means that in some cases, relying on them may restrict the size and scope of a bank's foreign operations below the desired level. If the profit potential of a particular location is great enough, and if a bank has the capacity to develop that potential with an alternative arrangement, it is probably well-advised to do so.

Representative Offices

Representative offices are established in foreign locations to conduct operations that do not require deposit and lending facilities in the host countries. Since such offices do not conduct deposit banking, they do not eliminate the need for correspondents. They do, however, improve the quality of the correspondent relationship by virtue of their physical presence in host countries.

Aside from their role in improving correspondent relationships, representative offices locate potential borrowers, furnish intelligence about local business conditions, and provide assistance to domestic and foreign clients who either do business in the host countries or are interested in doing business there. When, for example, a corporate executive from the home country visits a country in which a bank has a representative office, the views of an officer in that office may carry considerable weight with that executive's assessment of the local environment.

Several factors may tend to favor the establishment of a representative office rather than a more substantial presence. First, if a host country prohibits foreign banks from conducting deposit banking, the option of going beyond the representative office does not exist. Second, the expected business volume may be too small to justify a larger investment. Third, if the profit potential of deposit banking in a country is uncertain, establishing a representative office may be the appropriate way to explore this question further. Fourth, the political and economic environment of a country may be too risky to warrant the investment required to establish a greater presence than a representative office.

Foreign Branches

Despite these limitations, a more substantial presence than a representative office is often desirable. The issue then becomes whether to go with the branch format or with a separately incorporated unit, i.e., a subsidiary, affiliate, or joint venture. Branches are more numerous than separately incorporated units, but the latter are also common.

A **foreign bank branch** is a deposit banking unit that is legally an office of a corporation that is headquartered in a country other than the one in which the unit operates. In general, the branch format offers the best possibilities for achieving unified and efficient full-service banking across international boundaries. This is because a branch network can integrate its operations more completely than an organization composed of separately incorporated units. This advantage of the branch format is particularly important with respect to the mobility of funds. If its headquarters permits, a branch office can lend far greater sums than it can generate from its own resources because the resources that are potentially at its disposal are those of the entire corporation. Subsidiaries, affiliates, and joint ventures are, everything else the same, more constrained in making individual loans by the size of their capital bases. While they may be able to supplement their resources by enlisting the participation of associated companies, the process is more cumbersome than simply shifting funds internally from one corporate office to another.

It is commonly claimed that a major factor behind the extensive reliance on the branch format in foreign banking operations is that it provides greater security to a bank's customers than separately incorporated banking units. This assertion rests on the belief that the parent company or companies can always walk away from the liabilities of a separately incorporated banking unit without suffering legal consequences, but the entire resources of a company are legally committed to meeting the liabilities of a branch. In reality, however, it is *not* established that a bank is always legally responsible for a foreign branch's liabilities. As was demonstrated in a prominent case involving the Manila branch of Citibank, if a bank refuses to accept liabilities of a branch that is prevented from discharging its commitments by the action of a host-country government, it is not clear that it can be forced to accept those liabilities through legal action.[12] Nevertheless, while the precise extent of banks' legal responsibility for the obligations of foreign branches is in doubt, it remains generally true that the financial support for branches' liabilities is more solid than that for the liabilities of separately incorporated units. The main effect of the case of the Manila branch has been to provide an additional deterrent to the placement of funds in countries where governments may impose severe restrictions on international transactions.

While the branch format is the most common means of establishing full-service banking in foreign countries, this does not in itself explain why such facilities may be desirable. It is therefore necessary to ask how the establishment of full-service banking units abroad promotes the achievement of banks' objectives. Of the various answers to this question, five stand out. First, such units help banks to retain the business of domestic customers who have established foreign-based operations. Second, they attract business from new customers. The third answer is linked to the first two: they provide direct access to money markets that have captured a high percentage of the world's international financial activity. Fourth, they provide a partial escape from

---

[12]This case began in October 1983 when the Philippine government froze banks' forex outlays. Included in the freeze were about $600 million in dollar-denominated time deposits held by other banks with Citibank's Manila branch. These other banks, which were predominantly American and Japanese, had been induced to place money market funds with the Citibank branch by a combination of attractive interest rates and their assumption that the deposits were backed by the full resources of what was then the world's largest bank. After the freeze was imposed, however, Citibank refused to honor the maturing time deposits of its Manila branch with funds provided by other units, arguing that it was the Philippine government, not Citibank, that was responsible for the failure of the branch to honor its commitments. The prevailing view at the time was that Citibank was legally correct, but there were dissenting opinions among legal experts. The dispute was gradually resolved by the release of blocked funds by the Philippine government and the arrangement of compromises between Citibank and its Manila creditors. See *The Wall Street Journal,* January 24, 1984, p. 37; February 23, 1984, p. 40; and April 24, 1984, p. 39.

home-country regulations and, in some cases, confer tax advantages. Fifth, they contribute to the diversification of banks' earnings.

As nonbank firms have expanded abroad, their home-country banks have tended to accompany them with branches out of fear of losing some or all of those firms' business. This follow-the-customer explanation accounts for only part of the growth of foreign bank branches, however, as most of the business of foreign branches is usually conducted with customers other than home-country firms that do their banking with branches' home offices.[13] Evidently, therefore, much of the motivation for establishing foreign branches has been supplied by the prospects of finding new customers.

In general, banks find that, by comparison with their home-country operations, their foreign branches are more successful in finding suitable uses for funds than they are in attracting deposits. Foreign branches typically lack internal networks of branch offices within their host countries that would allow them to establish large host-country deposit bases, and they often encounter reluctance by host-country residents to deposit in banks that are identified as foreign. In addition, host country governments frequently discriminate against foreign branches in ways that discourage domestic residents from shifting funds to them. Because of their difficulties in attracting host-country deposits, foreign branches tend to rely heavily on money market borrowing and injections of funds from their home offices to finance their lending and other operations.

It should be noted that there have been cases in which foreign branches have succeeded in attracting host-country deposits, particularly time deposits. It remains true as a general proposition, nevertheless, that foreign branches are at a competitive disadvantage with host-country banks in attracting host-country deposits. This is one of the causes of the growing emphasis on acquiring foreign banking subsidiaries by purchasing controlling interests in well-established host-country banks.

Since foreign branches are not incorporated units, they are subject to home-country regulations that apply to the companies of which they are parts. Nevertheless, foreign branches are somewhat less restricted in their operations than home-country bank offices. For example, the foreign branches of U.S. banks are allowed to engage in some activities that are prohibited at home, and their deposit liabilities to foreigners have never been subject to the Federal Reserve System's reserve requirements.

Although the income earned by foreign branches is fully taxable by home-country governments, there are possible tax advantages associated with foreign branches. Some income tax concessions are allowed to prevent them from being at a competitive disadvantage, and the nonincome taxes that they have to pay are often lower than those levied at home.

Because of the great importance of stability of earnings to commercial banks, they generally have even more reason than most other corporations to

---

[13]Donald R. Marsh, "Foreign Branches," in William H. Baughn and Donald R. Mandich, eds., *The International Banking Handbook* (Homewood, Ill.: Dow Jones-Irwin, 1983), p. 558.

diversify their operations. While some diversification is achieved from the international operations of their home offices, foreign branches provide them with additional opportunities to diversify earnings. To the extent that branches operate in other currencies than those of their home countries, they provide additional possibilities for hedging the exchange risk. If, for example, the London branch of a U.S. bank has a net asset position in pounds sterling, this can offset a net liability position in pounds held by the home office. Foreign branches also allow banks to take advantage of the fact that systematic risk for the world as a whole tends to be lower than the systematic risk of any national economy.

Since the early 1980s, there has been a tendency for the number of foreign branches of U.S. banks to decline. Behind this decline have been such factors as the establishment of IBFs (which were first authorized in late 1981), mergers among U.S. banks, and a tendency for some U.S. banks to shift to the subsidiary form. At the end of 1990, there were 126 U.S. banks with 819 foreign branches.[14] By comparison, the comparable figures for the end of 1987 were 153 banks and 902 branches.[15] During most of the 1980s, there was also a tendency for the assets of foreign branches to decline, but this decline has been reversed in the past few years. Thus, from the end of 1988 to September 30, 1991, the total assets of foreign branches of U.S. banks, net of claims on the parent banks and their other branches, increased from $268.5 billion to $295.1 billion. On the latter date, $101.8 billion of the assets were held by branches in the United Kingdom, while $78.5 billion were held by branches in the Bahamas and the Cayman Islands.[16]

Foreign Banking Subsidiaries

While the branch is the most widely used form for establishing a full-service banking presence abroad, separately incorporated entities, usually subsidiaries, are also common. Banking affiliates and joint ventures are also used, but the parent-controlled subsidiary is the prevalent form for establishing a foreign banking presence with a separate corporation.

There are six prominent reasons for preferring subsidiaries over branches in foreign-based banking operations. First, in some situations, subsidiaries are preferred because of the limited liability feature of subsidiary ownership. Second, and partly because of the limited liability feature, foreign subsidiaries are less closely scrutinized and regulated by the parents' home-country governments than foreign branches. Third, some host-country governments,

---

[14]Board of Governors of the Federal Reserve System, *Annual Report 1990* (Washington, D.C.: Federal Reserve System, 1990), p. 199.

[15]Board of Governors of the Federal Reserve System, *Annual Report 1987* (Washington, D.C.: Federal Reserve System, 1987), p. 189.

[16]*Federal Reserve Bulletin,* January 1992, p. A55. According to the *Federal Reserve Bulletin,* July 1986, p. A55, the comparable figure at the end of 1982 was $316.9 billion. Part of the subsequent decline was due, however, to a decision in June 1984 to discontinue reporting the assets of foreign branches with total assets of less than $150 million.

such as those of Australia and Sweden, prefer that foreign banks operating within their jurisdictions be subsidiaries rather than branches because they find it easier to regulate and tax subsidiaries. Fourth, subsidiaries often offer better opportunities than branches for conducting retail banking and attracting large volumes of host-country deposits. Fifth, the banking laws of the host countries may allow subsidiaries to engage in operations, like investment banking, that are not permitted to branches by their home-country governments. Sixth, subsidiaries may offer tax advantages.

With respect to the first two reasons and the fifth, the subsidiary form is particularly attractive when a bank wants to engage in relatively risky, but profitable activities that are not permitted for branches under home-country restrictions. For U.S. banks in particular, the subsidiary form is sometimes chosen because it allows U.S. banks to circumvent the Glass-Steagall Act and engage in what would be construed as the securities business under that legislation.

In a country with a promising retail banking outlook and without either a public policy of discouraging residents from depositing in foreign-owned banks or a popular disinclination to deposit in them, the acquisition route offers a tempting alternative to relying on branches or building subsidiaries from scratch. The attractiveness of this alternative is borne out by the numerous acquisitions by foreign banks in recent years, not only in the United States, but also in other countries. In some well-publicized cases, however, bank acquisitions have turned out badly for the parent companies.[17] Parties have evidently lavished rather excessive attention on working out the deals required for acquisitions relative to the attention they have given to determining the value of the assets they have acquired and their capacity to generate earnings. In the aftermath of ill-advised acquisitions, a white-elephant syndrome has emerged that has encouraged caution, but foreign acquisitions of banks continue.

A joint venture with a local partner is sometimes used as an alternative to full control by a foreign parent. The domestic partner in a joint venture may bring to the arrangement important attributes that the foreign partner lacks, such as knowledge of local conditions, a well-established public image, and strong political connections. Nevertheless, the parties to joint ventures often have conflicting objectives, operating styles, and attitudes, and their history indicates that they are generally short-lived.

The primary tax advantage of subsidiaries is the possibility of deferring the taxation of income by the parent company's government. It is a general rule of

---

[17]The best-known example of a failed acquisition is the purchase of Crocker National Bank of California by Britain's Midland Bank in 1981. Midland ultimately paid over $1 billion to acquire all of Crocker's stock and invested several hundred million dollars more in an attempt to turn Crocker into a profitable operation. Nevertheless, Crocker continued to experience operating losses. In 1986, Midland sold Crocker to Wells Fargo Bank of California for about what it had paid to acquire the bank, but the net result of the venture was a huge loss, particularly in opportunity costs. See Alan C. Shapiro, *Multinational Financial Management*, 3d ed. (Boston: Allyn and Bacon, 1989), pp. 770–771; and Michael Kolbenschlag, "The Man with a Taste for Albatross," *Euromoney*, May 1986, pp. 23–25.

international taxation that subsidiaries' profits are not fully taxed by the parent companies' governments until they are remitted to the parents. By deferring profit remittances, the parents can often reduce their tax liabilities, at least temporarily. The profits of foreign branches, by contrast, are fully taxable by home country governments, although these governments often offer tax concessions to branches in order to avoid putting them at a competitive disadvantage. The tax deferral aspect suggests that while a branch may be the preferable format in the early stage of a foreign banking venture when profits are likely to be small or even negative, switching to the subsidiary format may be desirable when the venture has sufficiently matured. One scarcely need add that the choice between branch or subsidiary also hinges on host-country tax law and policy.

Edge Act Corporations

Since the World War I era, U.S. government policy has allowed banks greater operational leeway internationally than domestically. By forming *U.S.-based* subsidiaries known as **Edge Act corporations,** banks have long been allowed to engage in international operations both at home and abroad that would otherwise be prohibited. Edge Act subsidiaries have been authorized since 1919, but their widespread use is a comparatively recent phenomenon.

Sections 25 and 25(a) of the Federal Reserve Act Prior to World War I, international financial operations of U.S. banks were very limited. U.S. banks did not lend heavily to foreigners, and the financing of foreign trade was handled largely by British banks and discount houses. During the war, it was realized that, although Section 25 of the newly passed Federal Reserve Act (1913) allowed federally chartered banks to establish foreign branches, this did not meet the needs of banks desiring to engage in international banking. Section 25 was therefore amended to allow member banks of the Federal Reserve System, whether federally or state chartered, to have domestic subsidiaries that specialized in international banking. The subsidiaries that were subsequently established in accordance with Section 25 became known as *Agreement corporations* because any bank with a Section 25 subsidiary was required to enter into an agreement with the Federal Reserve authorities regarding the subsidiary's activities.

In 1919, the Federal Reserve Act was further amended by the addition of Section 25(a), which extended the scope of the activities allowed to international banking subsidiaries. This amendment became known as the Edge Act, in honor of its sponsor, Senator Walter Edge of New Jersey. The most fundamental difference between Section 25 and Section 25(a) was that the latter permitted banking subsidiaries, under certain conditions, to hold equity positions in foreign countries. These investments did not necessarily have to conform to the conventions of commercial banking, but could be for any purpose construed by the Fed to fall within the scope of Section 25(a).

In its original form, the Edge Act drew a sharp distinction between "banking" and "financing" activities. An Edge Act subsidiary could engage in one, but not both. Banking subsidiaries were allowed to conduct internationally oriented deposit banking in the United States and to hold equity interests in foreign banks, but they were prohibited from engaging in other activities. Financing subsidiaries were allowed, subject to regulations established by the Fed's Board of Governors, to engage in investment banking and other activities abroad not normally associated with commercial banking, but they were prohibited from conducting deposit banking. Either type of subsidiary was to be chartered by the federal government with approval by the Fed.

At no time since they were authorized has the number of Agreement corporations exceeded a handful. Almost all of those created have been state-chartered. The Edge Act alternative has always been the more popular of the two because of its federal charters (avoiding state regulation) and the possibility of engaging in financial activity. Even so, many years elapsed before a large number of Edge Act subsidiaries materialized. After World War II, the number of Edge Act companies gradually increased, with the main factor behind their growth being the possibility of conducting deposit banking, on a limited scale, across state boundaries. With Edge Act subsidiaries, regional banks could have deposit banking operations in New York, Chicago, Miami, and other financial centers, while money center banks could conduct deposit banking in financial centers outside their home states.

During most of the 1970s, the growth of Edge Act subsidiaries was slow because they remained subject to tight restrictions. They were required, for example, to meet a 10 percent reserve requirement on deposit liabilities and they were not allowed to have domestic branches. Thus, a New York bank desiring Edge Act operations in several U.S. cities had to set up a separate subsidiary in each location. Then came the International Banking Act of 1978, which was primarily concerned with the operations of foreign banks in the United States, but which contained provisions encouraging the growth of Edge Act subsidiaries. It was followed in 1979 by the issuance of Regulation K by the Fed's Board of Governors, which applies to the foreign operations of branches of U.S. banks and to Edge Act companies. Regulation K's liberal nature and its subsequent modifications stimulated a pronounced expansion of Edge Act operations both at home and abroad.

Current Status of Edge Act Subsidiaries   Under the provisions of Section 25(a) and Regulation K, Edge Act subsidiaries are allowed to mix banking with financing in their foreign operations.[18] A regulatory distinction still exists between the two types of activity in that capital and investment restrictions imposed on Edge Act companies deemed to be engaged in general banking are more stringent than those imposed on Edge Act companies engaged primarily in financial activity. If an Edge Act subsidiary has deposit and acceptance liabilities that exceed its capital and surplus, it is considered to be engaged in

---

[18]In actuality, such mixing was made possible in 1963, but later modifications in the governing laws and regulations have liberalized it.

banking and must maintain capital and surplus equal to at least 7 percent of its "risk assets," i.e., assets other than cash, amounts due from U.S. banks, U.S. government securities, and federal funds sold. Furthermore, whereas an Edge Act subsidiary engaged in financing may invest up to 50 percent of its capital and surplus in a single venture, an Edge Act banking subsidiary is subject to a 10 percent of capital and surplus limitation on loans to a single borrower.

Edge Act subsidiaries that conduct banking operations in the United States are still confined to activity that falls within the scope of "international business." It is now possible, however, for an Edge Act subsidiary to have branches in different states. Foreign banks are allowed to form Edge Act companies and to have branches, illustrating the principle that such banks are not discriminated against by U.S. government policy. Edge Act subsidiaries may take the form of joint ventures, which means that smaller banks can effectively join forces to engage in international banking on a scale that would be beyond the capacity of the individual banks acting independently.

Largely because of the reduction of barriers to interstate banking and the expansion of IBFs, the number of Edge Act corporations has been declining in the past few years. Whereas there were 140 Edge Act corporations with 124 branches at the end of 1985, the comparable figures at the end of 1990 were 100 Edge Act corporations and 40 branches.[19] At the end of 1987, U.S.-owned Edge Act companies accounted for only 1.5 percent of total U.S. banking claims on foreigners, compared with 49.6 percent for foreign branches, 21.8 percent for foreign subsidiaries, 14.0 percent for IBFs (other than those of Edge Act companies), and 13.1 percent for other U.S. banking claims.[20]

Foreign Banks in the United States

Simultaneously with the expansion of international activity by U.S. banks, foreign-controlled banking operations have expanded very rapidly in the United States. At the end of 1990, 307 foreign banks were operating in the country. These banks had a total of 597 banking offices in the form of branches and agencies and owned 18 Edge Act companies. In addition, these foreign banks owned 25 percent or more of 90 U.S. commercial banks. The importance of these operations is underscored by the fact that the banking assets held by these banks equalled approximately 22 percent of all U.S. banking assets.[21]

The greatly expanded foreign banking presence in the United States has contributed substantially to the current chorus of protest about the extent of foreign ownership and control of the U.S. economy. This presence is intimately connected with the growth of capital inflows into the United States that became so evident in the 1980s, but it also owes much to the general increase

---

[19]Board of Governors, *Annual Report 1985*, p. 179, and *Annual Report 1990*, p. 199.

[20]James V. Houpt, "International Trends for U.S. Banks and Banking Markets," Staff Study of the Board of Governors of the Federal Reserve System, no. 156, May 1988, p. 3.

[21]Board of Governors, *Annual Report 1990*, p. 189.

in financial integration among the world's leading industrial and financial powers. U.S. banks have expanded their presence abroad at the same time that foreign banks have increased their presence in the United States. The dilemma for those who sound alarms about the selling of America is that the United States is in a poor position to reverse a trend to which it has so greatly contributed by long extolling the merits of economic openness and contributing enormously through its ideology and its own example to placing doctrines of socialism and state control on the defensive. Moreover, given the performance of the U.S. economy during the 1980s, it is difficult to argue convincingly that the growing foreign financial presence merits legislation that would prevent American citizens from selling their assets to whomever they please.

The Sovereign Debt Problem

An important feature of the contemporary international banking scene is that bank lending to the governments of LDCs and Eastern Europe continues to be influenced by the loan-service difficulties of some of these governments that erupted into a full-blown crisis in 1982. The resulting problems have not been fully resolved since then. While it is true that some governments, such as those of Chile, Mexico, and Venezuela, have made great progress in dealing with their debt-service problems, it is also true that others remain in great difficulty. The operations of the creditor banks have been profoundly affected by this situation.

Origins of the Sovereign Debt Problem

For many years after the end of World War II, there was a gradual expansion of lending by banks in developed countries to the governments of LDCs and the member countries of the Soviet Bloc. The countries that received these loans were generally considered to have good prospects for economic growth. Loan payments almost always occurred on schedule, and more and more banks sought to participate in this type of lending. Sovereign loans were especially popular among Eurobanks, but many banks operating within the framework of traditional banking also participated in them.

Following the floating of the dollar in March 1973 and the subsequent decline in the dollar's exchange value, the members of the Organization of Petroleum Exporting Countries (OPEC), who customarily priced their product in dollars, decided to try to recoup their losses by substantially raising their price. When the price increases stood up without seriously eroding their sales volume, they decided to keep pushing the price up. By the end of 1974, OPEC had succeeded in quadrupling the world price of oil.

Oil-importing countries responded to the price increases by expanding their exports and borrowing dollars from banks. The oil-exporting countries expanded their imports, but some of them had enough oil revenue left over after spending on imports so that they were able to acquire large holdings of foreign assets. Overwhelmingly, the assets acquired were in developed countries, and they included large amounts of bank time deposits in Eurobanks, real estate, and securities.

The central banks of developed countries responded to this situation by allowing the reserves of commercial banks to expand rapidly. Accordingly, banks sought outlets for these resources, and prominent among the uses were sovereign loans to LDCs and members of the Soviet Bloc. Sovereign borrowers had established good credit records on previous borrowings, and the lending banks tended to ignore the fact that these credit records had been achieved by effectively using new loans to pay old ones. Public officials in developed countries encouraged banks to make sovereign loans in which banks would "recycle" the earnings (petrodollars) of OPEC countries by lending to oil-importing countries, thereby permitting these countries to maintain their momentum of economic growth.

LDCs had been exempted from the restrictions on capital outflows imposed by the U.S. government during the 1960s, and the governments of developed countries actively promoted bank lending to LDCs, even to Communist countries, in order to expand their exports and promote economic development in the borrowing countries. In the United States, the impressive profits obtained by money-center banks from sovereign loans induced many regional banks to obtain some of this business by participating in syndicated lending arrangements worked out by money-center banks.

Another factor contributing to the development of the sovereign loan problem was the preference of LDC and Communist governments for borrowing over equity investment by foreigners. In general, these governments were strongly biased against foreign ownership and free markets. Given the availability of bank loans on attractive terms, these governments saw little reason to welcome foreign owners. Furthermore, many of the fields in which foreign equity investors would have been interested were dominated by state-owned enterprises, which often operated at losses and had almost insatiable appetites for advanced technology and imported capital equipment. Foreign borrowing represented a way to partly satisfy that voracious appetite.

Floating Loan Rates   At the time of the OPEC price increases of 1973 and 1974, sovereign lending customarily occurred at fixed interest rates. As inflation increased, and with it interest rate uncertainty, banks began protecting themselves by inserting floating-rate provisions into their new sovereign loan agreements. The most popular benchmark interest rate for floating-rate bank loans was the 6-month LIBOR (London Interbank Offered Rate), but other rates, including the U.S. prime lending rate, were used. Under floating-rate provisions, loan rates were to be adjusted periodically to reflect what had happened to the benchmark rate.

During the latter part of the 1970s, nominal interest rate increases lagged behind increases in inflation rates, with the result that realized real interest rates tended to become negative. Coinciding with the negative turn in real interest rates, LDC exports expanded rapidly. Thanks to these developments, the debtor governments generally handled their obligations with what seemed to be surprising ease. By 1979, observers generally believed that the recycling problem had been handled smoothly and that debtor countries had additional borrowing capacity. Meanwhile, some oil-exporting countries, including Mexico, Venezuela, and Nigeria, had joined the ranks of heavily indebted nations because their governments' spending grew even faster than their oil revenues.

From Problem to Crisis   From 1974 to 1979, OPEC raised the price of oil several times by relatively small increments designed to keep pace with inflation and compensate for the downward trend in the dollar's exchange value. Earlier cartels in primary products had foundered within a few years after being launched because of disputes over market shares and an inability to weather declines in demand without breaking ranks. As the 1970s wore on, however, with little obvious evidence that OPEC had overreached itself, most observers concluded that OPEC was unlike past cartels. Despite the development of new sources of supply for oil and great improvements in fuel efficiency, most market forecasts assumed that the real price of oil would continue to rise.

In 1979 and 1980, the cartel decided to push again for large increases in the real price of oil. This time, however, it misjudged market conditions and the cohesiveness of its membership, and after some additional, though small, increases in 1981, the dollar price of oil began to decline. While the price declines were, in themselves, good news for oil importers, they occurred in combination with other developments that turned the debt problem into a crisis.

A major reason for the emergence of the sovereign debt crisis was that the United States and other leading countries decided, beginning in 1979, to follow a policy of monetary restraint in order to curb inflation. As a result, real interest rates rose sharply. In the United States, the realized real interest rate swung from being slightly negative during much of the 1970s to a positive 5 percent in 1982.[22] The increases in real interest rates reflected the behavior of market interest rates, and the increases in market interest rates led to large interest rate adjustments on outstanding floating-rate loans. Simultaneously, and largely because of the policy of monetary restraint, a worldwide recession developed that produced, among other things, a decline in the exports of heavily indebted countries. In addition, the exchange value of the dollar began moving upward, thereby causing difficulties for the many governments with large amounts of bank debt denominated in dollars. Some of the impact of these developments is seen in the fact that western hemisphere LDCs experienced an increase in the ratio of debt-service payments (including interest and amortization) to exports of goods and services from the already worrisome figure of 37.9 percent in 1978 to the staggering level of 49.6 percent in 1982.[23]

The first government to fail to meet its international debt-service obligations was Poland's in 1980. When confronted with the question of

---

[22]The real interest rate here is the nominal interest rate on U.S. Treasury bills minus the implicit GNP deflator.

[23]IMF, *World Economic Outlook*, April 1986, p. 242.

whether or not to declare the government of Poland in default, the governments of creditor nations backed down. To have declared Poland in default would have immediately endangered the solvency of some banks and would also have established a dangerous precedent. It was now clear that many countries had potential debt-service problems and that widespread defaults would be a catastrophe for the banking systems of developed countries. Consequently, the governments of the creditor countries allowed the Polish government to reschedule its debt-service payments.

Heavily indebted LDCs staved off international bankruptcy until August 1982, when Mexico's government announced that it could no longer honor its debt-service obligations. In short order, Mexico was joined by a number of other countries, including Brazil (in 1983), the LDC with the largest international indebtedness. Suddenly, most bank loans to LDC governments looked questionable. Some idea of the magnitude of the lending banks' problem is conveyed by the fact that in 1982, the nine largest money-center banks in the United States had outstanding LDC loans that exceeded 250 percent of their capital, while the U.S. commercial banking system as a whole had a ratio of LDC loans to capital that exceeded 150 percent.[24]

Managing the Sovereign Debt Problem

The general reaction of governments in both debtor and creditor countries to the sovereign debt crisis was to avoid declarations of default and to try to muddle through, hoping that the problem would be resolved with the passage of time. The Bank for International Settlements (BIS), an institution owned and operated by European central banks, provided short-term financial assistance to central banks in countries with acute debt-service problems until financing could be arranged from the IMF and other sources.[25] The IMF provided credit to financially troubled countries and began working out debt rescheduling programs with debtor governments that were to be supported by additional credits furnished by commercial banks. In addition, the World Bank and its "soft loan" affiliate, the International Development Association (IDA),

---

[24]Stanley Fischer, "Sharing the Burden of the International Debt Crisis," *American Economic Association Papers and Proceedings*, May 1987, p. 166.

[25]As was pointed out in Chapter 3, the BIS is a bank for central banks that performs services for European central banks and governments, including acting as a clearing agent for private Ecu clearing systems. The activities of the BIS extend beyond Europe, however, and it has become actively involved in helping central banks outside Europe and in promoting cooperation among central banks on a worldwide scale. Since the middle of the 1980s, the BIS has taken a leading role in promoting the establishment of uniform capital requirements for internationally operating commercial banks domiciled in the leading financial countries. At present, central banks in Europe, Japan, and North America are in the process of implementing the capital requirements that they have agreed to in meetings worked out under BIS auspices.

provided substantial credits to heavily indebted LDC governments.[26] Although the World Bank and the IDA provide long-term development financing, not short-term emergency credits, they arranged development loans that helped to alleviate the borrower's short-term financial problems.

The Policies of the Banks   Initially, and in cooperation with the IMF, creditor banks supplied additional funds to governments that were unable to service existing obligations. They did so in order to forestall defaults (which would have produced mandatory write-offs) and because they hoped to ultimately collect on loans that would otherwise have proved uncollectible. By 1986, however, banks' willingness to further increase their exposures to heavily indebted governments was rapidly diminishing.

The basic strategy of the creditor banks was to avoid write-offs while simultaneously increasing their capital. Their governments cooperated by avoiding official declarations of default and allowing uncollectible loans to be carried on the books at face value. An active market developed in trading past-due debt at deep discounts. Although the discounts provided a basis for writing down the book values of the debt remaining in banks' hands, the banks successfully resisted the implementation of write-down proposals for several years.

Soon after Mexico's government suspended its loan payments in 1982, it became evident to almost everyone that the creditor banks could not avoid large losses. It also became clear that the development prospects of heavily indebted countries would remain dismal as long as their debt problems remained unresolved. Accordingly, opinion tended to coalesce around the idea of allowing debtor governments to write off substantial amounts of their debt, provided that they adopted major structural economic reforms that would tend to encourage economic growth.

U.S. banks tended to be relatively resistant to the idea of negotiated write-offs. Their representatives argued, plausibly, that profound structural reforms should be in place *before* allowing large-scale debt write-offs. Less plausibly, they also argued that fairness to their stockholders required that write-off proposals be resisted. No one forced the banks to lend the money, however, and the stockholders who stood to gain from better-than-expected loan recoveries were not necessarily those who were hurt when the extent of

---

[26]Recall from Chapter 2 that the World Bank, known formally as the International Bank for Reconstruction and Development, grew out of the Bretton Woods Conference. It specializes in long-term development loans that are repayable in hard currency. Some of its capital has come from members' subscriptions and profits, but most of it has been raised by selling bonds in leading capital markets.

The IDA came into existence in 1980 for the purpose of making loans on a concessional basis, i.e., with below-market interest rates and very long repayment periods. Its loans tend to go to the poorer LDCs, whereas World Bank loans tend to go to comparatively wealthy LDCs. Since its lending is unprofitable, new capital is raised by the IDA from periodic contributions by the wealthier nations. In other words, IDA loans are fundamentally financed by contributions from the taxpayers of developed countries.

the sovereign loan problem first became clear. The stocks of money-center banks plunged sharply in price in the early 1980s, and there was a great turnover in bank stock ownership as investors adjusted their portfolios.

In order to increase their capital, the creditor banks launched all-out efforts to increase their profits, and they avoided making large dividend payments. The highly innovative behavior that has characterized money-center banks since 1982 has been due, in no small part, to their effort to recover from the sovereign debt problem. As banks' capital positions have improved, they have set aside portions of their capital as loan loss reserves. As things now stand, the sovereign debt problem is no longer a major threat to the solvency of money-center banks.

Four techniques stand out regarding how banks have managed their uncollectible debt: the sale of debt, debt-for-debt swaps, debt-equity swaps, and securitization. In addition, there have been debt write-downs independent of the use of these techniques. The resulting reductions in principal amounts have been large enough so that, notwithstanding the addition of unpaid interest to the amounts in arrears, the overall quantity of the problem debt is declining.

In debt-for-debt swaps, creditors exchange the delinquent debt of different countries. For example, Bank A might swap claims on the government of Brazil to Bank B in exchange for claims on one or more other governments. In debt-for-equity swaps, creditors surrender claims on governments in exchange for ownership rights, which they either exercise or convey to third parties. If a creditor acquires an enterprise, it gets a chance to recoup its loss if it can run the enterprise profitably. If it conveys all or part of the enterprise to a third party, it probably gets cash and/or another claim that has a high probability of being paid. A problem with debt-equity swaps is that they generally require an injection of local currency into an economy that already has a serious inflation problem. This is because the government involved must ordinarily come up with cash for the former owners and some of the creditors of the affected enterprise. A variation of this technique is to give the equity-receiving party shares in an investment fund.

In securitization, debt is discounted and replaced with securities whose soundness is guaranteed in full or in part. The debtor government may pledge some of its forex reserves as collateral, or the securities it issues may be supported by guarantees provided by one or more governments and/or an international agency.

The Brady Initiative   During the Reagan administration, the U.S. government opposed negotiated write-offs, but in 1989, the Bush administration's Secretary of the Treasury, Nicholas Brady, advanced a plan, known as the Brady Initiative, that substantially altered the no write-off position. Under this plan, debt-relief agreements are negotiated on a case-by-case basis with individual governments. Relief is conditional on the adoption of structural reforms and involves the joint participation of creditor banks, the IMF, and the World Bank.

The first concrete result of the Brady Initiative was an agreement with the government of Mexico in March 1990. Creditor banks could choose among three options: exchanging claims at a discount for highly collateralized bonds paying a market interest rate; exchanging claims on a one-for-one basis for less highly collateralized bonds paying a slightly below-market interest rate; and retaining their existing claims on Mexico, in which case the creditors were required to provide new loans to the Mexican government equivalent to 25 percent of the amount of the existing loans. The government of Mexico committed itself to providing debt-equity swaps, to a program of limited debt buybacks, to a recapture clause that allowed creditors who agreed to debt write-downs to receive additional compensation should the price of oil rise beyond a certain point by 1996, and to the continuation of the extensive structural reform program that it had already adopted.

The Mexican agreement cleared the way for Mexico to receive new credits from the IMF and the World Bank. Most creditors opted for either the par-value bonds or the discount bonds, but Mexico did receive some additional bank loans. Since the signing of the Mexican agreement, a number of other governments have worked out Brady Initiative proposals. Such agreements have not yet been reached with the governments of Brazil and Argentina, but those governments have reduced the volume of the problem loans through a combination of write-downs by banks and government buybacks at deep discounts.

Putting the Sovereign Loan Problem in Perspective

The sovereign loan problem has had disastrous effects on the economies of many LDCs and has profoundly affected international banking. This does not mean, however, that bankers in high-income countries have written off the developing world and decided to confine their lending to countries in their own category. Note, for example, that Exhibit 12.1 indicates that at the end of 1990, reporting area banks held $718.6 billion in claims on countries outside the reporting area, and that this figure represented 21.4 percent of the estimated $3,350.0 billion in net international bank credit. Some of this $718.6 billion represented credit extended to Middle Eastern oil exporting countries and to Australia and New Zealand, but the vast majority of it consisted of claims on developing countries other than Middle Eastern oil exporters. While Exhibit 12.1 indicates that the net expansion of bank lending to countries outside the reporting area from 1987 to 1990 was very modest, it should be taken into account that there were large write-downs of debt during this period. A fair conclusion, therefore, is that the bank loan spigot to the developing world has not been cut off.

Exhibit 12.6 furnishes data on the external indebtedness of developing countries from 1983 to 1991. The data are from the IMF's *World Economic Outlook* and include the former USSR and the countries of Eastern Europe among the developing countries. Particularly relevant as far as the sovereign debt problem is concerned are the 15 countries classified as heavily indebted:

| E X H I B I T | 12.6 | *External Debt Indicators of Developing Countries: Year-End, 1983–1991 (In Billions of U.S. Dollars)*

Indicator	1983	1985	1987	1989	1990	1991[a]
Total external debt of developing countries[b]	925.5	1,059.2	1,310.5	1,368.7	1,466.4	1,493.7
By type of creditor						
Official	283.7	358.5	501.7	540.6	601.4	597.3
Commercial banks	487.2	519.5	602.4	588.4	594.3	608.4
Other private	154.7	181.1	206.4	239.7	270.7	288.0
Fifteen heavily indebted countries	394.7	419.2	490.5	480.0	508.2	502.0
By type of creditor						
Official	63.0	88.3	132.0	151.6	181.9	174.9
Commercial banks	271.3	278.8	303.3	276.4	271.3	270.0
Other private	60.4	52.0	55.2	52.1	55.0	57.1
Eastern Europe and the USSR	99.5	114.2	141.5	153.1	174.8	174.6
By type of creditor						
Official	32.4	37.1	45.8	43.6	50.8	48.3
Commercial banks	56.2	65.8	86.5	94.1	98.9	89.7
Other private	10.9	11.3	9.2	15.5	25.1	36.6
Other developing countries	431.3	525.8	678.5	735.6	783.4	817.1
By type of creditor						
Official	188.3	233.1	323.9	345.4	368.7	374.1
Commercial banks	159.7	174.9	212.6	217.9	224.1	248.7
Other private	83.4	117.8	142.0	172.2	190.6	194.3
Debt-service ratios (percent)[c]						
All developing countries	17.0	19.3	18.3	15.4	14.1	16.1
Fifteen heavily indebted countries	41.6	40.9	37.8	31.0	27.9	37.1
Eastern Europe and the USSR	11.6	13.6	12.1	12.2	11.9	17.0
Sub-Saharan Africa	21.7	22.4	21.4	21.2	22.5	24.5
Four newly industrializing Asian economies	8.9	9.3	10.5	4.5	3.3	3.3

[a]All 1991 estimates are projections as of the fall of 1991.

[b]Excludes liabilities to the IMF.

[c]Ratios of interest payments on total debt plus amortization payments on long-term debt only to total exports of goods and services. Payments on debt owed to the IMF are excluded.

Source: IMF, *World Economic Outlook*, October 1991, pp. 147, 151, 154.

Argentina, Bolivia, Brazil, Chile, Colombia, Ecuador, Ivory Coast, Mexico, Morocco, Nigeria, Peru, the Philippines, Uruguay, Venezuela, and Yugoslavia. Accordingly, data for the countries in this category appear in Exhibit 12.6, which also includes external debt and debt-service data for Eastern Europe and the USSR, and debt-service data for sub-Saharan Africa and four newly industrializing countries in Asia: Hong Kong, Singapore, South Korea, and Taiwan.

From 1983 to 1991 there was a modest overall increase in bank lending to developing countries. All of this increase went to countries other than the 15 heavily indebted countries. In 1983, these 15 countries accounted for $271.3 billion of a total of $487.2 billion in liabilities to foreign commercial banks. In 1991, the comparable figures were $270.0 billion and $608.4 billion, respectively. Clearly, there was a substantial increase in bank lending to developing countries other than the 15 most heavily indebted countries. Exhibit 12.6 shows that the group of countries represented by Eastern Europe and the USSR substantially increased its net borrowings from foreign banks. Data not presented in Exhibit 12.6 make it clear that, in general, developing countries other than the 15 heavily indebted countries and the four newly industrializing countries in Asia increased their indebtedness to foreign commercial banks by amounts that ranged from modest to large. Exhibit 12.6 supports this statement by showing that other developing countries increased their borrowings from foreign commercial banks from $159.7 billion in 1983 to $248.7 billion in 1991. It is noteworthy that much of the increase indicated occurred because of guarantees provided to commercial bank lenders by the governments of developed countries for the purpose of promoting exports to developing countries.

The debt-service data from Exhibit 12.6 point to the persistence of fairly high ratios of interest and amortization payments to exports of goods and services for the developing countries as a whole. There has been some improvement in the debt-service ratios of the most heavily indebted countries, but these ratios remain high. The high debt-service ratios for sub-Saharan Africa imply continuing difficulty for that part of the world in terms of establishing creditworthiness, and, indeed, most developing countries are seriously constrained in terms of borrowing ability by their debt-service ratios. An inevitable conclusion from the data in Exhibit 12.6 is that the growth of commercial bank lending to developing countries depends greatly on the ability of developing countries to expand their exports.

In the future, the developing countries that are most successful in obtaining financial assistance from foreign commercial banks are going to be the countries that are most successful in expanding exports and attracting direct foreign investment. There is an enormous potential for the expansion of bank lending to the countries of Eastern Europe and the former Soviet Union, but the current economic chaos and political uncertainty in those countries had led to a wait-and-see attitude on the part of bankers. In any event, there is enough promise in the developing world so that one should not rule out the possibility of a great expansion of international banking activity in it.

Summary

Most international lending by banks occurs in the Eurocurrency market, but international lending within the framework of traditional banking continues to be important, particularly in connection with financing exports and loans for small amounts that are common in the Eurocurrency market. Much of the international activity of banks consists of interbank transactions, and the vast majority of international bank lending to non-bank borrowers goes to borrowers in economically developed countries. Commercial banks are, however, a very important credit source for developing countries.

In BA financing, which is generally associated with international trade, banks lend their good names rather than their money. Some BAs, however, are held by banks as investments. BA financing is generally cheaper than direct borrowing from banks, but there has been a tendency for it to decline. One reason for the decline is the growing importance of CP, which consists of unsecured notes that are sold, usually on a discount basis, either to CP dealers or in direct placements to investors. In the United States, CP dealers are primarily investment banks.

The alternative formats for establishing an international banking presence in foreign countries include correspondent relationships, representative offices, branches, and subsidiaries. These last two formats come under consideration when a bank desires to establish full-service operations. The importance of the practice of acquiring a foreign subsidiary by acquiring a controlling interest in a local bank is increasing. Edge Act companies are subsidiaries of U.S. or foreign banks that are located in the United States and engage in international banking. Their importance is relatively minor.

The sovereign debt problem afflicting commercial banks has been a major factor affecting international banking since 1982. It resulted from an unsound expansion of bank lending to the governments of developing countries that was brought to an abrupt halt by rising interest rates and other factors. Since 1982, the creditor banks have made much headway against this problem, but much of the problem remains unresolved. The sovereign debt problem has profoundly affected international banking and placed great pressure on money-center banks to increase their capital. Notwithstanding the sovereign loan problem, however, bank lending to developing countries has increased overall since 1982.

References

Ball, Clifford A., and Adrian E. Tschoegl. "The Decision to Establish a Foreign Bank Branch or Subsidiary: An Application of Binary Classification Procedures." *Journal of Financial and Quantitative Analysis*, September 1982, pp. 411–424.

Bank for International Settlements. *Annual Report*. Basle: BIS, annual.

Berglund, Milton E. "Representative Offices." In William Baughn and Donald R. Mandich, eds. *The International Banking Handbook*. Homewood, Ill.: Dow Jones-Irwin, 1983, pp. 594–602.

Board of Governors of the Federal Reserve System. *Annual Report*.

Bulow, Jeremy, and Kenneth Rogoff. "The Buyback Boondoggle." *Brookings Papers on Economic Activity* (1988), pp. 675–704.

Eiteman, David K., and Arthur I. Stonehill. *Multinational Business Finance*, 6th ed. Reading, Mass.: Addison-Wesley, 1992, Chapter 10.

Euromoney (Monthly).

Evans, Richard. "Are Barclays Days of Empire Over?" *Euromoney*, June 1986, pp. 55–64.

_____. "New Debts for Old—And the Swapper Is King." *Euromoney*, September 1987, pp. 72–91.

Federal Reserve Bulletin (Monthly).

Fischer, Stanley. "Sharing the Burden of the International Debt Crisis." *American Economic Association Papers and Proceedings,* May 1987, pp. 165–170.

Heller, H. Robert. "The Debt Crisis and the Future of International Bank Lending." *American Economic Association Papers and Proceedings,* May 1987, pp. 171–175.

Houpt, James V. "International Trends for U.S. Banks and Banking Markets." *Staff Study of the Board of Governors of the Federal Reserve System,* no. 156, May 1988.

Hurley, C. Keefe, Jr. "The Federal Reserve System and Regulation and International Banking." In William Baughn and Donald R. Mandich, eds. *The International Banking Handbook,* Homewood, Ill.: Dow Jones-Irwin, 1983, pp. 751–763.

International Monetary Fund. *World Economic Outlook* (several issues per year).

Jain, Arvind K., and Douglas Nigh. "Politics and the International Lending Decisions of Banks." *Journal of International Business Studies,* Summer 1989, pp. 349–359.

Jensen, Frederick H., and Patrick M. Parkinson. "Recent Developments in the Bankers' Acceptance Market." *Federal Reserve Bulletin,* January 1986, pp. 1–12.

Johnson, Ronald A., Venkat Srinivasan, and Paul J. Bolster. "Sovereign Debt Ratings: A Judgmental Model Based on the Analytic Hierarchy Process." *Journal of International Business Studies,* First Quarter 1990, pp. 95–117.

Kettell, Brian, and George R. Magnue. *The International Debt Game: A Study in International Banking Lending.* Cambridge, Mass.: Ballinger Publishing, 1986.

Khoury, Sarkis J. "Sovereign Debt: A Critical Look at the Causes and the Nature of the Problem." *Essays in International Business,* Columbia, S.C.: University of South Carolina, Center for International Business Studies, July 1985.

Krueger, Anne O. "Debt, Capital Flows, and LDC Growth." *American Economic Review Papers and Proceedings,* May 1987, pp. 159–164.

Makin, John H. *The Global Debt Crisis: America's Growing Involvement.* New York: Basic Books, 1984.

Marsh, Donald R. "Foreign Branches." In William H. Baughn and Donald R. Mandich, eds. *The International Banking Handbook.* Homewood, Ill.: Dow Jones-Irwin, 1983, pp. 557–579.

Naveja, Albert F. "Correspondent Banking." In William H. Baughn and Donald R. Mandich, eds. *The International Banking Handbook,* Homewood, Ill.: Dow Jones-Irwin, 1983, pp. 580–593.

Nigh, Douglas, Kang Rae Cho, and Suresh Krishnan. "The Role of Location-Related Factors in U.S. Banking Involvement Abroad: An Empirical Examination." *Journal of International Business Studies,* Fall 1986, pp. 59–72.

Shapiro, Alan C. "Currency Risk and Country Risk in International Banking." *Journal of Finance,* July 1985, pp. 881–891.

————. "International Banking and Country Risk Analysis." *Midland Corporate Finance Journal,* Fall 1986, pp. 56–64.

Stone, E. C. "Edge Act and Agreement Corporations." In William H. Baughn and Donald R. Mandich, eds. *The International Banking Handbook.* Homewood, Ill.: Dow Jones-Irwin, 1983, pp. 603–611.

Sutin, Steward. "Foreign Affiliates and Subsidiaries." In William H. Baughn and Donald R. Mandich, eds. *The International Banking Handbook.* Homewood, Ill.: Dow Jones-Irwin, 1983, pp. 580–593.

Tschoegl, Adrian E. "International Retail Banking as a Strategy: An Assessment." *Journal of International Business Studies,* Summer 1987, pp. 67–88.

Weaving, Rachel. "Measuring Developing Countries' External Debt." *Finance and Development*, March 1987, pp. 16–19.

Wood, John H., and Norma L. Wood. *Financial Markets*. San Diego: Harcourt, Brace, Jovanovich, 1985, Chapter 8.

Questions

1. While the concept of an international financial transaction applies to transfers of assets between residents of different nations, some international financial transactions take place between residents of the same nation. Give examples.
2. What are merchant banks? How do they differ from investment banks?
3. It can be determined from Exhibit 12.2 that as of the end of 1990, U.S. banks accounted for less than 10 percent of the external claims of banks in reporting area countries. Does a 10 percent share fairly reflect the relative importance of U.S. banks in international banking?
4. Banking protectionism means that a government restricts the ability of foreign banks to compete within its jurisdiction. What are the possible costs of such a policy?
5. Although interest rates are generally slightly lower in the Eurocurrency market than in traditional banking markets, much international lending by banks occurs through traditional channels. Why?
6. Compare the roles of commercial banks as sources of credit in the BA and CP markets in the United States.
7. Even though the interest cost of conventional bank borrowing is generally higher than the discount rates applied on commercial paper, borrowers often choose direct borrowing from banks over CP. Why?
8. Assuming that a bank already has a correspondent relationship with a bank in a certain foreign country, why might it wish to establish a representative office there?
9. Given a choice between setting up a foreign branch or having a foreign subsidiary, what circumstances would induce a bank to favor the branch? What circumstances would favor the subsidiary?
10. What are the differences between Edge Act and Agreement corporations, and why is neither a major factor in U.S. international banking at the present time?
11. Although OPEC oil price increases contributed greatly to the development of the sovereign debt crisis that erupted in 1982, the world price of oil decreased before the crisis occurred. Why did the oil price reductions fail to prevent the crisis from occurring?
12. Summarize the strategies and techniques used by creditor banks to cope with the sovereign loan problem.
13. Summarize the Brady Initiative agreement reached in 1990 with the government of Mexico.
14. Based on the data in Exhibit 12.6, analyze how the external indebtedness of developing countries has changed since 1982.

CHAPTER 13

The Eurocurrency Market

■

As was pointed out in the last chapter, most international banking occurs in the Eurocurrency market, whose operations are denominated in currencies other than those of the countries in which they are carried out. This market's origins were examined in Chapter 2, and Chapter 6 stressed its importance for interest arbitrage and the maintenance of IRP. Chapters 2 and 12 referred to the offshore banking centers that are attached to the Eurocurrency market. Chapters 4 and 12 referred briefly to IBFs, which are also a part of the Eurocurrency market. Chapter 6 provided a footnote reference to the offshoot of the Eurocurrency market known as the *Asia currency market*. Until now, however, this book has not provided a systematic account of the Eurocurrency market's composition and the nature of its operations. The purpose of this chapter is to provide such an account.

An Overview of the Eurocurrency Market

Earlier, it was indicated that Eurocurrencies are typically time deposits denominated in currencies other than those of the countries in which they are located. They come into being when parties shift bank deposits denominated in given currencies to banks in other countries without changing the currencies of denomination. If, for example, a Middle Eastern oil exporter accepts a $20 million demand deposit in a bank in the United States and then elects to exchange these funds for a dollar-denominated time deposit in a bank in the United Kingdom, the time deposit is a Eurodollar deposit. The ownership of the demand deposit in the United States passes from the exporter to a bank in the United Kingdom, which then turns the bulk of the funds into earning assets.

It was also indicated earlier that the Eurocurrency market's existence derives from its comparative freedom from government control, which allows it great flexibility and gives it competitive advantages in terms of deposit and loan rates. In addition, it was indicated that lending in the Eurocurrency market is relatively short-term by comparison with bond financing, but that the Eurocurrency market's maturities overlap those of bonds. Eurocurrency market lending is commonly on a floating-rate basis. The broad outline of the market's operation has thus been presented. All that remains is to fill in the details.

The Expansion of Eurocurrency Deposits

Assume that a Belgian firm, B, sells $4 million worth of precision medical equipment to a U.S. firm, M, receiving in payment a demand deposit of $4 million with Citibank of New York. Because B does not need to use the funds immediately and desires to earn interest on them, it places them in a 90-day Eurodollar deposit with National Westminster Bank in London. As a result, the ownership of the $4 million demand deposit in Citibank passes from B to National Westminster.

National Westminster now has a liability on which it must pay interest that is offset by a nonearning asset. It is thus under pressure to rapidly convert the demand deposit with Citibank into one or more earning assets. Like banks in domestic financial markets, its normal course of action would be to lend such surplus funds directly, but it may well choose an alternative. If it chooses direct lending, it has various possibilities in terms of currencies and lending locations. It could turn the funds over to a National Westminster branch in the United States for lending there, or it could exchange them for pounds and lend domestically. In either of these cases, our example would come to an end since we would no longer be in the Eurocurrency market. Assuming, however, that National Westminster chooses to use the funds in the Eurocurrency market, the possibilities include lending dollars from its London offices, purchasing dollar-denominated securities, lending dollars to another Eurobank, or converting the dollars into a currency other than the pound and using the funds in that form.

When a bank lends to another bank in the Eurocurrency market, the standard procedure is for the lending bank to exchange a demand deposit for a time deposit in the borrowing bank on which the lending bank receives the prevailing LIBOR rate for loans of the same maturity. This rate is normally a bit higher than the standard Eurocurrency deposit rate paid to nonbank depositors, the difference between the two rates commonly being 0.125 percent. If, for example, National Westminster pays 9.125 percent on its time deposit liability to B, it may well obtain 9.250 percent on a Eurodollar time deposit from a bank that is anxious to acquire additional funds. Note that if National Westminster elects to lend all $4 million to another bank at the LIBOR, the quantity of Eurodollars created up to this point rises to $8 million.

Assume, however, that National Westminster lends all $4 million to Firm U, a British company, and that U uses $1 million to pay for an import from Firm X in the United States and $2 million to pay for an import from Firm L in Brazil. Also assume that the remaining $1 million is exchanged at National Westminster for DM2 million and used to pay for an import from Firm G in Germany. Now assume that Firm X elects to place its $1 million in a demand deposit in Bank One of Ohio to cover payroll outlays, that Firm L places its $2 million in a dollar-denominated IBF account with Chase Manhattan Bank of New York, and that Firm G deposits the DM2 million in a mark-denominated deposit with the Luxembourg subsidiary of Deutsche Bank of Germany. To keep things "simple," assume that the marks sold by National Westminster were from a demand deposit in Deutsche Bank of Germany. The net effects of these transactions on the various banks are, at this point, as follows (in millions of dollars):

National Westminster		Citibank	
Demand deposit in Citibank+$1 Loan to U +$4 Demand deposit in Deutsche Bank of Germany −$1	Eurodollar time deposit of B +$4	Federal Reserve account −$3	Demand deposit of M −$4 Demand deposit of Na-tional West-minster +$1

Chase Manhattan		Bank One	
Federal Reserve acccount +$2	IBF time deposit of L +$2	Federal Reserve account +$1	Demand deposit of X +$1

Deutsche Bank, Luxembourg		Deutsche Bank, Germany	
Demand deposit in Deutsche Bank, Germany +$1	Euromark time deposit of G +$1		Demand deposit of National Westminster −$1 Demand deposit of Deutsche Bank, Luxem-bourg +$1

According to these T-accounts, the quantity of Eurodollars created is now $6 million, consisting of B's $4 million time deposit in National Westminster and L's $2 million IBF time deposit in Chase. Firm L's IBF deposit is counted as a Eurodollar deposit even though it is denominated in dollars and held in a bank in the United States because, as is explained later in the chapter, IBFs are basically treated as if they are located outside the United States. Since the DM2 million time deposit of Firm G with Deutsche Bank in Luxembourg, valued at $1 million in the T-accounts, is also a Eurocurrency deposit, the total quantity of such deposits created is, so far, $7 million.

As things now stand, some additional creation of Eurocurrency deposits may occur since Chase has, assuming it clears its claim on Citibank through the Federal Reserve banks, $2 million in additional reserves in its IBF account, while Deutsche Bank in Luxembourg has the equivalent of $1 million in reserves because of its DM2 million deposit with Deutsche Bank of Germany. In both cases, it is likely that the reserves will further increase the volume of Eurocurrency deposits.

Notice that $1 million in reserves leaked from the Eurocurrency market when Firm X elected to deposit the funds it received from Firm U with Bank One. In like manner, if G had chosen to deposit its DM2 million with Deutsche

Bank of Germany instead of the Luxembourg branch, another $1 million of reserves would have leaked from the Eurocurrency market. Thus, any time that funds that are lent or otherwise disbursed in the Eurocurrency market are deposited in a bank account denominated in the home currency of the bank involved, those funds leave the Eurocurrency market unless they are in IBFs (or the IBF-like "offshore market" of Japan).

It is evident that the process of Eurocurrency deposit expansion closely resembles the process of domestic bank deposit expansion with which the reader is presumably familiar. There are, however, important differences between the two processes. When, for example, the Fed provides new reserves for the U.S. banking system by purchasing securities in the open market, commercial banks and other depository institutions expand their deposits by a multiple of the amount of the new reserves. Given the quantity of reserves created, the ultimate expansion of deposits depends on the required reserve ratios of the different categories of deposits. It also depends on the quantity of excess reserves, if any, retained by depository institutions as they expand their deposits and the reserve drain or leakage caused by increases of currency in circulation.

In the Eurocurrency market, the reserves consist, for the most part, of deposits in home country commercial banks, not deposits in central banks. Also, there are no reserve requirements, and reserve leakage occurs when deposits denominated in the home country currency are made in home country banks, not because of increases of currency in circulation. Moreover, in domestic deposit expansion, some of the deposits created, namely demand deposits, can be used as a medium of exchange and are unambiguously money. In the Eurocurrency market, the deposits created are time deposits and are, therefore, excluded from the M1 money stock.

Since Eurocurrency deposits are not subject to reserve requirements, the potential expansion of such deposits after additions to the reserve stock would theoretically be very high if the leakages were small. Eurobanks need to hold some reserves for the redemption of maturing liabilities, but it is so easy for them to acquire needed currencies that they ordinarily need to hold very small amounts of reserves behind Eurocurrency time deposit liabilities, such as 1 or 2 percent of those liabilities. In reality, however, the leakages are normally so large that the Eurocurrency deposit multiplier is usually smaller than domestic deposit multipliers. Still, there is no doubt that the Eurocurrency market has substantially increased the world's volume of bank deposits.

Almost since economists became aware of the Eurocurrency market's significance, some have worried about the possibility that its unregulated creation of deposits would have inflationary and other adverse implications for the world economy. The market's apologists argue, however, that since Eurocurrency deposits are not a medium of exchange, and since governments can still control M1 money supplies, the inflationary implications of Eurocurrency deposit expansion, if any, are not serious. Moreover, they contend, the gains in the efficiency with which capital is used more than compensate for any other problems caused by the Eurocurrency market, notably problems associated with looser bank regulation.

The Structure of the Eurocurrency Market

Because of its freedom from regulation, the Eurocurrency market offers attractive interest rates to both borrowers and lenders, flexible financial arrangements, and tax advantages. The market's structure, however, bars small-scale borrowers from participating. At the retail level, deposits for small amounts can be obtained, but at the more significant wholesale level, Eurodollar deposits are customarily in multiples of $500,000. This $500,000 figure represents a virtual minimum for a Eurocurrency loan. At the other extreme, very large loans, possibly for a billion dollars or more, are made through syndicated loan arrangements, in which a number of banks participate as lenders. Eurodollar futures and option contracts are traded on the exchanges, but their contract size is so large as to inhibit participation by small-scale speculators and hedgers.

The Interest Rate Advantage   The Eurocurrency market is closely integrated with interbank forex operations, and both depend on an elaborate and efficient communications network that is expensive to operate in an absolute sense, but offers a low cost per unit of money in large transactions. Indeed, a major reason that the Eurocurrency market offers relatively attractive interest rates to both borrowers and depositors is that its unit transaction costs are relatively low because of the large scale of its transactions.

There are, of course, other reasons for the Eurocurrency market's relatively attractive interest rates. The absence of reserve requirements means that a higher percentage of banks' Eurobanking assets are in earning form as compared to their domestic banking assets, and the vigorous competition among Eurobanks assures that both borrowers and depositors share in the resulting gains. Costs arising from complying with government regulations are low, and there are no deposit insurance assessments. Borrowers in the Eurocurrency market are normally well-enough known that their creditworthiness need not be investigated extensively, if at all. Eurobanks are not required to make loans on concessionary terms to favored classes of borrowers, as banks operating in domestic markets are sometimes required to do, which frees them from the resulting pressure to raise the interest rates charged to other borrowers. No taxes are withheld from interest payments to Eurocurrency depositors, and the taxes and fees levied on Eurobanking operations are generally lower than those applied to domestic banking.

The fact that the interest rates paid on Eurocurrency deposits tend to be somewhat higher than those on domestic deposits is not entirely explained by the factors that have just been mentioned, though. The interest rate differential exists in part because Eurocurrency deposit rates *must* normally be higher than domestic deposit rates to attract funds. Eurocurrency deposits are not insured, and the governments of the countries in which they are located are less likely to rescue banks with problems arising from Eurobanking operations than they are to aid banks with problems related to domestic conditions. One reason for this is that Eurobanks are frequently foreign-owned, but a more basic reason is that the freedom of Eurobanks from regulation also frees governments from the responsibility to save them from the consequences of adverse events. The risk of holding Eurocurrency deposits thus appears to be greater than that of holding domestic deposits.

While holding Eurocurrency deposits may entail additional risk, the difference is ordinarily very small. The banks that participate most actively in Eurobanking tend to be highly rated, and the holders of Eurocurrency deposits have more incentive to seek out sound banks than the holders of government-insured deposits. Then, too, the governments of countries with Eurobanking facilities are not completely indifferent to these facilities' soundness since their expansion ultimately depends in part on reputations for soundness and integrity. Moreover, except in offshore banking centers, Eurobanks commonly have domestic operations, so host-country governments may not be able to wash their hands entirely of responsibility for Eurobanks without adverse implications for domestic banking. In short, there is little reason to believe that the risk premium factored into Eurocurrency deposit rates should normally be large unless a country with Eurocurrency deposits has a political risk problem.

While no set interest rate differential exists between Eurocurrency deposits and domestic deposits, a difference of 25 basis points (0.25 percent) is standard for deposits with comparable maturities and other characteristics. The differential can be considerably larger than 25 basis points when the Eurocurrency deposits are in a country with a political risk problem.[1] A similar, though generally smaller, interest rate differential exists between Eurocurrency and domestic bank lending rates. It is more difficult to compare lending rates than deposit rates, however, because of differences in loan characteristics and credit standings of borrowers.

Arbitrage Opportunities   Do interest rate differentials between the Eurocurrency and domestic markets for both loans and deposits give rise to arbitrage between them? The answer is emphatically yes! When an interest rate differential becomes large enough, a bank can profitably borrow in the Eurocurrency market and lend in a domestic market. Moreover, because the Eurocurrency market is so completely integrated into the forex market, an arbitraging bank may not have to borrow in the same currency as that in which it lends. If, for example, the interest rate differential were large enough, a bank might borrow U.S. dollars in the Eurocurrency market, convert them into Australian dollars in a spot exchange, lend the Australian dollars in the domestic money market, and cover by selling Australian dollars forward. This example is, of course, a case of interest arbitrage. Interest rate differentials between domestic markets and the Eurocurrency market are a major cause of such arbitrage.

---

[1]Grabbe indicates that before the Philippine government imposed restrictions on foreign currency transactions in 1983, the Manila branch of Citibank was purportedly paying 0.75 percent more than the normal 0.25 percent differential between Eurodollar and domestic dollar time deposits. See J. Orlin Grabbe, *International Financial Markets* (New York: Elsevier, 1986), p. 230.

Because of market segmentation between domestic money markets and the Eurocurrency market, interest arbitrage does not eliminate the interest rate differentials. It does tend, however, to limit them. An equilibrium tends to be reached in which the interest rate differentials are small enough to just offset the cost and risk of arbitrage. Because interest rates and exchange rates are constantly changing, however, a chance to engage in interest arbitrage may materialize at any moment.

The arbitrage opportunities presented in the Eurocurrency market are not limited to banks. This is particularly true of partial interest arbitrage. Thus, if domestic interest rates in Australia are sufficiently high relative to Eurodollar interest rates, a firm needing to borrow Australian dollars may find it advantageous to borrow U.S. dollars (or some other currency) in the Eurocurrency market, exchange them spot for Australian dollars, and sell Australian dollars forward. Similarly, an Australian firm seeking the highest locked-in, short-term return might find it advantageous to buy U.S. dollars spot, put them into a Eurodollar deposit, and sell U.S. dollars forward.

Since arbitrage via the Eurocurrency market affects exchange rates, interest rates, and money supplies, some governments have sought to prevent it by placing controls on banks' transactions. Both the Japanese and French governments, for example, have long employed such controls. Both have subsequently modified their policies, however, because of the realization that they were interfering with the ability of their banks to compete internationally.

The Role of Interbank Transactions In the Eurocurrency market, as in the forex market, most transactions are interbank. For this reason, the Eurocurrency market is often called an interbank market. It is more accurate to call it a wholesale market, however, because much of its activity consists of large-scale transactions between banks and their nonbank customers.

The importance of interbank transactions in the Eurocurrency market can be seen in Exhibit 12.1, which indicates that at the end of 1990, $3,866.6 billion out of a total of $7,216.6 billion in international claims of reporting area banks were claims on other banks in the reporting area. An additional $328.1 billion represented claims on banks outside the reporting area. While these figures include claims that should be assigned to traditional banking, the majority of these claims should be assigned to the Eurocurrency market. It seems fair to conclude, therefore, that most of the activity of the Eurocurrency market is interbank.

A major factor behind the largely interbank character of the Eurocurrency market is the typically small spread between interbank loan and deposit rates. Just as marketmaking banks in the forex market simultaneously quote bid and ask prices, marketmaking banks in the Eurocurrency market simultaneously quote bid and ask interest rates on Eurocurrency deposits. The bid rate indicates what a marketmaker will pay on a time deposit of a given maturity, while the ask interest rate indicates the rate at which a marketmaker will lend to other banks. The spread between these rates is typically ⅛ percent (12.5 basis points). As percentages of middle interest rates, these spreads are wider than the comparable spreads in the forex market, but narrower than interbank interest rate spreads in domestic markets.

Many of the banks in the Eurocurrency market are foreign branches and subsidiaries that have difficulty obtaining large amounts of resources from domestic depositors. Because of the relatively low cost of obtaining resources from other banks and the great quantity of funds available, it is possible for these banks to obtain funds through interbank borrowing without placing themselves at a great cost disadvantage relative to their local competition.

The Eurocurrency market's interest rate spreads reflect the risks and costs of interbank transactions. There is a forex risk because Eurobanks' assets and liabilities are denominated in different currencies. There is also an interest rate risk because the maturities of Eurocurrency assets and liabilities do not coincide. Both of these risks can be reduced or eliminated through hedging, but the cost of hedging affects the spreads. In addition, there is the risk that a party to an agreement may not perform through inability or unwillingness. Normally, however, the risk of nonperformance is very small.

Nonbank Use of the Eurocurrency Market   While most Eurobank assets and liabilities are interbank, a large portion is not. The Eurocurrency market is a major channel for conducting savings into the nets of corporations and governments, and this channel's flow is increasing. Even in the dark days from 1982 to 1985 when the sovereign debt crisis burst into full flower, there was some growth in the nominal amount of the Eurocurrency market's outstanding loans to nonbank borrowers. Realistically, however, there was probably some decrease in the real volume of such loans because of inflation and the overstatement of the actual market values of LDC debt. Since 1985, however, the real volume of Eurocurrency market lending has grown rapidly.

Exhibit 13.1 presents the BIS's summary of net international lending via banks, bond issues, and Euronotes from the end of 1985 to the end of 1990. Net international lending (Item E) equals total lending through these three vehicles minus those interbank positions that are not offset by equivalent loans to nonbank borrowers. This means, for example, that if an interbank position finances a domestic loan that would not otherwise be included in either total cross-border claims of reporting banks or local claims in foreign currency, it is included in net international lending. Item A, net international bank lending, therefore represents the BIS's estimate of international lending by banks to nonbank borrowers. Item A includes both Eurocurrency and domestic market lending, but it can safely be assumed that the figures for this item primarily reflect Eurocurrency market lending.

Obviously, the period indicated in Exhibit 13.1 was one of tremendous growth in net international lending, whose total amount (Item E) increased from $1,940 billion at the end of 1985 to $4,375 billion at the end of 1990. While there was some inflation during this period, the increase in the nominal amount of net international lending was so large that most of it was real. There is some overstatement of total net international bank lending due to carrying uncollectible sovereign loans on the books at higher-than-market values, but it

Item	Stocks at Year-End 1985	Changes, Excluding Exchange Rate Effects[a]					Stocks at Year-End 1990
	1985	1986	1987	1988	1989	1990	1990
Total cross-border claims of reporting banks[b]	$2,574.3	$509.5	$601.8	$436.1	$684.9	$480.0	$5,907.2
Local claims in foreign currency	562.8	147.7	163.0	74.8	122.2	109.0	1,309.4
Minus: Double-counting due to redepositing among the reporting banks	1,652.1	452.2	444.8	250.9	397.1	209.0	3,866.6
A = Net international bank lending[c]	1,485.0	205.0	320.0	260.0	410.0	380.0	3,350.0
B = Net new Euronote placements	16.0	13.4	23.4	19.5	6.9	32.0	111.2
Total completed international bond issues		220.5	180.0	220.7	263.6	239.4	
Minus: Redemptions and repurchases		64.6	73.0	82.6	89.4	108.4	
C = Net international bond financing	572.5	155.9	107.0	138.1	174.3	131.0	1,472.5
D = A + B + C = Total international financing	2,073.5	374.3	450.4	417.6	591.2	543.0	4,933.7
Minus: Double-counting[d]	133.5	79.3	50.4	67.6	76.2	78.0	558.7
E = Total net international financing	1,940.0	295.0	400.0	350.0	515.0	465.0	4,375.0

[a]Nondollar flow banking data are converted into dollars at constant end-of-quarter exchange rates. Stock data are converted at current exchange rates.

[b]Banks in the Group of Ten countries plus Luxembourg, Austria, Denmark, Finland, Ireland, Norway, Spain, the Bahamas, Bahrain, the Cayman Islands, Hong Kong, the Netherlands Antilles, and Singapore, and the branches of U.S. banks in Panama.

[c]In addition to direct cross-border claims on end-users, these estimates include certain interbank positions: firstly, claims on banks outside the reporting area—the assumption being that these "peripheral" banks will not, in most cases, borrow the funds from banks in the financial centers simply for the purpose of redepositing them with other banks in these centers; secondly, claims on banks within the reporting area to the extent that these banks switch funds into domestic currency and/or use them for direct foreign currency lending to domestic customers; thirdly, a large portion of the foreign currency claims on banks in the country of issue of the currency in question, e.g., dollar claims of banks in London on banks in the United States; here again the assumption is that the borrowing banks obtain the funds mainly for domestic purposes and not for relending abroad.

[d]International bonds taken up by the reporting banks, to the extent that they are included in the banking statistics as claims on nonresidents; bonds issued by the reporting banks mainly for the purpose of underpinning their international lending activities.

Source: Bank for International Settlements, *61st Annual Report* (Basle: BIS, 1991), p. 122.

should be taken into account that billions of dollars in sovereign debt write-downs occurred during the period.[2]

It can be determined from Exhibit 13.1 that, in percentage terms, the growth of net international bond financing was greater than that of net international bank lending from 1986 to 1990. After 1986, however, the growth rate of net international bank lending was, overall, about the same as that of net international bond financing. International bond financing grew rapidly in the years immediately after 1982 largely because the sovereign debt crisis encouraged a shift from bank financing to bond financing. Beginning in 1986, however, international bank lending staged a strong comeback.

Category B, net new Euronote placements, represents a type of lending that began in 1984 and has grown modestly since then. By the end of 1990, this type of lending accounted for only $111.2 billion of the total $4,375 billion in net international lending. Nevertheless, Euronotes are important enough to claim some of our attention. Because they are generally considered to be more closely associated with international banking than with international securities markets, they are explained later in this chapter.

The growth in the Eurocurrency market's nonbank lending depends, in part, on the general growth of international financial activity, in part on the market's ability to attract funds, and in part on its attractiveness relative to competing markets. The market does particularly well when (as in 1987) there is a rise in long-term interest rates and a high degree of uncertainty about exchange rates and future interest rates.

While borrowing from banks is an alternative to issuing securities, these two types of financing sometimes complement one another. In 1987 and 1988, for example, despite Japan's role as the largest net supplier of funds to international financial markets, there were large increases in foreign currency lending to nonbank Japanese borrowers for the purpose of financing purchases of securities denominated in currencies other than the yen. The borrowed funds, combined with the flow of Japanese savings directly into securities markets, caused a very large increase in Japanese holdings of foreign currency-denominated securities and yen-denominated securities issued outside Japan's domestic securities market.

The appeal of Eurocurrency market financing to nonbank borrowers rests on relatively low interest rates, arbitrage opportunities, freedom from government controls, easy management of the exchange risk, and the fact that loans can be arranged, if desired, for medium-term periods. The maturities of Eurocurrency loans thus overlap those of bond issues. Understandably, therefore, there is much competition between these two types of financing. Shifts between them are common, which tends to make the amount of each unstable.

---

[2]For example, banks wrote off $15 billion of the Mexican government's debt in 1990. Bank for International Settlements, *61st Annual Report* (Basle, 1990), p. 130.

Eurobanking Centers and Facilities

Although London is clearly the Eurocurrency market's leading center, the market has numerous other locations. The United States and Japan have become important Eurobanking countries since their governments began allowing resident banks to operate Eurobanking facilities legally separate from domestic banking. Several offshore banking centers have attained major status in the Eurocurrency market, including landlocked Luxembourg, and several western European countries other than the United Kingdom have significant Eurocurrency market operations.

While London is the most important Eurobanking center, this does not mean that British banks dominate the Eurocurrency market. In terms of both loan claims and deposit liabilities, Japanese banks clearly occupy the top position. U.S. banks are also very prominent in the Eurocurrency market, and banks from many other countries participate in that market as both borrowers and lenders.

Exhibit 13.2 presents BIS data on international bank assets and liabilities for reporting area banks allocated according to bank nationality. A glance at the exhibit suffices to demonstrate the enormous importance of Japanese banks, which had almost three times the international assets of second-place U.S. banks and almost as large a preponderance in liabilities at the end of 1990. Japanese banks accounted for 35 percent of the international assets of reporting area banks at the end of 1990 (as compared with 27 percent at the end of 1985), while the share of U.S. banks was only 11.9 percent (as compared with 21.9 percent at the end of 1985). Yet this comparison seems to overstate the relative importance of U.S. banks because Exhibit 13.2 includes the international positions of U.S. banks in offshore centers with the figures for U.S. banks, but (unlike Exhibit 13.1) otherwise excludes those centers. If the offshore positions of U.S. banks were excluded from Exhibit 13.2, the share of U.S. banks in the total international bank assets of the countries included there would be less than 8 percent and would be smaller than the shares of German and French banks.[3] Note, however, that Exhibit 13.2 excludes the cross-border assets and liabilities of U.S. banks denominated in foreign currencies.

It should be kept in mind, however, that the relative international importance of U.S. banks is not fully captured by data on banks' assets and liabilities. Many of the international operations of banks, including forex trading and financial swaps, are largely off the books, and U.S. banks are extremely prominent in such operations. Nevertheless, there is no denying that the relative importance of U.S. banks in international operations has tended to decline in recent years.

Exhibit 13.2 indicates that 1990 produced a large expansion in the international operations of banks located in Continental Europe. This expansion is largely a response to the emerging common market. Governments

---

[3]Ibid., p. 124.

| E X H I B I T | 13.2 | *International Bank Assets and Liabilities by Bank Nationality: Total Stocks in 1985 and 1990, and Changes in 1990ᵃ (billions of U.S. dollars)*

Parent Country of Banks	Change in Current Dollars, 1990				Total Stocks	
	Total	Related Offices	Non-Related Banks	Non-banks	Year-End 1985	Year-End 1990
Japan						
Assets	$153.0	$ 71.6	$ 49.9	$ 31.6	$ 707.0	$2,120.4
Liabilities	135.1	38.5	56.4	40.3	672.5	2,059.8
United States						
Assets	−15.3	10.1	−30.3	4.9	593.3	712.4
Liabilities	−2.7	14.3	−6.2	−10.9	555.2	741.6
Germany						
Assets	166.2	36.8	82.2	47.1	191.0	601.8
Liabilities	130.2	34.5	41.8	53.8	157.4	459.3
France						
Assets	122.3	39.3	49.8	33.1	245.2	555.2
Liabilities	154.2	52.6	49.0	52.6	248.9	610.9
Italy						
Assets	73.5	8.4	27.7	37.4	113.5	328.0
Liabilities	74.0	7.7	45.6	20.7	115.1	330.5
United Kingdom						
Assets	25.2	0.0	20.8	4.4	191.0	272.3
Liabilities	13.2	0.3	11.6	1.1	200.8	321.6
Other						
Assets	262.2	68.6	89.6	104.1	672.7	1,379.2
Liabilities	321.6	77.6	115.7	128.5	664.9	1,444.3
Total						
Assets	787.1	234.8	289.7	262.6	2,713.7	5,969.3
Liabilities	825.6	225.5	313.9	286.1	2,614.8	5,968.0

ᵃThis table shows the cross-border positions in all currencies plus the foreign currency positions vis-à-vis local residents of banks in the following 17 countries: Austria, Belgium, Luxembourg, Canada, Denmark, Finland, France, Germany, Ireland, Italy, Japan, the Netherlands, Spain, Sweden, Switzerland, the United Kingdom, and the United States (cross-border positions in domestic currency only). The figures for U.S. banks also include the cross-border positions reported by U.S. banks' branches in the Bahamas, the Cayman Islands, Panama, Hong Kong, and Singapore. The international assets and liabilities in this table are classified according to the nationality of ownership of the reporting banks. Nonbank positions include official monetary institutions and, on the liabilities side, banks' issues of CDs and other securities.

Source: Bank for International Settlements, *61st Annual Report* (Basle: BIS, 1991), p. 125.

in a number of European countries have been dismantling their restrictions on the operations of both domestic and foreign banks, and there have been mergers and acquisitions among European banks with different national identifications that have tended to expand international positions. In 1990, at least, the international positions of European banks grew relatively more rapidly than those of Japanese banks.

International Banking Facilities (IBFs)

IBFs have existed since late 1981 when they were authorized by the Federal Reserve System's Board of Governors. The primary motivation behind their authorization was the desire to take business away from offshore banking operations in the Caribbean. In effect, the IBFs were to be "onshore offshore" operations, i.e., banking facilities located in the United States with *some* of the characteristics of Eurobanking facilities operating outside the country.

An IBF is not a separate banking entity, but a separate group of accounts. A bank with IBF accounts may be a U.S.-chartered depository institution, including an Edge Act subsidiary, or it may be a U.S. branch of a foreign bank. Although IBFs are physically located in the United States, they are not subject to either reserve requirements or assessments for deposit insurance. Unlike other U.S. banking facilities, they may offer deposits denominated in currencies other than the dollar. IBFs of U.S. banks are exempt from federal taxes, their income becoming taxable only when transferred to the banks' regular accounts. IBFs in branches of foreign-owned banks are taxable on the same basis as the rest of those branches' operations.

IBFs' operations are subject to various restrictions designed to prevent their abuse to avoid regulations and controls that apply to domestic banking. IBFs may not lend to U.S. residents except other IBFs or their own parent entities. A bank's borrowing from its IBF accounts are subject to the same reserve requirements that apply to U.S. banks' borrowings from Eurobanks. In parallel fashion, IBFs may not hold deposits for U.S. residents except other IBFs or their own parents. IBFs are not allowed to issue negotiable instruments. The deposits they offer may only be nonnegotiable time deposits, and, to prevent them from being used as checking accounts, the minimum maturity for deposits is 2 business days.[4] While IBFs may lend to nonbank foreigners, the loan proceeds may not be used to finance the borrowers' operations in the United States. A $100,000 minimum applies to deposits and transactions involving nonbank customers of IBFs except for interest withdrawals and the closing of accounts.

As was shown in Exhibit 12.2, total IBF assets stood at $302.8 billion at the end of 1990 and accounted for more than half of the cross-border positions of banks located in the United States. To a considerable degree, IBFs have realized the Fed's intention of capturing business from offshore Caribbean banks. The Caribbean banks have continued to exist, however, and their branches owned by U.S. banks have achieved some nominal growth in assets and liabilities since 1981. These banks can legally lend to U.S. residents, which IBFs generally cannot do. They offer negotiable certificates of deposit, another thing that IBFs cannot do. While the possibility of having IBFs has increased the attractiveness of U.S. branches for many foreign banks, the fact that these banks can avoid U.S. taxes by operating out of the Caribbean has exercised a restraining influence.

---

[4]An exception exists for overnight deposits of overseas banks, other IBFs, and the parent bank.

Exhibit 12.2 also indicates that there was a slight net shrinkage in IBFs' assets (but not liabilities) in 1989 and 1990. The primary explanation for the asset shrinkage is that there were large write-downs in U.S. banks' claims on sovereign borrowers that were carried on IBFs' books. If U.S. banks had been achieving the expansion that they had recorded in earlier years, however, this would have carried over to the IBF accounts.

Some of the shrinkage of IBFs' assets in 1990 is explained by the fact that in December 1990, the Fed moved to eliminate reserve requirements against U.S. banks' Eurocurrency market liabilities. Prior to December 13, 1990, U.S. banks were subject to a 3 percent reserve requirement against Eurocurrency liabilities, including loans from their own branches, with maturities of less than 1½ years. From December 13, 1990 to January 17, 1991, these requirements were eliminated.[5] Their elimination means that banks in the United States have a reduced incentive to maintain IBF accounts. Nevertheless, considerable incentive to use IBFs remains.

While perhaps 30 percent of the assets and liabilities of IBFs consist of claims on and obligations to nonbank foreigners, most of their assets and liabilities are from interbank transactions. Like other banks in the Eurocurrency market, the banks with IBFs use interbank transactions to manage their exchange and interest rate risks, caused, for the most part, by transactions made to accommodate nonbank customers.

Particularly noteworthy is that the transactions of IBFs can be integrated with a bank's other transactions to reduce the interest rate risk. Consider, for example, the case where a bank's total dollar liabilities with 1 month to maturity exceed its total dollar assets of the same maturity by $4 million, while its dollar assets with 2 months to maturity exceed its dollar liabilities of the same maturity by $4 million. Although assets and liabilities for these maturities are matched overall, the bank is exposed to the interest rate risk. If an interest rate increase occurs during the next month when the bank has to borrow $4 million to meet its maturing liabilities, the higher interest rate it pays may wipe out its gain from the assets with the longer maturities. Accordingly, the bank might use its IBF accounts to arrange a swap in which it would acquire $4 million in assets with 1-month maturities and $4 million in liabilities with 2-month maturities. The swap could take the form of a 1-month IBF time deposit claim exchanged for a 2-month IBF time deposit liability. The swapping counterparty could be a bank with 1-month assets that exceed its 2-month liabilities. No forex transaction would be required.

The Offshore Market of Japan (JOM)

Although Japan has a long tradition of relying on pervasive government controls of its commercial, financial, and industrial life, the phenomenal expansion of the Japanese economy has resulted in growing pressure to loosen the controls. The situation is like an old earthen dam that is unable to contain

---

[5]*Federal Reserve Bulletin*, December 1991, p. A8.

an ever-growing volume of flood water. At some point, water must either be released or diverted if the dam is not to break. In the Japanese case, the flood water consists of an accumulation of savings without historical precedent. As the savings flow accumulated, it became increasingly evident that it could not be entirely contained within Japan's domestic financial markets. The relevant questions became how much of the flow to release and how to release it.

The Japanese government persisted for some years in following policies designed to minimize capital outflows, thus keeping Japan's real interest rate level relatively low. These policies meant, however, that Japanese financial firms were unable to match the overseas expansion of their counterparts in the United States, the United Kingdom, and several other countries. Over time, however, the pressure on the Japanese government to loosen its controls increased until the government felt compelled to respond positively, clearing the way for a dramatic expansion of the foreign operations of Japanese financial firms and a corresponding increase in Japan's capital outflows.

An important manifestation of the new policy of financial openness has been the establishment of the Japan Offshore Market (JOM) late in 1986. The JOM basically does for Japan what the IBFs do for the United States. Although it is called an "offshore" market, the JOM is physically located in Japan and is based on segregated accounts whose use is restricted to transactions with nonresidents, including the foreign subsidiaries of Japanese corporations.

The chief advantages offered by the JOM are exemption from the withholding tax on income earned from domestic deposits and freedom from the reserve requirements and interest rate controls that apply to domestic banking. Although foreign banks are allowed to participate in the JOM, they generally have not done so to any great extent because Singapore and Hong Kong offer them more than the JOM does. The chief beneficiaries of the JOM to date have been Japanese regional banks that have not established overseas branches.

Although the JOM began to operate 5 years after the IBFs did, it now surpasses the IBFs in size. As Exhibit 12.2 indicates, as of the end of 1990, the cross-border claims of the JOM equaled $495 billion, compared with $302.8 billion for the IBFs. In addition, the JOM held $92 billion in local claims denominated in foreign currency, while the comparable figure for the IBFs was zero. In other words, banks with JOM accounts are allowed to hold claims on Japanese residents, including banks, that are denominated in foreign currencies, but IBFs are not.

The Asia Currency Market

In 1968, the government of Singapore granted permission to the local branch of the Bank of America to offer dollar-denominated deposits and to participate freely in the Eurocurrency market. Other banks rapidly followed the Bank of America's lead, and in a short time Singapore emerged as a major Eurocurrency market center. Because of the time zone gap between it and banking centers in Europe and the Caribbean, and also because of the corresponding differences in market participants, the Singapore-based part of the Eurocurrency market became known as the *Asia dollar market* and, later, as the *Asia currency market.*

The immediate causes of the Asia currency market's development were the abundance of dollars circulating among Far Eastern residents as a by-product of the Vietnam War and the fact that owners of dollars were often reluctant to divulge the extent of their holdings to local authorities. Accordingly, the dollars tended to move to London. While many returned to the Far East via the lending process, there was an overall outflow of dollars from the region. This capital drain furnished a strong macroeconomic reason for developing the Asia currency market. The inconvenience of the time gap between the Far East and the banking centers of Europe and North America provided additional motivation.

In the 20-plus years of its existence, the Asia currency market has attained major status. It has expanded beyond its original base in Singapore, but Singapore remains its leading center in terms of the volume of cross-border positions carried on banks' books, a volume that rivals the IBFs and the JOM. To a large degree, however, transactions in the Asia currency market are "booked" in Singapore and arranged elsewhere, particularly in Hong Kong since Singapore offers a very hospitable environment for foreign banks, including exceptionally low taxes.

While the funds deposited with banks in the Asia currency market are generally lent to Asian borrowers, including the Far Eastern branches of European and North American banks, close links, including arbitrage transactions, join this market to non-Asian financial centers. With the Asia currency market, the Eurocurrency market, like the forex market, has come to operate on a 24-hour basis. Its prospects for continued growth are excellent, for while the financial future of Hong Kong may be in doubt because of its impending acquisition by the People's Republic of China in 1997, the combination of economic growth in a number of countries in the region and growing financial liberalization should fuel its expansion.

Offshore Banking Centers

In its purest form, an offshore banking center offers some banking services to local residents, but its reason for being is to allow nonresidents to conduct banking operations with minimal government control. The country in which such a center is located derives some income and employment from the center's activity, and its government obtains some revenues from the taxes, fees, and other charges levied on the banks that avail themselves of its hospitality. These revenues are, however, lower than those generated by a comparable volume of business conducted in London or in other financial centers located in countries with large domestic banking markets.

Singapore and Hong Kong are frequently classified as offshore centers, but each has a domestically oriented banking market of considerable size, which makes the offshore designation questionable. The most clear-cut examples of offshore banking centers are places such as the Cayman Islands, the Bahamas, Bahrain, Luxembourg, and various other small countries that lack large and well-developed domestic banking markets. In such locations, the vast majority of banking is international in character and involves parties who are either foreign residents or the offices of foreign-owned banks.

A common feature of offshore banking is the use of **shell branches,** which are nothing more than booking offices. Upon payment of fees as low as $10,000 to $15,000 per year, and after meeting capital requirements that are well below the already low capital requirements for establishing a London branch, a bank can set up an operation in, for example, the Cayman Islands that requires no more than a handful of employees and a small office with excellent communication facilities. Such an operation may carry on its books assets and liabilities totaling hundreds of millions of dollars. All of a shell's transactions are worked out elsewhere, and yet the country in which transactions are booked is considered, from the legal perspective, to be the home of the resulting financial obligations.

The ease with which banking can be conducted in offshore centers does not necessarily imply an anything-goes atmosphere. For example, one cannot assume that money flows associated with illegal drug trafficking receive the active or even tacit approval of local authorities who are eager to collect money for their favorite charities. An offshore center can expect sanctions if its banking authorities are regarded as too indifferent to the uses to which their banking facilities are put and if they refuse to cooperate with criminal investigations in other countries that point to the use of its facilities for flagrantly illegal activity. These actions may include restrictions on transfers of bank deposits to banks in that center, and without such deposits, an offshore center is deprived of its lifeblood. Moreover, if an offshore center has a reputation as a haven for criminals, the willingness of many Eurocurrency market participants to rely on it may be adversely affected, with the result that its interest rates may have to reflect an additional risk premium.

Offshore Banking and Tax Avoidance   While government officials in offshore banking countries generally seek to avoid having their countries regarded as playgrounds for criminals, they are also generally unwilling to serve as agents for the collection of other governments' taxes. Typically, offshore banking centers offer anonymous deposits, keeping the identities of depositors confidential. They also offer low or zero tax withholding rates on interest payments to foreigners. The generosity of the governments of offshore banking countries extends to income taxes on foreign companies, which encourages nonfinancial corporations as well as banks to maintain offices in these countries. For this reason, offshore banking countries are often called *tax havens*. When nonfinancial firms establish subsidiaries in offshore banking countries, the subsidiaries rely on the banking facilities that operate there. This creates a symbiotic relationship between offshore banking and the operations of nonfinancial multinational companies.

It is difficult for the governments of multinational companies' home countries to avoid some revenue loss because of the diversion of transactions to offshore banking countries. There are, however, limits to the willingness of governments to passively accept the revenue loss. If the loss comes to be regarded as excessive, action will be taken to hamper the operations of banks and other firms in tax haven countries, even at the risk of causing some competitive disadvantage to domestically based multinational firms.

Since 1962, the U.S. government has limited the ability of multinational firms to avoid taxes by setting up foreign subsidiaries to receive income. It has done this by treating the income of such subsidiaries, under certain conditions, as if it were received by the U.S. parent companies. If, for example, a foreign subsidiary derives income from investments in the United States; if it receives dividends, fees, royalties, or other such income; or if it derives income from reinvoicing operations, much or all such income may be taxed as if the subsidiary did not exist. In reinvoicing operations, a corporation uses a foreign subsidiary to book purchases of goods in one country for resale in a third country, pricing the goods so that most of the resulting profits are realized by the subsidiary.

In general, governments refrain from taxing foreign-source income of domestic corporations until it lands at home. Accordingly, if a domestic company's foreign subsidiary does not remit to the parent all of the income attributable to it, some of the income may escape taxation by the parent company's government. In the Revenue Act of 1962, however, the U.S. government established an income category known as **Subpart F** that applies to foreign-source income of certain types, including those given in the last paragraph. If a foreign company is classified under U.S. law as a **controlled foreign corporation (CFC)**, and if a substantial part of its income is of types included in Subpart F, some or all of the income received by the CFC may be taxable to the parent even if the parent does not receive it. In general, a CFC is a company that is more than 50 percent owned by U.S. stockholders, each of whom individually controls at least 10 percent of the company's voting stock. If, for example, a single U.S. stockholder owns over 50 percent of a foreign company's voting stock, or if five stockholders each own slightly more than 10 percent of a foreign company's voting stock, the company is a CFC. Even if a company is a CFC, however, the U.S. parent or parents will be taxed primarily or entirely on income received by them rather than income attributed to them unless a substantial part of the CFC's income is classified as Subpart F.

The law applying to CFCs and Subpart F income is complicated, and a full presentation of it would exceed the intended scope of this book. It illustrates the point, however, that a government can take effective action to restrain the use of foreign subsidiaries to avoid taxes. The governments of countries other than the United States, including the members of the EEC, employ similar measures to limit their revenue losses to tax havens. It remains true, nevertheless, that firms can often enjoy important tax savings by setting up subsidiaries in countries that combine low taxes with offshore banking.

Private Banking   In some offshore banking centers, including Luxembourg and Monaco, **private banks** play a prominent role. The clientele of these facilities consist largely of wealthy individuals who find it advisable to arrange for the management of at least some of their wealth outside their home countries. Banks that cater to such clientele are often specialized institutions whose primary activity is private banking, but much private banking is conducted by well-known commercial banks and financial service firms. American Express, for example, is prominent in private banking.

Although it is not normally classified as an offshore banking country, Switzerland has traditionally been important in private banking, and Geneva has long been regarded as the leading private banking center. In recent years, however, concessions to law enforcement officials in other countries have raised doubts about how much anonymity Swiss authorities can guarantee to private banking clients, and this has somewhat diminished Switzerland's luster as a private banking country.

The clients of private banks are often persons who do not want the nature and extent of their foreign asset holdings revealed to government officials in their home countries. In some cases, clients *are* government officials in their home countries. In January 1990, for example, the press reported that one of the officials of the Bank of Credit and Commerce International (BCCI) claimed that he had served as a personal banker for Manuel Noriega while he was president of Panama.[6] This admission followed the entering of a guilty plea by BCCI in a federal court in Tampa to the charge that it had laundered drug money. Subsequently, in 1991 the BCCI case developed into what is perhaps the greatest international banking scandal of all time. The case of BCCI, a Luxembourg-based bank with extensive private banking operations, is examined in the appendix to this chapter.

While secrecy is a very important factor in private banking, particularly when government officials are clients, the clients of private banks are often individuals, including expatriates, for whom secrecy is secondary in importance to lower taxes, freedom from exchange controls, and the expertise in asset management offered by private banks. As might be surmised from this, the services of private banks resemble the activities of the trust departments of domestic commercial banks and investment firms.

The foregoing comments are not intended to convey the impression that private bankers are indifferent to the sources of existing and prospective clients' wealth. If a private bank appears to be aiding and abetting activities that are criminal under the laws of most nations, particularly the laws of the wealthiest nations, the country in which the questionable operations are occurring runs the risk of provoking punitive measures by the offended governments. For this reason, and because reputations for integrity often matter to bankers and their clients, private banks and their host country governments generally desire to avoid the appearance of working hand-in-glove with criminals. Admittedly, however, a fine line sometimes separates what is criminal from what is not. Also, some private bankers are not greatly troubled by ethical issues raised by their clients' conduct. Money not only talks; it speaks all languages fluently.

---

[6]Paul M. Barrett and Richard B. Schmitt, "Noreiga-Linked Bank Admits Laundering," *The Wall Street Journal,* January 17, 1990, p. B4.

Offshore Banking and the Eurocurrency Market   Based on the analysis that has been presented, it appears that offshore banking can be broken down into three broad types of activity. First, some operations are part of the Eurocurrency market. For example, when U.S. residents hold foreign currency deposits in Caribbean banks, and when both U.S. and foreign residents hold dollar certificates of deposit in such banks these are considered Eurocurrency assets. Second, some offshore banking is incidental to the operations of nonbanking subsidiaries located in offshore tax havens. Thus, finance subsidiaries use offshore banking countries' facilities in connection with bond issues. Third, some off-shore banking is private banking, which focuses on money management.

Given the diversity of offshore banking, it is hardly surprising that offshore banking centers have different banking specialties. In Europe, for example, Monaco, Liechtenstein, Cyprus, Malta, Gibraltar, Madeira, the Channel Islands of Jersey and Guernsey, and the Isle of Man all feature offshore banking, but none of these locations is prominent in the Eurocurrency market. To some extent, offshore banking is regarded as an appropriate activity for encouraging the economic development of small nations and selected territories of larger nations. Its effectiveness in this regard seems to be considerable, and it can be expected that the scope and geographic extent of offshore banking will continue to grow.

Loans, Deposits, and Intermediation

Now that we have surveyed the general contour of the Eurocurrency market, it is time to examine those of its features that are directly associated with its financial intermediary function. This involves examining how the market raises and disposes of funds. It also involves examining operations of Eurobanks that closely resemble the operations of investment banks in the distribution of bond issues. Specifically, we shall examine Euronotes and Eurocommercial paper.

Eurocurrency Deposits

While it is customarily stated categorically that Eurocurrency deposits are *time* deposits, some Eurocurrency deposits, namely **overnight Eurodollars,** can be regarded as demand deposits that pay interest. Overnight Eurodollars closely resemble overnight repurchase agreements (repos) in which contracting parties arrange swaps of securities for cash that are carried out in the course of 2 business days.

Assume that early on Day 1, Firm X has $2 million in a demand deposit that it won't need for at least a day. In order to earn interest on these funds, X takes an overnight Eurodollar deposit with the Cayman Islands branch of Bank A that pays interest at the annual rate of 5.4 percent. Bank A obtains the use of the $2 million immediately; assuming that the transaction occurs early in the day, it has the use of funds for most of Day 1 and until the close of Day 2. In return, X collects $300 interest (based on a 360-day year) and is free to make some other disposition of the funds at the end of Day 2. In effect, X has collected interest on a demand deposit.

It is generally unnecessary for depositors to arrange overnight Eurodollar deposits or repos each time they want to earn interest on a demand deposit. A bank can arrange a standing agreement with such depositors in which it will *sweep* either the depositor's entire demand deposit balance or the excess over a specified minimum into repos, Eurodollars, or other appropriate assets overnight. In the money stock statistics of the United States, both overnight repos and overnight Eurodollars are included in M2.

Far more significant than overnight Eurodollars are straight **Eurocurrency time deposits,** whose maturities range from a few days to a few years and whose amounts can range from $1,000 or less to millions of dollars. Formerly, the interest rates paid on such deposits were fixed for the lifetimes of the contracts, but it is now common to have automatic interest rate adjustments every 3 or 6 months for Eurocurrency time deposits with relatively long maturities. This floating-rate feature of Eurocurrency time deposits improves the match between Eurobanks' liabilities and assets, for most of the latter are also floating rate. Having fixed-rate liabilities would be very troublesome for Eurobanks, for example, if the floating rates at which they lend were to decline below the rates paid on many of their time deposits.

An alternative to the straight time deposit is the **negotiable certificate of deposit (CD),** which differs from the straight time deposit in that it can be traded like a negotiable security without the loss of accumulated interest. At maturity, the issuing bank simply pays the face amount of the CD plus accumulated interest to whoever holds it. The advantage of the CD over the straight time deposit is, of course, its liquidity. A straight time deposit requires permission from the bank of deposit to cash it in before maturity. While such permission would probably be granted, liquidating a time deposit before maturity, in addition to the possible loss of accumulated interest, can damage a depositor's credit rating. The disadvantage of the negotiable CD is that it carries a lower interest rate than a Eurocurrency time deposit of the same maturity. The interest rate differential is normally 12.5 basis points.

The interest rates on Eurocurrency CDs may be either fixed or floating. The use of floating rates increases as a function of maturity and uncertainty about interest rates. Some Eurocurrency CDs are marketed much like bond issues. Thus, a bank may announce a CD issue that runs into millions of dollars and sell parts of it in relatively small denominations, such as $10,000 or $25,000. Such multiple-buyer CDs commonly have maturities of several years and resemble bond issues. In most cases, however, Eurocurrency CDs are, like time deposits, separately arranged with individual depositors. On average, CDs are for larger amounts and longer maturities than time deposits.

Eurocurrency Loans

Whereas interbank lending in the Eurocurrency market typically involves issues of time deposits or CDs by borrowing banks, nonbank lending typically entails issues of promissory notes. If a loan to a nonbank borrower is large, it will probably take the form of a syndicated loan, in which a number of banks participate as lenders. If the loan period exceeds a few months, the loan generally carries a floating rate whether it is between banks or to a nonbank borrower. The loan period may be either short-term or medium-term. In general, loans to nonbank borrowers are for longer terms than interbank loans.

The Loan Syndication Process   In syndicated Eurocurrency market lending, a bank known as the **lead manager** or loan arranger assumes primary responsibility for working out the loan terms and bringing in other banks, known as participating banks, to share in the loan. Frequently, one or more banks other than the lead manager play some role in these arrangements. Such banks are known as **co-lead managers** or receive some other designation that serves to distinguish them from the mass of participating banks. A co-manager's main distinction is often that it accepts a relatively large share of the loan. In addition, a bank known as the **agent bank,** which is likely to be a managing bank, oversees the loan by collecting payments due and distributing them to the other lending banks.

In a typical syndicated Eurocurrency loan, the lending process begins with the selection of a lead manager by the prospective borrower. The lead manager then prepares a **placement memorandum** that summarizes the borrower's financial condition and outlines the purposes and details of the proposed loan. The memorandum is circulated among the banks that are invited to participate. If the response is good, the loan amount may be increased, but if it is poor, the loan amount may be scaled down. The amount is not scaled down if the lead manager and the other managing banks, if any, have guaranteed the amount of the loan. In that event, the loan is said to be fully underwritten, and the managing bank or banks must lend what the other participating banks do not. Alternatively, the loan may be on a best efforts basis, in which case the managing bank or banks can scale down the loan amount if the response from participating banks is unfavorable.

To achieve and hold a high ranking as a syndicated Eurocurrency loan arranger is an important objective for banks that participate heavily in international lending. This is largely because of the fee income that is generated directly by the loan arrangement process. The borrower pays an up-front, one-time management fee that is allocated primarily to the lead manager and other managing banks. The amount of this fee is highly variable depending on market conditions, but it commonly ranges from 0.5 percent to 2.5 percent of the total loan amount. The borrower also periodically pays an agent fee to the managing bank. This provides an additional incentive to be a managing bank. Fee income has attained great importance for banks since the sovereign loan crisis emerged and, largely as a result, banks' capital requirements were raised, for it can be earned without incurring on-the-books assets. On the other hand, vigorous competition has tended to keep Eurocurrency market fees low.

Attaining prominence as a lead manager also appeals to banks because it enhances a bank's overall reputation, and this tends to attract additional business. A bank that gains such prominence is also likely to be depended on

| EXHIBIT | 13.3 | *The Top 25 Syndicated Loan Arrangers 1989 and 1990*

				1990	
Rank				Loan Amounts ($ billions) of dollars)	Number of Issues
1990	1989	Arranger	Nationality		
1	1	Citicorp	United States	$34.4	156
2	6	J.P. Morgan	United States	33.4	95
3	4	Chase Manhattan	United States	23.6	192
4	7	Chemical	United States	20.6	67
5	9	National Westminster	United Kingdom	19.9	113
6	8	First National Bank of Chicago	United States	18.5	94
7	5	Bank of America	United States	18.1	84
8	10	Barclays Bank Group	United Kingdom	17.8	108
9	2	Manufacturers Hanover	United States	15.6	139
10	12	CFSB/Crédit Suisse	Switzerland	11.4	49
11	11	S.G. Warburg	United Kingdom	9.2	29
12	3	Bankers Trust	United States	8.5	70
13	14	Midland	United Kingdom	7.8	46
14	16	Security Pacific	United States	7.8	64
15	17	Swiss Bank Corporation	Switzerland	7.5	41
16	29	Deutsche	Germany	7.0	31
17	26	Sumitomo	Japan	6.0	67
18	20	Continental	United States	5.4	32
19	95	Bayerische Landesbank	Germany	5.1	6
20	—	Chevron Corporation	United States	5.0	1
21	18	Crédit Lyonnais	France	4.9	28
22	32	Banque Nationale of Paris	France	4.8	20
23	23	Westpac Banking Corporation	United Kingdom	4.5	34
24	25	Dai-Ichi Kangyo	Japan	4.3	69
25	27	Bank of Tokyo	Japan	3.7	17

Source: "Annual Financing Report," Supplement to *Euromoney*, March 1991, p. 22.

for forex dealing, swaps, and other operations that provide income from fees, commissions, and spreads.

Exhibit 13.3 presents *Euromoney's* ranking of the top 25 syndicated loan arrangers for 1990. These banks are ranked according to the total amounts of loans arranged, not according to the amount of money lent. Thus, the top five syndicated lenders in 1990 were NatWest ($10.8 billion), Barclays ($8.9 billion), Citicorp ($8.7 billion), Fuji ($8.7 billion), and Sumitomo ($7.8

billion).[7] Of these, only Citicorp and NatWest were among the top five loan arrangers, and Fuji was not even among the top 25 arrangers.

Evident from Exhibit 13.3 is the fact that U.S. banks tend to dominate lead management activity in banks' syndicated lending and that British banks are also very prominent. The dominance of U.S. and, to a lesser extent, British banks reflects their extensive experience with syndicated lending, their network of contacts among lending banks, and the heavy concentration of borrowers in recent years among U.S. and British corporations.

The loan amounts indicated in Exhibit 13.3 are inflated by comparison with data provided by other sources on syndicated credits actually disbursed in the Eurocurrency market. The amounts of loans arranged often exceed the amounts actually lent, and many of the loans included in Exhibit 13.3 were not technically Euroloans. For example, if Citicorp arranges a syndicated loan for a U.S. corporation in dollars, the loan is a domestic loan, not an international loan to be included in Eurocurrency market statistics.

According to *Financial Market Trends,* a publication of the Office for Economic Cooperation and Development (OECD), the actual amount of international syndicated bank lending on a disbursements basis in 1990 was $121.5 billion, of which $119.3 billion were classified as Euroloans. The currency distribution of the loans was as follows: U.S. dollar, 57.9 percent; pound sterling, 17.9 percent; Ecu, 8.9 percent; mark, 6.9 percent; yen, 1.7 percent; and others, 6.7 percent. The percentage of dollar-denominated loans was considerably lower than in 1988 and 1989.[8]

The interest rates on syndicated Eurocurrency market loans are customarily referenced to the six-month LIBOR. When, as is often the case, a borrower does not utilize all of the authorized loan amount, it must pay a *commitment fee* that customarily ranges from 0.25 percent to 0.75 percent of the unused amount.

The Down and Up of Syndicated Lending   Until the early 1980s, the growth of syndicated lending was fuelled primarily by sovereign loans to LDC governments, including the governments of Soviet Bloc countries. The sovereign loan crisis caused a sharp shift away from syndicated lending to lending through issuing securities. In connection with this shift, investment banking firms and the investment banking arms of European commercial banks greatly expanded their international operations. Commercial banks responded to the shift by lending to investment banks, generating fee income from fees and commissions, promoting the use of CP, initiating Euronote financing, and setting up investment banking subsidiaries.

Since 1986, the syndicated loan market has staged a strong comeback. In 1988, 1989, and 1990, the amounts of syndicated lending processed through the Eurocurrency market were $116.2 billion, $114.5 billion, and $119.3

---

[7]"Annual Financing Report," Supplement to *Euromoney,* March 1991, p. 22.

[8]*Financial Market Trends,* October 1991, pp. 79, 82.

billion, respectively.[9] There was probably some drop off in 1991 due to such factors as a greater concern over credit quality by lenders, the slowdown in the world economy, and increasingly attractive interest rates on bonds, but the volume of syndicated lending was still large.

The recovery of syndicated lending has been accompanied by changes. In particular, whereas sovereign lending was the driving force behind the growth of syndicated lending until the early 1980s, its current growth depends primarily on corporate borrowing. Sovereign lending to LDC and eastern European governments still occurs. In some instances, however, it does so in connection with financial restructuring programs arranged with governments that are in arrears. In other instances, loans are made to LDC or eastern European governments that have managed to establish or retain good credit ratings. Overall, however, the volume of new syndicated lending to such governments is small. Moreover, while the governments of high-income countries are often large-scale international borrowers, they generally issue securities that carry below-LIBOR interest rates. Corporations also borrow by issuing securities, of course, but they rely less heavily on securities than their governments, primarily because corporations cannot borrow so cheaply.

For corporations, the syndicated loan is often comparable in cost to borrowing by issuing bonds, but the former offers greater flexibility as to timing and amount. Flexibility largely explains the extensive use of syndicated borrowing in connection with mergers and acquisitions. Such takeover financing has appealed to banks because it typically offers them large basis point spreads over the LIBOR. These spreads have seemed to be more than enough to warrant accepting the additional risk that such lending involves.

Another important influence on the resurgence of syndicated lending has been the innovation of **multiple option facilities,** in which a borrower receives various financing choices, including, possibly, a straight syndicated loan, issuing Euronotes or CP, and a menu of currencies in which to borrow. Another factor of some importance in syndicated lending is the use of government guarantees to promote exports. In financing for aircraft sales, for example, the amount lent is frequently large enough to warrant a syndicated loan, and the availability of government guarantees for the loans makes banks willing to undertake lengthy lending commitments.

Euronotes and Eurocommercial Paper

When, early in the 1980s, the sovereign debt crisis forced commercial banks to scramble for alternatives to syndicated lending, one of their most important moves was to develop a lending arrangement known as the **Euronote issuance facility (NIF).** In this type of arrangement, a bank or a bank syndicate makes a medium-term or even long-term underwriting commitment, usually to a well-known corporation, for notes that are usually short-term. The borrower issues notes as needed up to the total amount of the facility, and the notes are

---

[9]Ibid., p. 82.

distributed to investors by the underwriting bank or banks. An underwriting bank normally winds up holding some of the notes only if they cannot be satisfactorily placed with investors. An arranging bank receives a one-time underwriting fee for its services. In addition, a small **facility fee** is charged on a continuing basis on any unused portion of the NIF.

Although arranging NIFs is generally regarded as a commercial banking activity, investment banks also participate. In some cases, the notes are placed through a tender panel, which consists of banks that bid for newly issued notes with the intention of reselling them. In other cases, a single bank serves as the sole placing agent.

With an NIF, a borrower obtains a medium- or long-term commitment to allow short-term borrowing. Accordingly, the use of NIFs has been greatest when the interest rate yield curve has risen decidedly upward as a function of time. When short-term interest rates are equal to or, in a condition known as interest-rate inversion, higher than medium- and long-term rates, the use of NIFs tends to diminish. Their use also tends to diminish when current long-term rates are lower than short-term rates are *expected* to be in the near future, for borrowers then tend to favor long-term, fixed-rate bonds.

Banks highly prize NIFs because they provide opportunities to earn income from fees while simultaneously avoiding acquiring assets against which capital reserves must be maintained. For borrowers, NIFs offer an opportunity to obtain short-term funds at a lower cost than that of syndicated loans. In syndicated lending, banks generally cannot afford to lend at rates equal to or less than the LIBOR because that rate approximately measures their incremental cost of acquiring funds for lending. With NIFs, however, highly rated borrowers may be able to do slightly better than the LIBOR. Also, since the fees charged with NIFs are typically low, the overall cost of using an NIF is likely to be below that of a syndicated loan.

Notwithstanding their advantages, the use of NIFs dropped off sharply from 1987 to 1989. The primary cause of this decline was the advent of **Euro-commercial paper (Euro-CP)**, which tends to be an even lower-cost source of funds for highly rated corporate borrowers because it involves no underwriting fees. The commercial banks and investment banks that deal in Euro-CP depend heavily on deriving income from the spread between its buying and selling prices, and this spread is normally only a few basis points. Prime borrowers can therefore generally obtain funds more cheaply with Euro-CP than with underwritten Euronotes.

It may be too soon to post obituary notices for NIFs, however, because underwritten Euronotes made a modest comeback in 1990. This is shown in Exhibit 13.4, which indicates that the outstanding volume of NIFs and other, similar underwritten facilities declined in volume in 1988 and 1989, but increased sharply in 1990. It appears that the backup feature of the NIFs' underwriting commitment has considerable appeal when, as in 1990, potential borrowers have good reason to worry about their credit ratings.

It is clear from Exhibit 13.4, however, that Euro-CP programs have come to be far more significant than underwritten Euronotes. The existence of a large pool of investors in Europe and Asia interested in high-quality,

| EXHIBIT | 13.4 | *Euronote Financing: 1988–1990*
                            (in billions of U.S. dollars)

| | Net Change | | | Stocks at Year-End |
Type of Facility	1988	1989	1990	1990
New facilities announced				
Euro-commercial paper	$55.6	$49.3	$44.4	
Other short-term Euronotes[a]	10.6	10.3	3.0	
Medium-term notes[b]	17.0	12.9	25.4	
Total	83.2	72.5	72.8	
Net new issues				
Euro-commercial paper	19.9	5.3	11.8	$ 70.3
Other short-term Euronotes[a]	−3.4	−2.4	8.0	19.1
Medium-term notes[b]	3.0	4.0	12.3	21.9
Total	19.5	6.9	32.0	111.2

[a]Includes NIFs and similar underwritten facilities.
[b]Includes Euro-commercial paper programs with options to issue MTNs.
Source: Bank for International Settlements, *61st Annual Report* (Basle: BIS, 1991), p. 134.

short-term instruments, the extensive prior experience of U.S. banking firms with CP issues, the great flexibility of Euro-CP as to amount, maturity, and currency, and the low cost of Euro-CP have all contributed to the rapid emergence of this market. It appears, however, that the days of rampant cost-cutting by banks in order to establish a presence in this market are over. Approximately ten banking firms, led by Swiss Bank Corporation, Union Bank of Switzerland (UBS) Phillips & Drew, Lehman Brothers, J.P. Morgan, and Citicorp have established a commanding presence in the Euro-CP market.[10] These firms have recently increased the profitability of participating in the Euro-CP market by charging commissions on a scale based on the size and credit ratings of borrowers and by increasing the fees charged for arranging Euro-CP programs.[11]

One of the most promising developments in international financial markets in recent years, which dates from the fall of 1986, is the rise of **medium-term Euronotes (Euro-MTNs)**, whose maturities range from 9 months to 20 years, but generally do not exceed 10 years. MTNs were pioneered by U.S. investment banking firms. They closely resemble CP; the only essential difference is their longer maturities. Longer maturities mean that there is a greater liquidity problem with MTNs than with CP. There is little secondary trading in Euro-MTNs, but liquidity is provided by commitments from dealers to buy back paper before maturity at prices that allow them to receive their spreads.

---

[10]"The 1991 Euromoney Global Financing Guide," *Euromoney*, September 1991, p. 117.
[11]Bank for International Settlements, *Sixty-First Annual Report* (Basle: BIS, 1991), p. 134.

The fact that Euro-MTNs combine relatively long maturities with great flexibility as to amount, currencies, maturities, and interest rate characteristics (e.g., fixed or floating) makes them a very important alternative to Eurobonds, particularly Eurobonds that are privately placed. They are especially appealing to frequent borrowers because there are obvious cost savings involved in arranging a single Euro-MTN commitment as opposed to arranging a series of Eurobond issues.

Underlining the growing importance of Euro-MTNs is the fact that their outstanding volume increased more in 1990 than did that of Euro-CP (see Exhibit 13.4). Moreover, in the first eight months of 1991, the volume of new Euro-MTN programs was $27.2 billion, as compared with only $9.1 billion for the same period in 1990.[12] Merrill Lynch is the number one firm in Euro-MTN, but a number of other firms have established an important presence as Euro-MTN arrangers.[13]

Summary

The Eurocurrency market encompasses bank transactions that are denominated in currencies other than those of the countries in which the banks are located. London is the market's leading center, but the market has numerous other centers. The Asia currency market, centered in Singapore, is part of the Eurocurrency market, as are the operations conducted through accounts in U.S. banks known as International Banking Facilities (IBFs) and similar accounts in Japanese banks that are called the Japan Offshore Market (JOM). Also included in the Eurocurrency market are offshore banking operations conducted in numerous small countries. Most of the Eurocurrency market's transactions are between banks, but the market is also an important source of credit to nonbank borrowers.

Because of such factors as the lack of reserve requirements and deposit insurance assessments, Eurobanks tend to have an advantage over domestic banks in both the interest rates they pay to depositors and those they charge to borrowers, but the interest rates on Eurocurrency deposits include a risk premium since they are uninsured. The interest rate differentials between the Eurocurrency and domestic banking markets give rise to important arbitrage opportunities.

The growth of the Eurocurrency market has been a powerful influence on governments to loosen their control over domestic banking operations, as both the IBFs and the JOM illustrate. Offshore banking centers continue to prosper, not only because of their integration into the Eurocurrency market, but also because they provide tax havens for corporate subsidiaries and participate in private banking operations.

The sovereign debt crisis slowed the Eurocurrency market's growth and led to major changes in its operations. Syndicated loans have made a

---

[12] *Financial Market Trends*, October 1991, p. 85.

[13] "The 1991 Euromoney Global Financing Guide," *Euromoney*, September 1991, p. 117.

comeback, but few LDC governments are among the borrowers. The comeback has been associated with such developments as the financing of corporate takeovers and Eurobanks' offering of multiple option facilities. In addition, the Eurocurrency market has developed new lending techniques. Euronote issuing facilities (NIFs), which are underwritten by Eurobanks, developed as a technique for allowing Eurobanks to generate fee income by serving as intermediaries between borrowers and investors. Of greater importance is the Euro-CP market, which has become a major factor in Eurocurrency market activity. Medium-term Euronotes (Euro-MTNs), which resemble CP but have longer maturities, appear to have great promise as a competitor with Eurobonds.

References

Andersen, Torben Juul. *Euromarket Instruments.* New York: New York Institute of Finance, 1990, Chapters 2 and 3.

Bank for International Settlements. *Annual Report.* Basle: BIS, annual.

Euromoney: Annual Financing Report. March 1991 Supplement.

Financial Market Trends (Published three times annually by the Organization for Economic Cooperation and Development).

Grabbe, J. Orlin. *International Financial Markets.* New York: Elsevier, 1986, Chapters 12–15.

Hultman, Charles W. *The Environment of International Banking.* Englewood Cliffs, N.J.: Prentice-Hall, 1990.

———, and L. Randolph McGee. "International Banking Facilities: The Early Response." *The Bankers Magazine,* May/June 1984, pp. 82–86.

Key, Sydney J. "International Banking Facilities." *Federal Reserve Bulletin,* October 1982, pp. 567–577.

Mattingly, J. Virgil, Jr. "Statement before the Subcommittee on Consumer and Regulatory Affairs of the Committee on Banking, Housing, and Urban Affairs, U.S. Senate, May 23, 1991." *Federal Reserve Bulletin,* July 1991, pp. 572–581.

Moffett, Michael H., and Arthur Stonehill. "International Banking Facilities Revisited." *Journal of International Financial Management and Accounting,* Spring 1989, pp. 88–103.

"The 1991 Euromoney Global Financing Guide." *Euromoney,* September 1991, pp. 115–166.

Sarver, Eugene. *The Eurocurrency Market Handbook,* 2d ed. New York: New York Institute of Finance, 1990.

Saunders, Anthony. "The Eurocurrency Interbank Market: Potential for International Crisis?" Federal Reserve Bank of Philadelphia *Business Review,* January/February 1988, pp. 17–27. Reprinted in Robert W. Kolb, ed. *The International Finance Reader.* Miami: Kolb Publishing, 1991, pp. 278–287.

Questions

1. How does the expansion of Eurodollar deposits differ in essential respects from the expansion of the M1 money supply in the United States? In practice, which is likely to have the greater deposit multiplier on the basis of new reserves? Why?

2. Explain why the Eurocurrency market tends to have an interest rate advantage over domestic money markets with respect to both loan and deposit rates. What prevents this advantage from disappearing because of interest arbitrage?

3. Explain why the Eurocurrency market is primarily an interbank market. Using the approach of the BIS for measuring international bank lending, how would you go about measuring the extent to which the Eurocurrency market is a net supplier of credit to nonbank users?

4. What are IBFs, and what are their advantages? Why hasn't the existence of IBFs dried up the Eurocurrency market operations of Caribbean banks? Why is it that the operations of IBFs have recently shown little, if any, expansion?

5. What developments led to the creation of the JOM? Essentially, what does the JOM do, and how does it differ from the IBFs?

6. What is the significance of Subpart F of the Revenue Act of 1962?

7. What is the basic function of private banking? Is it fair to say that most private banking involves illegal activity?

8. Distinguish among overnight Eurodollars, straight Eurocurrency time deposits, and negotiable Eurocurrency CDs.

9. Since 1985, the syndicated lending part of the Eurocurrency market has rebounded from the consequences of the sovereign loan crisis. What have been the ingredients of this rebound?

10. What are the functions of lead managers and co-managers in Eurocurrency market syndicated loans? Why do U.S. banks tend to dominate the standings in *Euromoney's* listing of top syndicated loan managers?

11. What are Euronote issuance facilities (NIFs)? Explain both their sudden rise and their subsequent decline. In addition, explain why it may be premature to announce them as having died.

12. Explain the sudden emergence of Euro-CP as a major lending vehicle in the Eurocurrency market.

13. Why is it that medium-term Euronotes (MTNs) appear to be a rising star in the Eurocurrency market's constellation of lending instruments?

| A P P E N D I X | *Appendix 13.1* |

The BCCI Case and Its Implications

The following account of the Bank of Commerce and Credit International case relies heavily on a statement presented by J. Virgil Mattingly, General Counsel, Board of Governors of the Federal Reserve System, before a subcommittee of the U.S. Senate.[1]

Since the spring of 1991, much news coverage has been devoted to the international banking scandal associated with the operations of the Bank for

---

[1] J. Virgil Mattingly, Jr., "Statement before the Subcommittee on Consumer and Regulatory Affairs of the Committee on Banking, Housing, and Urban Affairs, U.S. Senate, May 23, 1991," *Federal Reserve Bulletin*, July 1991, pp. 572–581.

Credit and Commerce International (BCCI), a Luxembourg-based bank with widespread deposit operations and an extensive involvement in private banking. Based on information indicating that BCCI was operating in violation of British law, the government of the United Kingdom shut down BCCI's operation in London in July 1991 and assumed control over its assets. Banking authorities in the United States, Luxembourg, and numerous other countries have also closed the doors on BCCI's operations in their countries. Subsequent revelations have indicated that many of BCCI's depositors can expect to recover little from the bank's assets, and press reports have indicated that the chief stockholders of BCCI, the royal family of Abu Dhabi and the government of that country, stand to lose more than $1 billion of their investment. Press reports have also indicated that, on many occasions, officers of BCCI violated the banking laws of host countries and used the bank's assets to illegally enrich themselves and parties with whom they dealt.

In the United States, BCCI had never been authorized to directly engage in deposit banking, but it had been allowed to have representative offices. It was also authorized to operate as a bank holding company, subject to the approval by the Board of Governors of the Federal Reserve System under the terms of the Bank Holding Company Act. No acquisitions were so approved, but it was subsequently revealed that BCCI had gained control of the Independence Bank, headquartered in Encino, California, and the National Bank of Georgia without obtaining prior authorization to do so. The National Bank of Georgia became a subsidiary of First American Bankshares in 1987, and it is this relationship between BCCI and First American Bankshares that is at the center of the BCCI controversy in the United States.

Originally known as Financial General Bankshares, First American Bankshares owns banks in the District of Columbia and several states. As early as 1977, the chief executive of BCCI, Agha Hasan Abedi, expressed an interest in acquiring a controlling interest in Financial General. In late 1977 and early 1978, four prominent BCCI clients from Saudi Arabia and Kuwait acquired approximately 20 percent of Financial General's shares. The Securities and Exchange Commission ruled, however, that these investors were in violation of a statute known as the Williams Act. Under the terms of this act, the investors either had to divest their shares or make an offer for all the shares of Financial General. Three of the four investors then joined with a group of individual and corporate investors from the Middle East to form Credit and Commerce American Holdings, N.V. (CCAH), a Netherland Antilles corporation, for the purpose of making a tender offer for the shares of American General.

In October 1978, CCAH filed an application with the Board of Governors to acquire Financial General's shares, but the Board dismissed the application because Financial General's Maryland subsidiary opposed it, and Maryland law forbade the hostile acquisition of a Maryland bank. Subsequently, however, Financial General's management worked out an acceptable takeover proposal with CCAH, and in November 1980, CCAH again applied for approval to acquire Financial General. After an elaborate investigation of the proposed acquisition, which included consideration of the relationship between CCAH and BCCI, the acquisition was approved on April 19, 1982. In

August 1982, Financial General Bankshares was renamed First American Bankshares.

The application filed by CCAH stated that BCCI owned no shares in CCAH, either directly or indirectly, and that BCCI had not and would not lend for the purpose of acquiring stock in CCAH or in two subsidiaries related to the Financial General acquisition that CCAH had established. It was also indicated by the petitioners that the only relationship between BCCI and CCAH that existed or was intended was that BCCI would serve as an investment adviser to CCAH. The two subsidiaries created by CCAH were Credit and Commerce American Investment, B.V. (CCAI), a Netherlands company, and FGB Holding (subsequently renamed First American Corporation), a District of Columbia corporation wholly owned by CCAI. FGB Holding was used to acquire the shares of Financial General.

CCAH's application also specified that no role in the management or operation of Financial General was to be played by the Middle Eastern investors. Financial General's management was to be placed in the hands of a board of directors that was to include former U.S. Senator Stuart Symington, former Secretary of Defense, Clark Clifford, and retired Lieutenant General, Elwood R. Quesada.

When Financial General Bankshares became First American Bankshares, Clifford became chairman of its board of directors, Symington became chairman of the board of CCAH, and Clifford's law partner, Robert A. Altman, became president of First American Corporation as well as secretary and a managing director of CCAH. In short, the top management of the chain of companies involved in the Financial General acquisition, with the exception of CCAI, was placed in the hands of prominent American citizens.

In 1988, BCCI was indicted for money laundering, and early in 1989, it pleaded guilty to this charge in a federal court in Tampa. At that time, CCAH was preparing an application to acquire a bank in Florida. The combination of these developments led to an investigation by the Federal Reserve Bank of Richmond to determine the relationship between CCAH and BCCI. The Richmond Fed reported to the Board of Governors on February 8, 1989, that it had found no evidence of an irregular relationship between these two entities or of a failure by CCAH to live up to its commitments. The report indicated, however, that there were individuals who owned shares in both CCAH and BCCI. In spite of this discovery, The Board of Governors concluded that because the Bank Holding Company Act does not prohibit common ownership of banking firms by individuals as it does in the case of companies, there was no basis for acting against CCAH.

By this time, there was a growing concern in the United States that CCAH and BCCI were, in fact, linked. In late 1989, the Board of Governors was advised by a foreign banking supervisor that BCCI had outstanding loans to some stockholders of CCAH. The Board contacted BCCI about the matter and was assured that BCCI had played no role in the acquisition of Financial General and that BCCI held no stock of CCAH as loan collateral.

In November 1990, the office of the New York County District Attorney informed Federal Reserve authorities that a confidential source had indicated to it that BCCI had made substantial loans to CCAH stockholders secured by CCAH shares. This information led to an examination of records in BCCI's main office in London in December 1990, and the conclusion was reached that BCCI did indeed have substantial loans outstanding that were secured by CCAH stock. Further investigation provided additional proof of the link between CCAH and BCCI. On March 4, 1991, BCCI consented to a cease and desist order from the Department of Justice that required it to divest its holdings of stock in CCAH and its subsidiaries, to avoid future transactions with CCAH, and to submit a plan for closing down its operations in the United States.

Further developments suggest that the relationship between BCCI and CCAH was only the tip of a large iceberg. In July 1991, the British authorities closed BCCI's operations in their country, and since that time, numerous sensational revelations and charges about BCCI have been added to the mix. Perhaps U.S. residents should take comfort in the fact that the damage caused by the BCCI debacle in their country appears to have been relatively minor.

The BCCI case has raised a number of issues about the regulation of international banking. Particularly disturbing is that while there was good reason to suspect a link between BCCI and CCAH as early as 1978, the existence of the relationship was not exposed until 1990. Discovering the link was difficult because of supervisory agencies in one country lacking access to information held by supervisory agencies in other countries; the existence of bank secrecy laws; legal manuevers to prevent the disclosure of documents and other information of interest to regulatory authorities; and the fact that existing laws governing banks that operate internationally do not require banks to maintain consolidated records about their operations in any single country.

Without doubt, the BCCI debacle increases the likelihood that the U.S. government will pass legislation designed to place the operations of foreign banks in the United States under greater regulatory scrutiny. The greater the extent to which governments in other countries, including offshore banking centers, refuse to fully cooperate with U.S. authorities in matters pertaining to international banking, the more certain it is that the U.S. government will pass legislation designed to place the operations of foreign banks in the United States under stricter controls.

BCCI was able to operate as it did because it was able to prevent regulatory authorities from developing a comprehensive picture of its operations. As a Luxembourg corporation with headquarters in London, with its stockholders in the Middle East, with operations extended to many countries, and with friends who were often prominently placed, BCCI was able to avoid a regulatory judgment day for more than a decade. Above all, the lesson of the BCCI case should be that there is a need for an international agreement to ensure that every bank operating extensively internationally is subject to comprehensive supervision on a consolidated basis by *some* supervisory authority. Ordinarily, this authority should be in the hands of the governments of banks' home countries. Obviously, however, there are situations when this kind of authority should not be entrusted to the home country government. Luxembourg is certainly not the most lax country in the world in terms of bank supervision, but there is no reason why its government should be assigned the responsibility for overseeing the operations of a bank with a small office there that has operations all over the globe.

International Securities Markets

■

Just as the forex and international banking markets have undergone profound, even revolutionary, changes since 1973, so also have markets in internationally traded securities. Much of the basic structures of these markets have been retained, but the elaborations and refinements of those structures have been numerous and extensive. Moreover, it is clear that the momentum for change in these markets is far from exhausted. The complete international integration of bond and stock markets in the leading industrial countries has not yet been achieved, but a profound movement in that direction is likely to continue.

Most of our attention in this chapter will be directed to international bond markets, for they are much larger than international markets in equities and have proceeded farther down the road toward complete international financial integration. Toward the end of the decade of the 1980s, however, the internationalization of stock markets accelerated sharply. As a consequence, international markets in equities have now become, for the first time, a major component of the overall structure of international financial markets. Accordingly, a portion of this chapter is devoted to the developing international markets in equity securities.

International Bonds: An Overview

International bonds are bonds that are issued and distributed on behalf of nonresident borrowers. These bonds fall into two categories: foreign bonds and Eurobonds. **Foreign bonds** are issued in domestic capital markets and are distinguished from other bonds issued in those markets by having foreign borrowers. They are normally denominated in the national currencies of the countries in which they are issued. Host country governments commonly distinguish legally between them and bonds issued by domestic borrowers, but they are distributed and traded like domestic bonds.

Eurobonds are denominated in currencies other than those of the countries in which they are issued. For example, if the government of Sweden borrows dollars by issuing bonds that are initially distributed in the United States, the bonds are foreign bonds, but if it borrows dollars by issuing dollar-denominated bonds that are initially distributed in countries other than the United States, the bonds are Eurobonds.

Foreign bonds may be denominated in currencies other than those of the countries in which they are issued. For example, if Ecu-denominated bonds were to be issued in the United States, their issuer would have to satisfy SEC requirements for issuing bonds domestically, and their initial distribution would probably occur entirely in the United States. This means one would more accurately call such bonds *foreign bonds* rather than *Eurobonds*.

There is an international aspect even to domestic bond issues to the extent that such bonds are purchased by foreigners. The large budget deficits of the U.S. government have been financed in part by the sale of Treasury bonds to foreigners. Also, foreign investors have been prominent buyers of junk bonds issued in the U.S. domestic bond market in connection with corporate takeover attempts.

It has been suggested that it is fitting to speak of the forex *market* and the Eurocurrency *market,* but it is preferable to speak of international bond *markets.*[1] The point is that the international distribution and trading of bonds occurs in an environment of market segmentation. Increasingly, however, international financial integration is moving the world toward an essentially unified world bond market with blurred lines of demarcation between the Eurobond market and domestic bond markets. As Bruno Solnik has observed, "current differences in costs and trading procedures and other impediments are bound to disappear as the internationalization of the world bond market continues."[2]

Most international bond issues are distributed to the general public amidst many competitive issues through a network of investment banking firms that serve as underwriters. Increasingly, however, bonds are being distributed as **private placements,** in which the underwriting firms sell them directly to institutional investors, such as pension funds and insurance companies without offering them to the public. Privately placed bonds generally lack the liquidity of publicly offered bonds, and their terms often make them similar to longer-term bank loans. They offer advantages, however, in terms of time and cost. For example, because they can be sold with a minimum effort by the investment banks that serve as intermediaries, the fees charged to the borrowers by the intermediaries are relatively low.

The History of International Bonds

Foreign bonds have a fairly lengthy history, in fact, they antedate the rise of national stock markets. In the nineteenth century, governments discovered that bond issues could be used to deal with their long-standing problem of financing growing spending on public works in an era of low taxes and hard money. Private corporations found them to be a convenient vehicle for raising

---

[1]J. Orlin Grabbe, *International Financial Markets* (New York: Elsevier, 1986), p. 271.

[2]Bruno Solnik, *International Investments* 2d ed. (Reading, Mass.: Addison-Wesley, 1988), p. 161.

long-term capital without surrendering control. (The development of holding companies was basically a twentieth-century phenomenon.) Even today, in many countries the prevailing patterns of corporate ownership feature closely held companies whose stocks are not publicly traded. As domestic bond markets evolved, foreign bonds denominated in pounds sterling and other gold standard currencies began to be issued in London and other financial centers. Such bonds were generally issued by governments.

Foreign bonds have tended to be issued in countries with well-developed capital markets and currencies whose exchange values tend to hold up well over time. Accordingly, such countries as the United Kingdom, the United States, and, lately, Japan, have loomed relatively large in foreign bond statistics. Surprisingly, perhaps, Switzerland heads the list of countries in which foreign bonds are issued. The preeminence of Switzerland in this respect is explained by at least five factors. First, Switzerland has a long history of political and economic stability and a currency whose exchange value has weathered the test of time. Second, while Switzerland is small, it is wealthy and has a large volume of savings. Third, although the Swiss government has historically imposed severe restrictions on direct international lending by Swiss banks, it has allowed these same banks to engage freely in investment banking. Fourth, the Swiss government has encouraged foreign borrowers to issue bonds denominated in Swiss francs by imposing easily satisfied requirements and regulations for foreign bond issues and by exempting nonresidents from withholding of taxes on bond interest payments. Fifth, the Swiss central bank, known as the Swiss National Bank, has restricted transfers of Swiss franc bank deposits to prevent trading in Swiss franc-denominated Eurobonds. A borrower wishing to issue bonds denominated in Swiss francs must therefore issue them in Switzerland.

Incidentally, the exclusion of Swiss franc bonds from the Eurobond market has not prevented Swiss banks from being major participants in that market. Bonds denominated in currencies other than the Swiss franc are issued in Switzerland, and Swiss banks have used their expertise in bond underwriting and investment to establish a major presence in the distribution and trading of bonds issued in other countries. Moreover, a large but unknown proportion of Eurobonds are ultimately held in Switzerland in foreign individuals' fiduciary accounts that are administered by Swiss banks.[3]

The history of Eurobonds is much shorter than that of foreign bonds. As was pointed out in Chapter 2, Eurobonds did not become important until the 1960s, when they rose to prominence because of the interest equalization tax and other restrictions on foreign bond issues imposed by the U.S. government. Subsequently, the Eurobond market's development has followed a bumpy

---

[3]Although it is admittedly difficult to be certain, it is widely believed that in the past, up to 50 percent of all Eurobonds have been held in this manner. The proportion of Eurobonds so held is probably decreasing, however, because of increasing participation in the Eurobond market by institutional investors and other factors. See Torben Juul Andersen, *Euromarket Instruments* (New York: New York Institute of Finance, 1990), p. 96.

path. In 1973 and 1974, for example, the dollar's weakness and the upward movement of interest rates discouraged Eurobond financing. In the late 1970s, the upward movement of interest rates was again a discouraging factor. In 1987, a combination of uncertainty about the dollar, renewed inflation fears, and too many new Eurobond issues led to a market retrenchment. Overall, however, the Eurobond market has grown rapidly. The market is large and innovative, and as long as domestic bond markets continue to be separated from it by regulations and other factors, its continued existence seems assured.

A major factor behind the growth of Eurobond financing during the 1980s was the emergence of interest-rate and currency swaps, which are subjects of Chapter 16. By issuing Eurobonds and swapping the resulting obligations for obligations payable in other currencies and/or other types of interest payments, the issuers of Eurobonds have been able to achieve gains in terms of cost savings and hedging. The gains have been important enough that most Eurobond issues since around 1986 have been swap-driven.

Although the Eurobond market is much larger than all foreign bond markets combined, this does not mean that foreign bonds are being phased out. To the contrary, since 1984 when the U.S. government eliminated its withholding requirement for taxes on interest payments to foreign bondholders, foreign bond markets have enjoyed a new vitality. It should be kept in mind, however, that the distinctions between the two types of bond markets are becoming less significant. For some time now, and beginning well before 1984, a simplification process has been underway in which the restrictions on bond financing and trading in domestic markets have been relaxed and the techniques and practices employed by bond issuers, investment banking intermediaries, and bond investors have become increasingly standardized. Thus, as was suggested earlier, the world may be moving toward a single market in international bonds.

Some International Bond Statistics

Exhibit 14.1 presents data from *Financial Market Trends* on new interbond issues for the years 1988, 1989, and 1990 and for the first eight months of 1990 and 1991. It divides international bonds into two main classes: international issues and foreign issues. The international issues of Exhibit 14.1 can be considered to be Eurobonds. Included with the Eurobonds, however, are relatively small amounts of foreign currency bonds sold in domestic bond markets that are conceptually foreign bonds as the term is used in this book. The foreign issues of Exhibit 14.1 consist of bonds that are issued in a domestic bond markets and are denominated in the currencies of the countries in which they are issued. The vast majority of foreign bonds issued fall into this category.

Exhibit 14.1 also has a category called special placements, which are more often called private placements. The blanks for 1989, 1990, and 1991 for bonds of this category are misleading. They simply mean that private placements that would qualify to be called international bonds have not been separated from other issues in the data for these years.

| E X H I B I T | 14.1 | *International Bond Issues: 1988–August 1991*
(Billions of U.S. Dollars)

				January–August	
Type of Issue	1988	1989	1990	1990	1991
All issues					
International issues	178.8	212.8	180.1	118.3	161.7
Foreign issues	48.3	42.9	49.8	31.2	33.3
Special placements	2.5	—	—	—	—
Total	229.6	255.7	229.9	149.5	195.0
International issues by currency					
U.S. dollar	74.5	117.5	70.0	46.6	52.6
Yen	15.9	15.6	22.8	13.3	17.7
Sterling	23.6	18.5	20.9	13.8	19.2
Deutschemark	23.7	16.4	18.3	14.2	12.3
Ecu	11.2	12.6	17.9	12.4	24.7
French franc	2.3	4.5	9.4	5.5	8.7
Canadian dollar	13.1	12.5	6.4	3.5	14.0
Italian lira	1.5	3.5	5.4	2.7	6.1
Australian dollar	8.4	6.7	5.2	3.9	2.7
Dutch guilder	2.1	2.3	0.8	0.4	1.4
New Zealand dollar	0.8	0.7	0.5	0.4	0.3
Danish krone	1.0	0.2	0.2	—	0.1
Other	0.7	1.8	2.3	1.6	1.9
Total	178.8	212.8	180.1	118.3	161.7
Foreign issues by market					
Switzerland	26.3	18.6	23.2	15.7	14.6
United States	10.1	9.4	9.9	6.1	8.0
Japan	6.7	8.2	7.9	4.4	4.0
Luxembourg	1.8	1.7	4.4	2.7	3.8
Netherlands	0.7	—	0.6	0.3	0.1
United Kingdom	0.4	1.2	0.3	—	0.1
Other	2.3	3.8	3.5	2.0	2.7
Total	48.3	42.9	49.8	31.2	33.3

Source: *Financial Market Trends*, October 1991, p. 89.

It is clear from Exhibit 14.1 that the volume of Eurobonds issued is far greater than that of foreign bonds, and that among Eurobonds, the U.S. dollar is by far the most popular currency of denomination. There is no doubt that the relative popularity of dollar Eurobonds has tended to decline over the years, but on a year-to-year-basis, the effect of this trend is often masked by relatively short-term factors. The sharp decline in dollar Eurobond issues that occurred in 1990, for example, is surely not to be explained by investors' sudden desire to obtain the benefits of portfolio diversification of assets among currencies, but by shifts in the preferences of borrowers and investors based on changes in expectations. The proportion of Eurobonds that are dollar-denominated tends to increase when the dollar's exchange value is expected to hold up well, when the expected real interest rate in the United States is relatively high, and when the prospects for a low inflation rate in the United States are promising. It tends to decrease when the opposite circumstances prevail.

Among the factors influencing the currency composition of Eurobonds is the use of currency swaps. In 1987 and 1988, for example, there was a surge of Eurobond issues denominated in Australian dollars because of the attractions of currency swaps involving that currency. In 1989 there was a large increase in U.S. dollar Eurobond issues by Japanese firms because of the ability of those firms to issue such bonds on attractive terms and swap them for low-rate yen obligations.

The recent rise in the popularity of Ecu Eurobonds is also largely due to currency swaps. Sovereign borrowers are relatively prominent among the issuers of Ecu bonds, and most of the Ecu bonds that are issued by private borrowers are issued by multinational firms with high credit ratings. The bonds are popular with investors because they offer an attractive combination of yields and safety. While the use of the Ecu as a medium of exchange is growing, there tends to be a mismatch between the proceeds received from issuing Ecu bonds and the need for them in transactions. This is especially the case with sovereign borrowers and some of the relatively small corporate issuers. This mismatch is eliminated by using currency swaps. Note that in the first eight months of 1991, the Ecu rose to a strong second place among the currencies in which Eurobonds were denominated.

Exhibit 14.1 also highlights the previously mentioned importance of the Swiss bond market. Among other domestic bond markets, only those of the United States, Japan, and Luxembourg issued significant amounts of foreign bonds in the years surveyed.

Exhibit 14.2 presents BIS data on international bond issues for 1988, 1989, and 1990. It provides information on the different types of bond issues, which is a matter to be considered later in the chapter. The reason for including Exhibit 14.2 at this point is that it indicates the extent to which scheduled and early repayments reduced the net amount of borrowing from new bond issues. In 1989, for example, $263.6 billion in international bonds were issued, but repayments reduced the net amount of new borrowing to $174.3 billion.

Exhibit 14.3 provides data on the distribution of international bond issues among borrowing countries and international agencies from 1986 through the first eight months of 1991. It indicates that more than 90 percent of all new issues during the period were by borrowers in nations belonging to the OECD, whose members are overwhelmingly economically developed countries. It also indicates that, while international bond issues were widely distributed among OECD members, Japan led all other borrowers by a wide margin.

Outside the OECD, the predominant issuers of international bonds are international organizations, such as the World Bank, who use their relatively high credit standings (assured by government guarantees behind their debts) to fund loans to countries that are unable to issue foreign-currency bonds on their own. A few developing countries (mostly in the Far East, including India) have been able to issue foreign bonds in recent years. Very recently, a few Latin American countries have been able to issue international bonds.

| E X H I B I T | 14.2 | *Main Features of International Bond Market Activity: 1988–1990 (Billions of U.S. Dollars)*

| Classification | New Issues | | | Stocks at Year-End 1990 |
	1988	1989	1990	
Total announced gross new issues[a]	226.3	261.8	241.7	
Straight fixed-rate issues	160.8	149.5	166.5	
Floating-rate notes	23.5	27.1	42.1	
Equity-related issues[b]	42.0	85.2	33.2	
Total completed gross new issues	220.7	263.6	239.4	
Minus: Scheduled repayments	42.7	57.4	87.3	
Minus: Early repayments	39.9	32.0	21.1	
Equals total net new issues	138.1	174.3	131.0	1,472.5
Straight fixed-rate issues	99.0	89.0	80.7	1,008.1
Floating-rate notes	5.1	10.5	27.1	205.7
Equity-related issues[b]	34.1	74.8	23.2	258.7

[a]Nondollar bonds are converted into dollars at exchange rates prevailing on announcement dates.

[b]Convertible bonds and bonds with equity warrants.

Source: Bank for International Settlements, *61st Annual Report* (Basle: BIS, 1991), p. 135.

| E X H I B I T | 14.3 | *International Bond Issues by Countries and Groups of Borrowers: 1988–August 1991 (Billions of U.S. Dollars)*

| Country and Classification | 1988 | 1989 | 1990 | January–August | |
				1990	1991
OECD countries	213.4	240.4	208.4	136.9	181.1
Australia	8.4	7.2	3.5	2.3	2.3
Canada	13.1	13.2	12.9	7.9	15.7
France	16.5	13.7	17.4	11.7	16.0
Germany	12.3	10.0	9.6	7.9	8.6
Italy	7.9	9.3	13.2	9.0	8.2
Japan	51.3	97.5	55.4	30.4	49.1
Sweden	8.4	6.1	6.6	4.9	4.2
United Kingdom	26.5	20.3	20.0	12.7	20.2
United States	17.3	15.8	21.8	16.3	12.5
Other OECD	51.7	47.3	48.0	33.8	44.3
Developing countries	4.2	2.6	4.5	2.6	4.8
Eastern Europe	1.4	2.2	1.6	1.1	0.3
International development organizations	8.0	10.3	15.0	8.7	7.7
Other	0.1	0.2	0.4	0.2	1.1
Total	227.1	255.7	229.9	149.5	195.0

Source: *Financial Market Trends*, October 1991, p. 60.

The issuers of international bonds include governments, international organizations, well-known financial firms, and nonfinancial corporations. In general, investors strongly prefer the issues of borrowers with high credit ratings. Issuers of junk bonds need not apply. Increasingly, however, corporations that are not classified among the top-rated borrowers have successfully issued international bonds that were amply secured by such assets as mortgages, automobile paper, and credit card obligations. The highest-rated borrowers commonly issue international bonds in amounts ranging from $100 million to $500 million, but some private corporations have floated "jumbo" international bond issues of $1.5 billion or more. Borrowers with bond credit ratings as low as A are unlikely to issue international bonds in amounts exceeding $200 million.

The precise composition of the group of investors in international bonds is something of a mystery because all Eurobonds and many international bonds are in bearer form. It is widely believed that until very recently, most investors have been wealthy individuals. At present, however, international bonds are popular with institutional investors who have been attracted by improvements in secondary markets, the relaxation of investment controls by home country governments, and growing awareness of the advantages of portfolio diversification.

The Nuts and Bolts of International Bonds

Among the features of international bonds that merit inclusion in a survey of international financial markets are the different types of bond instruments, issuing procedures and costs, legal considerations including taxation, the relationship of international bonds to swap financing, and their role in portfolio strategy. International bonds are a complicated subject, and going deeply into all of their features would require writing another book. Of necessity, therefore, the focus here is on the features that distinguish them from domestic bonds. For details on the technical aspects of bond prices and yields, the reader should consult works that specialize in such matters. Because Chapter 16 covers financial swaps, their connections with bond financing are not explored in this chapter.

Types of Bond Instruments

A bewildering assortment of international bonds are available. The diverse talents and experience of financial engineers from different countries have been pooled to provide the Eurobond market with its highly innovative and adaptable environment. Much of this flexibility has spilled over into foreign bond issues. With respect to the form in which payments are made to bondholders, there are three main categories of international bonds: fixed-rate or straight bonds, floating-rate notes (FRNs), and zero-coupon bonds.

Straight bonds require periodic interest payments. In the Eurobond market the payment interval is 1 year, but in domestic bond markets it is generally 6 months. In the Eurobond market interest payments are based on a 360-day year and interest accrues on the basis of 30-day months. Most domestic issues of straight bonds also use a 360-day year, but some, most notably bonds issued in the United Kingdom, use a 365-day year. Some **perpetual bonds,** i.e., bonds that never mature, are issued, but most straight bonds have finite maturities. A **bullet bond** requires payment of the entire principal amount at a single maturity date. Bullet bonds are popular, but many bond issues allow full or partial redemption before their final maturity dates.

Floating-rate international bonds (FRNs) pay interest based on reference rates, usually the 6-month or 3-month LIBOR. The periodic interest payments depend on what happens to the reference rate between payment intervals. A common practice is to adjust the interest rate on an interest payment date to reflect any changes in the reference rate since the previous interest payment date or, in the case of the first interest payment, since the starting date. The interest rate for the next period is then known in advance. The interest rate paid during a payment interval may, however, be *postdetermined.* For example, the interest rate may be determined by averaging the reference rate for the interest payment period or by the reference rate on the interest payment date. Some FRNs are **index-linked bonds.** For such bonds, the coupon amount (interest payment) or even the principal to be repaid may be adjusted according to changes in an underlying price index, which may be an index of commodity prices, a stock market index, an index of interest rates, or some other type of index. A 360-day year is generally used for setting interest payments, but whereas fixed-rate Eurobonds use 30-day months in calculating accrued interest, accrued interest on floating-rate Eurobonds is calculated on the basis of actual days. There are some perpetual FRNs, but most FRNs have definite maturity dates.

Zero-coupon bonds do not pay interest, but are sold on a discount basis. They are popular with investors from countries that treat the difference between the purchase price of a security and its redemption price as a capital gain for tax purposes, provided, of course, that capital gains are taxed more leniently than ordinary income. They also appeal to issuers who do not wish to incur obligations to make periodic interest payments during bond issues' lives.

Exhibit 14.4 gives the OECD's estimate of new issues of international bonds from 1986 to August 1991, classified by types of bond instruments. Figures for five types of bonds are shown: straight bonds, FRNs, zero-coupon bonds, convertible bonds, and bonds with equity warrants. Convertibles and bonds with equity warrants are usually (but not always) fixed-interest bonds, but they have features that merit a separate listing in statistical compilations. As Exhibit 14.4 shows, both convertibles and bonds with equity warrants, particularly the latter, have attained considerable importance in recent years, certainly enough importance to "warrant" an examination of their characteristics.

Recall that Exhibit 14.2 also presents data on the types of international bonds issued, although in somewhat less detail than Exhibit 14.4 does. The differences in the amounts shown in the two tables are due, to some extent, to the use of different techniques for exchange rate conversion. Exhibit 14.2

| E X H I B I T | 14.4 | *Types of International and Foreign Bond*
Offerings: 1988–August 1991

	1988	1989	1990	January–August 1990	January–August 1991
New Issues by Major Instrument (billions of dollars)[a]					
Straights	160.2	154.6	158.9	105.6	147.8
Floating rate	22.3	17.8	37.1	21.9	11.5
Convertibles	11.3	14.1	10.6	8.0	8.0
Bonds with equity warrants	29.7	66.2	21.2	12.8	25.8
Zero coupons	1.1	2.3	1.5	0.8	1.8
Other	2.5	0.7	0.6	0.4	0.1
Total	227.1	255.7	229.9	149.5	195.0
Structure of the Market by Major Instrument (percent)					
Straights	70.5	60.5	69.1	70.6	75.8
Floating rate	9.8	6.9	16.1	14.6	5.9
Convertibles	5.0	5.5	4.6	5.4	4.1
Bonds with equity warrants	13.1	25.9	9.2	8.6	13.2
Zero coupons	0.5	0.9	0.7	0.5	0.9
Other	1.1	0.3	0.3	0.3	0.1
Total	100.0	100.0	100.0	100.0	100.0

[a]Nondollar bonds are converted into dollars at constant exchange rates during each period.
Source: *Financial Market Trends*, October 1991, p. 60.

converts nondollar bonds into dollars at the exchange rates prevailing on announcement dates. Exhibit 14.4 uses constant exchange rates to make the conversions.

Convertible Bonds   A **convertible bond** is exchangeable into some other asset. Typically, such a bond is exchangeable, at the option of the bondholder, into a predetermined number of shares of the common stock of the issuing corporation. Some are convertible into shares in one or more *other* companies. Some are convertible into bonds with different payment characteristics — fixed-interest bonds are sometimes convertible into floating-interest bonds or vice versa. Some convertible bonds have even been exchangeable for commodities, notably gold or oil. It is assumed here, however, that the term *convertible bonds* means bonds that are exchangeable for the stock of the issuing corporation.

While convertible bonds are normally convertible into shares of stock at a single predetermined price, the conversion price sometimes varies according to a formula. *Putable convertibles* allow the bondholders to sell the bonds back to the issuer without conversion, while *callable convertibles* allow the bond issuer the right of early redemption without conversion. There is often a *currency play,* in which a convertible bond issue is denominated in a currency different from the one in which the stock can be purchased.

The convertibility feature allows bond issuers to borrow at lower interest rates than would otherwise be available. In effect, the bondholder pays an option premium by accepting a lower interest rate than other issues would pay. Since the option the bondholder receives is a call option, the pricing of the convertibility feature follows the principles of call option pricing. The interest saving realized by the issuer of convertibles is greatest when the prospects for an upswing in the price of its stock are most promising.

Bonds with Equity Warrants   **Equity warrants** are negotiable certificates that give their owners the right to purchase predetermined numbers of common shares of the issuing corporation at specified prices during specified time periods. They are commonly attached to bond issues, but **naked warrants** are also issued that are not attached to bond issues. Bonds with warrants resemble convertibles, but offer greater flexibility since the warrants can be detached from the bonds and sold separately. The detachability feature also means that the warrants can be retained and the bonds sold separately.

Exhibit 14.4 shows that from 1988 through August 1991, the volume of bonds issued with warrants attached greatly exceeded the volumes of convertibles. The use of equity warrants was particularly great in 1989, when bonds with warrants attached accounted for more than one-fourth of all new international bond issues.

The popularity of bonds with equity warrants is largely due to the success of Japanese firms with this instrument. A bull market in Japanese stocks during much of the 1980s allowed Japanese firms to issue dollar Eurobonds with warrants at attractive interest rates and use currency swaps to convert the dollar obligations into medium- and long-term yen obligations carrying remarkably low interest rates. Toward the end of 1989, however, the Japanese stock market went into a downward spiral that continued through most of 1990. The market was fairly stable in 1991, and some recovery of bonds with equity warrants occurred.

Linked to the downward spiral of Japanese stocks in 1990 and also contributing to the decline in bond issues with equity warrants was a general rise in interest rates that set in around the beginning of the year and was particularly pronounced in such strong currencies as the yen, the mark, and the Swiss franc. A rise in interest rates lowers the present value of any future gains from common stock appreciation. Since the value of equity warrants hinges on the probability of such gains, that value also tends to diminish. If the value of the warrants diminishes, the interest-rate reductions that can be realized by issuing bonds with warrants also decline, reducing the incentive to issue the bonds.

Since equity warrants are detachable, the bonds to which they are attached are valued separately from the warrants, and since the bonds carry relatively low interest rates, they are sold at substantial discounts. This feature of the bonds appeals to investors who want to realize capital gains by buying discount bonds and holding them to maturity, or at least until they have substantially appreciated. For this reason, the clientele for bonds with equity warrants is not limited to investors who hope to gain from appreciating prices of underlying stocks.

The detachability of the warrants also means that the bonds can readily be used to arrange financial swaps. With convertible bonds, by contrast, the arrangement of swaps is hampered by uncertainty surrounding the possibility of conversion. For example, a problem would arise for an issuer of convertible bonds who used a swap to hedge the bond obligation if that obligation should be reduced or eliminated through conversion. Incidentally, whereas convertibles are often callable by the issuers, bonds with warrants attached are generally noncallable with respect to both the bonds themselves and the warrants. Some *redeemable warrants* allow the issuer to call them at a predetermined price if they have not been exercised by a certain date.

Other differences between convertibles and bonds with equity warrants include their effects on the issuer's cash flows and balance sheet. In the case of convertibles, conversion means a reduction in a liability and an offsetting increase in equity. Any cash flow occurring because of a difference between a bond's redemption price and the price of the stock acquired is likely to be very small. When equity warrants are exercised, however, there is a cash flow to the issuer together with an increase in the issuer's equity without a matching reduction in its liabilities.

Just as there are variations in the types of convertible bonds, there are also variations in the types of equity warrants. In addition to the redeemable warrants previously mentioned, *interest-bearing warrants* require investors to pay higher warrant premiums in exchange for receiving periodic interest payments from the issuer. Some issues of warrants are divided into *warrant classes*, each of which carries a different exercise period and/or a different strike price.

Straight Bonds and FRNs Returning to Exhibit 14.4, it is obvious that straight bonds are the backbone of international bond markets. Even in 1989, when the equity warrant fad reached its peak, straights accounted for 60.5 percent of all international bond issues. In the first eight months of 1990, the corresponding figure rose to 75.8 percent.

The distribution of international bond issues between straight bonds and FRNs depends on a number of factors. Among them, five seem worthy of mention. First, there is interest-rate uncertainty. The rise of FRNs to prominence approximately tracked the increase in interest-rate volatility that followed the collapse of the Bretton Woods System in 1973.[4] Second, the use of straight bonds is strongly affected by variations in the popularity of equity warrants and the convertibility feature. Third, FRNs are, to a considerable extent, substitutes for syndicated loans. Fourth, the use of straight bonds is strongly influenced by the use of financial swaps. Fifth, both straight and floating-rate international bonds are strongly affected by developments in domestic bond markets, particularly the U.S. domestic bond market.

---

[4]According to Andersen, *Euromarket Instruments*, p. 111, the first FRN issue actually occurred in 1970, when an Italian utility issued FRNs indexed to the 6-month LIBOR. Incidentally, the Andersen book is a comprehensive and easily readable treatment of Euromarkets that is highly recommended to the reader.

During the 1970s, FRNs appealed to investors who were anxious to avoid losses from holding fixed-rate securities during a period of rising interest rates. Until the early 1980s, however, when the sovereign debt crisis emerged, syndicated loans dominated floating-rate international lending, and FRNs were largely confined to longer-term maturities of from 10 to 15 years. In reaction to the debt crisis, banks cut back on their longer-term floating-rate loans and sought to improve their liquidity positions in ways that involved minimal losses of earnings. Given their predominantly floating-rate liabilities, they preferred assets that also featured floating rates. Investing in FRNs seemed admirably suited for banks and other financial institutions with floating-rate liabilities, for not only were FRNs liquid and responsive to interest rate changes but they also offered yields that were a little higher than those on other floating-rate assets of comparable liquidity and quality. Accordingly, investment in FRNs by banks and other financial institutions became the driving force behind the growing use of FRNs; this persisted even when the trend in interest rates moved downward. It was not difficult to find borrowers who were willing to accommodate an increased investment demand for FRNs at a time when interest rates seemed destined to fall. Increasingly, therefore, banks substituted investments in FRNs for syndicated lending. One consequence of this development was a reduction in the maturities of FRNs so that they typically ranged from 7 to 10 years.

The reader may wonder how the yield on FRNs could have exceeded that on other floating-rate assets of comparable liquidity and quality. The explanation is twofold. First, FRNs generally have longer maturities than most other high-quality bank assets. Second, the spread or markup between an FRN rate and its reference rate tends to increase as the life of the FRN lengthens because the longer the life increases the risk that some event will adversely affect its value. Examples of such events would be deterioration in the borrower's credit standing or an increase in the spread between FRNs and their reference interest rate. If, for example, an FRN carries a spread of 0.25 percent over the 6-month LIBOR and the spread on newly issued FRNs of comparable quality and maturity rises to LIBOR plus 0.5 percent, an investor holding the FRN with the 0.25 percent spread experiences an opportunity loss that becomes realized if the FRN is sold.

During the first half of the 1980s, the trend toward substitution of FRNs for syndicated loans drew strong support from changes in relative borrowing costs. The relative cost of syndicated loans rose for two reasons. First, as the creditworthiness of Eurobanks came increasingly into question, the banks increased their deposit rates relative to competitive interest rates in order to attract funds. The relatively higher deposit rates were then reflected in loan rates. Second, as competition for FRN business increased among banks, fee cutting lowered the relative cost of FRN financing.

The growing popularity of FRNs as an investment medium led to the introduction of perpetual FRNs, on which the spreads typically ranged from 35 to 50 basis points over LIBOR. Toward the end of 1986, however, a combination of interest rate uncertainty and too many issues pushed the prices of perpetual FRNs well below par value, providing painful evidence to investors that longer-term FRNs are, after all, vulnerable to price fluctuations. FRN financing declined sharply in 1987, made a modest comeback in 1988, and declined again in 1989. There was a robust recovery of FRN financing in 1990, when nondollar, long-term interest rates generally rose, but 1991 produced a sharp decline that was based primarily on the expectation of lower long-term interest rates.

An important factor in the market for Eurobond FRNs is that they are normally indexed to a different reference rate from that used for domestic FRNs issued in the United States. Eurobond FRNs are customarily indexed to the LIBOR, though some are indexed to the LIBID or the LIMEAN (an average of the LIBOR and the LIBID). Domestic FRNs in the United States are commonly indexed to Treasury bill rates. As a result, Eurobond FRNs tend to be more stable in price and less stable in terms of interest rates than U.S. domestic FRNs. The explanation for these facts flows from the variability of the spread between the LIBOR and T-bill rates. When loan risks are generally low, LIBOR rates may not be more than 1 percent higher than corresponding T-bill rates, but when conditions are more disturbed, and particularly when there are doubts about the soundness of the international banking system, this differential widens substantially and has even been known to exceed 4 percent.

When the LIBOR rises relative to the T-bill rate, investors holding FRNs indexed to a T-bill rate find that their FRNs *decline* in price because they do not receive the upward adjustment in interest payments that is obtained by the holders of FRNs that are indexed to the LIBOR (or the LIBID, etc.). As Bruno Solnik has observed, "domestic FRNs indexed to Treasury bill rates are not an attractive investment during panicky periods."[5] Largely because domestic FRNs have a price volatility problem, they commonly offer such features as adjustable interest rate spreads and put clauses that protect investors.

As with other types of international bond instruments, international FRNs come in a variety of types. While the 6-month LIBOR is the most commonly used reference rate, the quarterly LIBOR is also used, as are other reference rates, including price indexes. Also as we have seen, there are perpetual FRNs and FRNs with postdetermined interest payments. There are also FRNs (known as *drop lock FRNs*) on which the interest rate switches from floating to fixed if the floating rate would otherwise fall below a certain figure.

Among the types of bonds that can be either straights or FRNs, **callable bonds** allow issuers to redeem the bonds at predetermined prices after stated periods of time. **Putable bonds** allow investors to sell the bonds back to their issuers after stated periods of time at predetermined prices. With *partly paid bonds,* investors commit themselves to make additional purchases at predetermined future dates, and with *deferred purchase bonds,* the purchasers pay part of the principal amounts at issue and the rest later. These last two options appeal to investors who hope to take advantage of expected declines in the

---

[5]Solnik, *International Investments,* p. 209.

exchange values of the currencies in which the bonds are denominated. Paralleling such instruments on the issuer side are *multiple tranche issues,* in which a borrower issues part of an authorized quantity of bonds on one date and, if desired, the rest at a later date or dates.

While most straight bonds and FRNs are bullet bonds, many issues fall into the **sinking fund** category, which means that they are progressively amortized over the issues' lives. The bonds to be redeemed early may be chosen by lot, or the issuer may redeem parts of an issue by purchasing bonds in the market according to a prearranged schedule. In some cases, bonds are issued with serial numbers indicating the specific dates on which they will be redeemed. Compared to other progressively amortized bonds, such *serial bonds* offer the investor the advantage of knowing when redemption will occur, but this advantage is often more than offset by the loss of liquidity that results from the proliferation of maturities.

The maturities of newly issued straight bonds fall generally within the range of 5 to 15 years. When interest-rate uncertainty increases, maturities tend to be shorter. On the other hand, there have been times when perpetual straight bonds have been popular. In reality, however, the lives of perpetuals are often much shorter than might seem to be implied from the lack of a maturity date. Perpetual straight bonds are generally callable, and when they are not, the issuers can generally redeem them by buying them back if market conditions warrant doing so.

The great proliferation of bond types makes for complexity in the determination of bond yields and prices. When, for example, a bond issue has an option feature, that feature must be taken into account in determining the bond's price. Compounding the complexity resulting from the proliferation of bond types, bond issues differ in the frequency of interest payments, the ways in which interest is calculated, the ways in which bond prices are quoted, and taxation. For example, while the interest payments on straight Eurobonds are based on a 360-day year and are almost always made annually, some domestic bond markets use a 365-day year. Even when, as in the United States, a 360-day year is used, it is common to make the interest payments semiannually. Consequently, before a valid comparison can be made between the yield on a Eurobond and the yield on a foreign bond or a domestic bond, it may be necessary to make adjustments for different characteristics.

A similar problem arises in connection with accrued interest. In most cases, the prices of international bonds are quoted separately from any interest accrual since the last interest payment date, but there are cases in which accrued interest is incorporated into bond quotations. Accordingly, investors must be careful to be certain that when they compare yields, they are treating accrued interest consistently. As far as taxes are concerned, while Eurobond interest payments are generally free from withholding tax requirements, some countries have withheld taxes on interest payments on bonds issued by domestic borrowers. Investors in countries that allow favorable tax treatment of capital gains may gain tax advantages in buying discounted bonds, including zero-coupon bonds, even if their yields are lower than those of other bonds with comparable risks.

Dual-Currency Bonds and Currency Option Bonds   For students of international finance, a particularly interesting bond variant is the **dual-currency bond,** which is issued and pays interest in one currency but is redeemed at maturity in another. Usually, the redemption exchange rate is set in advance, but there are dual-currency bonds whose redemption exchange rates are indexed to the exchange rate in existence at the time of redemption. Dual-currency bonds are ordinarily straight bonds.

The primary motivation behind issuing dual-currency bonds has been the desire of borrowers to take advantage of the relatively low interest rates that tend to be associated with strong currencies. Accordingly, these bonds have tended to be issued in marks, Swiss francs, and, lately, yen. Prior to 1990, U.S. corporations often issued dual-currency bonds in a low-interest rate currency and redeemed them in dollars. The proceeds of such bond issues were generally converted into dollars spot, and the issuers then relied on various hedging techniques to protect themselves from the exchange risk associated with the interest payments. The interest rate paid on the bonds depended in part upon the redemption exchange rate. If, for example, the redemption exchange rate was the same as the spot rate at the time of issue, the coupon rate paid on the bonds was likely to be higher than on other bonds to compensate investors for the risk of dollar depreciation. On the other hand, if the redemption exchange rate was indexed to the current spot rate, or if the redemption exchange rate was set in advance to provide investors with a strong margin of protection, the interest rate paid was likely to be no higher than on other bonds denominated in the same currency as that of the interest payments.

Somewhat similar to dual-currency bonds are **currency option bonds,** which give bondholders the right to receive both interest payments and redemption payments in either of two currencies. If there is a high probability that the exchange rate between the two currencies will vary considerably during the life of the bond issue, the interest rate paid in either currency is likely to be substantially lower than the interest rate paid on single-currency bonds denominated in either of the two currencies. The issuer usually protects itself against a large exchange rate movement by inserting a call provision into the bond agreement. While the issuer can thus protect itself against excessive exchange rate movements, the popularity of currency option bonds has tended to diminish over time because issuers tend to regard them as being too risky.

Issuing Procedures and Costs

In the Eurobond market, the standard procedure is to distribute a public offering through an investment banking syndicate that may include subsidiaries of commercial banks and firms that are classified as merchant banks. The process begins when a prospective bond issuer approaches one or more investment banks about its plans. The issuer selects a firm to serve as the issue's lead manager, and the lead manager commonly selects one or more investment banking firms to serve as **co-lead manager(s).** The lead manager's functions, some of which are generally shared with the co-lead manager(s), include advising the issuer about the issue's features, composing the group of firms that are to underwrite and sell the bonds, preparing the appropriate material (circular and/or prospectus) describing the issue, and arranging the necessary documentation and payment procedures. Understandably, the lead manager is often called the **book runner.**

Another function of the lead manager, one that is likely to be shared with the co-lead manager(s), is to commit to the sale and support of the issue. Joining the lead manager and the co-lead manager(s) to complete the **managing syndicate** are the co-managers, whose primary functions are to make commitments to purchase the bonds and to provide assistance in organizing the sale of the bonds to the public.

There are three key dates in the process of bringing a Eurobond issue to market. On the **announcement date,** which occurs after the lead manager has arranged the managing syndicate, invitations are sent out describing the bond issue and inviting other firms to join the distribution process as underwriters and sellers. Based on the response, the lead manager and the co-lead manager(s) set the final terms, and the managing syndicate makes a firm commitment to the borrower. The final terms are announced and the necessary documents are signed on the **offering date.** At this point, the public placement of the bonds begins. Finally, on the **closing date,** the firms involved in the sale of the bonds buy them from the issuer and distribute purchased bonds to investors. Any bonds sold after this date are said to have been placed after the syndicate has *broken.*

In the traditional syndication process, the sale of the bonds to the public is handled by the *underwriting group* and the *selling group.* The basic distinction between the two is that underwriters commit themselves to buy specified quantities of the bonds before the closing date. Matters become somewhat complicated since members of the managing syndicate generally act as underwriters and sellers, and the underwriters generally act as sellers. Usually, some firms (generally small ones) belong only to the selling group.

The lead manager or one of the co-lead managers serves as the *principal paying agent,* whose primary duty is to receive interest and amortization payments from the borrower and distribute them to the investors. The payment function may be shared with *co-paying agents,* who are likely to be located near principal investors. The principal paying agent may also serve as the *fiscal agent,* whose primary functions are to authenticate the bonds and to make sure that the number issued equals the authorized quantity. The fiscal agent may also distribute the bonds to investors, though this function may alternatively be assigned to a *distribution agent.* Rather than use a fiscal agent, a *trustee* may perform its function, although the trustee acts on behalf of the investors, while the fiscal agent acts on behalf of the borrower.

Exhibit 14.5 provides an example of a *tombstone,* which is a public announcement distributed to financial publications after the closing date for a bond issue. It advertises the issue and gives publicity to the firms in the managing syndicate. The placement of Merrill Lynch International Limited at the head of the list of firms indicates that it was the lead manager. Notice that the first group of firms beginning with Credit Suisse First Boston Limited and ending with UBS Philips & Drew Securities Limited (a British affiliate of Union

| E X H I B I T | 14.5 | *An Example of a Tombstone Announcement*

The Bonds referred to below have not been registered pursuant to the United States Securities Act of 1933 and the Bonds
may not be offered or sold in the United States or to U.S. persons as part of the distribution of the Bonds
The announcement appears as a matter of record only.

New Issue   July 1990

EUROPEAN INVESTMENT BANK

U.S.$500,000,000
9¹/₈ per cent. Bonds due 2000

Merrill Lynch International Limited

Credit Suisse First Boston Limited	Deutsche Bank Capital Markets Limited
Goldman Sachs International Limited	IBJ International Limited
Morgan Stanley International	Nomura International
Paribas Capital Markets Group	Salomon Brothers International Limited
Swiss Bank Corporation Investment Banking	UBS Phillips & Drew Securities Limited
BNP Capital Markets Limited	Daiwa Europe Limited
The Nikko Securities Co., (Europe) Ltd.	Norinchukin International Limited
S.G. Warburg Securities	Yamaichi International (Europe) Limited

Bank of Switzerland) appear in alphabetical order above the remaining six firms beginning with BNP Capital Markets Limited (a British affiliate of Banque Nationale de Paris). This organization indicates that the firms in the first group were co-lead managers and those in the second group were co-managers. The large number of co-lead managers may seem strange, but the size of the issue ($500 million) and the nature of the borrower (the European Investment Bank) favored widely geographically distributed participating firms. Finally, note the statement at the top of the tombstone that the bonds were not to be offered or sold in the United States or to U.S. residents. This indicates that the bonds were Eurobonds.

The Duration of the Issuing Process   As of around 1985, the average time from the date on which the issuer chose the lead manager to the closing date was 5 to 6 weeks. Since then, the average length of time from start to finish has diminished because of changes in issuing procedures. One reason for this shorter time period has been the use of **bought deals,** in which the lead manager buys the entire issue from the borrower before the announcement date, puts the managing syndicate together, and sets the final terms of the issue as of the announcement date. Before bought deals appeared, the time from the announcement date to the closing date ran from 1 to 2 weeks, but bought deals may reduce this time to 1 or 2 days.

Another factor that has reduced the average time required to bring an issue to the public has been the introduction of the U.S. practice of **fixed price reoffering (FPRO),** in which the selling firms commit themselves to refrain from selling newly issued bonds below a specified price before the closing date. Without this system, underwriters and sellers may be tempted to oversubscribe to an issue in the knowledge that, if necessary, they can probably move the excess by discounting the price and sacrificing fee income. FPRO, however, prohibits price discounting before the closing date. Moreover, because the fees allowed to underwriters and sellers under FPRO are much smaller than those under other systems, there is not much margin for price discounting after the closing date. This gives the participating firms an incentive to sell the bonds as quickly as possible. Whatever the arrangement, the lead manager (along with any co-lead managers) usually makes some kind of commitment to prevent or moderate price swings by offering two-way price quotations to other bond dealers.

The Fee Structure   The costs of a bond issue to the borrower include interest payments and the fees charged by the firms that manage and sell the issue. The cost of the fees may be partly offset if the borrower's price for the bonds plus the fees exceed the principal amount of the bonds; if the price received plus the fees are less than the principal amount, the borrower incurs an additional cost from price discounting.

Traditionally, the fees paid by the borrower are broken down into four categories: the *praecipium,* which goes to the lead manager and may be shared with the co-lead manager(s); the *management fee,* which goes to the managing syndicate; the *underwriting fee;* and the *selling concession.* Without FPRO, the total fees on a dollar or yen Eurobond issue tend to run from about 1⅜ to 2 percent of the issue's principal, depending on its maturity. The total fees on Eurobonds denominated in other currencies tend to be slightly higher, and they are still higher on Swiss franc issues because of the oligopsonistic position enjoyed by Swiss banks. With FPRO, however, the total fees may be as low as 5/16 percent.[6] Thus, on a Eurobond issue of $500 million, the fees may be less than $2 million. This does not necessarily mean, however, that FPRO reduces the income to the firms that bring Eurobonds to market since, in the absence of this system, price discounts could erode most of the underwriting and selling fees.

[6]Andersen, *Euromarket Instruments,* p. 101.

In a standard fee structure without fixed price reoffering, the praecipium and the management fee are likely to be about ⅛ percent each. The underwriting fee and the selling concession, particularly the latter, tend to be considerably larger. Prior to the introduction of fixed price reoffering, a large **gray market** had developed in which bonds were sold at large discounts before their offering dates by members of the underwriting and selling groups. As was accurately predicted by Orlin Grabbe, the growth of the gray market inevitably meant that it would come to dominate the pricing of bonds after their offering date. Grabbe also foresaw that the gray market would tend to undermine the position of the lead manager, one of whose functions is to determine the appropriate price for a bond issue.[7] Both bought deals and FPRO are, in large part, responses to the situation that Grabbe foresaw. Bought deals drastically shorten the period for gray market trading and thus allow lead managers to assert more control over prices. FPRO eliminates gray market trading.

Although it is sometimes ignored, the conventional wisdom of the investment banking community holds that bought deals should not be combined with FPRO. The basic problem is that if the lead manager misprices an issue, the selling firms' inability to discount the bonds before the closing date may lead to a poor reception for the issue and sharp price discounts after the closing date. Since the selling concession on such issues is small, it may prove difficult for the selling firms to avoid losses. The lead manager and/or co-lead managers may allay the fears of the selling firms by offering price support after the closing date, but this increases their risk.

FPRO has now established itself as the dominant procedure used in issuing Eurobonds. The chief exception to this generalization is the mark part of the Eurobond market, and the reason for this exception is that the Bundesbank controls the issuing process to preserve a traditional fee structure and allow German banks to dominate the syndication process.[8]

FPRO is generally given credit for having improved the Eurobond market by giving it greater price certainty, stabilizing profits, and reducing the risk to selling firms. This does not mean, however, that the technique is without its critics. For one thing, because FPRO eliminates the role of the underwriter, it also eliminates the underwriting fee. This fact hardly endears the technique to firms that are unimportant as managers, but aspire to be underwriters. Another complaint is that the technique sometimes squeezes the profits of selling firms without eroding the managers' profits.

Consider the following example, keeping in mind that a bond's price is inversely related to its interest rate.[9] Assume that a certain new Eurobond issue should be priced to the market at 40 basis points (bp) over treasuries denominated in the currency of issue if the participating firms are to receive the standard profit margin on an FPRO issue, which is assumed to be 3 bp. Adding

---

[7]Grabbe, *International Financial Markets*, p. 293.

[8]"Financing in Foreign Markets," Supplement to *Euromoney*, November 1991, pp. 3, 6.

[9]This example has been adapted from one appearing in "The 1991 Euromoney Global Financing Guide," *Euromoney*, September 1991, p. 139.

the 3 bp to the 40 bp gives a cost to the issuer of 43 bp over the treasury rate. The management fee is to be included in the 3 bp margin, and, in keeping with standard practice in FPRO, there is to be no praecipium.

Now assume that competitive bidding for the lead manager role results in a commitment by the successful bidder to price the issue for market at 37 bp over treasuries. With the 3 bp margin included in the price to the issuer, the issuer's cost becomes 40 bp. The management fee, which is assumed to be 0.8 bp, is to be taken out of the 3 bp margin.

Since the correct market price is assumed to be 40 bp, the issue is *overpriced* to the market, resulting in fewer buyers at the fixed price announced by the managing syndicate. When the closing date is reached and the syndicate breaks, the sellers have to place the bonds at 40 bp, which means that they fail to realize a profit. The managing firms, however, still obtain the management fee of 0.8 bp.

While this example suggests that managing firms may be biased toward overpricing in using FPRO, one should remember that lead managers have incentives to price bonds correctly. The willingness of selling firms to participate depends on their profit expectations, and sellers will tend to avoid participating in issues led by firms with a reputation for overpricing. Moreover, managing firms are also sellers. Finally, in order to induce selling firms to participate, managing firms may have to agree to buy unsold bonds at a guaranteed price.

Private Placements   Another factor tending to reduce fees associated with Eurobond issues is the growth of private placements, which have very low fees. In the past, the lack of a strong secondary market for private placements was a major drawback to their use, since borrowers had to offer higher coupon rates than those on publicly placed issues in order to compensate. Increasingly, however, the liquidity problem is being reduced through improvements in over-the-counter trading. Moreover, U.S. institutional investors, particularly insurance companies, have developed a strong appetite for private placements. For many of these buyers, liquidity is a secondary consideration.

Private placements of dollar Eurobonds have received a strong boost from the adoption of the Securities and Exchange Commission's Rule 144A, which allows dollar Eurobonds to be distributed and traded in the United States under certain conditions without being subject to the restrictions applied to publicly placed Eurobonds. Under Rule 144A, for example, privately placed bonds may be sold in the United States in bearer form. To enhance liquidity, they may be sold with terms that allow buyers to register them and trade them as publicly traded securities.

While the volume of private placements has been growing rapidly,[10] their growth would undoubtedly be even more impressive were it not for the

---

[10]It is estimated that in the first half of 1991, private placements under Rule 144A equalled $8.48 billion, as compared with $1.51 billion for the first half of 1990. See Danielle Robinson, "Europe to the Rescue," *Euromoney*, December 1991, p. 74.

| EXHIBIT | 14.6 | *Lead and Co-Lead Managers for Eurobond Issues:*
1990–First Half of 1991 (Millions of Dollars)

Rank		
1991	**1990**	**Bank**
1	2	Nomura Securities
2	5	Merrill Lynch
3	7	J.P. Morgan
4	3	CSFB/Crédit Suisse
5	1	Deutsche Bank
6	12	Union Bank of Switzerland
7	14	Banque Paribas
8	6	Daiwa Securities
9	4	Salomon Brothers
10	8	Goldman Sachs
11	16	Swiss Bank Corporation
12	15	Yamaichi Securities
13	9	S.G. Warburg
14	13	Morgan Stanley
15	11	Nikko Securities
16	29	Westdeutsche Landesbank
17	27	Dresdner Bank
18	10	Industrial Bank of Japan
19	21	Barclays Bank Group
20	18	Commerzbank
21	28	Baring Brothers
22	20	Hambros
23	38	Lehman Brothers
24	23	Banque Bruxelles Lambert
25	36	Samuel Montagu

Each manager's apportionment depends upon the type of participation. A lead manager receives four units and a co-lead manager receives two units.

Source: "The 1991 Euromoney Global Financing Guide," *Euromoney,* September 1991, p. 138.

competition provided by MTNs, which can be tailored to have most of the characteristics of private placements, but offer greater flexibility. The provisions of Rule 144A apply to dollar-denominated Euro-MTNs as well as to privately placed dollar Eurobonds.

The Euromoney Rankings Exhibit 14.6 essentially reproduces a table appearing in the September 1991 issue of *Euromoney* that ranks the top 25 Eurobond managers based on the business volume in the first half of 1991. A lead manager received twice the weight of a co-lead manager in the allocation of an issue.

Obviously, there is enormous competition for the lead manager and co-lead manager roles. Although 25 firms are listed in Exhibit 14.6, they account for only about 70 percent of all Eurobond issues for the first half of 1991. Another indicator of competitiveness is pronounced differences in the rankings for the first half of 1991 as compared to 1990.

First Half 1991			1990		
Amounts	Number of Issues	Share (%)	Amounts	Number of Issues	Share (%)
$10,063.28	224	7.00%	$14,265.27	189	8.12%
7,972.84	143	5.54	7,203.43	134	4.10
7,720.73	91	5.37	6,604.61	131	3.76
7,635.95	150	5.31	10,183.31	184	5.80
6,808.37	136	4.74	14,265.27	189	8.12
5,930.17	119	4.12	4,824.03	147	2.75
4,787.20	79	3.33	4,141.95	124	2.36
4,342.17	104	3.02	6,857.77	162	3.90
4,261.55	55	2.96	9,202.90	63	5.24
4,244.27	101	2.95	6,510.12	87	3.71
3,777.85	119	2.63	3,010.92	119	1.71
3,606.78	94	2.51	4,121.32	97	2.35
3,370.76	57	2.34	5,741.72	72	3.27
3,356.86	58	2.33	4,415.30	90	2.51
3,248.29	82	2.26	4,849.97	91	2.76
3,246.39	47	2.26	1,845.47	59	1.05
3,197.95	53	2.22	2,000.86	62	1.14
3,167.60	106	2.20	4,906.29	139	2.79
2,889.17	43	2.01	2,453.57	42	1.40
1,957.23	44	1.36	2,700.89	61	1.64
1,848.05	28	1.29	1,878.67	32	1.07
1,760.19	43	1.22	2,496.13	81	1.42
1,706.50	51	1.19	1,452.32	43	0.83
1,704.13	103	1.19	2,305.30	179	1.31
1,661.27	34	1.16	1,628.24	47	0.93

Based on these rankings, Nomura Securities is the world's top Eurobond dealer. Note, however, that Nomura is shown to have tied with Deutsche Bank in 1990. Note also the impressive positions of Swiss firms in the rankings, and that U.S. firms, one a commercial banking firm (J.P. Morgan), held the second and third positions in the first half of 1991.

Eurobond dealers tend to develop specialties, resulting in a firm that is strong in one category, such as fixed-rate dollar Eurobonds, and weak in others. Dealers tend to be much stronger in some currencies than in others. Obviously, therefore, changes in the currency composition of Eurobonds and their other features can have profound effects on the rankings regardless of changes in the abilities of different firms. Firms that are strong in certain respects may fail to make a strong showing in the overall rankings. Thus, Goldman Sachs and Bankers Trust were rated as being by far the most innovative Eurobond lead managers in 1991, yet Goldman Sachs is ranked tenth in Exhibit 14.6, and Bankers Trust did not even make the list.

Legal Considerations   Various legal considerations, including taxes, affect international bond markets. For example, the fact that the United States generally requires the ownership of domestically issued securities to be registered has contributed enormously to the growth of the Eurobond market since Eurobonds are customarily issued in bearer form. Everything else remaining the same, if Eurobonds are purchased for the tax advantage offered by bearer bonds, their yields will tend to be somewhat lower than those on registered bonds. These lower yields tend to encourage borrowers to go to the Eurobond market rather than issue bonds in the domestic U.S. market.

Another tax-related factor that has been of great importance in promoting the growth of the Eurobond market has been the lack of withholding taxes on interest payments in the countries in which Eurobonds are issued. When governments have required the withholding of taxes on interest payments on bonds issued by domestic borrowers, the alternative of issuing Eurobonds has tended to become very attractive. Before 1984, for example, the United States required the withholding of a 30 percent tax on the interest payments on domestically issued bonds. In order to avoid this tax, numerous U.S. firms issued Eurobonds through subsidiaries incorporated in the Netherlands Antilles, with which the U.S. government had a tax treaty allowing this procedure. As the volume of Eurobonds issued through these subsidiaries increased, the U.S. government came under increasing pressure to abrogate the treaty. Instead, it chose to eliminate the withholding tax requirement on foreign-owned bonds issued by U.S. borrowers. This meant that U.S. firms could henceforth issue Eurobonds without going through a subsidiary. Several other governments then followed the U.S. government's lead, giving the Eurobond market a major boost.

Although the withholding of taxes on interest payments is diminishing, it still has relevance for international bonds. For example, Luxembourg is a moderately important center for international bond issues in part because it has no tax withholding requirement on interest payments, while Belgium does. This means that a highly rated borrower can issue bonds denominated in Luxembourg francs and sell them to tax-reducing Belgian investors at lower yields than bonds issued by the Belgian government. Since the Luxembourg franc circulates one-to-one with the Belgian franc, Belgian investors in Luxembourg bonds avoid the exchange risk. Luxembourg's tax leniency also encourages borrowers who might otherwise issue Belgian franc bonds for the purpose of entering into currency swaps to issue bonds denominated instead in Luxembourg francs.

In general, foreign bond issues are subject to greater procedural and paperwork requirements than Eurobonds, and this is an important part of the reason that the volume of Eurobonds exceeds that of foreign bonds. In the United States, for example, the SEC requires foreign borrowers who issue publicly distributed bonds in the United States to file prospectuses and to divulge information that would not be required from Eurobond issuers. The SEC has developed a simplified procedure for foreign bond issuers, but it has not yet brought itself to fully match the Eurobond market in this respect. Since ratings have been developed that appear to accurately assess Eurobond issuers' prospects, the rationale for requiring more information from these issuers than they have to divulge to issue Eurobonds is unclear, nor is it clear why it should take longer for a borrower to bring a foreign bond issue to market in the United States than to bring a Eurobond issue to market.

These examples give but a small sample of the legal complexities of international bonds. Despite the pressure for standardization being applied to the different bond markets, many differences still separate countries in terms of the requirements imposed on bond issuers, the practices followed by financial intermediaries, and the treatment of bond investors. Nevertheless, there is no doubt that the pressure for standardization is having its effects.

International Bonds in Portfolio Strategy

A powerful factor behind the growth in the volume of international bonds has been the increasing awareness of the risk-adjusted portfolio gains that can be achieved by investing in bonds denominated in various currencies. It is possible, of course, to achieve currency diversification of a bond portfolio by buying bonds in the domestic markets of different countries. Liquidity considerations and other factors, however, often lead portfolio managers to favor Eurobonds. The trading spreads in the Eurobond market are generally low (especially for FRNs), and an efficient clearing system allows trades to be effected quickly and at low cost. Most Eurobond trades are cleared through either Euroclear, located in Brussels, or Cedel, located in Luxembourg. These clearing systems do not make physical delivery of bonds to their purchasers. Ownership changes are registered electronically and the securities are left in trust under suitable arrangements. Most Eurobonds are listed at the Luxembourg Stock Exchange or in London, so the latest price information is readily available. In short, the Eurobond market is highly efficient and easily accessible to portfolio managers.

Numerous studies have indicated that diversification into foreign currency bonds can improve the risk-adjusted performance of an investment portfolio. This is true whether an American investor diversifies into nondollar bonds or investors in other countries diversify into bonds denominated in dollars and other foreign currencies. The basic reason for the diversification gains is the imperfect correlation among the yields on bonds denominated in different currencies. They are imperfectly correlated because interest rate variations between countries are imperfectly offset by exchange rate variations, and vice versa. Because bond yields in different currencies are imperfectly correlated, investors can follow portfolio theory, as explained in Chapter 11, to lower their risk without sacrificing expected rates of return.

Consider, for example, the case of a U.S. pension fund that elects to purchase straight bonds denominated in yen and Swiss francs even though their yields are lower than those on comparable dollar bonds. Based on the factors analyzed in Chapter 9, especially the IFE, the fund's managers could reasonably anticipate that appreciation in the yen and the franc should approximately offset the negative interest rate differential. Admittedly, situations can be envisioned in which buying the foreign currency bonds would work out unfavorably. Such could be the case if the yen and the franc failed to appreciate. On the other hand, it is arguable that a favorable outcome is equally likely and that portfolio diversification into foreign currency bonds provides protection against a rise in dollar bond yields and the resulting decline in bond prices. The weight of both economic theory and empirical evidence suggest that if dollar bond yields rise, holding yen and Swiss franc bonds should moderate the loss in terms of dollars from holding dollar bonds.

If a rise in dollar bond yields is nominal only, the dollar will tend to depreciate against the yen and the Swiss franc unless equally large increases occur in nominal interest rates in Japan and Switzerland. Because international changes in nominal interest rates are imperfectly correlated, however, chances are that Japan and Switzerland would not have equally large nominal interest rate increases, so their currencies would appreciate. This appreciation would tend to increase the dollar value of the foreign currency bonds in the portfolio. Also, while an increase in the U.S. real interest rate relative to the real interest rates of Japan and Switzerland would tend to cause the dollar to appreciate, such an increase would probably follow a prior *depreciation* of the dollar. This is because central banks are most likely to allow a real interest rate increase when it serves to correct a previous depreciation of the national currency or to prevent the national currency from depreciating. From the point of view of a U.S. investor, this means that a rise in the U.S. real interest rate need not be associated with a decline in the dollar yields from foreign currency bonds.

To illustrate the empirical support for the analysis that has been presented, consider a study by Haim Levy and Zvi Lerman. They found that, during the period 1960 through 1980, U.S. investors with bond portfolios that were heavily weighted toward foreign currency bonds would have attained more than twice the mean rate of return attained by investors with portfolios consisting of U.S. bonds only at about the same level of risk. They also found that because the correlations between bond markets were weaker than those between stock markets, U.S. investors with foreign asset portfolios that included both bonds and stocks would generally have fared better in terms of the risk−return tradeoff than U.S. investors with diversified portfolios of foreign stocks only, notwithstanding the fact that in nearly all the countries surveyed, stock yields were larger than bond yields. Only those investors with very little aversion to risk and very high concentrations of Japanese stocks would have fared better with stocks-only portfolios.[11]

Since the period covered by the Levy−Lerman study was one in which the dollar exhibited chronic weakness against numerous other currencies, the benefits of diversification may have been due to dollar yields being exaggerated by the behavior of exchange rates. Levy and Lerman argue, however, that because the low correlation between bond markets exhibited during the period 1960 through 1980 is likely to persist indefinitely into the future, it should still be possible to achieve future portfolio gains by diversifying into foreign currency bonds.

---

[11]Haim Levy and Zvi Lerman, "The Benefits of International Diversification in Bonds." in Robert W. Kolb, ed., *The International Finance Reader* (Miami: Kolb Publishing, 1991), pp. 190−198.

As Europe moves toward its goals of a fully integrated capital market and a unified monetary system, bond yields among the different European currencies will come to be more closely correlated. This suggests that U.S. portfolio strategists seeking to diversify the currency compositions of their bond holdings should look beyond bonds denominated in European currencies. Obvious candidates include bonds denominated in yen, Australian and New Zealand dollars, and Canadian dollars (though Canadian-dollar bond yields are closely correlated with U.S.-dollar bond yields), along with bonds denominated in other currencies that pass the marketability test.

Finally, it should be noted that achieving diversification gains through international bond investment is not just a matter of diversifying among currencies. Diversification among borrowers also matters. Thus, even when investing in U.S. dollar bonds, some diversification gains can be achieved by investing in bonds issued by non-U.S. borrowers.

International Stock Markets

Although the volume of international trading in bond issues far exceeds the volume of international trading in stocks, the latter has been growing at a faster rate. As a result, the subject of international trading in stocks is forcing its way into international finance textbooks. It is likely that in a few years, the study of international stock markets will consume as much of the student's time as the study of international bank financing and bonds. An illustration of the sudden increase in importance of the internationalization of stock trading is the fact that Orlin Grabbe's pathbreaking text on international financial markets, which examined those markets in detail in 1985, has five chapters on international bond markets and no material on the internationalization of stock markets. Since 1985, the Euroequities market has been added to the list of Euromarkets, foreign investors have greatly increased their presence in domestic stock markets, and corporations have greatly expanded their offerings of new issues in foreign stock markets. While some internationalization of stock markets had occurred before 1985 (foreign investors were present in U.S. stock markets from their inceptions), the present situation is different enough from what existed earlier that using 1985 as a benchmark is readily defensible.

The push for the internationalization of stock markets has come simultaneously from investors and capital-raising corporations and can be viewed as part of the process of international financial integration that is sweeping the world. Investors have been induced to buy foreign stocks by the prospects of diversification gains and the belief that the stocks of particular foreign firms and countries provide higher rates of return than are likely to be found domestically. Investor enthusiasm for foreign stocks was a major factor in the bullishness of most stock markets from early 1985 until late 1987 and from early 1988 until late 1989.

Under bullish conditions, dividend payouts become secondary in importance to prospective capital gains, and raising capital by issuing stock represents a cheap method for financing corporate expansion. In addition, international trading of a firm's stock helps it to increase world awareness of its existence with, presumably, beneficial effects. It has also been suggested that the diversification of a firm's investor base among foreign stockholders may help to stabilize the price of its stock, but it is probably wise to avoid taking a firm position on this point since foreign ownership of a firm's stock may, at times, accentuate the stock's price instability.[12]

The growing internationalization of stock markets has accompanied and been promoted by increased listings of foreign stocks with organized exchanges. This expansion has been general, but it is particularly noticeable in Europe, where it is closely associated with the process of economic integration. As this process moves forward and corporations struggle to maintain and enhance their positions in an increasingly competitive environment, the appeal of selling shares to nonresidents increases. Since, however, each European country has its own stock exchange or (especially in Germany) exchanges, and since most of these separate exchanges are likely to continue to exist, it makes sense for European firms to list their stocks with more than one European exchange and possibly with exchanges outside Europe. The growth of international trading in European equities has also been stimulated by the privatization of government enterprises in most European countries.

There are three primary means by which the internationalization of stock ownership is effected. First, if the shares of a foreign company are listed with a domestic exchange, they can be traded domestically in much the same way as domestic shares are traded. Second, if domestic securities firms trade foreign stocks in foreign stock markets, investors can buy and sell those stocks without having to engage in international transactions on their own accounts. Third, domestic investors may trade foreign stocks by working directly with brokers in foreign stock markets. The brokers may be either foreign firms or domestic firms that are members of the foreign stock exchanges. Which course of action is chosen depends on cost, risk, and convenience. The third alternative would not appeal to a small-scale American investor in European stocks who habitually sleeps later than the chickens, but it may be the hands-down choice for a U.S. pension fund that wants to effect a large trade in a European stock with a minimal effect on the stock's price, since a stock generally has its greatest liquidity in its home country stock market.

The term **international equities** is generally applied to only the first of these alternatives, i.e., to foreign stocks traded on domestic exchanges. **Euroequities** are international equities traded mainly outside the home country of the issuing corporation. New Euroequity issues have gone from zero in 1985 to an average of several billion dollars per year as of 1990. While the Euroequities market is growing, new Eurobond issues are currently running from 10 to 20 times the volume of new Euroequity issues.

Most international equities are not Euroequities, however. Generally, a newly issued stock to be distributed in foreign stock markets is part of an issue

---

[12]The problem is that, because foreign stockholders may be less informed about conditions in a firm's home country than domestic stockholders, they may react in a more volatile way to political and economic news affecting that country. This problem is likely to be especially serious in countries whose stock markets are small and illiquid.

that is distributed primarily in the domestic stock market of the issuing company. For example, the total dollar value of new international equities in 1989 was over $15.7 billion, of which only $1.6 billion consisted of Euroequities.[13] Moreover, many of the shares that are distributed domestically, and therefore excluded from statistics on international equities, are sold to foreigners. It is safe to conclude that Euroequities are but the tip of the international stocks iceberg.

Some of the international trading of stocks involves buying and selling participations in **equity country funds,** which are country-specific stock portfolios. Such funds are used to draw foreign capital into countries with weak stock markets and few well-known firms. Typically, the host country government wants to attract foreign equity capital and to promote the growth of the domestic stock market while simultaneously limiting the extent of foreign control of domestic firms. While the stocks included in country fund portfolios are generally previously existing shares rather than new issues, foreign purchases of equity fund participations provide additional capital to the host country if the previous owners are domestic residents. Moreover, to the extent that equity country funds enhance stock liquidity in secondary markets, they encourage domestic firms to finance their expansion plans with new stock issues.

Equity country funds have tended to be especially popular for investors wishing to make equity investments in Mexico and Pacific Rim countries. Following the collapse of communist governments in eastern Europe, equity funds materialized in that part of the world. In the first half of 1990, $2.7 billion flowed into new equity country fund issues traded on foreign stock markets. This represented an impressive proportion of the total flow of funds into new international equities, which was estimated (conservatively) at $8.4 billion for the same period.[14] Because country funds have demonstrated their viability, and because the number of countries offering them can be expected to increase, they are expected to continue to grow in popularity.

Euromoney has estimated the volume of new international equities brought to market in 1990 at $15.0 billion.[15] In the first half of 1991, the estimated volume was $12.5 billion, up by about $3 billion over the same period in 1990.[16] During both 1990 and the first half of 1991, the number one lead manager for international equities, by a wide margin, was Goldman Sachs.

The volume of international trading in stocks will probably grow enormously in the years ahead. While it is clear that the present world trend toward greater economic openness and greater reliance on market forces is meeting resistance, the trend is strong. Moreover, while the United States, Japan, and the United Kingdom have highly developed stock markets, in most other developed countries and in virtually all LDCs, the vast majority of

---

[13]Simon Brady, "Euro-Equity? Nein Danke," *Euromoney,* May 1990, pp. 68–69.

[14]"Global Financing Guide," *Euromoney,* September 1990, p. 228.

[15]"Annual Financing Report," Special Supplement to *Euromoney,* March 1991, p. 24.

[16]"The 1991 Euromoney Global Financing Guide," *Euromoney,* September 1991, p. 162.

Leading Stock Exchanges in Terms of Foreign Equity Turnover: 1988 and 1989

		Foreign Sector Turnover (Millions of U.S. Dollars)	
Rank	Exchange	1989	1988
1	ISE[a,b]	$138,518.3	$65,204.3
2	New York	67,389.3	53,389.2
3	Tokyo	20,309.5	5,773.2
4	Federation of German Exchanges[b,c]	16,013.2	10,320.8
5	American (AMEX)[d]	7,180.0	2,858.1
6	Paris and Province[e,f]	4,233.9	3,449.8
7	Brussels[e]	2,901.7	2,233.1
8	NASDAQ	2,572.0	1,856.0
9	Australian	1,091.7	n.a.
10	Johannesburg[g]	787.1	180.0
11	Vienna	629.3	377.8
12	Toronto	407.8	295.8
13	Amsterdam[b]	404.9	161.9
14	New Zealand[h]	261.5	102.3
15	Copenhagen	240.7	60.6
16	Kuala Lumpur	224.9	137.1
17	Stockholm	77.6	77.6
18	Montreal	49.2	30.4
19	Luxembourg	29.3	27.2
20	Hong Kong[i]	20.8	61.8

[a]The phasing in of the SEQUAL confirmation system by the second half of 1989 means turnover for some stocks reported before October 1989 may represent as little as 10 percent of actual trading.

[b]To compensate for the double-counting convention prevalent at the ISE and the German, Amsterdam, and Helsinki exchanges, the figures produced by these exchanges have been halved. However, in the case of the ISE, some purchase and sale transactions in overseas equities reported via SEQUAL are paired, with only the sales value of these transactions being included in the volume statistics. Halving of volume figures for comparison purposes thus results in underestimation of actual trading on the ISE.

[c]Data have been obtained directly from the Federation of German Stock Exchanges and its constituent members with the exceptions of the Hanover and Bremen exchanges. Estimates of double counting affecting turnover figures for individual foreign equities within Germany vary.

[d]Many foreign exchanges have estimated the value of turnover on a snapshot basis, i.e., by multiplying the number of transactions in each stock by its market price at the end of a given period, for example, 1 month in the case of the ISE and 1 year in the case of the AMEX.

[e]The figures given refer to official trading only.

[f]International equities are traded on the Paris stock exchange. The Province exchange trades domestic securities only.

[g]The figures given include turnover of US$26,703,351 for companies incorporated in Bophuthatswana, Ciskei, and Transkei.

[h]Of the 135 companies listed on the New Zealand Stock Exchange, only 22 have quotation rights and are traded on the exchange floor. Thus a significant amount of international equity trading is omitted from the figures because trades in nonquoted listed companies are not recorded by the exchange.

[i]Overseas incorporated companies whose main business is in Hong Kong are excluded from these figures.

n.a. = not available.

Source: "Who's Where on World Markets," *Euromoney*, May 1990, pp. 62–63.

Foreign Sector Market Share (Percent)		Foreign Sector Growth: 1988–1989 (Percent)
1989	1988	
29.98%	19.64%	112.44%
4.37	3.94	26.22
0.83	0.23	251.79
4.85	5.93	55.15
16.17	9.24	151.22
3.71	4.80	22.73
27.45	22.29	29.94
8.48	6.86	38.65
2.43	n.a.	n.a.
9.95	4.19	337.33
5.82	20.60	66.67
0.58	0.54	37.86
0.91	0.57	150.09
8.45	5.99	155.62
1.73	1.29	297.19
3.16	5.25	64.04
0.44	0.43	0.00
0.29	0.24	61.84
21.70	29.16	7.72
0.05	0.02	−66.34

private firms are closely held and rely heavily on bank financing. In these countries there are, in addition, many government-owned enterprises that are prime candidates for privatization and that also depend heavily on bank financing. In many cases, the survival and growth of both types of enterprises will depend on the ability to sell shares of stock, and it is highly likely that limited foreign ownership will often be welcome.

The Trading of International Equities

Exhibit 14.7 presents data from *Euromoney* on turnover in international equities for 20 different stock exchanges (three in the United States) in 1988 and 1989. Total turnover in international equities is shown in millions of dollars and as percentages of total stock turnover. Included among the international equities traded are the stocks of a relatively small number of firms incorporated in tax haven countries, but these stocks accounted for less than 5 percent of the total international equities turnover during the 2 years considered.

The premier exchange for trading international equities is the International Stock Exchange (ISE) of London, which trades international equities through its Stock Exchange Automated Quotation System International (SEQUAL). The ISE's great lead over other exchanges in international equities reflects its location, its long-standing preeminence among European stock exchanges, and the simplicity of SEQUAL's listing requirements. According to Exhibit 14.7, international equities provided 30 percent of the ISE's total stock turnover in 1989, which was a sharp rise over 1988. As is explained in the notes to Exhibit 14.7, the figures presented underestimate the ISE's international equities turnover, so the relative importance of this trade for the ISE was somewhat greater than 30 percent in 1989 and 20 percent in 1988.

While the trading volume in international equities on the German exchanges was much smaller in 1988 and 1989 than on the ISE, it is widely anticipated that the Frankfurt exchange will mount a serious challenge to the ISE as European economic integration proceeds. In the past, the growth of the German stock exchanges has been hampered by the closely held nature of most German companies and institutional arrangements between German banks and other German firms that have funneled savings into the banks rather than stocks traded on domestic exchanges. No doubt, however, Germany will expand its stock market activity, and the Frankfurt exchange intends to lead the way.

The New York Stock Exchange (NYSE) ranks second to the ISE in the trading of international equities; it holds a substantial lead over third-place Tokyo. Both the American Stock Exchange (AMEX) and the National Association of Securities Dealers Automated Quotation System (NASDAQ) are among the top 10 exchanges for international equities, but their combined figures for 1989 were less than one-sixth of the international equities trading volume of the NYSE.

Foreign stocks are traded on U.S. exchanges through the use of **American depository receipts (ADRs),** which are negotiable certificates representing ownership rights in foreign companies. One ADR may represent one share, or, when the price per share is below what is desirable for trading in the United States, one ADR may represent enough shares to bring the price to the desired level. ADRs are issued by U.S. banks that are authorized to serve as ADR depositories, and these banks either hold the equivalent foreign shares in trust or have them held in trust in a foreign bank. ADRs are traded like ordinary stocks and are listed among these stocks in the trading reports for U.S. stock exchanges that appear in *The Wall Street Journal* and elsewhere.

If ADRs are *sponsored,* they are issued under an agreement between the foreign company and a depository bank. The bank assumes responsibility for dividend payments to investors, and the expenses of handling ADR accounts are borne by the company and/or the bank. If ADRs are *unsponsored,* they are issued by a depository bank at the request of investors, and the investors are responsible for the attendant expenses. If a foreign company wants its stock listed on a U.S. exchange, it must have a sponsorship agreement and meet the listing requirements imposed by the exchange and the SEC. For example, a firm with sponsored ADRs pays fees to the listing exchange and furnishes financial reports in English that conform to SEC standards.

The SEC's Rule 144A applies to ADRs. This means that, under circumstances determined by the SEC, ADRs can be in bearer form. Ordinarily, however, their ownership must be registered.

Exhibit 14.7 indicates that, while trading in international securities is less important for American exchanges than for the ISE, the percentage of total stock turnover attributed to international equities increased on each of the three exchanges in 1989. A single year's performance does not establish a long-term trend, but it is clear that ADR listings are increasing and that U.S. investors are showing increased interest in foreign stocks. It should be noted, however, that ADR trading generally attracts relatively small-scale investors. The fees charged on ADR trades are higher than those charged on trades in domestic stocks, and, in general, a large ADR trade has a greater price effect than an equally large trade in the shares of the same company on the home country stock exchange. For large trades, therefore, it is generally preferable to go to the home exchange.

In Europe, Euroequities are commonly traded using European depository receipts (EDRs). These closely resemble ADRs, but differ from them in two major respects: they are usually quoted in the currency of a company's home country and they are generally issued in bearer form.

Considering that many U.S. and Japanese firms are included among the ranks of the world's largest enterprises, relatively few of these firms' shares are heavily traded on foreign stock exchanges. In 1989, only two Japanese stocks and six U.S. stocks were included in *Euromoney*'s listing of the 50 most heavily traded international equities. The leaders in this regard were the United Kingdom (11 firms plus 2 firms classified as Anglo/Dutch), Germany (9 firms), and Canada (7 firms).[17] Evidently, U.S. and Japanese firms are under less pressure to list their stocks on foreign stock exchanges than firms in other countries.

Some Observations on Investments in Foreign Stocks

It is now well-established that gains have resulted from the international diversification of stock portfolios, and it is widely believed that many additional opportunities for diversification gains exist. In choosing foreign stocks for their portfolios, however, investors consider not only diversification gains, but also such factors as nations' economic growth prospects, exchange rate expectations, and political risk. Market sentiment about such matters changes daily, leading to great volatility in the capital flows linked to purchases and sales of foreign stocks. Over periods of several years, some countries' stocks are likely to prove much more attractive than stocks in other countries,

[17]"Who's Where on World Markets," *Euromoney*, May 1990, pp. 56–57. However, the second-ranked firm was Schlumberger, a diversified energy company classified by *Euromoney* as from the Netherlands Antilles, but which is really a U.S. firm. First place, incidentally, went to Deutsche Bank.

as is clear when one compares the performances of different countries' stock indexes. Yet even in countries whose stock markets have performed relatively poorly, the relative participation of foreign investors is likely to have increased.

Exchange Rates Once Again   The increased international diversification of stock portfolios seemingly contradicts assertions that exchange rate volatility impacts negatively upon investments in foreign stocks. In earlier years, when confidence in PPP was higher than it is now, it was widely believed that a currency's depreciation did not necessarily harm foreign stockholders since their loss from currency depreciation would tend to be offset by gains in the local currency prices of the stocks held. This comforting notion of offsetting price movements has been strongly challenged by evidence that, as was noted in Chapter 3, nominal exchange rates tend to be closely correlated with real exchange rates, at least among leading currencies. This means that investors residing in countries with appreciating currencies tend to experience capital losses on their holdings of stocks in companies that are domiciled in countries with depreciating currencies. Thus, if the dollar is depreciating against the yen and most European currencies, foreigners holding U.S. stocks are likely to find that those stocks perform poorly in comparison with Japanese and European stocks.

The rule that stock investments in countries with depreciating currencies perform relatively badly is subject to at least three caveats. First, recall that PPP's validity tends to be greater over the long term than the short term. Second, what is true of a country's stocks overall may not be true for individual stocks. For example, the shares of a U.S. multinational firm that is strongly export-oriented and derives much of its income from foreign subsidiaries may hold up relatively well when the dollar depreciates. Third, when the investment horizon is extended to countries whose currencies are not among the leading currencies, the situation may change considerably. The mere fact that the Mexican peso is depreciating against the dollar is not necessarily bad news for U.S. investors in Mexican stocks. Given Mexico's relatively high inflation rate, PPP has greater relevance for the peso/dollar exchange rate than, say, the mark/dollar exchange rate. Also, the rate of depreciation of the peso may actually have diminished.

For an answer to why currency depreciation is often a negative factor in determining comparative returns on stocks, the reader is referred to the analysis of Chapters 9, 10, and 11. It would seem, however, that a decline in the exchange value of a leading currency often coincides with unfavorable news about economic growth, interest rates, political risk, or other factors that influence stock prices and returns.

Interest Rates and Other Factors   While an increase in a country's expected real interest rate relative to the rest of the world is (rightly) regarded as tending to cause its currency to appreciate, this is because more international capital flows are connected with transactions in debt instruments than with transactions in equities. A rise in a country's real interest rate level tends to move equity-related capital flows toward the outflow side of the ledger. A rise in the real interest rate lowers the present value of a given future income stream and increases the opportunity cost of borrowing money in order to buy stocks. Moreover, it has negative implications for economic growth. Foreign investors may not be significantly discouraged by the present value effect of a real interest rate increase since (presumably) they calculate present values in their own currencies, but they will be discouraged by worse prospects for economic growth. The growth factor may encourage domestic residents to substitute equity investment abroad for equity investment at home.

Complicating matters is the fact that when the everything-else-being-the-same assumption implicit in the last paragraph is dropped, offsetting factors may operate. An increase in a country's real interest rate may result from an improvement in its economic growth prospects that is not offset by an increase in the domestic money supply. In such a case, an increase in the real interest rate would not necessarily be followed by a shift toward capital outflows in the BOP's equity accounts. Note, however, that a negative correlation seems to exist between returns on stocks and changes in nominal interest rates. Solnik has found statistically significant evidence of such a correlation for all eight members of a group of developed countries during the period January 1971 through December 1989.[18] Yet it is fitting to recall that when both real and nominal interest rates in the United States increased sharply in the early 1980s, foreign purchases of U.S. stocks also increased.

The increase in foreign purchases of U.S. stocks in the early 1980s coincided with the appreciation of the dollar and reinforced that appreciation. The outlook for U.S. economic growth also improved at this time. Any negative effects of higher U.S. interest rates on foreign purchases of U.S. stocks were apparently offset by the prospects for exchange rate gains and for rising stock prices caused by increases in expected profits.

Of course, many factors besides exchange rates and interest rates influence equity-related capital flows, but to go into them in detail would require another entire book. As just one illustration of the many possibilities, consider the fact, noted by Solnik, that some financial analysts use lawyer intensity ratios (lawyers per 1,000 persons) to predict the outlook for a nation's stocks.[19] The rationale for this is that lawyer intensity seems to have a negative correlation with economic growth. For example, Japan and Germany, both of which have low lawyer intensities, have had higher economic growth rates than the United States and the United Kingdom, both of which (particularly the former) have high lawyer intensities. Similarly, the Pacific Rim countries, which are relatively lawyer poor, have had more rapid economic growth than India and Latin America, where lawyers are relatively more abundant, at least in the "modern" sectors of the economies. If there is, in fact, a causal linkage

---

[18]Solnik, *International Investments,* 2d ed., pp. 15–16.
[19]*Ibid.,* p. 56.

here, an increase in lawyer intensity has negative implications for a nation's stock market.[20]

Some Guiding Principles   In selecting foreign stocks, it is desirable to discard some rules of thumb for domestic markets. For example, the price/earnings (P/E) ratio, a "moldy oldie" technique of domestic stock picking, is a dangerous indicator for foreign stocks. The reasons are various. Accounting principles differ among nations, with the result that the true dollar equivalent of earnings in some countries is different (usually on the plus side) from what is indicated by translating reported earnings into dollars at current exchange rates. Thus, if reported income in Country X is only half what would be reported under U.S. accounting practice, then everything else being the same, a P/E ratio in X that is twice that of a U.S. firm would, in fact, be an equivalent indicator of value. But everything else is not likely to be the same. For example, Japan, whose P/E ratios are typically much higher than those of the United States, may offer advantages in terms of prospects for currency appreciation, economic growth, and risk that more than offset differences in P/E ratios.

Robert D. Arnott and Roy D. Henriksson suggest that the key to successful international investment is to accurately estimate a country's **equity risk premium,** which is the amount by which the expected rate of return on stocks exceeds that of either bonds or cash (by which they evidently mean M2 money).[21] They argue that this premium tends toward an equilibrium value in each country, but that it differs from country to country. When the premium is at its equilibrium level in each country, investors should be neutral toward investments in stocks. If a country's equity risk premium becomes abnormally large, however, this is a signal to investors to buy that country's stocks. The investment decision, they maintain, should be made independently of any currency hedging decision, and they also hold that the cost of currency hedging is small enough that if a foreign investment is otherwise desirable, this cost is readily absorbed. Assuming that it is indeed possible to measure each country's equity risk premium, the chief problem in implementing the Arnott–

---

[20]No doubt there is such a thing as optimal lawyer intensity to maximize economic growth, i.e., a country can have too few lawyers to achieve this objective. Also, it should be noted, as was pointed out to the author by Yutaka Horiba of Tulane University, that in Japan the usual measure of lawyer intensity considerably understates the use of legal services because Japanese firms have employees who perform extensive legal services and who should be treated as lawyers for the purpose of making comparisons between Japan and other countries.

Possibly more meaningful than lawyer intensity for stock forecasting would be an appropriate measure of bureaucratic intensity, i.e., a ratio of some or all public sector employees per 1,000 persons. Incidentally, famed historian William H. McNeill warned us 30 years ago that, war aside, the greatest threat to social progress in the modern world is bureaucratic routine, which can stifle any changes that tend to threaten the positions of entrenched bureaucracies. See McNeill's *The Rise of the West* (Chicago: University of Chicago Press, 1963), p. 803.

[21]Robert D. Arnott and Roy D. Henriksson, "A Disciplined Approach to Global Asset Allocation," *Financial Analysts Journal*, March/April 1989, pp. 17–28; reprinted in Robert W. Kolb, ed., *The International Finance Reader* (Miami: Kolb Publishing, 1991), pp. 161–172.

Henriksson approach is to determine if a change in the premium is, in fact, a departure from equilibrium or represents a new equilibrium.

Summary

The internationalization of securities markets is far advanced in bonds and is proceeding rapidly in stocks. There are three distinctly different dimensions to the internationalization of securities markets: issuing and trading foreign securities in domestic markets, the operations of Eurosecurities markets, and foreign participation in the trading of securities domestically.

The volume of Eurobonds in existence far exceeds that of foreign bonds. The leading country for foreign bonds is Switzerland, whose government prohibits issuing franc-denominated Eurobonds. Foreign bonds are also issued in several other countries. The distinctions between foreign bonds and Eurobonds are gradually being eroded. The U.S. dollar is the leading currency for Eurobond issues, but many Eurobonds are issued in other currencies, including the Ecu, which has recently reached second place.

International bonds are distributed to the public through a network of investment banks serving as managers, underwriters, and sellers. A relatively small (but growing) quantity of international bonds are private placements. Most international bonds are issued by the governments of developed countries or by highly rated private corporations, but some are issued by companies whose credit ratings are not among the highest. Historically, most international bonds have been purchased by wealthy individuals, but the popularity of such bonds with institutional investors has recently expanded rapidly. A major factor behind the growth in international bond financing has been the use of financial swaps.

There are numerous types of international bonds. A particularly important distinction is that between straight (fixed-rate) bonds and floating-rate bonds (FRNs). Most international bonds are straight bonds, but FRNs and bonds with equity conversion features (equity warrants and convertibles) are important alternatives.

Intense competition among the investment banks that manage and distribute international bond issues has recently led to modifications in fee structures and improvements in the efficiency with which such bonds are marketed. Most important in this regard has been the introduction of fixed-price reoffering (FPRO), in which the selling firms commit themselves to refrain from selling new issues below a specified price prior to the closing date. Also important has been the adoption of the SEC's Rule 144A, which allows Eurobonds to be privately issued in the United States.

The internationalization of stock markets is being spurred by various factors. The international distribution of stock issues allows corporations to raise large sums of money relatively cheaply. For investors, the internationalization of stock holdings provides diversification gains and opportunities for extraordinary rates of return. While there is a growing reliance on issues of international equities, most international stock transactions occur when foreigners trade stocks in the home countries of issuing firms. Reliance on international equities is particularly common among corporations domiciled in developed countries other than the United States or Japan.

References

Adler, Michael, and David Simon. "Exchange Risk Surprises in International Portfolios." *Journal of Portfolio Management*, Winter 1986, pp. 44–53.

Andersen, Torben Juul. *Euromarket Instruments*. New York: New York Institute of Finance, 1990.

"Annual Financing Report." Special Supplement to *Euromoney*, March 1991.

Arnott, Robert D., and Roy D. Henriksson. "A Disciplined Approach to Global Asset Allocation." *Financial Analysts Journal*, March/April 1989, pp. 17–28. Reprinted in Robert W. Kolb, ed. *The International Finance Reader*. Miami: Kolb Publishing, 1991, pp. 161–172.

Bank for International Settlements. *Sixty-First Annual Report*. Basle: BIS, 1991.

Brady, Simon. "Euro-Equity? Nein Danke." *Euromoney*, May 1990, pp. 68–69.

DeCaires, Bryan, ed. *The Guide to International Capital Markets*. London: Euromoney Publications, 1988.

Eiteman, David K., Arthur I. Stonehill, and Michael H. Moffett. *Multinational Business Finance*, 6th ed. Reading, Mass.: Addison-Wesley, 1992, Chapters 11–13.

Eun, Cheol S., and Bruce G. Resnick. "Currency Factor in International Portfolio Diversification." *Columbia Journal of World Business*, Summer 1985, pp. 45–53.

Financial Market Trends. (Periodical. Three issues annually).

"Financing in Foreign Markets." Supplement to *Euromoney*, November 1991.

Gallant, Peter. *The Eurobond Market*. New York: Woodhead-Faulkner, 1988.

"Global Financing Guide." *Euromoney*, September 1990, pp. 193–254.

Grabbe, J. Orlin. *International Financial Markets*. New York: Elsevier, 1986, Chapters 16–20.

Howe, John S., and Kathryn Kelm. "The Stock Price Impacts of Overseas Listings." *Financial Management*, Autumn 1987, pp. 51–56.

Humphreys, Gary. "The Belgian Dentist Bites Back." *Euromoney*, October 1990, pp. 54–60.

International Capital Markets: Developments and Prospects. Washington, D.C.: IMF, 1990.

Lee, Adrian S. "International Asset and Currency Allocation." *Journal of Portfolio Management*, Fall 1987, pp. 68–73.

Levy, Haim, and Zvi Lerman. "The Benefits of International Diversification in Bonds." *Financial Analysts Journal*, September/October 1988, pp. 56–64. Reprinted in Robert W. Kolb, ed. *The International Finance Reader*. Miami: Kolb Publishing, 1991, pp. 190–198.

"The 1991 Euromoney Global Financing Guide." *Euromoney*, September 1991, pp. 114–166.

Robinson, Danielle. "Europe to the Rescue." *Euromoney*, December 1991, pp. 73–76.

Rhee, S. Ghon, and Rosita P. Chang, eds. *Pacific Basin Capital Markets Research*. Amsterdam: North Holland, 1990.

———, Rosita P. Chang, and Peter E. Koveos. "The Currency-of-Denomination Decision for Debt Financing." *Journal of International Business Studies*, Fall 1985, pp. 143–150.

Roll, Richard. "The International Crash of October 1987." *Financial Analysts Journal*, September/October 1988, pp.

19–35. Reprinted in Robert W. Kolb, ed. *The International Finance Reader.* Miami: Kolb Publishing, 1991, pp. 173–189.

Shapiro, Alan C. "The Impact of Taxation on the Currency-of-Denomination Decision for Long-Term Borrowing and Lending." *Journal of International Business Studies,* Spring/Summer 1984, pp. 15–25.

Sarver, Eugene. *The Eurocurrency Market Handbook,* 2d ed. New York: New York Institute of Finance, 1990, Chapter 9.

Solnik, Bruno. *International Investments,* 2d ed. Reading, Mass.: Addison-Wesley, 1991, Chapters 2 and 4–7.

"Who's Where on World Markets." *Euromoney,* May 1990, pp. 56–76.

Questions

1. Among the countries in which foreign bonds are issued, Switzerland is preeminent. How is this fact explained?
2. What explains the rise of Ecu bonds to second place as the currency of denomination for Eurobond issues in 1991? Also, what is a plausible explanation for the decline in dollar-denominated Eurobond issues in 1990?
3. How are bullet bonds distinguished from sinking fund bonds, and why are most international bonds bullet bonds?
4. What are index-linked bonds? Under what circumstances would you advise issuing them?
5. What are zero-coupon bonds, and what advantages do they offer? How do you explain the fact that they are of rather minor importance in the Eurobond market?
6. Compare convertible bonds with bonds with equity warrants attached and explain why the latter have tended to be somewhat more popular in the Eurobond market.
7. What factors determine the relative popularity of straight Eurobonds as opposed to FRNs?
8. Why might some price risk be associated with holding FRNs, and why is this risk greater for FRNs referenced to the U.S. Treasury bill rate than for FRNs linked to the LIBOR?
9. Distinguish callable bonds from putable bonds and explain how these features affect bond yield rates.
10. What are dual currency bonds? What is the motivation behind their use? How do they differ from currency option bonds?
11. Explain both bought deals and fixed-price reoffering (FPRO). Why are the two techniques generally not combined?
12. A common complaint against FPRO is that it squeezes the profits of selling firms because their fees are lower than with the traditional method for issuing Eurobonds and lead managers allegedly tend to underprice the bonds under their control. What reasons exist for being skeptical about this complaint?
13. It can be argued that since bond interest rates in different currencies reflect exchange rate expectations, there is no good reason to believe that holding bonds denominated in different currencies should provide higher yields

over time than holding only domestic bonds. What is wrong with this argument?

14. How do international equities differ from Euroequities, and what are the leading exchanges for the trading of international equities?

15. What are the attractions for both host countries and investors of equity country funds?

16. Explain the nature of ADRs. What disadvantages do they have?

17. Evaluate the exchange risk as a deterrent to investing in foreign stocks.

18. Given that an increase in a country's real interest rate tends to cause a decline in its stock prices, why does such an increase not necessarily tend to reduce foreign participation in its stock market?

| C H A P T E R | *15* |

The Financing of
International Trade

■

Underlying the vast volume of financial transactions identified as international capital flows are the movements of real goods and services that we call *international trade*. This chapter deals with financing this trade, or "real" side of the international economy.

The need for trade financing arises fundamentally from the fact that it takes time to generate income from imports of goods and services. For business firms, the income generated becomes profits. For governments, it tends to take the form of revenues, mostly taxes, that are generated by the economic growth that imports make possible. Complicating matters is the fact that international trade has a currency dimension—the exporter wants to be paid in a convertible currency (usually the exporter's local currency if it is convertible), while the importer wants to choose the currency in which to pay, usually the importer's national currency. In both its credit and currency dimensions, trade finance is a natural area for commercial bank participation. Accordingly, banks are extensively involved in international trade as lenders, guarantors of credit provided by others, dealers in and brokers of trade-related financial paper, and participants in arranging and carrying out international trade. So extensive is this trade-related activity of commercial banks that for many of them, particularly for regional banks, most of their involvement in international finance is trade-related.

Because governments, *all* governments, consider international trade to be too important to be left entirely to the operation of market forces, there is a great deal of government involvement in the financing of international trade. Most of this involvement centers around the promotion of exports, despite the warnings of economists from Adam Smith on that favoring exports over imports is questionable policy. Of the ways in which governments favor exports, particularly relevant to our inquiry are their export insurance programs for exporters, their guarantees to banks on export-related loans, and their direct loans for export promotion. In addition, development loans by the World Bank and other international agencies are motivated in part by the desire to stimulate the exports of developed countries. Otherwise, those countries would not be putting up the money.

The scope of trade finance includes, paradoxically, trade that is essentially barter. Commonly called **countertrade,** the international swapping of goods for goods has at times accounted for more than 20 percent of all world merchandise trade. Its use stems from the fact that many countries would tend to have large trade deficits at existing exchange rates if their imports were not controlled. The volume of countertrade tends to vary according to the availability of foreign exchange in the countries that resort to it. When a government resorts to countertrade, it attempts to pay for some imports with goods that would not be exportable at existing exchange rates. Typically, the goods imported under countertrading arrangements are not those to which the importing country's government assigns the highest priority. Although it is by now almost universally recognized that countertrade is far less efficient economically than trading goods for money, its existence is a fact of life to which the participants in international trade have had to adapt.

The scope of trade finance also includes leasing as an alternative to conventional international trading arrangements. In some cases, international leasing entails the temporary use of equipment, such as aircraft, in exchange for periodic rental payments. In others, the leasing arrangement is really a sale set up in the leasing format because of tax advantages and/or other considerations.

Conventional Trade Financing Procedures

At one extreme, the exporter may require *payment in advance* before allowing the importer to obtain the goods. This technique allows the exporter to avoid granting credit when it is in a strong bargaining position. Its appeal is obvious when the importer is in a country where the government may, at any time, refuse to allow importers to comply with their international obligations. It is also used for goods that are customized to the specific requirements of the importer and/or could not readily be resold in case of default.

At the other extreme, in **open account selling,** the importer receives the goods before paying for them and is allowed a certain amount of time in which to pay. A down payment may be required, and the remainder may be paid in installments, but the exporter grants credit to the importer and bears the attendant risk unless another party provides financing and/or bears the risk. Despite this drawback, open account selling is widely used, especially with foreign affiliates and importers in countries with convertible currencies who have good records of meeting their obligations. An important consideration in the use of open account selling is whether or not exports occur on a recurring basis to the importer.

When the risk of the open account method is small, its flexibility and low cost may make it an attractive option for exporters. When the exporter provides the credit, the cost of doing so may be at least partly recovered in the price of the goods. Moreover, it may be possible for the exporter to sell (factor) its trade accounts receivable cheaply enough to make this a viable option if the exporter desires to be relieved of the obligation to provide credit.

Offering slightly more protection to exporters than open account selling is *selling by consignment,* in which the exporter retains title to the goods until the importer sells them. The exporter's retention of ownership may make a difference in some cases when an importer fails to honor its commitment, but collection may still prove difficult if the exporter has few or no liabilities to the importer that it can cancel in the event of nonperformance. For example, if the importer is not allowed to make an on-time payment because of exchange controls imposed by its government, the exporter's legally valid claim for payment may be worthless. Understandably, therefore, consignment selling is used primarily for exports to affiliated companies. Open account selling is likely to be preferable if the importer is unaffiliated and presents little risk; if the importer is unaffiliated and risky, the exporter should probably seek stronger protection than is provided by the retention of ownership rights to goods located in a foreign country.

While international finance is a fast-changing field, some characteristics have remained relatively stable. One is the use of bills of exchange or drafts to finance international trade. As was pointed out in Chapter 12, these instruments have long been used by exporters and are frequently converted into bank-guaranteed negotiable instruments known as bankers' acceptances (BAs).

Bills of Exchange and Bankers' Acceptances (BAs)

Recall that a bill of exchange or a draft is an order to pay addressed to a specific party that calls for payment of a specified sum on a specific or determinable date to a specified party. In international trade, bills of exchange are commonly drawn on banks that have agreed to honor them, but they may be drawn on importers instead. A bill of exchange drawn on a bank is a *bank bill,* while one drawn on an importer or other nonbank party is a *trade bill.* Banks serve as exporters' agents in preparing bills of exchange and handling the documentation pertaining to the goods. They also take care of delivering documents and collecting payments. The payment terms of a bill of exchange are known as its *tenor.*

A **sight draft** is a bill of exchange that is paid upon presentation to the party on which it is drawn, assuming that the accompanying documents, if any, are in proper order. A **time draft** is a bill of exchange that is payable at some specified future date. This date is usually 30, 60, 90, etc. days after the date on which the draft is drawn or after its sight, i.e., after it has been presented to and accepted by the drawee. Time drafts are often issued in conformance with terms specified in **letters of credit (L/Cs)**. Typically, an L/C is issued to an exporter by an importer's bank and indicates that the bank will honor a draft drawn by the exporter. A time draft becomes a bankers' acceptance (BA) upon its acceptance by the drawee bank. If a time draft is drawn upon an importer instead of a bank, it becomes a *trade acceptance* once the importer accepts it. As was explained in Chapter 12, BAs are negotiable instruments and can readily be discounted (sold) by the recipient exporters. Trade acceptances are also negotiable.

Drafts can be either clean or documentary. A **clean draft** is usually used to collect a payment that is not connected with a current shipment of goods by an exporter. For example, if an importer has not paid on time for a *previous* shipment of goods on an open account sale, the exporter might send a clean draft to the importer to apply pressure. Refusal to accept the draft could then be used to support a legal action against the importer. If a firm or government agency has failed to make an on-time payment because of the imposition of exchange controls, for example, sending a clean draft could be useful in prying the necessary forex permit from the authorities.

A draft that applies to a current shipment of merchandise is likely to be a **documentary draft,** i.e., one that is accompanied by various documents pertaining to the merchandise. Included among these documents, which are briefly examined a little later, are the bill of lading, the commercial invoice, insurance papers, and possibly other paperwork.

Letters of Credit

Many, but not all, documentary drafts are issued pursuant to L/Cs, which are issued by parties (usually banks) indicating the specific terms under which they will accept drafts issued by other named parties, usually exporters. Usually, but not always, an L/C is issued by a bank that represents the importer and is sent by that bank to the exporter or the exporter's bank.

In some situations, an exporter might be reluctant to rely solely on an L/C provided by an importer's bank, even if that bank were to promise to pay the desired amount in the currency chosen by the exporter on an acceptable date. An exporter may insist on a more ironclad arrangement. One possibility is to have the L/C issued by a bank of the exporter's choice. Another is to convert an L/C issued by one bank into a **confirmed L/C** by having a second bank add its guarantee. By confirming an L/C issued by another bank, the confirming bank indicates that it will accept a draft drawn by the exporter. The confirming bank receives assurance from the issuing bank that the latter will transfer funds to it before it pays out funds to the exporter.

L/Cs are either **revocable** or **irrevocable.** If an L/C is revocable, the issuing bank has the right to back out of the commitment at any time before the exporter's draft is presented. An irrevocable L/C cannot be cancelled unless all the parties involved agree.

Everything else being the same, a confirmed irrevocable L/C is better for an exporter than an L/C that is either unconfirmed or revocable or both. Even an unconfirmed revocable L/C may be quite acceptable, however, if the exporter has confidence in the issuing bank and the importer. An intermediate combination is an unconfirmed irrevocable L/C for which the exporter's bank acts as an **advising bank.** In this capacity, the exporter's bank indicates that, while it is not confirming an L/C issued by another bank, it will accept the exporter's draft. The advising bank reserves the right, however, to refuse to disburse funds to the exporter if it has not received prior compensation from the issuing bank.

L/Cs can readily be adapted to different circumstances. It is conceivable, for example, that an exporter might want a *negotiable L/C,* i.e., one that could be used with any bank willing to rely on it as the basis for accepting a draft from the exporter. The bank collects a fee for issuing such an L/C and the exporter receives the option of drawing its draft on a bank that may be, from its perspective, preferable to the issuing bank. Another alternative, the *transferable L/C,* is used when the identity of the exporter is not yet known. Suppose, for example, that a trading company, i.e., a company that acts as an intermediary between exporters and importers, has lined up an importer of wheat, but has not yet placed the export order. By securing a transferable L/C naming it as the beneficiary, the company can assure a prospective exporter that payment has been arranged and guaranteed. Upon notification, the issuing bank names the exporter as the L/C's new beneficiary.

A bank that issues or confirms an L/C is not legally required to fulfill its commitment unless the exporter complies *exactly* with the terms of the L/C and its confirmation, if any. If a bank issues an L/C indicating that it will accept a draft presented at its New York offices no later than July 20, the issuing bank may refuse to accept a draft presented on July 21 at its London offices. If the L/C states that any draft presented must be accompanied by a bill of lading and a commercial invoice, the bank is not obligated to accept a draft if those documents are not presented in accordance with the specifications stated or implied by the L/C.

The Documents of International Trade

The last paragraph calls attention to the documents required by L/Cs. Of these, the most important is the **bill of lading (B/L)**, a receipt issued by the carrier of goods that confers control over them. The B/Ls used in conjunction with L/Cs in international trade are almost always **order B/Ls,** which means that they are issued to exporters, or possibly to their banks, and can be assigned by the recipients to other parties. Since an order B/L establishes ownership of the goods and can be assigned to another party, it can be used as loan collateral. A bank that issues an L/C may thus require that the accompanying B/L be endorsed to its order, and it may not surrender the B/L to the importer until the importer has met its obligation to the bank.

Like L/Cs, B/Ls vary according to circumstances. If, for example, a parent firm ships goods to a European affiliate in an open account arrangement in which the parent has no reason to retain the goods' legal ownership, the parent might prefer a **straight B/L.** This type of B/L usually consigns the goods to the importer, and it cannot be transferred to another party. It would not be used, therefore, in a situation where a lender might want the goods as loan collateral.

B/Ls also differ in terms of the certification provided by the carriers of goods at the time they are issued. A B/L that indicates that goods have been received does not necessarily indicate that they are ready for shipment or that shipment is under way. A *clean B/L* means that the goods were apparently in good condition at the time the carrier took charge of them. A potential lender on the goods might require, however, that a B/L indicate not only that the goods were *apparently* in good condition, but also that they had been thoroughly inspected.

Virtually all significant international shipments of goods require insurance. Accordingly, the cost and coverage of insurance have important implications for the volume and location of international trade. For example, following the Iraqi occupation of Kuwait in August 1990, there was a sharp increase in the insurance charges on petroleum shipments from the Persian Gulf. This had a noticeable impact on the pattern of petroleum shipments. The participants in international trade were also reminded at that time that conventional shipping insurance policies may have war hazard clauses and other clauses that prevent recovery when the insured goods are lost or damaged under specified circumstances. For a bank that lends for international trade or provides a guarantee under an L/C, it is important, therefore, to know precisely the extent of coverage.

Numerous international trade documents are required by governments, particularly those of the importing countries. Standard is the requirement of a **consular invoice,** which is issued by a foreign office of the importing country's government to certify the amount and nature of the goods to be imported. In many cases, a *certificate of origin* is also necessary. This document verifies the country of origin of imports. Documentation may also be required certifying that imported goods do not violate health and safety regulations. Various other documents may be required by the governments of importing countries. Moreover, the governments of exporting countries often have documentary requirements. The U.S. government has numerous restrictions on exports designed to prevent the flow of goods that may have military value to potential enemies. Obviously, banks involved in trade financing require a great deal of expertise regarding the details of international trade if their operations are to show profits.

Providing Credit to Importers and Exporters

We have seen that when exporters provide credit to importers through the use of bank drafts and L/Cs, they can discount the resulting BAs to obtain cash for their exports before payments are made by importers. It has also been pointed out that exporters may provide credit to importers through open account selling and that governments are heavily involved in trade finance. At this point, we turn to the consideration of private financing techniques other than BAs and open account selling.

Financing for Importers   Importers often pay for imports simply by borrowing from local banks. The lending bank generally requires the importer to provide a *trust receipt,* which means that the bank retains title to the goods and the importer is legally the goods' trustee. The importer's arrangement with the lending bank may require repayment of the loan as the goods are sold.

Sometimes, the importer provides the lending bank with an **import draft,** which is drawn by the importer on a bank (usually the lending bank) and authorizes that bank to transfer funds from the importer's account to the lending bank on the date indicated on the draft.

Importers frequently obtain financing by raising capital through new issues of bonds or stocks. If, for example, a multinational company raises $250 million from a bond issue to finance an investment program, it is likely that part of the funds raised will fund purchases of imported capital goods. Although the goods may be paid for as they are received, effectively they are purchased on credit for the period of time represented by the life of the bond issue.

Financing for imports is frequently arranged by banks in exporting countries. Banks lend to importers in part to serve client exporters and in part because governments promote exports by guaranteeing loans made by banks to the buyers of the nation's exports. We shall be looking at export loan guarantees a little later in the chapter.

Financing for Exporters   Time drafts that are turned into BAs and discounted by exporters are a major source of financing for exporters, as was explained in Chapter 12. There are, however, other techniques for financing exports. Exporters do not necessarily have to convert their time drafts into BAs to obtain financing, for both trade drafts and bank drafts can often be discounted advantageously without conversion into BAs. In such cases, exporters often buy insurance against risks other than the exchange risk, and this coverage can be transferred to a financial institution that discounts time drafts. In most cases, drafts are discounted *without recourse,* which means that if a drawee fails to honor a draft, the party that discounted the draft cannot look to the exporter for payment. As an alternative to discounting individual drafts, an exporter may be able to bundle a collection of drafts as collateral for a bank loan.

The discounting of receivables is known as **factoring,** and the party that does the discounting is known as a **factor.** Factoring can be arranged with ordinary accounts and notes receivable as well as with outstanding bills of exchange. It is considerably more expensive than discounting high-quality BAs, but there are numerous situations in which exporters cannot finance with high-quality BAs. For example, if competition protects importers from any compulsion to provide L/Cs, or if no highly rated bank can be found to provide BA financing on good terms, the exporter may be well-advised to use factoring. Perhaps this cost can be recovered in the price of the exports. Also, while factoring costs more than BA financing, the cost differential is often small enough to make factoring an attractive alternative.

The factoring of exports is more highly developed in Europe than elsewhere, but it is a growing practice among exporters outside Europe. Factors charge fees to exporters that typically range from 1.75 to 2 percent of export value for factoring without recourse. In addition, the discount rate applied to factored exports is likely to represent a differential of 1 to 2 percent over the cost of conventional bank financing for exports.[1] These added costs are substantial, but they are often amply justified in view of the risks that exporters escape by factoring without recourse. The costs can be lowered by factoring with recourse, but nonrecourse financing is generally used because factors can lower and manage the relevant risks. This ability rests on their expertise in collecting debts from importers, their skill in evaluating relevant risks, and their reliance on the principle of risk diversification.

Forfaiting   Considerable attention has been focused of late on a type of factoring known as **forfaiting.** Derived from the French *à forfait,* which means to surrender a right (and which is obviously akin to the English *forfeit*), this term applies to the fixed-rate, medium-term (for 3 to 7 years) factoring of exports without recourse supported by guarantees provided by financial institutions in the importing countries. Forfaited exports are usually, but not always, capital goods, and almost all of them are exports to eastern Europe and LDCs. The exporters are generally located in developed countries, but some are located in LDCs. Although forfaiting was pioneered by banks in Switzerland and Germany, London has become its leading center. It has grown rapidly since the early 1980s, but it is doubtful that it applies to more than 1 percent of total world trade.[2] Nevertheless, because it has great potential for growth and provides an excellent illustration of the capacity of international banking institutions to adapt to a changing environment, it merits further examination.

In most cases, the financial institutions that act as **forfaiters** (factors) are the export financing divisions of large commercial banks, some of which are separately incorporated. Some forfaiters are relatively small financial institutions that may offer standard commercial banking operations, but that specialize in financing international trade. An outstanding example of this latter type of institution is the Hungarian International Bank, which operates out of London and has the majority of its stock is owned by the National Bank of Hungary, the Hungarian central bank.[3]

Forfaiting originated as a response to the use of countertrade by Soviet bloc governments. Because countertrade's limitations prevented these governments from satisfying their requirements for imported capital goods, an opportunity arose for the use of financial techniques to arrange hard currency imports on convenient terms. Forfaiting proved to be such a technique. When the sovereign debt crisis led to a (largely temporary) increase in countertrade, forfaiting began to be used extensively in trade with LDCs, and London speedily emerged as its leading center. Countertrade has receded in importance for heavily indebted LDCs, but forfaiting has continued to grow. At present, its

---

[1]Alan C. Shapiro, *Multinational Financial Management,* 3d ed. (Boston: Allyn and Bacon, 1989), p. 444.

[2]"Forfaiting," *Euromoney,* February 1988 Special Supplement, p. 4.

[3]*Ibid.,* p. 21.

greatest use is in trade with eastern Europe, but it is widely used in trade with the nations of north Africa, the Middle East, and the Pacific Rim and is spreading elsewhere.

Central to the use of forfaiting is the ability of the forfaiters to obtain suitable guarantees of payment from central banks or highly rated commercial banks in the importing countries. When an exporter asks a forfaiter to assume a credit it has granted or would like to grant to an importer, the forfaiter will ordinarily agree to discount the credit without recourse only if a reliable institution in the importing country guarantees the importer's obligation, which may be in the form of either a bill of exchange or a promissory note.

In most cases, the guarantee takes the form of an **aval,** which is simpler than a formal guarantee, but usually adequate for the forfaiter's needs. In an aval, the guarantor bank or **avalist** endorses each bill of exchange or note submitted to it by the importer by adding the words **per aval** and the signature of a responsible officer. In addition, the avalist writes the words *on behalf of* by the name of the drawee on bills of exchange. This simple procedure suffices to obligate the avalist if the importer fails to pay the forfaiter. A formal guarantee is considerably more complicated because it requires separate documentation.

If, however, there are any legal problems associated with the use of an aval, or if any changes in the importer's obligation arise from the provision of a guarantee, a formal guarantee becomes necessary. Some jurisdictions do not legally recognize avals. Also, because the use of avals developed in countries with civil law rather than English common law traditions, some legal questions pertaining to the use of avals have not been fully resolved in countries whose legal systems grew out of the latter.[4] Whether the guarantee takes the form of an aval or a formal guarantee, the guarantor's commitment is, in the vast majority of cases, to pay the forfaiter in hard currency. In some instances, however, guarantors have converted importers' hard currency obligations into local currency obligations.

Recall that forfaiting is used to provide fixed-rate, medium-term financing to importers. To protect against the interest rate risk and other risks, forfaiters generally require importers to make payments in 6-month floating-rate installments. There is a secondary market in forfaited paper, and this allows a forfaiter to liquidate a position if it seems desirable.

Because BAs are typically used for short-term export financing, it is misleading to compare the cost of forfaiting with that of BAs. One can much more appropriately compare the cost of forfaiting with that of extending medium-term credits to importers *in the same countries* under government-supported export promotion programs. Whether or not forfaiting is more expensive for exporters than the credits provided under such programs depends in part on the amount of government subsidy incorporated into the latter. Suppose, illustrating a common occurrence, an exporter wanting to

---

[4]*Ibid,* pp. 24–29.

extend medium-term credit to an importer can obtain commercial and political risk insurance at subsidized rates from a government-backed agency that guarantees payment of 90 percent of the amount of credit extended. Also assume that the exporter can finance the entire amount of the credit to the importer by using forfaiting. Because forfaiting generally involves obtaining a guarantee from a central bank or a commercial bank whose government would probably not allow it to fail, it would probably obviate the need for buying commercial risk insurance. Political risk insurance could probably be purchased from a private insurer at a price not greatly in excess of that charged by the government-backed agency. It does not necessarily follow, therefore, that forfaiting would be an inferior alternative to financing under the government-sponsored program. Moreover, forfaiting generally offers greater flexibility than governments' export-promotion programs, which tend to impose restrictions pertaining to such matters as the amount of financing that can be provided and the maturity profile of the repayment agreements.[5] It is hardly surprising, therefore, that government export promotion programs have begun to incorporate forfaiting into their operations.

While forfaiting attracts exporters because of its documentary simplicity, flexibility, and avoidance of outlays for commercial risk insurance, its greatest attraction for them is the chance to turn medium-term receivables into immediate cash on terms that are competitive with alternative financing vehicles. This allows importers to buy goods on relatively favorable terms that might otherwise be unattainable. Since a central bank or a commercial bank (which is subject, no doubt, to considerable government control) must guarantee payment, a guarantee is often equivalent to an import permit. When an importer would like to procure goods from more than one seller, located, perhaps, in more than one country, the purchases can be combined into a single financial package, simplifying the importer's financial arrangements. Because forfaiters are adept at managing payments in different convertible currencies, importers can choose the convertible currency in which they will pay.

One of the most intriguing aspects of forfaiting is that it has provided ample opportunity for financial innovators to demonstrate their remarkable skills. For example, forfaiting can be combined with an interest rate or currency swap (both of which are explained in the next chapter) to provide an appealing "synthetic security" for investors. To illustrate this point, Exhibit 15.1 shows how an aggressive bank could create a synthetic floating-rate security based on a transaction à forfait to avoid the risks involved in forfaiting and an interest rate swap to avoid the interest rate risk.

Exhibit 15.1 is a considerably modified version of an actual case in which Citibank played the central role represented by the dealer bank in the exhibit.[6]

---

[5] *Ibid.*, p. 27.
[6] *Ibid.*, p. 9.

| E X H I B I T | 15.1 | *Combining Forfaiting with an Interest-Rate Swap*

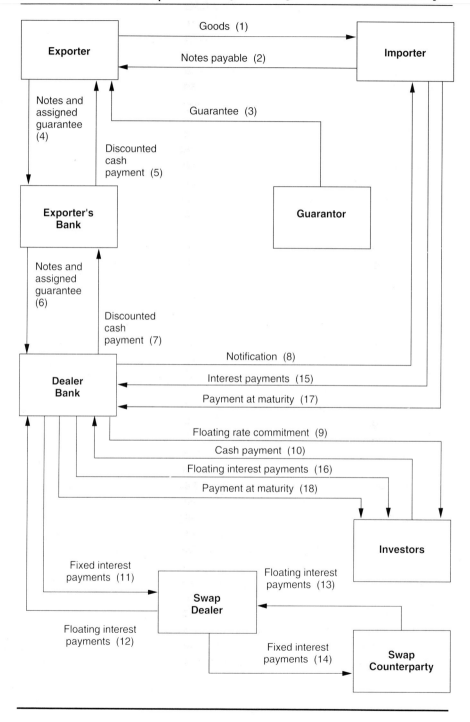

The 18 flows shown in Exhibit 15.1 can be broken down into 6 phases. In the first phase, Flows 1 through 5, the exporter's bank (the forfaiter) acquires notes payable from the importer and a guarantee from an appropriate bank in the importing country. In the second phase, Flows 6 through 8, the dealer bank replaces the forfaiter by buying the importer's notes and receiving the assignment of the guarantee. The dealer bank notifies the importer of the transfer of its obligation, and the importer becomes obligated to make fixed interest payments on its debt to the dealer bank. To simplify matters, the exhibit assumes that the importer pays for the goods at maturity instead of in stages.

In the third phase, Flows 9 and 10, the dealer bank sheds the risk involved in holding the importer's notes by selling participations in them to a group of investors, which might well be other banks. The dealer bank continues to hold the notes, however, and serves as their trustee. These participations constitute the synthetic security created by the dealer bank. It is assumed that the investors will only purchase them at a price acceptable to the dealer bank if they receive floating-rate interest payments. In the fourth phase, the dealer bank repairs the mismatch between its floating-rate interest payments and its fixed-rate interest receipts by entering into an interest rate swap with a swap dealer, which could conceivably be the swaps department of the same dealer bank. The swap dealer offsets this swap by locating a counterparty whose needs match those of the dealer bank. To simplify matters, Exhibit 15.1 does not show the commitments of the swap parties, but it does record the subsequent interest flows.

At this point, the dealer bank has eliminated most of the potential risks and presumably stands to profit from favorable interest-rate differentials. The fifth phase records the interest flows, Flows 11 through 16. The final phase is the repayment phase, represented by Flows 17 and 18. No repayment flows are associated with the swaps because they are exchanges of interest payments only; no principal changes hands.

Forfaiting has proved useful as a device for funneling badly needed imports into heavily indebted LDCs. For instance, a bank that holds rescheduled claims against a government that will be paid only after many years if ever, may elect to discount some of these claims in exchange for a participation in a forfaited trade deal with a shorter maturity. In general, an LDC government that has rescheduled much of its debt is more likely to repay a medium-term, trade-related debt than a long-term, rescheduled debt. Moreover, the interest rate on the trade-related debt is likely to be higher than the interest rate on the rescheduled debt. Additional security for the trade-related debt can be provided by securing a commitment from the government involved to channel specified amounts of its forex earnings into an escrow account in another country that is controlled by a third party. Some holders of trade-related claims against a country may want the option of accepting local currency at a favorable exchange rate instead of being paid in a convertible currency. This option becomes attractive when the holders of the claims have uses for local currency or can sell it for convertible currency.

Countertrade and Leasing

Very different in nature from standard trade practices, countertrade and leasing represent what can be called unconventional trade financing procedures. The former is widely used in eastern Europe and, to a lesser degree, among LDCs. The latter has a wider geographic application and occurs in response to entirely different circumstances.

Countertrade

As was pointed out a bit earlier, countertrade first came to prominence in trade with members of the Soviet bloc. With their command economies and doctrines denigrating reliance on market prices to determine the allocation of resources and the distribution of goods, the governments of these countries sought to force their international trade into bilateral goods-for-goods trading patterns as much as possible. In addition, as early as the 1960s trade financing problems led some LDCs, such as Brazil, to experiment with countertrade. Generally speaking, these experiments did not turn out well, but the emergence of the sovereign debt crisis spawned renewed interest in countertrade. The resulting countertrade boom has receded somewhat as eastern European countries have developed more flexible trading arrangements and financial conditions in some LDCs have improved, but countertrade remains an important fact of life with which bankers and other participants in international trade have to contend. In trade finance, as in other areas of international finance, bankers have shown great ability to adapt to changed conditions and opportunities.

Types of Countertrade   Narrowly construed, countertrade consists of goods-for-goods exchanges that conform to restrictions imposed by at least one country. The term also applies, however, to cases in which international movements of goods are linked to flows of money or credit in ways that cannot be classified as routine sales. For example, some heavily indebted governments have accepted arrangements in which creditor banks cancel some of their claims on those governments in exchange for taking some of the countries' exports. In a typical case of this type, First Interstate Bank of California wrote off claims against Peru in exchange for Peruvian exports of copper wire, fish products, clothing, wood products, and such vegetables as garlic, onions, and fresh asparagus.[7] This arrangement could also be called a *debt-for-exports swap,* but the countertrade label is applied to it because it involved arranging exports to avoid conventional trading procedures.

The simplest countertrade situation is *straight barter,* in which goods are simultaneously exchanged for goods of equivalent value so that no money changes hands. In other cases, foreign exporters may be required to accept

[7]Rosamund Jones, "Fishmeal? That'll Do Nicely," *Euromoney,* June 1988, p. 150.

partial payment for their goods in the form of exports from the countertrading country. In either of these situations, a foreign exporter that accepts goods for which it has no use may engage the services of a commodity broker to find buyers for the goods. If countertrade is a large enough factor in its operations, it may establish a countertrading subsidiary. Countertrading subsidiaries have also sometimes been established by prominent commercial banks, which may be prevented by law from direct participation in countertrade.

Another type of countertrade is the *clearing agreement,* whose use dates back to at least the 1930s when it was used by the governments of Germany and the Soviet Union. In this arrangement, each party agrees to exchange goods with the other over a period of time, i.e., the exchanges of goods are not necessarily simultaneous. The goods to be exchanged may be specified in detail, or considerable flexibility may be allowed in their composition as long as the quantities shipped reach a specified value. At the end of the trading period, any balance owed by one country to the other may be settled by providing additional goods or by making a cash payment, probably in a convertible currency.

Switch trading allows a party to transfer a claim arising from a clearing agreement to another party. If, for example, Country A finishes the trading period with a net claim on Country B, Country A is allowed to sell its claim to another party if Country B cannot provide it with additional acceptable goods on acceptable terms.

With the *buyback,* the countertrade agreement calls for the exchanges of goods to be separated in time. An outstanding example of such an arrangement is the agreement between several western European governments and the government of the Soviet Union in which European firms were to participate in the construction of natural gas pipelines in the Soviet Union in exchange for long-term commitments from western Europe to purchase some of the gas. Because the present value of the gas to be received exceeded the value of the European contribution to the Soviet pipeline development, the agreement required hard currency payments for the imported gas.

Somewhat similar to the buyback is the *counterpurchase,* which separates the exchanges in time, but does not specify the goods that one of the parties will receive. For example, a U.S. aircraft firm may export jet liners to a developing country's government in exchange for the government's commitment to allow it to obtain repayment over a specified time period by selecting goods of its choice that the government or private suppliers in that country are able to export. In such an arrangement, as in most other countertrading arrangements, it is necessary to specify how the prices of traded goods are to be determined.

There are, no doubt, other countertrading arrangements. The types given should be sufficient, however, to demonstrate that countertrade has numerous possible manifestations.

An Assessment of Countertrade   In terms of economic efficiency, an inherent problem with countertrade is that it entails some sacrifice of hard currency earnings for the countries that require it. Ideally, a countertrading government would use countertrade to export goods that could not be profitably exported for cash at existing exchange rates. It is obviously difficult, if not impossible, however, to avoid some displacement of hard currency exports. This means that unless the same goods would be imported under countertrading arrangements that would have been imported in their absence, there is a danger that countertrade may lead to suboptimal imports. Government bureaucracies in countertrading countries try to prevent this, but it is doubtful that allocating imports on the basis of bureaucratic preferences improves on market allocation. Moreover, by forcing their exporters to work through counter-trade, governments discourage them from learning how to operate in foreign markets. The commodity brokers who serve as countertrading intermediaries give some help in this regard, but the incentive to develop export knowledge would be much greater for local producers who were allowed to sell their products for scarce foreign exchange and keep most of the proceeds.

Most economists are skeptical that countertrade provides enough benefits to cover its costs. Even if it did not suboptimize imports, it would involve the costs of bureaucratic control. In addition, foreign exporters charge more for their goods when they are required to participate in countertrade to sell them. Against these points, countertrade's proponents argue that bureaucratic allocation may be superior to market allocation in some nations' particular circumstances. Moreover, as has been pointed out by Shapiro (who is highly critical of countertrade), when a government has entered into a price-fixing agreement with other governments, such as those engineered by OPEC, countertrade can be used to cut the price of the commodity involved without openly violating the agreement.[8]

Although the point is not often made explicitly, a factor behind the use of countertrade is the belief that the costs of bureaucratic control are low in terms of social opportunity cost. This belief stems from the assumption that adding workers to government payrolls does not significantly diminish private sector employment. If this assumption is valid, a corollary is that cutting back on those payrolls would lead to an increase in open unemployment and underemployment. This employment rationale for maintaining a large bureau-cracy has received ideological reinforcement, and once a large bureaucracy is in place, it tends to be highly resistant to suggestions that its role be curtailed. It seems unlikely, therefore, that countertrade will soon wither away.

Leasing

A *lease* is an agreement in which the owner (the lessor) of tangible property assigns the use of the property to another party (the lessee) in return for periodic rental payments, which are made in advance. Usually, a lease is for a definite time period, which may be considerably less than the expected useful life of the property. Leases have long been used, of course, for housing and business premises, and in recent years, they have become popular for capital

---

[8]Shapiro, *Multinational Financial Management*, p. 414.

equipment and consumer durables. Leasing of capital equipment has become common in international trade because of tax considerations, its usefulness in reducing risk, and the possibility of avoiding exchange controls.

Classified on the basis of their terms, leases are of two primary types: **operating leases** and **financial** or **capital leases.** Operating leases are normally for shorter periods of time than the expected lives of the leased equipment, and they are frequently renewable. It is common for operating leases to be cancellable at the option of the lessee. Some operating lease contracts call for lessors to bear the cost of maintenance and other expenses, such as repairs and insurance, of using leased equipment; in other cases, lessees bear these costs.

A financial or capital lease requires the lessee to bear the costs of using the property and is usually noncancellable. When a financial lease is cancellable, cancellation entails a substantial penalty. The term of a financial lease extends for all or most of the expected life of leased equipment, and the payments are designed to allow the lessor to recover the equipment's cost plus what amounts to an interest return. From this it follows that, economically, a financial lease is equivalent to a purchase on credit. Legally, however, there is often a difference between a financial lease and a credit purchase, and this can have tax consequences; differences in the tax treatment of financial leases from country to country create opportunities to use them internationally to lower taxes.

Leases are also classified on the basis of type of financing. In this regard, there are three primary types: direct leases, sale and leaseback agreements, and leveraged leasing.

Direct leasing is the traditional method for financing a lease. A firm that owns equipment, either the manufacturer of the equipment or an equipment dealer, simply leases the equipment to the lessee. Equipment dealers who use direct leasing usually finance many of their purchases of equipment through conventional borrowing. In the past, this type of lease financing has so often been associated with operating leases that the term *direct lease* is often regarded as being synonymous with *operating lease.* The lessor often takes the responsibility for maintaining the equipment and bearing most of the other expenses associated with its use.

In a sale and leaseback agreement, one party sells property to another party and then leases it from the new owner. The lessee receives both cash and the use of the property in return for periodic rental payments and whatever residual value the property may have when the lease expires. A particular advantage of this arrangement, which is commonly used with operating leases, is that the lessee can generally deduct the lease payments from its taxable income. When the lessee's country's taxes are higher than the lessor's, this arrangement can reduce the total taxes paid by the two parties. Moreover, if the leased property includes land, which is ordinarily not depreciable for tax purposes, the deductibility of the lease payments means that the lessee effectively amortizes the land's value. Understandably, sale and leaseback is a popular arrangement between affiliated companies located in different countries.

Leveraged leasing is a comparatively recent development associated with large purchases of capital equipment. A leveraged lease has three parties—a lender joins the lessor and the lessee. The lessor typically makes a substantial down payment on the purchase of equipment, but most of the purchase is financed by a loan from the lender to the lessor. The lender ordinarily secures the loan by obtaining a mortgage on the equipment and receiving an assignment of the lease payments sufficient to service the loan.

The Tax Advantages of International Leasing   As sale and leaseback agreements indicate, a lease between firms located in different countries may lower overall tax payments. The tax advantage rests on the transfer of ownership of the leased property, so the tax effects of a lease hinge on whom the tax authorities consider to be the property's owner.

U.S. tax law draws a sharp distinction between operating and financial leases with respect to determining the ownership of leased property for tax purposes. For property under an operating lease, the owner is the lessor; for property under a financial lease (called a *capital lease* by the IRS), the owner is the lessee. In an operating lease, therefore, the lessor deducts depreciation and receives whatever other tax advantages may be associated with ownership, including any investment tax credit. Also, however, the lessor reports the full amount of the lease payments as income. The lessee deducts the full amount of the lease payments. In a financial lease, the lease payments are treated as debt amortization, so the lessor includes as income only the interest portion of the payments. The lessee receives the tax benefits of ownership, including the depreciation deduction, but can only deduct the interest portion of the lease payments. The basic reason for this treatment of financial leases is to prevent parties from reducing taxes by disguising purchases of equipment as leases.

The difference in the taxation of operating and financial (capital) leases in the United States makes it essential to have a set of legal standards that distinguishes between them. The relevant standards have been provided by the Financial Accounting Standards Board (FASB), whose Statement No. 13, issued in 1976, specifies that a capital lease is one which meets any *one* of the following conditions:[9]

1. The lease transfers title to the asset to the lessee by the end of the lease period.
2. The lease contains an option to purchase the asset at a bargain price.
3. The lease period equals or exceeds 75 percent of the asset's estimated economic life.
4. At the beginning of the lease, the present value of the minimum lease payments equals or exceeds 90 percent of the fair value of the leased property to the lessor (minus any investment tax credit realized by the lessor).

If a lease meets none of these conditions, it is taxed as an operating lease. While the conditions appear to leave some room for interpretation (for example, the

---

[9]James C. Van Horne, *Financial Management and Policy*, 8th ed. (Englewood Cliffs, N.J.: Prentice-Hall, 1989), p. 516.

precise meaning of "90 percent of the fair value"), they appear to be comprehensive enough to make it difficult to construct a financial lease that allows the lessor to obtain the tax benefits of ownership.

The FASB–IRS conditions for distinguishing capital leases from operating leases mean that in the United States, the taxation of leases is based on economic reality rather than the legal distinction between a lease and a purchase. A number of countries use the economic reality approach, but others accept the legal distinction between a lease and a purchase as valid for tax purposes. Therefore, they tax what would be called a capital lease in the United States as if it were an operating lease. If, for example, Switzerland allows what would be called a capital lease in the United States to be taxed as an operating lease, a lease between a Swiss lessor and a U.S. lessee can allow both parties to claim depreciation deductions on the same equipment. A lease that allows both parties to claim the tax benefits of ownership is popularly known as a *double-dip lease*.

Double dipping can also occur when both the lessor and the lessee are located in countries that use the economic reality approach, but differ in how they determine what is a financial or a capital lease. An example of such a case is provided by Shapiro.[10] The Dutch airline KLM leased airplanes from a U.S. firm in an arrangement that qualified as an operating lease in the United States and a financial lease in the Netherlands. As a result, both the lessor and the lessee were able to claim depreciation deductions on the planes.

Shapiro also calls attention to the significance of the Tax Reform Act of 1986 for international leasing.[11] Among other things, this act increased income tax collections from corporations by reducing their deductions. Before 1986, U.S. multinationals could deduct almost all of their interest payments on general-purpose borrowings. Now, however, they must allocate the interest payments in proportion to the locations of their assets. A U.S. firm that has 50 percent of its assets located abroad can deduct 50 percent of its interest payments on its general-purpose borrowings from its income subject to U.S. income tax. On the other hand, when a U.S. company is the lessee in an international operating lease, the lease payments are fully deductible. On balance, therefore, U.S. multinationals now have more incentive than they had before 1986 to acquire property through international operating leases as opposed to purchasing assets financed by borrowing.

Other Advantages of International Leasing   While tax advantages account for most of the popularity of leasing in international trade, other factors contribute to this popularity. Among these factors are reducing political risk and avoiding credit and exchange controls.

Although credit insurance may be available for exports of equipment to buyers in countries with high political risk, it is sometimes advisable to supply

---

[10]Shapiro, *Multinational Financial Management*, p. 716.
[11]*Ibid.*, pp. 744–745.

equipment to such buyers through leases rather than sales. Suppose, for example, that a multinational firm has a subsidiary located in a country with high political risk and that the parent can either sell equipment to the subsidiary or lease to it. If the subsidiary is expropriated or goes bankrupt, the parent may be able to reclaim the equipment on the basis of ownership. Leasing is likely to be better when the risk is political rather than of another type because if business failure results from a nonpolitical cause, the parent may be subject to considerable pressure to make good on the subsidiary's debts. If, for example, a parent fails to stand behind the debts of a subsidiary that has failed because of bad management, the credit ratings of other subsidiaries and of the parent itself may be adversely affected. Reinforcing this political risk basis for using leases is the general proposition that a government that invokes exchange controls in order to limit foreign currency outlays is less likely to restrict lease payments than profit remittances or interest payments. A country with high political risk is unlikely to hesitate to resort to exchange control to manage its payment problems.

Finally, if a government uses exchange controls and/or credit controls to restrict foreign investment by its residents, leasing may be an effective means for avoiding the controls. A well-known example of this situation is Japanese experience with restrictions on long-term yen loans to foreign borrowers and on the percentages of assets of Japanese financial institutions that can be foreign. Operating and financial leases have allowed Japanese lenders to work around these restrictions. For example, financial leases amounting to conditional sales with longer terms than those allowed on yen loans have been used to finance sales of ships to foreign buyers.[12]

Government-Sponsored Trade Finance Activities

Virtually all governments actively promote their countries' exports. The techniques include tax breaks, direct subsidies, low-cost government loans, credit insurance, and loan guarantees. In addition, exchange control countries commonly allow exporters favorable conversion rates on forex earnings and/or the right to use some of those earnings as they see fit.

Among the most plausible rationales advanced in support of export promotion are the claims that the production of exports stimulates output and employment and allows a nation to finance a larger volume of imports. On balance, however, economists tend to be skeptical about export promotion programs, whose effects include the promotion of certain exports at the expense of other production, including exports that do not qualify for assistance. Moreover, because governments compete against each other in export promotion, some nullification of their efforts occurs. The clearest winners in this competition are foreign importers, while the clearest losers are the taxpayers who fund export promotion programs or the parties who might

---

[12]*Ibid.*, pp. 717–718.

have gained if their governments had found other uses for the money spent on export promotion. The most generous allocations of resources for export promotion are made by governments of developed countries, which can better afford the cost of export promotion than the governments of LDCs. Collectively, perhaps, the LDCs derive some net gain from this competition, but great doubt exists about whether or not it represents an efficient way to redistribute income internationally and promote economic development. Whatever export promotion's merits, however, it is apparently here to stay. As long as the governments of *some* developed countries make heavy commitments of resources to export promotion, we can rest assured that the governments of the rest will feel compelled to meet such "unfair competition" with export promotion programs of their own.

These pages focus on the export programs of the U.S. government, which primarily provides loan financing and export credit insurance. Other developed countries have similar (and often more comprehensive) programs.

Export Loan Financing

Two ways in which governments promote exports are by making direct loans that finance exports and by underwriting credits extended to foreign importers by exporters and financial institutions. In the United States, with its tradition of minimal direct lending by government agencies, the primary emphasis has been on underwriting credits extended by banks and exporters. The U.S. government is, however, in the direct lending business. Its primary agency for making export-related loans is the Export-Import Bank, which was created in 1934 as an independent executive-branch agency.[13] The word *Import* in the Eximbank's title is misleading—its mission has always been to promote U.S. exports.

The Eximbank's operations are overseen by five full-time directors, who are appointed by the president with the advice and consent of the Senate. Its operating capital is supplied by the U.S. Treasury in accordance with Congressional authorizations, and Congress establishes guidelines for its mission. Its activities fall under three main headings: lending on its own account, guaranteeing export-related loans by banking institutions, and making credit insurance available to U.S. exporters. In executing its guaranty function, it works with the Private Export Funding Corporation (PEFCO), a private corporation that lends and promotes lending to foreign buyers of U.S. products. In executing its credit insurance function, it works with the Foreign Credit Insurance Association (FCIA), an unincorporated association of private

---

[13]The main motivation behind the Eximbank's establishment was to expand exports to the Soviet Union. During the early years of the Great Depression, the U.S. government was desperate to increase exports and felt that the U.S.S.R. was a potentially important outlet for U.S. goods. It was feared, however, that the potential could not be realized without U.S. government intervention to make exports available to the Soviet Union on terms that were competitive with those offered by other governments. The Soviet government was, of course, adept at playing off one capitalist government against another.

insurance firms whose main activity is protecting U.S. exporters against commercial and political risks.

Eximbank Loans   The fundamental purpose of Eximbank loans is to finance U.S. exports that face subsidized competition from other governments' export-promotion activities. Accordingly, a general guideline is that the Eximbank does not lend when unsubsidized private financing is available. Eximbank loans are of two types: *direct loans* to foreign buyers of U.S. products and *intermediary loans* to banking institutions that lend to foreign buyers of U.S. products. The loan amounts are not to exceed 85 percent of U.S. export value. The loan periods may be either medium-term (1 to 7 years) or long-term (more than 7 years), and both types of loans are at fixed rates. The U.S. exporters that benefit from these loans commonly obtain *preliminary commitments* from the Eximbank that allow them to include information about available financing in negotiations with foreign importers.

The Eximbank's lending rates follow guidelines set by the OECD to limit interest rate subsidies by export financing agencies. Its direct loans and long-term intermediary loans carry the lowest rates permitted under these guidelines. Its medium-term intermediary loans are at rates ranging from 50 bp to 150 bp below the OECD minimum rates, but the intermediaries must relend to importers at the OECD minimum rates.

In setting its guidelines, the OECD divides importing countries into three categories based on per capita GNP: rich countries (Category I), intermediate countries (Category II), and poor countries (Category III). Loans to Category I borrowers are not to fall below the OECD's Commercial Interest Reference Rates (CIRRs), which are representative commercial lending rates in various currencies. The minimum rates for loans to other borrowers are based on a weighted average of government bond rates denominated in the U.S. dollar, the mark, the pound sterling, the French franc, and the yen. The minimum rate on loans to Category II borrowers is higher than that on loans to Category III borrowers. For the period July 14, 1990 to January 15, 1991, for example, the Category II minimum rate was 10.05 percent on loans of 5 years or less or 10.55 percent on loans of more than 5 years, while the Category III minimum rate was 9.20 percent on all loans.[14]

The Category II and Category III minimum loan rates are the same regardless of the currency lent. This means, for example, that if U.S. interest rates are lower than the interest rates in the other currencies in which direct loans are made, as has been the case since 1990, the subsidy element in Eximbank loans, if any, is less for loans in dollars than for loans in other currencies.

As a general rule, the Eximbank does not make direct long-term loans to Category I borrowers (long-term being defined as more than 5 years in this

---

[14]Export-Import Bank of the United States, "Medium- and Long-Term Export Loans and Guarantees," Rev. July 1990, p. 9.

instance). Indeed, the vast majority of the exports promoted by the Eximbank are to developing countries. It does, however, provide guarantees on long-term loans to Category I borrowers, and if a CIRR loan offer from another government exists that cannot be met competitively with an Eximbank guarantee, it will consider a matching loan.

A major factor in Eximbank lending is the upfront **exposure fee,** which varies with the length of loans and the risk classifications assigned by the Eximbank to borrowers and their countries. This fee is charged to exporters. It is collected as loans are disbursed and is paid directly by the exporters in direct loans and by them through the intermediaries in intermediary loans. The fee ranges from 0.5 percent on a 1-year loan made to or guaranteed by the government of a highly rated country to 8.0 percent or even more on loans of 10 or more years to borrowers in countries with the lowest ratings.[15] It is a one-time fee, however, and it can be added to the loan principal.

In addition, the Eximbank charges most borrowers a per annum **commitment fee** of 0.5 percent on the undisbursed amounts of their loans. Medium-term loans to intermediaries are exempt from this fee, however, unless such loans are combined with loan guarantees for the intermediaries, in which case the fee is charged.

Most of the Eximbank's direct loans are long term and are parts of large loan packages in which private lenders participate. The amount lent by the Eximbank averages more than $20 million per loan, but the Eximbank is required to make some direct loans that finance exports by relatively small firms. A controversial aspect of its direct lending, though one that is hardly surprising, is its many delinquent loans. On September 30, 1989, loan delinquencies totaled $898.6 million in principal and $579.1 million in accrued interest and were distributed among more than 37 countries.[16] Many other direct loans had been rescheduled at that time.[17]

Intermediary loans are typically for relatively small amounts and average less than $2 million each. For medium-term intermediary loans, Eximbank guarantees are often provided on the companion loans made by intermediaries. Intermediary loans are often made to banks outside the United States, some of them in third countries. For example, if the U.S. subsidiary of a Japanese manufacturing firm had an opportunity to sell goods to a buyer in Africa, the

---

[15]*Ibid.,* p. 8.

[16]Brazilian importers led the way with delinquencies of $578.4 million. Argentina held a distant second place with $186.1 million. Next came Cuba with $95.1 million, Nigeria with $94.8 million, and Zaire with $89.3 million. The Cuban figure included $58.8 million in accrued interest, indicating a very long delinquency period. Export-Import Bank of the United States, *Annual Report, 1989* (Washington, D.C.: Eximbank, 1990), p. 17. In its *Annual Report* for 1990, the Eximbank changed its reporting format and did not publish comparable data on delinquencies. The change reflected, among other things, the Eximbank's decision to generally discontinue the accrual of interest on delinquent and rescheduled loans for accounting purposes.

[17]On September 30, 1990, the outstanding balances on the Eximbank's rescheduled loans, including some capitalized interest, were $3,227.8 million. Export-Import Bank of the United States, *Annual Report, 1990* (Washington, D.C.: 1991), pp. 30–32.

Eximbank could lend to the London branch of a Japanese bank, and the branch could lend to the importer.

Eximbank Guarantees . The second major activity of the Eximbank is to guarantee export-related loans. The guarantees fall into two main categories: guarantees of loans by U.S. banks to foreign buyers of U.S. goods and guarantees of PEFCO's loans to foreign buyers of U.S. goods. The Eximbank also guarantees loans to small- and medium-sized U.S. exporters. These loans can fund working capital needs and thus do not need to be tied to specific exports.

In 1990, the Eximbank unveiled a new loan guaranty procedure, known as *bundling,* in which several Eximbank-guaranteed transactions are combined into a single loan facility. In the first such facility, First Interstate Bankcorp of Los Angeles provided a large line of credit to the Banco Nacional de Comercio Exterior (Bancomext), a state enterprise that was to be used to finance various purchases of capital goods and services by different Mexican firms. Bancomext was able to use the line of credit to support issues of securities in international capital markets. The amount of the Eximbank's guarantee authorized for this facility in 1990 was $205.7 million.[18]

The loan guarantees provided by the Eximbank follow the same 85 percent-of-export-value guideline as Eximbank loans. Similarly, the Eximbank charges *exposure fees* on guarantees that usually exactly match those charged on its loans, but when a medium-term intermediary loan is combined with a loan guarantee for the intermediary, the exposure fee is charged only for the guarantee. The exposure fee is charged to exporters, but it is collected from the guaranteed lenders.

The Eximbank charges lenders a per annum commitment fee of 0.125 percent on the undisbursed balances of guaranteed loans except when a loan guarantee for an intermediary is combined with an Eximbank loan to the intermediary. In that case, a commitment fee of 0.5 percent per annum is charged on the undisbursed portion of the loan.

Most of the guarantees provided by the Eximbank are for long-term loans. Guarantees are available on either fixed or floating-rate loans, and the loans may be in convertible currencies other than the dollar. Eximbank guarantees are transferable to other parties. International leases, whether operating or financial, are eligible for Eximbank guarantees.

Most Eximbank loan guarantees provide comprehensive coverage of both political and commercial risks. A guarantee covering political risks only is available for transactions with private firms or nonsovereign state enterprises and is the only type of guarantee available when there is common ownership between the exporter and the foreign buyer. Political risks include war, cancellation of import permits, expropriation, intervention in the importer's business, and restrictions on loan repayments in foreign currency. Commercial

---

[18]*Ibid.,* pp. 10, 18.

risks include nonpayment for other reasons than those specified as political risks, including changes in tariffs, natural disasters, the competitive situation, but they do not include exchange rate changes. When the coverage received is for political risks only, the exposure fee is correspondingly reduced.

Just as the Eximbank has had a problem with delinquent loans, it has also had a problem with delinquencies on guaranteed loans. When a borrower defaults, the Eximbank takes over the claim in what is known as *subrogation*. Subrogated claims also arise from defaults to exporters who are covered by Eximbank insurance. As of September 30, 1990, the Eximbank held $949.3 million in rescheduled subrogated claims, excluding accrued interest. The comparable figure for rescheduled and delinquent loans was $3,538.7 million.[19]

PEFCO was created in 1970 to promote high-value exports such as sales of aircraft. Its stockholders are mainly commercial banks, but include manufacturing and investment banking firms. PEFCO makes long-term loans (with terms of more than 5 years) and very long-term loans (with terms of 20 years or more) to foreign buyers of U.S. goods. It also has a Note Purchase Facility that factors exporters' medium- and long-term receivables without recourse. PEFCO frequently participates in loan packages with commercial banks and/or the Eximbank in which it takes the longer maturities. While some of PEFCO's operating capital comes from stockholder subscriptions, most of it comes from issuing its own debt securities, most of which are long term. Because the Eximbank guarantees all export loans by PEFCO and also guarantees PEFCO's borrowings, it can issue securities on very favorable terms.

Export Credit Insurance

The third major activity of the Eximbank is providing credit insurance to U.S. exporters. It shares the responsibility for this activity with the FCIA, which is an unincorporated association of private insurers. The FCIA actually administers the export insurance program and sells the policies. The insurance covers commercial and political risks and is classified as either short term (up to 180 days) or medium term (181 days to 5 years). When it is necessary to allow exporters to meet government-sponsored competition from other countries, the FCIA will provide credit insurance for up to 7 years on some big-ticket exports. Most of the insurance it issues is, however, short term. Parties can transfer coverage from exporters to financial institutions when exporters factor receivables. Credit insurance is also sold to U.S. lessors of equipment.

The FCIA was organized in 1961 with the idea of having private insurers bear the commercial risk portion of export credit insurance. The Eximbank assumed the political risk portion. The Eximbank underwrote the FCIA's

---

[19]*Ibid.*, p. 33. The figure of $3,538.7 million for delinquent loans is somewhat higher than that of $3,227.8 million given in note 17 because some loans included in the higher figure had not been rescheduled. Extensive rescheduling occurred in 1990.

operations by agreeing to cover overall operating losses should they occur, but the Eximbank did not agree to cover losses on individual policies.

The emergence of the sovereign debt crisis in 1982 led to sizable losses by some of the FCIA's insurers and to a restructuring of the export credit insurance program. In the restructuring, the Eximbank agreed to guarantee the commercial risk portion of the FCIA's medium-term policies, but the FCIA retained the commercial risks of the short-term policies.

The distinction between commercial and political risks was examined in connection with loan guarantees, but no mention was made of the problems that can arise in interpreting precisely what these risks mean. For example, sometimes an importer may be able to cancel its commitment to an exporter without necessarily giving rise to an enforceable claim against the FCIA or the Eximbank. A host-country government may use "creeping expropriation" to undermine an importer's solvency without giving rise to a claim that falls under the Eximbank's political risk umbrella. While it might seem that this case would then be covered by a policy's commercial risk coverage, assuming that the policyholder has such coverage, questions can also arise about what is included in that coverage. Such gaps in the coverage of FCIA policies sometimes induce exporters to buy private insurance that supplements the coverage provided by those policies.

The insurance premiums charged by the FCIA vary with a policy's coverage, the terms of the sale, the nature of the buyer, and the risk classification of the importing country. Because political risk is considered to be beyond the importer's control, it is insurable up to 100 percent of the amount owed in some cases, but in others, such as short-term, single-buyer policies, the political risk coverage may fall as low as 90 percent. In order to provide exporters with an incentive to correctly evaluate their customers, the maximum commercial risk coverage is generally set at a lower level than the corresponding political risk coverage, but the commercial risk coverage may be 100 percent when the buyer is a government. The minimum commercial risk coverage is also 90 percent.

Banking institutions are eligible to purchase FCIA insurance when they factor exporters' bills of exchange drawn on importers or their banks. A U.S. bank that confirms an L/C drawn on a foreign bank is eligible for insurance against the risk that the issuing bank will fail to honor a BA that it has accepted. The U.S. branches or subsidiaries of foreign banks are permitted to buy FCIA insurance.

Although the FCIA's insurance does not provide protection against every conceivable risk, its coverage is extensive enough to exercise considerable influence on U.S. exports. This insurance reduces the pressure on exporters to require importers to pay in cash or produce L/Cs from banks of impeccable standing. Also, exporters can allow importers longer payment periods than they would otherwise offer. In addition, when exports are insured, exporters can obtain bank financing more easily and on better terms.

Now that the damage done by the sovereign loan debt problem has been contained and largely absorbed, the risks entailed in offering credit to importers in developing countries appear to have diminished and become more calculable. Moreover, in arrangements in which one party accepts risk and another party bears it, the risk-bearing party tends to want a high degree of control over the other party's commitments. In light of these facts, it is not surprising that the Eximbank has indicated that it would like to effect some changes in its relationship with the FCIA. In its *Annual Report* for 1990, the Eximbank expressed a desire to separate its insurance coverage from that provided by the FCIA.[20] Presumably, if the Eximbank begins to write its own policies, it will tend to accept risks that the FCIA would be reluctant to accept if it were entirely on its own. Ultimately, however, it is up to Congress and the President to determine if and how the government's role in promoting credit insurance for U.S. exports is to be changed.

An Overview of the Eximbank's Operations

Exhibit 15.2 presents a summary of the Eximbank's main operations for fiscal 1990, which ended September 30, 1990. The exhibit summarizes authorizations for loans, guarantees, and export credit insurance. Total authorizations were $8,787.9 million, of which export credit insurance accounted for about 55 percent. Since the total value of the exports that benefitted from these programs was only about $9.3 billion, the role of the Eximbank in promoting U.S. exports may appear to be minimal. It should be taken into account, however, that many Eximbank loans and loan guarantees are generally parts of larger loan packages in which private financial institutions, including PEFCO, participate. It should also be taken into account that Exhibit 15.2 does not show the amount of export credit insurance for which the FCIA was the underwriter. Incidentally, the volume of authorizations shown in Exhibit 15.2 for fiscal 1990 represented a 38.2 percent increase over fiscal 1989.

In each fiscal year from 1983 through 1990, the Eximbank operated at a loss, and it is likely to continue to operate at a loss in the future. On September 30, 1991, it had a net capital deficiency of $5,413.2 million.[21] In other words, if the Eximbank were a private corporation, it would be bankrupt.

The continuing losses of the Eximbank reflect the loss of interest income and the writing off of claims in the aftermath of the sovereign debt crisis. They also reflect the consequences of a negative interest rate spread between the interest rates at which the Eximbank borrows and the interest rates at which it lends. In order to diminish its losses on the spread, the Eximbank has tended to shorten the average length of its borrowings. In addition, it has worked with the OECD to achieve guideline lending rates that more adequately mirror market interest rates than has been the case in the past. Moreover, these guidelines rates are now adjusted semiannually.

The Eximbank has unlimited borrowing authority with the Federal Financing Bank. Ultimately, however, if the Eximbank's losses are not brought to a halt, its obligations to the Federal Financing Bank will have to be written off at the expense of U.S. taxpayers.

---

[20]Ibid., p. 35.
[21]Ibid., p. 40.

| E X H I B I T | 15.2 | *Eximbank Authorizations: Fiscal 1990 (Millions of Dollars)*

All Programs	Number of Authorizations	Amount Authorized	Export Value
Loans[a]			
Direct loans	16	$318.0	$382.5
Intermediary loans	184	240.6	285.4
War Chest grants[b]	4	53.4	0
Interest Equalization Program[b]	2	2.1	0
Total	206	$614.1	$667.9
Guarantees[a]			
Long-term guarantees	30	2,713.1	3,211.4
Medium-term guarantees	182	531.0	434.0
Working capital guarantees	86	88.6	98.5
Total	298	3,332.7	3,743.9
Export credit insurance			
Short-term	1,043	4,214.7	4,214.7
Medium-term	66	626.4	666.6
Total	1,109	4,841.1	4,881.3
Grand total	1,613	$8,787.9	$9,293.1

[a]Export values for guarantees related to specific loans are included with the related loan.

[b]Export values for War Chest grants and the Interest Equalization Program are included with related authorizations.

Source: Export-Import Bank of the United States, *Annual Report, 1990* (Washington, D.C.: Eximbank, 1991), p. 15.

Summary

This chapter has explored the financing of international trade. Compared to other areas of international finance, trade finance is stable. As is illustrated by developments in forfaiting, however, trade financing practices are changing and are influenced by changes in other financial techniques.

Most international trade involves the use of what may be termed *conventional trade financing procedures.* Two techniques were singled out for detailed treatment: the use of bills of exchange and bankers' acceptances, which are frequently issued in conjunction with letters of credit, and the factoring of export receivables. Particular emphasis was given to forfaiting, a type of factoring that is widely used in connection with exports of capital goods and that has been growing in importance.

Among less conventional trade financing procedures, two were examined: countertrade and leasing. Countertrade, one form of which is straight barter, involves linking a country's exports to specific commitments by other parties that avoid traditional trading procedures. It is used by countries with weak currencies and governments that are heavily involved in the management of their countries' trade. International leasing is a growing practice that owes its popularity to tax advantages and other factors, including the reduction of political risks.

Also examined were the export promotion activities of the Export-Import Bank of the United States and its allied private-sector agencies. The Eximbank operates primarily in three areas: lending on its own account, guaranteeing loans by banking institutions, and providing export credit insurance. Overall, the volume of exports directly assisted by the Eximbank is small relative to total U.S. exports, but Eximbank assistance is often provided in association with private financial assistance for exports. A controversial aspect of the Eximbank's operations is that it operates at a loss.

References

Abdullah, Fuad A. *Financial Management for the Multinational Firm.* Englewood Cliffs, N.J.: Prentice-Hall, 1987, Chapter 7 and Appendices G and H.

Eiteman, David K., Arthur I. Stonehill, and Michael H. Moffett. *Multinational Business Finance,* 6th ed. Reading, Mass.: Addison-Wesley, 1992, Chapter 18.

Export-Import Bank of the United States. *Annual Report.*

_____. "Medium- and Long-Term Export Loans and Guarantees." Rev. July 1990.

Financing Foreign Operations. New York: Business International Corporation, various issues.

Foreign Credit Insurance Association. "Your Competitive Edge in Selling Overseas." Rev. November 1990.

"Forfaiting." Supplement to *Euromoney,* February 1988.

Francis, Dick. *The Countertrade Handbook.* Westport, Conn.: Quorum Books, 1987.

The Guide to Export Finance 1988. London: Euromoney Publications, 1988.

A Handbook on Financing U.S. Exports, 5th ed. Washington, D.C.: Machinery and Allied Products Institute, 1988.

Hennart, Jean-François. "Some Empirical Dimensions of Countertrade." *Journal of International Business Studies,* Second Quarter 1990, pp. 243–270.

Jones, Rosamund. "Fishmeal? That'll Do Nicely." *Euromoney,* June 1988, pp. 149–152.

Khoury, Sarkis J. "Countertrade: Forms, Motives, Pitfalls, and Negotiation Requirements." *Journal of Business Research,* June 1984, pp. 257–270.

Lecraw, Donald J. "The Management of Countertrade: Factors Influencing Success." *Journal of International Business Studies,* Spring 1989, pp. 41–59.

Rodriguez, Rita M., ed. *The Export-Import Bank at Fifty: The International Environment and the Institution's Role.* Lexington, Mass.: Lexington Books, 1987.

Shapiro, Alan C. *Multinational Financial Management,* 3d ed. Boston: Allyn and Bacon, 1989, Chapters 13, 21.

Van Horne, James C. *Financial Management and Policy,* 8th ed. Englewood Cliffs, N.J.: 1989, Chapter 18.

Venedikian, Harry M., and Gerald A. Warfield. *Export-Import Financing,* 2d ed. New York: Wiley, 1986.

Questions

1. What is a clean draft, and when does such an instrument tend to be used in international trade?
2. How does a negotiable L/C differ from a transferable L/C?
3. Assume that a U.S. exporter draws a dollar time draft on a bank

designated by the importer in accordance with the terms of an irrevocable L/C issued by that bank. The exporter's bank agrees to serve as the advising bank, but does not confirm the L/C. Assuming that the exporter does not wish to convert the draft into a BA and intends to hold it to maturity, from whom is it likely to collect? What obligations does the issuing bank have in this case? What must the exporter do to assure itself that it has a legally valid claim?

4. The B/Ls used in conjunction with L/Cs in international trade are almost always order B/Ls. Why?

5. When a bank or other financial institution finances an exporter without recourse and takes over control of the documents issued in connection with the export, including the B/L and the export insurance policy, what are some of the things that the bank should be concerned about other than the ability of the importer to pay?

6. What is an import draft, and of what use is such a document?

7. Explain the circumstances that may induce an exporter to obtain financing by factoring bills of exchange and importers' accounts and notes receivable instead of using BAs.

8. What are the distinguishing features of forfaiting, and why has forfaiting often been used in countries that rely extensively on countertrade?

9. How does an aval differ from a formal guarantee?

10. Why might an exporter prefer to rely on forfaiting to finance an export to an LDC or an eastern European country rather than pursue the alternative of buying export credit insurance from a government-backed agency and using the insurance coverage to obtain bank financing?

11. Although we do not examine financial swaps in detail until the next chapter, why do you think forfaiting is often compatible with the use of financial swaps?

12. If we define barter as the simultaneous exchange of goods of equivalent value, then how does countertrade differ from barter? Why do you think some governments require countertrade instead of relying more on exchange controls or other devices to restrict imports?

13. How do operating leases differ from financial leases? Why does this distinction matter for U.S. firms that export equipment under leasing arrangements? What is the meaning of the concept of a capital lease in the United States?

14. What could be the advantages for exporters of using either the sale and leaseback technique or leveraged leasing?

15. What is a double-dip lease, and how does such a phenomenon arise?

16. Who gains from the intergovernmental competition in export promotion programs, and who loses?

17. What is the nature of the OECD guidelines for the interest rates charged by governments in their loans for export promotion? Do you think that these guidelines tend to have the effect of favoring some countries' exports over others? Explain.

18. Explain the nature of the exposure fees charged by the Eximbank on loans and loan guarantees.

19. How does PEFCO fit into the U.S. government's export-promotion activities? Is it correct to say that PEFCO's stockholders are guaranteed a profit?

20. What are the key features of the joint export insurance program operated by the Eximbank and the FCIA? To what extent is the FCIA underwritten by the Eximbank?

Financial Swaps

■

In financial swaps, the contracting parties (counterparties) make exchanges which are separated in time and reverse each other. Such an exchange is generally arranged through an intermediary commercial bank or investment bank serving as a broker or dealer.

In one form or another, such swaps have been around for some time. During the 1960s, for example, the U.S. government frequently arranged intergovernmental currency swaps for the defense of the dollar. For example, the Fed would obtain a certain quantity of marks from the Bundesbank in exchange for an equivalent quantity of dollars with the understanding that the exchange would be reversed at the same exchange rate after a specified time interval. Also, as we saw in Chapter 6, most forward transactions are swaps that combine either spot exchanges with forward exchanges or forward exchanges with different maturities. In addition, private firms have long used swaps known as *parallel loans* or *back-to-back loans* to circumvent exchange controls and reduce their forex exposures.

The decade of the 1980s produced a spectacular expansion of swap financing that has yet to exhaust itself. This expansion occurred in response to arbitrage opportunities produced by market imperfections, the growing need for protection against the exchange and interest rate risks, improvements in computer technology, and lower market barriers to financial transactions. Excluding forward swaps, two categories of swaps have dominated the swap financing revolution: currency swaps and interest-rate swaps. Currency swaps are inherently linked to international financial operations. Interest-rate swaps may be entirely domestic in nature, but they are frequently international. Both types have numerous variations, and currency swaps often share characteristics with interest-rate swaps.

In the general pattern for currency swaps, the counterparties exchange currencies at the current spot rate and reverse the exchange at a later date at the *same* exchange rate. Between the beginning and ending dates, the counterparties exchange interest payments. In some cases, the counterparties do not actually exchange principals, but make interest payments to each other on hypothetical amounts known as *notional principals*. Currency swaps closely resemble forward swaps, but forward swap exchanges ordinarily occur at different exchange rates, and no interest payments are exchanged.

Furthermore, while most forward swaps are for less than a year (though they may be for as long as 3 ycars), currency swaps are generally for periods of 2 or more years.

In an interest-rate swap, the counterparties agree to exchange interest payments based on a notional principal; no actual exchange of principal amounts takes place. Very commonly, a counterparty with a fixed interest obligation contracts to make floating-rate interest payments to a counterparty with a floating-rate obligation in exchange for a commitment by the floating-rate payer to make fixed interest payments to it. The reciprocal interest payments may offset each other so that only the net difference is actually paid. Not all interest-rate swaps involve exchanges of fixed-rate payments for floating-rate payments, however.

Toward the end of the 1980s, another type of financial swap emerged that seems destined to attain considerable importance. This technique, the **commodity swap,** typically resembles a fixed-for-floating interest-rate swap. As will be explained, the primary function of commodity swaps is to provide protection against fluctuations in the prices of the underlying commodities for periods longer than those covered by commodity futures contracts.

The Evolution Of Financial Swaps

Currency swaps between private parties were a natural extension of the central bank swaps used to support the dollar and other currencies during the 1960s. Commonly, however, currency swaps are regarded as an outgrowth of experience with parallel and back-to-back loans. Both of these attained prominence in the 1970s when the British government tried to discourage capital outflows by taxing pound sterling forex transactions, and when their usefulness in maneuvering around comprehensive exchange controls was demonstrated.

Parallel Loans

Parallel loans involve at least four parties. Commonly, though not always, the parties consist of two pairs of affiliated companies. The parallel loans commonly consist of a loan by an affiliate of each company to an affiliate of the other company, with the loans being in different currencies.

Assume that a parent corporation in the Netherlands (DP) with a subsidiary in England (DS) wants a 1-year pound sterling loan. Also assume that a parent corporation in the United Kingdom (BP) with a subsidiary in the Netherlands (BS) wishes to obtain a 1-year loan in guilders. Each parent company has a higher credit rating in its home country than its subsidiary has in the country in which it is located.

One feasible course of action would be for each parent company to borrow in its local currency and lend to its subsidiary, which would then convert the loan proceeds into the needed currency at the current spot rate. Since the loan period is assumed to be 1 year, the subsidiaries could presumably hedge the exchange risk with forward swaps. Assume, however, that the British government taxes both spot and forward sales of pounds for foreign currencies, adding to the cost of the transaction. Also, note that since this course of action involves going through the forex market, each subsidiary will bear a cost in the form of the bid–ask spread on forex transactions, a cost which will increase if the subsidiaries cover the exchange risk with forward swaps. If, therefore, a way can be found to provide each subsidiary with the needed funds without going through the forex market, both can reduce their financing costs.

At first glance, it may seem that the forward covers would be unnecessary since a forex loss by a subsidiary would be offset by a forex gain by the parent, or vice versa. In reality, however, both sets of firms would have exchange risk problems. Suppose, for example, that BS does not hedge, and during the time it owes pounds to BP, the guilder declines against the pound, with the result that BS incurs a realized loss when it buys spot pounds to repay the loan. Since BP collects the same quantity of pounds from BS that it would have collected had the exchange rate not changed, BP does *not* realize an offsetting gain. On a consolidated basis, the result for BP is similar to its result had it bought guilders spot, invested them unhedged, and later bought spot pounds with guilders at a less favorable exchange rate. It is desirable, therefore, that BS hedge the exchange risk. Note that if the loan were for a period longer than a year and a forward contract were not available for the time period of the loan, the hedging problem would become more complicated. BS might then seek to protect itself with a series of forward contracts arranged sequentially, but this would further increase the cost of hedging.

The situation presented here is ideal for a parallel loan arrangement. Each parent company could borrow locally at a favorable interest rate and lend the proceeds to the other parent's subsidiary. This procedure would allow the subsidiaries to avoid forex transactions and the resulting hedging problem, and the cost savings realized could be allocated to effectively lower each subsidiary's borrowing cost. The resulting exchange of principals is shown in Exhibit 16.1. Conceivably, each parent could lend at the same rate at which it

| E X H I B I T | 16.1 | *Exchange of Principals in a Parallel Loan Arrangement*

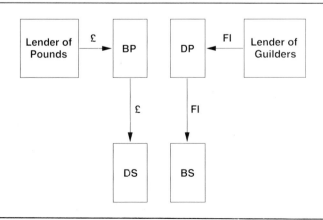

borrows, but it is also conceivable that the parents' lending rates could be slightly above their borrowing rates in order to cover their costs and, possibly, to generate some gain. The flows of interest payments and the repayments of principal would follow the lines in Exhibit 16.1, but with the directional arrows reversed.

Another situation in which a parallel loan arrangement might be desirable may arise when a government has comprehensive exchange controls. Assume, for example, that Argentina severely limits the right of subsidiaries of foreign corporations to remit profits to their parent companies, while a U.S. parent company (USP) with an Argentine subsidiary (USS) wants to obtain a profit remittance in dollars from the subsidiary. Also assume that a newly established Argentine subsidiary (FS) of a French parent company (FP) wants to borrow Argentine pesos to expand its operations, but is unable to do so on favorable terms because of credit controls imposed by the Argentine government to restrain inflation.

A feasible solution to the problems of these parties might be for USS to make a peso loan to FS while FP simultaneously lends dollars to USP. Alternatively, the four parties might simply exchange currencies and avoid the loans, but the circumstances could favor the parallel loan arrangement. With the parallel loan, USP obtains the dollars it wants without having to declare them as taxable income, and it can deduct the subsequent interest payments to FP against its taxable income. Also, the exchange rate could move against USP before the Argentine government relaxed its controls on profit remittances, reducing their value below the current values of the dollar loan. A priori, one cannot say that a parallel loan would always be superior to a simple currency exchange, but neither can one rule out the possibility that it would be superior in a particular instance.

Back-to-Back Loans

Back-to-back loans resemble parallel loans, but are simpler since they involve only two parties. Suppose, for example, that Purehex, a U.S.-based firm, and Schneckenhaus, a German firm, both conduct operations in various currencies. At the moment, Purehex wants to obtain marks and Schneckenhaus wants to obtain dollars, but assume that Purehex cannot borrow marks as favorably as Schneckenhaus can, and that Schneckenhaus cannot borrow dollars as favorably as Purehex can. In this situation, it would probably make sense for Purehex to borrow dollars and lend them to Schneckenhaus while Schneckenhaus borrows marks and lends them to Purehex. This is a **back-to-back loan,** i.e., one in which parties simultaneously lend to each other in different currencies. Given the presumed borrowing advantage of each firm in its home country currency and the fact that forex transactions would be avoided, it is likely that this arrangement would lower each firm's cost of borrowing. Without such an arrangement, Purehex would probably borrow dollars, convert them into marks at the current spot rate, and hedge the resulting mark exposure. With the back-to-back loan, Purehex avoids the costs incurred in forex transactions. While it is true that the back-to-back loan would give it a translation (on-the-books) exposure in marks, that exposure would probably be offset by the acquisition of mark-denominated assets.[1]

Absolute Advantage and Back-to-Back Loans   The statement that Purehex cannot borrow marks as favorably as Schneckenhaus and that Schneckenhaus cannot borrow dollars as favorably as Purehex indicates that each firm has an absolute borrowing advantage in its home country currency. Such advantages commonly exist because of market imperfections or differences in risk. Creditors who lend in one currency might not have the same information as those who lend in the other currency, or the two groups of creditors might evaluate information differently. For another possibility, tax considerations or some kind of government-sanctioned discrimination might cause foreign borrowers to be treated differently from domestic borrowers. Borrowers' risks might also be perceived to vary from currency to currency so that some firms may be considered to be riskier borrowers when they borrow in a currency other than that of their home country.

Comparative Advantage and Back-to-Back Loans   At this point, it is desirable to call upon that old war-horse of international trade theory, the principle of comparative advantage, which was unveiled to the world by David Ricardo in 1817 with the publication of his *Principles of Political Economy and Taxation*. Although Ricardo confined his presentation of comparative advantage to international trade, establishing a pattern that has prevailed to the present, many economists have long understood that the principle has much wider applicability.

When, for example, a football coach elects to start at quarterback an athlete who could play defensive back better than anyone else on the team, the soundness of the decision rests squarely on comparative advantage. The decision is objectively correct if the athlete's superiority over other team members in terms of points scored minus points given up is greater at quarterback than at defensive back. On the other hand, if the athlete's margin of superiority is slight at quarterback and pronounced at defensive back, the decision is probably wrong—the athlete should play defensive back, notwithstanding his slight superiority at the more glamorous quarterback position.

The principle of comparative advantage underlies much of the cost saving associated with financial swaps. This point is readily shown by inserting appropriate numbers into the Purehex–Schneckenhaus back-to-back loan

---

[1]Note that this translation exposure operates in the opposite way from the *transaction* exposure that occurs if Purehex borrows dollars and converts them into marks at the current spot rate. The translation exposure of the mark loan is a liability, while the transaction exposure from a spot purchase of marks is an asset. The dollar effects of an exchange rate change would, therefore, be in opposite directions in the two cases. Since, however, Purehex would probably use the proceeds of the mark loan to acquire mark-denominated assets, it would probably have no significant change in its net translation exposure in marks because of its participation in the back-to-back loan. With the alternative of borrowing dollars, however, it would probably continue to have a net mark exposure.

example. Recall that that example assumed that each firm had an absolute borrowing advantage in its home country currency. Now assume, however, that Schneckenhaus enjoys a higher credit rating than Purehex in both dollar and mark borrowings. Suppose, for example, that Schneckenhaus can borrow at 7.5 percent in marks and 10 percent in dollars, while Purehex can borrow at 9.5 percent in marks and 11 percent in dollars. As the following analysis explains, a back-to-back loan can still be advantageous for both parties, notwithstanding the fact that Schneckenhaus has an absolute borrowing advantage in both currencies.

Given these borrowing rates, there is a potential gain from arranging a back-to-back loan in which Schneckenhaus lends marks and Purehex lends dollars. In Ricardian terms, Schneckenhaus has a comparative cost advantage in marks and Purehex has a comparative cost advantage in dollars. The potential gain stems from the fact that the 2 percent (or 200 bp) difference in mark borrowing rates does not equal the difference in dollar borrowing rates, which is 1 percent (100 bp). Thus, let Schneckenhaus borrow marks at 7.5 percent and Purehex borrow dollars at 11 percent in a back-to-back loan arrangement in which Schneckenhaus lends marks to Purehex at its cost, 7.5 percent, and Purehex lends dollars to Schneckenhaus at 9.5 percent. Since this arrangement allows Schneckenhaus to cut its dollar borrowing rate from 10 percent to 9.5 percent, it realizes a gain of 50 points. Purehex loses 150 points in dollars since it borrows at 11 percent and lends at 9.5 percent, but it gains 200 points in marks by borrowing at 7.5 percent instead of 9.5 percent. Overall, therefore, Purehex also gains 50 points.

There are, of course, other possibilities. For example, Purehex could lend dollars to Schneckenhaus at 11 percent and borrow marks from it at 9 percent, in which case each party would again gain 50 points. Or they could meet each other halfway, with Schneckenhaus lending marks at 8.25 percent and Purehex lending dollars at 10.25 percent, once more achieving gains of 50 points each. Of course, an arrangement could be worked out in which the 100 point overall gain is not evenly shared.

The potential gains from a back-to-back loan are likely to be greater when each party has an absolute borrowing advantage in its home country currency than when one of the parties has an absolute borrowing advantage in both countries. As this example reveals, however, the gain from a back-to-back loan based only on comparative advantage may be significant.

From Parallel and Back-to-Back Loans to Swaps

While parallel and back-to-back loans offer definite benefits to the participants, three problems limit their usefulness: the necessity of finding parties with matching needs, the fact that failure by one party to fully comply with such an agreement does not legally relieve another party of its obligation to comply, and the fact that such loans are carried on the books of the participating parties. Each of these problems can be overcome fully or in part with currency swaps, and this explains their rapid emergence during the 1980s. Parallel and back-to-back loans still have roles to play, however, for they can be used to maneuver around exchange controls when a currency is not hooked into the currency swap network.

Both parallel loans and back-to-back loans can be regarded as currency swaps, but the prevailing usage of the term excludes them. Their exclusion is based on the fact that, whereas they are generally viewed as consisting of legally separate lending agreements, a currency swap is generally considered to be a single lending agreement. With parallel and back-to-back loans, a failure by one party to comply does not release a counterparty from its obligation to comply, i.e., they confer no automatic **right of offset.** Thus, in the Purehex–Schneckenhaus back-to-back loan, if Purehex fails to make a scheduled interest payment, Schneckenhaus is not automatically relieved of its obligation to pay interest to Purehex. Until Schneckenhaus can get the agreement legally dissolved, its obligation to Purehex continues. The parties could negotiate a separate agreement defining rights of offset to absolve a party of its obligation to comply if a counterparty fails to do so, but problems may still arise.[2] With currency swaps, however, the right of offset is generally recognized to be embodied in the agreement.

When a parallel or back-to-back loan goes into effect (viewing the former as a two-party agreement), the exchange of principals gives each side to the arrangement net increases in both assets and liabilities whose amounts are customarily recorded in full on the counterparties' books. With currency swaps, however, the principal amounts are not customarily shown on the books. Keeping the transactions off the books has been a major factor behind the use of currency swaps, particularly by commercial banks, which, in the aftermath of the sovereign loan crisis, have been striving to increase their earnings in ways that do not significantly increase their capital requirements under applicable regulations. While it is true that currency swaps are now being factored into banks' capital requirements, the weights assigned to them are far less than those assigned to banks' on-the-books assets.[3] The factoring of currency swaps into capital requirements has slightly reduced banks' incentive to use them, but the overall growth of currency swap volume has continued to be rapid.

In parallel and back-to-back loans, the counterparties must have matching needs with respect to currencies, principals, types of interest payments (fixed or floating rates), frequency of interest payments, and length of the loan period. Currency swaps largely resolve this problem of matching needs, however, because they are arranged by specialized swap dealers and brokers, usually money center banks, who recruit prospective counterparties and, when acting as dealers, accept temporary or easily hedged positions to fill gaps between prospective counterparties.

---

[2]See John A. M. Price, "The Technical Evolution of the Currency Swap Product," in Boris Antl, ed., *Swap Finance*, vol. I (London: Euromoney Publications, 1986), p. 54. According to Price, such an agreement must be registered if it is to provide the right of offset, but even the registration of a set-off agreement may not totally eliminate the problem.

[3]A brief account of the capital requirements applied to banks' interest-rate and currency swaps is provided toward the end of the chapter.

The first true currency swap was arranged in August 1981 by Salomon Brothers with the World Bank and IBM as counterparties. IBM had previously acquired fixed-rate obligations in marks and Swiss francs, and when the dollar appreciated, it obtained an unrealized capital gain in terms of dollars. Because its management believed (incorrectly) that the dollar's appreciation would not continue, IBM wanted to realize the capital gain and extricate itself from its mark–franc exposure. The World Bank wanted to issue Eurobonds at the lowest attainable interest cost. Under Salomon Brothers' direction, the World Bank put out two dollar Eurobond issues that matched the maturities and interest payment schedules of IBM's mark and Swiss franc obligations. The World Bank then swapped interest payments with IBM so that IBM made the Bank's dollar interest payments and the Bank made IBM's mark and franc interest payments.[4] This arrangement allowed the Bank to lower its borrowing cost because the mark and franc interest rates it paid were lower than the dollar interest rate. While IBM ended up paying the higher dollar interest rate, it was relieved of the exchange risk associated with paying interest in marks and Swiss francs.

The first interest-rate swaps appeared in London before 1981 had ended, and in 1982 their use spread to the United States. The motivating factor behind their use was their ability to convert fixed-rate interest payments into floating-rate interest payments, and vice versa. The volume of interest-rate swaps outstanding soon came to be larger than that of currency swaps, and interest-rate swaps continue to have a wide lead. At any given moment, however, even the volume of currency swaps is in the hundreds of billions of dollars.

Many individuals who plot financial strategy for banks, multinational firms, and governments believe that the swap revolution is far from having run its course. The recent emergence of commodity swaps has added to the bullish mood about the future of swap financing, but as we shall see, the obstacles facing commodity swaps are considerably greater than those confronting the users of currency and interest-rate swaps.

When the first currency swaps appeared, the commercial or investment banks that arranged them generally acted as brokers rather than dealers, i.e., they sought to match counterparties in return for generous commissions and avoided interposing themselves between the counterparties as principals. When U.S. dollar-denominated interest-rate swaps appeared, the arranging banks quickly found that the abundance of potential counterparties and the standardization of dollar-denominated financial markets made it feasible for them to act as marketmakers by entering into swaps as counterparties. They could then offset their positions by locating appropriate counterparties or taking other steps to hedge their positions. A similar transition of banks from serving as brokers to being marketmakers subsequently occurred in currency swaps as they experienced further growth and standardization. Banks take relatively fewer positions in commodity swaps, however, than in either currency or interest-rate swaps.

---

[4]J. Orlin Grabbe, *International Financial Markets* (New York: Elsevier, 1986), p. 310.

Currency Swaps

A currency swap can be viewed as a series of forward contracts, one for each cash flow.[5] When a currency swap entails an exchange of fixed-rate interest payments, it is like a relatively long-term forward contract except that the beginning and ending exchange rates are ordinarily identical. Periodic interest payments reflect the initial interest rate differential between the currencies. In a yen-dollar swap with a fixed yen interest rate of 6 percent and a fixed dollar interest rate of 8 percent, for example, the 2 percent differential compensates the swap's yen interest receiver for the lack of a forward premium in the reexchange of principals at the swap's termination. A currency swap and a forward contact thus both incorporate IRP, but their manners of doing so differ.

When the interest payments exchanged in a currency swap are fixed-for-floating or even floating-for-floating, the swap can be likened to a series of forward contracts in which the forward premium or discount is known in advance only for the first "contract." For each subsequent "contract," the parties know the spot rate in advance, but the forward premium or discount depends on what happens to the floating interest rate or rates that are incorporated into the swap.

There are at least three analytically distinct reasons for using financial swaps, whatever their type. The most important historically have been cost reductions and hedging. In addition, financial swaps are increasingly being used to create assets designed to raise investors' rates of return. Underlying the use of swaps for all three reasons is their flexibility.

Lower Costs

Market imperfections have spawned differences in comparative borrowing costs, supplying much of the momentum for growth in swap financing. Domestic borrowers have often had comparative advantages over foreign borrowers, though prestigious foreign borrowers have been known to have comparative borrowing advantages in domestic markets. Moreover, because banks' assessments of borrowers' creditworthiness have often differed from those of bond investors, comparative borrowing advantages between banking and bond markets have stimulated the use of swaps to take advantage of them. In many instances, these market discrepancies have allowed borrowing cost reductions of more than 50 basis points, notwithstanding the portion of the potential gains the banks and other financial firms that have acted as swap arrangers have siphoned off as compensation for their services. As in other free-market arbitrage situations, the gains from arbitraging on the basis of comparative borrowing costs have tended to diminish as borrowers have responded to the opportunities. Nevertheless, the volume of swap financing

---

[5]Solnik suggests that a currency swap can also be likened to a portfolio of two bonds in which a short position in one currency is combined with a long position in the other. Bruno Solnik, *International Investments,* 2d ed. (Reading, Mass.: Addison-Wesley, 1991), pp. 221–222.

has continued to grow and shows every indication of further expansion. The continued growth of swap financing makes it clear that there is much more behind the use of financial swaps than comparative borrowing costs.

Among these factors behind the growth of financial swaps are cost savings arising for reasons other than comparative borrowing costs. Such savings may arise as by-products of hedging with swaps or from what has been called "tax and regulatory arbitrage."[6] In addition, sometimes swaps have lowered borrowing costs by developing new markets or allowing borrowers access to markets that were previously closed to them.

Lowering Costs through Hedging   Hedging can lower a firm's borrowing costs because it reduces the uncertainty of cash flows and the probability of unfavorable changes in the values of assets and liabilities, thereby making the firm more creditworthy. In addition, because it increases the total amount that a firm can borrow, it facilitates economies of scale, which can reduce operating costs. The willingness of lenders to lend to a private firm depends on such factors as the ratio of the borrower's assets to equity capital and the volatility of its earnings. Higher volatility of earnings and greater variations in asset values increase the amount of equity that a borrower is expected to hold. Since hedging reduces earnings volatility, it permits a firm to acquire a larger volume of assets (by increasing the volume of liabilities) with a given volume of capital. With a larger volume of assets, a firm is better positioned to realize economies of scale.

Tax and Regulatory Arbitrage   The use of a currency swap to effect tax and regulatory arbitrage is illustrated by the following example. Assume that a Japanese firm wants to float a 10-year, fixed-interest bond issue, but there is a tax on bond interest income received by residents of Japan. Also assume that the regulations imposed on such issues are considerably more stringent than those applying to Eurobond issues, whether denominated in yen or dollars, and that the firm expects the Eurobond market to be more receptive to a bond issue denominated in dollars than to one denominated in yen. In this situation, it could be advantageous to issue dollar Eurobonds and enter into a currency swap to exchange dollars for yen, agreeing to pay fixed interest in yen in exchange for receiving fixed interest in dollars. With this procedure, the firm should be able to fully hedge its dollar bond issue while obtaining the desired yen financing on more favorable terms than a domestic bond issue would have offered.

Would the firm be able to find a swap counterparty on satisfactory terms? It is quite conceivable that it would. Suppose, for example, that a second Japanese firm wants to borrow dollars long-term at a fixed interest rate.

---

[6]This term is suggested in Clifford W. Smith, Jr., Charles W. Smithson, and Lee M. Wakeman, "The Evolving Market for Swaps," *Midland Corporate Finance Journal*, Winter 1986, pp. 20–32; reprinted in *Financial Management Collection*, August 1986, pp. 1–8. This article provides an excellent, though now slightly dated, overview of the subject of swap finance that brings out in easily understandable fashion the essential features of both currency and interest-rate swaps.

| E X H I B I T | 16.2 | *Interest Flows in a Yen–Dollar Swap*

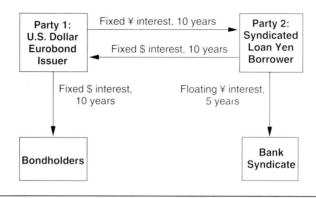

Although dollar interest rates exceed yen interest rates, the firm prefers to borrow dollars because it anticipates a long-term decline in the dollar's exchange value. It wants to pay a fixed rate on its dollar borrowing because it expects that dollar interest rates will tend to move slightly upward during the next 10 years. Assume that this second firm could issue dollar-denominated Eurobonds, but prefers to finance its planned dollar expenditures by borrowing yen from a bank syndicate on a floating-rate basis and arranging a swap in which it exchanges yen for dollars and agrees to pay fixed interest in dollars in exchange for receiving fixed interest in yen. Although the firm would be paying floating-rate yen interest and receiving fixed-rate yen interest, assume that it is willing to accept this apparent mismatch because of an expected decline in yen interest rates. Besides, let's assume, most of its yen receivables are at floating interest rates, which means that borrowing yen at a floating rate provides a better match against assets than would borrowing yen at a fixed rate. The floating rate financing could be arranged for a shorter time period than the swap to leave open the possibility of shifting to fixed-rate financing should the expected yen interest rates be revised upward.

A swap might be arranged between the two Japanese firms by a bank acting as a broker rather than as a marketmaker. The bank would receive an upfront commission for its services and would not be involved in the subsequent flows of interest payments. Exhibit 16.2 presents the flows of interest payments from the swap counterparties to each other and to their lenders. It is assumed that the swap is for 10 years, i.e., the same period as Party 1's Eurobond issue. Party 2, it is assumed, arranges its syndicated loan for 5 years. The flows of principals at the inception of the swap would, of course, be in opposite directions from those of the interest payments. Ideally, the interest payments in the swap would be set to coincide with the interest payments on the bonds and the bank loan. The yen interest payments by Party 1 to Party 2 could be offset against the dollar interest payments from Party 2 to Party 1 at the current spot rate so that only the net difference between them would actually be paid.

Numerous variations of this example would be possible, but it should be evident that a firm wishing to use a swap to escape taxes and the cost of complying with regulations has a good chance of finding a counterparty or counterparties willing to take the other side of the desired swap. Moreover, whereas arbitrage based on comparative borrowing costs may prove temporary because of competition, tax and regulatory arbitrage tends to last as long as the taxes and regulations. Ultimately, however, the taxes and regulations tend to be undermined by the arbitrage process.

The Development of New Markets   The use of swaps to lower borrowing costs by developing new markets or allowing borrowers access to previously unavailable markets is illustrated by the sudden emergence of Eurobond issues denominated in Australian dollars during the middle 1980s. Previously, Australian firms and government entities were virtually unable to borrow long-term at fixed rates by issuing bonds denominated in Australian dollars because of the undeveloped domestic bond market. Moreover, Australian banks were unwilling to lend at fixed rates beyond very short time periods, and their interest rates on floating-rate loans for other than short periods were quite high. Many Australian borrowers found that their best alternative for obtaining medium- and long-term financing was to rely on floating-rate Eurodollar loans, converting the proceeds into Australian dollars.

Bonds denominated in Australian dollars appealed to many investors because nominal Australian-dollar interest rates were so high relative to nominal U.S.-dollar interest rates that they expected that the interest differential would more than offset the future depreciation of the Australian dollar. Accordingly, it proved feasible to arrange currency swaps in which highly rated borrowers, including European public sector entities, issued fixed-rate Australian dollar Eurobonds and swapped their receipts of Australian dollars for U.S. dollars on which they agreed to pay floating-rate interest. The arranging banks offset these swaps by finding counterparties, usually Australian firms or public sector entities with outstanding floating-rate Eurodollar loans, who agreed to pay fixed-rate interest in Australian dollars.

The reductions in borrowing costs achieved by both sides to these swaps were large. The counterparties issuing Australian dollar Eurobonds obtained floating-rate U.S. dollars at 35 basis points or more below what they could achieve with other currency swaps. The Australian counterparties obtained fixed-rate Australian dollars for medium- and long-term periods at interest rates well below the short-term rates charged by Australian banks.[7]

It is arguable that the emergence of swap-driven Australian dollar Eurobonds provides another illustration of the operation of comparative advantage. Conceivably, the Australian borrowers could have issued such bonds, but deferred to borrowers who could capitalize on their high credit ratings and name recognition to achieve comparative borrowing advantages in

---

[7]See "The Global Swaps Market," *Euromoney* supplement, June 1986, pp. 34–35.

the Eurobond market. Since, however, the Australian borrowers were effectively precluded from issuing Australian dollar bonds by high interest rates, and since the swap counterparties who issued such bonds had never issued them before, it seems desirable to distinguish such new market activity from currency swaps that exploit *existing* comparative advantages in established markets.

Currency Swaps as Hedging Instruments

Currency swaps are used much like forward and futures contracts for hedging forex exposure, but for longer terms. Whereas forwards and futures are used primarily for short-term hedging, currency swaps usually hedge forex exposures of more than 2 years' duration. Currency swaps can also be used for shorter-term hedging, however, and are increasingly being used for that purpose. To some extent, therefore, currency swaps compete with forwards and futures rather than complement them.

When currency swaps compete head-to-head with forwards and futures, the governing factors in choosing among alternatives include flexibility, cost, and familiarity. Currency swaps have the edge over forwards and futures in terms of flexibility, but forwards and futures have the edge in terms of familiarity. Forwards and futures also generally have a cost advantage over currency swaps, though this advantage is usually small.

While some currency swaps are brokered (meaning that the arranging bank matches counterparties and avoids serving as a counterparty itself), most are now handled much like outright forwards, i.e., the arranging bank accommodates a customer without having previously lined up a counterparty to take an offsetting position. After entering into a swap, the arranging bank generally seeks to hedge its position by entering into an offsetting swap with one or more other customers, though it may hedge by other means.

Such bank dealers cover their transaction costs and risks by charging what amounts to a bid–ask spread in terms of interest basis points, i.e., the interest rates they pay are slightly lower than those they charge. Typically, this currency swap spread amounts to from 15 to 25 basis points per year, but when customers use currency swaps for hedging, the spread tends to gravitate toward the lower end of this range because hedging reduces the credit risk that banks accept when they act as swap counterparties. If, for example, a swap counterparty is using a currency swap to hedge an exposure in yen, the swap reduces the chance that the counterparty will be unable to meet its financial obligations since it reduces the probability of loss from an unfavorable exchange rate movement.

Forwards and futures differ from fixed-interest currency swaps in the timing of cash flows. With forwards, the interest rate differential between currencies is paid/received only at contract maturity. With futures, it is paid/received periodically and is intermingled with the cash flows that result from daily marking to market. The interest flows of currency swaps can be timed to coincide closely with those being hedged. Thus, if a potential swap counterparty has an outstanding obligation with 2 years to maturity that provides for the payment of interest in Swiss francs every 6 months, a swap might be arranged that provides the counterparty with a covering receipt of Swiss francs every 6 months. The flexibility of swaps may thus allow more perfect matching of cash flows than can be achieved with forwards or futures.

Finally, it should be noted that currency swaps have an advantage over forwards or futures in that they can be arranged when forwards or futures are unavailable. Suppose that a country's government prohibits forward transactions in the local currency or imposes unacceptable terms on them. Also assume that a firm in the country is obligated to make floating-rate interest payments in dollars during the following 2 years. Conceivably, the firm might enter into a currency swap in which it receives floating-rate dollars in exchange for making either floating-rate or fixed-rate payments in the local currency. Such an arrangement would differ from a back-to-back loan in being legally a single agreement instead of two agreements.

The Use of Currency Swaps to Create Assets

Most financial swaps are motivated by the opportunity to reduce costs or the desire to hedge existing liabilities. Increasingly, another motivation for using them has been to create *synthetic assets,* which are combinations of financial instruments that provide the same payoff characteristics as other assets. Suppose, for example, that a U.S. investment firm desires to increase its portfolio holdings of Swiss franc bonds because of expected long-term gains from diversification. It may not be happy, however, with the available Swiss franc bonds because of their characteristics, such as call provisions, or because of doubts about the creditworthiness of issuers. In this situation, it may be possible to create a synthetic Swiss franc bond issue by arranging a currency swap in which a bank intermediary agrees to serve as the swap counterparty. The firm could exchange a commitment to pay dollar interest for the receipt of interest in Swiss francs. In such an arrangement, it would not be necessary to exchange principals, i.e., the exchange of principals between the firm and the arranging bank would be notional. The arranging bank could then offset its position with one or more other swaps or through alternative arrangements.

Note that if the arranging bank is willing to accommodate the firm, the synthetic security created may have characteristics that exactly fit the firm's specifications. Note also that since the bank acts as a swap principal rather than as a broker, the credit risk accepted by the firm is that of nonperformance by the bank rather than nonperformance by another party. Obviously, therefore, the desirability of the arrangement depends to some extent on the creditworthiness of the arranging bank. This point serves to remind us that, as a general proposition, the use of swap financing techniques in which banks act as counterparties depends greatly on the soundness of the arranging banks.

The potential for using swaps to create synthetic assets is enormous. In fact, some observers believe that the creation of synthetic assets will become more important in medium- and long-term financing than the placement of standard bond issues. Should such a development materialize, bond markets would be dominated by the issues of governments with high credit ratings because of their liquidity and safety.

If the use of swaps is to develop to such proportions, it is essential to have a large secondary swap market. The owner of a freely traded bond can sell it if cash is needed or if it appears that the bond's price is going to fall substantially. It is normally not such a simple matter to liquidate a synthetic bond, however, although there are several possibilities for doing so.

Among these possibilities is *voluntary termination,* in which a counterparty liquidates a swap by making a lump-sum payment to the other counterparty. The voluntary feature of this approach can be eliminated by inserting a *buy-back provision* into the swap agreement, but swap counterparties are unlikely to agree to this free of charge. A third possibility is for a swap counterparty to write a *mirror swap* with the other counterparty. In this arrangement, the existing swap is reversed with a second swap that reflects current market conditions. Both swaps are carried to maturity, and the differences in cash flows caused by the second swap are reflected in the periodic settlements of interest payments between the counterparties. Still another possibility is the *reverse swap,* in which a counterparty offsets the original swap by entering into a swap with a third party. With both the mirror swap and the reverse swap, there is some credit risk, the nature of which is examined a little later.

A fifth possibility is for a swap counterparty to sell its position to a third party, but this alternative requires the approval of the counterparty on the other side of the swap since the buyer may not be as creditworthy as the original counterparty. This problem can be overcome if the swap dealer requires counterparties to furnish adequate collateral. Moreover, it is highly likely that exchange trading in standardized interest-rate and currency swaps will materialize in which swaps are traded much like futures contracts. Note that in the sale of a swap whose value has turned against the selling party, that party has to pay the other party to take on its obligation.

Types of Currency Swaps[8]

The workhorse of the currency swaps market is the *fixed-for-floating rate nonamortizing currency swap,* which is the plain vanilla variety of currency swap financing. The counterparties exchange principals at the outset, usually at the current spot rate, and reverse the exchange at the swap's termination at the same exchange rate. Periodically, usually either semiannually or annually, the counterparties exchange interest payments. One party pays fixed-rate interest in one currency, while the other party pays floating-rate interest in the other currency. Such swaps are nonamortizing because the principal repayments occur at termination.

Another popular type of currency swap is the *fixed-for-fixed rate nonamortizing currency swap,* which is identical to the fixed-for-floating swap except that both parties pay fixed rates. A fixed-for-fixed currency swap can be created by combining a fixed-for-floating currency swap with a fixed-for-

---

[8]The material in this section is largely based on John F. Marshall and Kenneth R. Kapner, *Understanding Swap Finance* (Cincinnati: South-Western Publishing, 1990), pp. 46–47.

floating interest-rate swap. Suppose, for example, that Great White Whale Corporation (GWW) participates in a plain vanilla fixed-for-floating rate currency swap as a floating-rate payer of dollars and a fixed-rate receiver of yen. GWW can convert its floating-rate obligation into a fixed-rate obligation by entering into an interest-rate swap in dollars in which it accepts floating-rate payments and makes fixed-rate payments.

There are also *floating-for-floating rate nonamortizing currency swaps*, which are identical to fixed-for-floating swaps except that both parties pay floating interest rates. Such a swap may be arranged in a single agreement, or it may be created by combining a fixed-for-floating currency swap with an interest-rate swap in which the fixed-rate payer in the currency swap becomes the floating-rate payer in the interest-rate swap.

Circus swaps are combinations of currency swaps and interest-rate swaps in which the floating rates are based on the LIBOR. Either a fixed-for-fixed nonamortizing currency swap or a floating-for-floating nonamortizing currency swap becomes a circus swap if it combines a plain vanilla currency swap with a fixed-for-floating interest-rate swap and the floating portion of each swap is LIBOR-based.

Also, there are *amortizing currency swaps,* in which the principals that were originally exchanged are reexchanged in stages. These swaps can be fixed-for-floating, fixed-for-fixed, or floating-for-floating. In addition, as was noted in connection with the explanation of the use of currency swaps to create assets, it is possible to arrange currency swaps in which only notional principals are exchanged.

Various other currency swap arrangements have been used, and new ones are constantly being developed. In an example of such arrangements, the *off-market swap*, the initially exchanged principals are not of equal value, i.e., they differ from the current spot rate. The gap between the amounts is then subsequently made up either during the interest payment period or upon the swap's termination. Such a swap may be used for tax reasons.

Pricing Currency Swaps

When banks act as dealers in currency swaps, they furnish potential customers with bid and ask prices stated in terms of interest rates, and exchange rates that reflect bid–ask spreads. The prices quoted depend on various factors, including the length of life of a swap, its complexity, the availability of counterparties with whom the arranging bank can offset positions, the creditworthiness of a potential customer, the stability of current market conditions, expectations about future market conditions, and any regulatory constraints on transactions related to swap financing. Since the creditworthiness and reputation of an arranging bank are likely to matter to potential customers, and since arranging banks are likely to differ considerably in these respects, the pricing of a swap also depends on the arranging bank's standing among potential customers. A bank with an outstanding reputation is likely to be able to obtain more favorable pricing terms than one whose reputation is less strong.

The Risks of Dealing in Currency Swaps   The spread obtained by swap dealers reflects the risks and costs of dealing in them and managing the resulting positions. Because the risks involved in dealing in currency swaps are considerably greater than those involved in dealing in interest-rate swaps, the bid–ask spreads for currency swaps tend to be considerably greater than the bid–ask spreads of interest-rate swaps. Currency swaps involve both exchange risk and interest-rate risk, but interest-rate swaps involve no exchange risk. As a general proposition, because the market for currency swaps is thinner than that for interest-rate swaps, currency swaps are subject to a greater **mismatch risk,** the risk that a swap dealer will not be able to exactly offset a swap to avoid taking a position. More significantly, credit risk is normally greater with currency swaps than with interest-rate swaps.

The **credit risk** of a swap is the probability that a counterparty will default. With currency swaps, this risk is smaller than the credit risk of lending, but it can still be substantial. If a loan is never repaid, the lender loses the amount of the loan plus any accrued interest. If a counterparty to a currency swap defaults, the other counterparty does not lose all of the principal since, assuming principals were exchanged at the outset of the swap, it will have received a sum equivalent (usually) to what it gave up. Nevertheless, if a counterparty defaults and the relevant exchange rate has moved in favor of the nondefaulting party in the interim or would do so before the swap's termination, the loss from a default can be large.

Suppose, for example, that Bank T enters into a 7-year yen/dollar swap with Firm X at an exchange rate of ¥150/dollar in which the bank swaps yen for dollars. Under the terms of the swap, the exchange is to be reversed at the end of 7 years at the same exchange rate. Now assume that Firm X defaults after 3 years when the spot exchange rate is ¥136/dollar. Also assume that if the swap had been carried to its contracted termination date, the spot exchange rate would have been ¥120/dollar. Assuming dollar interest rates are generally higher than yen interest rates, the default would mean that Bank T would now be faced with a realized loss in terms of interest payments that would not be compensated by the receipt of yen at a favorable exchange rate. Moreover, the default would cost the bank the opportunity to gain from the upward movement of the yen during the last 4 years of the swap's projected life.

Once the default occurs, Bank T would probably seek to enter into a *replacement swap,* which ideally would replicate the terms of the swap in which Firm X defaulted without imposing an additional cost on Bank T. Bank T would not be able to enter into a replacement swap at ¥150/dollar without paying dearly for the privilege, however, since with the spot rate at ¥136/dollar, a swap at ¥150/dollar would be off-market. Bank T would thus experience a loss of principal as a consequence of the rise in the yen's exchange value.

By its nature, the credit risk of a swap is not hedgeable. Some protection against this risk can be obtained by entering into swaps whose values are likely to change in opposite directions. The credit risk cannot be diversified away, however, because defaults by a dealer's counterparties are far more likely to occur when swaps have positive values for dealers (and negative values for counterparties) than when their values for dealers are negative. Thus, even if a counterparty is nearing bankruptcy, it will probably try to avoid default on a swap that has a positive value to it by selling the swap, entering into a reverse swap, or some other manuever. If a counterparty goes bankrupt, it may still be able to unload a swap with a positive value, and even if it doesn't, the fact that a swap dealer's claim arising from the swap is likely to be subordinate to other claims against the counterparty means that the chances of recovery are probably dim.[9]

Dealing in currency swaps entails running other risks. Of these, the most noteworthy is the **spread risk,** the chance of an adverse movement in the swap spread. This spread, like the swap rate spread of forward exchange rates, can vary independently of changes in exchange rates and interest rates. Thus, if a counterparty defaults, and a dealer enters into a replacement swap, the dealer is hurt if it has to enter into the replacement swap with a less favorable spread than that on the swap that has been prematurely terminated.

Summing up, currency swap dealers face substantial risks. The small size of the spreads for currency swaps (normally 20 bp or less) indicates, however, that these risks are decidedly manageable.

Indication Pricing Schedules   The commercial banks and investment banks that serve as swap dealers prepare *indication pricing schedules* for their personnel to use in making offers to customers. Take, for example, a plain vanilla fixed-for-floating nonamortizing swap between the mark and the dollar in which the mark interest rate is fixed and the dollar interest rate floats with the 6-month LIBOR. The indication pricing schedule used by a dealer might well look like the form in Exhibit 16.3, which matches various possible maturities with their corresponding mark interest rates. The interest rates shown are midrates, i.e., they do not reflect the spread. The spread is assumed to be a constant 20 points and is obtained by adjusting the mark midrate according to whether the dealer bank pays or receives marks. The interest rates shown are annual rates, but the interest payment periods are 6 months. The swaps are assumed to be nonamortizing, which it will be recalled means that exchanges of principal occur only at the beginning and end of the swap. Principal repayments in such lump-sum amounts are known as *bullet transactions*. A normal yield curve is assumed, i.e., the mark interest rate rises as a function of the term of a swap.

A similar indication pricing schedule could be developed for swaps in which the dollar interest rate is fixed and the mark rate floats. Other such schedules could be developed for swaps involving other currencies and for swaps of different types, such as amortizing swaps.

---

[9]Legally, swaps are classified as executive contracts and stand below on-the-books liabilities in the hierarchy of claims against a bankrupt firm. The author was alerted to this point by his former student, Joseph Fung. Joseph K. W. Fung, "The Pricing of Vulnerable Interest-Rate Swap Contracts" (unpublished Ph.D. dissertation, University of Alabama, 1991), pp. 9–10.

| EXHIBIT | 16.3 | *Indication Pricing Schedule for Mark/Dollar Swaps*

Maturity	Midrate
2 years	8.40
3 years	8.54
4 years	8.67
5 years	8.79
6 years	8.90
7 years	8.99
10 years	9.16

Deduct 10 basis points (0.10 percent) if the bank is paying the mark rate, and add 10 basis points if the bank is receiving the mark rate. The midrates are annual mark interest rates with semiannual interest payments. Principal repayments are on a bullet basis.

Source: Based on John F. Marshall and Kenneth R. Kapner, *Understanding Swap Finance* (Cincinnati: South-Western Publishing, 1990), p. 75.

Interest-Rate Swaps And Commodity Swaps

While currency swaps are inherently international in nature, interest-rate swaps can be strictly domestic. Often, particularly when they are arranged in the Eurocurrency market, interest-rate swaps have counterparties from different countries or foreign arranging banks. As we have seen, they are frequently combined with currency swaps. Commodity swaps commonly arise in connection with international trade, particularly in oil.

Interest-Rate Swaps

Recall that the counterparties in interest-rate swaps exchange interest rate payments based on notional principals, not actual principals, and that in pure interest-rate swaps there is no exchange of currencies (notional or actual). If the reciprocal interest payments are timed so that their payment dates coincide, as they commonly are, only the net difference need be paid. Spreads on interest-rate swaps are quite narrow (5 to 10 bp), reflecting the low risks involved and the huge and liquid financial markets in the currencies in which most interest-rate swaps are denominated (dollars, yen, sterling, and marks). The narrow spreads, in turn, provide additional incentive to use interest-rate swaps.

Because there are numerous situations in which interest-rate swaps meet potential users' financial requirements, and because the cost of using them is low, they have become a major financial instrument in a remarkably short time. At the end of 1989, the total outstanding notional principal amount of interest rate swaps was estimated at $1,502.6 billion, 50 percent more than at the end of 1988. During the first half of 1990, the notional principal value of new interest rate swaps was estimated at $561.5 billion. By comparison, the total outstanding notional principal amount of currency swaps at the end of 1989 was estimated at $450 billion, an increase of 40 percent over the previous year, and the volume of new currency swaps arranged during the first half of 1990 was estimated at $94.6 billion.[10] Most interest-rate swaps are in U.S. dollars, and the U.S. dollar is also one of the currencies involved in most currency swaps.

The Uses of Interest-Rate Swaps   Interest-rate swaps have the same basic uses as currency swaps. Like currency swaps, they owe much to comparative advantage. As a general rule, investors in fixed-rate instruments are more sensitive to borrowers' credit ratings and general reputations than are the banks that engage in large-scale lending at floating rates. Accordingly, the interest-rate differentials among borrowers have tended to be greater in fixed-rate lending (bonds) than in bank lending, with the result that interest-rate swaps based on comparative advantage have often been feasible. Similarly, interest-rate swaps also provide cost reductions as by-products of hedging, through tax and regulatory arbitrage, and by providing borrowers with access to markets that were previously closed to them. Also, like currency swaps, they are used for hedging (particularly of liabilities) and for the creation of synthetic assets.

One of the most appealing uses of interest-rate swaps is when a borrower with an outstanding bond issue wishes to alter this liability without having to engage in the costly and time-consuming process of retiring the existing issue and coming out with a new one. Suppose, for example, that a firm with an outstanding floating-rate dollar bond issue with 4 years to maturity would like to switch to a fixed-rate issue. Rather than call or otherwise buy back the outstanding bonds, the firm could enter into a 4-year interest-rate swap, accepting floating-rate interest payments and paying fixed-rate interest. This procedure would allow the firm to hedge the outstanding bond issue and lock in a fixed interest rate which it expects to be lower than future interest rates. Moreover, this could be accomplished at a cost of only 5 to 10 basis points per year.

The use of interest-rate swaps appeals in similar fashion to portfolio managers wishing to protect their assets. Consider, for example, the case of an investment firm holding fixed-rate bonds denominated in a currency, such as the Ecu, for which interest-rate futures are not readily available. Assume that short-term interest rates in the relevant currency are rising, causing concern that longer-term interest rates will soon rise also. The firm could, of course, sell the bonds and convert the proceeds into an asset denominated in another currency, or it could place the proceeds of the sale in short-term assets

---

[10]Bank for International Settlements, *61st Annual Report* (Basle: BIS, 1991), pp. 142–143. Based on data provided by the International Swap Dealers Association (ISDA).

denominated in the same currency. Alternatively, it could retain the bonds, avoiding the cost of liquidating them, and enter into an interest-rate swap in which it would accept floating-rate interest payments and make fixed-rate interest payments.

Interest-rate swaps are also useful in arbitraging differences in interest rates in different markets. Such differences arise, for example, between the Eurodollar market and the market for U.S. Treasury securities, as the following example illustrates. In September 1986, Chemical Bank International entered into an asset swap with a private firm in which it obtained $150 million of a floating-rate note (FRN) issue of the government of the United Kingdom. The FRN was dollar-denominated, and its interest rate was the LIBID (London Interbank Bid rate) minus ⅛ percent.[11] Chemical then located a swap counterparty willing to pay 65 basis points over the current rate on 5-year U.S. Treasury securities in exchange for receiving the floating rate of LIBID minus ⅛ percent. After agreeing to a swap with this counterparty, Chemical located two investors who were willing to purchase the right to receive the 5-year U.S. Treasury rate plus 65 basis points, provided that Chemical collateralized the purchase with its holdings of the U.K. FRN issue. The investors obtained a fixed-interest rate well above the going U.S. Treasury rate without a significant sacrifice of investment quality. The interest flows associated with this arrangement are shown in Exhibit 16.4. It can be presumed that Chemical pocketed some fee income for its services.

In another common use of interest-rate swaps, an investor can combine them with currency swaps to exploit a comparative borrowing advantage in a currency other than the one in which a borrower actually wants to borrow. This procedure is common in connection with bonds denominated in Ecus and pounds sterling and in dollar-denominated bonds issued by Japanese borrowers.

Recall from the material on currency swaps an example in which a Japanese firm issued dollar Eurobonds with a fixed interest rate and then entered into a currency swap with another Japanese firm through which it converted the fixed-rate dollar obligation into a fixed-rate yen obligation. The same basic result could be attained by combining an interest-rate swap with a currency swap, and in fact, this combination is more likely to be used. Typically, a Japanese firm issues fixed-rate dollar Eurobonds intending to enter into a currency swap with a Japanese bank in which the firm would swap fixed-rate yen payments for fixed-rate dollar receipts. Because Japanese banks normally do not wish to hold fixed-rate obligations in a foreign currency, the bank would enter into a dollar interest-rate swap with a foreign bank, probably one with a Tokyo branch, in which the Japanese bank would receive fixed-rate dollars and pay floating-rate dollars. The resulting arrangement is shown in Exhibit 16.5.

---

[11]The LIBID is the deposit rate that London banks offer to pay to other banks. It is slightly lower than the LIBOR.

| E X H I B I T | 16.4 | *Chemical Bank's FRN-Asset Swap: Interest Flows*

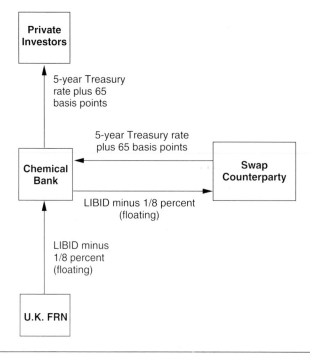

Source: "Financial Innovations Made to Measure," *Euromoney*, January 1987 supplement, p. 26.

| E X H I B I T | 16.5 | *Interest Flows in a Currency Swap Combined with an Interest-Rate Swap*

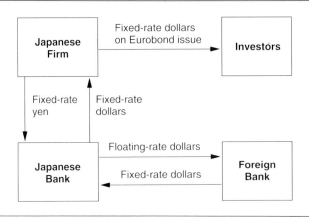

Incidentally, this type of arrangement has contributed greatly to the achievement of low-cost financing for prominent Japanese firms. Such firms have often enjoyed comparative borrowing advantages in the dollar Eurobond market because of the high esteem in which investors hold them. They have capitalized (literally) on this esteem to issue bonds with attractive features, most frequently equity warrants, which have allowed them to further reduce their dollar interest rates. They have then passed on some of their dollar savings to the banks with which they have entered into interest-rate swaps to obtain fixed-rate yen financing at remarkably low cost.

There are numerous other possible illustrations of interest-rate swaps, but considerations of space dictate that they not be presented. By this time, however, it should be abundantly clear that interest-rate swaps are a financial instrument of outstanding importance. It should be remembered, however, that their greatest strength lies in the area of medium-term and long-term financing.

Types of Interest-Rate Swaps[12] The plain vanilla interest-rate swap is the fixed-for-floating swap in which both interest payments are denominated in the same currency and are based on a notional principal. The floating rate is typically (though not always) based on the LIBOR, and the fixed rate is typically based on the comparable rate on government securities. The counterparties typically make simultaneous and offsetting periodic interest payments to each other so that only the net difference is paid.

In a *zero-coupon-for-floating swap,* the floating-rate payer makes periodic interest payments, but the fixed-rate payer makes only a single payment at the swap's termination. The notional principal is obtained by discounting this single payment at the appropriate rate of discount. This type of swap is used by parties who hold zero-coupon assets and desire to avoid cash outlays for interest payments during the lives of those assets.

Floating-for-floating swaps, also known as *basis swaps,* specify floating rates for each side of a swap that are not identical. Different rates may be used, such as the LIBOR and a stated margin over the U.S. Treasury rate. Alternatively, the rates may be referenced to the same basic indicator, but differ as to time periods. For example, one party may make monthly payments referenced to the 1-month LIBOR while the other party makes semiannual payments referenced to the 6-month LIBOR. It is also possible to combine these two variations so that two indicators are used and the frequency of interest payments differs.

Forward swaps (also known as **deferred swaps** to avoid confusion with the forward swaps we examined earlier) and **delayed rate-setting swaps** (also known as **deferred rate-setting swaps**) postpone the beginning of a swap or the

---

[12]The material in this section is based largely on Marshall and Kapner, *Understanding Swap Finance,* pp. 42–45.

determination of the applicable interest rates. In a forward or deferred swap, the interest rates are set at the outset, but the start of the swap is delayed. Such a swap accommodates the need of one of the parties to use an interest-rate swap in the near future, but not immediately. This arrangement provides protection against an unfavorable interest-rate movement in the interim. In a delayed rate-setting swap, the interest rates applying to a swap are determined after its starting date in accordance with an agreed-upon formula. Needless to say, a party that concedes the right of deferral to another party expects to be compensated.

In *rate-capped swaps,* ceilings are set on the floating rate or rates in interest-rate swaps. The party receiving the cap pays a fee to its counterparty. Closely related to this type of swap is the **mini–max swap,** which states both a ceiling and a floor on the floating rate or rates used.

As with currency swaps, there are amortizing interest-rate swaps, in which the notional principal gradually declines according to a pre-set schedule. In **roller-coaster swaps,** the notional principal increases to some maximum figure and then amortizes to zero over a swap's remaining life. Roller-coaster swaps are commonly used by mortgage firms to hedge portfolios of fixed-rate, graduated-payment mortgages that are financed with floating-rate liabilities.

Increasingly important are *asset-based swaps,* which are used to create synthetic securities. Interest-rate swaps of this type are similar to the asset-based currency swaps that were examined earlier. Such swaps may duplicate existing assets or create assets that previously did not exist.

Finally, a **terminable swap** gives the fixed-rate payer the option to cancel a swap agreement before its maturity date. Since these swaps have an option feature, they are examined later in the chapter in the section dealing with swaptions, as options on swaps are now commonly called.

Other types of interest-rate swaps have been devised in the past and will, no doubt, be devised in the future. As long as financial needs exist that can best be met by varying from the norm, and as long as swap dealers can obtain adequate compensation for meeting those needs, financial architects will continue to apply their fertile imaginations to financial swaps.

Pricing Interest-Rate Swaps   Since interest-rate swaps do not, in themselves, involve exchanges of currencies or principals, they are less risky than currency swaps and more easily priced. The pricing process involves setting the relevant interest rates and interest payment schedules and adding any fees that swap dealers require for their services. The interest rates are set to provide a spread, which, as has been noted previously, commonly runs from 5 to 10 basis points. Any fees are usually collected upfront and are received only when a dealer's services are more extensive than normal. Most interest-rate swaps are standardized and do not generate fee income.

As in the case of currency swaps, dealers in interest-rate swaps provide their capital markets personnel with indication pricing schedules to guide negotiations with potential customers. Since there are numerous possible variations in interest-rate swaps, there are numerous possible indication pricing schedules. Exhibit 16.6 gives an example of such a schedule involving

| EXHIBIT | 16.6 | *Indication Pricing Schedule for Interest-Rate Swaps*

Maturity	Bank Pays Fixed Rate	Bank Receives Fixed Rate	Current TN Rate
2 years	2-years TN + 22 bps	2-years TN + 32 bps	8.10%
3 years	3-years TN + 26 bps	3-years TN + 35 bps	8.30
4 years	4-years TN + 32 bps	4-years TN + 40 bps	8.49
5 years	5-years TN + 38 bps	5-years TN + 46 bps	8.61
6 years	6-years TN + 42 bps	6-years TN + 51 bps	8.71
7 years	7-years TN + 45 bps	7-years TN + 55 bps	8.78
10 years	10-years TN + 52 bps	10-years TN + 62 bps	8.86

The schedule assumes semiannual compounding at the above rates and bullet transactions. The differences in basis points (bp) between the rates the bank pays and the rates it receives are the dealer spreads. TN means the Treasury security rate based on a 365-day year, compounded semiannually.

Source: Based on John F. Marshall and Kenneth R. Kapner, *Understanding Swap Finance* (Cincinnati: South-Western Publishing, 1990), p. 61.

the relatively simple case of plain vanilla fixed-for-floating swaps. The floating rate is assumed to be the 6-month LIBOR. The interest rates shown are fixed rates based on the current yields on U.S. Treasury securities stated as semiannual bond-equivalent yields, i.e., bond yields on which interest is compounded semiannually for a 365-day year. The swap spreads are the differences in basis points between the rates that the dealer bank pays and the rates it receives. This spread amounts to 10 basis points or less. Variations in the spread reflect market conditions and the dealer's existing positions. The yield rate on Treasury securities (the TN rate) increases as a function of time, indicating a normal yield curve, and the premium over the TN rate also increases as a function of time to reflect risk.

Now suppose that a client requests from the bank a 4-year plain vanilla swap in which the client would pay the 6-month LIBOR (a floating rate) and the bank would pay the fixed rate. Assuming that the client's creditworthiness is not in question and that the appropriate interest rate shown in Exhibit 16.6 is applied to the swap, the bank would wind up with an obligation to pay a fixed rate of 8.81 percent on a semiannual bond-equivalent basis.[13]

---

[13]Because the LIBOR is based on a 360-day year, it is necessary to use a simple conversion formula in order to make an exact comparison with a yield stated on a bond-equivalent basis with a 365-day financial year. The formula involves multiplying the bond-equivalent yield by 360/365 to obtain a yield based on 360 days. Alternatively, the LIBOR can be converted into a bond-equivalent yield by multiplying it by 365/360. It is necessary to remember, however, that the 6-month LIBOR should be compared with a bond-equivalent yield on which the interest is compounded semiannually.

Although interest-rate swaps involve less risk than currency swaps, interest-rate swaps do have risks.[14] In general, there is greater risk on the fixed-rate side of an interest-rate swap than on the floating-rate side. Dealer banks commonly hedge the interest-rate risk and take the same basic steps to protect against the credit risk that they take with currency swaps.

Commodity Swaps

Since 1987, commodity swaps have emerged as the newest major category of financial swaps. While it is doubtful that they will ever attain the importance of either interest-rate swaps or currency swaps, they appear to have found a permanent niche among the tools of financial management. They help firms cope with the problem of fluctuating prices of primary products, particularly oil; and although commodity producers and users have other avenues available for hedging commodity prices, they are a useful addition. Commodity futures can be used for short-term hedging, and commodity-linked bonds can be used for longer-term hedging. With the latter, a commodity producer issues bonds with call options (or possibly warrants), thereby obtaining a lower interest rate. If the commodity price remains below the option strike price, the interest rate does not change. If the commodity price rises and the options are exercised, the producer pays a higher interest rate that is linked to the commodity price. The producer can do this without difficulty since the higher commodity price means an increase in its revenues. By buying such bonds, a commodity user gains medium- or long-term protection against a price increase.

While commodity-linked bonds have features that appeal to the potential clientele for commodity swaps, they also have limitations. Specifically, they are not issued unless producers need to raise funds and find them to be an attractive way to do so, their purchase is not confined to commodity users, and a *commodity* hedge that operates through an interest rate is unlikely to fully satisfy either producers or users.

Commodity swaps may be a far more satisfactory way to hedge commodity prices on a medium- or long-term basis than commodity-linked bonds. Such swaps work much like plain vanilla interest-rate swaps and are usually for 5 years or less. Just as interest-rate swaps normally do not involve any exchange of principals, commodity swaps normally do not result in the delivery of a commodity. Suppose, for example, that an oil producer wants to lock in the price of oil. It can enter into a swap with an arranging bank that

---

[14]This point was driven home in 1990 and 1991 by the failure of Drexel-Burnham Lambert, a giant U.S. investment banking firm, by other bank failures in the United States and the United Kingdom, and by the downgrading of the credit ratings of a number of banking institutions. In addition, in January 1991, the House of Lords, Britain's highest court of appeal, ruled that local authorities in the United Kingdom were not empowered to enter into financial swaps and that any such contracts entered into by them were null and void. This decision had the effect of causing losses for swap dealers who had entered into interest-rate swaps with local governments in the United Kingdom.

guarantees it a fixed price per barrel for a specified number of barrels. In return, it agrees to make floating-rate payments to the arranger if an indexed price of oil moves above the fixed price. The indexed price is then multiplied by the number of barrels to determine the amount due. If the price of oil remains unchanged, no money changes hands; if it moves downward, the arranger makes a payment to the producer. In effect, therefore, the producer is a floating-rate payer and the bank is a fixed-rate payer. The producer receives protection against a price decrease, but gives up any possible gain from a price increase. It is possible to structure a swap so that the producer can obtain some gain if the price goes up.

The swap arranger in this case faces the problem of protecting itself against a price decrease. Ideally, it would probably want to locate one or more potential swap counterparties interested in gaining protection against a price increase. Needless to say, there are many such potential counterparties. An airline, for example, might be very interested in a swap that would guarantee it a fixed price for oil in return for making a floating payment commitment that would cost it money only if the price of oil should decrease.

There are obvious advantages in commodity swaps, and it is hardly surprising that they have suddenly emerged (1987 being their first big year) as an important new financial instrument. They received a very big boost from the Iraqi invasion of Kuwait in August 1990. Before that event, the total notional amount of commodity swaps was estimated at between $7 and $10 billion, but following the invasion of Kuwait, their amount is estimated to have soared to the range of $40 to $50 billion.[15] U.S. regulatory authorities have cleared the way for the use of commodity swaps in the United States. Nevertheless, the obstacles to their use are considerably greater than the obstacles to the use of interest-rate swaps. One problem is that commodities may not be of uniform quality. Another is the lack of liquidity in the market for commodity swaps. In still another problem, if an arranger fails to exactly offset its commodity swaps with matched swaps, it is likely to be more difficult to satisfactorily hedge the resulting position than would be the case with a position taken in either a currency swap or an interest-rate swap. One more problem is that commodity producers may have bullish outlooks that make them reluctant to foreclose the possibility of gaining from increases in the price of their commodity.

Notwithstanding these problems, commodity swaps have a promising future. Already, commodity swaps have been arranged in gold, copper, aluminum, and nickel, and other commodities could conceivably be added to the list. Given the history of price instability in the markets for primary products and the evident inability of producers to control prices, both producers and users have ample incentives to hedge with commodity swaps. These incentives give rise to a profit potential in commodity swaps that should provide financial institutions with the incentive to clear away the obstacles to their expanded use. Moreover, because a number of heavily indebted LDCs are

---

[15]Bank for International Settlements, *61st Annual Report* (Basle: BIS, 1991), p. 145.

major exporters of commodities whose prices are notoriously unstable, it stands to reason that commodity swaps can alleviate their debt service problems. Such swaps could provide these countries with protection against price declines, improving their ability to service their debts during periods of price weakness, and the swaps could be structured to allow them to derive some benefit from upward price swings.

Two Final Topics

In wrapping up this survey of financial swaps, there are two final matters that, in the writer's judgment, merit some consideration. One is the emergence of *swaptions*, as options on financial swaps are commonly called. The other is the treatment of financial swaps under the new international capital standards that have been set for banks in the industrial countries.

Swaptions

The standard swaption is an option to enter into a plain vanilla interest-rate swap. In a **call swaption**, the buyer obtains the right to *receive* fixed-interest payments, and in a **put swaption**, the buyer obtains the right to *make* fixed-interest payments. Call swaptions are attractive when interest rates are expected to fall, and put swaptions are attractive when interest rates are expected to rise. For example, if a firm buys a call swaption before an interest-rate decline of sufficient magnitude, it exercises the swaption and gains by receiving a locked-in, fixed interest rate while paying a now lower floating rate. As with other options, the buyers of swaptions pay upfront premiums to the writers. A premium is normally equivalent to from 20 to 40 basis points per annum.

The banks and investment firms in the business of arranging swaptions generally act as dealers rather than as brokers, i.e., they stand ready to enter into swaptions on either the buying or selling side. In buying swaptions, as they often do, they accommodate customers who write them in order to use the premium income to lower their borrowing cost or increase the effective interest rate they receive on assets.

Swaptions versus Caps, Floors, and Collars   Using swaptions is an alternative to using interest-rate caps, floors, and collars, all of which are traded by the same bank personnel who trade swaptions. An *interest-rate cap* sets a maximum rate on floating-rate interest payments, while an *interest-rate floor* sets a minimum rate. An *interest-rate collar* combines a cap with a floor. A buyer of one of these instruments pays a one-time, up-front premium to the seller that is a percentage of the *notional principal,* i.e., there is no actual flow of principal. The premium amount depends on such factors as the length of life of the instrument and the probability that the buyer will be able to take advantage of it. The lives of these instruments commonly range from 1 to 10 years.

The buyer of a cap receives a cash payment from the seller when the floating reference rate for the cap is higher than the cap's strike rate on a given date when the two rates are matched against each other. Suppose that a firm buys a 5-year cap whose strike rate is a 6-month LIBOR of 10.5 percent. If the 6-month LIBOR is at 11 percent on a date when the two rates are to be compared, say 6 months from the start of the cap's term, the seller becomes obligated to pay the buyer an amount equal to 0.5 percent times the notional principal of the cap for a 6-month period. Similarly, if a firm buys an interest-rate floor and the reference rate falls below the strike rate of the floor, the seller makes a cash payment to the buyer. Frequently, a firm that wants to buy a cap will enter into a collar in which it simultaneously buys a cap and sells a floor. The premium from the floor helps to offset the cost of the cap. Also, of course, a firm could enter into a collar in which it simultaneously buys a floor and sells a cap. This might be done, for example, by an investment firm that wishes to assure itself that the interest rate it receives on floating-rate assets will not fall below a certain level.

It is commonly stated that buying swaptions is cheaper than buying caps and floors, but whether or not this is true depends on such factors as the strike rate in the cap or floor, the interest rates specified in a swaption, and the time periods of the alternatives being compared. For example, buying a cap with a 5-year exercise period may be considerably more expensive than buying a swaption which gives, for 1 year, the right to enter into a 4-year swap. Whereas the cap would provide protection for 5 years, the protection provided by the swaption would be lost after 1 year if it were not exercised. In other words, the apparent cheapness of swaptions relative to caps and floors may be deceptive. Moreover, when a bank enters into a swaption, it has to consider the credit risk problem, which is something it does not have to worry about in setting the premium for a cap or a floor. Since a credit risk problem exists with swaptions that does not affect caps and floors, one would expect this difference to be reflected in their relative costs.

There are still other complications involved in comparing swaptions with caps and floors. For example, it is possible to buy or write *captions,* which are options on the purchase of caps. A caption is cheaper than a cap if it is not exercised, but more expensive if it is exercised. Complicating matters further, it is possible to buy options on captions! In conclusion, it is probably wise to avoid stating flatly that swaptions are cheaper than caps and floors, and one should keep in mind that both types of instruments are traded by the same people. In particular circumstances, one type may be superior to the other, but in different circumstances, the balance may tip in the other direction.

The Uses of Swaptions   Two uses of swaptions stand out: to hedge interest rates and to realize the embedded value of a call provision on a bond issue. In addition, the term *swaption* is sometimes applied to options to cancel swaps, i.e., to terminable swaps.[16] The first of these uses is the most easily explained. Suppose, for example, that the interest yield curve in a particular currency is

---

[16]See "When the Swap Meets the Option," *Euromoney* supplement, April 1989, pp. 32, 37, and 43.

unusually steep and that some firms have reacted to this situation by borrowing short-term at floating rates rather than borrowing long-term at fixed rates. Assume, however, that there is a high probability that both short-term and long-term interest rates will rise. A firm might well consider entering into a plain vanilla interest-rate swap as the fixed-rate payer. Alternatively, it could buy a cap. As a third alternative, it could buy a swaption, i.e., an option on a swap in which it would be the fixed-rate payer. The swaption would preserve the possibility of gaining should interest rates decline instead of going up, but it would cost more than entering into a swap immediately if it should subsequently be exercised. The choice between a swaption and a cap would hinge on their relative costs and the firm's interest-rate expectations.

The second use of swaptions, to monetize the value of a call provision in a bond issue, is illustrated by the following example, which was furnished to *Euromoney* by Citibank of New York.[17] Assume that Company XYZ has just issued DM100 million of fixed-rate bonds with 10 years to maturity and an interest rate of 6.70 percent. XYZ has the right to call the bonds after 5 years and will exercise the right if the relevant interest rate in 5 years is below 6.70 percent. If it calls the bonds, it plans to replenish its funds by borrowing for 5 years at the 6-month LIBOR. XYZ can monetize the call feature by writing a 5-year call swaption that gives the buyer the right to enter into a 5-year interest-rate swap that would go into effect on the date, 5 years later, when XYZ could call the bonds. To simplify matters, assume that the fixed rate that XYZ would pay in the event that the swaption should be exercised would be 6.70 percent and that it would receive the 6-month LIBOR in return. If, therefore, the bonds were called and the swaption were exercised, XYZ would, in effect, still be paying 6.70 percent for 5 years, but its borrowing cost would be reduced by the swaption premium. Should interest rates in 5 years be high enough to prevent the exercise of the call swaption, its borrowing cost of 6.70 percent would still be effectively lowered by the amount of the swaption premium.

Assume that XYZ writes the swaption and that Citibank buys it, paying an upfront premium of DM1 million. The possible outcomes are shown in Exhibit 16.7. Notice that the upfront premium of DM1 million is equivalent to a reduction of 33 basis points per annum in XYZ's borrowing cost for each of the last 5 years, whether or not the swaption is exercised. (An interest rate of 6.70 percent has been used for this calculation.) Although it appears that XYZ loses from this arrangement only if it could borrow at a rate below 6.37 percent in 5 years, it should be taken into account that if XYZ had originally issued bonds without the call feature, it could probably have borrowed at a lower rate than 6.70 percent.

While the term *swaption* generally refers to options that confer the right to enter into swaps, it sometimes refers to options that confer the right to

---

[17]See Ron Cooper, "They're Teaching the Old Swap New Tricks," *Euromoney*, April 1989, p. 49.

| EXHIBIT | 16.7 | *Possible Outcomes with the XYZ–Citibank Swaption*

A. Interest rate below 6.7 percent on call date; swaption exercised

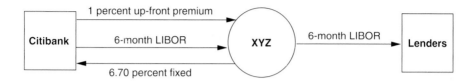

Net cost to XYZ:

−6.70% Fixed swap rate
+0.33% Up-front premium converted to per annum basis for previous 5 years
+LIBOR Floating swap rate
−LIBOR Floating rate paid to lenders who substitute for bondholders
−6.37%

B. Interest rate above 6.7 percent on call date; swaption not exercised

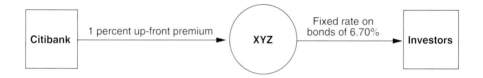

Net cost to XYZ:

−6.70% Fixed rate on bonds
+0.33% Up-front premium converted to per annum basis for previous 5 years
−6.37%

Source: "They're Teaching the Old Swap New Tricks," *Euromoney*, April 1989, p. 49.

terminate swaps. In a *callable swap* (or swaption), the fixed-rate payer in a fixed-for-floating interest-rate swap has the option of terminating the swap before its maturity date. The fixed-rate payer customarily pays a somewhat higher interest rate than it would otherwise pay and may be required to pay a termination fee if the call privilege is exercised. A *putable swap* (or swaption) gives the floating-rate payer the right to terminate before maturity, and the floating-rate payer customarily pays for this right by accepting a lower fixed rate than it would otherwise receive and may be required to pay a termination fee if the option is exercised. Related to callable and putable swaps, **extendable swaps** give one of the parties the right to lengthen the life of a swap beyond its scheduled maturity. In reality, such a swap can be viewed as either a callable swap or a putable swap, depending on who receives the extension privilege.

Terminable swaps (or swaptions) are commonly used in connection with deferred swaps, i.e., swaps with set interest rates, but whose start is delayed until a specified date. Suppose, for example, that Purehex Corporation has arranged a deferred swap in which it is the fixed-rate payer. Because it feels that there is a good chance that interest rates will fall before the swap is activated, it has arranged to have a call feature that allows it to cancel the swap if interest rates decline before the date on which the swap is to be activated. To get this feature, it agrees to pay a higher interest rate if the swap is activated than it would otherwise have paid. If interest rates fall sufficiently, Purehex exercises its call and cancels the swap, paying a termination fee to the arranger. Note that if the swap goes into effect and the call premium is paid in the form of a higher interest rate rather than in the form of an explicit premium payment, this may have advantages for tax and accounting purposes. In truth, securing such advantages is a major reason for the use of terminable swaps.

Swaps and the New International Capital Standards

A major factor drawing banks into swap financing has been the off-balance-sheet aspect of swap transactions. As governments have increased banks' base capital requirements in the aftermath of the sovereign debt problem, the fact that these requirements have traditionally been expressed as percentages of banks' on-the-books assets has given banks a strong incentive to generate earnings (and increase capital) without increasing their book assets. Financial swaps have benefitted strongly from this incentive.

As we have seen, however, banks' off-balance-sheet operations involve accepting additional risk. For this reason, soon after the sovereign debt bubble burst, a consensus developed among regulators that these operations should be taken into account in the revision of banks' capital requirements that was widely regarded as essential in light of the debt debacle. Some regulators, reflecting an almost total lack of understanding of the nature of the risks associated with off-the-books operations, suggested that in setting capital requirements for such items as option and swap contracts, banks' claims should be valued at 100 percent of face value or notional value and be subjected to the same capital requirements as loans of the same amounts. Such suggestions induced the money-center banks of different countries to launch large-scale education campaigns, with considerable success.

In December 1987, central bankers from the G-10 countries agreed to the **Basle Accord**, which was formalized in 1988. Under its provisions, which are being implemented by national central banks, uniform bank capital require-ments for internationally operating banks are to be established in the leading industrial nations. By the end of 1992, these banks are to have minimum 8 percent ratios of recognized capital to aggregate risk-weighted credit expo-sures, which will include off-the-books assets. At least half of the recognized capital must be "core" (Tier 1) capital, which includes disclosed reserves, common stock, and noncumulative preferred stock. The rest (Tier 2 capital) consists of such items as undisclosed reserves, asset revaluation reserves, hybrid capital instruments, and subordinated debt.[18]

As far as financial swaps are concerned, the new capital requirement guidelines work as follows. The first major step is to determine the credit-risk equivalent of individual swaps. This involves ascertaining a swap's principal amount and what it would cost to replace it in case of default, plus an add-on factor to take future volatility into account. Typically, the credit-risk equivalent for an interest-rate swap is less than 1 percent of the swap's notional principal; it is even possible that the credit-risk equivalent calculation can reduce a bank's capital requirements if the bank would gain from default. For currency swaps, the credit-risk equivalent is likely to amount to at least several percentage points of a swap's principal amount.

The next major step is *risk weighting,* which involves adjusting the credit-risk equivalent according to the risk rating of a swap counterparty. In most cases, risk weighting results in a reduction of 50 percent or more in the amount of the credit-risk equivalent. The third major step is to multiply the risk-weighted value by the *capital ratio* set by the Basle Accord, which is to be 8 percent by 1993.

Most capital requirements imposed on financial swaps under the new guidelines are small. Even for currency swaps, the capital requirements are likely to remain much smaller than those for loans of the same principal amounts. Moreover, it is likely that the final Basle Accord guidelines will allow extensive scope for **netting,** which allows banks to assess their capital requirements for swaps with particular customers on the basis of all their swaps with these customers. At present, however, the use of netting is contingent upon the existence of mutual cancellation agreements in swap contracts that end each counterparty's obligation if the other counterparty defaults.

It appears that the new capital guidelines reduce, but do not significantly impair, banks' incentive to serve as swap arrangers. In fact, it is arguable that the guidelines encourage the use of swaps since they have removed uncertainty. It should be kept in mind, however, that capital guidelines are not the only serious problem that has arisen in connection with the use of swaps. There are still legal issues pertaining to them that remain unresolved to the satisfaction of swap arrangers. Moreover, at the beginning of 1992, the U.S. Treasury Department announced that it would like to require brokerage firms to value their end-of-year holdings of securities, including swaps, at market prices. The adoption of this measure would increase the taxation of swaps since it would require swap dealers to include unrealized gains from them in their taxable income. At present, following the principle of valuing assets at cost or market value, whichever is lower, swap dealers can deduct unrealized losses on swaps without having to report unrealized gains.

---

[18]Bank for International Settlements, *61st Annual Report* (Basle: BIS, 1991), p. 115.

Summary

Financial swaps evolved from experience with parallel and back-to-back loans, which allowed firms to work around exchange controls and capitalize on comparative borrowing advantages. These techniques had inherent problems that prevented banks from promoting their widespread use, but the problems were largely overcome with currency swaps, which first appeared in the early 1980s. The appearance of currency swaps was immediately followed by that of interest-rate swaps, which soon surpassed currency swaps in volume. Commodity swaps have recently emerged as a third type of financial swap, but one that is much less important than its predecessors. These three types of swaps are primarily medium-term instruments. Commodity swaps have recently emerged as a third type of financial swap, but one of much less importance.

Currency swaps are used to lower borrowing costs, to hedge risk, and to create synthetic assets. Competition has whittled away at the gains derived from swaps based on comparative borrowing advantages, but such gains continue to occur. Currency swaps also provide cost savings because of other factors, such as tax reductions and avoiding government regulations. In hedging, currency swaps have a strong advantage over forwards in avoiding exchange risks of 2 or more years' duration. Their remarkable flexibility should guarantee the expansion of their use.

Most currency swaps involve actual exchanges of principals and exchanges of fixed-rate interest payments for floating-rate interest payments in a different currency. There are, however, numerous types of currency swaps. It is now standard practice for commercial banks and investment banks to act as swap dealers and to make markets. Swap dealers face various risks. Notable among them is the credit risk, which is much smaller than the credit risk on loans, but which can constitute a serious problem.

Most interest-rate swaps involve exchanges of notional principals. They have the same basic uses, except for hedging the exchange risk, as currency swaps and are often combined with currency swaps. The dealer spreads on interest-rate swaps are considerably smaller than those on currency swaps. Plain vanilla interest-rate swaps are very popular, providing for exchanges of fixed-for-floating interest payments based on equal notional principal amounts, but there are even more varieties of interest-rate swaps than of currency swaps. An important recent development is the emergence of swap options, or swaptions, which are typically options on plain vanilla interest-rate swaps.

The primary appeal of commodity swaps is their capacity to hedge medium- and long-term price fluctuations in oil and other primary products. Greater obstacles exist to their use than for currency or interest-rate swaps, but there is great potential for their growth, nevertheless.

As bank regulators have moved to increase and standardize banks' capital requirements, financial swaps have come under close regulatory scrutiny. To date, it appears that, while the risk-weighted capital requirements that have been applied to banks' financial swaps may have had some restraining effect on the growth of swap financing, that growth is almost certain to continue.

References

Antl, Boris, ed. *Swap Finance,* Vol. 1. London: Euromoney Publications, 1986.

———. *Swap Finance,* Vol. 2. London: Euromoney Publications, 1986.

Bank for International Settlements. *Sixty-First Annual Report* (Basle: BIS, 1991).

Brady, Simon. "Dressing Up, without a Killing." *Euromoney,* April 1989, pp. 77–80.

———. "How to Tailor Your Assets." *Euromoney,* April 1989, pp. 83–89.

Cooper, Ian, and Antonio S. Mello. "The Default Risk of Swaps." *Journal of Finance,* June 1991, pp. 597–620.

Cooper, Ron (with Beth McGoldrick). "They're Teaching the Old Swap New Tricks." *Euromoney,* April 1989, pp. 43–49, 52–55.

Fung, Joseph K. W. "The Pricing of Vulnerable Interest-Rate Swap Contracts." Unpublished Ph.D. dissertation: University of Alabama, 1991.

"The Global Swaps Market." Supplement to *Euromoney,* June 1986.

Henderson, Schuyler K. "A Legal Eye on Hedging's Newest Club." *Euromoney,* May 1990, pp. 95–96.

Hull, John C. "Assessing Credit Risk in a Financial Institution's Off-Balance Sheet Commitments." *Journal of Financial and Quantitative Analysis,* December 1989, pp. 489–502.

———. *Introduction to Futures and Options.* Englewood Cliffs, N.J.: Prentice-Hall, 1991, Chapter 6.

"Innovation in the International Capital Markets." Supplement to *Euromoney,* January 1986.

Lewis, Julian. "The Bandwagon Starts to Roll." *Euromoney,* May 1990, pp. 87–94.

Marshall, John F., and Kenneth R. Kapner. *Understanding Swap Finance.* Cincinnati: South-Western Publishing, 1990.

Price, John A. M. "The Technical Evolution of the Currency Swap Product." In Boris Antl, ed. *Swap Finance,* Vol. 1. London: Euromoney Publications, 1986, pp. 53–59.

Smith, Clifford W., Jr., Charles W. Smithson, and Lee M. Workman. "The Evolving Market for Swaps." *Midland Corporate Finance Journal,* Winter 1986, pp. 20–32.

Solnik, Bruno. *International Investments,* 2d ed. Reading, Mass.: Addison-Wesley, 1991, Chapters 6, 7.

Turnbull, Stuart M. "Swaps: A Zero Sum Game?" *Financial Management,* Spring 1987, pp. 15–21.

"When the Swap Meets the Option." Supplement to *Euromoney,* April 1989, pp. 26–46.

Wilford, D. Sykes. "Strategic Risk Exposure Management." Working paper no. 3 in *Working Papers in Risk Management.* New York: Chase Manhattan Bank, February 1987.

Questions

1. Why are parallel loan arrangements especially likely to occur these days when at least one of the countries involved is an exchange control country?
2. Why have currency swaps generally replaced parallel and back-to-back loans in transactions involving freely traded currencies?
3. A plain vanilla currency swap involves an exchange of fixed-rate interest payments in one currency for floating-rate interest payments in another currency. How do such swaps differ from forward contracts?
4. Assume that a party has outstanding a 4-year floating-rate borrowing arrangement in which it pays interest in a foreign currency based on the

6-month LIBOR. Under what circumstances should this party consider entering into a plain vanilla currency swap as the fixed-rate payer?

5. The savings achieved with currency swaps in terms of basis point reductions in borrowing costs have declined greatly since currency swaps were introduced in the early 1980s, but the volume of currency swaps outstanding continues to grow. How do you explain that fact?

6. Explain how Australian borrowers were able to use currency swaps to borrow in Australian dollars at fixed interest rates for medium- and long-term periods.

7. Explain how an investment firm, for example a firm managing pension funds for college teachers, might use a currency swap to create a synthetic fixed-rate Swiss franc bond issue with 6 years to maturity. What might be the advantages of doing this instead of simply buying Swiss franc bonds? What are the possible disadvantages?

8. Explain an off-market currency swap. What circumstances are likely to lead to the use of such an arrangement?

9. In discussions of the risks to which currency swaps are subject, references are sometimes made to the *market risk,* which is the risk that such variables as interest rates, the exchange rate, and the swap spread will move adversely and cause a swap to have a negative value. How is this risk related to the credit risk of a currency swap, and what is the relevance of the market risk to a strategy of trying to minimize losses from the credit risk?

10. How does the credit risk of a plain vanilla currency swap compare with the credit risk of a loan of the same principal amount, assuming the parties involved have the same creditworthiness in either case?

11. What is a plain vanilla interest-rate swap? Why is the bid–ask spread on such a swap likely to be much smaller than the spread on a plain vanilla currency swap? How is the spread commonly incorporated into the pricing structure of an interest-rate swap?

12. It is commonly stated that plain vanilla interest-rate swaps are frequently based on market imperfections that lead to different ratings of borrowers in different credit markets. Explain the nature of these alleged market imperfections and why their existence can lead to the use of interest-rate swaps.

13. Japanese firms have often been able to lower their cost of fixed-rate yen financing by issuing *dollar-denominated* Eurobonds and using interest-rate and currency swaps. Explain how this procedure works.

14. What is a deferred interest-rate swap?

15. Explain how a standard commodity swap involving oil is likely to work.

16. What are call swaptions and put swaptions? Also, compare a call swaption with an interest-rate cap.

17. What is an interest-rate collar, and how is it likely to be used?

18. Explain how a swaption can be used to realize the embedded value of a call provision in a bond issue. Under what circumstances would writing a call swaption turn out to be advantageous for a writer who has an outstanding issue of callable bonds?

19. Under what circumstances might a firm buy a putable swap or swaption giving it the right to terminate a deferred swap before or after the swap goes into effect? How is the swap premium likely to be paid?

Problems

1. Puromex, the Mexican subsidiary of Purehex, a U.S. firm, wants to borrow Mexican pesos for 2 years, while Casa de Caracoles, a Mexican firm that manufactures food products, has a U.S. subsidiary, Nutrimex, that wants to borrow dollars for 2 years. Puromex can borrow pesos at 20 percent, provided that Purehex guarantees the loan, while Casa de Caracoles can borrow pesos at 21 percent. Nutrimex can borrow dollars at 12.5 percent, while Purehex can borrow dollars at 10 percent. Show how a parallel loan arrangement could be used to lower the borrowing cost for each side to allow the parties to share equally in the cost saving. In addition, and considering the matter from the perspective of the parent companies, explain how the parallel loan arrangement changes the forex exposure of the parents by comparison with the alternative of a parent-to-subsidiary loan.

2. Assume that Mighty Bank has entered into a 5-year currency swap with Firm T in which Mighty Bank pays 9.5 percent interest in dollars semiannually and receives floating-rate interest in pounds sterling at the 6-month LIBOR plus 1 percent. In this swap, Mighty Bank received $4 million in exchange for an equivalent amount of pounds at the exchange rate of $1.8475/pound. Now assume that Mighty Bank can offset the swap by entering into a 4-year, $4 million swap with Firm Z in which Mighty Bank would receive 9.0 interest in dollars semiannually and pay the 6-month pound sterling LIBOR. The exchange rate for this second swap is assumed to be $1.8350/pound. Assuming that Mighty Bank enters into the swap with Z, how would you go about estimating the dollar amount of its gain? How could you protect the dollar value of the difference between the sterling LIBOR rate it receives and the rate it pays?

Glossary

■

Absolute purchasing power parity (Absolute PPP) The concept of PPP that finds the exchange rate between two currencies by dividing the local currency price of a good in one country by its local currency price in another country. Alternatively, the absolute PPP exchange rate is the ratio between the local currency prices of a given market basket of goods and services.

Absorption A nation's total expenditure on goods and services including imports. Absorption differs from GNP in that GNP includes a nation's exports and excludes imports, absorption does the reverse.

Accommodating transactions Balance of payment (BOP) transactions that finance autonomous transactions recorded in the BOP. Because it is difficult to determine precisely the boundary between accommodating and autonomous transactions, there are various measures of both.

Accounting exposure *See* Translation exposure

Adjustable peg An exchange rate system, for which the Bretton Woods System provides a notable example, in which official exchange rates are subject to periodic changes. The European Monetary System (EMS) provides another notable example of such a system.

Advising bank A bank which, while not confirming a L/C issued by another bank which has been sent to it, agrees to honor a draft drawn on the issuing bank. The advising bank reserves the right to refuse to pay the drawer if it has not received prior compensation from the issuing bank.

Agent bank A bank that collects payments due from borrowers and distributes them to lenders or investors in connection with, for example, a syndicated Eurocurrency market loan or a Eurobond issue. In some cases, the agency function is divided among the participating institutions in the management syndicate.

American Depository Receipts (ADRs) Certificates of ownership issued by U.S. banks to investors in foreign stocks in lieu of providing them with shares to which the ADRs confer title. The shares are held in trust for the investors, and the ADRs are negotiable at U.S. stock exchanges.

American-style option An option that can be exercised at any time before its expiration date. Exchange-traded currency options are generally American style.

American terms The pricing of currencies against the U.S. dollar so that the resulting exchange rates are in dollars per unit of foreign currency; for example, $0.7083/SF American terms are commonly used in pricing the pound sterling and Irish punt and for currency options and futures.

Amortizing swap A currency swap in which the principal amounts exchanged at the outset of the swap are reexchanged in stages.

Announcement date The date on which the lead manager of a new issue of securities reveals the final terms of the issue and the managing syndicate's commitment to support it.

Appreciation An increase in a currency's value in the forex market.

Arbitrage In broad terms arbitrage includes any situation in which a party (the arbitrageur or arbitrager) realizes a gain by taking advantage of discrepancies in market prices. Interest arbitrage and currency arbitrage are two prominent types encountered in international finance. Traditionally, arbitrage has been viewed as involving little, if any, risk; however, there is a tendency to apply the term to cases in which considerable risk is involved.

Article VIII One of the Articles of Agreement of the IMF, this article requires countries that have accepted it to avoid the use of exchange controls on current account transactions. Countries that have accepted Article VIII are generally classified as developed countries.

Article XIV One of the Articles of Agreement of the IMF, this article allows countries with existing exchange controls on current account transactions to retain them.

Asset management theory of exchange rate determination *See* Portfolio balance theory

Asia currency market Centered in Singapore but including Hong Kong, the Japan Offshore Market, and other locations, this market consists of banking operations that are fully integrated into the Eurocurrency market.

Autonomous transactions BOP transactions considered to occur for reasons independent of other BOP transactions. *See also* Accommodating transactions

Aval A type of guarantee used in forfaiting simpler than a formal guarantee. In an aval, the guarantor bank, known as the *avalist,* endorses each draft or note it discounts with the words *per aval* and an appropriate signature. The avalist also writes *on behalf of* by the name of the drawer of any draft submitted to it for discount.

Back-to-back loan An arrangement in which one party lends in a particular currency to another party, receiving in return a reciprocal loan in another currency. Typically such loans are based on comparative borrowing advantages and/or the desire to avoid forex transactions that are subject to exchange controls or other impediments.

Balance of international indebtedness (BII) An estimate of the reciprocal claims between a nation and the rest of the world as of a specific date. In the United States, this statement is officially called the International Investment Position of the United States.

Balance of payments (BOP) A summary of the economic transactions of the residents and government of a country with the residents and governments of the rest of the world during a certain period of time, usually a quarter or a year. It is an accounting statement and follows the principles of double-entry bookkeeping.

BOP deficit The amount, if any, by which the quantity of foreign exchange autonomously demanded at existing exchange rates exceeds the quantity autonomously supplied, with the result that the prices of foreign currencies tend to rise in the absence of central bank intervention.

BOP surplus   The amount, if any, by which the quantity of foreign exchange autonomously supplied at existing exchange rates exceeds the quantity autonomously demanded, with the result that the prices of foreign currencies tend to fall in the absence of central bank intervention.

Balance of trade   *See* Balance on trade in goods and services

Balance on current account   In the BOP, this is the net balance on all transactions involving trade in goods and services and also unilateral transfers.

Balance on goods, services, and income   In the BOP, this is the net balance on transactions in goods and services, including flows of investment income. It differs from the current account balance in its exclusion of unilateral transfers. As in the case of the merchandise trade balance, an excess of credits over debits is called a surplus or favorable balance, whereas an excess of debits over credits is called a deficit or unfavorable balance.

Balance on merchandise trade   In the BOP, this is the net balance derived by subtracting total merchandise imports from total merchandise exports. Conventionally, an excess of merchandise exports over merchandise imports is called a surplus or favorable merchandise trade balance, whereas an excess of imports over exports is called a deficit or unfavorable balance.

Bank draft   *See* Draft

Banker's acceptance (BA)   A bill of exchange or draft drawn on a bank that has been accepted by the bank and has therefore become a negotiable instrument eligible for discounting in a money market.

Bank for International Settlements (BIS)   An official banking institution, located in Basle, Switzerland, that is owned by central banks and managed by European central bankers. The BIS fosters international cooperation in banking and monetary matters, provides financial assistance to central banks in other countries, promotes the non-official use of Ecus, and otherwise supports the EMS.

Bank note exchange rate   This rate applies to exchanges of currencies in the form of paper money and traveler's checks. These exchanges result in immediate delivery and are typically for small amounts.

Basis   A term employed in futures trading, basis is the cash or spot price of a good, currency, financial instrument, or index minus the corresponding futures price. It corresponds to the forward swap rate and generally declines as the time to maturity diminishes.

Basle Accord   A 1987 agreement among representatives of the G-10 nations to work toward the establishment of uniform bank capital requirements to be applied internationally.

Bearer securities   Unregistered securities, i.e., securities whose ownership is not a matter of legal record. They are used in the Eurobond market and in the domestic capital markets of many nations.

Biased predictor   An indicator of a future value that varies in a nonrandom fashion from that value. For example, if a forward rate is a biased predictor of the future spot rate, there is a greater than 50 percent chance that it will deviate on one particular side of the spot rate.

Bilateral par value exchange rate This refers to the reference exchange rates between pairs of currencies that participate in the joint float of the EMS. The bilateral par value exchange rate between two jointly floating currencies is the cross rate between those currencies' Ecu central rates.

Bill of exchange *See* Draft

Bill of lading (B/L) A receipt issued by the carrier of goods that also serves as a contract between the carrier and the shipper (exporter). In international trade, B/Ls are generally *order B/Ls*, which can be assigned to other parties and used as loan collateral because they confer control over the goods. A *straight B/L* cannot be assigned and is ordinarily used in transactions between affiliates.

Book runner *See* Lead manager

Bought deal In this arrangement, the lead manager for an issue of securities buys the entire issue from the borrower before the announcement date, puts the managing syndicate together, and sets the terms of the issue as of the announcement date.

Brady Initiative Advanced by Secretary of the Treasury Nicholas Brady in 1989, this plan has become the basis for working out debt relief agreements with LDC governments that have fallen behind in their interest and amortization payments. Brady initiatives are worked out on a case-by-case basis and involve the joint participation of a debtor government, creditor banks, the IMF, and the World Bank. Relief is conditional on the adoption of structural economic reform programs and takes several forms, including debt-for-equity swaps and securitization.

Branch *See* Foreign bank branch

Bretton Woods Conference Held at a resort hotel in New Hampshire in 1944 and attended by the representatives of more than forty governments, this historic conference authorized the post–World War II establishment of international organizations concerned with exchange rates and BOP problems, the financing of reconstruction and economic development, and the reduction of barriers to international trade.

Bretton Woods System An international monetary system based on the concept of the adjustable peg, the Bretton Woods System was in operation from 1947 until August 1971. The Smithsonian Agreement of December 1971 attempted to preserve a modified version of this system but it was finally abandoned in March 1973.

Bubble *See* Rational speculative bubble

Bullet bonds Bonds whose entire principal amounts are repaid on a single maturity date.

Bureaucratic hedging The technique of obtaining expert opinion in support of managerial decisions so that criticism may be blunted if a decision turns out badly.

Callable bonds Bonds that can be redeemed by their issuer at a specified price before the scheduled redemption date.

Callable swap Also known as a *callable or call swaption,* a plain vanilla (fixed-for-floating) interest-rate swap in which the fixed-rate payer has the option of early termination.

Call option A contract in which a party has the right to buy an asset at a strike price fixed in advance on or before a specified date.

Capital accounts In the BOP, items that represent flows of assets. Individual capital accounts are recorded on a net basis.

Capital flight The large-scale and sudden transfer of wealth abroad because of domestic political risk.

Capital inflows Credit entries in the BOP that indicate either an increase in foreigners' claims on a nation or a reduction in that nation's claims on foreigners.

Capital lease *See* Financial lease

Capital markets A term that encompasses the issuing and trading of stocks and bonds. In general the term applies to the trading of assets with medium and long-term maturities or with no maturities; but medium and long-term bank loans are generally classified as belonging to money markets.

Capital outflows Debit entries in the BOP that indicate either an increase in a nation's claims on foreigners or a reduction in foreign claims on that nation.

Central bank swap An arrangement in which central banks authorize a reciprocal exchange of their national currencies that is to be reversed at a later date. The purpose of such a swap is to provide additional forex reserves for the support of their currencies.

Chicago Board of Trade (CBOT) An exchange specializing in the trading of futures and options. Although the CBOT is the world's largest futures exchange in terms of trading volume, it is much less important in the trading of currency futures than the Chicago Mercantile Exchange.

Chicago Mercantile Exchange (CME) An exchange specializing in the trading of futures and options. Its International Monetary Market (IMM) division dominates world trading in currency futures, and its Index and its Index and Option Market (IOM) is one of the world's two leading exchanges in the trading of currency options.

CHIPS *See* Clearing House Interbank Payments System

Clean draft A draft without accompanying documents. In international trade, clean drafts are used to collect payments that are unrelated to *current* shipments. If, for example, payment is overdue on an open account purchase or some other obligation incurred earlier, an exporter or other creditor may draw a clean draft in order to put pressure on the debtor.

Clearinghouse An agency of an organized exchange through which trades are confirmed, matched, and settled. A clearinghouse guarantees performance by acting as a party to each trade. It protects itself by requiring trading parties to post margins when contracts are opened and when the margins posted initially become inadequate.

Clearing House Interbank Payments System (CHIPS) Operated by the New York Clearing House Association in cooperation with the Federal Reserve Bank of New York, CHIPS processes and clears interbank transfers of dollars as a consequence of forex transactions in New York City.

Clearing member A firm qualified to clear trades and make end-of-the-day settlements with a clearinghouse. At organized exchanges, brokers and traders who are not clearing members must have their trades processed through the clearinghouse by clearing members.

Closing date In connection with issues of securities, this is the date on which the underwriting and selling firms buy securities from the issuer and distribute to investors those that have been sold.

Co-lead manager A term commonly applied to an investment bank that shares with the lead manager of a securities issue some of the responsibilities for arranging the terms of the issue and the composition of the managing syndicate. The term is also applied to commercial banks that participate in similar fashion in arranging syndicated loans.

Co-manager A firm that participates in the managing syndicate of a syndicated loan or an issue of securities but which does not play an important part in arranging the terms. A co-manager is often a firm that receives this classification by virtue of taking a large participation in the loan or issue.

Commercial paper This consists of unsecured short-term notes sold on a discount basis either through dealers (usually investment banks) or via direct placements with investors. Commercial banks commonly provide guarantees of commercial paper to investors.

Commitment fee A fee charged by a lending institution to the borrower on the authorized but uncommitted amount of a loan.

Commodity arbitrage In international trade, the process of gaining from the price discrepancy that results when the exchange rate between two currencies allows a good to be significantly cheaper in one country than in another.

Commodity Futures Trading Commission (CFTC) An agency of the U.S. government that regulates futures exchanges. It also regulates the trading of options by the IOM division of the CME since these options are on futures contracts traded by the CME's IMM division. The currency options traded at the PHLX are, however, regulated by the SEC.

Commodity swap Similar in structure to a plain vanilla interest-rate swap, a commodity swap provides protection against price fluctuations in a particular commodity. In return for being guaranteed a fixed price for the relevant commodity, a producer or user pays a floating amount based on a price index for the commodity that offsets variations in the commodity's market price. Normally, there is no delivery of the commodity between the swap counterparties.

Compensating balances Minimum bank balances required by banks of customers in return for receiving loans and other benefits. The requirement of such balances is particularly common in the United States for corporate customers.

Compensatory Financing Facility *See* IMM special lending facilities

Complete interest arbitrage *See* Interest arbitrage

Compound option Used in OTC trading, an option on an option that gives the buyer the right to enter into a call or put option.

Conditionality A term employed by the IMF, the principle that borrowers from the IMF must accept restrictions imposed by it to be eligible for a loan and must continue to abide by those restrictions in order to receive the total authorized amount of IMF lending.

Confirmed L/C A L/C accepted by one bank and guaranteed by another. The drawer of a draft based on the L/C can collect payment from either bank.

Consignment selling In international trade, this occurs when the exporter of goods retains the title to them until they are sold by the importer and funds are made available to the exporter. This technique is widely used in sales to affiliates.

Consular invoice A document issued by a representative office of the government of the country to which goods are to be shipped certifying the quantity and nature of the goods to be imported.

Contract reversal A technique used to close out trading positions at organized exchanges. For example, a party that is short six mark futures contracts eliminates its position by going long six mark futures contracts having the same maturity and making or receiving a payment for the difference in value.

Controlled foreign corporation (CFC) A company that is incorporated outside the United States and has at least 50 percent of its voting stock held by U.S. stockholders, each of whom must control at least 10 percent of the voting stock to be counted. If a substantial part of a CFC's income is classified as Subpart F, the income of the CFC is taxed as if it had all been remitted to the U.S. stockholders.

Convertible bonds Bonds that are exchangeable, at the bondholder's option, into some other asset, usually shares of stock in the company that issued them. Usually, but not always, the amount of stock obtainable per bond is predetermined. Sometimes convertible bonds are also called *callable*. In some cases, convertibles offer a *currency play* in that bonds issued on one currency are convertible into stocks that are priced in another currency.

Correspondent bank In international finance, a bank located in a foreign country that holds deposits for and provides services to a domestic bank.

Countertrade A term applied to various international trading arrangements that fundamentally amount to barter. In some cases, exporters to a country must make payment in currently provided goods; but in some cases, they may receive partial payment in convertible foreign exchange. In the *buyback* variation of countertrade, the exchanges of goods are separated in time.

Covered interest arbitrage The movement of short-term funds from one currency into another at the spot exchange rate in combination with a reverse currency exchange at the forward rate so as to take advantage of a divergence between the interest-rate differential and the forward premium or discount.

Covering Generating a foreign currency cash flow to offset a commitment to make or receive a cash flow in the same currency. It is a form of hedging commonly used in interest arbitrage.

Credit tranche The amount of quota-based borrowings under stand-by agreements which the IMF may authorize to a member government in excess of what is available to that member from its reserve tranche position with the IMF.

Cross rate of exchange The exchange rate between two currencies derived from the exchange rates between these currencies with a third currency. Cross rates are often derived by using the U.S. dollar as the third currency.

Currency arbitrage The process of taking advantage of price discrepancies in the forex market other than the bid−ask spread so as to profit from them. *Triangular currency arbitrage* involves taking advantage of disparate cross rates involving a third currency.

Currency option bonds Bonds that give bondholders the right to receive both interest payments and redemption payments in either of two currencies. They are usually callable.

Currency swap An arrangement in which two parties exchange principals in different currencies at the outset and re-exchange the principal amounts subsequently, usually on a single date. The exchanges of principals are usually actual rather than notional, and they are usually made at the spot rate in existence at the time of the initial exchange. During the swap's life, the parties exchange interest payments in the two currencies. A *plain vanilla currency swap* is a non-amortizing swap in which one party pays fixed interest and the other pays floating interest. Currency swaps are generally viewed as medium-term financial instruments.

Currency warrants   Financial instruments that are in effect, a type of currency option. They are freely negotiable and often issued with bond issues but may be detached and sold. Some currency warrants *(naked warrants)* are not attached to bonds. Currency warrants have smaller face values and typically longer terms than currency options.

Current accounts   In the BOP, items that represent flows of goods and services or unilateral transfers. Included among the flows of services are payments of interest, dividends, and other income from capital. The unilateral transfers are recorded on a net basis, but the flows of goods and services are recorded on a gross basis.

Daily settlement   The process of determining net position changes for brokers and traders at futures and other exchanges which mark to market daily. Those parties with gains receive cash payments from the exchange clearinghouse; those with losses may be required to post additional margin.

Day traders   In futures trading, refers to speculative traders in futures who execute numerous complete round turns in a day. Their trading helps to provide the market liquidity essential for hedging.

Debt-equity swap   A commonly used technique for reducing the indebtedness of heavily indebted LDC governments. In such a swap, a creditor, usually a bank, exchanges some of its claims on a government at a discount from their face value in return for acquiring an equity claim, such as ownership rights in a formerly state-controlled enterprise.

Debt-for-debt swap   As applied to the management of delinquent bank claims on debtor governments, this technique involves the exchange of claims on different countries.

Deferred swap   *See* Forward swap

Delayed or deferred rate-setting swap   An interest rate swap in which the applicable interest rates are determined after the swap's starting date in accordance with a prior agreement. The party receiving the right of deferral compensates the other swap party.

Dependent economy   An economy for which exchange rate variations can be so damaging that its government is well advised to try to stabilize the exchange value of its currency against the dollar, some other national currency, or a currency composite.

Depreciation   A decrease in a currency's value in the forex market.

Destabilizing speculation   Forex market speculation that drives an exchange rate farther away from its underlying equilibrium position and sets up an eventual corrective movement.

Devaluation   A reduction in the officially defined value of a currency whose value is stated in terms of gold, a national currency, a composite currency, or some other standard of value. When a currency's market value is based on its official value, devaluation leads to an immediate decline in its market value.

Direct basis (for exchange rate quotations)   The practice of quoting the price of a currency as the amount of another currency per unit of that currency.

Direct foreign investment (DFI) Foreign equity investment which confers either control of or a substantial voice in the management of a foreign enterprise or property. The Department of Commerce classifies foreign investment as DFI when a single investor holds an equity claim equal to 10 percent or more of the book value of a foreign enterprise or property.

Dirty float The manipulation of the forex value of a currency through central bank intervention so as to maintain a market value for a currency which differs significantly from the value that would otherwise exist.

Disciplinary effect In relation to the BOP, this is the restraining effect that a BOP deficit exercises upon the conduct of domestic monetary policy.

Discounting without recourse This occurs when the buyer of financial paper or receivables surrenders any right to collect payment from a party other than the debtor party whose obligation is purchased. Applied to factoring, for example, discounting without recourse means that the factor buying the paper gives up any right to claim payment from the exporter who is selling the paper.

Divestment The process of liquidating foreign investment in a country because of the perception of increasing risks, particularly political risk.

Documentary draft Commonly used in international trade, it is accompanied by a bill of lading, a commercial invoice, insurance papers, and other documents.

Dollar index A trade-weighted exchange rate index used by the FINEX in the trading of its dollar index futures and options contracts. The index is derived from the Federal Reserve's trade-weighted dollar index.

Double dip lease An international leasing arrangement effectively treated as an operating lease in one country and a capital lease in another, so that both parties are treated as owners of the leased equipment for tax purposes.

Draft Also known as a *bill of exchange*, it is an order to pay addressed to a specific party that calls for the payment of a specified sum on a specific or determinable date to a specified party. In international trade, the drawer of a draft usually orders a bank or importer to pay it rather than another party.

Dual-currency bonds Bonds that pay interest in one currency but are redeemed in another. The redemption exchange rate is usually set in advance but may be variable. Dual-currency bonds are generally straight bonds.

Dual trading A term applied to trading at organized exchanges when a broker is allowed to trade simultaneously for the firm's customers and for its own account.

Econometric models Mathematical formulations of theoretical relationships which incorporate relevant statistical data to make economic forecasts. Their forecasts differ from forecasts based on technical analysis in that the latter do not rely on fundamental relationships incorporated into formal economic theories, but on statistical patterns of correlation presumed to repeat themselves.

Economic exposure The risk of loss in the net present value of a firm or an investment as a result of an unhedged exchange rate change.

Ecu central rates The official par value exchange rates of members of the EMS, which are expressed in currency units per Ecu. From these central rates are derived the bilateral par value exchange rates between pairs of currencies in the EMS joint float.

Edge Act Corporation   A subsidiary of a U.S. bank or banks that is located in the United States and specializes in certain types of international banking. Edge Act subsidiaries are useful in helping banks cross state lines and in permitting relatively small banks to engage in international banking. Some Edge Act subsidiaries are permitted to hold foreign subsidiaries and engage in investment-banking type operations abroad.

Effective exchange rate   An exchange rate index calculated as a weighted average of exchange rates between a currency and selected foreign currencies. Weights are based on the relative importance of the foreign currencies in transactions against the currency whose effective exchange rate is being calculated.

Efficient market   A market in which access to information about market conditions is widely enough distributed so that new information is quickly processed, eliminating arbitrage opportunities and extraordinary speculative gains.

Elasticities approach   The body of economic theory that attempts to explain BOP adjustment and exchange rate determination in terms of the various supply and demand functions from which the demand for and the supply of foreign exchange are derived. This approach primarily incorporates the elasticities pertaining to current account flows.

Equilibrium theory of exchange rates   A theory in which exchange rates that are freely determined by the interplay of market forces and are heavily influenced by capital flows should be regarded as equilibrium rates even if they differ substantially from long-term PPP rates. According to the equilibrium theory, exchange rates tend to behave so that real exchange rate variations closely mirror nominal exchange rate variations even over substantial time periods.

Equity country fund   A country-specific stock portfolio traded at one or more stock exchanges.

Equity risk premium   The amount by which the expected rate of return on stocks exceeds that of bonds or of some other asset, such as M2 money.

Equity warrants   Negotiable certificates that give their owners the right to purchase a predetermined number of shares of the issuing corporation at a specified price during a specified time period. They are commonly tied to bond issues but are detachable. They may be issued as *naked warrants*.

Errors and omissions (E&O)   *See* Statistical discrepancy

Eurobonds   Bonds issued in currencies other than those of the countries in which they are initially distributed.

Euro-commercial paper (Euro-CP)   Commercial paper denominated in a different currency from that of the country or countries in which it is sold.

Eurocurrencies   Bank time deposits denominated in a currency other than that of the banks in which they are held.

Eurodollars   Eurocurrency deposits denominated in U.S. dollars.

Euroequities   Issues of corporate stocks primarily traded outside the home countries of the issuing companies.

Euronote issuance facility (NIF)   An arrangement in which a bank or a bank syndicate makes a medium-term or long-term commitment to a borrower to support short-term notes. The notes are distributed to investors by the underwriting bank or banks.

Euronotes Short-term notes distributed through commercial and investment banks outside the countries of the currencies in which they are denominated. Euro-CP is a type of Euronote.

European currency unit (Ecu) A currency composite, composed of various amounts of the currencies of the member countries of the EMS, which is used as the official unit of account and *numeraire* for the EMS. Members of the EMS hold some of their official reserves in Ecu balances, and Ecus are widely used in non-official transactions.

European Economic Community (EEC) An organization dedicated to the economic integration of Europe. Members include Belgium, Denmark, France, Germany, Greece, Ireland, Italy, Luxembourg, the Netherlands, Portugal, Spain, and the United Kingdom.

European Monetary System (EMS) The arm of the EEC that fosters intra-European monetary cooperation. Most of the EMS's members participate in its joint float arrangement, the exceptions being Greece, Portugal, and the United Kingdom.

European Options Exchange (EOE) Located in Amsterdam, this exchange is concerned primarily with the trading of options on the stocks of European companies.

European-style option An option that can be exercised only on its expiration date; widely used in OTC trading.

European terms The pricing of currencies against the U.S. dollar so that the resulting exchange rates are in foreign currency units per dollar; for example, SF2.4118/dollar. European terms are commonly used in interbank forex trading, though the pound sterling is habitually quoted in American terms, i.e., dollars per pound.

Exchange controls Government-imposed restrictions on purchases and/or sales of foreign currencies. They range from mild restrictions that do not prevent a currency from being considered convertible to comprehensive controls intended to give the government monopoly control over forex receipts and their allocation.

Exchange rate mechanism (ERM) The system of rules and procedures for maintaining the joint float of the EMS against the dollar and other currencies. The ERM is based on the Ecu as the numeraire.

Exchange rate points One exchange rate point has an absolute value of one in the last digit in which an exchange rate is customarily stated. Often, but not always, the mathematical value of a point is .0001; but in an exchange rate quotation such as ¥136.21/$, the value of a point would be .01.

Exchange risk The possibility of loss due to an unhedged exchange rate variation.

Expected exchange rate (EER) In exchange rate theory, this is the forward rate or an exchange rate that is closely linked to the forward rate.

Export-Import Bank (Eximbank) A U. S. government agency whose function is to promote exports so as to meet competition from the subsidized export-promotion agencies of other governments. It makes direct loans to importers, guarantees export-related loans by banking institutions, and assists in providing credit insurance to exporters.

Exposure fee A fee charged by a lender on the basis of the risk classifications assigned to borrowers and their countries. For example, the Eximbank charges an exposure fee on the loans it guarantees that varies sharply according to these classifications.

Extendable swap   A swap in which one of the parties has the right to extend the swap's life beyond the scheduled maturity.

Extended facility   *See* IMF special lending facilities

External balance   The situation that exists when a country's international payments position is in the condition desired by its government. Normally, this means that the country is in BOP equilibrium.

Facility fee   *See* Commitment fee

Factoring   The discounting of receivables including drafts as well as notes and accounts receivable by firms (known as *factors*) that specialize in buying such paper.

Financial Instrument Exchange (FINEX)   A division of the New York Cotton Exchange (CTN). Known in international finance for its dollar index futures and options contracts.

Financial lease   Known as a capital lease by the IRS, this is a lease that extends for all or most of the expected life of leased equipment and is non-cancelable. Economically, a financial lease is equivalent to a credit purchase; and the IRS regards such a lease as a sale for tax purposes. The tax laws of some countries, however, permit the lessor to enjoy the tax benefits of ownership.

Fisher effect   The proposition that the nominal interest rate of a country equals its expected real interest rate plus the expected inflation rate.

Fixed exchange rate   An exchange rate held within narrow limits by government policy. The permitted fluctuations may amount to several percentage points on either side of a par value exchange rate.

Fixed price reoffering   A procedure used in issuing Eurobonds in which

the selling firms commit themselves to refrain from selling bonds below a specified price before the managing syndicate's closing date.

Floating exchange rate   An exchange rate basically allowed to be determined by market forces. There may be some central bank intervention to reduce daily fluctuations and/or (in a "dirty" float) to influence the amount of movement.

Floating-rate bonds (FRNs)   Bonds whose interest rate is referenced to a bank rate, commonly the six-month LIBOR, and adjusted according to changes in the reference rate. The adjustment is usually based on what has happened to the reference rate since the last interest reset date and is applied to the next interest payment period. Sometimes, however, it is postdetermined; and it may be subject to a cap and/or a floor.

Floor brokers   Representatives of brokerage houses who trade on the floor of an exchange on behalf of their firms' customers.

Floor traders   Individuals who trade on the floor of an exchange on their own account or for the account of firms they represent.

Foreign bank branch   A deposit banking unit that is legally a part of a corporation headquartered in a country other than the one in which the unit operates.

Foreign banking subsidiary   A separately incorporated entity of a parent corporation located in a different country. The subsidiary may be fully or partly owned by the parent, and its activities may differ substantially from those of the parent.

Foreign bonds   Bonds issued and traded in domestic capital markets by foreign borrowers. Normally denominated in the currency of the country in which they are issued.

Foreign Credit Insurance Association (FCIA) An association of private insurers that provides credit insurance to U. S. exporters in cooperation with the Eximbank. The Eximbank bears the political risks and the commercial risks on medium-term policies issued by the FCIA, while the FCIA bears the commercial risks on its short-term policies.

Foreign Credit Restraint Program (FCRP) Introduced in 1965 on a voluntary basis, it was designed to restrain U.S. banks from lending to U.S. multinational firms for the purpose of financing acquisitions of foreign firms and properties. It became mandatory in 1968 and was eliminated in 1974.

Foreign exchange speculation The act of accepting an open (unhedged) position denominated in a foreign currency. In a broad sense, the acceptance of any such position is speculative but the term is often applied narrowly to refer to the act of accepting an unhedged forex exposure because of an expected exchange rate change.

Foreign repercussion effect An important concept in the Keynesian theory of BOP adjustment, this is the feedback effect on a nation's exports that follows from a change in its imports.

Forfaiting Factoring that involves the fixed-rate, medium-term nonrecourse discounting of export receivables on the basis of guarantees provided by a financial institution in the importing country. Forfaited exports are usually capital goods. The discounters of forfaited paper are known as *forfaiters*.

Forward exchange rate An exchange rate applying to an exchange of bank demand deposits that is to take place three or more business days in the future. Forward contracts are infor-mal agreements arranged by banks and are offered as either *outright forwards* or as *forward swaps*.

Forward option contract A forward contract that allows a party to choose any date within specified limits as the date for settling the exchange. The option period is usually ten days on either side of the maturity date.

Forward premium or discount Commonly stated on an annualized basis, the percentage of difference between a forward rate and the corresponding spot rate.

Forward swap An arrangement in which two parties agree to exchange specific amounts of currencies on one date and to reverse the exchange, usually at a different exchange rate, on a later date. One c f the exchanges is often a spot exchange, in which case the arrangement is a *spot-forward swap*. In *forward-forward swaps,* both exchanges are forward exchanges. These forward swaps differ from currency swaps in that there are no exchanges of interest payments and are usually for shorter time periods than currency swaps. The term forward swap is also applied to *deferred interest-rate swaps,* in which the beginning of a swap is postponed until after the outset of the swap.

Fungibility The ability of a good or an asset to be substituted into different uses.

Futures exchange rate An exchange rate applicable to a currency futures contract traded on an organized exchange. Like forwards, futures contracts effectively fix exchange rates in advance.

Gambler's ruin A losing streak that exhausts a speculator's capital.

General Agreement on Tariffs and Trade (GATT) An informal arrangement for negotiating reciprocal reductions in trade barriers that came into existence after World War II and is still in existence.

General Agreements to Borrow (GAB) An informal arrangement among the G-10 nations, Saudi Arabia, and Switzerland under which the participants stand ready to lend through the IMF for the mutual support of their currencies. At present, the GAB is little used.

Glass-Steagall Act of 1933 A landmark legislative act that, among other things, established the separation of commercial banking from investment banking in the United States.

Gold bullion standard A form of the gold standard in which domestic money of a participating country would be convertible into a standard quantity of gold bullion instead of gold coins.

Gold coin standard A form of the gold standard in which domestic money of a participating country would be convertible, either directly or indirectly, into gold coins containing a standard amount of gold.

Gold exchange standard A form of the gold standard in which the domestic money of a participating country would be convertible at a fixed exchange rate into the currency of a country whose money was convertible into gold.

Gold points The limits to which exchange rates could move under the gold standard without giving rise to international gold flows. These limits were determined by the cost of transacting in and shipping gold.

Gold Reserve Act of 1934 An act that officially devalued the U. S. dollar in terms of gold so as to increase gold's official price from $20.67 to $35 per ounce. It also committed the U. S. government to buy all gold offered to it at that price and to sell gold at that price in exchange for dollars held by foreign governments.

Gold standard A fixed exchange rate system in which the participating governments defined their currencies in terms of gold, bought and sold gold at the prices determined by these definitions, allowed the convertibility of currencies into gold at the fixed price, and allowed free private gold markets. The gold standard passed from the scene in the 1930s.

Gold standard adjustment mechanism The process by which exchange rates between gold standard countries would be brought into equilibrium with each other. This mechanism relied, in large part, on adjustments in money supplies and interest rates.

Gold tranche *See* Reserve tranche

Gray market The term applied to the practice of investment banking firms selling Eurobonds at discounted prices to selected buyers before the offering date.

Group of Five (G-5) An informal association of the governments of France, Germany, Japan, the United Kingdom, and the United States for the purpose of promoting cooperation on exchange rate policy and other matters of mutual economic concern.

Group of Seven (G-7) Similar in purpose to the G-5, the G-7 also includes Canada and Italy.

Group of Ten (G-10) Similar in purpose to the G-5 and the G-7, the G-10 also includes Belgium, the Netherlands, and Sweden.

Hedging As it pertains to forex exposure, hedging involves obtaining an asset or incurring a liability denominated in foreign currency to fully or partly offset an existing or prospective forex exposure.

Historical volatility In the trading of currency options, this is the standard deviation of past exchange rate volatility. This measure is used in determining option premiums.

IMF special lending facilities These are different types of arrangements under which the IMF lends. Examples include the *compensatory financial facility* for countries with temporary declines in export earnings and the *extended facility,* which allows loans for larger amounts and longer time periods than *credit tranche* borrowings. Other facilities include the *supplementary financing facility* and the *structural and enlarged structural adjustment facilities.* Facility loans are quota-based, but some are on concessionary terms.

Implied volatility The expected volatility incorporated into currency option premiums. It is the residual that remains after eliminating the other factors that determine premiums. *Historical volatility* influences implied volatility.

Import draft Drawn by an importer on a bank (often the bank that lends to the importer) authorizing the bank to transfer funds from the importer's account to the lending bank in accordance with the draft's *tenor.*

Importer's letter of credit (L/C) Issued by a bank on which an import draft is to be drawn authorizing the drawing of the draft.

Index-linked bonds Bonds for which coupon payments or even the principal may be adjusted according to an underlying price index.

Index and Option Market (IOM) The CME's option trading division. The options it trades are on IMM futures contracts.

Indication pricing schedule A listing of the interest rates and maturities at which a swap dealer stands ready to enter into either interest-rate or currency swaps.

Indirect basis (for exchange rate quotations) The practice of quoting the price of a currency as the amount of that currency per unit of another currency.

Inexact IRP A simplified process for calculating if IRP effectively holds. The annualized forward premium or discount is compared with the difference in interest rates between the countries whose currencies appear in the exchange rate.

Initial margin The margin required of clearing members of the IMM when they enter into futures contracts on behalf of customers.

Interest arbitrage The process of profiting from a discrepancy between the interest rate differential between two currencies and the forward premium or discount between the same two currencies. In *complete interest arbitrage* the arbitrageur borrows in one currency, buys the currency spot, buys an asset or lends with the proceeds, and covers with a forward sale of the purchased currency. In *partial interest arbitrage,* a forward contract is used to lock in a gain but there is only an acquisition or a use of funds, not both.

Interest Equalization Tax (IET) A tax imposed in 1963 on foreign bonds issued in the United States and extended in 1964 to foreign loans by U.S. financial institutions with maturities of a year or more. It was repealed in 1974.

Interest rate parity (IRP) The condition that exists when the interest rate differential between two currencies is exactly or approximately equal to the forward premium or discount between the same two currencies.

Interest-rate swap An agreement in which parties trade interest payments on a principal sum that is usually notional. Such swaps are usually medium-term. In a *plain vanilla* interest-rate swap, one party pays fixed interest and the other pays floating interest.

International Banking Facilities (IBFs) Authorized since 1981, these are "onshore offshore" operations that allow U. S. banks to engage in some Eurobanking activity. IBFs are accounts of U. S. banks segregated from their domestic accounts and used for international banking, subject to restrictions designed to prevent their use by nonbank U. S. residents. They offer substantial tax and other benefits.

International Bank for Reconstruction and Development Known as the World Bank, this organization makes development loans on terms considered to be fairly stringent. It has a "soft loan window," the International Development Association (IDA), and a venture capital affiliate, the International Finance Corporation (IFC). It raises capital from member subscriptions and by issuing government-guaranteed bonds.

International bonds Bonds issued and distributed on behalf of nonresident borrowers. *Foreign bonds* and *Eurobonds* are types of international bonds.

International equities Foreign stocks issued and traded on domestic exchanges. *Euroequities* are international equities traded primarily or entirely on exchanges outside the issuing firms' home countries.

International Fisher effect (IFE) The proposition that the nominal interest rate differential between two countries tends to be an unbiased predictor of changes in the spot exchange rate between their currencies.

International Investment Position of the United States *See* Balance of international indebtedness

International Monetary Fund (IMF) A product of the Bretton Woods Conference in 1944, this organization is primarily concerned with assisting LDCs in dealing with their international payments problems and promoting international cooperation in exchange rate policy. It also oversees the use of SDRs as an international reserve asset.

International Monetary Market (IMM) The division of the CME that trades financial futures. IMM members may also trade at the IOM.

International reserves Assets held by governments that can be freely used in support of their currencies in the forex market. They consist mostly of convertible currencies but also include governments' reserve tranche positions at the IMF, their SDR holdings, and their holdings of gold.

International Stock Exchange (ISE) A London exchange that is the world's leading exchange for the trading of international equities. The trading of international equities is handled through its Stock Exchange Automated Quotation System International (SEQUAL).

Intervention currency A currency used as an international reserve currency for the purpose of influencing market exchange rates.

In-the-money The amount by which current premium value of an option is above the strike price of a call or below the strike price of a put.

Intrinsic value The amount by which an option is in the money.

IRP neutral band The range of possible combinations of interest rate differentials and forward premiums or discounts within which IRP effectively holds. Within this band, either of these variables can change without giving rise to interest arbitrage.

Irrevocable letter of credit (L/C) A L/C in which the issuing bank guarantees that it will accept a properly drawn draft from a named party.

Japan Offshore Market (JOM) An arrangement, similar to the IBFs of the

United States, which allows Japanese banks to participate in the Asia currency and Eurocurrency markets. The participating banks use segregated accounts like the IBFs and receive similar benefits.

J Curve The relationship presumed to exist between a nation's current account balance and time following a depreciation/devaluation of its currency. Initially, this balance worsens but it then improves because of increases in the relevant supply and demand elasticities.

Law of one price *See* Purchasing power parity

Lead manager A commercial or investment bank that takes the primary role in arranging the terms for and the participation in a syndicated bank loan or a new issue of securities. It also arranges the relevant publicity and documentation. A lead manager is sometimes called a *book runner*.

Letter of credit (L/C) A document issued to the potential drawer of a bank draft in which the bank promises to honor a draft drawn according to the terms specified in the letter. The L/C may be either *revocable* or *irrevocable*. In international trade, L/Cs are commonly issued to exporters, but they may also be issued to importers.

Locals Professional speculators on organized exchanges. Their operations are invaluable in providing market liquidity.

Locking in The process of protecting an existing borrowing position or investment portfolio.

London gold pool An arrangement among the governments of the United States and other leading nations lasting from 1960 until 1968 whose purpose was to stabilize the world price of gold at about $35 per ounce.

London interbank bid rate (LIBID) The rate paid on interbank deposits in London in the Eurocurrency market. It is slightly below the LIBOR and is used much less frequently for reference purposes than that rate.

London interbank offer(ed) rate (LIBOR) Widely used as the reference rate for floating interest rate arrangements, this is the rate at which London banks lend to each other in the Eurocurrency market.

London International Financial Futures Exchange (LIFFE) Although it has suspended the trading of currency futures and options, its trading in interest-rate futures, including Eurodollars and sterling, make this one of the most important futures exchanges outside the United States.

Long-term capital flows Net changes in reciprocal claims between a nation and the rest of the world with maturities exceeding one year or, as in the case of shares of stock, with no definite maturity. Elsewhere in international finance, long term refers to time periods of more than five or seven years.

Louvre Accord An agreement by the governments of the G-7 countries reached in February 1987 for the purpose of maintaining their exchange rates within a broad range referenced to the dollar.

Maintenance margin The margin amounts beyond the initial margin, which CME clearing members must collect from their customers in order to satisfy the minimum margin requirements for trading at the IMM.

Managed float The floating of exchange rates with some central bank intervention to affect exchange rate levels. A widespread practice, it is sometimes called "dirty" floating.

Managing syndicate The group of investment banking firms that manages an issue of securities, obtains commitments from underwriting and selling firms, and organizes the sale of the securities to the public.

Marginal propensity to import A key relationship in the Keynesian theory, the proposition that a nation's imports tend to vary directly with changes in its income.

Margin requirements Amounts of money or other acceptable collateral placed on deposit to assure performance on a contract. In currency futures trading both buyers and sellers post margin. In the trading of currency options at exchanges margin is posted by option writers.

Marketmaker A financial intermediary, such as a dealer bank in the forex market, which provides market liquidity by making simultaneous offers to buy and sell.

Marking to market The revaluation of contractural obligations at organized exchanges so as to reflect current or closing prices.

Marshall-Lerner condition States that a nation with a trade deficit can reduce it by lowering its relative price level through depreciation/devaluation or relative deflation if the absolute sum of its elasticities of demand for imports and the foreign elasticity of demand for its exports exceeds one.

Medium-term Euronotes Euronotes which, like Euro-CP, are not underwritten. Their maturities are longer than those of Euro-CP.

Merchant bank A firm that combines commercial and investment banking functions in offering assistance to business firms and governments. Typically, the retail operations of merchant banks are limited in scope. Merchant banking is particularly popular in the United Kingdom.

MidAmerica Commodity Exchange (MCE) An affiliate of the CBOT that trades financial futures in competition with the IMM.

Middle exchange rate The exchange rate obtained by averaging bid and ask exchange rates.

Mini-max swap A swap with both a floor and a cap on the floating rate.

Mismatch risk The risk faced by dealers in forex swaps and other financial markets that they will not be able to achieve a perfect matching of assets and liabilities as to amount and maturity.

Monetary base This equals the reserves of domestic banks plus currency in circulation and is one of the targets of central banks in the conduct of monetary policy. It is affected by official reserve transactions in the BOP.

Monetary theory Applied internationally, this theory holds that BOP payments adjustment and exchange rate determination work through changes in the demand for and the supply of domestic money. Money demand works through k (the fraction of nominal income held in money form), the price level, and real output. Money supply is determined primarily by government policy.

Money market A general term applied to markets for bank loans and short-term securities.

Money market hedging Hedging by combining borrowing or lending transactions in foreign currencies with a spot exchange of currencies. It is a leading alternative to hedging with forward contracts.

Money market speculation The combining of a borrowing or lending transaction with a spot exchange of currencies so as to take advantage of an expected exchange rate change.

Multiple option facility Arrangement made in connection with a Eurocurrency market loan in which the borrower receives various choices, such as having either a syndicated loan or an issue of Euro-CP or receiving a choice of currencies in which funds can be borrowed or repaid.

National Futures Association (NFA) A private association of futures traders and brokers that implements and oversees codes of professional behavior at futures exchanges.

Netting A technique in which a multinational company offsets the foreign currency positions of its different operating units against each other so as to minimize the exchange risk and the volume of transactions required to manage it.

Neutral band *See* IRP neutral band

Neutralization *See* Sterilization

News This refers to unanticipated developments that have an immediate impact on financial markets and portfolio investment.

New York Cotton Exchange (CTN) *See* Financial Instrument Exchange (FINEX)

Nominal exchange rate An actual exchange rate, either realized or expected.

Nonamortizing swap A currency swap in which the repayments of principal occur at the swap's termination. Most currency swaps are nonamortizing.

Nonstochastic In financial theory, this is the characteristic of being predictable or nonrandom.

Nontradable goods Goods and services that do not ordinarily enter into international trade because of transportation costs and other factors.

Note issuance facility (NIF) An arrangement in which a bank or bank syndicate makes a medium-term or long-term commitment to support short-term note issues. The borrower issues notes as needed up to the amount of the facility, and the notes are distributed to investors by the underwriting bank or banks. NIFs have been declining in popularity. Competition from Euro-CP has reduced their popularity, but they continue to be used.

Offering date The date on which the public placement of an issue of securities handled by a managing syndicate begins.

Official reserve accounts A subcategory of the capital accounts section of the BOP which records changes in a nation's official reserve assets and in claims against that nation which are regarded as official reserve assets by the governments of other countries. For example, changes in foreign governments' holdings of U. S. dollar balances are included in the official reserve accounts of the U. S. BOP.

Official reserves *See* International reserves

Official reserve transactions balance Also known as the *official settlements balance,* this balance is widely regarded as the best approximate measure of a BOP deficit or surplus because of its implications for domestic bank reserves and money supplies.

Off-market swap As applied to currency swaps, this is a swap in which the initial exchange of principals does not occur at the current spot rate. The gap is made up in interest payments or at the swap's termination.

Offshore banking centers Banking centers whose primary function is to provide banking services to nonresidents of the countries in which they are located. The services include participation in the Eurocurrency market, specialized services for tax haven subsidiaries, and private banking.

Open account selling In international trade, this is a procedure in which an importer receives goods on credit from the exporter. No draft is drawn by the exporter.

Operating lease A lease for a period of time shorter than the expected life of the leased equipment. The lessor retains the tax benefits of ownership.

Operation Twist The term applied to the U. S. Treasury's efforts during the period 1961 to 1964 to alter the term structure of interest rates by raising short-term rates relative to long-term rates. The policy was designed to defend the dollar while simultaneously promoting real investment domestically. It is generally considered to have failed.

Optimum currency area An area, possibly larger than a country, in which economic efficiency is enhanced if there is a single currency or permanently fixed exchange rates.

Options Clearing Corporation (OCC) Centered in Chicago, this company serves as the clearinghouse for five U. S. options exchanges and NASDAQ. Included among the exchanges is the PHLX.

Option spread In option trading, a combination of a purchase of one option and the sale of another.

Organization for Economic Cooperation and Development (OECD) A cooperative arrangement among the governments of all economically developed countries and including a few LDCs, such as Turkey, which promotes economic cooperation and investment among the affiliated countries

Outright agreement. A forward transaction in which there is a single exchange of currencies. In offering outright forward contracts, forex dealers quote forward rates in full (*outright rates*) rather than as *swap rates*.

Overnight Eurodollars Eurodollar deposits with an effective maturity of one day. They provide a way to earn interest on demand deposits. Funds are transferred from a U. S. bank to a Eurobank early on day one and received back at the end of day two, with interest. These deposits are closely related to, and competitive with, overnight repurchase agreements.

Overvalued currency A currency whose market exchange value exceeds its equilibrium value as a result of exchange controls, a speculative bubble, or other cause.

Parallel loan A lending arrangement involving four parties in two countries. Commonly, the parties consist of two pairs of affiliated companies, and the loans are made in different currencies by an affiliate of one company to an affiliate of the other. Like back-to-back loans, they are used to avoid exchange controls and other impediments to the free exchange of currencies.

Partial interest arbitrage *See* Interest arbitrage

Perpetual bonds Also known as *consols,* perpetual bonds have no maturity. They are eliminated by exercising call provisions or by the issuer buying them back in bond markets.

Perverse elasticities case The (unusual) situation in which the relevant supply and demand elasticities are so low that the depreciation/devaluation of a nation's currency worsens its trade balance.

Philadelphia Board of Trade (PBOT) A subsidiary of the PHLX, it trades currency futures contracts in competition with the IMM. Its trading volume is much lower than that of the IMM, however.

Philadelphia Stock Exchange (PHLX) An exchange that has achieved great prominence in the trading of options. In currency options, it rivals the CME. The PHLX's currency options are options on spot, while those of the CME's IOD division are options on IMM futures contracts.

Placement memorandum A statement issued by the lead manager of a syndicated loan summarizing the borrower's financial condition and outlining the purposes and details of the proposed loan.

Plain vanilla A term applied to a relatively simple way of using a financial technique with more complicated applications. For example, using a put option with no special features is a plain vanilla technique. So is using a fixed-for-floating nonamortizing currency swap with standard interest payment intervals and no special options.

Plaza Agreement An agreement reached in September 1985 by the G-5 nations which provided for a coordinated program to lower the dollar's exchange value.

Points *See* Exchange rate points

Political risk The risk that government action will have an adverse effect on a firm's value.

Portfolio balance theory Applied internationally, this theory views exchange rates as being dominated by capital flows that occur in response to investors' changing perceptions of risks and returns. The theory has numerous points of difference with the monetary theory, one of the most important of which is that portfolio theory rejects the idea that assets can be perfect substitutes for each other internationally.

Portfolio indifference curve In portfolio theory, a curve that connects various combinations of asset risks and returns that provide an investor with equal utility.

Portfolio investment Investment for income only, i.e., which provides no managerial voice. Most portfolio investment is in interest-paying assets, but some is in equities. Sometimes, short-term investment is excluded from portfolio investment.

Position trader In futures trading, this is a trader who carries an open position over to the next trading day.

Praecipium The fee collected by the lead manager and/or the co-lead manager/s for services rendered in connection with a new issue of securities or a syndicated loan.

Primary financial market A market in which assets are initially sold.

Private banking Banking operations centering around the management of the wealth of individuals, many of whom reside in other countries. The services rendered are similar to those provided by the trust departments of commercial banks and investment firms. Private banking is often conducted in offshore locations.

Private Export Funding Corporation (PEFCO) A private corporation that works with the Eximbank to provide medium-term and long-term financing to importers of high-value U. S. goods. The loans are at fixed interest rates and are guaranteed by the Eximbank.

Private placements Issues of securities that are sold directly by investment banks to a restricted number of institutional investors without being offered to the general public.

Purchasing power parity (PPP) This is an extension of the *law of one price* into international trade. According to PPP, the exchange rate between two currencies tends to maintain this law, which holds that after allowance for transactions costs and other impediments to the movement of goods, goods tend to sell at the same price in each country. *See* Absolute PPP and Relative PPP

Putable swap An interest-rate swap in which the floating-rate payer has the option of early termination.

Put–call parity theorem The proposition that puts and calls of the same face value with a common strike price that equals the current forward or futures exchange rate tend to have identical premiums.

Rational speculative bubble An exchange rate movement away from the exchange rate's underlying or long-term value that is supported by speculators who believe they can detect the approximate timing of its reversal. Such bubbles are said to result in exchange rate *overshooting*.

Real exchange rate A market exchange rate adjusted for changes in relative price levels since a base period. If relative PPP held at all times, the real exchange rate would be constant. Real exchange rate movements have major significance for international trade and capital flows.

Reciprocity The principle of allowing firms owned by foreigners in particular countries to compete on an equal basis with domestically owned firms only if the governments of those countries extend reciprocal treatment to domestically owned firms that oprate in those countries.

Registered options traders (ROTs) This term applies to traders at the PHLX who either trade for the account of the firms they represent or broker orders for other parties. They also sometimes serve as market-makers.

Registered securities Securities that are subject to the requirement of registration of ownership with the issuing corporation or government. The United States follows the general practice of requiring the registration of ownership.

Regulation Q A regulation of the Federal Reserve System, which has been rescinded, that set maximum interest rates to be paid on domestic time and saving deposits. It was an important factor in promoting the development of the Eurodollar market.

Relative purchasing power parity (PPP) The proposition that a change in an exchange rate tends to have a perfect negative correlation with a change in nations' price levels. In the *traditional version of relative PPP,* historical variations in nations' price levels are referenced to a base period exchange rate to determine the exchange rate that should exist currently or should have existed at some time in the past. In the *efficient markets version of relative PPP,* the existing exchange rate is assumed to be an equilibrium rate and expected changes in price levels are used to derive the expected future exchange rates.

Representative office A banking office established in a foreign location to conduct operations that do not involve deposit and lending operations at that location. The activities of such offices include improving correspondent relationships, locating potential borrowers from a bank's lending offices, and providing information of use to the bank and its customers.

Reserve currency A national currency, such as the U. S. dollar or a composite currency (the SDR or the Ecu), which is included in the international reserves of a government that holds it.

Revaluation An increase in the officially defined value of a currency whose value is stated in terms of gold, a national currency, a composite currency, or some other standard of value. When a currency's market value is based on its official value, revaluation leads to an immediate increase in its market value.

Revocable letter of credit (L/C) A L/C issued by a bank which reserves the right to back out of its commitment at any time before a draft written in accordance with the L/C is presented to it.

Right of offset The right of a party to legally refuse to comply with its financial obligation under a contract if the other party to the agreement defaults.

Round turn The complete process of opening and closing a futures contract. Futures commissions are ordinarily charged on round-turn basis.

Rules of the game The term used to refer to the practices that the governments of gold standard countries were supposed to follow so as to facilitate the operation of the gold standard adjustment mechanism. Thus, a gold-losing country was expected to allow its money supply to decline and its real interest rate to increase.

Scalpers Floor traders at a futures exchange who execute round turns within a few minutes in the hope of profiting from small exchange rate movements.

Second Amendment An outgrowth of an agreement reached in Jamaica in 1976, this amendment to the IMF's Articles of Agreement was designed to bring the IMF's operations into conformity with the reality of floating exchange rates. *Article IV* of the Second Amendment sets forth the general principles which IMF members are expected to follow with respect to exchange rate policy.

Secondary financial market A market in which assets can be resold.

Securitization A technique used in managing delinquent sovereign debt in which outstanding debt is exchanged at discount for fully or partially collateralized securities.

Semistrong efficiency The category of market efficiency in which current prices reflect all publicly available information, but government agencies or corporate insiders who have first access to key information may conceivably profit by trading on their superior information.

Settlement date *See* Value date

Settlement margin Also known as *variation margin,* this is the additional margin required of clearing members of the CME when their margin accounts with the clearinghouse fall below the required levels. It is calculated twice daily.

Shell branches Booking offices of banks located in offshore banking centers. These offices may carry many millions of dollars of assets and liabilities on their books, but their transactions are arranged by offices in other banking centers.

Short-term capital flows In BOP terminology, these are international flows of claims with one year or less to maturity. They are recorded in the BOP on a net basis.

Sight draft A draft that is payable upon presentation to the party on which it is drawn.

Singapore International Monetary Exchange (SIMEX) An exchange that trades futures and options, the SIMEX operates a mutual offset system with the CME that allows contracts in some currencies to be opened at one exchange and closed at the other.

Sinking fund bonds Bonds that are progressively amortized over the life of a bond issue. The bonds amortized before maturity may be selected by lot or according to a prearranged schedule. Some of these bonds are *serial bonds*, which are amortized according to the numbers assigned to them.

Smithsonian Agreement An agreement among the G-10 governments reached in December 1971 which provided for a realignment of the participating countries' exchange rates and the maintenance of their currencies within 2.25 percent on either side of a currency's official par value.

The Snake An arrangement among European governments dating from early in 1972 which provided that the participating governments would keep the market values of their currencies within 2.25 percent of each other. The inadequacies of this arrangement prompted the establishment of the EMS in 1979.

Society for Worldwide Interbank Financial Telecommunications (SWIFT) Headquartered in Brussels, SWIFT is an international message transfer system owned and operated by more than 2,000 members. Most of the messages it transfers relate to forex transactions, but it is used to effect other financial transactions as well.

Special Drawing Rights (SDRs) An international reserve asset created and supported by the IMF, authorized in 1967 and introduced in 1970. No new SDRs have been created since 1981. An SDR is composed of specified amounts of five leading currencies.

Specialist In the trading of options at the PHLX, a specialist guides and controls the trading process of a particular line of option contracts by serving as a marketmaker, determining the order in which option contracts are traded, and executing orders.

Speculation *See* Foreign exchange speculation and Swap rate speculation

Spot exchange rate The exchange rate at which transfers of bank deposits are effected which occur two business days (or in some cases one business day) after an agreement to exchange is reached.

Spread *See* Option spread. The term has many other applications. For example, the difference between forex dealers' bid and ask prices is a spread; and so is the difference between Eurobanks' deposit and loan rates.

Spread risk A term with various applications, including the risk of an adverse change in the trading spreads received by dealers in financial swaps or in the trading of currencies.

Stabilizing speculation Speculation that tends to drive an exchange rate closer to its underlying value and to reduce the amplitude of its fluctuations.

Standby agreement An arrangement in which the IMF provides a line of credit to a borrowing government specifying the amount that can be borrowed during a specified time period, provided that the borrower satisfies the conditions specified by the IMF.

Statistical discrepancy (SD) Known generally as *errors and omissions*, this is a balancing account in the BOP used to assure equality between total debits and total credits. The SD designation is employed by the Department of Commerce in its BOP statements. A large balance in this account or a sharp swing in its balance is often indicative of an underlying trend affecting the U. S. BOP and the exchange value of the dollar.

Sterilization Also known as *neutralization*, this is central bank action to eliminate the monetary effects of central bank intervention in the forex market. For example, if the Fed's dollar support operations in the forex market lead to a reduction in the reserves of U. S. banks, the Fed could sterilize this effect by buying securities in the open market.

Stochastic Having the characteristic of being random or unpredictable. In finance, the term is often used in reference to the behavior of interest rates.

Straddle The combination of a call and a put with the same strike price and expiration date.

Straight bonds The most prevalent bond type, these are fixed-rate bonds with periodic interest payments.

Strike price The price at which an option can be exercised.

Strong-form efficiency The category of market efficiency in which there is no inside information—all market participants have access to all relevant information.

Subpart F A provision of the Revenue Act of 1962 applying to certain categories of foreign-source income received by foreign subsidiaries of U. S. firms which may be taxable as if it were wholly received by the parent companies. *See also* Controlled foreign corporation

Subsidiary *See* Foreign banking subsidiary

Swap position As applied to the forward market, this refers to a situation in which purchases of a currency match sales in amount but not as to maturities. Such a position is subject to the (small) risk of variations in swap rates.

Swap rate The difference between a forward rate and the corresponding spot rate expressed in points. It is analogous to the concept of basis in futures trading.

Swap rate speculation Speculation based on expected changes in forward swap rates. Such changes are prima-

rily due to changes in the interest rate differential between two currencies.

Swaps *See* Central bank swap, Commodity swap, Currency swap, Forward swap, and Interest-rate swap

Swaption An option to enter into an interest-rate swap. In a *call swaption,* the buyer gets the right to receive fixed-rate interest payments; and in a *put swaption,* the buyer gets the right to make fixed-rate interest payments.

SWIFT *See* Society for Worldwide Interbank Financial Telecommunications

Syndicated loan A type of lending arrangement often worked out in the Euro-currency market in which a group of banks participates. The loans extended are generally floating rate and referenced to the LIBOR.

Synthetic assets Combinations of derivative financial instruments that are used to provide the same payoff characteristics as bonds and other conventional financial assets.

Synthetic options Combinations of options and forward or futures contracts that effectively constitute options that are the reverse of those bought or sold. For example, combining a long put with a long futures position constitutes a *synthetic long call,* while combining a long call with a short futures position constitutes a *synthetic long put.*

Systematic risk The risk common to all available assets. It cannot be eliminated by portfolio diversification within a country, but the systematic risk of a national economy can be reduced by international investment since the systematic risks of different economies are not perfectly correlated.

Tax haven country A country, usually one with a very small population, which offers a low-tax environment for many types of foreign firms. Such countries are often offshore banking centers.

Technical analysis A method of economic forecasting based on the statistical analysis of the past behavior of seemingly relevant variables. In short-term forex rate forecasting, technical analysis seems to have performed better than forecasting based on econometric models.

Tender panel An arrangement in which banking institutions bid for participations in issues of securities, commercial paper, or NIFs.

Tenor A term applied to the terms of a draft.

Terminable swap A swap that can be terminated before its maturity date. If a fixed-rate payer holds the option to terminate, it is a *callable swap;* and if a floating-rate payer holds this option, it is a *putable swap.*

Threshold of divergence The point beyond which the currency of an EMS joint float member, expressed on an adjusted basis as currency units per Ecu, is not supposed to move without central bank intervention by the member's central bank to restrain further movement away from the currency's Ecu central rate. The threshold of divergence is 75 percent of the maximum allowable divergence of a currency's adjusted market value from its Ecu central rate.

Time draft A draft which is payable at a specified future date.

Time value (of an option) The amount by which an option's current premium (its price) exceeds its intrinsic value.

Tradable goods That part of a nation's output of goods and services that either compete against imports or are capable of being exported at current exchange rates.

Trade draft In international trade, this is a draft or bill of exchange drawn on an importer by the exporter.

Trade-weighted exchange rate *See* Effective exchange rate

Transaction by agreement The term used by the IMF for a situation in which two authorized holders of SDRs agree, at their initiative, to a spot exchange of SDRs for an equivalent amount of foreign exchange.

Transaction by designation The term used by the IMF for a situation in which the IMF informs a government that it must accept a certain quantity of SDRs from another government and give up an equivalent amount of its currency.

Transaction exposure The exchange risk associated with existing commitments to make or receive payments in foreign currencies.

Transfer prices The prices at which goods, services, and assets are transferred internationally between affiliated companies. Within limits determined by laws and regulations and their enforcement, transfer prices can be used to some degree to effect remittances of profits and to achieve tax advantages.

Translation exposure Also known as *accounting exposure,* this is the exchange risk associated with having assets and liabilities denominated in foreign currencies. Losses because of translation exposure appear on the books but may not be actual losses in terms of present or future cash flows.

Triangular (or three-point) arbitrage Arbitrage between two currencies that involves taking advantage of a disparate cross rate between the two currencies which is derived from their exchange rates with a third currency.

Two-tiered gold market An arrangement in effect from 1968 until 1971 in which intergovernmental transfers of gold among the governments of occurred at $35 per ounce and the participating governments refrained from intervention to affect gold's free market price.

Unbiased predictor   A market indicator whose deviations from a future price are equally likely to be on either side of that price and are, therefore, random.

Underlying price   As applied to currency options, the underlying price is the current exchange rate that is relevant to the option's exercise and premium value. The concept of an underlying price is also applied to the long-run exchange value of a currency, which may differ considerably from the currency's current market value.

Underwriters   Applied to new issues of securities, these are the firms that make commitments to buy specified amounts of a new issue before the closing date. They differ from sellers of securities in that they make specific commitments in advance.

Unilateral transfers   These are international transfer payments and consist of goods and services as well as money. The country making a unilateral transfer receives no quid pro quo for doing so. In the BOP, the unilateral transfer accounts are balancing entries which are recorded on a net basis.

Unsystematic risk   Risk that is not common to all available assets and which can therefore be diversified away.

Value (or delivery) date   The date on which an exchange of currencies actually occurs. It is also known as the *settlement date*. In spot transactions, the value date is normally two business days after an agreement to exchange is made; and in other transactions, it is typically two or more business days after the maturity date.

Variation margin   *See* Settlement margin

Vehicle currency   A currency in which international transactions are commonly denominated. The U. S. dollar is the most widely used vehicle currency.

Weak-form efficiency   The category of market efficiency in which current prices reflect all relevant historical information. As a result, no market participant obtains extraordinary profits by analyzing past behavior.

World Bank   *See* International Bank for Reconstruction and Development

Zero-coupon bonds   Bonds that pay no interest and are issued and traded on a discount basis from their maturity value.

Index

■